SERVICES MARKETING

Integrating Customer Focus Across the Firm

CANADIAN
EDITION

Valarie A. Zeithaml
University of North Carolina

Mary Jo Bitner
Arizona State University

Dwayne Gremler
Bowling Green State University

Tom Mahaffey
St Francis Xavier University

Bobbi Hiltz
St Francis Xavier University

Toronto   Montreal   Boston   Burr Ridge IL   Dubuque IA   Madison WI   New York
San Francisco   St. Louis   Bangkok   Bogatá   Caracas   Kuala Lumpur   Lisbon   London   Madrid
Mexico City   Milan   New Delhi   Santiago   Seoul   Singapore   Sydney   Taipei

Services Marketing
Canadian Edition

Statistics Canada information is used with the permission of the Minister of Industry, as Minister responsible for Statistics Canada. Information on the availability of the wide range of data from Statistics Canada can be obtained from Statistics Canada's Regional Offices, its World Wide Web site at <http://www.statcan.ca>, and its toll-free access number 1-800-263-1136.

ISBN-13: 978-0-07-096452-5
ISBN-10: 0-07-096452-1

1 2 3 4 5 6 7 8 9 10 QPV 0 9 8 7

Printed and bound in the USA.

Care has been taken to trace ownership of copyright material contained in this text; however, the publisher will welcome any information that enables them to rectify any reference or credit for subsequent editions.

Editorial Director: Joanna Cotton
Publisher: Lynn Fisher
Senior Sponsoring Editor: Leanna MacLean
Senior Marketing Manager: Joy Armitage Taylor
Developmental Editor: Emma Gain
Editorial Associate: Marina Seguin
Copy Editor: Rodney Rawlings
Senior Production Coordinator: Paula Brown
Cover and Interior Design: Michelle Losier, FineLines Design & Formatting
Cover Image Credit: © Digital Vision
Page Layout: Lynda Powell
Printer: Quebecor Printing Versailles

Library and Archives Canada Cataloguing in Publication

Services marketing/Valarie Zeithaml ... [et al.].—Canadian ed.

Includes index.
ISBN 978-0-07-096452-5 (bound)

1. Service industries—Marketing—Textbooks. 2. Customer services—Textbooks. 3. Marketing—Textbooks. I. Zeithaml, Valarie A.

HD9980.5.Z45 2007   658.8   C2007-900365-6

To Hugo, my lifelong friend.

V.A.Z.

To my family
—husband, Rich, and daughters Andrea and Christa
—for their unfailing love and support.

M.J.B.

To my mother, Pat, for her years of support,
and in memory of my father, David.

D.D.G

To Verna, Connor and Mia
—I am truly blessed to have them in my life.

T. M.

To Mike, Gavin and Lauren for their love and patience
and my parents, Michael and Josephine,
for their endless support.

B. H.

About the Authors

Valarie A. Zeithaml

University of North Carolina—Chapel Hill

VALARIE ZEITHAML received her MBA and PhD in marketing from the University of Maryland. She is the co-author of *Delivering Quality Service: Balancing Customer Perceptions and Expectations* (Free Press, 1990); and *Driving Customer Equity: How Customer Lifetime Value Is Reshaping Corporate Strategy* (with Roland Rust and Katherine Lemon, Free Press, 2000). In 2002, *Driving Customer Equity* won the first Berry—AMA Book Prize for the best marketing book of the past three years.

Professor Zeithaml has won five teaching awards and is also the recipient of numerous research awards, including awards from the *Journal of Consumer Research*, the *Journal of Marketing*, the *Journal of the Academy of Marketing Science*, and the *Journal of Marketing Research*. She has consulted with more than 50 service and product companies.

Mary Jo Bitner

Arizona State University

MARY JO BITNER serves as Academic Director for the Center for Services Leadership at ASU. Dr. Bitner was a founding faculty member of the Center for Services Leadership created for the study of services marketing and management. Dr. Bitner has published more than 50 articles and has received a number of awards for her research in leading journals, including the *Journal of Marketing, Journal of the Academy of Marketing Science, Journal of Business Research, Journal of Retailing, International Journal of Service Industry Management*, and *Academy of Management Executive*. She has consulted with and presented seminars and workshops for numerous businesses. In 2003, Dr. Bitner was honoured with the Career Contributions to the Services Discipline award by the American Marketing Association's Services Special Interest Group.

Dwayne D. Gremler

Bowling Green State University

DWAYNE D. GREMLER received his MBA and PhD degrees from Arizona State University. He is a passionate advocate for the research and instruction of services marketing issues. He has served as Chair of the American Marketing Association's Services Marketing Special Interest Group and has helped organize services marketing conferences in Australia, the Netherlands, France, and the United States. He has been the recipient of several research awards, and while a professor at the University of Idaho, Dr. Gremler received the First Interstate Bank Student Excellence in Award for teaching, an award determined by students in the College of Business and Economics.

Thomas D. Mahaffey

Saint Francis Xavier University

TOM MAHAFFEY has degrees from St. Francis Xavier University, the University of Alberta, the Ivey Business School at the University of Western Ontario, and Queen's University. While studying at Queen's, he was first introduced to the seminal work of Valarie Zeithaml, A. Parasuraman and Leonard Berry, and relied heavily on the SERVQUAL scale for his dissertation. He immediately adopted the first U.S. edition of *Services Marketing*. Besides his teaching, he is engaged in research and consulting activities related to retailing and the marketing of services, and is the president of Xavier Consulting Group, Inc.

Bobbi Hiltz

Saint Francis Xavier University

BOBBI HILTZ has degrees from the University of Prince Edward Island and Dalhousie University. She began her career with a national retailer before joining the faculty of St. Francis Xavier. She is involved in business education through both her teaching and her consulting activities. Besides her work in retailing, she is actively engaged in a research program related to customer relationship management.

Brief Contents

Contents

PART FIVE   Delivering and Performing Service   297

CHAPTER 12   Employees' Roles in Service Delivery   299

CHAPTER 13   Customers' Roles in Service Delivery   331

EXERCISES, MINI CASES, AND DECISION CASES

Preface

The Canadian economy, like other advanced economies around the world, is dominated by services. Within these economies, companies increasingly view services as critical to present and future success. Of pivotal importance to current and future managers of these companies is having the tools and knowledge they need. This text is for students and businesspeople who recognize the vital role services play in our economy and who also recognize the unique challenges that services marketing creates. Even manufacturing companies that, in the past, have depended on their physical products for their livelihood, now recognize that service provides key competitive advantages.

Why a Services Marketing Text?

We strongly believe that services marketing is different from goods marketing in significant ways, and that it requires strategies and tactics that traditional marketing texts do not fully reflect. This text is therefore unique in both structure and content.

Conceptual and Research Foundations

We synthesized research and conceptual material from many talented academics and practitioners to create this text. We relied on pioneering work of researchers and businesspeople from diverse disciplines such as marketing, human resources, operations, and management. Because the field of services marketing is international in its roots, we also drew from work originating around the globe. The framework of the book is managerially focused, with every chapter presenting numerous company examples and strategies for addressing issues in the chapter.

Unique Structure: The Gaps Model of Service Quality

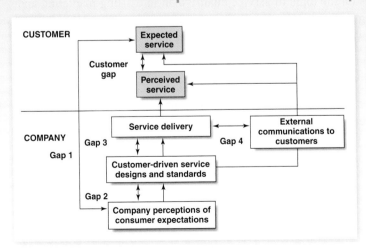

The text features a structure completely different from the standard 4P (marketing mix) structure of introductory marketing texts. The text is organized around the Gaps model of service quality, which is described fully in Chapter 2. Beginning with Chapter 3, the text is organized into parts around the Gaps model. For example, Chapters 3, 4, and 5 each deal with an aspect of the customer gap—customer behaviour, expectations, and perceptions respectively —to form the focus for services marketing strategies. The managerial content in the rest of the chapters is framed by the Gaps model using Part openers that build the model gap by gap. Each Part in the book includes multiple chapters with strategies for understanding and closing these critical gaps.

CONTENT OVERVIEW

The foundation of the text is the recognition that services present special challenges that must be identified and addressed. Issues commonly encountered in service organizations—the inability to inventory, difficulty in synchronizing demand and supply, and challenges in controlling the performance quality of human interactions—need to be articulated and tackled by managers.

In fact, one of the most interesting characteristics of services marketing is the need to integrate elements of the human resources and operations functions under a customer-focused umbrella. Just as leading business schools around the world are moving to integrating their courses by taking a cross-enterprise approach, so too have we integrated the core concepts needed to achieve service excellence.

The development of strong customer relationships through quality service (and services) are at the heart of this book's content. The topics covered are equally applicable to organizations whose core product is service (such as banks, transportation companies, hotels, hospitals, educational institutions, professional services, and telecommunication) and to organizations that depend on service excellence for competitive advantage (high-technology manufacturers, automotive and industrial products, and so on).

Rarely do we repeat material from marketing principles or marketing strategy texts. Instead, we adjust, when necessary, standard content on topics such as distribution, pricing, and promotion to account for service characteristics of intangibility, heterogeneity, inseparability, and perishability.

Further Distinguishing Content Features

Some of the distinguishing features of our text are:

↦ Greater emphasis on the topic of service quality than in existing marketing and service marketing texts, including detailed material on customer expectations and perceptions and what these expectations and perceptions imply for marketers.

↦ An entire chapter that recognizes human resource challenges and human resource strategies for delivering customer-focused services.

↦ Coverage of new service development processes and a detailed and complete introduction to service blueprinting—a tool for describing, designing, and positioning services.

↦ A chapter on the role of physical evidence, particularly the physical environment or "servicescape."

➡ Coverage of the customer's role in service delivery and strategies for making customers productive partners in service creation.

What's New to the Canadian Edition?

➡ New two-colour design that dramatically improves the visual appeal of the text, making it easier to read and navigate.

➡ Expanded treatment of key services marketing principles including the roles of people, processes and physical evidence; SERVQUAL; the services marketing triangle; customer lifetime value; and the fascinating role that customers themselves play in the co-production of the service.

➡ Revised and rewritten chapter opening vignettes that help students see the importance of closing each of the gaps that can lead to service failure.

➡ Increased emphasis on readability with the addition of many current Canadian advertisements from leading service firms that students will recognize, including Air Canada, Delta Hotels, WestJet, and Rogers. Advertisements have been chosen to illustrate key chapter content and material. As well, satirical cartoons are included that help to further illustrate core service principles and increase the text's accessibility.

➡ Revised and updated "Technology Insight" boxes that showcase the critical role that innovative technology plays in services today.

➡ Up-to-date "Global Feature" boxes in recognition of the work being done in services internationally.

➡ New "Exercises and Mini Cases" that, in addition to the full-length "Decision Cases" at the end of the text, provide additional application materials for in-class use (23 exercises and mini cases in total—10 new and 13 adapted "Strategy Insight" boxes from the U.S. edition).

➡ Thirteen full-length "Decision Cases," 12 of which are new to this edition, of varying complexity and length to provide extended practice of concepts. Cases from the U.S. edition have been retained and can be accessed on the Online Learning Centre at **www.mcgrawhill.ca/olc/zeithaml**.

➡ An exciting selection of video clips featuring Canadian and international firms to illustrate key chapter content in a relevant context.

➡ More examples vividly illustrating the theoretical ideas presented in the text, and dozens of real-world advertisements and marketing materials chosen from across Canada, allowing students to apply their learning to the realities of Canada's marketing environment.

PEDAGOGICAL SUPPORT

Chapter Objectives

Each chapter begins with a list of objectives to summarize the coverage and identify the pedagogical intentions of the chapter.

Chapter

16

Integrated Services Marketing Communications

Closing Provider Gap 4

THIS CHAPTER'S OBJECTIVES ARE TO

1. Discuss the key reasons for service communication challenges.
2. Introduce the concept of integrated service marketing communications.
3. Present four ways to integrate marketing communications in service organizations.
4. Present specific strategies for managing promises, managing customer expectations, educating customers, and managing internal communications.

"WE CAN EXPLAIN"—SCIENCE WORLD'S INTEGRATED MARKETING COMMUNICATIONS GENERATE INTEREST

Think of the last time you visited a museum. Did you consider that experience "fun"? Not likely, though it was probably interesting and worthwhile. Science World, a not-for-profit science museum located in Vancouver, British Columbia, was plagued with just that attitude and sought to change it. Despite having very high awareness, many of Science World's target audiences of 6-to-12-year-olds, their parents, and educators felt it was stodgy and serious. Then, in 2003, advertising agency Rethink stepped in and developed a campaign that changed people's perception and continues to inspire and generate positive results.

The integrated marketing communications strategy that resulted includes some creative outdoor, print, point-of-sale, radio and TV advertisements

Chapter Opening Vignette

All of the vignettes have been rewritten or revised for the Canadian edition. Each provides real-life context and provokes thought and discussion around the chapter topic.

310   Part 5 *Delivering and Performing Service*

Technology Spotlight

The High Price of Work Extension Technology

The goal of many companies has been achieving a real-time enterprise in which employees can access company information and be accessible to clients and employers continuously. The belief is that by employing work extension technologies (WET) such as email, laptops, cell phones, and PDAs, people will work more efficiently and be more productive. And some companies are thrilled with the results. As Derek Smith, a partner with the global law firm of Paul, Hastings, Janofsky & Walker puts it, "Technology has changed and enabled us to serve our clients better. One of the things we try to do at Paul Hastings is equip our attorneys so that wherever or whenever they are, they can access their clients."*

is an underlying cause. In particular, part of Duxbury's study examines WET users. And, while the study shows that the majority of technology users say technology has increased their productivity and interest in work, more than 60 percent experience more stress, and 70 percent have increased workloads. Further, those who were classified as frequent WET users worked more hours, had more job stress and stress in general, had a higher intent to turn over, had higher burnout, and had lower job and life satisfaction than employees using WET less frequently.

Duxbury's study points up a real area of concern. Creating an effective culture and thereby maintaining

Technology Spotlight Boxes

This feature provides up-to-date coverage of the advances in technology and the use of the Internet in the services arena.

106   Part 2   *Focus on the Customer*

Global Feature Boxes

In-depth examples of services marketing in an international context provide students with the complete picture of current global advances in the services marketing arena.

SUMMARY

This chapter presented the integrated gaps model of service quality (shown in Figure 2.6), a framework for understanding and improving service delivery. The entire text is organized around this model of service quality, which focuses on five pivotal gaps in delivering and marketing service:

The customer gap: Difference between customer expectations and perceptions

Provider Gap 1: Not knowing what customers expect

Provider Gap 2: Not selecting the right service designs and standards

Summary, Discussion Questions, and Exercises

Each chapter ends with a brief summary of key concepts, followed by topic-related questions to encourage and focus class discussion at the end of each chapter. Students are then offered an opportunity to further apply their knowledge with pertinent exercises.

Discussion Questions

1. Think about a service you receive. Is there a gap between your expectations and perceptions of that service? What do you expect that you do not receive?
2. Consider the "wish mode" discussion about IKEA. Think about a service that you receive regularly and put yourself in the wish mode. How would you change the service and the way it is provided?

Exercises

1. Choose an organization to interview, and use the integrated gaps model of service quality as a framework. An audit form is provided in Exhibit 2.1. Ask the manager whether the organization suffers from any of the factors listed in the figures in this chapter. Which factor in each of Figures 2.2 through 2.5 does the manager consider the most troublesome? What does the company do to try to address the problems?

Comprehensive Cases Section

The cases section has been expanded for the Canadian edition to include "Exercises and Mini Cases," as well as full-length decision cases. The "Exercises and Mini Cases" section contains a selection of short cases (1–2 pages in length), which are intended to be assigned in class as discussion starters, focus on analysis of the Gaps model and were specifically written for this edition to assist students in understanding the root causes of the four Provider Gaps that must be closed to achieve services excellence. The text ends with 13 full-length decision cases set in Canada and written to address key topics within services marketing.

SUPPLEMENTARY MATERIALS

For the Instructor

Instructor's CD-ROM

The CD-ROM contains a complete support package made up of the following elements:

- Instructor's Manual. The Instructor's Manual includes sample syllabi, suggestions for in-class activities, teaching notes for each of the cases included in the text, and answers to end-of-chapter discussion questions and exercises, as well as video teaching notes.

- Microsoft® PowerPoint® Presentations. The slides, completely redesigned and revised for the Canadian edition, include brief summaries of key concepts discussed in the text and visuals to support learning.

- Computerized Test Bank. Featuring numerous multiple choice, true/false, short-answer, and essay questions for every chapter of text, the test bank enables instructors to create effective assessment tools quickly and efficiently.

DVD, Including CBC Videos

This collection of videos not only features highly relevant material from CBC programming, but also a number of videos showcasing services firms from both the United States and Canada.

Online Learning Centre

Both students and instructors will find the text's online learning centre (OLC) to be an invaluable learning support tool. The OLC contains both a student section and a secure, password-protected instructor section. The instructor section will contain all the features available to students (relevant news headlines, quizzes, and videos), plus the Instructor's Manual and Microsoft® PowerPoint® presentations. The OLC is located at **www.mcgrawhill.ca/olc/zeithaml**.

Superior Service

iLearning Sales Specialist

Your Integrated Learning (iLearning) Sales Specialist is a McGraw-Hill Ryerson representative with the experience, product knowledge, training, and support to help you assess and integrate any of the following products, technology, and services into your course for optimum teaching and learning performance. Whether it is using our test bank software, helping your students improve their grades, or putting your entire course online, your iLearning Sales Specialist is there to help you do it. Contact your local iLearning Sales Specialist today to learn how to maximize all of McGraw-Hill Ryerson's resources.

iLearning Services Program

McGraw-Hill Ryerson offers a unique *i*Learning Services package designed for Canadian faculty. Our mission is to equip providers of higher education with superior tools and resources required for excellence in teaching. For additional information, please visit **www.mcgrawhill.ca/highereducation/iservices**.

Course Management

To create a Web page for your course using our resources, visit PageOut, the McGraw-Hill Ryerson website development centre, at www.mhhe.com/pageout. This Web page–generation software, free to adopters, is designed to help faculty create an online course complete with assignments, quizzes, links to relevant websites, and more—all in a matter of minutes.

In addition, content cartridges are available for the course management systems WebCT and Blackboard. These platforms provide instructors with user-friendly, flexible teaching tools. Please contact your local McGraw-Hill Ryerson *i*Learning Sales Specialist for details.

Teaching, Technology & Learning Conference Series

The educational environment has changed tremendously in recent years, and McGraw-Hill Ryerson continues to be committed to helping you acquire the skills you need to succeed in this new milieu. Our innovative Teaching, Technology & Learning Conference Series brings faculty together from across Canada with 3M Teaching Excellence award winners to share teaching and learning best practices in a collaborative and stimulating environment. Preconference workshops on general topics, such as teaching large classes and technology integration, will also be offered. We will also work with you at your own institution to customize workshops that best suit the needs of your faculty.

Research Reports on Technology and Student Success in Higher Education

These landmark reports, undertaken in conjunction with academic and private sector advisory boards, are the result of research studies into the challenges professors face in helping students succeed and the opportunities that new technology presents to impact teaching and learning.

For the Student

Online Learning Centre

In addition to viewing the videos that accompany the text, students can also benefit from the following features for every chapter of the text at the online learning centre (OLC):

- True/false quizzes
- Multiple choice quizzes
- Web links
- Essay questions with instant feedback

The OLC is located at **www.mcgrawhill.ca/olc/zeithaml**.

ACKNOWLEDGEMENTS

We wish to thank all those faculty who participated in both the preliminary and manuscript reviews for their thoughtful and constructive comments:

Richard Appleby, *Okanagan College*
Patricia Browne, *Kwantlen University College*
Rick Burjaw, *University of Western Ontario*
Doris Fulton, *Seneca College*
Stephen Grant, *University of New Brunswick*
Mike Guolla, *University of Ottawa*
Sarah Holding, *Malaspina University-College*
Simon Hudson, *University of Calgary*
Peter Jurczak, *Humber College*
David Mosley, *University of Ottawa*
Shelley Rinehart, *UNB Saint John*
Barry Wallace, *George Brown College*
Robert Warren, *University of Manitoba*

We especially wish to thank Stephen Grant, University of New Brunswick, and Simon Hudson, University of Calgary, for their work on the supplementary materials for this text, as well as all of the researchers who kindly gave their permission to use their cases—in particular, G. H. G. McDougall and Rita Lyn Spencer for permission to use multiple cases.

We would also like to acknowledge our debt to Professor Ian Spencer, colleague, mentor, and friend. Ian epitomized the central message of this book, and the need to have a customer (and learner) focus in all that we do.

Finally, we would like to thank the talented group at McGraw-Hill Ryerson, who worked very hard to make this project a reality, including Leanna MacLean, Senior Sponsoring Editor; Denise Foote, Senior Developmental Editor; Emma Gain, Developmental Editor; Kelly Dickson, Manager, Editorial Services; Paula Brown, Senior Production Coordinator; as well as Rodney Rawlings, Copy Editor, and Sarah Fulton, Associate Developmental Editor. It was a great pleasure working with this team.

Tom Mahaffey
Bobbi Hiltz

PART 1

Foundations for Services Marketing

This first Part of the text provides you with the foundations needed to begin your study of services marketing. The first chapter identifies up-to-date trends, issues, and opportunities in services as a backdrop for the strategies addressed in remaining chapters. The second chapter introduces the gaps model of service quality, the framework that provides the structure for the text. The remaining parts of the book will include information and strategies to address specific gaps, giving you the tools and knowledge to become a services marketing leader.

Chapter

1

Introduction to Services

THIS CHAPTER'S OBJECTIVES ARE TO

➝ 1. Explain what services are and identify important trends in services.

➝ 2. Explain the need for special services marketing concepts and practices and why the need has developed and is accelerating.

➝ 3. Explore the profound impact of technology on service.

➝ 4. Outline the basic differences between goods and services and the resulting challenges and opportunities for service businesses.

➝ 5. Introduce the expanded marketing mix for services and the philosophy of customer focus, as powerful frameworks and themes that are fundamental to the rest of the text.

NEW WAVE OF SERVICES: IBM TRANSFORMS INTO A SERVICES POWERHOUSE

IBM (www.ibm.ca) has transformed itself into a service provider. Like many businesses that were once viewed as manufacturing giants, IBM is shifting its focus. Back in 2001, Louis Gerstner, IBM's former CEO, predicted that soon "hardware and software will be sold inside a services wrapper." A headline in *eWeek* in early 2005 confirmed his prediction, proclaiming that IBM now sells services first, boxes second.

In a company brochure, IBM states that it is the largest *service* business in the world. Through its Global Services Canada division, IBM offers product support services, professional consulting services, and network computing services around the world. Many businesses have outsourced entire service functions to IBM. IBM Canada has won major multiyear service contracts with Scotiabank (worth about $900 million), TD Bank Financial Group ($720 million), and National Bank ($200 million). Although service are less lucrative than its other lines—operating margins are about 25 percent, as against 31 percent in hardware and a heady 87 percent in software—only services are capable of delivering the growth the company wants.

Going forward, IBM's strategy is to focus on total solutions and to be a truly valued, trusted, and indispensable partner for its key clients. This strategy means providing clients with total service solutions in such wide-ranging areas as human resources, marketing, product design, and customer relationship management.

No one in IBM would suggest that these positive results have been easily achieved. Switching from a manufacturing to a service and customer focus requires changes in management mindset, culture, and the way people work and are rewarded, and requires finding new ways of implementing customer solutions. At IBM this change has evolved over decades. It is suggested that Lou Gerstner's legacy at IBM may well be the definitive switch that the company has made from hardware to services and the strategic focus on customers.

Many of IBM's competitors have viewed the company's success and are attempting to make the same transformation. Underscoring its own commitment to the service sector, Hewlett-Packard recently signed a seven-year $2 billion outsourcing contract with CIBC. The agreement, at the time, was the largest in HP's history. Switching to services is not as easy as it looks, though. In moving into services, companies discover what service businesses such as hospitality, consulting, health care, financial services, and telecommunications have known for years: services marketing and management are different—not totally unique, but different. Selling and delivering a computer is not the same as selling and delivering a service that solves a customer's problem.[1]

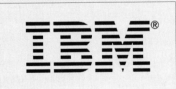

As the opening vignette suggests, services are not limited to service industries, services can be very profitable, and services are challenging to manage and market. Services represent a huge and growing percentage of the world economy; yet customer perceptions of service are not good.[2] Given the economic growth in services, their profit and competitive advantage potential, and the overall decline in customer satisfaction with services, it seems that the potential and opportunities for companies who can excel in services marketing, management, and delivery have never been greater.

This text will give you a lens with which to approach the marketing and management of services. What you learn can be applied in a company like IBM with a traditional manufacturing history or in pure service businesses. You will learn tools, strategies, and approaches for developing and delivering profitable services that can provide competitive advantage to firms. At the base of services marketing and management you will find a strong customer focus that extends across all functions of the firm—hence the subtitle of this book, "Integrating Customer Focus Across the Firm."

WHAT ARE SERVICES?

Put in the most simple terms, *services are deeds, processes, and performances.* Our opening vignette illustrates what is meant by this definition. The services offered by IBM are not tangible things that can be touched, seen, and felt, but rather are intangible deeds and performances. To be concrete, IBM offers repair and maintenance service for its equipment, consulting services for IT and e-commerce applications, training services, Web design and hosting, and other services. For the most part, the entire service is represented to the client through problem analysis activities, meetings with the client, follow-up calls, and reporting—a series of deeds, processes, and performances. Similarly, the core offerings of hospitals, hotels, banks, and utilities comprise primarily deeds and actions performed for customers.

Services include "all economic activities whose output is not a physical product or construction, is generally consumed at the time it is produced, and provides added value in forms (such as convenience, amusement, timeliness, comfort, or health) that are essentially intangible concerns of its first purchaser."[3] The breadth of industries making up the service sector of the Canadian economy is illustrated in Figure 1.1.

Service Industries, Services as Products, Customer Service, and Derived Service

As we begin our discussion of services marketing and management, it is important to draw distinctions between *service industries and companies, services as products, customer service,* and *derived service.* Sometimes when people think of service, they think only of customer service, but service can be divided into four distinct categories. The tools and strategies you will learn in this text can be applied to any of these categories.

Service industries and companies include those industries and companies typically classified within the service sector whose core product is a service. All of the following companies and organizations can be considered pure service companies: Marriott International (lodging), WestJet (transportation), Sun Life Financial (financial services), Athabasca University (education). The total services sector comprises a wide range of service industries, as suggested by Figure 1.1. Companies in these industries sell services as their core offering.

FIGURE 1.1   Contributions of Service Industries to Canadian Gross Domestic Product, 2004

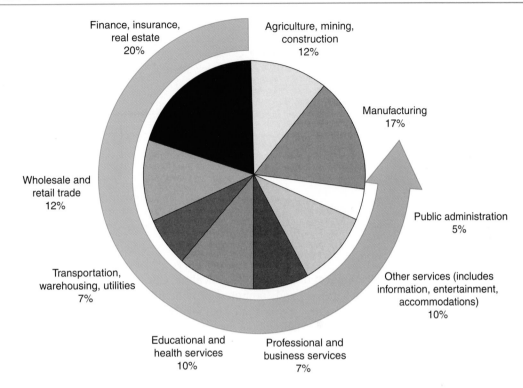

Source: Adapted from Statistics Canada website: www.statcan.ca. Accessed August 8, 2006.

Services as products represent a wide range of intangible product offerings that customers value and pay for in the marketplace. Service products are sold by service companies and by nonservice companies such as manufacturers and technology companies. For example, IBM and Hewlett-Packard offer information technology consulting services to the marketplace, competing with firms such as EDS and Accenture, which are traditional pure service firms. Other industry examples include department stores, like Chapters, that sell services such as gift wrapping and shipping, and pet stores, like Petcetera, that sell pet grooming and photography and training services.

Customer service is also a critical aspect of what we mean by "service." Customer service is the service provided in support of a company's core products. Companies typically do not charge for customer service. Customer service can occur onsite (as when a retail employee helps a customer find a desired item or answers a question), or it can occur over the phone or via the Internet. Many companies operate customer service call centres, often staffed around the clock. Quality customer service is essential to building customer relationships. It should not, however, be confused with the services provided for sale by the company.

Derived service is yet another way to look at what service means. In a recent article in the *Journal of Marketing*, Steve Vargo and Bob Lusch argue for a new dominant logic for marketing that suggests that all products and physical goods are valued for the services they provide.[4] Drawing on the work of respected economists, marketers, and philosophers, the two authors suggest that the value derived from physical goods is really the service provided by the good, not the good itself. For

FIGURE 1.2 **Tangibility Spectrum**

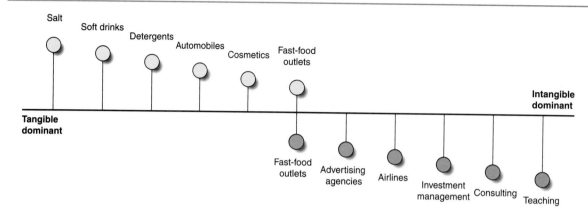

Source: G. Lynn Shostack, "Breaking Free from Product Marketing," *Journal of Marketing* 41 (April 1977), pp. 73–80. Reprinted with permission of the American Marketing Association.

example, they suggest that a pharmaceutical provides medical services, a razor provides barbering services, and computers provide information and data manipulation services. Although this view is somewhat abstract, it suggests that in the future we may think even more broadly about services than we currently do.

Tangibility Spectrum

The broad definition of services implies that intangibility is a key determinant of whether an offering is a service. Although this is true, it is also true that very few products are purely intangible or totally tangible. Instead, services tend to be *more intangible* than manufactured products, and manufactured products tend to be *more tangible* than services. For example, the fast-food industry, while classified as a service, also has many tangible components such as the food, the packaging, and so on. Automobiles, while classified within the manufacturing sector, also supply many intangibles, such as transportation. The tangibility spectrum shown in Figure 1.2 captures this idea. Throughout this text, when we refer to services we will be assuming the broad definition of services and acknowledging that there are very few "pure services" or "pure goods." The issues and approaches we discuss are directed toward those offerings that lie on the right side, the intangible side, of the spectrum shown in this figure.

WHY SERVICES MARKETING?

Why is it important to learn about services marketing, service quality, and service management? What are the differences in services versus manufactured-goods marketing that have led to the demand for books and courses on services? Many forces have led to the growth of services marketing, and many industries, companies, and individuals have defined the scope of the concepts, frameworks, and strategies that define the field. The field of services marketing and management has evolved as a result of these combined forces.

Service-Based Economies

First, services marketing concepts and strategies have developed in response to the growth of service industries and their increased importance to Canadian and other world economies. Although Canada has traditionally been viewed as a production-based economy that relies heavily on natural resources processing, our service sector is far more substantial than many may think, and it has recently been increasing in importance. Today, service industries in Canada account for almost 75 percent of our country's output and employment, having increased from a 50 percent share of each in the 1960s, and are attracting significantly more research and development dollars.[5]

Another indicator of the economic importance of services is that trade in services is growing worldwide and Canada's share of international share of service trade is increasing accordingly. The United States is the world's largest exporter of services and Canada's largest services trading partner as well. While, in contrast to the U.S., which generates a large trade surplus in services, Canada generates slight deficits, we are still the 12th-largest service exporter worldwide and our export rates have been increasing steadily since the 1980s.[6] And Canadian-based services available internationally may be more important still; many of our services are sold and delivered by affiliates based in foreign countries that are not accounted for in the trade balance calculation.

Finally, there is an increasing dominance of services in economies worldwide, as Table 1.1 indicates. The tremendous growth and economic contributions of the service sector have drawn increasing attention to the issues and challenges of service sector industries worldwide.

Service as a Business Imperative in Manufacturing and IT

Early in the development of the field of services marketing and management, most of the impetus came from service industries such as banking, transportation, and health care. As these traditional service industries evolve and become more competitive, the need for effective services management and marketing strategies continues. Now, however, manufacturing and technology industries such as automobiles, computers, and software are also recognizing the need to provide quality service and revenue-producing services in order to compete worldwide.

TABLE 1.1

Service Sector Contribution to Selected Economies Worldwide

Source: Central Intelligence Agency, *The World Factbook 2004*, available www.umsl.edu/services/govdocs/wofact2004/index.html, accessed September 14, 2006.

Country	Percent of GDP Attributed to Services
Bahamas	90
United States	79
Japan	74
United Kingdom	73
France	73
Canada	71
Sweden	69
Australia	68
Germany	68
Singapore	67
Brazil	51
India	48
China	33

From IBM and HP to President's Choice Financial, and General Motors, companies are recognizing the opportunity to grow and profit through services.[7] Why? Because the quick pace of developing technologies and increasing competition make it difficult to gain strategic competitive advantage through physical products alone. Plus, customers are more demanding. Not only do they expect excellent, high-quality goods and technology, they also expect high levels of customer service and total service solutions along with them.

At GE the services strategy began in the mid-1990s under then-CEO Jack Welch when he launched what has been termed the "third revolution." A major thrust of the third revolution was to push GE's growth strategies even deeper into services such as aftermarket services, financial services, broadcasting, management consulting, and other services as far afield as health care and utilities. GE now generates more than 75 percent of its revenues from services.[8] At General Motors, the services strategy is absolutely critical. Since 2002, GM has *lost* US$5.2 billion manufacturing vehicles but *earned* US$9.8 billion selling loans, insurance, and (even) mortgages. As noted by the *Globe and Mail*, during that time the Bank of GM made more money than the Bank of Nova Scotia!

Besides differentiating themselves with financial services such as GMAC Automotive, Insurance, and Mortgages, full-featured online banking, and educational loans, GM offers their On-Star in-vehicle safety and security system.[9] (See Figure 1.3.) Visit GM's website for a tour of its varied services (www.gm.com/company/financial_svc).

As manufacturers such as GM and IT companies such as IBM (see the opening vignette) transition to become services organizations, the need for special concepts and approaches for managing and marketing services is increasingly apparent.[10]

Deregulated Industries and Professional Service Needs

Specific demand for services marketing concepts has come from deregulating industries and professional services as both these groups have gone through rapid changes in the ways they do business. Over the past several decades, many very large service industries have been deregulated. While this is more pronounced in the United States than in Canada, the impacts are international. At the time of the publication of this book, major uncertainty existed in Canada related to possible bank mergers, CRTC reviews of digital services, and a whole spectrum of possible regulatory changes regarding telecommunications. Deregulation typically means that marketing decisions once made by the government are now partially or totally controlled by the industry.

Providers of professional services (such as physicians, lawyers, accountants, engineers, and architects) have also demanded new concepts and approaches for their businesses as these industries have become increasingly competitive and as professional standards have been modified to allow advertising. Whereas traditionally the professions avoided even using the word *marketing*, they are now seeking better ways to understand and segment their customers, to ensure the delivery of quality services, and to strengthen their positions amid a growing number of competitors.

Services Marketing Is Different

As the forces described above coincided and evolved, businesspeople realized that marketing and managing services presented issues and challenges not faced in manufacturing and packaged goods companies. These differences and challenges were captured in a series of interviews by management consultant Gary Knisely in 1979.[11] For example, when a firm's core offering is a deed performed by an employee (such

FIGURE 1.3

Services such as OnStar are critical to GM's future success.

Source: Reprinted with permission of *OnStar* magazine.

as engineering consulting), how can the firm ensure consistent product quality to the marketplace? As service businesses began to turn to marketing and decided to hire marketing people, they naturally recruited from the best marketers in the world—Procter & Gamble, General Foods, Kodak. People who moved from marketing in packaged goods industries to marketing in health care, banking, and other service industries found that their skills and experiences were not directly transferable. They faced issues and dilemmas in marketing services that their experiences in packaged goods and manufacturing had not prepared them for. These people realized the need for new concepts and approaches for marketing and managing service businesses.

Service Equals Profits

A dedication to quality service has been the foundation for success for many firms, across industries. In his book *Discovering the Soul of Service*, Leonard Berry describes in detail 14 such companies.[12] The companies featured in his book had been in business an average of 31 years in 1999 when the book was written. These companies had been profitable in all but five of their combined 407 years of existence due to nine common service themes, among them values-driven leadership, commitment to investments in employee success, and trust-based relationships with customers and other partners at the foundation of the organization.

Researchers are building a convincing case that service strategies, implemented appropriately, can be very profitable. Work sponsored by the Marketing Science Institute

suggests that corporate strategies focused on customer satisfaction, revenue generation, and service quality may actually be more profitable than strategies focused on
cost cutting or strategies that attempt to do both simultaneously.[13] Research out of the
Harvard Business School builds a case for the "service–profit chain," linking internal
service and employee satisfaction to customer value and ultimately to profits.[14] And
considerable research shows linkages from customer satisfaction (often driven by
service outcomes) to profits.[15] From the University of Michigan American Customer
Satisfaction Index (ACSI) even comes data suggesting that customer satisfaction is
directly linked to shareholder value. Firms in the top 50 percent of the ACSI rankings
show significantly higher shareholder value than firms in the bottom 50 percent.[16]
Finally, research from Canada's National Quality Institute (NQI) found that from
1990 to 2005, CAE winners achieved a 143.1 increase in shareholder value. This is in
contrast to an overall gain of 88.1 for the TSE 300 index.[17]

An important key to these successes is that the right strategies are chosen and that
these strategies are implemented appropriately and well. Much of what you learn
from this text will guide you in making such correct choices and in providing superior implementation. Throughout the text we will point out the profit implications
and tradeoffs to be made with service strategies. In Chapter 18 we will come back
to this issue by providing integrated coverage of the financial and profit impact of
service.

But "Service Stinks"

Despite the importance of service and the bottom-line profit potential for service,
consumers perceive that overall the quality of service is declining.[18] We see *BusinessWeek* magazine blatantly condemning service in its cover story "Why Service
Stinks."[19] And although there are exceptions in every industry, American Customer
Satisfaction Index (ACSI) scores for service industries are generally lower than the
average for all industries. Particularly low are ACSI scores in the transportation, communications, and utilities sectors. For example, whereas the national ACSI average
across all industries has risen to 74.4, cable and satellite television and the wireless
telecommunication industries overall receive ratings in the low-to-mid-60s, and most
airlines score in the mid-60s.[20]

Halifax-based author Laura Penny, in her book *Your Call Is Important to Us: The
Truth About Bullshit*, expresses the mood well: "If my call is so important, why isn't
anyone answering the damn phone?"[21]

This condemnation of service is troubling when, at some level, service has never
been better. For example, think of just one industry—health care. The ability to prevent and treat diseases has never been greater, resulting in an ever-increasing life
expectancy in most industrialized countries. So clearly, in some ways and in many
industries, services are better than ever.

Despite these obvious improvements, there is hard evidence that consumers perceive a lower quality of service overall and are less satisfied. There are many theories
as to why this decline in customer satisfaction with services has occurred. Plausible
theories include:

- With more companies offering tiered service based on the calculated profitability
  of different market segments, many customers are in fact getting less service than
  they have in the past.

- Increasing use by companies of self-service and technology-based service is perceived
  as less service, because no human interaction or human personalization is provided.

- Technology-based services (automated voice systems, Internet-based services, technology kiosks) are hard to implement, with many failures and with poorly designed systems in place.

- Customer expectations are higher because of the excellent service they receive from some companies. Thus, they expect the same from all and are frequently disappointed.

- Organizations have cut costs to the extent that they are too lean and too understaffed to provide quality service.

- The competitive job market results in less-skilled people working in front-line service jobs; talented workers soon get promoted or leave for better opportunities.

- Many companies give lip service to customer focus and service quality, but they fail to provide the training, compensation, and support needed to actually deliver quality service.

- Delivering consistent, high-quality service is not easy, yet many companies promise it.

For managers, students, and teachers of services marketing and management, the message is clear: services can be profitable, and yet overall quality perceptions and customer satisfaction are declining. In this text we will provide many examples of best practices—companies that understand how to get it right and are succeeding with service. We will also delineate many tools, concepts, and strategies that can help to reverse the "service stinks" mindset.

SERVICE AND TECHNOLOGY

The preceding sections examined the roots of services marketing and the reasons why the field exists. Another major trend—technology, specifically information technology—is currently shaping the field and profoundly influencing the practice of services marketing. In this section we explore trends in technology (positive *and* negative) to set the stage for topics that will be discussed throughout this text. In each chapter you will find a Technology Spotlight box that highlights the influence of technology on issues related to the particular chapter. We will also raise technology and service issues as appropriate throughout the general discussion in the text and have included several cases that explore the opportunities and challenges of services and technology. Together with globalization, the influence of technology is the most profound trend affecting services marketing today.

Potential for New Service Offerings

Looking to the recent past, it is apparent how technology has been the basic force behind service innovations now taken for granted. Automated voice mail, interactive voice response systems, fax machines, ATMs, and other common services were possible only because of new technologies. Just think how dramatically different your world would be without these basic technology services.

More recently, people have seen the explosion of the Internet, resulting in a host of new services. Internet-based companies like Amazon.ca and eBay offer services previously unheard of. And established companies find that the Internet provides a way to offer new services as well.[22] For example, the *Globe and Mail* offers an interactive version called *Insider Edition* that allows customers to organize the newspaper's content to suit their individual preferences.

Many new technology services are on the horizon. For example, some researchers project that the "connected car" will allow people to access all kinds of existing and new services while on the road. Already many cars are equipped with map and routing software that direct drivers to specific locations. In the future, in-car systems may provide recommendations for shopping by informing drivers when they are within a certain number of kilometres of their preferred retailer. On a road trip, the system may provide weather forecasts and warnings, and when it is time to stop for the night, the car's system might book a room at a nearby hotel, recommend a restaurant, and make dinner reservations.[23]

New Ways to Deliver Service

In addition to providing opportunities for new service offerings, technology is providing vehicles for delivering existing services in more accessible, convenient, productive ways. Technology facilitates basic customer service functions (bill paying, questions, chequing account records, tracking orders), transactions (both retail and business-to-business), and learning or information seeking. Our Technology Spotlight traces how, through history, evolving technologies have changed customer service forever. Companies have moved from face-to-face service to telephone-based service to widespread use of interactive voice response systems to Internet-based customer service and now wireless service. Interestingly, many companies are coming full circle and now offer human contact as the ultimate form of customer service.

Technology also facilitates transactions by offering a direct vehicle for making purchases. Technology giant Cisco Systems offers virtually all its customer service and ordering functions to its business customers via technology. Over 90 percent of its transactions with customers are completed online. On the consumer side, online shopping and transactions have already revolutionized the music and book businesses. Predictions suggest that online ordering will also rewrite the rules for purchasing jewellery, real estate, hotel rooms, and software.

Finally, technology, specifically the Internet, provides an easy way for customers to learn and research. Access to information has never been easier. For example, over 20,000 websites currently offer health-related information. Many provide answers to specific disease, drug, and treatment questions.[24]

Enabling Both Customers and Employees

Technology enables both customers and employees to be more effective in getting and providing service.[25] Through self-service technologies, customers can serve themselves more effectively. Via online banking, customers can access their accounts, check balances, apply for loans, shift money among accounts, and take care of just about any banking need they might have—all without the assistance of the bank's employees. All of Canada's financial institutions have moved increasing amounts of their business online. These services are just one example of the types of self-service technologies that are proliferating across industries.

For employees, technology can provide tremendous support in making them more effective and efficient in delivering service. Customer relationship management and sales support software are broad categories of technology that can aid front-line employees in providing better service. By having immediate access to information about their product and service offerings as well as about particular customers, employees

Technology Spotlight

The Changing Face of Customer Service

Excellent customer service—the daily, ongoing support of a company's offerings—is critical in creating brand identity and ultimate success. It includes answering questions, taking orders, dealing with billing issues, handling complaints, scheduling appointments, and similar activities. These essential functions can make or break an organization's relationships with its customers. The quality of customer care can significantly impact brand identity for service, manufacturing, and consumer products companies. Because of its importance in creating impressions and sustaining customer relationships, customer service has sometimes been called the "front door" of the organization or its "face."

So how has the "face" of customer service changed with the influx of technology? Long ago all customer service was provided face-to-face through direct personal interaction between employees and customers. The telephone changed this, allowing customers to call companies and speak directly with employees. Customer service became less personal, but without a doubt more efficient. With the evolution of computer technology, customer service representatives (CSRs) became even more efficient. Through computer information systems and customer data files, CSRs are able to call up customer records at their workstations to answer questions on the spot.

Over time, because communication and computer technologies allowed it, large organizations began to centralize their customer service functions, consolidating into a few large call centres that could be located anywhere in the world. For example, a large percentage of IBM's customer service calls in North America are handled out of its sales and service centre in Toronto, 24 hours a day. But still, in these types of call centres, customer service is for the most part an interpersonal event with customers talking directly, one-on-one with an employee.

The advent and rapid proliferation of the efficient, but much-maligned, automated voice response systems have changed personal customer service in many organizations into menu-driven, automated exchanges. In almost every industry, consumers encounter these types of systems, and many are quite frustrating—for example, when a system has a long, confusing set of menu options or when no menu option seems to fit the purpose of the call. Similarly, consumers become angry when they cannot get out of the system easily, or when there is no option to speak to a live person.

Some companies have overcome these obstacles, however, and have well-designed automated telephone systems that work well for customers. For instance, Rogers has recently redesigned their Customer Service Phone Line on the basis of customer feedback. The new system is available 24 hours a day, is easier to navigate, and allows callers to connect with a human when necessary. At Charles Schwab, the vice-president of retail voice technology occupies a senior management position, thereby communicating the importance of this function throughout the company. This may be partly why their customer satisfaction is rated among the highest in any industry.

Beyond automated telecom systems, the explosion of the Internet is also dramatically changing customer service for many companies. Service can now be provided on the Internet via email, website robots, FAQs, and online chats. In these cases there is no direct human interaction, and customers actually perform their own service. Ford Motor Company's dealership customers can set their own service appointments, send messages regarding their specific repair needs, and monitor the status of their vehicles, all online.

Why do companies continue to invest? One answer is that customers are demanding choice in how they get customer service. However, the cost to companies cannot be ignored. The typical service phone call involving human interaction is estimated to cost $7. Internet transactions involving human response cost $2.25. But a self-service phone call—no human interaction—costs less than $0.50. Although customers often enjoy technology-based service, and even demand it in many cases, it often doesn't work reliably,

continued

Source: Reproduced/used with permission of Rogers Communications Inc.

Technology Spotlight

The Changing Face of Customer Service—continued

doesn't seem to have any advantages over the interpersonal service alternatives, and lacks systems to recover from failures. Interestingly, when things don't work as they are supposed to on an Internet site or through an automated response system, customers are quick to look for more traditional interpersonal (in-person or via telephone) options, coming back to where they started!

Sources: J. A. Nickell, "To Voice Mail Hell and Back," *Business 2.0,* July 10, 2001, pp. 49–53; D. Ward, "The Web's Killer App: A Human Being," *Revolution,* March 2000, pp. 82–88; M. L. Meuter, A. L. Ostrom, R. I. Roundtree, and M. J. Bitner, "Self-Service Technologies: Understanding Customer Satisfaction with Technology-Based Service Encounters," *Journal of Marketing* 64 (July 2000), pp. 50–64; B. Horovitz, "Whatever Happened to Customer Service?" *USA Today,* September 25, 2003, available www.usatoday.com/money/economy/services/2003-09-25-services-frontcover_x.htm, accessed September 14, 2006.

are better able to serve them. This type of information allows employees to customize services to fit the customer's needs. They can also be much more efficient and timely than in the old days when most customer and product information was in paper files or in the heads of sales and customer service representatives.

Extending the Global Reach of Services

Technology infusion results in the potential for reaching out to customers around the globe in ways not possible before. The Internet itself knows no boundaries, and therefore information, customer service, and transactions can move across countries and across continents, reaching any customer who has access to the Web. Technology also allows employees of international companies to stay in touch easily—to share information, to ask questions, to serve on virtual teams together. All this technology facilitates the global reach as well as the effectiveness of service businesses. Our Global Feature focuses on the migration of service jobs and the ability to produce services almost anywhere.

The Internet *Is* a Service

An interesting way to look at the influence of technology is to realize that the Internet is just "one big service." All businesses and organizations that operate on the Internet are essentially providing services—whether they are giving information, performing basic customer service functions, or facilitating transactions. Thus all the tools, concepts, and strategies you learn in studying services marketing and management have direct application in an Internet or e-business world. Although technology and the Internet are profoundly changing how people do business and what offerings are possible, it is clear that customers still want basic service. They want what they have always wanted: dependable outcomes, easy access, responsive systems, flexibility, apologies, and compensation when things go wrong. But now they expect these same outcomes from technology-based businesses and from e-commerce solutions.[26] With hindsight it is obvious that many dot-com startups suffered and even failed because of lack of basic customer knowledge and failure of implementation, logistics, and service follow-up.[27]

Global Feature

The Migration of Service Jobs

With the ever-growing sophistication of information technology, the global reach of organizations is increasing at a spectacular rate. Activities that used to require close proximity and personal contact can now often be accomplished via the Internet, video, and telecommunication technologies. This advancement means that the jobs that produce and support these activities can be done almost anywhere in the world. The result has been referred to as a "migration of service jobs" out of countries such as Canada, the United States, and the United Kingdom to countries such as India, Pakistan, the Philippines, and Eastern European countries.

This globalization of services is in many ways inevitable, but it comes with considerable controversy. One clear concern is that some of the highest-paying service jobs are being "lost" to lower-wage countries, and this concern is very real for the individuals whose jobs are lost. However, the numbers are not as large as perhaps imagined. Critics of the global outsourcing of service jobs tend to be much more vocal in the United States than in Canada, though the Canadian media has not been silent on the issue. Some of the difference in concern noted between the two countries may be warranted. U.S.-based companies account for 70 percent of services outsourcing, and Forrester Research estimates that by the year 2015, 3.3 million high-tech and service jobs will move from the united States. Similarly, PricewaterhouseCoopers warns that 75,000 Canadian IT service jobs could be exported by 2010. However, in contrast with the United States, Canada is viewed as a "prime destination" for outsourced service jobs, and it currently ranks third worldwide as an outsourcing destination for information technology and business processes totalling $5.7 billion. Global outsourcing of service jobs can also be viewed as beneficial, because doing so can increase gross domestic product through increased innovation and job creation in other areas.

Although the specific outcomes of service job migration are not totally known, it is safe to say that the globalization of services will continue, resulting in further shrinking of the boundaries among people and countries.

Why is service job migration happening now? The root of the acceleration is the rapid development and accessibility of sophisticated information technologies. Services are information-intensive, and information can now be shared readily without direct personal contact. For example, researchers worldwide can work on a project simultaneously and share information instantaneously. Other services can easily be performed without regard for national boundaries. Canadian Imperial Bank of Commerce outsources its credit card processing to the United States; Indian financial analysts digest the latest disclosures of U.S. companies and file reports the next day; and other workers in India sort through mounds of consumer data provided by non-Indian company clients to determine behaviour patterns and develop ideas for marketing. In each of these cases, *where* the work is done is not important or meaningful to the client as long as it is done well and on time.

continued

Source: Indranil Mukerjee/Getty Images.

Global Feature

The Migration of Service Jobs—continued

A major reason that this movement of jobs is possible is that countries outside the developed world are now producing highly skilled, well-educated workforces, particularly in China and India. These workers typically work for far less compensation, allowing global companies to reduce labour costs on the one hand and increase overall productivity on the other. The quality of the work can be very high as well, with many companies citing quality and performance among their reasons for moving service jobs overseas.

Sources: U. Karmarkar, "Will You Survive the Services Revolution?" *Harvard Business Review,* June 2004, pp. 100–107; D. Goldfarb, "How Canada Wins from Global Services Outsourcing," *Commentary* (C. D. Howe Institute), November 2004, p. 1. M. Kripalani and P. Engardio, "The Rise of India," *BusinessWeek,* December 8, 2003; "Mapping Offshore Markets," white paper by neoIT, at www.neoIT.com; S. A. Teicher, "A Not So Simple Path," *Christian Science Monitor,* February 23, 2004; M. N. Baily and D. Farrell, "Exploding the Myths of Offshoring," *The McKinsey Quarterly,* online at www.mckinseyquarterly.com, July 2004.

The Paradoxes and Dark Side of Technology and Service

Although there is clearly great potential for technology to support and enhance services, there are potential negative outcomes as well. Mick and Fournier, well-regarded consumer researchers, have pointed out the many paradoxes of technology products and services for consumers, as shown in Table 1.2.[28] This section highlights some of the general concerns.

Customer concerns about privacy and confidentiality raise major issues for firms as they seek to learn about and interact directly with customers through the Internet. These types of concerns are what have stymied and precluded many efforts to advance technology applications in the health care industry, for example. Nor are all customers equally interested in using technology as a means of interacting with companies. Research exploring "customer technology readiness" suggests that some customers are simply not interested or ready to use technology.[29] Employees can also be reluctant to accept and integrate technology into their work lives—especially when they perceive, rightly or wrongly, that the technology will substitute for human labour and perhaps eliminate their jobs.

With technology infusion comes a loss of human contact, which many people believe is detrimental purely from a quality of life and human relationships perspective. Parents may lament that their children spend hours in front of computer screens, interacting with games, seeking information, and relating to their friends only through instant messaging without any face-to-face human contact. And workers in organizations become more and more reliant on communicating through technology—even communicating via email with the person in the next office!

Finally, the payback in technology investments is often uncertain. It may take a long time for an investment to result in productivity or customer satisfaction gains. Sometimes it never happens. For example, McKinsey & Company reports that a firm projected a $40 million savings from moving its billing and service calls to the Web. Instead it suffered a $16 billion loss as a result of lower usage by customers than projected, unanticipated follow-up calls and emails to the call centre from those who

TABLE 1.2 Eight Central Paradoxes of Technological Products

Paradox	Description
Control/chaos	Technology can facilitate regulation or order, and technology can lead to upheaval or disorder.
Freedom/enslavement	Technology can facilitate independence or fewer restrictions, and technology can lead to dependence or more restrictions.
New/obsolete	New technologies provide the user with the most recently developed benefits of scientific knowledge, and new technologies are already or soon to be outmoded as they reach the marketplace.
Competence/incompetence	Technology can facilitate feelings of intelligence or efficacy, and technology can lead to feelings of ignorance or ineptitude.
Efficiency/inefficiency	Technology can facilitate less effort or time spent in certain activities, and technology can lead to more effort or time in certain activities.
Fulfils/creates needs	Technology can facilitate the fulfilment of needs or desires, and technology can lead to the development or awareness of needs or desires previously unrealized.
Assimilation/isolation	Technology can facilitate human togetherness, and technology can lead to human separation.
Engaging/disengaging	Technology can facilitate involvement, flow, or activity, and technology can lead to disconnection, disruption, or passivity.

Source: D. G. Mick and S. Fournier, "Paradoxes of Technology: Consumer Cognizance, Emotions, and Coping Strategies," *Journal of Consumer Research* 25 (September 1998), pp. 123–47. © 1998 University of Chicago Press. Reprinted by permission.

had used the Web application initially, and loss of revenue from lack of cross-selling opportunities.[30]

 ## CHARACTERISTICS OF SERVICES COMPARED TO GOODS

There is general agreement that there is a difference between goods and services and that the distinctive characteristics discussed in this section result in challenges (as well as advantages) for managers of services.[31] But it is also important to realize that each of these characteristics can be arranged on a continuum similar to the tangibility spectrum shown in Figure 1.1. That is, although services tend to be more heterogeneous, more intangible, more difficult to evaluate than goods, the differences between goods and services are not black and white by any means.[32]

Table 1.3 summarizes the differences between goods and services and the implications of these characteristics. Many of the strategies, tools, and frameworks in this text were developed to address these characteristics, which, until the 1980s, had been largely ignored by marketers. Recently it has been suggested that these distinctive characteristics should not be viewed as unique to services but that they are also relevant to goods, that "all products are services," and that "economic exchange is fundamentally about service provision."[33] Although this view is rather abstract, it does suggest that all types of organizations may be able to gain valuable insights from services marketing frameworks, tools, and strategies.

Intangibility

The most basic distinguishing characteristic of services is intangibility. Because services are performances or actions rather than objects, they cannot be seen, felt, tasted,

TABLE 1.3 Goods vs. Services

Goods	Services	Resulting Implications
Tangible	Intangible	Services cannot be inventoried. Services cannot be easily patented. Services cannot be readily displayed or communicated. Pricing is difficult.
Standardized	Heterogeneous	Service delivery and customer satisfaction depend on employee and customer actions. Service quality depends on many uncontrollable factors. There is no sure knowledge that the service delivered matches what was planned and promoted.
Production separate from consumption	Simultaneous production and consumption	Customers participate in and affect the transaction. Customers affect each other. Employees affect the service outcome. Decentralization may be essential. Mass production is difficult.
Nonperishable	Perishable	It is difficult to synchronize supply and demand with services. Services cannot be returned or resold.

Source: A. Parasuraman, V. A. Zeithaml, and L. L. Berry, "A Conceptual Model of Service Quality and Its Implications for Future Research," *Journal of Marketing* 49 (Fall 1985), pp. 41–50. Reprinted by permission of the American Marketing Association.

or touched in the same manner that you can sense tangible goods. For example, health care services are actions (such as surgery, diagnosis, examination, and treatment) performed by providers and directed toward patients and their families. These services cannot actually be seen or touched by the patient, although the patient may be able to see and touch certain tangible components of the service (like the equipment or hospital room). In fact, many services such as health care are difficult for the consumer to grasp even mentally. Even after a diagnosis or surgery has been completed the patient may not fully comprehend the service performed, although tangible evidence of the service (e.g., incision, bandaging, pain) may be quite apparent.

Resulting Marketing Implications Intangibility presents several marketing challenges. Services cannot be inventoried, and therefore fluctuations in demand are often difficult to manage. For example, there is tremendous demand by Canadians to visit Florida in the winter, and much less demand in July. Yet resort owners have the same number of rooms to sell year-round. Services cannot be easily patented, and new service concepts can therefore easily be copied by competitors. Services cannot be readily displayed or easily communicated to customers, so quality may be difficult for consumers to assess. Decisions about what to include in advertising and other promotional materials are challenging, as is pricing. The actual costs of a "unit of service" are hard to determine, and the price–quality relationship is complex.

Heterogeneity

Because services are performances, frequently produced by humans, no two services will be precisely alike. The employees delivering the service frequently are the service in the customer's eyes, and people may differ in their performance from day to day or even hour to hour. Heterogeneity also results because no two customers are precisely alike; each will have unique demands or experience the service in a unique way. Thus the heterogeneity connected with services is largely the result of human interaction (between and among employees and customers) and all of the vagaries that accompany it. For example, a tax accountant may provide a different service experience to two different customers on the same day depending on their individual needs and personalities and on whether the accountant is interviewing them when he or she is fresh in the morning or tired at the end of a long day of meetings.

Resulting Marketing Implications   Because services are heterogeneous across time, organizations, and people, ensuring consistent service quality is challenging. Quality actually depends on many factors that cannot be fully controlled by the service supplier, such as the ability of the consumer to articulate his or her needs, the ability and willingness of personnel to satisfy those needs, the presence (or absence) of other customers, and the level of demand for the service. Because of these complicating factors, the service manager cannot always know for sure that the service is being delivered in a manner consistent with what was originally planned and promoted. Sometimes services may be provided by a third party, further increasing the potential heterogeneity of the offering.

Simultaneous Production and Consumption

Whereas most goods are produced first, then sold and consumed, most services are sold first and then produced and consumed simultaneously. For example, an automobile can be manufactured in Windsor, shipped to Vancouver, sold two months later, and consumed over a period of years. But restaurant services cannot be provided until they have been sold, and the dining experience is essentially produced and consumed at the same time. Frequently this situation also means that the customer is present while the service is being produced and thus views and may even take part in the production process. Simultaneity also means that customers will frequently interact with each other during the service production process and thus may affect each others' experiences. For example, strangers seated next to each other in an airplane may well affect the nature of the service experience for each other. That passengers understand this fact is clearly apparent in the way business travellers will often go to great lengths to be sure they are not seated next to families with small children. Another outcome of simultaneous production and consumption is that service producers find themselves playing a role as part of the product itself and as an essential ingredient in the service experience for the consumer.

Resulting Marketing Implications   Because services often are produced and consumed at the same time, mass production is difficult. The quality of service and customer satisfaction will be highly dependent on what happens in "real time," including actions of employees and the interactions between employees and customers. Clearly the real-time nature of services also results in advantages in terms of opportunities to customize offerings for individual consumers. Simultaneous production and consumption also means that it is not usually possible to gain significant economies of scale through centralization. Often, operations need to be relatively decentralized so that the service can be delivered directly to the consumer in convenient locations, although the growth of technology-delivered services is changing this requirement for many services. Also, because of simultaneous production and consumption, the customer is involved in and observes the production process and thus may affect (positively or negatively) the outcome of the service transaction.

Perishability

Perishability refers to the fact that services cannot be saved, stored, resold, or returned. A seat on an airplane or in a restaurant, an hour of a lawyer's time, or telephone line capacity not used cannot be reclaimed and used or resold at a later time. Perishability is in contrast to goods that can be stored in inventory or resold another day, or even returned if the consumer is unhappy. Wouldn't it be nice if a bad haircut could be returned or resold to another consumer? Perishability makes this action an unlikely possibility for most services.

Resulting Marketing Implications   A primary issue that marketers face in relation to service perishability is the inability to inventory. Demand forecasting and creative planning for capacity utilization are therefore important and challenging decision areas. The fact that services cannot typically be returned or resold also implies a need for strong recovery strategies when things do go wrong. For example, although a bad haircut cannot be returned, the hairdresser can and should have strategies for recovering the customer's goodwill if and when such a problem occurs.

Challenges and Questions for Service Marketers

Because of the basic characteristics of services, marketers of services face some very real and distinctive challenges. Answers to questions such as the ones listed here still elude managers of services:

How can service quality be defined and improved when the product is intangible and nonstandardized?

How can new services be designed and tested effectively when the service is essentially an intangible process?

How can the firm be certain it is communicating a consistent and relevant image when so many elements of the marketing mix communicate to customers and some of these elements are the service providers themselves?

How does the firm accommodate fluctuating demand when capacity is fixed and the service itself is perishable?

How can the firm best motivate and select service employees who, because the service is delivered in real time, become a critical part of the product itself?

How should prices be set when it is difficult to determine actual costs of production and price may be inextricably intertwined with perceptions of quality?

How should the firm be organized so that good strategic and tactical decisions are made when a decision in any of the functional areas of marketing, operations, and human resources may have significant impact on the other two areas?

How can the balance between standardization and personalization be determined to maximize both the efficiency of the organization and the satisfaction of its customers?

How can the organization protect new service concepts from competitors when service processes cannot be readily patented?

How does the firm communicate quality and value to consumers when the offering is intangible and cannot be readily tried or displayed?

How can the organization ensure the delivery of consistent quality service when both the organization's employees and the customers themselves can affect the service outcome?

➤ SERVICES MARKETING MIX

The preceding questions are some of the many raised by managers and marketers of services that will be addressed throughout the text through a variety of tools and strategies. Sometimes these tools are adaptations of traditional marketing tools, as with the services marketing mix presented here. Other times they are radically new, as in the case of service blueprinting presented in Chapter 9.

Traditional Marketing Mix

One of the most basic concepts in marketing is the marketing mix, defined as the elements an organization controls that can be used to satisfy or communicate with customers. The traditional marketing mix is composed of the four Ps: *product, price, place* (distribution), and *promotion*.[34] These elements appear as core decision variables in any marketing text or marketing plan. The notion of a mix implies that all the variables are interrelated and depend on each other to some extent. Further, the marketing mix philosophy implies an optimal mix of the four factors for a given market segment at a given point in time.

Key strategy decision areas for each of the four Ps are captured in the first four columns in Table 1.4. Careful management of product, place, promotion, and price will clearly also be essential to the successful marketing of services. However, the strategies for the four Ps require some modifications when applied to services. For example,

TABLE 1.4

Expanded Marketing Mix for Services

Product	Place	Promotion	Price
Physical good features	Channel type	Promotion blend	Flexibility
Quality level	Exposure	Salespeople	Price level
Accessories	Intermediaries	Selection	Terms
Packaging	Outlet locations	Training	Differentiation
Warranties	Transportation	Incentives	Discounts
Product lines	Storage	Advertising	Allowances
Branding	Managing channels	Media types	
		Types of ads	
		Sales promotion	
		Publicity	
		Internet/Web strategy	

People	Physical Evidence	Process
Employees	Facility design	Flow of activities
Recruiting	Equipment	Standardized
Training	Signage	Customized
Motivation	Employee dress	Number of steps
Rewards	Other tangibles	Simple
Teamwork	Reports	Complex
Customers	Business cards	Customer
Education	Statements	involvement
Training	Guarantees	

traditionally promotion is thought of as involving decisions related to sales, advertising, sales promotions, and publicity. In services these factors are also important, but because services are produced and consumed simultaneously, service delivery people (such as clerks, ticket takers, nurses, and phone personnel) are involved in real-time promotion of the service even if their jobs are typically defined in terms of the operational function they perform.

Expanded Mix for Services

Because services are usually produced and consumed simultaneously, customers are often present in the firm's factory, interact directly with the firm's personnel, and are actually part of the service production process. Also, because services are intangible, customers will often be looking for any tangible cue to help them understand the nature of the service experience. For example, in the hotel industry the design and decor of the hotel as well as the appearance and attitudes of its employees will influence customer perceptions and experiences.

Acknowledgment of the importance of these additional variables has led services marketers to adopt the concept of an expanded marketing mix for services shown in the three remaining columns in Table 1.4.[35] In addition to the traditional four Ps, the services marketing mix includes *people, physical evidence,* and *process.*

> **People**   All human actors who play a part in service delivery and thus influence the buyer's perceptions: namely, the firm's personnel, the customer, and other customers in the service environment.

All the human actors participating in the delivery of a service provide cues to the customer regarding the nature of the service itself. How these people are dressed, their personal appearance, and their attitudes and behaviours all influence the customer's perceptions of the service. The service provider or contact person can be very important. In fact, for some services, such as consulting, counselling, teaching, and other professional relationship-based services, the provider *is* the service. In other cases the contact person may play what appears to be a relatively small part in service delivery—for instance, a telephone installer, an airline baggage handler, or an equipment delivery dispatcher. Yet research suggests that even these providers may be the focal point of service encounters that can prove critical for the organization.

In many service situations, customers themselves can also influence service delivery, thus affecting service quality and their own satisfaction. For example, health care patients greatly affect the quality of service they receive when they either comply or don't comply with health regimens prescribed by the provider.

Customers not only influence their own service outcomes, but they can influence other customers as well. In a theater, at a ball game, or in a classroom, customers can influence the quality of service received by others—either enhancing or detracting from other customers' experiences.

> **Physical evidence**   The environment in which the service is delivered and where the firm and customer interact, and any tangible components that facilitate performance or communication of the service.

The physical evidence of service includes all the tangible representations of the service such as brochures, signage, and equipment. In some cases it includes the physical facility where the service is offered—the "servicescape"—for example, the retail bank branch facility. In other cases, such as telecommunication services, the physical facility may be irrelevant. In this case other tangibles such as billing statements and appearance of the repair truck may be important indicators of quality. Physical evidence cues provide

WestJet: Aligning People, Processes, and Physical Evidence

WestJet, founded only 10 years ago, has quickly come to occupy a solid position in the minds of Canadian travellers. Modelled on the success of Southwest Airlines, WestJet positions itself on value, and all aspects of its services marketing mix must sing from the same page if it hopes to remain successful.

Since its inception as a regional carrier flying to five cities with three used planes, WestJet now flies to more than 30 cities across North America with five times as many planes—many of which are new 737-700s. Besides expansion itself, other tangible demonstrations of its successful service strategy include being named Canada's third-most-respected corporation in a 2004 survey conducted by Ipsos Reid (it placed second in the same survey a year earlier).

Success has come for a number of reasons. The cornerstone of the value proposition is, of course, low pricing, which is made possible by having the lowest cost structure coupled with an engaged, high-performing staff. The combination makes for great value. It is clear that all of WestJet's marketing mix is aligned around this value proposition. The three new marketing mix variables all reinforce the same message:

- *People.* WestJet has a unique employee culture—so unique that it placed first in the 2005 Canadian Corporate Culture study conducted by *Canadian Business* magazine and Waterstone Human Capital, Ltd. It was especially singled out for its "entrepreneurial spirit," "delivering what they promise," and "winning attitude." Employees are carefully selected, well trained, and empowered to get the job done. The company celebrates its success, provides the necessary tools and training, promotes from within, shares its profits, and encourages employees to become owners through a generous matching share-purchase program. All advertisements seem to be targeted as much at its own employees ("An Important Message from an Owner") as its customers. In 2004, WestJet was rated first in customer service.

- *Processes.* The service delivery process must also reinforce value. Like Southwest, WestJet reduces pilot training and maintenance costs by buying only one type of aircraft. They also focus on short average flight durations and quick airport turnaround times, permitting them to fly more people more cheaply. WestJet does not transfer baggage to connecting flights, charges for all food, and encourages "guests" to buy their tickets online and use Web Check-In or Self-Serve Check-In Kiosks. Unlike Southwest, though, they do permit travellers to pre-select their seats. To date, WestJet's processes have been rated first in providing high-quality products and services, and on-time performance hovers in the low 90 percent range—good enough to be ranked number two in North America. Even its Investors Relations group is well regarded for its efficiency, being voted "Best Communication within the Retail Industry" by *IR Magazine*.

- *Physical evidence.* WestJet's tangible evidence reinforces its low-cost, fun atmosphere. Employees dress casually to reinforce the fun and to further emphasize the airline's commitment to its employee's comfort; advertisements stress the corporate culture and the key role of the employee; and the website plays up the fun image with amazing trivia—did you know for instance, that Canadians eat more KD (Kraft Dinner) per capita than any other nation on earth or that WestJet has 31 Karens, 39 Lisas, 61 Jens, 67 Davids, 46 Michelles, 86 Michaels, and 1 Yoga?

But as it continues to expand, WestJet's services marketing mix is gradually changing. Some observers are beginning to wonder if these changes are putting WestJet's strategy at risk. Consider the following decisions: purchasing new Boeing 737-700s; leather seats; seatback ExpressVu TVs; and Air Miles rewards and the launch of an expensive TV campaign rather than continuing to rely on print and radio. As well, with the addition of long-haul flights (including Honolulu, Maui, Miami, and Orlando), the company is moving away from its strategy of short-haul, point-to-point, rapid turnaround, no-layover flights. With Air Canada bringing down its services (removal of free meals and charging for pillows and blankets in economy class) and WestJet increasing its services, is WestJet at risk of losing its differentiation?

Source: Courtesy of WestJet.

Sources: CCNMatthews, "WestJet Corporate Culture Most Admired in Canada Independent Study Reveals," news release, October 20, 2005, available www2.ccnmatthews.com/scripts/dnrp/release.asp?d=/cnrpxml/2005/10/20/292445_1_1020200583810AM.xml&t=WJA, accessed September 14, 2006; N. Ramage, "WestJet on the Fly," *Marketing* 110, no. 22 (June 20, 2005), p. 13; www.westjet.com.

excellent opportunities for the firm to send consistent and strong messages regarding the organization's purpose, the intended market segments, and the nature of the service.

Process The actual procedures, mechanisms, and flow of activities by which the service is delivered—the service delivery and operating systems.

The actual delivery steps that the customer experiences, or the operational flow of the service, also give customers evidence on which to judge the service. Some services are very complex, requiring the customer to follow a complicated and extensive series of actions to complete the process. Another distinguishing characteristic of the process that can provide evidence to the customer is whether the service follows a production-line/standardized approach or whether the process is an empowered/customized one. For example, two successful airline companies, WestJet and Singapore Airlines, follow very different process models. WestJet is a no-frills, low-priced airline that offers mostly frequent, relatively short flights. All the evidence it provides is consistent with its vision and market position, as illustrated in Exhibit 1.1. Singapore Airlines, on the other hand, focuses on the business traveller and is concerned with meeting individual traveller needs. Thus, its process is highly customized to the individual, and employees are empowered to provide nonstandard service when needed. Both airlines have been very successful.

The three new marketing mix elements (people, physical evidence, and process) are included in the marketing mix as separate elements because any or all of them may influence the customer's level of satisfaction and repurchase decisions. The traditional elements as well as the new marketing mix elements will be explored in depth in future chapters.

STAYING FOCUSED ON THE CUSTOMER

A critical theme running throughout this text is *customer focus.* In fact, the subtitle of the book is "Integrating Customer Focus Across the Firm." From the firm's point of view, all strategies are developed with an eye to the customer, and all implementations are carried out with an understanding of their impact on the customer. From a practical perspective, decisions regarding new services and communication plans will integrate the customer's point of view; operations and human resource decisions will be considered in terms of their impact on customers. All the tools, strategies, and frameworks included in this text have customers at their foundation. The services marketing mix just described is clearly an important tool that addresses the uniqueness of services, keeping the customer at the centre.

In this text, we also view customers as assets to be valued, developed, and retained. The strategies and tools we offer thus focus on customer relationship building and loyalty as opposed to a more transactional focus in which customers are viewed as one-time revenue producers. This text looks at customer relationship management not as a software program but as an entire architecture or business philosophy. Every chapter in this text can be considered a component needed to build a complete customer relationship management approach.

SUMMARY

This chapter has set the stage for further learning about services marketing by presenting information on changes in the world economy and business practice that have driven the focus on service: the fact that services dominate the modern economies of the world; the focus on service as a competitive business imperative; specific needs of the deregulated and professional service industries; the role of new service concepts growing from technological advances; and the realization that the characteristics of services result in unique challenges and opportunities. The chapter presented a broad definition of services as deeds, processes, and performances, and it drew distinctions between pure services, value-added services, customer service, and derived service.

Building on this fundamental understanding of the service economy, the chapter went on to present the key characteristics of services that underlie the need for distinct strategies and concepts for managing service businesses. These basic characteristics are that services are intangible, heterogeneous, produced and consumed simultaneously, and perishable. Because of these characteristics, service managers face a number of challenges in marketing, including the complex problem of how to deliver quality services consistently.

The chapter ended by describing two themes that provide the foundation for future chapters: the expanded marketing mix for services; and customer focus as a unifying theme. The remainder of the text focuses on exploring the unique opportunities and challenges faced by organizations that sell and deliver services and on developing solutions that will help you become an effective services champion and manager.

Discussion Questions

1. What distinguishes service offerings from customer service? Provide specific examples.
2. How is technology changing the nature of service?
3. What are the basic characteristics of services vs. goods? What are the implications of these characteristics for IBM Global Service or for WestJet?
4. One of the underlying frameworks for the text is the services marketing mix. Discuss why each of the three new mix elements (process, people, and physical evidence) is included. How might each of these communicate with or help to satisfy an organization's customers?
5. Think of a service job you have had or currently have. How effective, in your opinion, was or is the organization in managing the elements of the services marketing mix?
6. Again, think of a service job you have had or currently have. How did or does the organization handle relevant challenges listed in Table 1.3?
7. How can quality service be used in a manufacturing context for competitive advantage? Think of your answer to this question in the context of automobiles or computers or some other manufactured product you have actually purchased.

Exercises

1. Roughly calculate your budget for an average month. What percentage of your budget goes for services vs. goods? Do the services you purchase have value? In what sense? If you had to cut back on your expenses, what would you cut out?
2. Visit two local retail service providers that you believe are positioned very differently (such as Dollarama and The Bay or Burger King and a fine restaurant). From your own observations, compare their strategies on the elements of the services marketing mix.

3. Try a service you have never tried before on the Internet. Analyze the benefits of this service. Was enough information provided to make the service easy to use? How would you compare this service to other methods of obtaining the same benefits?

⟶ Notes

1. D. Kirkpatrick, "Inside Sam's $100 Billion Growth Machine," *Fortune*, June 14, 2004, pp. 80–98; D. Kirkpatrick, "IBM, from Big Blue Dinosaur to E-Business Animal," *Fortune*, April 26, 1999, pp.116-26; W.M. Bulkeley, "These Days, Big Blue Is About Big Services Not Just Big Boxes," *The Wall Street Journal*, June 11, 2001, p. A1; David Kirkpatrick, "IBM Shares Its Secrets," *Fortune* 152, no. 5 (September 5, 2005), p. 128; Darryl K. Taft, "Research to the Rescue: IBM Research Unit Turns to Services to Help Propel High-Value Business Opportunities," *eWeek* 21, no. 26 (June 28, 2004), p. 20; Shane Schick, "IBM Inks TD Desktop Deal for $720M," *Computing Canada* 29, no. 21, p. 1.
2. D. Brady, "Why Service Stinks," *BusinessWeek,* October 23, 2000, pp. 118–28.
3. J. B. Quinn, J. J. Baruch, and P. C. Paquette, "Technology in Services," *Scientific American* 257, no. 6 (December 1987), pp. 50–58.
4. S. L. Vargo and R. F. Lusch, "Evolving to a New Dominant Logic for Marketing," *Journal of Marketing* 68 (January 2004), pp. 1–17.
5. International Trade Canada, "Canada and Trade in Services," March 29, 2006, available www.dfait-maeci.gc.ca/tna-nac/TS/canada-ts-en.asp, accessed September 14, 2006, and Anonymous, "Meeting the Challenges of a Services Economy," *Micro: The Micro-Economic Research Bulletin* 10, no. 1 (Winter/Spring 2005), p. 1.
6. International Trade Canada, "Canada and Trade in Services"; Industry Canada, "Services Industries," 2003, available www.strategis.gc.ca, accessed November 8, 2005.
7. M. Sawhney, S. Balasubramanian, and V. V. Krishnan, "Creating Growth with Services," *Sloan Management Review,* Winter 2004, pp. 34–43.
8. T. Smart, "Jack Welch's Encore," *BusinessWeek,* October 28, 1996, pp. 155–60; and GE company data, 2000.
9. D. Decloet, "Selling the Bank of GM Is Probably a Sign of Desperation," GlobeandMail.com, October 20, 2005.
10. J. A. Alexander and M. W. Hordes, *S-Business: Reinventing the Services Organization* (New York: SelectBooks, 2003); R. Oliva and R. Kallenberg, "Managing the Transition from Products to Services," *International Journal of Service Industry Management* 14, no. 2 (2003), pp. 160–72.
11. This discussion is based on interviews conducted by Gary Knisely that appeared in *Advertising Age* on January 15, 1979; February 19, 1979; March 19, 1979; and May 14, 1979.
12. L. Berry, *Discovering the Soul of Service* (New York: The Free Press, 1999).
13. R. T. Rust, C. Moorman, and P. R. Dickson, "Getting Return on Quality: Revenue Expansion, Cost Reduction, or Both?" *Journal of Marketing* 66 (October 2002), pp. 7–24.
14. J. L. Heskett, T. O. Jones, G. W. Loveman, W. E. Sasser Jr., and L. A. Schlesinger, "Putting the Service–Profit Chain to Work," *Harvard Business Review,* March/April 1994, pp. 164–74.

15. E. W. Anderson and V. Mittal, "Strengthening the Satisfaction–Profit Chain," *Journal of Service Research* 3, no. 2 (November 2000), pp. 107–20.

16. "Predictive Capabilities," www.theacsi.org, accessed October 13, 2004.

17. Adam J. Stoehr, "Impressive Stock Performance of CAE Winners from 1990–2005," November 1, 2005, available www.nqi.ca/articles/article_details.aspx?ID=547, accessed September 14, 2006.

18. C. Fishman, "But Wait, You Promised . . . ," *Fast Company,* April 2001, pp. 116–27.

19. D. Brady, "Why Service Stinks," *BusinessWeek,* October 23, 2000, pp. 116–28.

20. "Latest Increase in ACSI Bodes Well for the Economy," www.theacsi.org releases. Posted June 4, 2004, accessed October 13, 2004.

21. Laura Penny, *Your Call Is Important to Us: The Truth About Bullshit* (Toronto: McClelland & Stewart Ltd., 2005), back cover.

22. L. P. Willcocks and R. Plant, "Getting from Bricks to Clicks," *Sloan Management Review,* Spring 2001, pp. 50–59.

23. "Revolution Digital Tomorrow Report: Technologies That Will Change Marketing," *Revolution,* February 2001, pp. 51–65.

24. S. Fox and L. Rainie, "Vital Decisions," Washington, DC: The Pew Internet & American Life Project, available at www.pewinternet.org, 2002, accessed September 25, 2006.

25. M. J. Bitner, S. W. Brown, and M. L. Meuter, "Technology Infusion in Service Encounters," *Journal of the Academy of Marketing Science* 28 (Winter 2000), pp. 138–49.

26. M. J. Bitner, "Self-Service Technologies: What Do Customers Expect?" *Marketing Management,* Spring 2001, pp. 10–11.

27. R. Hallowell, "Service in E-Commerce: Findings from Exploratory Research," Harvard Business School, Module Note, N9-800-418, May 31, 2000.

28. D. G. Mick and S. Fournier, "Paradoxes of Technology: Consumer Cognizance, Emotions, and Coping Strategies," *Journal of Consumer Research* 25 (September 1998), pp. 123–47.

29. A. Parasuraman and C. L. Colby, *Techno-Ready Marketing: How and Why Your Customers Adopt Technology* (New York: The Free Press, 2001).

30. D. Khandelwal and S. Kell, "Customer Care in a New World," North American Contact Center Summit, January 23, 2002.

31. Discussion of these issues is found in many services marketing publications. The discussion here is based on V. A. Zeithaml, A. Parasuraman, and L. L. Berry, "Problems and Strategies in Services Marketing," *Journal of Marketing* 49 (Spring 1985), pp. 33–46.

32. For research supporting the idea of goods–services continua, see D. Iacobucci, "An Empirical Examination of Some Basic Tenets in Services: Goods–Services Continua," in *Advances in Services Marketing and Management,* ed. T. A. Swartz, D. E. Bowen, and S. W. Brown (Greenwich, CT: JAI Press, 1992), vol. 1, pp. 23–52.

33. S. L. Vargo and R. F. Lusch, "The Four Service Marketing Myths," *Journal of Service Research* 6 (May 2004), pp. 324–35.

34. E. J. McCarthy and W. D. Perrault Jr., *Basic Marketing: A Global Managerial Approach* (Burr Ridge, IL: Richard D. Irwin, 1993).

35. B. H. Booms and M. J. Bitner, "Marketing Strategies and Organizational Structures for Service Firms," in *Marketing of Services,* ed. J. H. Donnelly and W. R. George (Chicago: American Marketing Association, 1981), pp. 47–51.

Chapter 2

Conceptual Framework of This Book: The Gaps Model of Service Quality

THIS CHAPTER'S OBJECTIVES ARE TO

→ 1. Introduce a framework, called the gaps model of service quality, which is used to organize this textbook.

→ 2. Demonstrate that the gaps model is a useful framework for understanding service quality in an organization.

→ 3. Demonstrate that the most critical service quality gap to close is the customer gap, the difference between customer expectations and perceptions.

→ 4. Show that four gaps that occur in companies, which we call provider gaps, are responsible for the customer gap.

→ 5. Identify the factors responsible for each of the four provider gaps.

SERVICE QUALITY AT DELTA HOTELS

Source: Courtesy of Delta Hotels.

Delta Hotels (www.deltahotels.ca) is one of the largest and most successful hotel chains in Canada. Rising from humble beginnings as a single unit motor inn in British Columbia over 40 years ago, Delta boasts 40 properties, 11,300 rooms, and 7,000 employees nationwide. The chain has become a recognized service leader in North America—a rare distinction among hotel operators. It received two Canada Awards for Excellence—for quality (2000) and for a healthy workplace (2004)—from the National Quality Institute. It has also been voted one of "The 50 Best Employers in

Canada" by the *Globe and Mail*'s magazine Report on Business, in five of the past six years. The company prides itself on its innovative service offerings, including its famous "One-Minute Check-In" that guarantees free rooms to members of Delta Privilege, its guest recognition program, who wait longer than one minute for check-in service; its "Blue Ribbon" guarantee that promises rooms in perfect order at check-in; its pet policy that allows animals to stay onsite; and its chain-wide family program.

Take a moment to examine Delta's mission statement:

The mission of Delta Hotels is to be the full service, Canadian, hotel management company of choice with the dominant first-class brand. In carrying out this mission, Delta will be guided by our Quality Approach, and will be known:

To Owners as:
- The brand of choice for the hotel owner of first-class hotels
- An efficient operator who generates superior returns on their assets

To Guests as:
- A hotel company that offers great value
- A hotel company that has warm, friendly, sincere, customer-focused employees
- A hotel company that offers consistent delivery of products and services, is innovative, and [is] consistently improving service

To Employees as:
- A company where employees can contribute and grow
- A great place to work where a culture exists that recognizes "the way we deal with our employees will be reflected in the manner that they interact with our guests"
- A company that demonstrates and encourages an attitude that is supportive of the social needs of the community[1]

You may now be wondering why other North American hotels haven't been recognized with awards similar to Delta. This textbook is focused on highlighting strategies and tactics that companies can use to minimize any gaps that might occur between what customers expect in a service encounter and what they believe they have received in that encounter. Delta Hotels' mission statement, its more innovative service offerings briefly highlighted here, and its recent accolades indicate that the company values its customers and employees, invests a great deal of importance in service design and standards, and can deliver on its promises. As you will read in this chapter and throughout the text, each of these plays an important strategic part in matching customer perceptions with expectations.

Effective services marketing is a complex undertaking that involves many different strategies, skills, and tasks. Executives have long been confused about how to approach this complicated topic in an organized manner. This textbook is designed around one approach: viewing services in a structured, integrated way called the *gaps model of service quality.*[2] Sections of the book are tied to each of the gaps described in this chapter.

⟼ THE CUSTOMER GAP

The *customer gap* is the difference between customer expectations and perceptions (see Figure 2.1). Customer expectations are standards or reference points that customers bring into the service experience, whereas customer perceptions are subjective assessments of actual service experiences. Customer expectations often consist of what a customer believes should or will happen. For example, when you visit an expensive restaurant, you expect a high level of service, one that is considerably superior to the level you would expect in a fast-food restaurant. Closing the gap between what customers expect and what they perceive is critical to delivering quality service; it forms the basis for the gaps model.

Because customer satisfaction and customer focus are so critical to the competitiveness of firms, any company interested in delivering quality service must begin with a clear understanding of its customers. This understanding is relatively easy for an organization as small as the Island Hotel but very difficult for a large organization in which managers are not in direct contact with customers. For this reason, we will devote the first section of the textbook to describing the relevant customer concepts so that the focus of everything can relate back to these concepts. Considerable evidence exists that consumer evaluation processes differ for goods and services and that these differences affect the way service providers market their organizations. Unfortunately, much of what is known and written about consumer evaluation processes pertains specifically to goods. The assumption appears to be that services, if not identical to goods, are at least similar enough in the consumer's mind that they are chosen and evaluated in the same manner. We will detail what is known about customer behaviour in services in Chapter 3.

The sources of customer expectations are marketer-controlled factors (such as pricing, advertising, sales promises) as well as factors that the marketer has limited ability to

FIGURE 2.1

The Customer Gap

The Customer Gap

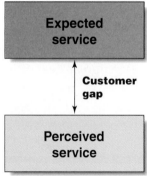

affect (innate personal needs, word-of-mouth communications, competitive offerings). In a perfect world, expectations and perceptions would be identical. In practice, there is often a gap between what customers expect and what they receive, and we will devote virtually the entire textbook to describing strategies and practices designed to close this customer gap. We will describe customer expectations in detail in Chapter 4 and customer perceptions in Chapter 5.

⟶ THE PROVIDER GAPS

To close the all-important customer gap, the gaps model suggests that four other gaps—the *provider gaps*—need to be closed. These gaps occur within the organization providing the service (hence the term *provider gaps*) and include

Gap 1: Not knowing what customers expect

Gap 2: Not selecting the right service designs and standards

Gap 3: Not delivering to service designs and standards

Gap 4: Not matching performance to promises

The rest of this chapter is devoted to a description of the full Gaps model.

Provider Gap 1: Not Knowing What Customers Expect

Provider Gap 1 is the difference between customer expectations of service and company understanding of those expectations. A primary cause for not meeting customers' expectations is that the firm lacks accurate understanding of exactly what those expectations are. Many reasons exist for managers not being aware of what customers expect: they may not interact directly with customers, they may be unwilling to ask about expectations, or they may be unprepared to address them. In this text, we broaden the responsibility for the first provider gap from managers alone to any employee with the authority to influence service policies. In today's organizations, the authority to make adjustments in service delivery is often delegated to empowered teams and front-line people.

Figure 2.2 shows the key factors responsible for Provider Gap 1. An inadequate marketing research orientation is one of the critical factors. When management or empowered employees do not acquire accurate information about customers' expectations, Provider Gap 1 is large. Formal and informal methods to capture information about customer expectations must be developed through marketing research. This chapter's Global Feature discusses techniques that IKEA and other companies have used to identify customer expectations.

Another key factor that is related to Provider Gap 1 is lack of upward communication. Front-line employees often know a great deal about customers; if management is not in contact with frontline employees and does not understand what they know, the gap widens.

Also related to Provider Gap 1 is a lack of company strategies to retain customers and strengthen relationships with them, an approach called relationship marketing. When organizations have strong relationships with existing customers, Provider Gap 1 is less likely to occur. Relationship marketing is distinct from transactional marketing, the term used to describe the more conventional emphasis on acquiring new customers rather than retaining them. When companies focus too much

FIGURE 2.2

Key Factors Leading
to Provider Gap 1

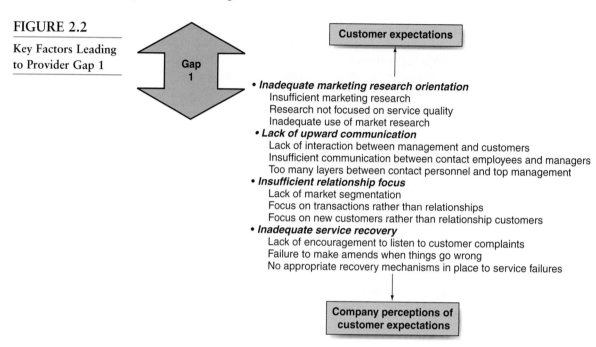

Customer expectations

- *Inadequate marketing research orientation*
  Insufficient marketing research
  Research not focused on service quality
  Inadequate use of market research
- *Lack of upward communication*
  Lack of interaction between management and customers
  Insufficient communication between contact employees and managers
  Too many layers between contact personnel and top management
- *Insufficient relationship focus*
  Lack of market segmentation
  Focus on transactions rather than relationships
  Focus on new customers rather than relationship customers
- *Inadequate service recovery*
  Lack of encouragement to listen to customer complaints
  Failure to make amends when things go wrong
  No appropriate recovery mechanisms in place to service failures

**Company perceptions of
customer expectations**

on attracting new customers, they may fail to understand the changing needs and expectations of their current customers. Technology affords companies the ability to acquire and integrate vast quantities of data on customers that can be used to build relationships. Frequent-flyer travel programs conducted by airlines, car rental companies, and hotels are among the most familiar programs of this type.

The final key factor associated with Provider Gap 1 is lack of service recovery. Even the best companies, with the best of intentions and clear understanding of their customers' expectations, sometimes fail. It is critical for an organization to understand the importance of service recovery—why people complain, what they expect when they complain, and how to develop effective service recovery strategies for dealing with inevitable service failures. Such strategies might involve a well-defined complaint-handling procedure and an emphasis on empowering employees to react on the spot, in real time, to fix the failure; other times it involves a service guarantee or ways to compensate the customer for the unfulfilled promise.

To address the factors in Provider Gap l, this text will cover topics that include how to understand customers through multiple research strategies (Chapter 6), how to build strong relationships and understand customer needs over time (Chapter 7), and how to implement recovery strategies when things go wrong (Chapter 8). Through these strategies, Provider Gap 1 can be minimized.

Provider Gap 2: Not Having the Right Service Designs and Standards

Accurate perceptions of customers' expectations are necessary, but not sufficient, for delivering superior quality service. Another prerequisite is the presence of service designs and performance standards that reflect those accurate perceptions. A recurring theme in service companies is the difficulty in translating customer expectations into service quality specifications that employees can understand and execute. These problems are reflected in Provider Gap 2, the difference between

Global Feature

An International Retailer Puts Customers in the Wish Mode to Begin Closing the Gaps

Finding out what customers expect is the first step in closing all the gaps in the organization to provide service excellence. In Chapter 6 we will talk about many ways that companies determine customer perceptions, including customer surveys and complaints, but understanding what customers expect can often be more challenging. Putting customers in the "wish mode" is an innovative approach to closing Gap 1 that proved successful for IKEA (www.ikea.ca), the world's largest furniture retailer, when it opened its Chicago retail outlet.

In this approach, nine groups of a dozen customers each were asked to dream up their ideal IKEA shopping experience. They were told to pretend that all IKEA stores had been destroyed and that new ones had to be designed from scratch. How would the store look? What would the shopping experience be like? Jason Magidson, who helped IKEA create the process, reported that customers responded with statements like the following:

> "I never feel disoriented because I always know exactly where I am in relation to every department."

> "If I am buying one item, all of the other items that go with it are nearby."

> "Shopping is a pleasant, relaxing experience."

Even though they were not technical experts, customers were asked to actually draw up a design for a store that would satisfy their needs.

What is significant about IKEA's approach is not just that the company asked customers what they expected but that they subsequently incorporated these expectations into the service design for the store. Designers created a multistorey octagonal building with an atrium in the centre that formed a home base for shoppers, addressing their concern about being able to find items easily. In keeping with another customer expectation, items were grouped together with related products. When shoppers were tired or hungry, they could go to the cafeteria-style restaurant on the upper floor that served Swedish food. IKEA's customers were so satisfied with the store (85% rated it as "excellent" or "very good") that they returned more and spent about an hour longer than they did in other IKEA stores. These actions close Gap 2, because service design was based on customer expectations.

IKEA has done an excellent job of closing all four provider gaps. The company's supplier network is carefully chosen and managed to ensure quality and consistency. Despite the fact that the company has stores in more than 34 countries, it keeps standards, designs, and approaches very consistent everywhere, thereby reducing Gap 2. Servicescapes—the indoor and outdoor physical environments—are unique and customer-focused, further closing Gap 2. IKEA is also well known for its strong employee culture and careful hiring and training, factors that help reduce Gap 3. In Chapter 13, we will tell you about another way the company closes Gap 3: its innovative service concept that involves customers in the delivery, assembly and creation of its products. To accomplish this service, the company educates its customers thoroughly with its scriptlike catalogues, thereby helping to close Gap 4.

Source: Michael Newman/Photo Edit.

Sources: Jason Magidson and Gregg Brandyberry, "Putting Customers in the 'Wish Mode,'" *Harvard Business Review,* September 2001, pp. 26–27; Barbara Solomon, "A Swedish Company Corners the Business: Worldwide," *Management Review,* April 1991, pp. 10–13; Richard Normann and Rafael Ramfrez, "From Value Chain to Value Constellation: Designing Interactive Strategy," *Harvard Business Review,* July/August 1993, pp. 65–77; www.ikea.ca.

company understanding of customer expectations and development of customer-driven service designs and standards. Customer-driven standards are different from the conventional performance standards that companies establish for service in that they are based on pivotal *customer* requirements that are *visible* to and *measured* by customers. They are operations standards set to correspond to customer expectations and priorities rather than to company concerns such as productivity or efficiency.

As shown in Figure 2.3, Provider Gap 2 exists in service organizations for a variety of reasons. Those people responsible for setting standards, typically management, sometimes believe that customer expectations are unreasonable or unrealistic. They may also believe that the degree of variability inherent in service defies standardization and therefore that setting standards will not achieve the desired goal. Although some of these assumptions are valid in some situations, they are often only rationalizations of management's reluctance to tackle the challenges of creating standards to deliver excellent service.

Because services are intangible, they are difficult to describe and communicate. This difficulty becomes especially evident when new services are being developed. It is critical that everyone (managers, front-line employees, and behind-the-scenes support staff) work with the same concepts of the new service. For a service that already exists, any attempt to improve it will also suffer unless everyone has the same vision of the service. One of the most important ways to avoid Provider Gap 2 is to clearly design services without oversimplification, incompleteness, subjectivity, and bias. To do so, tools are needed to ensure that new and existing services are carefully developed and improved. Chapter 9 describes the tools that are most effective in service development and design, including service blueprinting, a unique tool for services.

The quality of service delivered by customer contact personnel is critically influenced by how they are evaluated and compensated. Standards signal to contact personnel what the management priorities are and which types of performance really count. When service standards are absent or when standards do not reflect

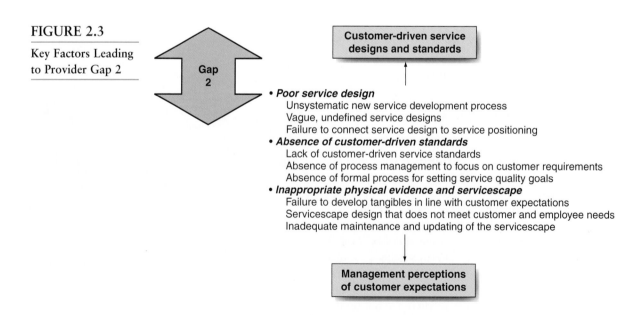

FIGURE 2.3

Key Factors Leading
to Provider Gap 2

Gap
2

**Customer-driven service
designs and standards**

• *Poor service design*
  Unsystematic new service development process
  Vague, undefined service designs
  Failure to connect service design to service positioning
• *Absence of customer-driven standards*
  Lack of customer-driven service standards
  Absence of process management to focus on customer requirements
  Absence of formal process for setting service quality goals
• *Inappropriate physical evidence and servicescape*
  Failure to develop tangibles in line with customer expectations
  Servicescape design that does not meet customer and employee needs
  Inadequate maintenance and updating of the servicescape

**Management perceptions
of customer expectations**

customers' expectations, quality of service is likely to suffer. When standards do reflect what customers expect, the quality of service they receive is likely to be enhanced. The Technology Spotlight in this chapter shows how Amazon.com uses customer-defined standards as the basis for its excellent service performance. Chapter 10 develops the topic of customer-defined service standards and shows that if they are developed appropriately they can have a powerful impact on closing both Provider Gap 2 and the customer gap.

In Chapter 11 we focus on the roles of physical evidence in service design and in meeting customer expectations. The *servicescape,* the physical setting where the service is delivered, is a particular focus of Chapter 11. Think of a restaurant, a hotel, a theme park, a health club, a hospital, or a school. The servicescape—the physical facility—is critical in these industries in terms of communicating about the service and making the entire experience pleasurable. In these cases the servicescape plays a variety of roles, from serving as a visual metaphor for what the company stands for to actually facilitating the activities of both consumers and employees.

Provider Gap 3: Not Delivering to Service Designs and Standards

Once service designs and standards are in place, it would seem that the firm is well on its way to delivering high-quality services. This assumption is true, but is still not enough to deliver excellent service. The firm must have systems, processes, and people in place to ensure that service delivery actually matches (or is even better than) the designs and standards.

Provider Gap 3 is the discrepancy between development of customer-driven service standards and actual service performance by company employees. Even when guidelines exist for performing services well and treating customers correctly, high-quality service performance is not a certainty. Standards must be backed by appropriate resources (people, systems, and technology), and employees must be measured and compensated on the basis of performance along those standards. Thus, even when standards accurately reflect customers' expectations, if the company fails to provide support for those standards—if it does not facilitate, encourage, and require their achievement—standards do no good. When the level of service delivery falls short of the standards, it falls short of what customers expect as well. Narrowing Gap 3—by ensuring that all the resources needed to achieve the standards are in place—reduces the customer gap.

Research has identified many of the critical inhibitors to closing Gap 3 (see Figure 2.4). These factors include employees who do not clearly understand the roles they are to play in the company, employees who experience conflict between customers and company management, poor employee selection, inadequate technology, inappropriate compensation and recognition, and lack of empowerment and teamwork. These factors all relate to the company's human resource function and involve internal practices such as recruitment, training, feedback, job design, motivation, and organizational structure. To deliver better service performance, these issues must be addressed across functions (such as with both marketing and human resources).

Another important variable in Provider Gap 3 is the customer. Even if contact employees and intermediaries are 100 percent consistent in their service delivery, the uncontrollable variables of the customer can introduce variability in service delivery. If customers do not perform their roles appropriately—if, for example, they fail to

FIGURE 2.4

Key Factors Leading
to Provider Gap 3

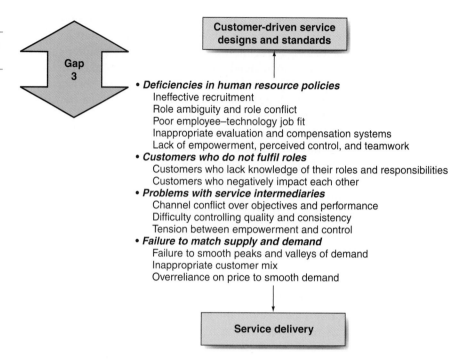

**Customer-driven service
designs and standards**

• *Deficiencies in human resource policies*
   Ineffective recruitment
   Role ambiguity and role conflict
   Poor employee–technology job fit
   Inappropriate evaluation and compensation systems
   Lack of empowerment, perceived control, and teamwork
• *Customers who do not fulfil roles*
   Customers who lack knowledge of their roles and responsibilities
   Customers who negatively impact each other
• *Problems with service intermediaries*
   Channel conflict over objectives and performance
   Difficulty controlling quality and consistency
   Tension between empowerment and control
• *Failure to match supply and demand*
   Failure to smooth peaks and valleys of demand
   Inappropriate customer mix
   Overreliance on price to smooth demand

Service delivery

provide all the information necessary to the provider or neglect to read and follow instructions—service quality is jeopardized. Customers can also negatively influence the quality of service received by others if they are disruptive or take more than their share of a service provider's time. Understanding customer roles and how customers themselves can influence service delivery and outcomes are critical.

A third difficulty associated with Provider Gap 3 involves the challenge in delivering service through such intermediaries as retailers, franchisees, agents, and brokers. Because quality in service occurs in the human interaction between customers and service providers, control over the service encounter by the company is crucial, yet it rarely is fully possible. Most service (and many manufacturing) companies face an even more formidable task: attaining service excellence and consistency in the presence of intermediaries who represent them and interact with their customers yet are not under their direct control. Franchisers of services depend on their franchisees to execute service delivery as they have specified it. And it is in the execution by the franchisee that the customer evaluates the service quality of the company. With franchises and other types of intermediaries, someone other than the producer is responsible for the fulfilment of quality service. For this reason, a firm must develop ways to either control or motivate these intermediaries to meet company goals.

Another issue in Provider Gap 3 is the need in service firms to synchronize demand and capacity. Because services are perishable and cannot be inventoried, service companies frequently face situations of overdemand or underdemand. Lacking inventories to handle overdemand, companies lose sales when capacity is inadequate to handle customer needs. On the other hand, capacity is frequently underutilized in slow periods. Most companies rely on operations strategies such as cross-training or varying the size of the employee pool to synchronize supply and demand. Marketing strategies for managing demand—such as price changes, advertising, promotion, and alternative service offerings—can supplement approaches for managing supply.

Technology Spotlight

Amazon.ca Closes the Gaps

Can an online company be an excellent service provider, identifying customer expectations and meeting them by closing the four provider gaps? Amazon (www.amazon.ca) is a company that exemplifies the use of the strategies needed to provide consistent, accurate, and even personalized service.

Understanding customer expectations is a strategy that Amazon begins when a customer first starts shopping at its online store. From the very first time customers make choices, the company's computers begin profiles on them, offering selections based on a database of previous customers that read similar books or listened to similar music. In the beginning some offerings may not seem on target, but the longer customers shop at Amazon, the more accurately the company identifies their preferences and the more appropriate suggestions become. In time, the company even begins to send emails that are so specific ("We noticed that you purchased the last book by Jonathan Kellerman and we want you to know that he has just published a new book") that it almost seems like the local librarian is calling to let you know your new book is in. One of the company's unique features is "Your Store," a tab on the home page that sends customers to a selection of items that past purchases indicate would be of interest to them.

Customer-defined standards exist for virtually all activities at Amazon, from delivery to communication to service recovery. When you buy a product from Amazon, you select the mode of delivery and the company tells you the expected number of days it will take to receive your merchandise. Standard shipping is three to five days, but two- and one-day shipping are also available. The company has standards for how quickly you are informed when a product is unavailable (immediately), how fast you find out whether an out-of-print book can be located (three weeks), how long you can return items (30 days), and whether you pay return shipping costs (not if it is Amazon's error).

Service performance is where Amazon excels. Orders almost always arrive ahead of the promised date, are accurate, and are in excellent condition because of careful shipping practices. The company's copyrighted 1-Click Ordering allows regular customers to make purchases instantaneously without creating a shopping cart. Customers can track packages and review previous orders at any time. Amazon also makes sure that all its partners, who sell used and new books and other items direct to customers, perform to Amazon's standards. The company verifies performance of each purchase by asking the customer how well the merchant performed, then it posts scores where customers can see them easily.

Managing promises is handled by clear and careful communication on the website. Virtually every page is easy to understand and navigate. For example, the page dealing with returns eliminates customer misunderstanding by clearly spelling out what can be returned (almost everything) and what cannot (items that are gas powered or have flammable liquids, large televisions, opened CDs). The page describes how to repack items and when refunds are given. The page dealing with a customer's account shows all previous purchases and exactly where every ordered item is in the shipping process.

amazon.ca™

Source: Amazon, Amazon.com, the Amazon.com logo, and 1-Click are registered trademarks of Amazon.com, Inc. or its affiliates.

Now visit Chapters' Canadian-owned online store (www.chapters.indigo.ca) to see how it handles each of these provider gaps. Is Chapters as effective as Amazon in closing each gap?

Source: www.Amazon.ca.

We will discuss strategies to deal with the roles of employees in Chapter 12, customers in Chapter 13, intermediaries in Chapter 14, and demand and capacity in Chapter 15.

Provider Gap 4: Not Matching Performance to Promises

Provider Gap 4 illustrates the difference between service delivery and the service provider's external communications. Promises made by a service company through its media advertising, sales force, and other communications can raise customer expectations. The discrepancy between actual and promised service therefore has an adverse effect on the customer gap. Broken promises can occur for many reasons: overpromising in advertising or personal selling, inadequate coordination between operations and marketing, and differences in policies and procedures across service outlets. Figure 2.5 shows the key factors that lead to Provider Gap 4.

In addition to elevating expectations through exaggerated claims, there are other, less obvious ways in which external communications influence customers' assessments. Service companies frequently fail to educate customers appropriately. They also neglect to manage customer expectations of what will be delivered in service transactions and relationships.

One of the major difficulties associated with Provider Gap 4 is that communications to consumers involve issues that cross organizational boundaries. Because service advertising promises what people do, and because what *people* do cannot be controlled like machines, this type of communication involves more than the marketing department. This type of marketing is what we call *interactive marketing*—the marketing between contact people and customers—and it must be coordinated with the conventional types of *external marketing*. When employees do not understand the reality of service delivery, they are likely to make exaggerated promises or fail to communicate well. The result is poor service quality perceptions. Effectively coordinating actual

FIGURE 2.5

Key Factors Leading to Provider Gap 4

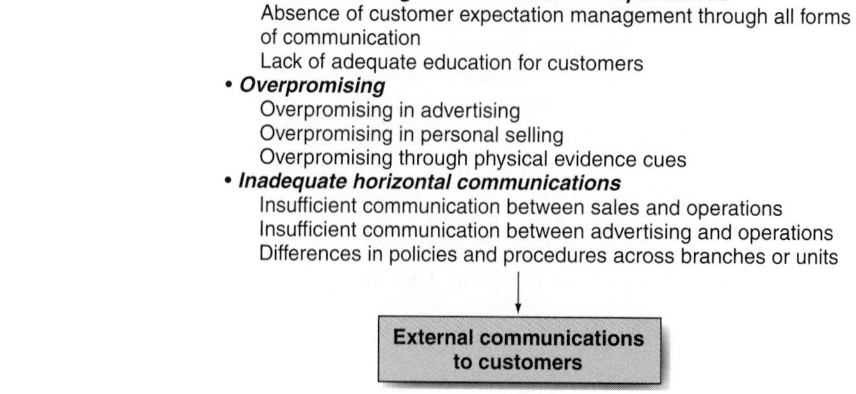

Service delivery

Gap 4

- *Lack of integrated services marketing communications*
  Tendency to view each external communication as independent
  Absence of interactive marketing in communications plan
  Absence of strong internal marketing program
- *Ineffective management of customer expectations*
  Absence of customer expectation management through all forms of communication
  Lack of adequate education for customers
- *Overpromising*
  Overpromising in advertising
  Overpromising in personal selling
  Overpromising through physical evidence cues
- *Inadequate horizontal communications*
  Insufficient communication between sales and operations
  Insufficient communication between advertising and operations
  Differences in policies and procedures across branches or units

External communications to customers

service delivery with external communications, therefore, narrows Provider Gap 4 and favourably affects the customer gap as well.

Another issue in Provider Gap 4 is associated with the pricing of services. With goods, customers possess enough price knowledge before purchase to be able to judge whether a price is fair. With services, customers often have no internal reference points for prices before purchase and consumption. Pricing strategies such as discounting, "everyday prices," and couponing obviously need to be different in services in which the customer has no initial sense of prices. Techniques for developing prices for services are more complicated than those for pricing tangible goods.

In summary, external communications—whether from marketing communications or pricing—can create a larger customer gap by raising expectations about service delivery. In addition to improving service delivery, companies must also manage all communications to customers so that inflated promises do not lead to higher expectations. Chapter 16 will discuss integrated services marketing communications, and Chapter 17 will cover pricing to accomplish these objectives.

⟼ PUTTING IT ALL TOGETHER: CLOSING THE GAPS

The full conceptual model shown in Figure 2.6 conveys a clear message to managers wishing to improve their quality of service: the key to closing the customer gap is to close Provider Gaps 1 through 4 and keep them closed. To the extent that one or more Provider Gaps exist, customers perceive service quality shortfalls. The gaps model of service quality therefore serves as a framework for organizations attempting to improve quality service and services marketing. Exhibit 2.1 provides a service quality gaps audit based on the model.

The model begins where the process of improving service quality begins: with an understanding of the nature and extent of the customer gap. Given the service organization's need to focus on the customer and to use knowledge about the customer to drive business strategy, we believe that this emphasis is warranted.

FIGURE 2.6

Gaps Model of
Service Quality

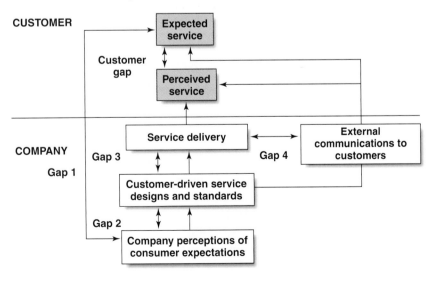

Gaps Model of Service Quality

Using the Gaps Model to Assess an Organization's Service Strategy

The gaps model featured in this chapter and used as a framework for this textbook is a useful way to audit the service performance and capabilities of an organization. The model has been used by many companies as an assessment or service audit tool, because it is comprehensive and offers a way for companies to examine all the factors that influence service quality. To use the tool, a company documents what it knows about each gap and the factors that affect the size of the gap. Although you will learn much more about each of these gaps throughout the book, we provide here a basic gaps audit. In Exercise 1 at the end of this chapter, we propose that you use this audit with a company to determine its service quality gaps.

Service Quality Gaps Model Audit

For each of the following factors in the gaps, indicate the effectiveness of the organization on that factor. Use a 1 to 10 scale where I is "poor" and 10 is "excellent."

Customer Gap	*1 = poor* *10 = excellent*
1. How well does the company understand customer expectations of service quality?	
2. How well does the company understand customer perceptions of service?	

Provider Gap I	*1 = poor* *10 = excellent*
1. **Market Research Orientation** Is the amount and type of market research adequate to understand customer expectations of service? Does the company use this information in decisions about service provision?	
2. **Upward Communication** Do managers and customers interact enough for management to know what customers expect? Do contact people tell management what customers expect?	
3. **Relationship Focus** To what extent does the company understand the expectations of different customer segments? To what extent does the company focus on relationships with customers rather than transactions?	
4. **Service Recovery** How effective are the service recovery efforts of the organization? How well does the organization plan for service failures? **Score for Provider Gap 1**	

Provider Gap 2	*1 = poor* *10 = excellent*
5. **Systematic Service Design** How effective is the company's service development process? How well are new services defined for customers and employees?	
6. **Presence of Customer-Defined Standards** How effective are the company's service standards? Are they defined to correspond to customer expectations? How effective is the process for setting and tracking service quality goals?	

7. **Appropriate Physical Evidence and Servicescape**

   How appropriate, attractive, and effective are the company's physical facilities, equipment, and other tangibles?

   Score for Provider Gap 2

Provider Gap 3	*1 = poor* *10 = excellent*

8. **Effective Human Resource Policies**

   How effectively does the company recruit, hire, train, compensate, and empower employees?

   Is service quality delivery consistent across employees, teams, units, and branches?

9. **Effective Role Fulfilment by Customers**

   Do customers understand their roles and responsibilities?

   Does the company manage customers to fulfil their roles, especially customers that are incompatible?

10. **Effective Alignment with Service Intermediaries**

    How well are service intermediaries aligned with the company?

    Is there conflict over objectives and performance, costs and rewards?

    Is service quality delivery consistent across the outlets?

11. **Alignment of Supply and Demand**

    How well is the company able to match supply with demand fluctuations?

    Score for Provider Gap 3

Provider Gap 4	*1 = poor* *10 = excellent*

12. **Integrated Services Marketing Communications**

    How well do all company communications—including the interactions between company employees and customers—express the same message and level of service quality?

13. **Effective Management of Customer Expectations**

    How well does the company communicate to customers about what will be provided to them?

14. **Accurate Promising in Advertising and Personal Selling**

    Does the company avoid overpromising and overselling?

15. **Adequate Horizontal Communications**

    How well do different parts of the organization communicate with each other so that service quality equals what is promised?

    Score for Provider Gap 4

The score for each gap should be compared to the maximum score possible. Are certain gaps weaker than others? Which areas in each gap need attention?

SUMMARY

This chapter presented the integrated gaps model of service quality (shown in Figure 2.6), a framework for understanding and improving service delivery. The entire text is organized around this model of service quality, which focuses on five pivotal gaps in delivering and marketing service:

The customer gap: Difference between customer expectations and perceptions

Provider Gap 1: Not knowing what customers expect

Provider Gap 2: Not selecting the right service designs and standards

Provider Gap 3: Not delivering to service designs and standards

Provider Gap 4: Not matching performance to promises

The gaps model positions the key concepts in services marketing in a manner that begins with the customer and builds the organization's tasks around what is needed to close the gap between customer expectations and perceptions. The final chapter in the book, Chapter 18, discusses the financial implications of service quality, reviewing the research and company data that indicates linkages between service quality and financial performance.

Discussion Questions

1. Think about a service you receive. Is there a gap between your expectations and perceptions of that service? What do you expect that you do not receive?
2. Consider the "wish mode" discussion about IKEA. Think about a service that you receive regularly and put yourself in the wish mode. How would you change the service and the way it is provided?
3. If you were the manager of a service organization and wanted to apply the gaps model to improve service, which gap would you start with? Why? In what order would you proceed to close the gaps?
4. Can Provider Gap 4 be closed prior to closing any of the other three provider gaps? How?
5. Which of the four provider gaps do you believe is hardest to close? Why?

Exercises

1. Choose an organization to interview, and use the integrated gaps model of service quality as a framework. An audit form is provided in Exhibit 2.1. Ask the manager whether the organization suffers from any of the factors listed in the figures in this chapter. Which factor in each of Figures 2.2 through 2.5 does the manager consider the most troublesome? What does the company do to try to address the problems?
2. Use the Internet to locate the website of Walt Disney, Marriott, Ritz-Carlton, or any other well-known, high-quality service organization. Which provider gaps has the company closed? How can you tell?

3. Interview a nonprofit or public sector organization in your area (it might be some part of your school). Find out if the integrated gaps model of service quality framework makes sense in the context of its organization.

⟼ Notes

1. "Our Mission," Delta Hotels site, www.deltahotels.ca/en/about/mission.html, accessed September 18, 2006.
2. The gaps model of service quality that provides the structure for this text was developed by and is fully presented in Valarie A. Zeithaml, A. Parasuraman, and Leonard L. Berry, *Delivering Quality Service: Balancing Customer Perceptions and Expectations* (New York: The Free Press, 1990).

PART

2

Focus on the Customer

The Customer Gap

The Customer Gap

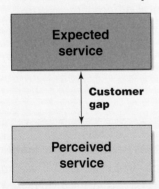

The figure here shows a pair of boxes from the gaps model of service quality that correspond to two concepts—*customer expectations* and *customer perceptions*—that play a major role in services marketing. Customer expectations are the standards of performance or reference points for performance against which service experiences are compared, and are often formulated in terms of what a customer believes should or will happen. Customer perceptions are subjective assessments of actual service experiences.

We devote this Part of the textbook to describing this gap and other relevant customer concepts because excellent services marketing requires a focus on the customer. We detail what is known about customer behaviour relative to services in Chapter 3, customer expectations in Chapter 4, and customer perceptions in Chapter 5. Knowing what customers want and how they assess what they get is the foundation for designing effective services.

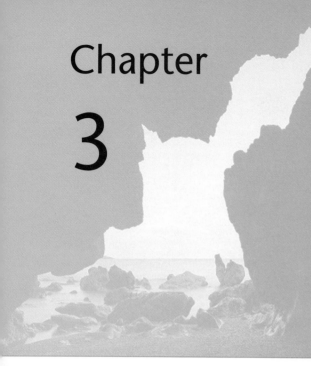

Chapter

3

Consumer Behaviour in Services

Customer Gap

THIS CHAPTER'S OBJECTIVES ARE TO

➡ 1. Enhance understanding of how consumers choose and evaluate services, through focusing on factors that are particularly relevant for services.

➡ 2. Describe how consumers judge goods versus services in terms of search, experience, and credence criteria.

➡ 3. Develop the elements of consumer behaviour that a services marketer must understand: choice behaviour, consumer experiences, and postexperience evaluation.

➡ 4. Explore how differences among consumers (cultural differences, group decision making) affect consumer behaviour and influence services marketing strategies.

CONSUMER PROBLEM: TIME DEFICIENCY

Today's dual-career couples, single-parent families, and two-job families are realizing a burning consumer need: more time. Individuals in these and other nontraditional family configurations are overstressed with their work and home obligations and find that dealing with many of life's everyday tasks is overwhelming. As depicted in the Time Crunch Meter, created from a recent Ipsos Reid survey, feeling that there is not enough time in the day to do what is needed to be done is a global phenomenon (see Figure 3.1). And, although Canada was not included in the survey, the situation is similar

FIGURE 3.1

Ipsos Reid Time Crunch Meter
Do you agree strongly, agree somewhat, disagree somewhat, or disagree strongly with the statement "There is never enough time in the day to get done what I want to get done."

*Urban-only samples.
**China's urban-only sample includes Hong Kong.

Source: Courtesy of Ipsos.

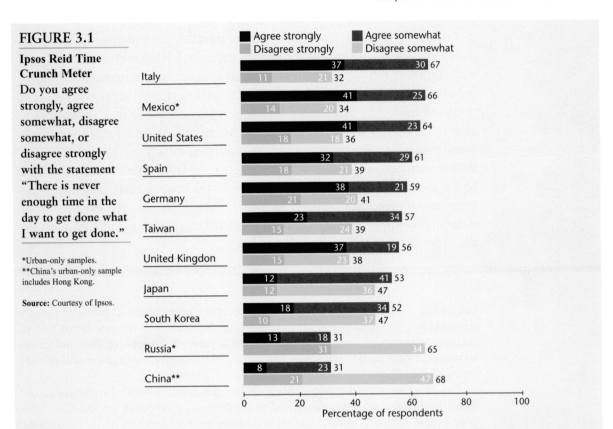

Legend:
- Agree strongly
- Agree somewhat
- Disagree strongly
- Disagree somewhat

Country	Agree strongly	Agree somewhat	Total Agree	Disagree strongly	Disagree somewhat	Total Disagree
Italy	37	30	67	11	21	32
Mexico*	41	25	66	14	20	34
United States	41	23	64	18	18	36
Spain	32	29	61	18	21	39
Germany	38	21	59	21	20	41
Taiwan	23	34	57	15	24	39
United Kingdon	37	19	56	15	23	38
Japan	12	41	53	12	36	47
South Korea	18	34	52	10	37	47
Russia*	13	18	31	31	34	65
China**	8	23	31	21	47	68

Percentage of respondents

here. As John Torella from Toronto's J. C. Williams Group remarked about the time-poor customer, "They just don't have the time to do the kind of conventional shopping they've done in the past. It's particularly that young married segment—husband and wife working, a couple of kids."[1] For many customers, all types of shopping have become "drudgery or worse."[2] Faced with this dilemma, consumers have choices: They can continue to do all these tasks for themselves, or they can decide to employ the services of professionals or friends and relatives to help them out.[3]

The antidote to this time deficiency is found in many new services and service features that recover time for consumers. Innovative new services—plant watering, wedding advising, baby-proofing, executive organizing, and personal shopping—are emerging to deal with tasks that used to be performed by the household but now can be purchased by the time-buying consumer.[4] Conventional services such as retailing, banking, and restaurants[5] are also adding peripheral services to make shopping easier, increasing their hours to suit customer schedules, reducing transaction time, improving delivery, and providing merchandise or services at home or work. Increased use of the Internet is also saving time for customers. With the Web and home delivery, many shopping tasks can be carried out by customers without even leaving the house and at any time of the day or night.

And there is an increasingly popular parallel phenomenon in business today known as *outsourcing*, which means purchasing whole service functions (such as billing, payroll, secretarial support, maintenance, inventory, network operations, and marketing) from other firms rather than executing them in-house. The motivation for corporations is not so much saving time as it is saving money, better use of limited resources, and focusing on core competencies. Companies that use outsourcing effectively have discovered that in many cases purchasing services outright from another company can be far more economical than the payroll and capital costs of performing them inside. Another benefit, particularly for smaller businesses, is that outsourcing allows the company to focus on its core competencies without the distraction of less central tasks.

The primary objectives of services producers and marketers are identical to those of all marketers: to develop and provide offerings that satisfy consumer needs and expectations, thereby ensuring their own economic survival. To achieve these objectives, service providers need to understand how consumers choose, experience, and evaluate their service offerings.

This chapter shows that services' characteristics result in some differences in consumer evaluation processes compared to those used in assessing goods. Consumers have a more difficult time evaluating and choosing most services partly because services are intangible and nonstandardized and partly because consumption is so closely intertwined with production. These characteristics lead to differences in consumer evaluation processes for goods and services in all stages of the buying and consumption process.

FIGURE 3.2

Service tasks contribute to consumers' time deficiency.

Source: Ryan McVay/ Photodisc/Getty Images.

SEARCH, EXPERIENCE, AND CREDENCE PROPERTIES

One framework for isolating differences in evaluation processes between goods and services is a classification proposed by economists.[6] Economists first distinguished between two categories of properties of consumer products: **search qualities**, attributes that a consumer can determine before purchasing a product; and **experience qualities**, attributes that can be discerned only after purchase or during consumption. Search qualities include colour, style, price, fit, feel, hardness, and smell; experience qualities include taste and wearability. Products such as automobiles, clothing, furniture, and jewellery are high in search qualities because their attributes can be almost completely determined and evaluated before purchase. Products such as vacations and restaurant meals are high in experience qualities because their attributes cannot be fully known or assessed until they have been purchased and are being consumed. A third category, **credence qualities**, includes characteristics that the consumer may find impossible to evaluate even after purchase and consumption.[7] Examples of offerings high in credence qualities are treatments for some medical conditions and brake relinings on automobiles. Few consumers possess medical or mechanical skills sufficient to evaluate whether these services are necessary or are performed properly, even after they have been prescribed and produced by the seller. The ad shown in Figure 3.3 vividly shows that cholesterol treatment is strong in credence properties. People often don't know the extent of the condition until it is too late.

Figure 3.4 arrays products high in search, experience, or credence qualities along a continuum ranging from easy to evaluate to difficult to evaluate. Products high in search qualities are the easiest to evaluate (left end of the continuum). Products high in experience qualities are more difficult to evaluate, because they must be purchased and consumed before assessment is possible (centre of continuum). Products high in credence qualities are the most difficult to evaluate, because

FIGURE 3.3

Cholesterol treatment is high in credence properties.

Source: © 2006 Pfizer Canada Inc.

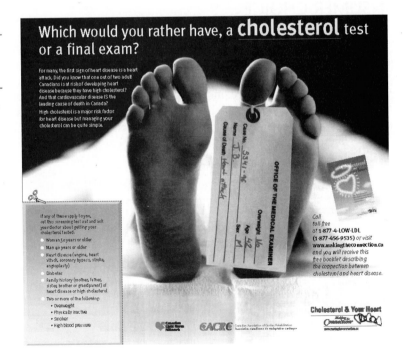

FIGURE 3.4

Continuum of
Evaluation for
Different Types of
Products

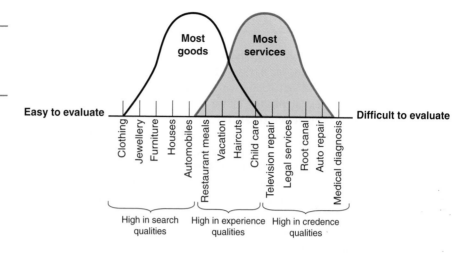

the consumer may be unaware of whether the offerings satisfy given wants or needs even after consumption (right end of the continuum). The major premise of this chapter is that most goods fall to the left of the continuum, whereas most services fall to the right because of the distinguishing characteristics described in Chapter 1. These characteristics make services more difficult to evaluate than goods, particularly in advance of purchase. Difficulty in evaluation, in turn, forces consumers to rely on different cues and processes when assessing services.

The next sections of this chapter build from these basic differences to explore the stages of consumer decision making and evaluation for services. This discussion is organized around three broad stages of consumer behaviour, as shown in Figure 3.5: consumer choice, consumer experience, and postexperience evaluation. Within each of these stages, you will see similarities and differences between goods and services.

CONSUMER CHOICE

The first important area of consumer behaviour is how customers choose and make decisions and the steps that lead to the purchase of a particular service. This process is similar to that used for goods in some ways and different in others. Customers follow a logical sequence, including need recognition, information search, evaluation of alternatives, and purchase. The following sections discuss this sequence, particularly focusing on the ways in which services decision making is different from goods decision making.

FIGURE 3.5 Stages in Consumer Decision Making and Evaluation of Services

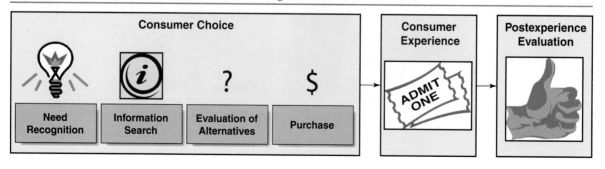

Need Recognition

The process of buying a service begins with the recognition that a need or want exists. Although there are many different ways to characterize needs, the most widely known is Maslow's hierarchy, which specifies five need categories arranged in a sequence from basic lower-level needs to higher-level needs. Services can fill all these needs, and they become increasingly important for higher-level social, ego, and self-actualization needs (see Figure 3.6).

The hierarchical nature of Maslow's need categorization has been disputed, and evidence exists that people with unfilled basic needs can be motivated to self-actualize. We are not concerned with the hierarchical nature in this section; we use it only as a way to discuss different drives that lead customers to the next stages of consumer behaviour in services.

Information Search

Once they recognize a need, consumers obtain information about goods and services that might satisfy this need. Seeking information may be an extensive, formalized process if the service is important to the consumer (e.g., a European vacation package). In other cases, the information search may be quick (e.g., a restaurant for a quick lunch). Consumers use both personal sources (e.g., friends or experts) and nonpersonal sources (e.g., mass media and websites) to gain information about goods and services. Seeking information is a way of reducing risk, helping consumers feel more confident about their choices.

Personal and Nonpersonal Sources

When purchasing goods, consumers make use of both personal and nonpersonal sources because both convey information about search qualities. When purchasing services, on the other hand, consumers seek and rely to a greater extent on *personal* sources for several reasons.

First, mass and selective media can convey information about search qualities but can communicate far less about experience qualities. By asking friends or experts about services, however, the consumer can obtain information vicariously about experience qualities.

FIGURE 3.6

Teeth whitening is a growing service that is driven by consumers' ego needs.

Source: Courtesy BriteSmile.

A second reason for greater use of personal sources of information for services is that many types of nonpersonal sources of information are not as readily available for services. Many service providers are local, independent merchants without the funds to advertise. Furthermore, cooperative advertising is used infrequently with services because most local providers are both producer and retailer of the service. And, because professional associations banned advertising for so long, both professionals and consumers tend to resist its use even though it is now permitted.

Finally, because consumers can assess few attributes *before* purchase of a service, they may feel greater risk in selecting a little-known alternative. Personal influence becomes pivotal as product complexity increases and when objective standards by which to evaluate a product decrease (i.e., when experience qualities are high).[8] Managers in service industries clearly recognize the strong influence of word-of-mouth communication (Figure 3.7).

Interestingly, consumers are now able through the Internet to seek more nonpersonal information about services in the form of visuals, photographs, and even virtual tours.[9] In addition to these tangible representations of the service experience, consumers can also seek the personal opinions of others via the Web through chat rooms, online ratings, and consumer complaint websites. Some consumer complaint websites even target a specific firm's current and prospective customers, offering unsolicited information.[10]

Perceived Risk

Although some degree of perceived risk may be inevitable, more risk appears to be involved in the purchase of services, because services are more intangible, variable, and perishable. Risk can come in the form of financial risk, time risk, performance risk, social risk, or psychological risk.

The intangible nature of services and their high level of experience qualities imply that services generally must be selected with less prepurchase information. There is clear evidence that greater intangibility increases perceptions of risk.[11] And because services are nonstandardized, the consumer will feel some uncertainty about the outcome and consequences each time a service is purchased. In addition, services purchases may involve more perceived risk than other purchases because, with some exceptions, services are not accompanied by warranties or guarantees. Dissatisfied

FIGURE 3.7

Consumers seek and rely on personal sources in purchasing experience goods and services.

Source: Mark Lewis/Getty Images.

customers can rarely "return" a service; they have already consumed it by the time they realize their dissatisfaction. Finally, many services are so technical or specialized that consumers often can't evaluate whether they are satisfied, even after they have consumed the service.

The increase in perceived risk in purchasing services suggests the use of strategies to reduce risk. Risk reduction can be accomplished through tactics that reduce risk directly (e.g., guarantees) or by addressing the factors that contribute to the perception of risk (e.g., making the service more tangible).[12] For example, Canada Post and FedEx provide tracking numbers for customers so they can follow their shipments online and know exactly where a package is. This system helps reduce the risk for consumers. Offering a free or reduced-cost trial period for a service would be another means to reduce risk. For example, child care centres often encourage a free trial day for prospective clients and their children to reduce the sense of risk in this important decision. To the extent possible, service providers should emphasize employee training and other procedures to standardize their offerings so that consumers learn to expect a given level of quality, again reducing perceived risk.

Evaluation of Service Alternatives

The evoked set of alternatives—that group of products that a consumer considers acceptable options—is likely to be smaller with services. One reason involves differences in retailing between goods and services. To purchase goods, consumers generally shop in retail stores that display competing products in close proximity, clearly demonstrating the possible alternatives. To purchase services, on the other hand, the consumer visits an establishment (such as a bank, a dry cleaner, or a hair salon) that almost always offers only a single "brand" for sale. A second reason for the smaller evoked set is that consumers are unlikely to find more than one or two businesses providing the same services in a given geographic area, whereas they may find numerous retail stores carrying the identical manufacturer's product. A third reason for a smaller evoked set is the difficulty of obtaining adequate prepurchase information about services.

Faced with the task of collecting and evaluating experience qualities, consumers may simply select the first acceptable alternative rather than searching many alternatives. The Internet has the potential to widen the set of alternatives and already has done so in some industries. This trend is most notable in airlines and hotels where comparable information is available through providers such as Travelocity, Orbitz, and Expedia.

For nonprofessional services, consumers' decisions often entail the choice between performing the services for themselves or hiring someone to perform them.[13] Working people may choose between cleaning their own homes or hiring housekeepers, or even between staying home to take care of their children or engaging a day care centre to provide child care. Consumers may consider themselves as sources of supply for many services, including lawn care, tax preparation, and preparing meals. Thus, the customer's evoked set frequently includes self-provision of the service. Self-service via technology is also a viable alternative for many services, as the Technology Spotlight demonstrates.

Service Purchase

Following consideration of alternatives, consumers decide to purchase a particular service or to do it themselves. One of the most interesting differences between goods and services is that most goods are fully produced (at the factory) prior to being purchased by consumers. Thus, consumers, prior to making their decision, can see and frequently

Technology Spotlight

Self-Service Technologies: How Much Do Customers Like Providing Their Own Services?

One major change in consumer behaviour is the growing tendency for consumers to interact with technology to create services instead of interacting with a live service firm employee. *Self-service technologies (SSTs)* are technological interfaces that allow customers to produce services independent of direct service employee involvement. Examples of SSTs that you are probably very familiar with are automated teller machines, pay-at-the-pump terminals at gas stations, automated hotel checkout and check-in, and any service over the Internet. Some Internet-based companies have begun selling divorce kits to speed up processing time, and some online divorce services will send all the legal paperwork after an individual completes a series of short questions over the Internet. Electronic self-ordering is being developed at fast-food chains, and self-scanning at grocery stores is available through companies such as Loblaws.

The table here shows a comprehensive set of categories and examples of SSTs in use today. The columns of the matrix represent the types of technologies that companies are using to interface with customers in self-service encounters, and the rows show purposes of the technologies from the customer perspective. As you can see, customers use the technologies to provide customer service, to conduct transactions, and to provide self-help.

A recent study asked customers across a wide range of industries and applications what they think of SSTs and found that customers have very strong feelings about them. They both love and hate SSTs, depending on a few key conditions. Customers love them when:

- *SSTs bail them out of difficult situations.* A single parent with a sleeping child in the car needs to get gas and money for work the following morning. Using a pay-at-the-pump gas station and drive-up ATM allows the parent to accomplish these tasks without leaving the sleeping child.

- *SSTs are better than the interpersonal alternative.* SSTs have the potential to save customers time, money, and psychological costs. The Internet allows customers to shop at any time and complete transactions

Source: Reproduced with the permission of Air Canada.

more quickly than they could in person. Internet loans and mortgages allow customers to avoid the anxiety of meeting a banker in person and feeling judged.

- *SSTs work.* When SSTs work as they are supposed to, customers are impressed. When these transactions work smoothly, as they usually do after the proper setup, the transactions are satisfying.

On the other hand, customers hate SSTs when the following problems occur:

- *SSTs fail.* The researchers found that 60 percent of the negative stories they heard stemmed from failures of SSTs. Broken machines, failed PINs, websites that were down, and items not shipped as promised all frustrate consumers.

- *SSTs are poorly designed.* Poorly designed technologies that are difficult to use or understand create hassles for customers, making them feel as though

continued

Technology Spotlight

Self-Service Technologies: How Much Do Customers Like Providing Their Own Services?—continued

the SST is not worth using. Websites that are difficult to manoeuvre are particularly troublesome. If customers cannot reach information they need within a few clicks (some researchers say that two clicks are all that customers will tolerate), customers shun the website.

- *The customer messes up.* Customers dislike using technologies that they feel they cannot perform adequately. Even though they feel partial responsibility, they will avoid using them in the future. A common frustration today is having various usernames and passwords for different websites.

- *There is no service recovery.* When the process or technology fails, SSTs rarely provide ways to recover on the spot. In these cases customers must then call or

visit the company, precisely what they were trying to avoid by using the self-service technology.

It is increasingly evident that these technological innovations will be a critical component of customer–firm interactions. If these SSTs are to succeed, the researchers contend, they must become more reliable, be better than the interpersonal alternatives, and have recovery systems in place when they fail.

Sources: M. L. Meuter, A. L. Ostom, R. I. Roundtree, and M. J. Bitner, "Self-Service Technologies: Understanding Customer Satisfaction with Technology-Based Service Encounters," *Journal of Marketing* 64 (July 2000), pp. 50–64; M. J. Bitner, "Self-Service Technologies: What Do Customers Expect?" *Marketing Management,* Spring 2001, pp. 10–11.

Interface \ Purpose	**Categories and Examples of SSTs in Use**			
	Telephone/Interactive Voice Response	**Online/Internet**	**Interactive Kiosks**	**Video/CD**
Customer Service	• Telephone banking • Flight information • Order status	• Package tracking • Account information	• ATMs • Hotel checkout	
Transactions	• Telephone banking • Prescription refills	• Retail purchasing • Financial transactions	• Pay at the pump • Hotel checkout • Car rental	
Self-Help	• Information telephone lines	• Internet information search • Distance learning	• Blood pressure machines • Tourist information	• Tax preparation software • Television/CD-based training

try the exact object that they will buy. For services, much is still unknown at the point of purchase. In many cases, the service is purchased and produced almost simultaneously—as with a restaurant meal or live entertainment. In other cases, consumers pay all or part of the purchase price up-front for a service they will not fully experience until it is produced for them much later. This situation arises with services such as vacation tours or home remodelling, or ongoing services such as health club memberships or university educations. In business-to-business situations, long-term contracts for services (such as payroll, network integration, or landscaping) may be signed prior to anything being produced at all.

Because of the inherent risk in the purchase decision for services, some providers offer "free" (or "deeply discounted") initial trials or extensive tours of their facilities (e.g., prospective student and parent tours at universities) in order to reduce risk in the final purchase decision. In business-to-business situations, trust in the provider is paramount when customers sign long-term service contracts, and frequently the contracts themselves spell out in detail the service-level agreements and penalties for nonperformance.

CONSUMER EXPERIENCE

Because the choice process for services is inherently risky with many unknowns, the experience itself often dominates the evaluation process. As noted, services are high in experience and credence qualities relative to goods; thus, how consumers evaluate the actual experience of the service is very critical in their evaluation process and their decision to repurchase later. In fact, noted customer experience experts have stated that "the experience is the marketing."[14]

Much has been written recently about customer experiences and their important role in influencing consumer behaviour. Goods and services companies alike are being admonished to create "memorable experiences for their customers."[15]

In this section we describe elements of consumer behaviour that are relevant to understanding service experiences and how customers evaluate them. We do not limit our discussion to fun, exciting, or memorable experiences only. Instead, we use the term *customer experience* to encompass service processes that span the mundane to the spectacular. Customers purchasing building maintenance and dry cleaning services still have experiences, albeit less exciting ones than customers of entertainment or travel services. All services *are* experiences—some are long in duration and some are short; some are complex and others are simple; some are mundane, whereas others are exciting and unique. Creating and managing effective processes and experiences are always essential management tasks for service organizations. Many subsequent chapters in this book will provide you with tools and approaches for managing specific elements of the customer experience—the heart of services marketing and management.

Services as Processes

Because services are performances done for and with customers, they typically involve a sequence of steps. Consider medical services. Some of the steps in medical care involve patients interacting with their physician, other steps may be carried out by the customers themselves (e.g., "following the doctor's orders," taking medications), and other steps may involve third parties (e.g., going to a lab for blood work). The combination of these steps, and many others along the way, constitute a process, a service experience that is evaluated by the consumer. It is the combination of steps, or the "experience," that is evaluated by the customer. In many cases, the customer's experience comprises interactions with multiple, interconnected organizations, as in the case of medical services or home buying. Diverse sets of experiences across the network of firms (e.g., a doctor's office, medical laboratory, hospital, and physical therapy clinic) will likely influence consumers' overall impressions of their experience.[16] Whether or not the provider acknowledges it, it is inevitable that the customer will have an experience—good, bad, or indifferent.

Service Provision as Drama

The metaphor of a theatre is useful for analyzing service performances. Both the theatre and service organizations aim to create a desirable impression before an audience and recognize that the way to accomplish this is by carefully managing the actors and the physical setting.[17] The service marketer must play many drama-related roles—including director, choreographer, and writer—to be sure the performances of the actors are pleasing to the audience. The Walt Disney Company (Figure 3.8) explicitly considers its service provision a "performance," even using show business terms such as *cast member*, *onstage*, and *show* to describe the operations at Disneyland and Walt Disney World.[18]

The skill of the service **actors** in performing their routines, the way they appear, and their commitment to the "show" are all essential to service delivery. Although service actors are present in most service performances, their importance increases in three conditions. First, service actors are critical when the degree of direct personal contact is high. Consider the difference between a visit to Denny's and a trip to a Japanese restaurant like Benihana. In many cases customers go to Japanese steakhouses as much for the show as for the food, and they eagerly anticipate the performance of the real-time chef who twirls knives, jokes with the guests, and even flips shrimp into his hat or onto guests' plates. The second condition in which service actors' skills are critical is when the services involve repeat contact. Nurses in hospitals, favourite waiters, or captains on cruises are essential characters in service theatre, and their individual performances can make or break the success of the services. The third condition in which contact personnel are critical is when they have discretion in determining the nature of the service and how it is delivered. When you consider the quality of the education you are receiving in college, you are certain to focus much of your evaluation on your professors' delivery of classes. In education, as in other services such as medical and legal services, the professional is the key actor in the performance.[19]

Ray Fisk and Steve Grove, two experts in the area of service dramaturgy, point out that service actors' performances can be characterized as sincere or cynical.[20] A sincere performance occurs when an actor becomes one with the role that she is playing, whereas a cynical performance occurs when an actor views a performance only

FIGURE 3.8

At Disney World the delivery of service is conceived as drama.

Source: Freelance Consulting Services/Corbis.

as a means to an end, such as getting paid for doing the job. When a service employee takes the time to listen and help, the performance is sincere and often noteworthy. Unfortunately, too many examples of cynical performances exist in which front-line "actors" seem to care little about the "audience" of customers. As Grove and Fisk point out, a single employee can ruin the service experience by ridiculing other cast members' efforts, failing to perform his role correctly, or projecting the wrong image. To create the right impression, three characteristics are necessary: loyalty, discipline, and circumspection.[21]

The **physical setting** of the service can be likened to the staging of a theatrical production, including scenery, props, and other physical cues. Among a setting's features that may influence a service are the colours or brightness of the surroundings; the volume and pitch of sounds in the setting; the smells, movement, freshness, and temperature of the air; the use of space; the style and comfort of the furnishings; and the setting's design and cleanliness.[22] As an example, the service provided by a cruise ship features its layout (broad and open), decor and comfort (large, cushioned deck chairs), furnishings (lots of polished wood and brass), and cleanliness ("shipshape"). The setting increases in importance when the environment distinguishes the service. Consider how critical the setting is for a downtown law firm, which must appear professional, capable, even imposing.[23] In essence, the delivery of service can be conceived as drama, where service personnel are the actors, service customers are the audience, physical evidence of the service is the setting, and the process of service assembly is the performance.[24]

The drama metaphor offers a useful way to improve service performances. Selection of personnel can be viewed as auditioning the actors. An actor's personal appearance, manner, facial expression, gestures, personality, and demographic profile can be determined in large part in the interview or audition. Training of personnel can become rehearsing. Clearly defining the role can be seen as scripting the performance. Creation of the service environment involves setting the stage. Finally, deciding which aspects of the service should be performed in the presence of the customer (onstage) and which should be performed in the back room (backstage) helps define the performances the customer experiences.

Service Roles and Scripts

Roles are combinations of social cues that guide and direct behaviour in a given setting.[25] Just as there are roles in dramatic performances, there are roles in service delivery. For example, the role of a hostess in a restaurant is to acknowledge and greet customers, find out how many people are in their group, and then lead them to a table where they will eat. The success of any service performance depends in part on how well the role is performed by the service actor and how well the team of players—employees and customers—act out their roles.[26] Service employees need to perform their roles according to the expectations of the customer; if they do not, the customer may be frustrated and disappointed. If customers are informed and educated about their roles and if they cooperate with the provider in following the script, successful service provision is likely.

One factor that influences the effectiveness of role performance is the **script**—the logical sequence of events expected by the customer, involving her as either a participant or an observer.[27] Service scripts consist of sequences of actions associated with actors and objects that, through repeated involvement, define what the customer expects.[28] (See Figure 3.9 for a "service script" that was misread!)

Receiving a dental checkup is a service experience for which a well-defined script exists. For a checkup the consumer expects the following sequence: Enter the

reception area, greet a receptionist, sit in a waiting room, follow the dental hygienist to a separate room, recline in a chair while his teeth are cleaned by the hygienist, be examined by the dentist, then pay for the services. When the service conforms to this script, the customer has a feeling of confirmed expectations and satisfaction. Deviations from the service script lead to confusion and dissatisfaction. Suppose, on moving to a new town, you went to a dentist who had no receptionist and no waiting area, only a doorbell in a cubicle. Suppose, on answering the doorbell, an employee in shorts took you to a large room where all patients were in dental chairs facing each other. These actions and objects are certainly not in the traditional service script for dentistry and might create considerable uncertainty and doubt in patients.

Some services are more scripted than others. Customers would expect very expensive, customized services such as spa vacations to be less scripted than mass-produced services such as fast food ("Have a nice day!") and airline travel.

The Compatibility of Service Customers

We have just discussed the roles of employees and customers receiving service. We now want to focus on the role of *other customers* receiving service at the same time. Consider how central the mere presence of other customers is in churches, restaurants, dances, bars, clubs, and spectator sports.[29] The way other customers behave with many services—such as airlines, education, clubs, and social organizations—exerts a major influence on a customer's experience.[30] In general, the presence, behaviour, and similarity of other customers receiving services has a strong impact on the satisfaction and dissatisfaction of any given customer.[31]

Customers can be incompatible for many reasons—differences in beliefs, values, experiences, abilities to pay, appearance, age, and health, to name just a few. The service marketer must anticipate, acknowledge, and deal with heterogeneous consumers who have the potential to be incompatible. The service marketer can also bring homogeneous customers together and solidify relationships between them, which increases the cost to the customer of switching service providers.[32] Customer compatibility is a factor that influences customer satisfaction, particularly in high-contact services. Recently, for instance, Westin Hotels decided to ban smoking in all their Canadian hotels—not just in certain rooms. For nonsmokers this is likely to be considered very good news. But smokers may not be so pleased.

Customer Coproduction

In addition to being audience members, as suggested by the drama metaphor, service customers also play a coproduction role that can have profound influence on the service experience.[33] For example, counselling, personal training, or educational services have little value without the full participation of the client, who will most likely have extensive work to do between sessions. In this sense, the client coproduces the service. In business-to-business contexts such as consulting and architecture, customers also coproduce the service.[34] It has been suggested that customers therefore need to understand their roles and be "trained" in ways that are similar to the training of service employees, so that they will have the motivation, ability, and role clarity to perform.[35] The customer coproduction role is particularly relevant in self-service situations, as noted in this chapter's Technology Spotlight.

The idea of customers as "partners" in the cocreation of products is gaining ground across all industries, not just services.[36] Postmodern consumer behaviour experts propose an even broader interpretation of this idea. They suggest that a fundamental characteristic of the postmodern era is consumers' assertiveness as active participants in creating their world—often evidenced in their demands to adjust, change, and use products in customized ways.[37]

Emotion and Mood

Emotion and mood are feeling states that influence people's (and therefore customers') perceptions and evaluations of their experiences. Moods are distinguished from emotions in that *moods* are transient feeling states that occur at specific times and in specific situations, whereas *emotions* are more intense, stable, and pervasive.[38]

Because services are experiences, moods and emotions are critical factors that shape the perceived effectiveness of service encounters. If a service customer is in a bad mood when she enters a service establishment, service provision will likely be interpreted more negatively than if she were in a buoyant, positive mood. Similarly, if a service provider is irritable or sullen, his interaction with customers will likely be colored by that mood. Furthermore, when other customers in a service establishment are cranky or frustrated, whether from problems with the service or from existing emotions unrelated to the service, their mood affects the provision of service for all customers who sense the negative mood.

In what specific ways can mood affect the behaviour of service customers? First, positive moods can make customers more obliging and willing to participate in behaviours that help service encounters succeed.[39]

A second way that moods and emotions influence service customers is to bias the way they judge service encounters and providers. Mood and emotions enhance and amplify experiences, making them either more positive or more negative than they might seem in the absence of the moods and emotions.[40] The positive mood of a customer at a dance will heighten the experience, leading to positive evaluations of the service establishment (Figure 3.10). The direction of the bias in evaluation is consistent with the polarity (positive or negative) of the mood or emotion.

Finally, moods and emotions affect the way information about service is absorbed and retrieved in memory. As memories about a service are encoded by a consumer, the feelings associated with the encounter become an inseparable part of the memory. If travellers fall in love during a vacation in the Bahamas, they may hold favourable assessments of the destination due more to their emotional state than to the destination itself.

FIGURE 3.10

Positive moods of customers in a dance club heighten their service experiences.

Source: Mark Richards/Photo Edit.

Because emotions and moods play such important roles in influencing customer experiences, "organizations must manage the emotional component of experiences with the same rigor they bring to the management of product and service functionality."[41] Organizations may observe customers' emotional responses and attempt to create places, processes, and interactions to enhance certain emotions. Some firms believe that consumers' emotional responses may be the best predictors of their ultimate loyalty. Thus, many companies are now beginning to measure emotional responses and connections as well—going beyond traditional measures of satisfaction and behavioural loyalty.

POSTEXPERIENCE EVALUATION

Following the service experience, customers form an evaluation that determines to a large degree whether they will return or continue to patronize the service organization (see Figure 3.5). Historically within the field of marketing, more attention has been paid to *prepurchase* evaluations and consumer choice. Yet *postpurchase* and postexperience evaluations are typically most important in predicting subsequent consumer behaviours and repurchase, particularly for services.

Postexperience evaluation is captured by companies in measures of satisfaction, service quality, loyalty, and sometimes emotional engagement. We devote an entire chapter (Chapter 5) to exploring the specifics of customer satisfaction and service quality. Another chapter (Chapter 7) will examine the topic of relationships and loyalty.

Word-of-Mouth Communication

Postexperience evaluations will significantly impact what consumers tell others about the service. Because service consumers are strongly influenced by the personal opinions of others, understanding and controlling word-of-mouth communication becomes even more important for service companies. When service is dissatisfactory, it is critical to have an effective service recovery strategy (see Chapter 8) to curb negative word of mouth.

Attribution of Dissatisfaction

When consumers are disappointed with purchases, they may attribute their dissatisfaction to the producers, the retailers, or themselves. Because consumers participate to a greater extent in services, they may feel more responsible for their dissatisfaction when they purchase services than when they purchase goods. As an example, consider a consumer purchasing a haircut; receiving the cut she desires depends in part on her clear specifications of her needs to the stylist. If disappointed, she may blame either the stylist (for lack of skill) or herself (for choosing the wrong stylist or for not communicating her own needs clearly).

The quality of many services depends on the information the customer brings to the service encounter: a doctor's accurate diagnosis requires a conscientious case history and a clear articulation of symptoms; and a dry cleaner's success in removing a spot depends on the consumer's knowledge of its cause. Dissatisfaction may not be blamed completely on the retailer or producer, because consumers must adequately perform their part in the production process also.

With products, on the other hand, a consumer's main form of participation is the act of purchase. The consumer may attribute failure to receive satisfaction to her own decision-making error, but she holds the producer responsible for product performance. Goods usually carry warranties or guarantees with purchase, emphasizing that the producer believes that if something goes wrong, it is not the fault of the consumer.

Positive or Negative Biases

Research suggests that people remember negative events more than positive ones and are more influenced by negative information than by positive information, and that it is easier for consumers to remember the negative service experiences they have than to think of the many routine, or even positive, experiences.

Research also that says that customers will weigh negative information about a product attribute more heavily than positive information in forming their overall brand attitudes. Yet some very interesting and recent research suggests "positivity bias" for services.[42] The research showed that consumers tend to infer positive qualities for the firm and its employees if they have a good experience with one service employee. When individual service providers are regarded positively, customers' positive perceptions of other service providers in the company are also raised. On the other hand, customers who have a negative experience with one employee are less likely to draw a negative inference about all employees or the firm. That is, customers are more likely to attribute that negative experience to the individual provider, not the entire firm. Although this is just one study, the results and implications are intriguing.

Brand Loyalty

The degree to which consumers are committed to particular brands of goods or services depends on a number of factors: the cost of changing brands (switching cost), the availability of substitutes, social ties to the company, the perceived risk associated with the purchase, and the satisfaction obtained in the past. Because it may be more costly to change brands of services, because awareness of substitutes is limited, and because higher risks may accompany services, consumers are more likely to be loyal to services than to goods.

The difficulty of obtaining information about services means that consumers may be unaware of alternatives or substitutes for their brands. Monetary fees may accompany brand switching in many services: physicians often require complete physicals on the initial visit; dentists sometimes demand new X-rays; and health clubs frequently charge "membership fees" at the outset to obtain long-term commitments from customers.

If consumers perceive greater risks with services, as is hypothesized here, they probably depend on brand names to a greater extent than when they purchase products. Brand loyalty, described as a means of economizing decision effort by substituting habit for repeated, deliberate decision, functions as a device for reducing the risks of consumer decisions.

A final reason that consumers may be more brand-loyal with services is the recognition of the need for repeated patronage in order to obtain optimum satisfaction from the seller. Becoming a "regular customer" allows the seller to gain knowledge of the customer's tastes and preferences, ensures better treatment, and encourages more interest in the consumer's satisfaction. Thus a consumer may exhibit brand loyalty to cultivate a satisfying relationship with the seller.

Brand loyalty has two sides. The fact that a service provider's own customers are brand-loyal is, of course, desirable. The fact that the competitors' customers are difficult to capture, however, creates challenges. Marketers can also facilitate switching from competitors' services by reducing switching costs, as was done by TD Canada Trust with its Easy Switch program.

UNDERSTANDING DIFFERENCES AMONG CONSUMERS

To this point in the chapter, we have discussed consumer decision making and evaluation processes that are applicable across a wide range of consumers and types of services. In these last sections of the chapter, we examine the role of national and ethnic cultures in shaping consumer behaviour.

Global Differences: The Role of Culture

Culture represents the common values, norms, and behaviours of a particular group and is often identified with nations or ethnicity. Culture is learned, shared, multidimensional, and transmitted from one generation to the next. Understanding cultural differences is important in services marketing because of its effects on the ways that customers evaluate and use services. Culture also influences how companies and their service employees interact with customers. Culture is important in international services marketing—taking services from one country and offering them in others—but it is also critical within countries. More and more, individual countries are becoming multicultural, and organizations need to understand how this factor affects evaluation, purchase, and use of services even within countries.

Research provides considerable evidence that there are differences in how consumers perceive services across cultures. For example, a study of service quality perceptions in Taiwan revealed that much greater emphasis is placed on the interpersonal dimensions of service than is generally true in studies of U.S. consumers.[43] Another study showed notable differences in how fast-food and grocery consumers in eight different countries (Australia, China, Germany, India, Morocco, the Netherlands, Sweden, and the United States) evaluate these services.[44] Research also recommends that firms carefully consider global differences in the ways they measure service quality in

Global Feature

Differences in the Service Experience in the United States and Japan

As we emphasize in this chapter, the way service experiences differ across cultures influences how consumers evaluate service. Until recently, service differences across cultures were observed anecdotally rather than systematically, and researchers had few guidelines or criteria on which to evaluate these differences. One notable exception is a study that examined differences in the service experience across two cultures, in the United States and Japan, and provided both vivid examples and solid evidence of cultural subtleties that affect service encounters. The examples came from interviews with Japanese students studying at an American university and are categorized by dimensions of service behaviour. Following these examples, which come directly from the study, are a few of the interesting research findings.

- *Authenticity.* In Japan, "every clerk has the same type of smile ... the smile is not natural," and "everything is done according to the manual." In the United States, clerks "act independently," and "there is more variation in treatment."

- *Caring.* Caring or concern is the most important dimension in Japan, where "The customer is God." In the United States, sales clerks are always answering "I don't know"; another comment was that "they don't seem to care."

- *Control.* Control seems very important to Americans. In Japan, on the other hand, customers are "kind of timid or nervous. They tend to give the controlling interest to the clerk." Control is not important in Japan.

- *Courtesy.* In Japan, "if we find something bad about the service like, for example, they didn't apologize for spilling water, we never go back there again." Courtesy is very important in Japan.

- *Formality.* In Japan, formal treatment is a requirement for all service. Treatment in the United States is much more informal.

- *Friendliness.* "In the U.S. I feel like I'm supposed to treat serving people as equals. In Japan, that is not so." In Japan, friendliness can be disrespectful, and

formality is usually preferred. In the United States, friendliness is expected.

- *Personalization.* "In Japan, you are treated the same." The waiters "are almost faceless, too businesslike and whoever comes, they treat them like the same person." In the United States, service is much more personalized and names are used more frequently.

- *Promptness.* "In the U.S., the sales clerk and the customer expect to have a nice little chat ... in Japan, many people would prefer a sales clerk who is quick but unfriendly."

After measuring and testing cultural dimensions across samples from the two countries, the study's author developed several compelling insights that are critical for understanding what service providers need to do to influence perceptions and evaluations of service encounters.

First, themes of friendliness, being personal, authenticity, and promptness dominate in the United States, whereas caring and concern are central in Japan. This difference can be explained by the cultural focus on individualism in the United States and the emphasis on empathy (being attentive, caring, and kind) in Japan. Civility, an important dimension in both countries, had different meanings: in the United States it meant paying attention and providing good service, whereas in Japan it due to being patient and fair. Authenticity is a relevant dimension in the United States but not in Japan, likely due to the Japanese focus on playing a role rather than expressing individual feelings.

It is evident from this study, and from others like it, that understanding culture is pivotal to being evaluated as an effective service provider. Providing the same service experience offered in the home country may not be successful when a service is extended to other cultural groups.

Source: Reprinted with permission of Elsevier Science Limited from K. F. Winsted, "The Service Experience in Two Cultures," *Journal of Retailing* 73, no. 3 (1997), pp. 337–60.

order to make valid comparisons across cultures.[45] Because of the importance of the global dimensions of business and cultural differences among consumers, we include a Global Feature in every chapter to illustrate how global differences affect services management as well as consumer behaviour. Our Global Feature in this chapter illustrates differences in how consumers experience and evaluate services in the United States compared to Japan.

Despite the clear differences in cultures, human nature dictates that people tend to view other cultures through the often cluttered lens of their own.[46] These prejudices are important, because they reflect a fundamental issue in services. As we discuss in Chapters 4 and 5, the intangibility of services makes their evaluation very much a matter of individual perception. And perceptions, at least when it comes to cultural differences, are what count, even if these perceptions are wrong.

In a recent study reported in *Science*, researchers looked at 30 personality traits among college students in 49 countries—everything from openness, agreeableness, conscientiousness, and warmth to straightforwardness, modesty, and competence. They then compared the stereotypes that subjects in each country would use to describe themselves using actual personality traits as measured using standardized tests. The result? We all have stereotypes of our own cultures, but our actual personalities are quite different.

Canadians, for instance, believe we are quite different from Americans. We describe ourselves as extremely agreeable. Americans describe themselves as very disagreeable. We believe we are calm and not irritable. Americans think they are more anxious and more hostile. According to the principal investigator, though, Canadians and Americans have almost identical personality traits. Time after time, the researchers found that people from all cultures hold strong stereotypes of themselves but that their own responses to the personality tests don't match the stereotype.[47]

So the truth of the matter is that, at the level of individual personality, we aren't very different from other people. But because we think we are, we have a tendency to evaluate things from our preexisting stereotypes. Another expert, Geert Hofstede, sums up the message of one of his books as follows:

> Everybody looks at the world from behind the windows of a cultural home, and everybody prefers to act as if people from other countries have something special about them (a national character) but home is normal. Unfortunately, there is no normal position in cultural matters."[48]

Differences in how services are evaluated across cultures can be traced to basic factors that distinguish cultures from each other. In the next sections, we highlight some of the major differences that can influence how people choose, use, and evaluate services, including values and attitudes, manners and customers, material culture, aesthetics, and educational and social institutions. Language, another obvious cultural difference particularly important for services, is discussed in Chapter 16.

Values and Attitudes Differ Across Cultures

Values and attitudes help determine what members of a culture think is right, important, and/or desirable. Because behaviours, including consumer behaviours, flow from values and attitudes, services marketers who want their services adopted across cultures must understand these differences.

Although North American brands often have an "exotic" appeal to other cultures, firms should not count on this appeal as a long-term strategy. In the late 1990s Wal-Mart found that the cachet of U.S. brands was falling in Mexico. The Mexican news media alerted consumers to shoddy foreign goods, and some Wal-Mart customers turned to a spirit of nationalism. The retailer responded with an "Hecho en Mexico" program similar to the "Made in the Canada" program that was successful here. In some situations it is more than a case of nationalism: brand attitudes are negatively influenced by specific prejudices toward "dominating" cultures. The Korean ban on Japanese movies and the French phobia about Euro Disney are good examples of the latter.

Manners and Customs

Manners and customs represent a culture's views of appropriate ways of behaving. It is important to monitor differences in manners and customs because they can have a direct effect on the service encounter. Central and Eastern Europeans are perplexed by Western expectations that unhappy workers "put on a happy face" when dealing with customers. As an example, McDonald's requires Polish employees to smile whenever they interact with customers. Such a requirement strikes many employees as artificial and insincere. The fast-food giant has learned to encourage managers in Poland to probe employee problems and to assign troubled workers to the kitchen rather to the food counter.[49]

Habits are similar to customs, and these tend to vary by culture. Japanese take very few vacations, and when they do they like to spend 7 to 10 days. Their vacations are unusually crammed with activities—Rome, Geneva, Paris, and London in 10 days is representative.[50]

Material Culture

Material culture consists of the tangible products of culture, or as comedian George Carlin puts it, "our stuff." Cars, houses, clothes, and furniture are examples of material culture.

The majority of Mexicans do not own cars, limiting retailers' geographic reach. Further, most Mexicans own small refrigerators and have limited incomes that restrict the amount of groceries they can purchase at one time. Instead of the once-per-week shopping trip typical in North America, Mexicans make frequent, smaller trips. Promotional programs in Mexico are also constrained by the availability of media. Limited ownership of televisions and radios affects the ability of services marketers to reach target audiences.

Terms of mortgages are another interesting area of cross-cultural differences in financial services. The typical mortgage in Canada is issued for five years with repeated financing every five years, whereas in the United States mortgages are issued for thirty years at the outset. In Mexico, most people pay cash for houses because mortgages are virtually unavailable. And in Japan, 100-year mortgages are quite common and often pass along with the house or flat to the next generation.

Aesthetics

Aesthetics refers to cultural ideas about beauty and good taste. These ideas are reflected in music, art, drama, and dance as well as the appreciation of colour and form (Figure 3.11).

Perhaps Alanis Morissette and MuchMusic sell well internationally, but even so, the adage "There's no accounting for taste" still rings quite true with most consumers around the world. A summer stroll through one of Madrid's important tourist attractions, Parque de Retiro, provides a simple but memorable lesson in how aesthetics vary across cultures. Trash cans are everywhere, but somehow the refuse doesn't make it into them. From the North American perspective, the litter detracts from the

FIGURE 3.11

Ideas about aesthetics differ across cultures.

Source: Ryan McVay/ Photodisc/Getty Images.

otherwise beautiful park. German tourists, used to the clean organization of their own fastidiously tidy forests, react negatively.

Educational and Social Institutions

Both educational and social institutions are affected by and transmit culture. Culture manifests itself most dramatically in the people-to-people contact of social institutions. Classroom interactions, for example, vary substantially around the world. Notice if the student from Japan sitting next to you in class verbally disagrees with your instructor. Japanese students are used to listening to lectures, taking notes, and asking questions only after class, if at all. In Japan the idea of grading class participation is nonsense. Alternatively, because Spaniards are used to huge undergraduate classes (hundreds rather than dozens), they tend to talk to their friends even when the instructor is talking.

Like education, health care delivery systems and doctor–patient interactions also reflect cultural differences. Canadians ask questions and get second opinions about medical care. Alternatively, the social hierarchy is heavily reflected in the Japanese health care system; instead of patients being most important, the doctors command deference. Thus the Japanese health care system, while delivering the best longevity statistics of any country, is relatively unresponsive to concerns of patients.

Group Decision Making

A group is defined as two or more individuals who have implicitly or explicitly defined relationships to one another such that their behaviour is interdependent.[51] When groups make decisions about services—a household purchasing a family vacation or an organization purchasing marketing research services—many of the same issues arise as for individuals: greater perceived risk; more reliance on word-of-mouth communication; greater difficulty in comparing alternatives; and often a higher level of customer participation. For example, although many large organizations have very clear evaluation processes for buying goods, their processes and decision rules for purchasing services are often not as well defined. The intangibility and variability of business services make them more risky and often difficult to compare. Thus, organizations often rely on established partnerships, long-term relationships, or referrals from others when it comes to major service purchases. Similar issues arise for households who rely heavily on personal referrals in making significant services purchases such as home repair, remodelling, landscaping, medical care, and vacation trips. Even smaller household decisions—where to eat dinner or choice of a dry cleaner—may be influenced by referrals and may involve a great deal of risk, depending on the occasion. Where to have Grandma's 40-year-old wedding dress drycleaned can be a decision that carries considerable risk.

Despite these similarities, aspects that are different for group buying are collective decision making, mixed motives or goals, roles in the purchasing process, and group culture. We will highlight some of these differences for two major groups: households and organizations.

Households

When a family makes a service purchase decision, it has a collective style of decision making that often differs from what any of the individuals would use if making an independent choice. When a family chooses a vacation destination, for example, its style may involve one of the following: (1) one parent makes a unilateral decision that the family will go on vacation to Disneyland; (2) the family discusses possible vacation destinations at the dinner table, taking each person's ideas and suggestions into account, and selects three locations that a parent will investigate further; (3) the parents provide a budget and a list of the destinations that can be visited within that budget, then allow the children to choose among them. Once a destination has been chosen, the mix of motives or goals of the group comes into play. The mother may want to sightsee, the father to rest, and the children to visit local theme parks. In this and other group purchasing decisions, the needs and goals of the various members must be balanced so that the service (in this case the vacation) delivers optimal satisfaction for as many members as possible. Group roles are also a key consideration. In a household, one individual often identifies a need and initiates the purchase, someone else may influence which service provider is selected, someone else may pay, and someone else may become the ultimate user of the service. For example, the father may decide that the family needs to visit the dentist, a teenager may recommend a dentist that her friend uses, the mother may pay the bills, and all the family members may go to the dentist to receive treatment. Finally, national and ethnic culture affects household purchase and consumption behaviours. For example, ethnic groups vary, with some being very patriarchal, others egalitarian, and still others autocratic.

Organizations

Organizational consumers are a special category of group consumers. These days, companies spend millions on information technology services, call centres, travel management, and payroll services, and outsourced services for human resource management. Making the right decision on services purchases can be absolutely critical for an organization's success. How do companies make these important decisions?

For routine and even complex purchases, organizations often rely on a small number of buyers within the company, many of whom specialize in purchasing. These buyers are typically organized either formally or informally into buying centres, which include all people involved in the decision process.[52] Each of these roles may be taken by a different person, or one person may assume all roles in some cases.

- The *initiator* identifies the organization's service needs.

- The *gatekeeper* collects and controls information about the purchase.

- The *decider* determines what service to purchase.

- The *buyer* or purchasing agent physically acquires the service.

- The *user* consumes the service and may or may not have any influence over the purchase decision.

Among the characteristics that distinguish organizational from individual decision making are economic forces such as current business climate and technology trends; organizational strategies and culture; whether purchasing is a centralized or decentralized function; and the group forces that influence purchasing decisions.[53] Organizational purchases also tend to differ by magnitude and include new task purchases (large purchases that require careful consideration of needs and evaluation of alternatives), straight rebuys (simple reorders of past service purchases), and modified rebuys (a mix of new and straight rebuy features).[54]

As companies outsource more services and particularly when these services are outsourced around the globe, purchase decisions become complex and difficult. Often companies must rely on outside expertise to help them with these multifaceted and financially risky decisions.

Organizational purchasers also rely on references and the experience of other organizations in making their service purchase decisions. Referrals and testimonials can be very helpful to other organizations considering similar business service purchases. In fact, many business service providers have customer stories, cases, and testimonials on their websites to help reduce the risk of these complex decisions.

SUMMARY

The intent of this chapter was to provide understanding for how consumers choose and evaluate services. Services possess high levels of experience and credence properties, which in turn make them challenging to evaluate, particularly prior to purchase. The chapter isolated and discussed three stages of consumer behaviour for services, and it looked at how experience and credence properties result in challenges and opportunities in all three stages. The three stages are consumer choice (including need recognition, information search, evaluation of alternatives, and service purchase); consumer experience; and postexperience evaluation. Consumer behaviour theories, current research, and insights for managers were highlighted in each of these sections.

Although the three stages are relevant for all types of consumer behaviour in services, important differences exist in behaviour across global cultures and for groups vs. individuals. Global differences in consumer behaviour were presented, particularly as they relate to service consumption. The chapter ended with a discussion of the differences in group versus individual consumer decision making related to households and organizations.

Discussion Questions

1. Based on the chapter, which aspects of consumer behaviour are similar and which are different for services versus goods?

2. Where does a college education fit on the continuum of evaluation for different types of products? Where does computer software fit? Consulting? Retailing? Fast food? What are the implications for consumer behaviour?

3. What are examples (other than those given in the chapter) of services that are high in credence properties? How do high credence properties affect consumer behaviour for these services?

4. For what types of services might consumers depend on mass communication (nonpersonal sources of information, including the Internet) in the purchase decision?

5. Which of the aspects discussed in the chapter describe your behaviour when it comes to purchasing services? Does your behaviour differ for different types of services?

6. Why are consumer experiences so important in the evaluation process for services?

7. Using the service drama metaphor, describe the services provided by a health club, a fine restaurant, or a vacation cruise line.

8. What are some differences in service choice, purchase, and consumption processes for organizations and households compared to individuals? What are some similarities?

Exercises

1. Choose a particular end-consumer services industry and one type of service provided in that industry (such as the financial services industry for mortgage loans, the legal services industry for wills, or the travel industry for a vacation package). Talk to five customers who have purchased that service and determine to what extent the information in this chapter described their behaviour in terms of consumer choice, consumer experience, and postexperience evaluation for that service.

2. Choose a particular business-to-business service industry and one type of service provided in that industry (such as the information services industry for computer maintenance services or the consulting industry for management consulting). Talk to five customers in that industry and determine to what extent the information in this chapter described their behaviour in terms of consumer choice, consumer experience, and postexperience evaluation for that service.

3. Visit a service provider of your choice. Experience the service firsthand if possible and observe other customers for a period of time. Describe the consumer (service) experience in detail in terms of what happened throughout the process and how customers, including yourself, felt about it. How could the service experience be improved?

4. Interview three people who come from countries other than your own. Ask them about their consumer behaviour patterns. Note the differences and similarities to your own consumer behaviour. What are possible causes of the differences?

Notes

1. S. Okalow, "Marketers Go Mobile," *Strategy Magazine*, March 22, 2004.
2. E. H. Fram, "Stressed-Out Consumers Need Timesaving Innovations," *Marketing News,* March 2, 1992, p. 10.
3. M. J. Dorsch, S. J. Grove, and W. R. Darden, "Consumer Intentions to Use a Service Category," *Journal of Services Marketing* 14, no. 2 (2000), pp. 92–117.
4. L. L. Berry, "The Time-Buying Customer," *Journal of Retailing* 55, no. 4 (Winter 1979), pp. 58–69.
5. A. Spector, "Menu Marketers Deliver Dinner, Incremental Sales," *Nation's Restaurant News,* May 19, 2003, p. 154.
6. P. Nelson, "Information and Consumer Behavior," *Journal of Political Economy* 78, no. 20 (1970), pp. 311–29.
7. M. R. Darby and E. Karni, "Free Competition and the Optimal Amount of Fraud," *Journal of Law and Economics* 16 (April 1973), pp. 67–86.
8. T. S. Robertson, *Innovative Behavior and Communication* (New York: Holt, Rinehart & Winston, 1971).
9. P. Berthon, L. Pitt, C. S. Katsikeas, and J. P. Berthon, "Virtual Services Go International: International Services in the Marketspace," *Journal of International Marketing* 7, no. 3 (1999), pp. 84–105.
10. J. C. Ward and A. L. Ostrom, "Online Complaining via Customer-Created Web Sites: A Protest Framing Perspective," working paper, W. P. Carey School of Business, Arizona State University, 2004.
11. M. Laroche, G. H. G. McDougall, J. Bergeron, and Z. Yang, "Exploring How Intangibility Affects Perceived Risk," *Journal of Service Research* 6, no. 4 (May 2004), pp. 373–89; K. B. Murray and J. L. Schlacter, "The Impact of Services versus Goods on Consumers' Assessment of Perceived Risk and Variability," *Journal of the Academy of Marketing Science* 18 (Winter 1990), pp. 51–65; M. Laroche, J. Bergeron, and C. Goutaland, "How Intangibility Affects Perceived Risk: The Moderating Role of Knowledge and Involvement," *Journal of Services Marketing* 17, no. 2 (2003), pp. 122–40.
12. M. Laroche et al., "Exploring How Intangibility Affects Perceived Risk."
13. R. F. Lusch, S. W. Brown, and G. J. Brunswick, "A General Framework for Explaining Internal vs. External Exchange," *Journal of the Academy of Marketing Science* 10 (Spring 1992), pp. 119–34; Dorsch, Grove, and Darden, "Consumer Intentions to Use a Service Category."
14. J. H. Gilmore and B. J. Pine II, "The Experience Is the Marketing," report from Strategic Horizons LLP, 2002.
15. See, for example, B. J. Pine II and J. H. Gilmore, *The Experience Economy* (Boston: Harvard Business School Press, 1999); B. H. Schmitt, *Experiential Marketing* (New York: The Free Press, 1999); B. H. Schmitt, *Customer Experience Management* (Hoboken, NJ: John Wiley & Sons, 2003).
16. S. S. Tax and F. N. Morgan, "Toward a Theory of Service Delivery Networks," working paper, W. P. Carey School of Business, Arizona State University, 2004.
17. S. J. Grove and R. P. Fisk, "Service Theater: An Analytical Framework for Services Marketing," in *Services Marketing,* 4th ed., ed. Christopher Lovelock (Englewood Cliffs, NJ: Prentice Hall, 2001), pp. 83–92.

18. S. J. Grove, R. P. Fisk, and M. J. Bitner, "Dramatizing the Service Experience: A Managerial Approach," in *Advances in Services Marketing and Management,* vol. 1, ed. T. A. Swartz, D. E. Bowen, and S. W. Brown (Greenwich, CT: JAI Press, 1992), pp. 91–121.
19. Grove, Fisk, and Bitner, "Dramatizing the Service Experience."
20. Grove and Fisk, "Service Theater."
21. Ibid.
22. Grove, Fisk, and Bitner, "Dramatizing the Service Experience."
23. Ibid.
24. Ibid.
25. M. R. Solomon, C. Surprenant, J. A. Czepiel, and E. G. Gutman, "A Role Theory Perspective on Dyadic Interactions: The Service Encounter," *Journal of Marketing* 49 (Winter 1985), pp. 99–111.
26. Ibid.
27. R. F. Abelson, "Script Processing in Attitude Formation and Decision Making," in *Cognition and Social Behavior,* ed. J. S. Carroll and J. S. Payne (Hillsdale, NJ: Erlbaum, 1976).
28. R. A. Smith and M. J. Houston, "Script-Based Evaluations of Satisfaction with Services," in *Emerging Perspectives on Services Marketing,* ed. L. Berry, G. L. Shostack, and G. Upah (Chicago: American Marketing Association, 1982), pp. 59–62.
29. J. E. G. Bateson and M. K. M. Hui, "Crowding in the Service Environment," in *Creativity in Services Marketing: What's New, What Works, What's Developing,* ed. M. Venkatesan, D. M. Schmalensee, and C. Marshall (Chicago: American Marketing Association, 1986), pp. 85–88.
30. J. Baker, "The Role of the Environment in Marketing Services: The Consumer Perspective," in *The Services Challenge: Integrating for Competitive Advantage,* ed. J. A. Czepiel, C. A. Congram, and J. Shanahan (Chicago: American Marketing Association, 1987), pp. 79–84.
31. C. L. Martin and C. A. Pranter, "Compatibility Management: Customer-to-Customer Relationships in Service Environments," *Journal of Services Marketing* 3 (Summer 1989).
32. Ibid.
33. N. Bendapudi and R. P. Leone, "Psychological Implications of Customer Participation in Co-Production," *Journal of Marketing* 67 (January 2003), pp. 14–28.
34. L. A. Bettencourt, A. L. Ostrom, S. W. Brown, and R. I. Roundtree, "Client Co-production in Knowledge-Intensive Business Services," *California Management Review* 44, no. 4 (Summer 2002), pp. 100–128.
35. S. Dellande, M. C. Gilly, and J. L. Graham, "Gaining Compliance and Losing Weight: The Role of the Service Provider in Health Care Services," *Journal of Marketing* 68 (July 2004), pp. 78–91; M. L. Meuter, M. J. Bitner, A. L. Ostrom, and S. W. Brown, "Choosing Among Alternative Service Delivery Modes: An Investigation of Customer Trial of Self-Service Technologies," *Journal of Marketing* 69, no. 2, p. 61.
36. C. K. Prahalad and V. Ramaswamy, "The New Frontier of Experience Innovation," *Sloan Management Review,* Summer 2003, pp. 12–18.
37. A. F. Firat and A. Venkatesh, "Liberatory Postmodernism and the Reenchantment of Consumption," *Journal of Consumer Research* 22, no. 3 (December 1995), pp. 239–67.

38. M. P. Gardner, "Mood States and Consumer Behavior: A Critical Review," *Journal of Consumer Research* 12 (December 1985), pp. 281–300.

39. Ibid., p. 288.

40. S. S. Tomkins, "Affect as Amplification: Some Modifications in Theory," in *Emotion: Theory, Research, and Experience,* ed. R. Plutchik and H. Kellerman (New York: Academic Press, 1980), pp. 141–64.

41. L. L. Berry, L. P. Carbone, and S. H. Haeckel, "Managing the Total Customer Experience," *Sloan Management Review*, Spring 2002, pp. 85–89.

42. V. S. Folkes and V. M. Patrick, "The Positivity Effect in Perceptions of Services: Seen One, Seen Them All?" *Journal of Consumer Research* 30 (June 2003), pp. 125–37.

43. B. Imrie, J. W. Cadogan, and R. McNaughton, "The Service Quality Construct on a Global Stage," *Managing Service Quality* 12, no. 1 (2002), p. 10–18.

44. B. D. Keillor, G. T. M. Hult, D. Kandemir, "A Study of the Service Encounter in Eight Countries," *Journal of International Marketing* 12, no. 1 (2004), pp. 9–35.

45. A. M. Smith and N. L. Reynolds, "Measuring Cross-Cultural Service Quality: A Framework for Assessment," *International Marketing Review* 19, no. 5 (2001), pp. 450–81.

46. R. B. Money, M. C. Gilly, and J. L. Graham, "Explorations of National Culture and Word-of-Mouth Referral Behavior in the Purchase of Industrial Services in the United States and Japan," *Journal of Marketing* 62 (October 1998), pp. 76–87.

47. A. Terracciano et al., "National Character Does Not Reflect Mean Personality Trait Levels in 49 Cultures," *Science* 310, no. 5745 (October 7, 2005), pp. 96–100.

48. G. Hofstede, *Culture and Organizations: Software of the Mind* (New York: McGraw-Hill, 1991), p. 235.

49. D. E. Murphy, "New East Europe Retailers Told to Put on a Happy Face," *Los Angeles Times,* November 26, 1994, pp. A1, A18.

50. "Japanese Put Tourism on a Higher Plane," *International Herald Tribune*, February 3, 1992, p. 8.

51. E. Arnould, L. Price, and G. Zinkhan, *Consumers*, 2nd ed. (New York: McGraw-Hill, 2004).

52. For excellent coverage of buyer behaviour in organizations, see M. D. Hutt and T. W. Speh, *Business Marketing Management,* 8th ed. (Mason, OH: South-Western, 2004), ch. 3.

53. Ibid., pp. 68–69.

54. Ibid., pp. 62–67.

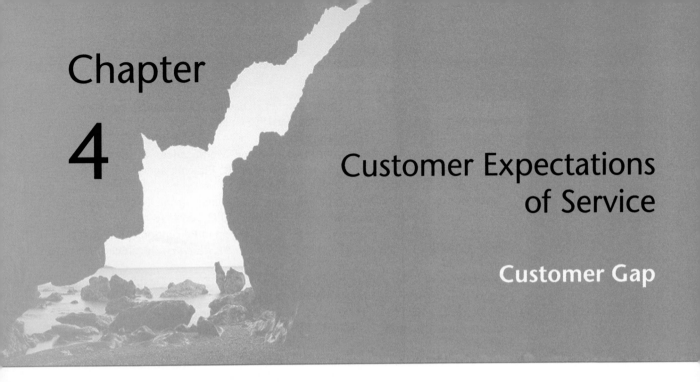

Chapter 4

Customer Expectations of Service

Customer Gap

THIS CHAPTER'S OBJECTIVES ARE TO

⟼ 1. Recognize that customers hold different types of expectations for service performance.

⟼ 2. Discuss the sources of customer expectations of service, including those that are controllable and uncontrollable by marketers.

⟼ 3. Acknowledge that the types and sources of expectations are similar for end consumers and business customers, for pure service and product-related service, for experienced customers and inexperienced customers.

⟼ 4. Delineate the most important current issues surrounding customer expectations.

APPRECIATING A CUSTOMER'S SERVICE EXPECTATIONS

Undoubtedly, the greatest gap between customer expectations and service delivery exists when the Japanese meet Russians. In Japan the customer is supreme. At the morning opening of large department stores in Tokyo, sales personnel line up to welcome patrons and bow as they enter! When one of us—who could speak no Japanese—visited Tokyo recently, as many as eight salespeople willingly tried to help me find a calligraphy pen. Although the pen was a very low-priced item, several attendants rushed from counter to counter to find someone to translate, several others spread out to find pens that might serve as the perfect gift, and still others searched for maps to other stores where the perfect pen could be found.

FIGURE 4.1

Tokyo sales personnel provide excellent customer service.

Source: © Charles Gupton/Stock Boston Inc./ PictureQuest.

Because of the wonderful treatment Japanese customers are used to in their home country, they often have service expectations that exceed service delivery even when shopping in "civilized" countries such as Great Britain: "Hideo Majima, 57, a Japanese tourist, looked puzzled and annoyed. He was standing in a London department store while two shop assistants conversed instead of serving him. He left without buying anything."[1] His annoyance is understandable when you realize the standard of service treatment in Japan.

Given how our friend Majima-san felt about shopping in Britain, try to imagine his perceptions of this actual dining experience in many Russian restaurants. Remember that in Russia's economy, products are still so scarce that suppliers rule. Sellers decide who gets what, and the concept of customer service is virtually meaningless. In a real-life experience from the nineties, a customer visiting the Izmailova Hotel had to excuse the waiters if they were too busy to serve customers—they were playing chess. "'Can't you see we're one move away from checkmate?' yelled waiter Oleg Shamov, surrounded by six other waiters in a restaurant back room. The match kept customers waiting for 40 minutes."[2] Free enterprise is apparently having strong effects in the former Soviet Union. Professor Peter Shikkirev at the Graduate School of International Business in Moscow assures us that some Russian restaurants are now providing service comparable to that of fine American restaurants. However, even that level of service would likely not delight Japanese customers.

Customer expectations are beliefs about service delivery that serve as standards or reference points against which performance is judged. Because customers compare their perceptions of performance with these reference points, thorough knowledge about customer expectations is critical to services marketers. Knowing what the customer expects is the first and possibly most critical step in delivering quality service. Being wrong about what customers want can mean losing a customer's business when another company hits the target exactly. Being wrong can also mean expending money, time, and other resources on things that do not count to the customer. Being wrong can even mean not surviving in a fiercely competitive market.

Among the aspects of expectations that need to be explored and understood for successful services marketing are the following: What types of expectation standards do customers hold about services? What factors most influence the formation of these expectations? What role do these factors play in changing expectations? How can a service company meet or exceed customer expectations?

In this chapter we provide a framework for thinking about customer expectations.[3] The chapter is divided into three main sections: (1) the meaning and types of expected service, (2) factors that influence customer expectations of service, and (3) current issues involving customer service expectations.

MEANING AND TYPES OF SERVICE EXPECTATIONS

To say that expectations are reference points against which service delivery is compared is only a beginning. The level of expectation can vary widely depending on the reference point the customer holds. Although most everyone has an intuitive sense of what expectations are, service marketers need a very clear definition of expectations in order to comprehend, measure, and manage them.

Let's imagine that you are planning to go to a restaurant. Figure 4.2 shows a continuum along which different possible types of service expectations can be arrayed from low to high. On the left of the continuum are different types or levels of expectations, ranging from high (top) to low (bottom). At each point we give a name

FIGURE 4.2

Possible Levels of Customer Expectations

Source: R. K. Teas, "Expectations, Performance Evaluation and Consumers' Perceptions of Quality," *Journal of Marketing*, October 1993, pp. 18–34. Reprinted by permission of the American Marketing Association.

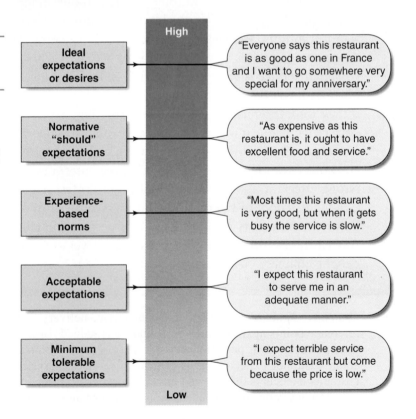

to the type of expectation and illustrate what it might mean. Note how important the expectation you held will be to your eventual assessment of the restaurant's performance. Suppose you went into the restaurant for which you held the minimum tolerable expectation, paid very little money, and were served immediately with good food. Next suppose that you went to the restaurant for which you had the highest (ideal) expectations, paid a lot of money, and were served good (but not fantastic) food. Which restaurant experience would you judge to be best? The answer is likely to depend a great deal on the expectations that you brought to the experience.

Because the idea of customer expectations is so critical to evaluation of service, we start this chapter by talking about the levels of expectations.

Expected Service: Levels of Expectations

As we showed in Figure 4.2, customers hold different types of expectations about service. In the rest of this chapter, we focus on two types. The highest can be termed *desired service*: the level of service the customer hopes to receive—the "wished for" level of performance. Desired service is a blend of what the customer believes "can be" and "should be."[4] For example, consumers who sign up for a computer dating service expect to find compatible, attractive, interesting people to date. The expectation reflects the hopes and wishes of these consumers; without these hopes and wishes and the belief that they may be fulfilled, consumers would probably not purchase the dating service. In this situation and in general, customers hope to achieve their service desires but recognize that this is not always possible. We call the threshold level of acceptable service *adequate service*—the level of service the customer will accept.[5] In the economic slowdown following the dot-com meltdown, many college graduates who were trained for high-skilled jobs accepted entry-level positions at fast-food restaurants or internships for no pay. Their hopes and desires were still high, but they recognized that they could not attain those desires in the market that existed at the time. Their standard of adequate service was much lower than their desired service. Adequate service represents the "minimum tolerable expectation,"[6] the bottom level of performance acceptable to the customer.

Figure 4.3 shows these two expectation standards as the upper and lower boundaries for customer expectations. This figure portrays the idea that customers assess service performance on the basis of two standard boundaries: what they desire and what they deem acceptable.

Among the intriguing questions about service expectations is whether customers hold the same or different expectation levels for service firms in the same industry.

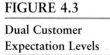

FIGURE 4.3

Dual Customer
Expectation Levels

Consider the following quotation:

> Levels of expectation are why two organizations in the same business can offer far different levels of service and still keep customers happy. It is why McDonald's can extend excellent industrialized service with few employees per customer and why an expensive restaurant with many tuxedoed waiters may be unable to do as well from the customer's point of view.[7]

Customers typically hold *similar desired* expectations *across* categories of service, but these categories are not as broad as whole industries. Among subcategories of restaurants are expensive restaurants, ethnic restaurants, fast-food restaurants, and airport restaurants. A customer's desired service expectation for fast-food restaurants is quick, convenient, tasty food in a clean setting. The desired service expectation for an expensive restaurant, on the other hand, usually involves elegant surroundings, gracious employees, candlelight, and fine food. In essence, desired service expectations seem to be the same for service providers within industry categories or subcategories that are viewed as similar by customers.

The *adequate* service expectation level, on the other hand, may *vary* for different firms *within* a category or subcategory. Within fast-food restaurants, a customer may hold a higher expectation for McDonald's than for Burger King. This chapter's Global Feature further discusses how culture influences expectations.

The Zone of Tolerance

As we discussed in earlier chapters of this textbook, services are heterogeneous in that performance may vary across providers, across employees from the same provider, and even with the same service employee. The extent to which customers recognize and are willing to accept this variation is called the *zone of tolerance*, illustrated in Figure 4.4. If service drops below adequate service—the minimum level considered acceptable—customers will be frustrated and their satisfaction with the company will be undermined. If service performance is higher than the zone of tolerance at the top end—where performance exceeds desired service—customers will be very pleased and probably quite surprised as well. You might consider the zone of tolerance as the range or window in which customers do not particularly notice service performance. When it falls outside the range (either very low or very high), the service gets the customer's attention in either a positive or negative way. As an example, consider the service at a checkout line in a grocery store. Most customers hold a range of acceptable times for this service encounter—probably somewhere between 5 and 10 minutes. If service consumes that period of time, customers probably do not pay much attention to the wait. If a customer enters the line and finds sufficient checkout personnel to serve her in the first two or three minutes, she may notice the service and judge

FIGURE 4.4

The Zone of
Tolerance

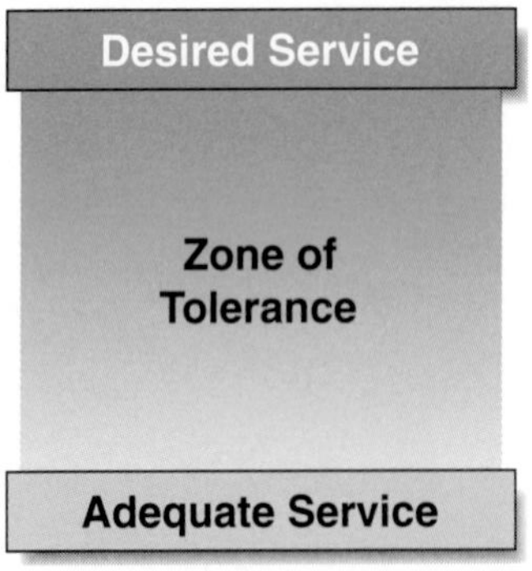

Desired Service

Zone of
Tolerance

Adequate Service

Global Feature

Cultural Influences on Service Expectations

To understand how consumers behave across cultures, we can identify five universal values across cultures. These universal values are well documented; they are based on a study using 72,215 employees working in 66 different national subsidiaries of IBM Corporation. The universal values, which collectively distinguish members of different cultures, include power distance, uncertainty avoidance, individualism–collectivism, masculinity–femininity, and Confucian dynamic or long-term orientation.[8] Here we explain how Hofstede, the author of this research, defined each of these subdimensions, and then we describe one of many ways they might affect consumer expectations in services.

- *Power distance* involves the way that the less powerful members of institutions and organizations within a country expect and accept that power is distributed unequally. Part of power distance involves human inequality in areas such as prestige, wealth, power, and law. People from cultures high in power distance are comfortable with power hierarchy, discrimination, and tolerance of inequalities.

- *Uncertainty avoidance* is the extent to which the members of a culture feel threatened by uncertain or unknown situations. People with high uncertainty avoidance like clear rules and explicit situations; people with low uncertainty avoidance can accept uncertainty without discomfort and tolerate inexplicit rules.

- *Individualism* exists in societies in which the ties between individuals are loose; all individuals are expected to look after themselves and their immediate family. *Collectivism,* the opposite, exists in societies in which people from birth onward are integrated into strong, cohesive groups that offer lifetime protection in exchange for loyalty. This subdimension can be summed up in three words: I vs. we.

- *Masculinity* and *femininity* are the dominant sex role patterns in the vast majority of both traditional and modern societies. Masculine societies value assertiveness, performance, ambition, and independence, whereas feminine societies value nurturance, quality of life, service, and interdependence.

- The *Confucian dynamic,* or *long-term versus short-term orientation dimension,* refers to the way people look at the future. Long-term orientation emphasizes perseverance, ordering relationships by status, thrift, and a sense of shame. On the other hand, short-term orientation focuses on personal steadiness and stability, saving face, respect for tradition, and reciprocation of greetings, favours, and gifts.

The impact of culture on consumer expectations can be illuminated using these five subdimensions of values and attitudes. In one study, for example, researchers found the following:[9]

- Consumers low on power distance have high overall expectations of service and particularly expect responsive and reliable service.

- Individualistic consumers have high overall service quality expectations and expect empathy and assurance from the service provider.

- Consumers high on uncertainty avoidance and short-term-oriented consumers have high overall service quality expectations.

As the authors of the study point out, marketing efforts will perform better when matched with cultural characteristics. This and other typologies that help us understand the differences in values across cultures will be of immense importance as service marketers develop and market service offerings.

Source: Based on background research and a study conducted by N. Donthu and B. Yoo, *Journal of Service Research* 1, no. 2 (November 1998), pp. 178–86.

it as excellent. On the other hand, if a customer has to wait in line for 15 minutes, he may begin to grumble and look at his watch. The longer the wait is below the zone of tolerance, the more frustrated he becomes.

Customers' service expectations are characterized by a range of levels (like those shown in Figure 4.3), bounded by desired and adequate service, rather than a single level. This tolerance zone, representing the difference between desired service and the level of service considered adequate, can expand and contract within a customer. An airline customer's zone of tolerance will narrow when she is running late and is concerned about making her plane. A minute seems much longer, and her adequate-service level increases. On the other hand, a customer who arrives at the airport early may have a larger tolerance zone, making the wait in line far less noticeable than when he is pressed for time. This example shows that the marketer must understand not just the size and boundary levels for the zone of tolerance but also when and how the tolerance zone fluctuates with a given customer.

Different Customers Possess Different Zones of Tolerance

An individual customer's zone of tolerance increases or decreases depending on a number of factors, including company-controlled factors such as price. When prices increase, customers tend to be less tolerant of poor service. In this case, the zone of tolerance decreases because the adequate service level shifts upward. Later in this chapter we will describe many different factors, some company-controlled and others customer-controlled, that lead to the narrowing or widening of the tolerance zone.

Zones of Tolerance Vary for Service Dimensions

Customers' tolerance zones also vary for different service attributes or dimensions. The more important the factor, the narrower the zone of tolerance is likely to be. In general, customers are likely to be less tolerant about unreliable service (broken promises or service errors) than other service deficiencies, which means that they have higher expectations for this factor. In addition to higher expectations for the most important service dimensions, customers are likely to be less willing to relax these expectations than those for less important factors, making the zone of tolerance for the most important service dimension smaller and the desired and adequate service levels higher.[10] Figure 4.5 portrays the likely difference in tolerance zones for the most important and the least important factors.[11]

FIGURE 4.5

Zones of Tolerance for Different Service Dimensions

Source: L. L. Berry, A. Parasuraman, and V. A. Zeithaml, "Ten Lessons for Improving Service Quality," *Marketing Science Institute,* Report No. 93-104 (May 1993).

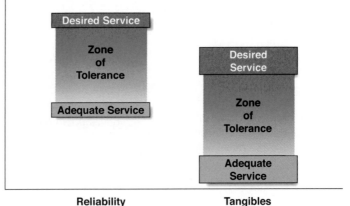

The fluctuation in the individual customer's zone of tolerance is more a function of changes in the adequate service level, which moves readily up and down because of situational circumstances, than in the desired service level, which tends to move upward incrementally because of accumulated experiences. Desired service is relatively stable compared with adequate service, which moves up and down and in response to competition and other factors. Fluctuation in the zone of tolerance can be likened to an accordion's movement, but with most of the gyration coming from one side (the adequate service level) rather than the other (the desired service level).

In summary, we can express the boundaries of customer expectations of service with two different levels of expectations: desired service and adequate service. The desired service level is less subject to change than the adequate service level. A zone of tolerance separates these two levels. This zone of tolerance varies across customers and expands or contracts with the same customer.

FACTORS THAT INFLUENCE CUSTOMER EXPECTATIONS OF SERVICE

Because expectations play such a critical role in customer evaluation of services, marketers need and want to understand the factors that shape them. Marketers would also like to have control over these factors as well, but many of the forces that influence customer expectations are uncontrollable. In this section of the chapter we try to separate the many influences on customer expectations.

Sources of Desired Service Expectations

As is shown in Figure 4.6, the two largest influences on desired service level are personal needs and philosophies about service. *Personal needs* are pivotal factors that shape what customers desire in service. They include physical, social, psychological, and functional categories. A fan who regularly goes to baseball games right from work, and is therefore thirsty and hungry, desires that the food and drink vendors pass by his section frequently, whereas a fan who regularly has dinner elsewhere has a low level of desired service from the vendors.

Some customers are more demanding than others, having greater sensitivity to, and higher expectations of, service. *Lasting service intensifiers* are individual, stable factors that lead the customer to a heightened sensitivity to service. One of the most important of these factors can be called *derived service expectations*, which occur

FIGURE 4.6

Factors That
Influence Desired
Service

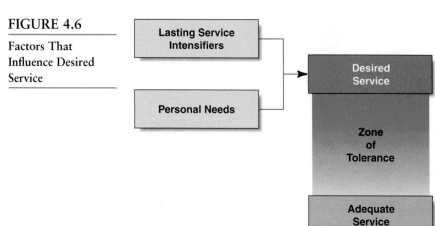

when customer expectations are driven by another person or group of people. The expectations of a parent choosing a vacation for the family or an employee choosing an office for the firm are intensified, because they represent and must answer to other parties who will receive the service. In the context of business-to-business service, customer expectations are driven by the expectations of their own customers.

Business-to-business customers may also derive their expectations from their managers and supervisors. For example, purchasing agents may increase demands for faster delivery at lower costs when company management is emphasizing cost reduction in the company.

Another lasting service intensifier is *personal service philosophy*—the customer's underlying generic attitude about the meaning of service and the proper conduct of service providers. If you have ever been employed as a wait person in a restaurant, you are likely to have standards for restaurant service that were shaped by your training and experience in that role. In general, customers who are themselves in service businesses or have worked for them in the past seem to have especially strong service philosophies.

To the extent that customers have personal philosophies about service provision, their expectations of service providers will be intensified. Personal service philosophies and derived service expectations elevate the level of desired service.

Sources of Adequate Service Expectations

A different set of determinants affects adequate service, the level of service the customer finds acceptable. In general, these influences are short-term and tend to fluctuate more than the factors that influence desired service. In this section we explain the five factors shown in Figure 4.7 that influence adequate service: (1) temporary service intensifiers, (2) perceived service alternatives, (3) customer's self-perceived service role, (4) situational factors, and (5) predicted service.

The first set of elements, *temporary service intensifiers,* consists of short-term, individual factors that make a customer more aware of the need for service.

FIGURE 4.7

Factors That
Influence Adequate
Service

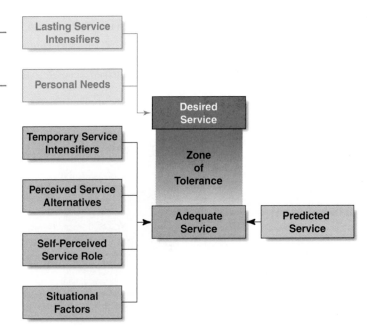

Personal emergency situations in which service is urgently needed (such as an accident and the need for automobile insurance or a breakdown in office equipment during a busy period) raise the level of adequate service expectation, particularly the level of responsiveness required and considered acceptable. The impact of temporary service intensifiers is evident in these comments by two participants:

> An automobile insurance customer: The nature of my problem influences my expectations, for example, a broken window versus an accident requiring brain surgery.

> A business equipment repair customer: I had calibration problems with the X-ray equipment. They should have come out and fixed it in a matter of hours because of the urgency.[12]

Problems with the initial service can also lead to heightened expectations. Performing a service correctly the first time is very important, because customers value service reliability above all other dimensions. If the service fails in the recovery phase, fixing it right the second time (i.e., being reliable in service recovery) is even more critical than it was the first time. Automobile repair service provides a case in point. If a problem with your automobile's brakes sends you to a car repair provider, you expect the company to fix the brakes. If you experience further problems with the brakes after the repair (a not-uncommon situation with car repair), your adequate service level will increase. In these and other situations where temporary service intensifiers are present, the level of adequate service will increase and the zone of tolerance will narrow.

Perceived service alternatives are other providers from whom the customer can obtain service. If customers have multiple service providers to choose from, or if they can provide the service for themselves (such as lawn care or personal grooming), their levels of adequate service are higher than those of customers who believe it is not possible to get better service elsewhere. It is important that service marketers fully understand the complete set of options that customers view as perceived alternatives. In general, service marketers must discover the alternatives that the customer views as comparable rather than those in the company's competitive set. In particular, companies must fully understand customer views of new service technologies (see our Technology Spotlight).

A third factor affecting the level of adequate service is the *customer's self-perceived service role*. We define this as customer perceptions of the degree to which they themselves exert an influence on the level of service they receive. In other words, customers' expectations are partly shaped by how well they believe they are performing their own roles in service delivery.[13] One role of the customer is to specify the level of service expected. A customer who is very explicit with a waiter about how rare he wants his steak cooked in a restaurant will probably be more dissatisfied if the meat is overcooked than a customer who is not so explicit. The customer's active participation in the service also affects this factor.

A final way the customer defines his or her role is in assuming the responsibility for complaining when service is poor. A dissatisfied customer who complains will be less tolerant than one who does not voice his or her concerns. An automobile insurance customer acknowledged his responsibility in service provision this way: "You can't blame it all on the insurance agent. You need to be responsible too and let the agent know what exactly you want."[14]

Customers' zones of tolerance seem to expand when they sense they are not fulfilling their roles. When, on the other hand, customers believe they are doing their part in delivery, their expectations of adequate service are heightened and the zone of tolerance contracts.

Technology Spotlight

Customer Expectations of New Technology Services at the Airport

One of the most difficult tasks that marketers face is understanding what customers expect from completely new services, and nowhere is this problem more evident than when these new services involve technology. Customers almost always resist new technology initially—perhaps because they do not understand it, perhaps because they fear change—even when the technology leads to improved service. Technology that makes obtaining service easier and faster is springing up all over, even in airports around the country. Customers are accepting some new service technologies and resisting others. Here we discuss some innovations that are meeting different fates.

Airlines have had success in customer adoption of self-check-in kiosks like those mentioned in the Technology Spotlight in Chapter 3. With these kiosks, passengers can check-in, select their seats, and even check baggage. Travellers tend to like these systems, because they save time and are easy to use. Not only is the service faster than working with an attendant, check-in is now faster also, because airlines have more kiosks than they used to have lines with attendants.

Exit Express, a technology substitute for toll booths in airport parking lots, has not been met with the same success in customer adoption. With this technology customers pay their parking fees at a machine before leaving, and simply insert their receipt at an Exit Express lane and then leave.

The Canada Border Security Agency (CBSA) has also been increasing technology use at airports to help move international travellers more efficiently through customs. Biometric iris scanners have been instituted at seven international airports across the country between 2003 and 2006. Low-risk Canadian or American travellers who wish to be expedited through the customs process at these Canadian airports can purchase a CANPASS Air membership for $50 annually. After swiping their membership card at the self-service CANPASS Air kiosk, members look into a camera and a digital black-and-white image of their iris is captured for comparison against

Source: Image courtesy of *Winnipeg Men* magazine.

their scan on record. Once their identification is made, travellers can simply leave the customs area.

Whether this technology will be readily accepted by travellers remains to be seen. In January 2006, after two years of availability, there were 13,500 active CANPASS Air members. While not all international travellers processed by CBSA are eligible for a CANPASS, the 20 million

Source: Canada Border Services Agency, Reproduced with Permission of the Minister of Public Works and Government Services Canada, 2006.

fliers clearing customs annually indicates that adoption of this technology has been sluggish.

So why have travellers so readily adopted some self-service technologies but remained more resistant to others that can also meet their expectations of faster service? The answer may have to do with implementation. When airlines introduced self-check-in kiosks, many staffed the terminals with attendants to help passengers use the technology. Exit Express systems do not have employees nearby to help customers through the process and deal with possible failures. CANPASS Air members can seek help from CBSA agents, but the terminals are not staffed.

There may be other factors also. Perhaps travellers do not think it is worth the decreased waiting time, or perhaps awareness of the technology's availability is low. Privacy concerns are also probably high, reducing travellers' trust of the technology. Customers may be wary of the screening process required to get a CANPASS and uncomfortable with biometric data being stored by the government.

Source: M. L. Meuter, M. J. Bitner, A. L. Ostrom, and S. W. Brown, "Choosing Among Alternative Service Delivery Modes: An Investigation of Customer Trial of Self-Service Technologies," *Journal of Marketing*, April 2005. Reprinted by permission of the American Marketing Association; Canada Border Services Agency, "CANPASS AIR Fact Sheet," 2005-08-29, www.cbsa-asfc.gc.ca/newsroom/factsheets/2005/0419-e.html, accessed September 20, 2006; and "CBSA National Statistics," *Canada Newswire*, June 15, 2005.

Levels of adequate service are also influenced by *situational factors,* defined as service performance conditions that customers view as beyond the control of the service provider. For example, where personal emergencies such as serious automobile accidents would likely intensify customer service expectations of insurance companies (because they are temporary service intensifiers), catastrophes that affect a large number of people at one time (tornadoes or earthquakes) may lower service expectations, because customers recognize that insurers are inundated with demands for their services. During the days following Hurricane Juan in Nova Scotia, telephone and Internet service was poor because so many people were trying to get in touch with friends and relatives. However, customers were forgiving—they understood the source of the problem. Customers who recognize that situational factors are not the fault of the service company may accept lower levels of adequate service given the context. In general, situational factors temporarily lower the level of adequate service, widening the zone of tolerance.

The final factor that influences adequate service is *predicted service* (Figure 4.8), the level of service that customers believe they are likely to get. For example, full-time residents in a college town usually predict faster restaurant service during the summer months when students are not on campus. This prediction will probably lead them to have higher standards for adequate service in restaurants during the summer than during school months. On the other hand, customers of telephone companies and utilities know that installation service from these firms will be difficult to obtain during the first few weeks of school when myriad students are setting up their apartments for the year. In this case, levels of adequate service decrease and zones of tolerance widen.

A good example of what firms need to do when they know that service levels may be temporarily impaired is provided in the newspaper advertisement used by the Halifax International Airport, shown in Figure 4.9. Notice how the airport tells its customers why upgrades are needed (to maintain safety), why the work must be done during the summer, and finally that customers should expect some delays especially during periods of low visibility.

FIGURE 4.8

Factors That
Influence Desired
and Predicted Service

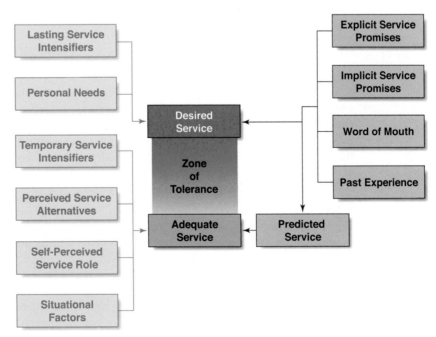

FIGURE 4.9

This firm is trying to manage expectations.

Source: Courtesy of Halifax International Airport Authority.

Predicted service is typically related to an individual transaction rather than the overall relationship with a service provider. Whereas desired and adequate service expectations are global assessments comprising many individual transactions, predicted service is almost always an estimate of what will happen in the next service encounter. For this reason, predicted service is viewed in this model as an influencer of adequate service.

Service Encounter Expectations vs. Overall Service Expectations

In Chapter 5 we discuss how customers hold expectations of the quality of *each* service encounter, just as they hold expectations about the *overall* service quality of a firm. When the expectations are about individual service encounters, they are likely to be more specific and concrete (such as the number of minutes one must wait for a front-desk clerk) than the expectations about overall service quality (such as speedy service).

Sources of Both Desired and Predicted Service Expectations

When consumers are interested in purchasing services, they are likely to seek or take in information from several different sources. This section discusses one internal and three external sources that influence both desired service and predicted service expectations: (1) explicit service promises, (2) implicit service promises, (3) word-of-mouth communications, and (4) past experience.

Explicit service promises are personal and nonpersonal statements about the service made by the organization. The statements are personal when they are communicated by salespeople or service or repair personnel; they are nonpersonal when they come from advertising, brochures, and other written publications. Explicit service promises are one of the few influences on expectations that are completely in the control of the service provider.

Being realistic would seem a logical and appropriate way to manage customer expectations and ensure that reality fits the promise. The Halifax Airport was being realistic in its newspaper ad shown in Figure 4.9. However, companies and the personnel who represent them often deliberately overpromise to obtain business, or inadvertently overpromise by stating their best estimates about delivery of a service in the future. In addition to overpromising, company representatives may not know when or in what final form the service will be delivered.

All types of explicit service promises have a direct effect on desired service expectation. If the sales visit portrays a banking service that is available 24 hours a day, the customer's desires for that service (as well as the service of competitors) will be shaped by this promise. A particularly dangerous promise that many companies today make to their business customers is to provide a "total solution" to their business needs. This promise is very difficult to deliver.

Explicit service promises influence the levels of both desired service and predicted service. They shape what customers desire in general as well as what they predict will happen in the next service encounter. Figure 4.10 shows how, in response to criticisms concerning power outages related to Hurricane Juan, Nova Scotia Power explicitly

FIGURE 4.10

Nova Scotia Power's Management of Customer Expectations

Source: Reprinted by permission of Nova Scotia Power.

What Happens When You Call Us?

If your power goes out you can call Nova Scotia Power at **1 (877) 428-6004, or 428-6004 (in Metro Halifax)**. Here's the kind of information you can expect along the way.

NSPI OUTAGE LINE 1 (877) 428-6004
- Open 24-hours a day

AUTOMATIC INFORMATION SYSTEM
- Provides information based on your calling area
- Automatically provides information about known outages in your area
- Improved messaging now includes:
  - Location of outage;
  - Cause, if known;
  - Estimated time when power will be back on
- To report a power outage stay on the line

AUTOMATIC REPORTING MENU
Press 1 – Report public hazard / emergency
Press 2 – Report loss of power
Press 3 – Listen to outage info from your calling area
Press 4 – Listen to outage info from other calling areas
Press 0 – Speak with a customer service representative
Press * – Repeat menu options
Press 7 – Return to main customer service menu
Press 9/Hang Up – End call

SPEAK TO CUSTOMER SERVICE REPRESENTATIVE
- Customer service representatives are here to assist you
- During extreme weather or large outages, when many people are calling, you may be asked to call back. If you hear this message, it means that thousands of customers are trying to reach a customer service representative at the same time
- We thank you for your patience

tried to manage customer expectations about what happens when customers call to report a power outage. This is also a good example of educating customers on their role in services—a topic we cover in Chapters 13 and 16.

Implicit service promises are service-related cues other than explicit promises that lead to inferences about what the service should and will be like. These quality cues are dominated by price and the tangibles associated with the service. In general, the higher the price and the more impressive the tangibles, the more a customer will expect from the service. A customer who stays at a posh hotel is likely to desire and predict a higher standard of service than from a hotel with less impressive facilities.

The importance of *word-of-mouth communication* in shaping expectations of service is well documented.[15] It conveys to customers what the service will be like and influence both predicted and desired service. Word-of-mouth communication carries particular weight as an information source because it is perceived as unbiased. Word of mouth tends to be very important in services that are difficult to evaluate *before* purchase. Experts (including *Consumer Reports,* friends, and family) are also word-of-mouth sources that can affect the levels of desired and predicted service.

Past experience is another force in shaping predictions and desires. (See Figure 4.11.) For example, you probably compare every stay in a particular hotel with all previous stays there. But past experience with the hotel is likely to be a very limited view of your past experience. You may also compare each stay with your experiences in other hotels and hotel chains. Customers also compare across industries: hospital patients, for example, compare hospital stays against the standard of hotel visits. Cable service customers tend to compare cable service with the standards set by telephone service, one reason cable service is often judged to be poor. In a general sense, past experience may incorporate previous experience with the focal brand, typical performance of a favourite brand, experience with the brand last purchased or the top-selling brand, and the average performance a customer believes represents similar brands.[16]

FIGURE 4.11

How Past Experience Shapes Predictions and Desires

Source: © Baby Blues Partnership. King Features Syndicate.

How might a manager of a service organization use the information we have developed in this chapter to create, improve, or market services? First, managers need to know the pertinent expectation sources and their relative importance. They need to know, for instance, the relative weight of word of mouth, explicit service promises, and implicit service promises in shaping desired service and predicted service. Some of these sources are more stable and permanent in their influence (such as lasting service intensifiers and personal needs) than the others, which fluctuate considerably over time (like perceived service alternatives and situational factors).

The different sources vary in terms of their credibility as well as their potential to be influenced by the marketer. Exhibit 4.1 shows the breakdown of various factors and how services marketers can influence them. Chapter 16 will detail these and other strategies that services marketers can use to match delivery to promises and thereby manage expectations.

ISSUES INVOLVING CUSTOMER SERVICE EXPECTATIONS

In this section we discuss four of the most frequently asked questions about customer expectations:

1. What does a service marketer do if customer expectations are "unrealistic"?

2. How does a company exceed customer service expectations?

3. Do customer service expectations continually escalate?

4. How does a service company stay ahead of competition in meeting customer expectations?

What Does a Services Marketer Do If Customer Expectations Are "Unrealistic"?

One inhibitor to learning about customer expectations is the fear of asking. This apprehension often stems from the belief that customer expectations will be extravagant and unrealistic and that by asking about them a company will set itself up for even loftier expectation levels (i.e., "unrealistic" levels). Yet compelling evidence suggests that customers' main expectations of service are quite simple and basic: "Simply put, customers expect service companies to do what they are supposed to do. They expect fundamentals, not fanciness; performance, not empty promises."[17] Customers want service to be delivered as promised. They want planes to take off on time, hotel rooms to be clean, food to be hot, and service providers to show up when scheduled. Unfortunately, many service customers are disappointed and let down by companies' inability to meet these basic service expectations.

Asking customers about their expectations does not so much raise the levels of the expectations themselves as heighten the belief that the company will do something with the information that surfaces. Arguably the worst thing a company can do is show a strong interest in understanding what customers expect and then never act on the information. At minimum, a company should acknowledge to customers that it has received and heard their input and that it will try to address their issues. The company may not be able to—and indeed does not always have to—deliver to expressed expectations. An alternative and appropriate response would be to let customers know the reasons desired service is not being provided and describe the efforts planned to address them. Another approach could be a campaign to educate customers about ways to use and improve the service they currently receive. Giving

 EXHIBIT 4.1

How Services Marketers Can Influence Factors

FACTOR	POSSIBLE INFLUENCE STRATEGIES
Explicit service promises	Make realistic and accurate promises that reflect the service actually delivered rather than an idealized version of the service.
	Ask contact people for feedback on the accuracy of promises made in advertising and personal selling.
	Avoid engaging in price or advertising wars with competitors because they take the focus off customers and escalate promises beyond the level at which they can be met.
	Formalize service promises through a service guarantee that focuses company employees on the promise and that provides feedback on the number of times promises are not fulfilled.
Implicit service promises	Ensure that service tangibles accurately reflect the type and level of service provided.
	Ensure that price premiums can be justified by higher levels of performance by the company on important customer attributes.
Lasting service intensifiers	Use market research to determine sources of derived service expectations and their requirements. Focus advertising and marketing strategy on ways the service allows the focal customer to satisfy the requirements of the influencing customer.
	Use market research to profile personal service philosophies of customers and use this information in designing and delivering services.
Personal needs	Educate customers on ways the service addresses their needs.
Temporary service intensifiers	Increase service delivery during peak periods or in emergencies.
Perceived service alternatives	Be fully aware of competitive offerings, and where possible and appropriate, match them.
Self-perceived service role	Educate customers to understand their roles and perform them better.
Word-of-mouth communications	Simulate word of mouth in advertising by using testimonials and opinion leaders.
	Identify influencers and opinion leaders for the service and concentrate marketing efforts on them.
	Use incentives with existing customers to encourage them to say positive things about the service.
Past experience	Use marketing research to profile customers' previous experience with similar services.
Situational factors	Use service guarantees to assure customers about service recovery regardless of the situational factors that occur.
Predicted service	Tell customers when service provision is higher than what can normally be expected so that predictions of future service encounters will not be inflated.

customers progress updates as service is improved to address their needs and desires is sensible, because it allows the company to get credit for incremental efforts to improve service (see the airport ad earlier in the chapter).

Some observers recommend deliberately underpromising the service to increase the likelihood of meeting or exceeding customer expectations.[18] While underpromising makes service expectations more realistic, narrowing the gap between expectations and perceptions, it also may reduce the competitive appeal of the offer. Also, some research has indicated that underpromising may have the effect of lowering customer *perceptions* of service, particularly in situations in which customers have little experience with a service.[19]

The second option is for the provider to follow a sale with a "reality check" about service delivery. One of us bought a new house from a builder. Typical sales promises were made about the quality of the home, some less than accurate, in order to make the sale. Before closing on the house, the builder and I conducted a final check on the house. At the front door, the builder turned to me and pointed out that every new home has between 3,000 and 5,000 individual elements and that in his experience the typical new home had 100 to 150 defects. Armed with this reality check, I thought the 32 defects found in my house seemed minor. Consider my response in the absence of that reality check.

How Does a Company Exceed Customer Service Expectations?

Many companies today talk about exceeding expectations—delighting and surprising customers by giving more than they expect. This philosophy raises the question, Should a service provider try simply to meet customer expectations or to exceed them?

First, it is essential to recognize that exceeding customer expectations on the basics is virtually impossible. Honouring promises—having the reserved room available, meeting deadlines, showing up for meetings, delivering the core service—is what the company is supposed to do. Companies are *supposed* to be accurate and dependable and provide the service they promised to provide.[20] Ask yourself if a provider doing any of these things would delight you. The conclusion you should reach is that it is very difficult to surprise or delight customers consistently by delivering reliable service.

How, then, does a company exceed their expectations? In virtually any service, developing a customer relationship is one approach for exceeding service expectations. Ritz-Carlton Hotels provides highly personalized attention to its customers. The company trains each of its employees to note guest likes and dislikes and to record these into a computerized guest history profile. The company now has information on the preferences of more than 240,000 repeat Ritz-Carlton guests, resulting in more personalized service. The aim is not simply to meet expectations of guests but to provide them with a "memorable visit." The company uses the guest history information to exceed customers' expectations of the way they will be treated. When a repeat customer calls the hotel's central reservations number to book accommodations, the reservation agent can call up the individual's preference information. The agent then sends this information electronically to the particular hotel at which the reservation is made. The hotel puts the data in a daily guest recognition and preference report that is circulated to employees. Employees then greet the repeat guest personally at check-in and ensure that the guest's needs/preferences are anticipated and met.[21]

How well does this approach work? According to surveys conducted for Ritz-Carlton by an independent research firm, 92 to 97 percent of the company's guests go away satisfied.[22]

Do Customer Service Expectations Continually Escalate?

As we illustrated in the beginning of this chapter, customer service expectations are dynamic. In the credit card industry, as in many competitive service industries, battling companies seek to best each other and thereby raise the level of service above that of competing companies. Service expectations—in this case adequate service expectations—rise as quickly as service delivery or promises rise. In a highly competitive and rapidly changing industry, expectations can thus rise quickly. For this reason companies need to monitor adequate service expectations continually—the more turbulent the industry, the more frequent the monitoring needed.

Desired service expectations, on the other hand, are far more stable. Because they are driven by more enduring factors, such as personal needs and lasting service intensifiers, they tend to be high to begin with and remain high.

How Does a Service Company Stay Ahead of Competition in Meeting Customer Expectations?

All else being equal, a company's goal is to meet customer expectations better than its competitors. Given the fact that adequate service expectations change rapidly in a turbulent environment, how can a company ensure that it stays ahead of competition?

The adequate service level reflects the minimum performance level expected by customers after they consider a variety of personal and external factors (Figure 4.7), including the availability of service options from other providers. Companies whose service performance falls short of this level are clearly at a competitive disadvantage, with the disadvantage escalating as the gap widens. These companies' customers may well be "reluctant" customers, ready to take their business elsewhere the moment they see an alternative.

If they are to use service quality for competitive advantage, companies must perform above the adequate service level. This level, however, may signal only a temporary advantage. Customers' adequate service levels, which are less stable than desired service levels, will rise rapidly when competitors promise and deliver a higher level of service. If a company's level of service is barely above the adequate service level to begin with, a competitor can quickly erode that advantage. Companies currently performing in the region of competitive advantage must stay alert to the need for service increases to meet or beat competition.

To develop a true customer franchise—immutable customer loyalty—companies must not only consistently exceed the adequate service level but also reach the desired service level. Exceptional service can intensify customers' loyalty to a point at which they are impervious to competitive options.

SUMMARY

Using a conceptual framework of the nature and determinants of customer expectations of service, we showed in this chapter that customers hold different types of service expectations: (1) desired service, which reflects what customers want; (2) adequate service, or what customers are willing to accept; and (3) predicted service, or what customers believe they are likely to get.

Customer expectations are influenced by a variety of factors. The types and sources of expectations are the same for end consumers and business customers, for pure service and product-related service, and for experienced customers and inexperienced customers.

Discussion Questions

1. What is the difference between desired service and adequate service? Why would a services marketer need to understand both types of service expectations?
2. Consider a recent service purchase that you have made. Which of the factors influencing expectations were the most important in your decision? Why?
3. Why are desired service expectations more stable than adequate service expectations?
4. How do the technology changes discussed in the Technology Spotlight in this chapter influence customer expectations?
5. Describe several instances in which a service company's explicit service promises were inflated and led you to be disappointed with the service outcome.
6. Consider a small business preparing to buy a computer system. Which of the influences on customer expectations do you believe will be pivotal? Which factors will have the most influence? Which factors will have the least importance in this decision?
7. What strategies can you add to Exhibit 4.1 in this chapter for influencing the factors?
8. Do you believe that any of your service expectations are unrealistic? Which ones? Should a service marketer try to address unrealistic customer expectations?
9. In your opinion, what service companies have effectively built customer franchises (immutable customer loyalty)?
10. Intuitively, it would seem that managers would want their customers to have wide tolerance zones for service. But if customers do have these wide zones of tolerance for service, is it more difficult for firms with superior service to earn customer loyalty? Would superior service firms be better off to attempt to narrow customers' tolerance zones to reduce the competitive appeal of mediocre providers?

Exercises

1. What factors do you think influenced your professor to adopt this text? In the case of text adoption, what do you think are the most important factors? After you have formulated your ideas, ask your professor in class to talk about the sources of his or her expectations.
2. Keep a service journal for a day and document your use of services. Ask yourself before each service encounter to indicate your predicted service of that encounter. After the encounter, note whether your expectations were met or exceeded. How does the answer to this question relate to your desire to do business with that service firm again?
3. List five incidents in which a service company has exceeded your expectations. How did you react to the service? Did these incidents change the way you viewed subsequent interactions with the companies? In what way?

Notes

1. "Japanese Put Tourism on a Higher Plane," *International Herald Tribune*, February 3, 1992, p. 8.
2. J. Kelley, "Service Without a Smile: Russians Find a Friendly Face Works Better," *USA Today*, January 22, 1992, p. 1.

3. The model on which this chapter is based is taken from V. A. Zeithaml, L. L. Berry, and A. Parasuraman, "The Nature and Determinants of Customer Expectations of Service," *Journal of the Academy of Marketing Science* 21 (Winter 1993), no. 1 (1993), pp. 1–12.

4. See sources such as C. Gronroos, *Strategic Management and Marketing in the Service Sector* (Helsingfors, Sweden: Swedish School of Economics and Business Administration, 1982); U. Lehtinen and J. R. Lehtinen, "Service Quality: A Study of Quality Dimensions," unpublished working paper, Helsinki, Finland OY, Service Management Institute, 1982; and S. W. Brown and T. A. Swartz, "A Dyadic Evaluation of the Professional Services Encounter," *Journal of Marketing* 53 (April 1989), pp. 92–98.

5. R. B. Woodruff, E. R. Cadotte, and R. L. Jenkins, "Expectations and Norms in Models of Consumer Satisfaction," *Journal of Marketing Research* 24 (August 1987), pp. 305–14.

6. J. A. Miller, "Studying Satisfaction, Modifying Models, Eliciting Expectations, Posing Problems, and Making Meaningful Measurements," in *Conceptualization and Measurement of Consumer Satisfaction and Dissatisfaction,* ed. H. K. Hunt (Bloomington, IN: Indiana University School of Business, 1977), pp. 72–91.

7. W. H. Davidow and B. Uttal, "Service Companies: Focus or Falter," *Harvard Business Review,* July/August 1989, pp. 77–85.

8 G. Hofstede, *Cultures and Organizations: Software of the Mind* (Berkshire, UK: McGraw-Hill, 1991).

9. N. Donthu and B. Uttal, "Cultural Influences on Service Quality Expectations," *Journal of Service Research* 1 (November 1998), pp. 178-86

10. A. Parasuraman, L. L. Berry, and V. A. Zeithaml, "Understanding Customer Expectations of Service," *Sloan Management Review* 32 (Spring 1991), p. 42.

11. L. L. Berry, A. Parasuraman, and V. A. Zeithaml, "Ten Lessons for Improving Service Quality," *Marketing Science Institute*, Report No. 93-104 (May 1993).

12. Zeithaml, Berry, and Parasuraman, "The Nature and Determinants," p. 8.

13. D. Bowen, "Leadership Aspects and Reward Systems of Customer Satisfaction," speech given at CTM Customer Satisfaction Conference, Los Angeles, March 17, 1989.

14. Zeithaml, Berry, and Parasuraman, "The Nature and Determinants," p. 8.

15. D. L. Davis, J. G. Guiltinan, and W. H. Jones, "Service Characteristics, Consumer Research, and the Classification of Retail Services," *Journal of Retailing* 55 (Fall 1979), pp. 3–21; and W. R. George and L. L. Berry, "Guidelines for the Advertising of Services," *Business Horizons* 24 (May/June 1981), pp. 52–56.

16 E. R. Cadotte, R. B. Woodruff, and R. L. Jenkins, "Expectations and Norms in Models of Consumer Satisfaction," *Journal of Marketing Research* 14 (August 1987), pp. 353–64.

17. Parasuraman, Berry, and Zeithaml, "Understanding Customer Expectations," p. 40.

18. Davidow and Uttal, "Service Companies."

19. W. Boulding, A. Kalra, R. Staelin, and V. A. Zeithaml, "A Dynamic Process Model of Service Quality: From Expectations to Behavioral Intentions," *Journal of Marketing Research* 30 (February 1993), pp. 7–27.

20. Parasuraman, Berry, and Zeithaml, "Understanding Customer Expectations," p. 41.

21. "How the Ritz-Carlton Hotel Company Delivers 'Memorable' Service to Customers," *Executive Report on Customer Satisfaction* 6, no. 5 (March 15, 1993), pp. 1–4.

22. Ibid.

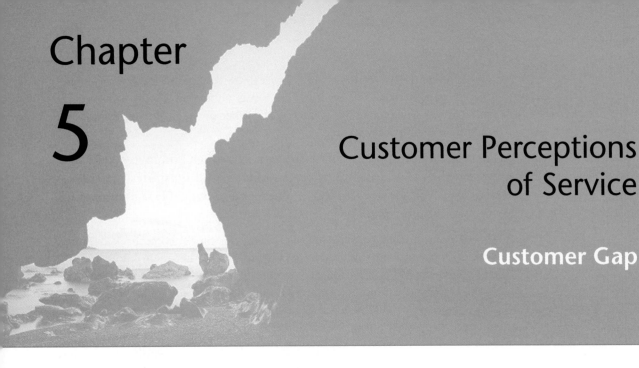

Chapter 5

Customer Perceptions of Service

Customer Gap

THIS CHAPTER'S OBJECTIVES ARE TO

1. Show what influences customer perceptions of service and the relationships among customer satisfaction, service quality, and individual service encounters.

2. Demonstrate the importance of customer satisfaction—what it is, the factors that influence it, and the significant outcomes resulting from it.

3. Develop critical knowledge of service quality and its five key dimensions: reliability, responsiveness, empathy, assurance, and tangibles.

4. Show that service encounters or the "moments of truth" are the essential building blocks from which customers form their perceptions.

EXCEEDING CUSTOMER EXPECTATIONS

Try to think of an example of great customer service you have received. What made the service you received so special?

Now, what if someone told you the service they received at Wal-Mart (www. walmart.ca) was great? Would you be surprised? Maybe—it all depends on your expectations of the service and your perception of how well the service provider has met or exceeded those expectations. Consider these examples provided by Wal-Mart customers.[1]

Sheila risked her own safety when she jumped in front of a car to prevent a little boy from being struck, Phyllis administered CPR to a customer who had suffered a heart attack in her store, Joyce threw a plate on the floor to assure a young mother that a set of dishes truly was unbreakable, and Annette gave up the Power Ranger she had on layaway for her own son so a customer's son could have his birthday wish.

Each of these examples demonstrates times when employees were able to exceed the expectations of those customers, and illustrates the kind of service Sam Walton expected his employees to provide. He summarized his service philosophy as follows:

> Exceed your customers' expectations. If you do, they'll come back over and over. Give them what they want—and a little more. Let them know you appreciate them. Make good on all your mistakes, and don't make excuses ... apologize. Stand behind everything you do. The two most important words I ever wrote were on that first Wal-Mart sign, "Satisfaction Guaranteed." They're still up there, and they have made all the difference.

Great prices, good merchandise quality and selection, friendly service, and unexpected over-the-top gestures by employees all add up to the satisfaction of shoppers at Wal-Mart. The same is true for other landmark service companies such as Lands' End, Delta Hotels, and IBM Global Services. In all of these companies the quality of the core product and exemplary customer service result in high customer service ratings.

So what is it that brings about customer satisfaction? How do customers evaluate service quality? How do they form their perceptions of service? Answers to these questions are the subjects of this chapter.

Source: Courtesy Wal-Mart Canada Corp.

CUSTOMER PERCEPTIONS

How customers perceive services, how they assess whether they have experienced quality service, and whether they are satisfied are the subjects of this chapter. We will be focusing on the *perceived service* box in the Gaps model. As we move through this chapter, keep in mind that perceptions are always considered relative to expectations. Because expectations are dynamic, evaluations may also shift over time—from person to person and from culture to culture. The things that satisfy customers today may be different tomorrow. Also keep in mind that the entire discussion of quality and satisfaction is based on *customers' perceptions of the service*—not some predetermined objective criteria of what service is or should be.

Satisfaction vs. Service Quality

Practitioners and writers in the popular press tend to use the terms *satisfaction* and *quality* interchangeably, but researchers have attempted to be more precise about the meanings and measurement of the two concepts, resulting in considerable debate.[2] Consensus is that the two concepts are fundamentally different in terms of their underlying causes and outcomes.[3] Although they have certain things in common, **satisfaction** is generally viewed as a broader concept, whereas **service quality** focuses specifically on dimensions of service. Based on this view, **perceived service quality** is a component of customer satisfaction. Figure 5.1 graphically illustrates the relationships between the two concepts.

As shown in the figure, service quality is a focused evaluation that reflects the customer's perception of: reliability, assurance, responsiveness, empathy, and tangibles.[4] Satisfaction, on the other hand, is more inclusive: it is influenced by perceptions of service quality, product quality, and price as well as situational factors and personal factors. For example, *service quality* of a health club is judged on attributes such as whether equipment is available and in working order when needed, how responsive the staff are to customer needs, how skilled the trainers are, and whether the facility is well maintained. *Customer satisfaction* with the health club is a broader concept that will certainly be influenced by perceptions of service quality but that will also include perceptions of product quality (such as quality of products sold in the pro shop), price of membership,[5] personal factors such as the consumer's emotional state, and even uncontrollable situational factors such as weather conditions and experiences driving to and from the health club.[6]

Transaction vs. Cumulative Perceptions

In considering perceptions, it is also important to recognize that customers will have perceptions of single, transaction-specific encounters as well as overall perceptions of a company based on all their experiences.[7] For example, a bank customer will

FIGURE 5.1

Customer
Perceptions
of Quality
and Customer
Satisfaction

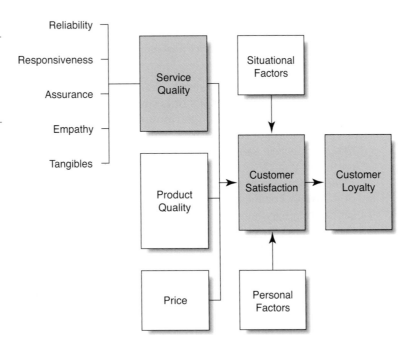

have a perception of how he or she was treated in a particular encounter with a bank employee at a branch. That perception is at a very micro, transaction-specific level. That same bank customer will also have overall perceptions of the bank based on all his encounters over a period of time. These experiences might include online banking experiences and experiences using the bank's ATMs. At an even more general level, the customer may have perceptions of the whole banking industry as a result of all his or her experiences with banks.

Research suggests that it is important to understand all these types of perceptions for different reasons and that the viewpoints are complementary rather than competing.[8] Understanding perceptions at the transaction-specific level is critical for diagnosing service issues and making immediate changes. These isolated encounters are also the building blocks for overall, cumulative experience evaluations, as you will learn later in this chapter. On the other hand, cumulative experience evaluations are likely to be better predictors of overall loyalty to a company. That is, customer loyalty most often results from the customer's assessment of all experiences, not just a single encounter.

In this chapter, we will begin with an overview of the broadest of these perceptions—satisfaction—and then turn our attention to the more specific concept of service quality. Finally, we will discuss the most specific concept—service encounters. These encounters, or "moments of truth," are the building blocks for the more general assessments of quality and satisfaction.

CUSTOMER SATISFACTION

What Is Customer Satisfaction?

"Everyone knows what satisfaction is, until asked to give a definition. Then, it seems, nobody knows."[9] This quote from Richard L. Oliver expresses the challenge of defining this most basic of customer concepts. Building from previous definitions, Oliver offers his own formal definition (p. 13):

> Satisfaction is the consumer's fulfillment response. It is a judgment that a product or service feature, or the product or service itself, provides a pleasurable level of consumption-related fulfillment.

We interpret this to mean simply that *satisfaction* is the customer's evaluation of whether a service has met his or her needs and expectations. Failure to meet needs and expectations is assumed to result in *dissatisfaction* with the product or service.

In addition to a sense of *fulfilment* in the knowledge that one's needs have been met, satisfaction can also be related to other types of feelings, depending on the particular context or type of service.[10] For example, satisfaction can be viewed as *contentment*—more of a passive response. It may also be associated with feelings of *pleasure*. For those services that really surprise the consumer in a positive way, satisfaction may mean *delight*. In some situations, involving removal of a negative, the consumer may associate a sense of *relief* with satisfaction. Finally, satisfaction may be associated with feelings of *ambivalence* when there is a mix of positive and negative experiences associated with the product or service.

Although consumer satisfaction tends to be measured at a particular point in time as if it were static, satisfaction is a dynamic, moving target that may evolve over time, influenced by a variety of factors.[11] Particularly when the service experience takes place over time, satisfaction may be highly variable depending on which experience cycle one is focusing on. Similarly, in the case of a service not previously experienced, customer expectations may be barely forming at the point of initial purchase; these expectations will solidify as the process unfolds and the consumer begins to form his or her perceptions. Through the service cycle the consumer may have a variety of different experiences—some good, some not good—and each will ultimately impact satisfaction.

What Determines Customer Satisfaction?

As shown in Figure 5.1, customer satisfaction is influenced by specific product or service features, perceptions of product and service quality, and price. In addition, personal factors such as the customer's mood or emotional state and situational factors such as family member opinions will also influence satisfaction.

Product and Service Features

Customer satisfaction is influenced significantly by the customer's evaluation of service features.[12] For a service such as a resort hotel, important features might include the pool area, access to golf facilities, restaurants, room comfort and privacy, helpfulness and courtesy of staff, room price, and so forth. In conducting satisfaction studies, most firms will determine what the important features and attributes are for their service and then measure perceptions of those features as well as overall service satisfaction. Research has shown that customers make tradeoffs among different service features (e.g., price level vs. quality vs. friendliness of personnel), depending on the type of service being evaluated and the criticality of the service.[13]

Consumer Emotions

Customers' emotions can also affect their perceptions of satisfaction.[14] These emotions can be stable, preexisting ones—for example, mood state or life satisfaction. Think of times when you are very happy (such as when you are on vacation), and your happy mood and positive frame of mind have influenced how you feel about the services you experience. Alternatively, when you are in a bad mood, your negative feelings may carry over into how you respond to services, causing you to respond negatively to any little problem.

Specific emotions may also be induced by the consumption experience itself, influencing a consumer's satisfaction with the service. Research done in a river-rafting context showed that the river guides had a strong effect on their customers' emotional responses to the trip and that those feelings (both positive and negative) were linked to overall trip satisfaction.[15] Positive emotions such as happiness, pleasure, elation, and a sense of warmheartedness enhanced customers' satisfaction with the rafting trip. In turn, negative emotions such as sadness, sorrow, regret, and anger led to diminished customer satisfaction. Overall, in the rafting context, positive emotions had a stronger effect than negative ones (as is apparent in Figure 5.2.) Similar effects of emotions on satisfaction were found in a Finnish study that looked at consumers' satisfaction with a government labour bureau service.[16] In that study, negative emotions including anger, depression, guilt, and humiliation had a strong effect on customers' dissatisfaction ratings.

Attributions for Service Success or Failure

Attributions—the perceived causes of events—influence perceptions of satisfaction as well.[17] When they have been surprised by an outcome (the service is either much better or much worse than expected), consumers tend to look for the

FIGURE 5.2

River rafters experience many positive emotions, increasing their satisfaction with the service.

Source: River Odysseys West, www.rowinc.com.

reasons, and their assessments of the reasons can influence their satisfaction. For example, if a customer of a weight-loss organization fails to lose weight as hoped for, she will likely search for the causes—was it something she did, was the diet plan ineffective, or did circumstances simply not allow her to follow the diet regimen—before determining her level of satisfaction or dissatisfaction with the weight-loss company.[18] For many services, customers take at least partial responsibility for how things turn out.

Even when customers do not take responsibility for the outcome, customer satisfaction may be influenced by other kinds of attributions. For example, research done in a travel agency context found that customers were less dissatisfied with a pricing error made by the agent if they felt that the reason was outside the agent's control or if they felt that it was a rare mistake, unlikely to occur again.[19]

Perceptions of Equity or Fairness

Customer satisfaction is also influenced by perceptions of equity and fairness.[20] Customers ask themselves: Have I been treated fairly compared with other customers? Did other customers get better treatment, better prices, or better quality service? Did I pay a fair price for the service? Was I treated well in exchange for what I paid and the effort I expended? Notions of fairness are central to customers' perceptions of satisfaction with products and services, particularly in service recovery situations. As you will learn in Chapter 8, satisfaction with a service provider following a service failure is largely determined by perceptions of fair treatment.

Other Consumers, Family Members, and Coworkers

In addition to product and service features and one's own individual feelings and beliefs, consumer satisfaction is often influenced by other people.[21] For example, satisfaction with a family vacation trip is a dynamic phenomenon, influenced by the reactions and expressions of individual family members over the duration of the vacation. Later, what family members express in terms of satisfaction or dissatisfaction with the trip will be influenced by stories that are retold among the family and selective memories of the events. Similarly, the satisfaction of the rafters in Figure 5.2 is certainly influenced by individual perceptions, but it is also influenced greatly by the experiences, behaviour, and views of the other rafters.

National Customer Satisfaction Indexes

Because of the importance of customer satisfaction to firms, many countries have a national index that measures customer satisfaction at a macro level.[22] Many public policymakers believe that these measures could and should be used as tools for evaluating the health of the nation's economy, along with traditional measures of productivity and price. Customer satisfaction indexes begin to get at the *quality* of economic output, whereas more traditional economic indicators tend to focus only on *quantity.* The first such measure was the Swedish Customer Satisfaction Barometer introduced in 1989.[23] Throughout the 1990s similar indexes were introduced in Germany (Deutsche Kundenbarometer, or DK, in 1992), the United States (American Customer Satisfaction Index, ACSI, in 1994), and Switzerland (Swiss Index of Customer Satisfaction, SWICS, in 1998).[24] Canada has not yet developed a national satisfaction index. Although the National Quality Institute devotes its resources to assisting its members improve the overall quality of its products and services, it does not have a national scoring system. NQI does have a scoring system for healthy workplaces, however, which we will return to in a later chapter.

In the United States, data compiled by the ACSI shows that consumers tend to be most satisfied with non-durables (like soft drinks and personal care products), somewhat less satisfied with durables (like automobiles and appliances), and least satisfied with services. This trend has been consistently observed over the entire history of the ACSI index.

We can only conjecture about the reasons for lower satisfaction with services in general. Perhaps it is because downsizing and right-sizing in service businesses has resulted in stressed and overworked front-line service providers who are unable to provide the level of service demanded. Perhaps it is due to the inherent heterogeneity of services discussed in Chapter 1; in other words, because services are difficult to standardize, and each customer has his or her own unique expectations, the result may be greater variability and potentially lower overall satisfaction. Perhaps it is due to difficulty finding qualified front-line service providers for consumer-service businesses. Perhaps it is due to rising customer expectations rather than any real or absolute decline in actual service. Whatever the reason, there is much room for improvement in customer satisfaction ratings across service industries.

Outcomes of Customer Satisfaction

Why all this attention to customer satisfaction? Satisfaction is an important indicator of quality of life. Further, customer satisfaction is correlated with other measures of economic health such as corporate earnings and stock value.

Individual firms have discovered that increasing levels of customer satisfaction can be linked to customer loyalty and profits.[25] As shown in Figure 5.3, there is an important relationship between customer satisfaction and customer loyalty. This relationship is particularly strong when customers are very satisfied. Xerox Corporation was one of the first companies to pinpoint this relationship. In the 1980s Xerox discovered through its extensive customer research that customers giving Xerox a 5 (very satisfied) on a satisfaction scale were six times more likely to repurchase Xerox equipment than were those giving the company a 4 (somewhat satisfied).[26] As another example, Enterprise Rent-A-Car learned through its research that customers who gave

FIGURE 5.3

Relationship
Between Customer
Satisfaction
and Loyalty in
Competitive
Industries

Source: J. L. Heskett, W.
E. Sasser Jr., and L. A.
Schlesinger, *The Service
Profit Chain: How Leading
Companies Link Profit and
Growth to Loyalty, Satisfaction,
and Value* (New York: The Free
Press, 1997), p. 83. © 1997
by J. L. Heskett, W. E. Sasser,
Jr., and L. A. Schlesinger.
Reprinted with the permission
of The Free Press, a Division of
Simon & Schuster, Inc.

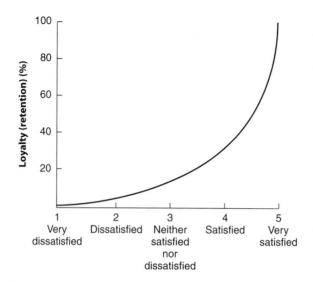

the highest rating to their rental experience were three times more likely to rent again than those who gave the company the second-highest rating.[27] Many other companies have drawn similar conclusions.

At the opposite end of the satisfaction spectrum, researchers have also found that there is a strong link between dissatisfaction and disloyalty—or defection. Customer loyalty can fall off precipitously when customers reach a particular level of dissatisfaction or when they are dissatisfied with critically important service attributes.[28] We discuss these relationships and the implications for relationship and loyalty marketing in Chapter 7. Thus, many companies are spending more time and money understanding the underpinnings of customer satisfaction and ways that they can improve.

SERVICE QUALITY

We now turn to *service quality,* a critical element of customer perceptions. In the case of pure services (e.g., health care, financial services, education), service quality will be the dominant element in customers' evaluations. In cases in which customer service or services are offered in combination with a physical product (e.g., IT services, auto services), service quality may also be very critical in determining customer satisfaction. Figure 5.1, which is our model of the relationship between quality and satisfaction, highlighted these relationships. We will focus here on the left side of that figure, examining the underlying factors that form perceptions of service quality. First we discuss *what* customers evaluate; then we look specifically at the five dimensions of service that customers rely on in forming their judgments.

Outcome, Interaction, and Physical Environment Quality

What is it that consumers evaluate when judging service quality? Researchers have suggested that consumers judge the quality of services according to the technical outcome provided, the process by which that outcome was delivered, and the quality of the physical surroundings where the service is delivered.[29] For example, a restaurant customer will judge the service on her perceptions of the meal (technical outcome quality) and on how the meal was served and how the employees interacted with her (interaction quality). The decor and surroundings (physical environment quality) will also impact perceptions of overall service quality.

This depiction of service quality as outcome quality, interaction quality, and physical environment quality is most recently captured by Michael Brady and Joseph Cronin in their empirical research published in the *Journal of Marketing*.[30] Other researchers have defined similar aspects of service in their examinations of service quality.[31]

Service Quality Dimensions

Research suggests that customers do not perceive quality in a unidimensional way but rather judge quality based on multiple factors. The dimensions of service quality have been identified through the pioneering research of Parsu Parasuraman, Valarie Zeithaml, and Leonard Berry. Their research identified five specific dimensions of service quality that apply across a variety of service contexts.[32] The five dimensions defined here are shown in Figure 5.1 as drivers of service quality. These five dimensions appear again in Chapter 6, along with the scale developed to measure them, SERVQUAL.

- *Reliability.* Ability to perform the promised service dependably and accurately

- *Responsiveness.* Willingness to help customers and provide prompt service

- *Assurance.* Employees' knowledge and courtesy and their ability to inspire trust and confidence

- *Empathy.* Caring, individualized attention given to customers

- *Tangibles.* Appearance of physical facilities, equipment, personnel, and written materials

These dimensions represent how consumers organize information about service quality in their minds. On the basis of exploratory and quantitative research, these five dimensions were found relevant for banking, insurance, appliance repair and maintenance, securities brokerage, long-distance telephone service, automobile repair service, and others. Sometimes customers will use all the dimensions to determine service quality perceptions, at other times not. For example, for an ATM, empathy is not likely to be a relevant dimension. And in a phone encounter to schedule a repair, tangibles will not be relevant. Research suggests that cultural differences will also affect the relative importance placed on the five dimensions, as discussed in our Global Feature. In the following pages we expand on each of the dimensions and provide illustrations of how customers judge them.

Reliability: Delivering on Promises

Of the five dimensions, reliability has been consistently shown to be the most important determinant of perceptions of service quality.[33] **Reliability** is defined as the ability to perform the promised service dependably and accurately. In its broadest sense, reliability means that the company delivers on its promises—promises about delivery, service provision, problem resolution, and pricing. Customers want to do business with companies that keep their promises, particularly their promises about the service outcomes and core service attributes.

One company that effectively communicates and delivers on the reliability dimension is FedEx. The reliability message of FedEx—"When it absolutely, positively has to get there overnight"—reflects the company's service positioning. See also Home

FIGURE 5.4

This ad demonstrates the "reliability" dimension of service quality.

Source: Reprinted by permission of Home Depot, Canada.

Depot's use of TV celebrity Mike Holmes to position its installation services on quality and reliability dimensions, illustrated in Figure 5.4.

Responsiveness: Being Willing to Help

Responsiveness is the willingness to help customers and to provide prompt service. This dimension emphasizes attentiveness and promptness in dealing with customer requests, questions, complaints, and problems. Responsiveness is communicated to customers by the length of time they have to wait for assistance, answers to questions, or attention to problems. Responsiveness also captures the notion of flexibility and ability to customize the service to customer needs. In Figure 5.5 on the next page, we see how one of Canada's biggest law firms, Borden Ladner Gervais, humorously positions itself on responsiveness.

To excel on the dimension of responsiveness, a company must view the process of service delivery and the handling of requests from the customer's point of view rather than from the company's point of view. Standards for speed and promptness that reflect the company's view of internal process requirements may be very different from the customer's requirements for speed and promptness. To truly distinguish themselves on responsiveness, companies need well-staffed customer service departments as well as responsive front-line people in all contact positions. Responsiveness perceptions diminish when customers wait to get through to a company by telephone, are put on hold, are put through to a complex voice mail system, or have trouble accessing the firm's website.

Assurance: Inspiring Trust and Confidence

Assurance is defined as employees' knowledge and courtesy and the ability of the firm and its employees to inspire trust and confidence. This dimension is likely to be particularly important for services that customers perceive as high risk or for services of which they feel uncertain about their ability to evaluate outcomes—for example, banking, insurance, brokerage, medical, and legal services.

FIGURE 5.5

This ad stresses the "responsiveness" dimension of service quality.

Source: Cartoon Bank, a division of the New Yorker/ Danny Shanahan, Cartoonist/ Mary Secord, Copy Writer, FCB Canada/Annie Lee, Art Director, FCB Canada.

"Could you give me a minute to collect my thoughts? My old law firm never called me back this quickly."

For the best legal solutions delivered in a way that exceeds your expectations, contact Sean Weir, National Managing Partner at 416.367.6040 or sweir@blgcanada.com.

CALGARY   MONTRÉAL   OTTAWA   TORONTO   VANCOUVER   WATERLOO REGION

Borden Ladner Gervais LLP - Lawyers • Patent & Trade-mark Agents • Avocats • Agents de brevets et de marques de commerce
Borden Ladner Gervais LLP is an Ontario Limited Liability Partnership

BORDEN LADNER GERVAIS

IT BEGINS WITH SERVICE

www.blgcanada.com

Trust and confidence may be embodied in the person who links the customer to the company, such as securities brokers, insurance agents, lawyers, or counsellors. In such service contexts the company seeks to build trust and loyalty between key contact people and individual customers. The "personal banker" concept captures this idea: customers are assigned to a banker who will get to know them individually and who will coordinate all their banking services.

In other situations, trust and confidence are embodied in the organization itself. Insurance companies such as Allstate ("You're in good hands with Allstate") and Prudential ("Own a piece of the rock") illustrate efforts to create trusting relationships between customers and the company as a whole. A recent ad campaign by FedEx uses the tag line "Relax, it's FedEx," going beyond its traditional reliability message to focus on assurance and trust.

Empathy: Treating Customers as Individuals

Empathy is defined as the caring, individualized attention that the firm provides its customers. The essence of empathy is conveying, through personalized or customized service, that customers are unique and special and that their needs are understood. Customers want to feel understood by and important to firms that provide service to them. Personnel at small service firms often know customers by name and build relationships that reflect their personal knowledge of customer requirements and preferences. When such a small firm competes with larger firms, the ability to be empathetic may give the small firm a clear advantage.

Tangibles: Representing the Service Physically

Tangibles are defined as the appearance of physical facilities, equipment, personnel, and communication materials. Service industries that emphasize tangibles in their strategies include hospitality services in which the customer visits the establishment

Global Feature

Importance of Service Quality Dimensions Across Cultures

The development of the service quality dimensions of reliability, responsiveness, assurance, empathy, and tangibles was based on research conducted across multiple contexts within the United States. As a general rule, reliability comes through as the most important dimension of service quality in the United States, with responsiveness also being relatively important when compared to the remaining three dimensions. But what happens when we look across cultures? Are the service quality dimensions still important? Which ones are most important? Answers to these questions can be extremely valuable for companies delivering services across cultures or in multicultural environments.

Researchers have used Hofstede's well-established cultural dimensions to assess whether service quality importance would vary across different cultural orientations. For example, *power distance* refers to

the extent to which status differences are expected and accepted within a culture. Research has suggested that most Asian countries are characterized by high power distance, whereas many Western countries score lower on power distance measures. Broadly speaking, *individualism* reflects a self-orientation that is characteristic of Western culture whereas its opposite, *collectivism,* is more typical of the East. Similar comparisons across cultures have been made for the other dimensions: *masculinity, uncertainty avoidance,* and *long-term orientation.* The question is whether these types of cultural differences may affect the importance consumers place on the service quality dimensions.

The figure shown here from research published by Furrer, Liu, and Sudharshan suggests strong differences in the importance of service quality dimensions across clusters of customers defined by different

continued

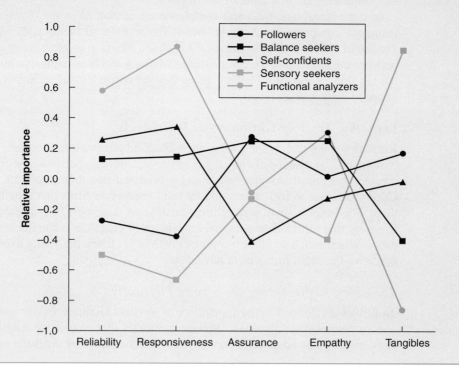

Global Feature

Importance of Service Quality Dimensions Across Cultures—continued

cultural dimensions. The cultural profile of the clusters is described here:

Followers: Large power distance, high collectivism, high masculinity, neutral uncertainty avoidance, and short-term orientation.

Balance seekers: Small power distance, high collectivism, neutral masculinity, high uncertainty avoidance, and medium-term orientation.

Self-confidents: Small power distance, high individualism, medium femininity, low uncertainty avoidance, and long-term orientation.

Sensory seekers: Large power distance, medium individualism, high masculinity, low uncertainty avoidance, and short-term orientation.

Functional analyzers: Small power distance, medium individualism, high femininity, high uncertainty avoidance, and long-term orientation.

From this figure it is clear that the service quality dimensions are important across cultures, but their relative importance varies depending on cultural value orientation. For example, small power distance cultures with high to medium individualism and long-term orientation (self-confidents and functional analyzers) rate reliability and responsiveness as most important. On the other hand, cultures with large power distance and high masculinity (followers and sensory seekers) rate these same dimensions as less important. The tangibles dimension shows the widest variation, with sensory seekers rating it most important and functional analyzers rating it least important.

The researchers in this study suggest a number of implications for companies serving multiple cultures. For example, if the target market has a follower cultural profile, service providers may want to emphasize training their employees to have professional knowledge and be trustworthy to gain the trust of these customers, combined with tangibles and empathy to convey service quality. On the other hand, to serve self-confidents, providers should emphasize equipping and empowering the employees so they are capable of providing reliable, responsive service.

Sources: G. Hofstede, *Cultures and Organizations: Software of the Mind* (New York, McGraw-Hill, 1991); O. Furrer, B. Shaw-Ching Liu, and D. Sudharshan, "The Relationships Between Culture and Service Quality Perceptions," *Journal of Service Research* 2, no. 4 (May 2000), pp. 355–71.

to receive the service, such as restaurants and hotels, retail stores, and entertainment companies.

Although tangibles are often used by service companies to enhance their image, provide continuity, and signal quality to customers, most companies combine tangibles with another dimension to create a service quality strategy for the firm. For example, Mr. Lube emphasizes both responsiveness and tangibles—providing fast, efficient service and a comfortable, clean waiting area.

Table 5.1 provides examples of how customers judge each of the five dimensions of service quality across a variety of service contexts.

TABLE 5.1 Examples of How Customers Judge the Five Dimensions of Service Quality

	Reliability	Responsiveness	Assurance	Empathy	Tangibles
Car repair (consumer)	Problem fixed the first time and ready when promised	Accessible; no waiting; responds to requests	Knowledgeable mechanics	Acknowledges customer by name; remembers previous problems and preferences	Repair facility; waiting area; uniforms; equipment
Airline (consumer)	Flights to promised destinations depart and arrive on schedule	Prompt and speedy system for ticketing, in-flight baggage handling	Trusted name; good safety record; competent employees	Understands special individual needs; anticipates customer needs	Aircraft; ticketing counters; baggage area; uniforms
Medical care (consumer)	Appointments are kept on schedule; diagnoses prove accurate	Accessible; no waiting; willingness to listen	Knowledge; skills; credentials; reputation	Acknowledges patient as a person; remembers previous problems; listens well; has patience	Waiting room; exam room; equipment; written materials
Architecture (business)	Delivers plans when promised and within budget	Returns phone calls; adapts to changes	Credentials; reputation; name in the community; knowledge and skills	Understands client's industry; acknowledges and adapts to specific client needs; gets to know the client	Office area; reports; plans themselves; billing statements; dress of employees
Information processing (internal)	Provides needed information when requested	Prompt response to requests; not "bureaucratic"; deals with problems promptly	Knowledgeable staff; well trained; credentials	Knows internal customers as individuals; understands individual and departmental needs	Internal reports; office area; dress of employees
Internet brokerage (consumer and business)	Provides correct information and executes customer requests accurately	Quick website with easy access and no down time	Credible information sources on the site; brand recognition; credentials apparent on site	Responds with human interaction as needed	Appearance of the website and collateral

e-Service Quality

The growth of e-tailing and e-services has led many companies to wonder how consumers evaluate service quality on the Web and whether the criteria are different from those used to judge the quality of non-Internet services.[34] A study sponsored by the Marketing Science Institute has been conducted to understand how consumers judge e-service quality.[35] In that study, e-SQ is defined as the extent to which a website facilitates efficient and effective shopping, purchasing, and delivery. Through exploratory focus groups and two phases of empirical data collection and analysis, this research identified seven dimensions that are critical for core service evaluation (four dimensions) and service recovery evaluation (three dimensions).

The four core dimensions that customers use to judge websites at which they experience no questions or problems are listed below. Do you agree with them?

- *Efficiency.* The ability of customers to get to the website, find their desired product and information associated with it, and check out with minimal effort

- *Fulfilment.* The accuracy of service promises, having products in stock, and delivering the products in the promised time

- *Reliability.* The technical functioning of the site, particularly the extent to which it is available and functioning properly

- *Privacy.* The assurance that shopping behaviour data are not shared and that credit information is secure

The study also revealed three dimensions that customers use to judge recovery service when they have problems or questions:

- *Responsiveness.* The ability of e-tailers to provide appropriate information to customers when a problem occurs, to have mechanisms for handling returns, and to provide online guarantees

- *Compensation.* The degree to which customers are to receive money back and are reimbursed for shipping and handling costs

- *Contact.* The availability of live customer service agents online or through the phone

SERVICE ENCOUNTERS: THE BUILDING BLOCKS FOR CUSTOMER PERCEPTIONS

We have just finished a discussion of customer perceptions, specifically customer satisfaction and service quality. Here we turn to the building blocks for customer perceptions—service encounters, or "moments of truth." Service encounters are where promises are kept or broken and where the proverbial rubber meets the road—sometimes called "real-time marketing." It is from these service encounters that customers build their perceptions.

Service Encounters or Moments of Truth

From the customer's point of view, the service encounters in a hotel include checking in, being taken to a room by a bellperson, eating a restaurant meal, requesting a wakeup call, and checking out. You might think of the linking of these moments of truth as a service encounter cascade (see Figure 5.6). It is in these encounters that

FIGURE 5.6

A Service Encounter
Cascade for a Hotel
Visit

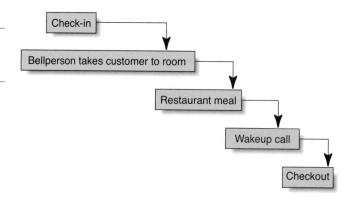

customers receive a snapshot of the organization's service quality, and each encounter contributes to the customer's overall satisfaction and willingness to do business with the organization again. From the organization's point of view, each encounter thus presents an opportunity to prove its potential as a quality service provider and to increase customer loyalty, as suggested by the ad for Doubletree Hotels shown in Figure 5.7 on the next page.

Some services have few service encounters, and others have many. The Disney Corporation estimates that each of its amusement park customers experiences about 74 service encounters and that a negative experience in any one of them can lead to a negative overall evaluation. Mistakes or problems that occur in the early levels of the service cascade may be particularly critical. Marriott Hotels learned this through their extensive customer research to determine what service elements contribute most to customer loyalty. They found that four of the top five factors came into play in the first 10 minutes of the guest's stay.[36]

The Importance of Encounters

Although early events in the encounter cascade are likely to be especially important, *any* encounter can potentially be critical in determining customer satisfaction and loyalty. If a customer is interacting with a firm for the first time, that initial encounter will create a first impression of the organization. In these first-encounter situations, the customer frequently has no other basis for judging the organization, and the initial phone contact or face-to-face experience can take on excessive importance in the customer's perceptions of quality. Even if the technical quality of the firm's repair service is superior, the firm may not get the chance to demonstrate it if the initial telephone encounter drives the customer away.

Logic suggests that not all encounters are equally important in building relationships. For every organization, certain encounters are probably key to customer satisfaction. For Marriott Hotels, as noted, the early encounters are most important. In a hospital context, a study of patients revealed that encounters with nursing staff were more important than encounters with meal service or patient discharge personnel.[37] And research at GTE Laboratories documented that small business customers' relationships with GTE depended on specific installation, repair, and sales encounters.[38]

In addition to these key encounters, there are some momentous encounters that, like the proverbial "one bad apple," simply ruin the rest and drive the customer away no matter how many or what type of encounters have occurred in the past. These momentous encounters can occur in connection with very important events (such

FIGURE 5.7

Every service encounter is an opportunity to build satisfaction and quality.

Source: Reprinted with permission, Hilton Hospitality, Inc./Doubletree ® Hotels, Suites, Resorts, Clubs. Photographer: Chris Schrameck.

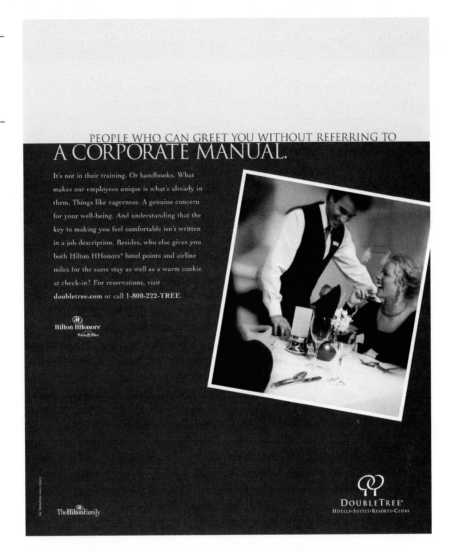

as the failure to deliver an essential piece of equipment before a critical deadline), or they may seem inconsequential, as in the story of the bank customer described in Exhibit 5.1. Similarly, momentous positive encounters can sometimes bind a customer to an organization for life.

Sources of Pleasure and Displeasure in Service Encounters

Because of the importance of service encounters in building perceptions, researchers have extensively analyzed service encounters in many contexts to determine the sources of customers' favourable and unfavourable impressions. The research uses the critical incident technique to get customers and employees to provide verbatim stories about satisfying and dissatisfying service encounters they have experienced.[39] With this technique, customers (either internal or external) are asked the following questions:

> Think of a time when, as a customer, you had a particularly *satisfying* (or *dissatisfying*) interaction with _____.

One Critical Encounter Destroys 30-Year Relationship

"If you have $1 in a bank or $1 million, I think they owe you the courtesy of stamping your parking ticket," said John Barrier. One day in 1989 Mr. Barrier paid a visit to his bank in Spokane, Washington. He was wearing his usual shabby clothes and pulled up in his pickup truck, parking in the lot next to the bank. After cashing a cheque, he went outside to drive away and was stopped by a parking attendant who told him there was a 60 cent fee, but that he could get his parking slip validated in the bank and park for free. No problem, Barrier thought, and he went back into the bank (where, by the way, he had been banking for 30 years). The teller looked him up and down and refused to stamp his slip, telling him that the bank

validated parking only for people who have transactions with the bank and that cashing a cheque wasn't a transaction. Mr. Barrier then asked to see the bank manager, who also looked him up and down, stood back, and "gave me one of those kinds of looks," also refusing to validate the parking bill. Mr. Barrier then said, "Fine. You don't need me, and I don't need you." He withdrew all his money and took it down the street to a competing bank, where the first cheque he deposited was for $1,000,000.

Source: "Shabby Millionaire Closes Account, Gives Bank Lesson About Snobbery." Reprinted with permission of United Press International from *The Arizona Republic* issue of February 21, 1989, p. A3.

When did the incident happen?

What specific circumstances led up to this situation?

Exactly what did the employee (or firm member) say or do?

What resulted that made you feel the interaction was *satisfying* (or *dissatisfying*)?

What could or should have been done differently?

Sometimes contact employees are asked to put themselves in the shoes of a customer and answer the same questions: "Put yourself in the shoes of *customers* of your firm. In other words, try to see your firm through your customers' eyes. Now think of a recent time when a customer of your firm had a particularly *satisfying/unsatisfying* interaction with you or a fellow employee." The stories are then analyzed to determine common themes of satisfaction/dissatisfaction underlying the events. On the basis of thousands of service encounter stories, four common themes—recovery (after failure), adaptability, spontaneity, and coping—have been identified as the sources of customer satisfaction/dissatisfaction in memorable service encounters.[40] Each of the themes is discussed here, and sample stories of both satisfying and dissatisfying incidents for each theme are given in Exhibit 5.2. The themes encompass service behaviours in encounters spanning a wide variety of industries.

Recovery—Employee Response to Service Delivery System Failures

The first theme includes all incidents in which there has been a failure and an employee is required to respond to consumer complaints. The failure may be, for example, a hotel room that is not available, an airplane flight that is delayed six hours, or a critical error on an internal document. The content or form of the employee's response is what causes the customer to remember the event favourably or unfavourably.

Adaptability—Employee Response to Customer Needs and Requests

A second theme underlying satisfaction/dissatisfaction is the adaptability of the service delivery system when the customer has special needs that make demands

Service Encounter Themes

THEME 1: RECOVERY

Satisfactory

They lost my room reservation but the manager gave me the VIP suite for the same price.

Even though I did not make any complaint about the hour-and-a-half wait, the waitress kept apologizing and said the bill was on the house.

Dissatisfactory

We had made advance reservations at the hotel. When we arrived we found we had no room—no explanation, no apologies, and no assistance in finding another hotel.

One of my suitcases was all dented up and looked like it had been dropped from 30,000 feet. When I tried to make a claim for my damaged luggage, the employee insinuated that I was lying and trying to cheat them.

THEME 2: ADAPTABILITY

Satisfactory

I did not have an appointment to see a doctor; however, my allergy nurse spoke to a practitioner's assistant and worked me into the schedule. I received treatment after a 10-minute wait. I was very satisfied with the special treatment I received, the short wait, and the quality of the service.

It was snowing outside—my car broke down. I checked 10 hotels and there were no rooms. Finally, one understood my situation and offered to rent me a bed and set it up in a small banquet room.

Dissatisfactory

My young son, flying alone, was to be assisted by the flight attendant from start to finish. At Toronto she left him alone in the airport with no one to escort him to his connecting flight.

Despite our repeated requests, the hotel staff would not deal with the noisy people partying in the hall at 3 a.m.

THEME 3: SPONTANEITY

Satisfactory

We always travel with our teddy bears. When we got back to our room at the hotel we saw that the cleaning person had arranged our bears very comfortably in a chair. The bears were holding hands.

The anaesthesiologist took extra time to explain exactly what I would be aware of and promised to take special care in making sure I did not wake up during surgery. It impressed me that the anaesthesiologist came to settle my nerves and explain the medicine I was getting because of my cold.

Dissatisfactory

The lady at the front desk acted as if we were bothering her. She was watching TV and paying more attention to that than to the hotel guests.

I needed a few more minutes to decide on a dinner. The waitress said, "If you would read the menu and not the road map, you would know what you want to order."

THEME 4: COPING

Satisfactory

A person who became intoxicated on a flight started speaking loudly, annoying the other passengers. The flight attendant asked the passenger if he would be driving when the plane landed and offered him coffee. He accepted the coffee and became quieter and friendlier.

Dissatisfactory

An intoxicated man began pinching the female flight attendants. One attendant told him to stop, but he continued and then hit another passenger. The copilot was called and asked the man to sit down and leave the others alone, but the passenger refused. The copilot then "decked" the man, knocking him into his seat.

on the process. In these cases, customers judge service encounter quality in terms of the flexibility of the employees and the system. Incidents categorized within this theme contain an implicit or explicit request for customization of the service to meet a need. Much of what customers see as special needs or requests may actually be rather routine from the employee's point of view; what is important is that the customers perceive that something special is being done for them according to their individual needs. External customers and internal customers alike are pleased when the service provider puts forth the effort to accommodate and adjust the system. On the flip side, they are angered and frustrated by an unwillingness to try to accommodate and by promises that are never followed through. Contact employees also see their abilities to adapt the system as being a prominent source of customer satisfaction, and often they are equally frustrated by constraints that keep them from being flexible.

Spontaneity—Unprompted and Unsolicited Employee Actions

Even when there is no system failure and no special request or need, customers can still remember service encounters as being very satisfying or very dissatisfying. Employee spontaneity in delivering memorably good or poor service is the third theme. Satisfying incidents in this group represent very pleasant surprises for the customer (special attention, being treated like royalty, receiving something nice but not requested), whereas dissatisfying incidents in this group represent negative and unacceptable employee behaviours (rudeness, stealing, discrimination, ignoring the customer).

Coping—Employee Response to Problem Customers

The incidents categorized in this group came to light when employees were asked to describe service encounter incidents in which customers were either very satisfied or dissatisfied. In addition to describing incidents of the types outlined under the first three themes, employees described many incidents in which customers were the cause of their own dissatisfaction. Such customers were basically uncooperative—that is, unwilling to cooperate with the service provider, other customers, industry regulations, and/or laws. In these cases nothing the employee could do would result in the customer feeling pleased about the encounter. The term *coping* is used to describe these incidents, because coping is the behaviour generally required of employees to handle problem customer encounters. Rarely are such encounters satisfying from the customers' point of view.[41]

Table 5.2 on page 116 summarizes the specific employee behaviours that cause satisfaction and dissatisfaction in service encounters according to the four themes just presented: recovery, adaptability, spontaneity, and coping. The left side of the table suggests what employees do that results in positive encounters, whereas the right side summarizes negative behaviours within each theme.

Technology-Based Service Encounters

All the research described thus far is based on interpersonal services. Recently researchers have also begun to look at the sources of pleasure and displeasure in technology-based service encounters.[42] These types of encounters involve customers interacting with Internet-based services, automated phone services, kiosk services, and services delivered via CD or video technology. Often these systems are referred to as *self-service technologies* (SSTs), because the customer essentially provides his or her own service.

Technology Spotlight

Customers Love Amazon.com

Although its stock price suffered in 2000–2001, along with that of just about every other Internet-based company, and although the company had never reported a profit until-early in 2002, just prior to entering Canada, customers have always loved Amazon.com. In 2003 the company completed its first full year of profitable quarters and the stock price was back up. The 2004 American Customer Satisfaction Index reflected a rating of 88 for Amazon—one of the highest ratings of any company in any industry, and certainly much higher than the 80 average rating for e-commerce endeavours and the 60–75 ratings for many other service businesses. And, although Amazon's ACSI rating fell to 84 in 2005, it is still one of the highest scores recorded.

Jeff Bezos, CEO of Amazon, whose name has become a household word worldwide, believes that his customers come first. With a continued focus on customers, relationships, value, and the brand itself, Bezos and others believe that sales will continue to grow (almost $7 billion in 2004) and profits will continue. According to Bezos, "Customers come first. If you focus on what customers want and build a relationship, they will allow you to make money."

Few would deny that Amazon is a master of technology and technology-based services for consumers. In fact, other companies, such as Toys "R" Us and Office Depot have sought a technology partnership with Amazon in order to benefit from the company's experience and success with customers. Amazon now provides Internet retail services for both these companies.

Amazon has taken a historically interpersonally dominated transaction and successfully transformed it to a Web-based service experience. Let's take a closer look at what the company is doing and why customers love it so much. Since its inception in July 1995, Amazon has grown to the point where it offers more book titles than any bricks-and-mortar bookstore could ever hope to stock. So selection and availability of titles are one key to its popularity with customers. But that is just the beginning.

In addition to a wide selection, Amazon has invested significant effort to simulate the feel of a neighbourhood bookstore, where a patron can mingle with other customers, discuss books, and get recommendations from bookstore employees. Amazon allows customers to find related books on virtually any topic by simply typing keywords and initiating a search of its massive database. Its one-to-one marketing system allows the company to track what individual consumers buy and let them know of additional titles that might interest them. This marketing is done while the customer is shopping as well as through periodic direct email that identifies books specifically related to the customer's past purchase patterns and interests.

Currently, customers can buy much more than books from Amazon. In fact, Bezos hopes that they can buy just about anything they want through the Amazon website. His goal from the beginning was "to create the world's most customer-centric company, the place where you can find and buy anything you want online." Bezos continues to take risks that are combined with a long-term view of success, and to reflect all new ideas against a customer-focused filter. It is hard to predict where these basic strategies may lead in the future, but even doubters are beginning to believe that Amazon will continue to succeed and be around for a long time. As noted in our Technology Spotlight in Chapter 2, Amazon is a great example of a technology company that addresses all the gaps in the service quality gaps model.

amazon.com®

Source: Amazon, Amazon.com, the Amazon.com logo, and 1-Click are registered trademarks of Amazon.com, Inc. or its affiliates.

Sources: S. Alsop, "I'm Betting on Amazon.com," *Fortune,* April 30, 2001, p. 48; ACSI results at www.theacsi.org; Robert D. Hof, "How Amazon Cleared That Hurdle," *BusinessWeek,* February 4, 2002, pp. 60–61; A. Deutschman, "Inside the Mind of Jeff Bezos," *Fast Company,* August 2004, pp. 52–58.

TABLE 5.2 General Service Behaviours Based on Service Encounter Themes—Dos and Don'ts

Theme	Do	Don't
Recovery	Acknowledge problem Explain causes Apologize Compensate/upgrade Lay out options Take responsibility	Ignore customer Blame customer Leave customer to fend for himself or herself Downgrade Act as if nothing is wrong "Pass the buck"
Adaptability	Recognize the seriousness of the need Acknowledge Anticipate Attempt to accommodate Adjust the system Explain rules/policies Take responsibility	Ignore Promise, but fail to follow through Show unwillingness to try Embarrass the customer Laugh at the customer Avoid responsibility "Pass the buck"
Spontaneity	Take time Be attentive Anticipate needs Listen Provide information Show empathy	Exhibit impatience Ignore Yell/laugh/swear Steal from customers Discriminate
Coping	Listen Try to accommodate Explain Let go of the customer	Take customer's dissatisfaction personally Let customer's dissatisfaction affect others

The research on SSTs reveals some different themes in terms of what drives customer satisfaction and dissatisfaction. The following themes were identified from analysis of hundreds of critical incident stories across a wide range of contexts, including Internet retailing, Internet-based services, ATMs, automated phone systems, and others.

For Satisfying SSTs

- *Solved an intensified need.* Customers in this category were thrilled that the technology could bail them out of a difficult situation—for example, a cash machine that came to the rescue, allowing the customer to get cash to pay a cab driver and get to work on time when a car had broken down.

- *Better than the alternative.* Many SST stories related to how the technology-based service was in some way better than the alternative—easy to use, saved time, available when and where the customer needed it, saved money.

- *Did its job.* Because there are so many failures of technology, many customers are simply thrilled when the SST works as it should!

For Dissatisfying SSTs

- *Technology failure.* Many dissatisfying SST stories relate to the technology simply not working as promised—it is not available when needed, PINs do not work, or systems are offline.

- *Process failure.* Often the technology seems to work, but later the customer discovers that a back-office or follow-up process, which the customer assumed was connected, does not work. For example, a product order seems to be placed successfully, but it never arrives or the wrong product is delivered.

- *Poor design.* Many stories relate to the customer's dissatisfaction with how the technology is designed, in terms of either the technical process (technology is confusing, menu options are unclear) or the actual service design (delivery takes too long, service is inflexible).

- *Customer-driven failure.* In some cases the customers told stories of their own inabilities or failures to use the technology properly. These types of stories are (of course) much less common than stories blaming the technology or the company.

For all of the dissatisfying SST stories, there is clearly an element of service failure. Interestingly, the research revealed little attempt in these technology-based encounters to recover from the failure—unlike the interpersonal service encounters described earlier, in which excellent service recovery can be a foundation for retaining and even producing very satisfied customers. As companies progress further with SSTs and become better at delivering service this way, we expect that growing numbers will be able to deliver superior service via technology. Many are doing it already, as our Technology Spotlight on Amazon.com illustrates. In the future we believe that many firms will be able to deliver highly reliable, responsive, customized services via technology and will offer easy and effective means for service recovery when failure does occur.[43]

The Evidence of Service

Because services are intangible, customers are searching for evidence of service in every interaction they have with an organization.[44] Figure 5.8 depicts the three major categories of evidence as experienced by the customer: people, process, and physical evidence. These categories together represent the service and provide the evidence that makes the offering tangible. Note the parallels between the elements of evidence of service and the new marketing mix elements presented in Chapter 1. The new mix elements essentially *are* the evidence of service in each moment of truth.

FIGURE 5.8

The Evidence of Service (from the Customer's Point of View)

Source: M. J. Bitner, "Managing the Evidence of Service," *The Service Quality Handbook,* ed. E. E. Scheuing and W. F. Christopher. Reprinted by permission of the American Marketing Association.

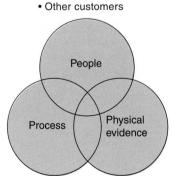

- Contact employees
- Customer him/herself
- Other customers

People

- Operational flow of activities
- Steps in process
- Flexibility vs. standard
- Technology vs. human

Process

Physical evidence

- Tangible communication
- Servicescape
- Guarantees
- Technology
- Website

SUMMARY

This chapter described customer perceptions of service by first introducing you to two critical concepts: customer satisfaction and service quality. These critical customer perceptions were defined and discussed in terms of the factors that influence each of them. You learned that customer satisfaction is a broad perception influenced by features and attributes of the product as well as by customers' emotional responses, their attributions, and their perceptions of fairness. Service quality, the customer's perception of the service component of a product, is also a critical determinant of customer satisfaction. Sometimes, as in the case of a pure service, service quality may be the *most* critical determinant of satisfaction. You learned that perceptions of service quality are based on five dimensions: reliability, assurance, empathy, responsiveness, and tangibles.

Another major purpose of the chapter was to introduce the idea of service encounters, or "moments of truth," as the building blocks for both satisfaction and quality. You learned that every service encounter (whether remote, over the phone, or in person) is an opportunity to build perceptions of quality and satisfaction. The underlying themes of pleasure and displeasure in service encounters were also described. The importance of managing the evidence of service in each and every encounter was discussed.

Chapters 3, 4, and 5 have provided you with a grounding in customer issues relevant to services. The three chapters together are intended to give you a solid understanding of customer behaviour issues and of service expectations and perceptions. Through the rest of the book, we illustrate strategies that firms can use to close the gap between customer expectations and perceptions.

⟼ Discussion Questions

1. What is customer satisfaction, and why is it so important? Discuss how customer satisfaction can be influenced by each of the following: product attributes and features, customer emotions, attributions for success or failure, perceptions of fairness, and family members or other customers.

2. Why do service companies generally receive lower satisfaction ratings than non-durable and durable product companies?

3. Discuss the differences between perceptions of service quality and customer satisfaction.

4. List and define the five dimensions of service quality. Describe the services provided by a firm you do business with (your bank, your doctor, your favourite restaurant) on each of the dimensions. In your mind, has this organization distinguished itself from its competitors on any particular service quality dimension?

5. Describe a remote encounter, a phone encounter, and a face-to-face encounter that you have had recently. How did you evaluate the encounter, and what were the most important factors determining your satisfaction/dissatisfaction in each case?

6. Describe an "encounter cascade" for an airplane flight. In your opinion, what are the most important encounters in this cascade for determining your overall impression of the quality of the airline?

7. Why did the gentleman described in Exhibit 5.1 leave his bank after 30 years? What were the underlying causes of his dissatisfaction in that instance, and why would that cause him to leave the bank?

8. Assume that you are a manager of a health club. Discuss general strategies you might use to maximize customers' positive perceptions of your club. How would you know if you were successful?

Exercises

1. Keep a journal of your service encounters with different organizations (at least five) during the week. For each journal entry, ask yourself the following questions: What circumstances led up to this encounter? What did the employee say or do? How did you evaluate this encounter? What exactly made you evaluate the encounter that way? What should the organization have done differently (if anything)? Categorize your encounters according to the four themes of service encounter satisfaction/dissatisfaction (recovery, adaptability, spontaneity, coping).

2. Interview someone with a different cultural background from you. Ask the person about service quality, whether the five dimensions of quality are relevant, and which are most important in determining quality of banking services (or some other type of service) in the person's country.

3. Think of an important service experience you have had in the last several weeks. Analyze the encounter according to the evidence of service provided (see Figure 5.8). Which of the three evidence components was (or were) most important for you in evaluating the experience, and why?

4. Interview an employee of a local service business. Ask the person to discuss each of the five dimensions of quality with you as it relates to the person's company. Which dimensions are most important? Are any dimensions *not* relevant in this context? Which dimensions does the company do best? Why? Which dimensions could benefit from improvement? Why?

5. Interview a manager, owner, or president of a business. Discuss with this person the strategies he or she uses to ensure customer satisfaction. How does service quality enter into the strategies, or does it? Find out how this person measures customer satisfaction and/or service quality.

6. Visit Amazon.com's website. Visit a traditional bookstore. How would you compare the two experiences? Compare and contrast the factors that most influenced your satisfaction and perceptions of service quality in the two different situations. When would you choose to use one rather than the other?

Notes

1. "Exceeding Customer Expectations," Wal-Mart Stores site, www.walmartstores. com, accessed September 25, 2006.

2. For more discussion of the debate on the distinctions between quality and satisfaction, see A. Parasuraman, V. A. Zeithaml, and L. L. Berry, "Reassessment of Expectations as a Comparison Standard in Measuring Service Quality: Implications for Future Research," *Journal of Marketing* 58 (January 1994), pp. 111–24;

R. L. Oliver, "A Conceptual Model of Service Quality and Service Satisfaction: Compatible Goals, Different Concepts," in *Advances in Services Marketing and Management,* vol. 2, ed. T. A. Swartz, D. E. Bowen, and S. W. Brown (Greenwich, CT: JAI Press, 1994), pp. 65–85; M. J. Bitner and A. R. Hubbert, "Encounter Satisfaction vs. Overall Satisfaction vs. Quality: The Customer's Voice," in *Service Quality: New Directions in Theory and Practice,* ed. R. T. Rust and R. L. Oliver (Newbury Park, CA: Sage, 1993), pp. 71–93; and D. Iacobucci et al., "The Calculus of Service Quality and Customer Satisfaction: Theory and Empirical Differentiation and Integration," in *Advances in Services Marketing and Management,* vol. 3, ed. T. A. Swartz, D. E. Bowen, and S. W. Brown (Greenwich, CT: JAI Press, 1994), pp. 1–67; P. A. Dabholkar, C. D. Shepherd, and D. I. Thorpe, "A Comprehensive Framework for Service Quality: An Investigation of Critical Conceptual and Measurement Issues through a Longitudinal Study," *Journal of Retailing* 7, no. 2 (Summer 2000), pp. 139–73; J. J. Cronin, Jr., M. K. Brady, and G. T. M. Hult, "Assessing the Effects of Quality, Value, and Customer Satisfaction on Consumer Behavioral Intentions in Service Environments," *Journal of Retailing* 7 (Summer 2000), pp. 193–218.

3. See in particular Parasuraman, Zeithaml, and Berry, "Reassessment of Expectations"; Oliver, "A Conceptual Model of Service Quality"; and M. K. Brady and J. J. Cronin Jr., "Some New Thoughts on Conceptualizing Perceived Service Quality: A Hierarchical Approach," *Journal of Marketing* 65 (July 2001), pp. 34–49.

4. A. Parasuraman, V. A. Zeithaml, and L. L. Berry, "SERVQUAL: A Multiple-Item Scale for Measuring Consumer Perceptions of Service Quality," *Journal of Retailing* 64 (Spring 1988), pp. 12–40.

5. Parasuraman, Zeithaml, and Berry, "Reassessment of Expectations."

6. Oliver, "A Conceptual Model of Service Quality."

7. See V. Mittal, P. Kumar, and M. Tsiros, "Attribute-Level Performance, Satisfaction, and Behavioral Intentions over Time," *Journal of Marketing* 63 (April 1999), pp. 88–101; L. L. Olsen and M. D. Johnson, "Service Equity, Satisfaction, and Loyalty: From Transaction-Specific to Cumulative Evaluations," *Journal of Service Research* 5 (February 2003), pp. 184-95.

8. Olsen and Johnson, "Service Equity, Satisfaction, and Loyalty."

9. R. L. Oliver, *Satisfaction: A Behavioral Perspective on the Consumer* (New York: McGraw-Hill, 1997).

10. For a more detailed discussion of the different types of satisfaction, see E. Arnould, L. Price, and G. Zinkhan, *Consumers,* 2nd ed., ch. 18, "Consumer Satisfaction" (New York: McGraw-Hill, 2004), pp. 754–96.

11. S. Fournier and D. G. Mick, "Rediscovering Satisfaction," *Journal of Marketing* 63 (October 1999), pp. 5–23.

12. Oliver, *Satisfaction,* ch. 2.

13. A. Ostrom and D. Iacobucci, "Consumer Trade-offs and the Evaluation of Services," *Journal of Marketing* 59 (January 1995), pp. 17–28.

14. For more on emotions and satisfaction, see Oliver, *Satisfaction,* ch. 11; and L. L. Price, E. J. Arnould, and S. L. Deibler, "Consumers' Emotional Responses to Service Encounters," *International Journal of Service Industry Management* 6, no. 3 (1995), pp. 34–63.

15. L. L. Price, E. J. Arnould, and P. Tierney, "Going to Extremes: Managing Service Encounters and Assessing Provider Performance," *Journal of Marketing* 59 (April 1995), pp. 83–97.

16. V. Liljander and T. Strandvik, "Emotions in Service Satisfaction," *International Journal of Service Industry Management* 8, no. 2 (1997), pp. 148–69.

17. For more on attributions and satisfaction, see V. S. Folkes, "Recent Attribution Research in Consumer Behavior: A Review and New Directions," *Journal of Consumer Research* 14 (March 1988), pp. 548–65; and Oliver, *Satisfaction,* ch. 10.

18. A. R. Hubbert, "Customer Co-creation of Service Outcomes: Effects of Locus of Causality Attributions," doctoral dissertation, Arizona State University, Tempe, Arizona, 1995.

19. M. J. Bitner, "Evaluating Service Encounters: The Effects of Physical Surrounding and Employee Responses," *Journal of Marketing* 54 (April 1990), pp. 69–82.

20. For more on fairness and satisfaction, see E. C. Clemmer and B. Schneider, "Fair Service," in *Advances in Services Marketing and Management,* vol. 5, ed. T. A. Swartz, D. E. Bowen, and S. W. Brown (Greenwich, CT: JAI Press, 1996), pp. 109–26; Oliver, *Satisfaction,* ch. 7; and Olsen and Johnson, "Service Equity, Satisfaction, and Loyalty."

21. Fournier and Mick, "Rediscovering Satisfaction."

22. C. Fornell, M. D. Johnson, E. W. Anderson, J. Cha, and B. E. Bryant, "The American Customer Satisfaction Index: Nature, Purpose, and Findings," *Journal of Marketing* 60 (October 1996), pp. 7–18.

23. E. W. Anderson, C. Fornell, and D. R. Lehmann, "Customer Satisfaction, Market Share, and Profitability: Findings from Sweden," *Journal of Marketing* 58 (July 1994), pp. 53–66.

24. M. Bruhn and M. A. Grund, "Theory, Development and Implementation of National Customer Satisfaction Indices: The Swiss Index of Customer Satisfaction (SWICS)," *Total Quality Management* 11, no. 7 (2000), pp. S1017–S1028; A. Meyer and F. Dornach, "The German Customer Barometer," www.servicebarometer.de.or.

25. J. L. Heskett, W. E. Sasser Jr., and L. A. Schlesinger, *The Service Profit Chain* (New York: Free Press, 1997).

26. M. A. J. Menezes and J. Serbin, *Xerox Corporation: The Customer Satisfaction Program,* case no. 591-055 (Boston: Harvard Business School, 1991).

27. F. F. Reichheld, "The One Number You Need to Grow," *Harvard Business Review,* December 2003, pp. 47–54.

28. E. W. Anderson and V. Mittal, "Strengthening the Satisfaction–Profit Chain," *Journal of Service Research* 3 (November 2000), pp. 107–20.

29. Brady and Cronin, "Some New Thoughts on Conceptualizing Perceived Service Quality."

30. Ibid.

31. See C. Gronroos, "A Service Quality Model and Its Marketing Implications," *European Journal of Marketing* 18, no. 4 (1984), pp. 36–44; R. T. Rust and R. L. Oliver, "Service Quality Insights and Managerial Implications from the Frontier," in *Service Quality: New Directions in Theory and Practice,* ed. R. T. Rust and R. L. Oliver (Thousand Oaks, CA: Sage, 1994), pp. 1–19; M. J. Bitner, "Managing the Evidence of Service," in *The Service Quality Handbook,* ed. E. E. Scheuing and W. F. Christopher (New York: AMACOM, 1993), pp. 358–70.

32. Parasuraman, Zeithaml, and Berry, "SERVQUAL: A Multiple-Item Scale." Details on the SERVQUAL scale and the actual items used to assess the dimensions are provided in Chapter 6.

33. Ibid.

34. For a review of what is known about service quality delivery via the Web, see V. A. Zeithaml, A. Parasuraman, and A. Malhotra, "Service Quality Delivery Through Web Sites: A Critical Review of Extant Knowledge," *Journal of the Academy of Marketing Science* 30, no. 4 (2002), pp. 362–75.

35. V. Zeithaml, A. Parasuraman, and A. Malhotra, "A Conceptual Framework for Understanding e-Service Quality: Implications for Future Research and Managerial Practice," Marketing Science Institute working paper, Report No. 00-115, 2001.

36. "How Marriott Makes a Great First Impression," *The Service Edge* 6, no. 5 (May 1993), p. 5.

37. A. G. Woodside, L. L. Frey, and R. T. Daly, "Linking Service Quality, Customer Satisfaction, and Behavioral Intention," *Journal of Health Care Marketing* 9 (December 1989), pp. 5–17.

38. R. N. Bolton and J. H. Drew, "Mitigating the Effect of Service Encounters," *Marketing Letters* 3, no. 1 (1992), pp. 57–70.

39. For detailed discussions of the Critical Incident Technique, see J. C. Flanagan, "The Critical Incident Technique," *Psychological Bulletin* 51 (July 1954), pp. 327–58; M. J. Bitner, J. D. Nyquist, and B. H. Booms, "The Critical Incident as a Technique for Analyzing the Service Encounter," in *Services Marketing in a Changing Environment,* ed. T. M. Bloch, G. D. Upah, and V. A. Zeithaml (Chicago: American Marketing Association, 1985), pp. 48–51; S. Wilson-Pessano, "Defining Professional Competence: The Critical Incident Technique 40 Years Later," presentation to the Annual Meeting of the American Educational Research Association, New Orleans, 1988; I. Roos, "Methods of Investigating Critical Incidents," *Journal of Service Research* 4 (February 2002), pp. 193–204; D. D. Gremler, "The Critical Incident Technique in Service Research," *Journal of Service Research* 7 (August 2004), pp. 65–89.

40. For a complete discussion of the research on which this section is based, see M. J. Bitner, B. H. Booms, and M. S. Tetreault, "The Service Encounter: Diagnosing Favorable and Unfavorable Incidents," *Journal of Marketing* 54 (January 1990), pp. 71–84; M. J. Bitner, B. H. Booms, and L. A. Mohr, "Critical Service Encounters: The Employee's View," *Journal of Marketing* 58, no. 4 (1994), pp. 95–106; D. Gremler and M. J. Bitner, "Classifying Service Encounter Satisfaction across Industries," in *Marketing Theory and Applications,* ed. C. T. Allen et al. (Chicago: American Marketing Association, 1992), pp. 111–18; and D. Gremler, M. J. Bitner, and K. R. Evans, "The Internal Service Encounter," *International Journal of Service Industry Management* 5, no. 2 (1994), pp. 34–56.

41. Bitner, Booms, and Mohr, "Critical Service Encounters."

42. This discussion is based on research and results presented in M. L. Meuter, A. L. Ostrom, R. I. Roundtree, and M. J. Bitner, "Self-Service Technologies: Understanding Customer Satisfaction with Technology-Based Service Encounters," *Journal of Marketing* 64 (July 2000), pp. 50–64.

43. M. J. Bitner, S. W. Brown, and M. L. Meuter, "Technology Infusion in Service Encounters," *Journal of the Academy of Marketing Science* 28, no. 1, pp. 138–49.

44. Bitner, "Managing the Evidence of Service."

PART 3

Understanding Customer Requirements

The Listening Gap

Provider Gap 1

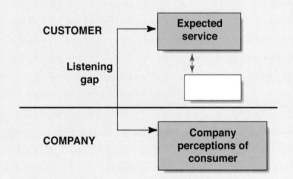

Not knowing what customers expect is one of the root causes of not delivering to customer expectations. Provider Gap 1 is the difference between customer expectations of service and company understanding of those expectations. Note that in the accompanying figure we created a link between the customer and the company, showing customer expectations above the line that dissects the model and provider perceptions of those expectations below the line. This alignment signifies that what customers expect is not always the same as what companies believe they expect.

Part 3 describes three ways to close Provider Gap 1. In Chapter 6, we detail ways that companies listen to customers through research. Both formal and informal methods of customer research are described, including surveys, critical incident studies, and complaint solicitation. Upward communication from front-line employees to managers, another key factor in listening to customers, is also discussed.

Chapter 7 covers company strategies to retain customers and strengthen relationships with them, an approach called relationship marketing. Relationship marketing is distinct from transactional marketing, the more conventional approach that tends to focus on acquiring new customers rather than retaining them. As you will discover in Chapter 7, having a relationship focus forces companies to pay attention to retaining their customers. This, in turn, requires them to pay attention to their customers' expectations. To retain customers you must satisfy them. To satisfy them, you must know what they expect.

Chapter 8 describes service recovery, the other major strategy needed to close Provider Gap 1. Service recovery involves understanding why customers complain, what they expect when they complain, and how to deal with service failures. Firms engaged in service recovery must, along with other approaches, create a complaint-handling procedure, empower employees to react in real time to fix failures, and guarantee service. Excellent service recovery strategies seek to gain insight from service failures, allowing firms to better understand customers and their expectations.

Chapter

6

Listening to Customers Through Research

Provider Gap 1

THIS CHAPTER'S OBJECTIVES ARE TO

→ 1. Present the types of and guidelines for marketing research in services.

→ 2. Show how marketing research information can and should be used for services.

→ 3. Describe the strategies by which companies can facilitate interaction and communication between management and customers.

→ 4. Present ways that companies can and do facilitate interaction between contact people and management.

TD Bank Financial Group Excels at Research in Services

Toronto-Dominion Bank Financial Group (TDBFG, www.td.com), head-quartered in Toronto, has the best customer service among the five major banks in the country. TDBFG, ranking number one overall on a 2005 customer service index kept by independent market research company Synovate (www.synovate.com), outperformed competitors in eight of eleven categories, including "overall quality of customer service" and "staff service at my branch." And the accolades do not stop there. The 150-year-old company has won numerous awards for having the best customer Internet bank in the nation, and has been honoured with SQM's Contact Centre Industry Service Quality Award for Excellence.

The SQM award constitutes recognition that the company's focus is on the customer. As TDBFG's 2004 Corporate Responsibility Report indicates,

"Our customers are why we exist so paying attention to what counts to them is the overarching focus that propels our business." However, with 52,000 employees and 14 million customers worldwide, knowing just what the customer expects can be a challenge. TDBFG uses a variety of research sources to listen to their customers.

Among the company's most detailed customer research initiatives is the Voice of the Customer study, which entails administering hundreds of thousands of customer surveys annually within a few days of a banking experience. The results are used to tabulate a Customer Satisfaction Index (CSI), providing an internal measure of how the company is performing in the eyes of the customer. As with the external validation the company has received on their customer-focused initiatives, customers are increasingly satisfied with their Toronto-Dominion experience. The CSI has increased every year from 81.9 in 2002 to 86.8 in 2005.

Other customer-focused research initiatives at TDBFG are focus groups conducted with front-line employees and a formal Customer Problem Resolution process. Additionally, the company maintains a comprehensive data warehouse and employs a team of analysts to sift through the reams of data for further insight.

TD Bank Financial Group has been successful in satisfying customers because their research lets them know what customers expect so that strategies can be implemented to provide customers with the service they desire, resolve problems as they arise, and, in turn, maintain a loyal customer base.[1]

 Bank Financial Group

Source: Courtesy of TD Bank Financial Group.

Despite a genuine interest in meeting customer expectations, many companies miss the mark by thinking inside out—they believe they know what customers *should* want, rather than finding out what they *do* want. (See Figure 6.1 for a humorous take on "listening to customers.") When this happens, companies provide services that do not match customer expectations. Because services have few clearly defined and tangible cues, this difficulty may be considerably larger than it is in manufacturing firms. A better approach involves thinking outside in—determining customer expectations and then delivering to them. Thinking outside in uses research to understand customers and their requirements fully. Research, the subject of this chapter, involves far more than conventional surveys. It consists of a portfolio of listening strategies that allow companies to deliver service to customer expectations.

USING RESEARCH TO UNDERSTAND CUSTOMER EXPECTATIONS

In this section we discuss the elements of services research programs that help companies identify customer expectations and perceptions. In the sections that follow, we

FIGURE 6.1

An example of how *not* to listen to your customers.

Source: © Graham Harrop.

will discuss ways in which the tactics of general research may need to be adjusted to maximize its effectiveness in services.

Research Objectives for Services

The first step in designing services research is the most critical: defining the problem and research objectives. This is where the services marketer poses the questions to be answered with research. In spite of the importance of this first stage, many research studies are initiated without adequate attention to objectives.

Research objectives in services are similar in many ways to the research conducted for physical products. However, they incorporate additional elements that require specific attention.

First, services research must continually track service performance, because performance is subject to human variability and heterogeneity. Conducting performance research at a single point in time, as might be done for a physical product, would be insufficient in services. Another focus of services research involves documenting the process by which service is performed. Even when service employees are performing well, a service provider must continue to track performance, because the potential for variation in service delivery always exists.

A second distinction in services research is the need to consider and monitor the gap between expectations and perceptions. This gap is dynamic because both perceptions and expectations fluctuate. Does the gap exist because performance is declining, because performance varies with demand and supply level, or because expectations are escalating?

Exhibit 6.1 lists a number of services research objectives. Once objectives such as these have been identified, they will point the way to decisions about the most appropriate type of research, methods of data collection, and ways to use the information. The additional columns in this table are described in sections of this chapter.

Elements in an Effective Marketing Research Program for Services

Type of Research	Primary Research Objectives	Qualitative/Quantitative	Costs of Information		Frequency
			Monetary	Time	
Complaint solicitation	To identify/attend to dissatisfied customers To identify common service failure points	Qualitative	Low	Low	Continuous
Critical incident studies	To identify "best practices" at transaction level To identify customer requirements as input for quantitative studies To identify common service failure points To identify systemic strengths and weaknesses in customer-contact services	Qualitative	Low	Moderate	Periodic
Requirements research	To identify customer requirements as input for quantitative research	Qualitative	Moderate	Moderate	Periodic
Relationship surveys and SERVQUAL surveys	To monitor and track service performance To assess overall company performance compared with that of competition To determine links between satisfaction and behavioural intentions To assess gaps between customer expectations and perceptions	Quantitative	Moderate	Moderate	Annual
Trailer calls	To obtain immediate feedback on performance of service transactions To measure effectiveness of changes in service delivery To assess service performance of individuals and teams To use as input for process improvements To identify common service failure points	Quantitative	Low	Low	Continuous

Technique	Research objective	Type of research			Frequency
Service expectation meetings and reviews	To create dialogue with important customers To identify what individual large customers expect and then to ensure that it is delivered To close the loop with important customers	Qualitative	Moderate	Moderate	Annual
Process checkpoint evaluations	To determine customer perceptions of long-term professional services during service provision To identify service problems and solve them early in the service relationship	Quantitative	Moderate	Moderate	Periodic
Market-oriented ethnography	To research customers in natural settings To study customers from cultures other than North America in an unbiased way	Qualitative	Moderate	High	Periodic
Mystery shopping	To measure individual employee performance for evaluation, recognition, and rewards To identify systemic strengths and weaknesses in customer-contact services	Quantitative	Low	Low	Quarterly
Customer panels	To monitor changing customer expectations To provide a forum for customers to suggest and evaluate new service ideas	Qualitative	Moderate	Moderate	Continuous
Lost customer research	To identify reasons for customer defection To assess gaps between customer expectations and perceptions	Qualitative	Low	Low	Continuous
Future expectations research	To forecast future expectations of customers To develop and test new service ideas	Qualitative	High	High	Periodic
Database marketing research	To identify the individual requirements of customers using information technology and database information	Quantitative	High	High	Continuous

FIGURE 6.2

Criteria for an
Effective Services
Research Program

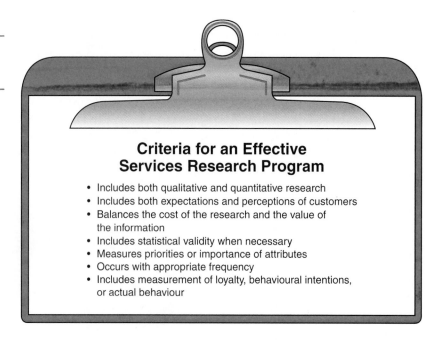

**Criteria for an Effective
Services Research Program**

- Includes both qualitative and quantitative research
- Includes both expectations and perceptions of customers
- Balances the cost of the research and the value of
  the information
- Includes statistical validity when necessary
- Measures priorities or importance of attributes
- Occurs with appropriate frequency
- Includes measurement of loyalty, behavioural intentions,
  or actual behaviour

Criteria for an Effective Services Research Program

A **services research program** can be defined as the composite of all research needed to address the objectives and execute an overall measurement strategy. Understanding the criteria for an effective services research program (see Figure 6.2) will help a company evaluate different types of research and choose the ones most appropriate for its research objectives. In this section we discuss these criteria.

Includes Qualitative and Quantitative Research

Research is not limited to surveys and statistics. Some forms of research, called *qualitative research*, are exploratory and preliminary, and are conducted to clarify problem definition, to prepare for more formal research, or to gain insight when more formal research is not necessary. Insights gained through one-on-one conversations, customer focus groups, critical incidents research, and direct observation of service transactions show the marketer the right questions to ask of consumers. Because the results of qualitative research play a major role in designing quantitative research, it is often the first type of research done. Qualitative research can also be conducted after quantitative research to make the numbers in computer printouts meaningful by giving managers the perspective required for interpreting data and initiating improvement efforts.[2]

Quantitative research in marketing is designed to describe the nature, attitudes, or behaviours of customers empirically and to test specific hypotheses that a services marketer wants to examine. These studies are key for quantifying the customers' satisfaction, the importance of service attributes, the extent of service quality gaps, and perceptions of value. Such studies also provide managers with benchmarks for evaluating competitors. Finally, results from quantitative studies can highlight specific service deficiencies that can be more deeply probed through follow-up qualitative research.

Includes Both Perceptions and Expectations of Customers

As we discussed in Chapter 4, expectations serve as standards or reference points for customers. In evaluating service quality, customers compare what they perceive they get in a service encounter with their expectations of that encounter. For this reason, a measurement program that captures only perceptions of service is missing a critical part of the service quality equation. Companies need also to incorporate measures of customer expectations.

Measurement of expectations can be included in multiple ways. First, research that relates to customers' requirements—that identifies the service features that matter to customers—can be considered expectation research. In this form, the *content* of customer expectations is captured, initially in some form of qualitative research such as focus group interviews. Research on the *levels* of customer expectations also is needed. This type of research assesses the levels of customer expectations and compares these with perception levels, usually by calculating the gap between expectations and perceptions.

Balances the Cost of the Research and the Value of the Information

An assessment of the cost of research compared with its benefits is another key criterion. One cost is monetary, including costs to marketing research companies, payments to respondents, and internal costs incurred by employees collecting the information. Time costs are also important, including the time needed by employees to administer the research and the interval between data collection and availability for use by the firm. These costs must be weighed against the gains to the company in improved decision making, retained customers, and successful new service launches. As in many other marketing decisions, costs are easier to estimate than the value of the information. For this reason, we include only costs, not value, in Exhibit 6.1. In later chapters we describe approaches to estimating the value of customers to a company, approaches that are useful as input to the tradeoff analysis needed to address this criterion.

Includes Statistical Validity When Necessary

We have already shown that research has multiple objectives. These objectives determine the research methodology. To illustrate, some research is used by companies to build relationships with customers—to allow contact employees to find out what customers desire, to diagnose the strengths and weaknesses of the firm, to prepare a plan to meet requirements, and to confirm that the company has executed the plan. The underlying objective of this type of research is to allow contact people to identify specific action items that will gain the maximum return in customer satisfaction. This type of research does not need sophisticated quantitative analysis, anonymity of customers, careful control of sampling, or strong statistical validity.

On the other hand, research used to track overall service quality that will be used for bonuses and salary increases must be carefully controlled for sampling bias and statistical validity. Not all forms of research have statistical validity, and not all forms need it. Most forms of qualitative research, for example, do not possess statistical validity.

Measures Priorities or Importance

Customers have many service requirements, but not all are equally important. One of the most common mistakes managers make in trying to improve service is spending resources on the wrong initiatives, only to become discouraged because the firm's

Technology Spotlight

Conducting Marketing Research on the Web

One of the most intriguing applications of the Internet is online research, replacing comment cards and intrusive telephone calls with cyber-surveys that are challenging and fun for consumers. The application is growing rapidly, for obvious reasons: Internet research has been touted to have many benefits to marketers besides more willing respondents, including the following:

- *Speed.* Rather than months required to collect data through mail questionnaires, or weeks needed to train interviewers and obtain data from telephone questionnaires, online surveys can be prepared and executed quickly. A sample of 300 to 400, large enough for many studies, can be completed in a weekend and available for viewing by clients on a secure website.

- *Ability to target hard-to-reach populations.* One of the traditional difficulties in research, particularly segmentation research, is to identify and access hard-to-reach consumers. One firm overcoming this difficulty is Toronto's In-Sync (www.insyncresearch.com), which conducts Virtual Roundtables (online focus groups). About 12 participants stay together (virtually) for a week, and visit a designated website where they respond to questions and perform exercises. Another Canadian firm doing interesting work is Tangency (www.tangency.ca), whose findings suggest that young males are more comfortable in virtual focus groups than they would be in traditional ones. The resulting richer conversations lead to increased understanding of both group and individual expectations and perceptions.

- *Ability to target customers with money.* Online research allows service companies to reach customers who have higher incomes, higher education levels, and greater willingness to spend. Consumers with computers who use online services regularly tend to be in these demographic target groups, and they can be effectively surveyed with online research. Compared with the sample that would be obtained from traditional research using all telephone subscribers, the sample of online users is far better in terms of marketing potential.

- *Opportunity to use multimedia to present video and audio.* Telephone surveys are limited to voice alone, whereas mail surveys are constrained to two-dimensional visuals. In the past, to present the full range of audio and video needed to give respondents the true sense of a service being researched, surveys had to be conducted in person and were therefore very expensive ($30 to $150 per person depending on the topic and sample). Online research offers broader stimuli potential through all multimedia possibilities at a fraction of the cost.

- *No interviewers.* And therefore no interviewer errors or interviewer bias. Bias occurs when the interviewer is in a bad mood, tired, impatient, or not objective. These problems occur with human interviews but not cyber-interviews. Interviewer error is another age-old research problem, described well by a research professional:

  > The first survey I ever designed was on the subject of home heating systems. When I went to observe the first day of field, I was surprised and horrified to realize that most of my interviewers could not pronounce many of the technical terms that I had used in the survey, and virtually none of them knew what those terms meant. It wasn't exactly the best way to collect data.

- *Control over data quality.* This can eliminate contradictory or nonsensical answers. With traditional surveys, researchers need a step called "data cleaning and editing" in which all data are checked for such problems; electronic checks can be built into online surveys that take care of this problem as it occurs.

- *Inexpensive research.* Data collection costs can be the most expensive part of a study, and the

continued

Technology Spotlight

Conducting Marketing Research on the Web—continued

most expensive part of data collection can be paying subjects to participate. Online marketing research, astonishingly, is 10 to 80 percent less expensive than other approaches. The Internet also eliminates postage, phone, labour, and printing costs that are typical with other survey approaches. Respondents also seem to complete Web-based surveys in half the time it would take an interviewer to conduct the survey, perhaps contributing to the lack of need for incentives.

One additional but to date undersubstantiated benefit is higher response rate—reportedly as high as 70 percent—possibly stemming from the fact that the interactive nature of cyber-research can make answering surveys fun for respondents. While it is getting more difficult to get consumers to answer traditional surveys, the entertainment value of cyber-surveys makes it easy to recruit participants. One study shows that consumers are five times more likely to complete an electronic survey as they are to do the same survey with written materials and that researchers obtain the following three additional benefits: (1) consumers "play" an e-survey longer, answering more questions than in a traditional survey; (2) people tend to concentrate more fully on their answers; and (3) the entertainment value of an e-survey actually lowers the respondent's perceived time to complete the survey.

The advantages of online research likely far outnumber the disadvantages. However, marketers need to be aware of certain drawbacks. Perhaps the major problem is the composition of the sample. Unlike the process used with most telephone and mail surveys, the population of responders is not usually selected but is a matter of convenience, consisting of whoever responds to the survey. This is a particular problem when respondents are recruited from other websites and click through to the survey. In these cases marketers may not even know who the responders are and whether they in fact fit the profile for answering the survey. To address this problem, companies are prequalifying respondents by telephone or email, then asking for enough demographic information to ensure that the respondents meet the desired requirements.

Sources: A. Hogg, "Online Research Overview," MarketingPower.com, updated 2004; D. McCullough, "Web-Based Market Research Ushers in New Age," *Marketing News*, September 14, 1998, p. 28; R. Weible and J. Wallace, "Cyber Research: The Impact of the Internet on Data Collection," *Marketing Research*, Fall 1998, pp. 19–24; R. Nadilo, "On-Line Research Taps Consumers Who Spend," *Marketing News*, June 8, 1998, p. 12; and S. Yaffe, "Going Deep: Getting to Know Customers Better Than They Know Themselves Means Asking Different Questions Differently," *Strategy Magazine*, February 2005, p. 55.

service does not improve! Measuring the relative importance of service dimensions and attributes helps managers to channel resources effectively; therefore, research must document the priorities of the customer. Prioritization can be accomplished in multiple ways. *Direct importance measures* ask customers to prioritize dimensions of service. One effective approach involves asking respondents to allocate a total of 100 points across the various service dimensions. *Indirect importance measures* are estimated using the statistical procedures of correlation and regression analysis, which show the relative contribution of questionnaire items or requirements to overall service quality. Both indirect and direct importance measures provide evidence of customer priorities.

Occurs with Appropriate Frequency

Because customer expectations and perceptions are dynamic, companies need to institute a research *process*, not just do isolated studies. A single study provides only a snapshot of one moment in time. For full understanding, marketing research must be ongoing.

Just what does "ongoing research" mean in terms of frequency? As we discuss the different types in the following section, you will see the frequency with which each type of research could be conducted.

Includes Measures of Loyalty, Behavioural Intentions, or Behaviour

An important trend in services research involves measuring the positive and negative consequences of service quality along with overall satisfaction or service quality scores. Among the most important generic behavioural intentions are willingness to recommend the service to others and repurchase intent. Positive behavioural intentions include saying positive things about the company, recommending the company to others, remaining loyal, spending more with the company, and paying a price premium. Negative behavioural intentions include saying negative things to others, doing less business with the company, switching to another company, and complaining to outside organizations such as the Better Business Bureau.

Summary

The research criteria discussed here should be incorporated into a services marketing research program. As we discuss the elements in such a program, we will indicate how these approaches satisfy the criteria. In addition to the types and techniques of research shown in Exhibit 6.1, the boxes in this chapter also show how electronic and other technologies add to the information that managers can collect.

ELEMENTS IN AN EFFECTIVE SERVICES RESEARCH PROGRAM

A good services research program includes multiple types of research studies. If a company were to engage in virtually all types of service research, the portfolio would look like Exhibit 6.1, but few companies do all types of research. The particular portfolio for any company will match company resources and address the key areas needed to understand its customers. So that it will be easier for you to identify the appropriate type of research for different research objectives, we list the objectives in column 2 of Exhibit 6.1. In the following sections we describe each major type of research and show the way each type addresses the criteria associated with it. The Technology Spotlight discusses research conducted online.

Complaint Solicitation

Many of you have complained to employees of service organizations, only to find that nothing happens with your complaint. No one rushes to solve it, and the next time you experience the service the same problem is present. How frustrating! Good service organizations take complaints seriously. Not only do they listen to complaints—they also seek complaints as communications about what can be done to improve their service and their service employees.

Firms that use complaints as research use the information to identify dissatisfied customers, correct individual problems where possible, and identify common service

FIGURE 6.3

Participants in a focus group discuss services using the critical incidents technique.

Source: Getty Images.

failure points. Although this research is used for both goods and services, it has a critical real-time purpose in services—to improve failure points and to improve or correct the performance of contact personnel. Research on complaints is one of the easiest types of research for firms to conduct, leading many companies to depend solely on complaints to stay in touch with customers. Unfortunately, research provides evidence that customer complaints alone are a woefully inadequate source of information: only a small percentage of customers with problems actually complain. The rest will stay dissatisfied, telling other people about their dissatisfaction.

To be effective, complaint solicitation requires rigorous recording of numbers and types of complaints through many channels, and then working to eliminate the most frequent problems. Complaint channels include employees at the front line, intermediary organizations like retailers who deliver service, managers, and complaints to third parties such as customer advocate groups. Companies must both solve individual customer problems and seek overall patterns to eliminate failure points.

Critical Incidents Studies

In Chapter 5, we discussed the critical incident technique (CIT), a qualitative interview procedure in which customers are asked to provide verbatim stories about satisfying and dissatisfying service encounters they have experienced (Figure 6.3). According to a recent summary of the use of the technique in services, CIT has been reported in hotels, restaurants, airlines, amusement parks, automotive repair, retailing, banking, cable television, public transportation, and education.[3] The studies have explored a wide range of service topics: consumer evaluation of services, service failure and recovery, employees, customer participation in service delivery, and service experience.

CIT has many benefits. First, data are collected from the respondent's perspective and are usually vivid because they are expressed in consumers' own words and reflect the way they think. Second, the method provides concrete information about the way the company and its employees behave and react, thereby making the research easy to translate into action. Third, like most qualitative methods, the research is particularly useful when the topic or service is new and very little other information exists. Finally, the method is well suited for assessing perceptions of customers from different cultures because it allows respondents to share their perceptions rather than answer researcher-defined questions.[4]

Requirements Research

Requirements research involves identifying what customers expect in a service. Because these studies are so foundational, qualitative techniques are appropriate to begin them. Quantitative techniques may follow, usually during a pretest stage of survey development. Unfortunately, many companies do inadequate requirements research, often developing surveys on the basis of intuition or company direction rather than thorough customer probing.

An example of requirements research is *structured brainstorming*, a technique developed by researchers in IBM's Advanced Business Systems unit.[5] In this technique a sample of customers and potential customers is assembled. A facilitator leads the group through a series of exercises on creativity and then has the customers describe the ideal provider of the service—what they would want if they could have their ideal service. The facilitator asks "what" customers want (to elicit fundamental requirements), "why" they want it (to elicit the underlying need or benefit sought), and "how" they will know when they receive it (to elicit specific service features). IBM's Global Banking Industry used a similar format, with 100 audience members looking on. Ontario's The Glasgow Group assisted with the subsequent breakout sessions in which discussions with the audience members reflected on the roundtable topics.

Some researchers, though, suggest there are limits to what can be achieved with this approach. Jake McCaul, founder of Toronto-based Second Sight Innovation, says, "You can't ask customers what they want anymore; technology is moving too fast and there are too many [variables] at play."[6] Instead, many researchers, including Second Sight and Toronto-based InSync, believe the best way to understand the targets is to empower them to research themselves. "We charge them with exercises that direct them to become reflective of their needs and their relationships to a brand."[7]

Burger King tried taking their customers to lunch. Customers visited both Burger King and competitors' locations. In each case they went through the entire process from ordering to paying to eating (and leaving). Then they attended a full-day session devoted to understanding customer expectations and how the company might respond.

Relationship and SERVQUAL Surveys

Relationship surveys pose questions about all elements in the customer's relationship with the company (including service, product, and price). This comprehensive approach can help a company diagnose its relationship strengths and weaknesses. These surveys typically track service performance annually with an initial survey providing a baseline. Relationship surveys are also effective in comparing company performance with that of competitors, often focusing on the best competitor's performance as a benchmark. When used for this purpose, the sponsor of the survey is not identified and questions are asked about both the focal company and one or more competitors.

A good example of a relevant satisfaction survey is the *Globe and Mail*'s University Report Card, which, unlike the university rankings used by *Maclean's*, surveys students nationwide asking them how satisfied they are with their university experience.

(To see the respective studies, go to www.theglobeandmail.com/generated/realtime/specialReportCard2005.html and www.macleans.ca/universities.)

A sound measure of service quality is necessary for identifying needed performance improvement and evaluating the impact of improvement efforts. Unlike goods quality, which can be measured objectively by such indicators as durability and number of defects, service quality is abstract and is best captured by surveys that measure customer evaluations of service. One of the first measures to be developed specifically to measure service quality was the SERVQUAL survey.

The SERVQUAL scale involves a survey containing 21 service attributes, grouped into the five service quality dimensions (discussed in Chapter 5) of reliability, responsiveness, assurance, empathy, and tangibles. The survey sometimes asks customers to provide two different ratings on each attribute—one reflecting the level of service they would expect from excellent companies in a sector and the other reflecting their perception of the service delivered by a specific company within that sector. The difference between the expectation and perception ratings constitutes a quantified measure of service quality. Exhibit 6.2 shows the items on the basic SERVQUAL scale as well as the phrasing of the expectations and perceptions portions of the scale.[8]

Data gathered through a SERVQUAL survey can be used for a variety of purposes:

- To determine the average gap score (between customers' perceptions and expectations) for each service attribute

- To assess a company's service quality along each of the five SERVQUAL dimensions

- To track customers' expectations and perceptions (on individual service attributes and/or on the SERVQUAL dimensions) over time

- To compare a company's SERVQUAL scores against those of competitors

- To identify and examine customer segments that differ significantly in their assessments of a company's service performance

- To assess internal service quality (i.e., the quality of service rendered by one department or division of a company to others within the same company)

SERVQUAL is used all over the world in service industries. Published studies have used it, and adaptations of it, in a variety of contexts: real estate brokers, physicians in private practice, public recreation programs, dental schools, business school placement centres, and higher education. Many of the findings are unpublished and/or proprietary. However, from our knowledge of some of these applications, one example will be briefly described here.

The Ceramic Products Division of Corning, Inc., developed a systematic process for monitoring and improving its service quality as perceived by its customers, and the SERVQUAL approach was an integral component of this process. Corning's Ceramic Products Division began its service improvement process by focusing on its largest client, a multinational company. This division modified the SERVQUAL instrument for assessing its service quality as perceived by multiple levels within this company. The SERVQUAL survey was re-administered a year later to assess the impact of the corrective actions. Results indicated significant improvements in most of the targeted attributes and also identified additional areas for further corrective action. The success of SERVQUAL in this pilot application prompted Corning to make this process an ongoing activity in the Ceramics Product Division and to expand its implementation to other divisions and customer groups.

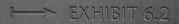 EXHIBIT 6.2

SERVQUAL: A Multidimensional Scale to Capture Customer Perceptions and Expectations of Service Quality

The SERVQUAL scale was first published in 1988 and has undergone numerous improvements and revisions since then. The scale currently contains 21 perception items that are distributed throughout the five service quality dimensions. The scale also contains expectation items. Although many different formats of the SERVQUAL scale are now in use, we show here the basic 21 perception items as well as a sampling of ways the expectation items have been posed.

PERCEPTIONS

	Strongly disagree					Strongly agree

Perceptions Statements in the Reliability Dimension

1. When XYZ Company promises to do something by a certain time, it does so.   1 2 3 4 5 6 7
2. When you have a problem, XYZ Company shows a sincere interest in solving it.   1 2 3 4 5 6 7
3. XYZ Company performs the service right the first time.   1 2 3 4 5 6 7
4. XYZ Company provides its services at the time it promises to do so.   1 2 3 4 5 6 7
5. XYZ Company insists on error-free records.   1 2 3 4 5 6 7

Statements in the Responsiveness Dimension

1. XYZ Company keeps customers informed about when services will be performed.   1 2 3 4 5 6 7
2. Employees in XYZ Company give you prompt service.   1 2 3 4 5 6 7
3. Employees in XYZ Company are always willing to help you.   1 2 3 4 5 6 7
4. Employees in XYZ Company are never too busy to respond to your request.   1 2 3 4 5 6 7

Statements in the Assurance Dimension

1. The behaviour of employees in XYZ Company instils confidence in you.   1 2 3 4 5 6 7
2. You feel safe in your transactions with XYZ Company.   1 2 3 4 5 6 7

	Strongly disagree					Strongly agree

3. Employees in XYZ Company are consistently courteous with you.   1 2 3 4 5 6 7
4. Employees in XYZ Company have the knowledge to answer your questions.   1 2 3 4 5 6 7

Statements in the Empathy Dimension

1. XYZ Company gives you individual attention.   1 2 3 4 5 6 7
2. XYZ Company has employees who give you personal attention.   1 2 3 4 5 6 7
3. XYZ Company has your best interests at heart.   1 2 3 4 5 6 7
4. Employees of XYZ Company understand your specific needs.   1 2 3 4 5 6 7
5. XYZ Company has operating hours that are convenient to all its customers   1 2 3 4 5 6 7

Statements in the Tangibles Dimension

1. XYZ Company has modern-looking equipment.   1 2 3 4 5 6 7
2. XYZ Company's physical facilities are visually appealing.   1 2 3 4 5 6 7
3. XYZ Company's employees appear neat.   1 2 3 4 5 6 7
4. Materials associated with the service (such as pamphlets or statements) are visually appealing at XYZ Company.   1 2 3 4 5 6 7

EXPECTATIONS: Several Formats for Measuring Customer Expectations Using Versions of SERVQUAL

Matching Expectations Statements (Paired with the Previous Perception Statements)

	Strongly disagree					Strongly agree
When customers have a problem, excellent firms will show a sincere interest in solving it.	1 2 3 4 5 6 7

Referent Expectations Formats

1. Considering a "world class" company to be a "7," how would you rate XYZ Company's performance on the following service features?

	Low	High
Sincere, interested employees	1 2 3 4 5 6 7
Service delivered right the first time	1 2 3 4 5 6 7

2. Compared with the level of service you expect from an excellent company, how would you rate XYZ Company's performance on the following?

	Low	High
Sincere, interested employees	1 2 3 4 5 6 7
Service delivered right the first time	1 2 3 4 5 6 7

Combined Expectations/Perceptions Statements

For each of the following statements, circle the number that indicates how XYZ Company's service compares with the level you expect:

	Lower than my desired service level			The same as my desired service level			Higher than my desired service level		
1. Prompt service	1	2	3	4	5	6	7	8	9
2. Courteous employees	1	2	3	4	5	6	7	8	9

Expectations Distinguishing Between Desired Service and Adequate Service

For each of the following statements, circle the number that indicates how XYZ Company's performance compares with your *minimum service level* and with your *desired service level*.

When it comes to . . .	Compared with my *minimum* service level XYZ's service performance is:			Compared with my *desired* service level XYZ's service performance is:		
	Lower	Same	Higher	Lower	Same	Higher
1. Prompt service	1 2 3	4 5 6	7 8 9	1 2 3	4 5 6	7 8 9
2. Employees who are consistently courteous	1 2 3	4 5 6	7 8 9	1 2 3	4 5 6	7 8 9

Source: A. Parasuraman, V. A. Zeithaml, and L. L. Berry, "SERVQUAL: A Multiple-Item Scale for Measuring Consumer Perceptions of Service Quality," *Journal of Retailing* 64, no. 1 (Spring 1988). Reprinted by permission of C. Samuel Craig.

Corning's use of SERVQUAL touches on virtually all the potential applications of the instrument listed earlier. It also illustrates the fact that SERVQUAL can be adapted for use in a variety of contexts, including industrial product and internal service contexts.

Trailer Calls or Posttransaction Surveys

Whereas the purpose of SERVQUAL surveys is usually to gauge the overall relationship with the customer, the purpose of transaction surveys is to capture information about the key service *encounters* with the customer. In this method, customers are asked a short list of questions immediately after a particular transaction (hence the name *trailer calls*) about their satisfaction. Because the surveys are administered continuously to a broad spectrum of customers, they are more effective than complaint solicitation (in which the information comes only from dissatisfied customers).

At checkout, immediately after staying at Fairfield Inns, customers are asked to use a computer terminal to answer four or five questions about their stay in the hotel. This novel approach has obvious benefits over the ubiquitous comment cards left in rooms—the response rate is far higher, because the process engages customers and takes only a few minutes. In other companies, transaction surveys are administered by telephone several days after a transaction. Because they occur close to service transactions, these surveys are useful in identifying sources of dissatisfaction and satisfaction. For example, Enterprise Rent-A-Car often calls customers a day after a car has been rented (and is still in the customer's possession) to ensure that customers are satisfied.

A strong benefit of this type of research is that it often appears to customers that the call is following up to ensure that they are satisfied; consequently the call does double duty as a market research tool and as customer service. This type of research is simple and fresh and provides management with continuous information about interactions with customers. Further, the research allows management to associate service quality performance with individual contact personnel so that high performance can be rewarded and low performance corrected. It also serves as an incentive for employees to provide better service because they understand how and when they are being evaluated.

Service Expectation Meetings and Reviews

In business-to-business situations, research that is highly effective involves eliciting the expectations of the client at a specified time of the year and then following up later (usually after a year) to discuss whether the expectations were fulfilled. Unlike other forms of research, these meetings are not conducted by unbiased researchers but are instead facilitated by senior members of the account team so that they can listen carefully to the client's expectations. You may be surprised to find that such interaction does not come naturally to sales teams who are used to talking to clients rather than listening carefully to their needs. Consequently, teams have to be carefully trained not to defend or explain but instead to comprehend. One company found that the only way it could teach its salespeople not to talk on these interviews was to take a marketing researcher along to gently kick the salesperson under the table whenever he or she strayed from the format!

The format, when appropriate, consists of (1) asking clients what they expect in terms of 8 to 10 basic requirements determined from focus group research, (2) inquiring what particular aspects of these requirements the account team performed well in the past as well as what aspects need improvement, and (3) requesting that the client rank the relative importance of the requirements. After getting the input, senior account members go back to their teams and plan their goals for the year around client requirements. The next step is verifying with the client that the account plan will satisfy requirements or, when it will not, managing expectations to let the client know what cannot be accomplished. After executing the plan for the year, the senior account personnel then return to the client, determine whether the plan has been successfully executed and expectations met, then establish a new set of expectations for the coming year.

Process Checkpoint Evaluations

With professional services such as consulting, construction, and architecture, services are provided over a long period, and there are not obvious ways or times to collect customer information. Waiting until the entire project is complete—which could last years—is undesirable because unresolvable problems could have occurred by then. But discrete service encounters to calibrate customer perceptions are also not usually available. In these situations, the smart service provider defines a process for delivering the services and then structures the feedback around the process, checking in at frequent points to ensure that the client's expectations are being met. For example, a management consulting firm might establish the following process for delivering its services to clients: (1) collect information, (2) diagnose problems, (3) recommend alternative solutions, (4) select alternatives, and (5) implement solutions. Next, it could agree with the client up front that it will communicate at major process checkpoints—after diagnosing the problem, before selecting the alternative, and so on—to make certain that the job is progressing as planned.

Market-Oriented Ethnography

Many of the types of research we discuss in this section are particularly relevant for Canada and cultures similar to it. Structured questionnaires, for example, make key assumptions about what people are conscious of or can recall about

In professional services, evaluations are made at important checkpoints in the process.

Source: Digital Vision/Getty Images.

their behaviour and what they are willing to explain to researchers about their opinions. These assumptions are based on our own culture. Even focus group interviews are inherently culture-based, because they depend on norms of participation, or what people are willing to say in front of others and to researchers. To fully understand how customers of other cultures assess and use services, it is necessary and effective to use other approaches, such as market-oriented ethnography. This set of approaches allows researchers to observe consumption behaviour in natural settings. The goal is to enter the consumer's world as much as possible—observing how and when a service is used in an actual home environment.

LeoShe—a research division made up of female employees of Toronto-based Leo Burnett—has conducted year-long studies in which women participants are invited to ask six to eight female friends to have regular dinner dates in which they talk about specified topics. These "friendship groups" show that deeper insights are possible when people are in natural settings.

Observation can also involve entering the experience as a participant observer and watching what occurs rather than asking questions about it. One-on-one interviews, particularly with key informants in the culture rather than consumers themselves, can provide compelling insights about culture-based behaviour. Studying existing documents and cultural artifacts can also provide valuable insights, especially about lifestyles and usage patterns.[9]

Best Western International used this technique to better understand its senior market. Rather than bringing participants into focus group facilities and asking them questions, the company paid 25 over-55 couples to videotape themselves on cross-country journeys. The firm was able to listen to how couples actually made decisions rather than the way they reported them. The insights they gained from this research were decidedly different from what they would have learned otherwise. Most noteworthy was the finding that seniors who talked hotel clerks into better deals on rooms did not need the lower price to afford staying at the hotel—they were simply after the thrill of the deal, as illustrated in this description:

> The 60-ish woman caught on the grainy videotape is sitting on her hotel bed, addressing her husband after a long day spent on the road. "Good job!" she exults. "We beat the s—t out of the front desk and got a terrific room."[10]

These customers then spent their discount money on better dinners elsewhere, contributing nothing to Best Western. "The degree of discount clearly isn't what it used to be in importance—and we got that right out of the research," claimed the manager of programs for Best Western.[11] This finding would be highly unlikely using traditional research and asking customers directly, for few customers would admit to being willing to pay a higher price for a service!

Mystery Shopping

In this form of research, which is unique to services (including retailing),[12] companies hire outside research organizations to send people into service establishments and experience the service as if they were customers. These "mystery shoppers" are trained in the criteria important to customers of the establishment. They deliver objective assessments about service performance by completing questionnaires about service standards. Questionnaires contain items that represent important quality or service issues to customers. Central, a regional chain of home improvement retail stores located in Nova Scotia, and Canadian Tire Automotive are just two examples of firms that use this technique. The mystery shoppers ask questions of service personnel and/or purchase products, then fill out a form detailing the level of service they received. The service experience might be evaluated on any number of predetermined criteria, such as employee helpfulness, employee knowledge, promptness of service, and store cleanliness.

Mystery shopping keeps workers on their toes, because they know they may be evaluated at any time. They know they are being judged on the company's service standards and therefore carry out the standards more consistently than if they were not going to be judged.

Customer Panels

Customer panels are ongoing groups of customers assembled to provide attitudes and perceptions about a service over time. They offer a company regular and timely customer information—virtually a pulse on the market. Firms can use customer panels to represent large segments of end customers.

Customer panels are used in the entertainment industry to screen movies before they are released. After a rough cut of a film has been created, the movie is viewed by a panel of consumers that matches the demographic target. In the most basic of these panels, consumers report on their responses to the movie. On the basis of these panels, movies are revised and edited to ensure that they will succeed in the marketplace. In extreme situations, entire endings of movies have been changed to be more consistent with customer attitudes. In some of the most sophisticated consumer panel research on movies (also used for television shows and commercials) consumers have digital devices in their seats through which they indicate their responses as they watch films. This instantaneous response allows the producers, directors, and editors to make changes at the appropriate places in the film to ensure that the story line, characters, and scenery are "tracking."

Lost Customer Research

This type of research involves deliberately seeking customers who have dropped the company's service to inquire about their reasons for leaving. Some lost customer research is similar to exit interviews with employees in that it asks open-ended, in-depth questions to expose the reasons for defection and the particular events that led to dissatisfaction. For example, Sobeys, a leading national grocer, had store managers telephone customers who had suddenly stopped shopping in their stores. It is also possible to use more standard surveys on lost customers.

One benefit of this type of research is that it identifies failure points and common problems in the service and can help establish an early-warning system for future defectors. Another benefit is that the research can be used to calculate the cost of lost customers.

Future Expectations Research

Customer expectations are dynamic and can change very rapidly. As competition increases, as tastes change, and as consumers become more knowledgeable, companies must continue to update their information and strategies. One such "industry" is interactive video, representing the merger of computer, telecommunications, and cable television. The technologies available in this industry are revolutionary. In dynamic market situations, companies want to understand not just current customer expectations but also future expectations—the service features desired in the future. Future expectations research is new and includes different types. First, *features research* involves environmental scanning and querying of customers about desirable features of possible services. *Lead user research* brings in customers who are opinion leaders/innovators and asks them what requirements are not currently being met by existing products or services. Another form of this research is the *synectics approach*, which defines lead users more broadly than in standard lead user research.

The question of customer involvement in expectation studies is often debated. Designers and developers claim that consumers do not know what they might want, especially in industries or services that are new and rapidly changing. Consumers and marketing researchers, on the other hand, counter that services developed independent of customer input are likely to be targeted at needs that do not exist. To study this question, researchers assessed the contributions made by users compared with professional developers for end-user telecom services. Three groups were studied: users alone, developers alone, and users with a design expert present to provide information on feasibility. Findings showed that users created more original but less producible ideas. However, inviting users to test and explore possibilities once a prototype has been created can produce positive results.[13]

ANALYZING AND INTERPRETING RESEARCH FINDINGS

One of the biggest challenges facing a researcher is converting a complex set of data to a form that can be read and understood quickly by employees who will make decisions. Many of the people who use marketing research findings have not been trained in statistics and have neither the time nor the expertise to analyze computer printouts and other technical research information. The goal in this stage of the research process is to communicate information clearly to the right people in a timely fashion. Among considerations are the following: Who gets this information? Why do they need it? How will they use it? Does it mean the same thing across cultures? (See the Global Feature box.) When users feel confident that they understand the data, they are far more likely to apply it appropriately. When managers do not understand how to interpret the data, or when they lack confidence in the research, the investment of time, skill, and effort will be lost.

Depicting research findings graphically is a powerful way to communicate research information. Here are a sample of graphic representations of the types of research data we have discussed throughout this chapter.

Tracking of Performance, Gap Scores, and Competition

A simple way of tracking performance is shown in Figure 6.4. Both expectations and perceptions are plotted, and the gap between them shows the service quality shortfall. Although any attribute or dimension of service can be tracked, Figure 6.4 shows only the scores for service reliability. Competitor service performance is another frequently tracked service quality measurement. It allows managers to have a better grasp of service improvement priorities for their firm by comparing the firm's service strengths and weaknesses against those of key competitors.[14]

Zones of Tolerance Charts

When companies collect data on the dual expectation levels described in Chapter 4 —desired service and adequate service—along with performance data, they can

FIGURE 6.4

Tracking of Customer Expectations and Perceptions of Service Reliability

Source: E. Sivadas, "Europeans Have a Different Take on CS [Customer Satisfaction] Programs," *Marketing News*, October 26, 1998, p. 39. Reprinted by permission of the American Marketing Association.

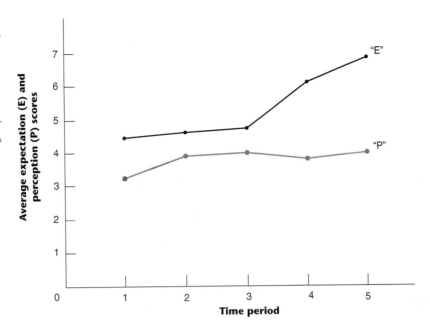

convey the information concisely on zones of tolerance charts. Figure 6.5 plots customer quality perceptions relative to customers' zones of tolerance. Perceptions of company performance are indicated by the circles, and the zones of tolerance boxes are bounded on the top by the desired service score and on the bottom by the adequate service score. When the perception scores are within the boxes, as in the figure, the company is delivering service that is above customers' minimum level of expectations. When the perception scores are below the boxes, the company's service performance is lower than the minimum level, and customers are dissatisfied with the company's service.[15]

FIGURE 6.5

Service Quality Perceptions Relative to Zones of Tolerance by Dimensions

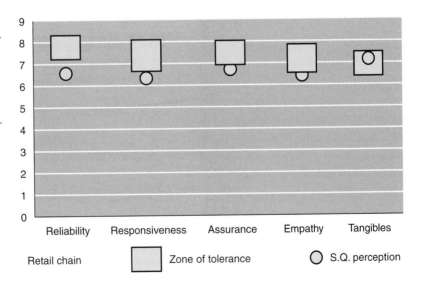

Global Feature

Culture Influences Marketing Research

Marketing research practices that are developed in North America are not always directly transferable to other cultures. Customer satisfaction measurement and CRM (customer relationship management), both created in the United States, are easily used in Canada with little modification. They do, however, have relevance in other countries and geographies but must be adapted to key differences that require a deep understanding of culture. In this box, we discuss how customer research, and specifically CRM, must be adapted in Asia.

CUSTOMER RELATIONSHIP MANAGEMENT IN ASIA

Don Peppers and Martha Rogers, consultants in CRM and related areas, have noted the Western orientation of CRM and have emphasized that inherent values in the CRM literature do not fit with Asian values. Whereas CRM literature in the United States assumes that customers will "unerringly respond [on] the basis of self-interest and self-gratification," Asian values—such as delayed gratification, loyalty to family and clan, and *Guanxi* (networks of obligations and connections)—must be taken into account if CRM is to succeed in Asia. As the consultants point out, customer relationships are different in Asia in these ways:

- Language preferences are more complex in China than in the United States. Chinese/Malaysian customers may speak one Chinese dialect

formally, transact business in Bahasa Malay, and complete legal documents in English. Knowing these differences customizes a relationship, but very few CRM systems can accommodate this level of customization.

- Customer names are very different in societies that are racially diverse. Some names are very long and do not have surnames. Chinese names start with the last (family) names and then are followed by the first and second given names. As you probably know from your Chinese classmates, Chinese people also sometimes give themselves Western names. Recognizing all these differences is very difficult for a CRM system.

- Some Asian customers have more than one marriage, family, and address. Sending information, such as for life insurance or financial services, to the wrong address violates privacy and can create very difficult situations!

- Asians will rarely tell anyone their net worth, because of a cultural bias against flaunting wealth. Therefore, it is difficult to find out which customers are most valuable on the basis of their income.

For these and other reasons, CRM has been adopted much more slowly in Asia than in Canada and the U.S.

Source: A. Berhad and T. Tyler, "Customer Relationship Management in Asia: A Cross Cultural Case Study Based on Aetna Universal Insurance" (Norwalk, CT: Peppers & Rogers Group, 2001).

Importance/Performance Matrices

One of the most useful forms of analysis in marketing research is the importance/performance matrix. Such a chart combines information about customer perceptions and importance ratings. An example is shown in Figure 6.6. Attribute importance is represented on the vertical axis from high (top) to low (bottom). Performance is shown on the horizontal axis from low (left) to high (right). There are many variations of these matrices; some companies define the horizontal axis as the gap between expectations

FIGURE 6.6

Importance/
Performance Matrix

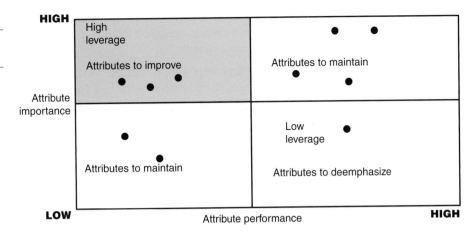

and perceptions, or as performance relative to competition. The shading on the chart indicates the area of highest leverage for service quality improvements—where importance is high and performance is low. In this quadrant are the attributes that most need to be improved. In the adjacent upper quadrant are attributes to be maintained, ones that a company performs well and that are very important to customers. The lower two quadrants contain attributes that are less important, some of which are performed well and others poorly. Neither of these quadrants merit as much attention in terms of service improvements as the upper quadrants because customers are not as concerned about the attributes that are plotted in them as they are the attributes in the upper quadrants.

MODEL SERVICES RESEARCH PROGRAMS

We have chosen three companies to illustrate comprehensive and effective programs that have sustained close customer–company relationships.

Disney

Most visitors to Walt Disney theme parks see magic, but the magic is based on solid research discipline. Disney conducts over 200 different external surveys a year, tracking satisfaction along with demographic profiles of its customers. The company also conducts price-sensitivity analysis to determine the tolerance of guests for various levels of pricing. One recent outcome of this analysis was the FastPass, a premium-priced ticket to the park that allows its purchasers to avoid lines and expedite their access to rides and other attractions. The company also has guests evaluate its different attractions, noting the aspects that are pleasing or troublesome and changing aspects to ensure that the attractions run as smoothly as possible. In addition, the company monitors tens of thousands of letters and comment cards it receives and practises "management by walking around." By doing so, Disney gathers critical information and enables the design of a service experience that delights its guests.[16]

FedEx

FedEx, the first major service company to win the U.S. Malcolm Baldridge National Quality Award, has a strong and comprehensive program of marketing and customer satisfaction research.[17] Its program includes:

- Customer requirements and expectations, gleaned from multiple qualitative and quantitative research studies, feedback from sales professionals, and feedback from customer service professionals.

- Toll-free numbers for complaints, which are systematically captured and dispatched to responsible parties. Trends are also tracked and analyzed.

- Customer satisfaction studies, with objectives of assessing satisfaction, identifying reasons for dissatisfaction, and monitoring satisfaction over time. This involves 2,400 telephone interviews per quarter measuring 17 domestic service attributes, 22 export service attributes, eight drop-box attributes, and eight service centre attributes.

- Ten targeted satisfaction studies on specialized business functions. These are direct-mail, self-administered surveys.

- Satisfaction monitoring at every point of interaction with the customer, some through transaction-based studies and others using operational measures driven by customer requirements.

- A comment card program, monitoring satisfaction with counter service.

- Customer satisfaction studies in world markets, focusing on understanding how service delivery must be adapted to global markets.

MuchMusic

MuchMusic, recently dubbed *Strategy Magazine*'s "Overall Brand of the Year," has taken listening to its customers to a whole new level, and that can't be easy when its target customers are changing as quickly as Canadian teenagers.

Listening closely to its audience is a core brand value at MuchMusic (Figure 6.7). The policy is based not only on traditional marketing research, but also—and even more so—on interacting with the audience and letting the audience set the agenda. MuchMusic has perfected listening with its MuchOnDemand program. Razer is a brand extension that lets customers program, select, and even host shows. PunchMuch lets customers request videos and join onscreen chats and polling—naturally, the polls drive the program.

FIGURE 6.7

MuchMusic is an industry leader in listening to its customers.

Source: Courtesy of MuchMusic.

Now MuchMusic has formalized its listening with an online research panel of 2,000 viewers aged 12 to 34. "It's an opportunity to have access to our viewers. ... [Moreover] it provides us with a framework on a balanced research level."[18]

Conducting research about customer expectations is only the first part of understanding the customer, even if the research is appropriately designed, executed, and presented. A service firm must also use the research findings in a meaningful way—to drive improvement in the way service is delivered. The misuse (or even nonuse) of research data can lead to a large gap in understanding customer expectations. Understanding how to make the best use of research—to apply what has been learned to the business—is a key way to close Provider Gap 1, the gap between customer expectations and management perceptions of customer expectations.

→ UPWARD COMMUNICATION

In some service firms, especially small ones, owners or managers may be in constant contact with customers. But in large service organizations, managers do not always get the opportunity to experience firsthand what their customers want.

The larger a company is, the more difficult it will be for managers to interact directly with the customer and the less firsthand information they will have about customer expectations. To truly understand customer needs, management benefits from hands-on knowledge of what really happens in stores, on customer service telephone lines, in service queues, and in face-to-face service encounters. If Gap 1 is to be closed, managers in large firms need some form of customer contact.

Objectives for Upward Communication

Exhibit 6.3 shows the major research objectives for improving upward communication. These objectives can be met by two types of interactive activities in the organization: one designed to improve the type and effectiveness of communications from customers to management, and the other designed to improve communications between employees and management.

Research for Upward Communication

Executive Visits to Customers

This approach is frequently used in business-to-business services marketing. In some visits, executives of the company make sales or service calls with customer contact personnel (salespeople). In other situations, executives of the selling company arrange meetings with executives at a similar level in client companies. When Lou Gerstner became CEO of IBM, one of his first actions was to arrange a meeting with 175 of the company's biggest customers for a discussion of how IBM can better meet their needs.

Executive or Management Listening to Customers

The marketing director at Milliken, a textile and chemicals firm, called his experience working the swing shift "naive listening," and he described its benefits as follows:

> Getting close to the customer is a winner! ... I worked the second shift (3:00 p.m. to midnight) and actually cleaned carpeting as well as hard-surface floors. I operated all the machinery they used daily, plus handled the same housekeeping problems .... Now I can put together my trade advertising as well as my entire merchandising program based directly upon the needs of my customers as I observed them. ... I'm learning—from new-product introduction to maintenance of existing products—exactly what our health care customers require.[19]

Elements in an Effective Program of Upward Communication

Type of Interaction or Research	Research Objective	Qualitative/ Quantitative	Cost of Information		
			Money	Time	Frequency
Executive visits to customers	To gain firsthand knowledge about customers	Qualitative	Moderate	Moderate	Continuous
Executive listenings	To gain firsthand knowledge about customers	Qualitative	Low	Low	Continuous
Research on intermediate customers	To gain in-depth information on end customers	Quantitative	Moderate	Moderate	Annual
Employee internal satisfaction surveys	To improve internal service quality	Quantitative	Moderate	Moderate	Annual
Employee visits or listenings	To gain firsthand knowledge about employees	Qualitative	Moderate	Moderate	Continuous
Employee suggestions	To obtain ideas for service improvements	Qualitative	Low	Low	Continuous

As this example illustrates, direct interaction with customers adds clarity and depth to managers' understanding of customer expectations and needs.

Managers can also spend time on the line, interacting with customers and experiencing service delivery. A formal program for encouraging informal interaction is often the best way to ensure that the contact takes place. At Loyalty Marketing Group Canada Inc., which operates Canada's most widely recognized loyalty program, the AIR MILES® Reward Program (Figure 6.8), the entire marketing department "double-jacks" on the phones in the customer care centre. AIR MILES president Bryan Pearson also meets with call centre specialists during regular lunchtime meetings.[20]

Research on Intermediate Customers

Intermediate customers (such as contact employees, dealers, distributors, agents, and brokers) are people the company serves who serve the end customer. Researching the needs and expectations of these customers *in serving the end customer* can be a useful and efficient way to both improve service to and obtain information about end users. It can also help the company learn about and satisfy the service expectations of intermediate customers, a process critical in their providing quality service to end customers.

FIGURE 6.8

Air Miles®
marketing staff
"double-jack"
on the call centre
phones to ensure
they know what
their customers
expect.

Source: Reprinted by permission
of The Loyalty Group.

Research on Internal Customers (Employees)

Employees who perform services are themselves customers of internal services on which they depend heavily to do their jobs well. There is a strong and direct link between the quality of internal service that employees receive and the quality of service they provide. For this reason it is important to conduct employee research that focuses on the service that internal customers give and receive. In many companies this focus requires adapting existing employee opinion research to focus on service satisfaction. Employee research complements customer research when service quality is the issue being investigated. Customer research provides insight into what is occurring, whereas employee research provides insight into why. The two types of research play unique and equally important roles in improving service quality. Companies that focus service quality research exclusively on external customers are missing a rich and vital source of information.[21]

Executive or Management Listening Approaches to Employees

Employees who actually perform the service have the best possible vantage point for observing the service and identifying impediments to its quality. Customer contact personnel are in regular contact with customers and thereby come to understand a great deal about customer expectations and perceptions.[22] If the information they know can be passed on to top management, top managers' understanding of the customer may improve. In fact, it could be said that in many companies, top management's understanding of the customer depends largely on the extent and types of communication received from customer contact personnel and from noncompany contact personnel (like independent insurance agents and retailers) who represent the company and its services. When these channels of communication are closed, management may not get feedback about problems encountered in service delivery and about how customer expectations are changing.

Sam Walton, the late founder of Wal-Mart, once remarked, "Our best ideas come from delivery and stock boys."[23] To stay in touch with the source of new ideas, Walton spent endless hours in stores working the floor, helping clerks, or approving personal cheques, even showing up at the loading dock with a bag of doughnuts for a surprised crew of workers.[24] He was well known for having his plane drop him next to a wheat field where he would meet a Wal-Mart truck driver. Giving his pilot instructions to meet him at another landing strip more than 320 kilometres down the road, he would make the trip with the Wal-Mart driver, listening to what he had to say about the company.

Managers who stay close to their contact people benefit not only by keeping their employees happy but also by learning more about their customers.[25] These companies encourage, appreciate, and reward upward communication from contact people. VIA Rail is instituting face-to-face meetings of cross-functional teams and meetings between customer relations and marketing staff to get deeper insights into the customers' experience. Through these important channels, management learns about customer expectations from employees in regular contact with customers and can thereby reduce the size of Gap 1.

Employee Suggestions

Most companies have some form of employee suggestion program whereby contact personnel can communicate to management their ideas for improving work. Suggestion systems have come a long way from the traditional suggestion box. Effective suggestion systems are ones in which employees are empowered to see their suggestions through, where supervisors can implement proposals immediately, where employees participate for continuous improvement in their jobs, where supervisors respond quickly to ideas, and where coaching is provided in ways to handle suggestions. (Recall the chapter opening vignette featuring Toronto-Dominion Bank Financial Group, which illustrated the value placed on employee insight for that firm.) In today's companies, suggestions from employees are facilitated by self-directed work teams that encourage employees to identify problems and then work to develop solutions to those problems.

SUMMARY

This chapter discussed the role of marketing research in understanding customer perceptions and expectations. After first describing criteria for effective services research, the chapter defined key forms of services research including critical incidents studies, mystery shopping, service expectation meetings and reviews, process checkpoint evaluations, and database research. Important topics in researching services—including developing research objectives and presenting data—were also described. Finally, upward communication, ways in which management obtains and uses information from customers and customer contact personnel, was discussed. These topics combine to close Provider Gap 1 between customer expectations and company understanding of customer expectations, the first of four Provider Gaps in the Gaps model of service quality.

⟼ Discussion Questions

1. Give five reasons why research objectives must be established before marketing research is conducted.

2. Why are both qualitative and quantitative research methods needed in a services marketing research program?

3. Why does the frequency of research differ across the research methods shown in Exhibit 6.1?

4. Compare and contrast the types of research that help a company identify common failure points (see column 2 in Exhibit 6.1). Which of the types do you think produces better information? Why?

5. In what situations does a service company need requirements research?

6. What reasons can you give for companies' lack of use of research information? How might you motivate managers to use the information to a greater extent? How might you motivate front-line workers to use the information?

7. Given a specific marketing research budget, what would be your recommendations for the percentage to be spent on customer research versus upward communication? Why?

8. What kinds of information might be gleaned from research on intermediate customers? What would intermediate customers know that service providers might not?

9. For what types of products and services would research on the Internet be preferable to traditional research?

⟼ Exercises

1. Choose a local services organization to interview about marketing research. Find out what the firm's objectives are and the types of marketing research it currently uses. Using the information in this chapter, think about the effectiveness of its marketing research. What are the strengths? Weaknesses?

2. Choose one of the services you consume. If you were in charge of creating a survey for that service, what questions would you ask on the survey? Give several examples. What type of survey (relationship vs. transaction-based) would be most appropriate for the service? What recommendations would you give to management of the company about making such a survey actionable?

3. If you were the marketing director of your college or university, what types of research (see Exhibit 6.1) would be essential for understanding both external and internal customers? If you could choose only three types of research, which ones would you select? Why?

4. Using the SERVQUAL scale in this chapter, create a questionnaire for a service firm that you use. Give the questionnaire to 10 people, and describe what you learn.

5. To get an idea of the power of the critical incidents technique, try it yourself with reference to restaurant service. Think of a time when, as a customer, you had a particularly satisfying interaction with a restaurant. Follow the instructions here,

which are identical to the instructions in an actual study, and observe the insights you obtain about your requirements in restaurant service:

a. When did the incident happen?

b. What specific circumstances led up to this situation?

c. Exactly what did the employee (or firm) say or do?

d. What resulted that made you feel the interaction was satisfying?

e. What could or should have been done differently?

➤ Notes

1. TD Bank annual report, 2005, available at www.td.com.

2. A. Parasuraman, L. L. Berry, and V. A. Zeithaml, "Guidelines for Conducting Service Quality Research," *Marketing Research: A Magazine of Management and Applications*, December 1990, pp. 34–44.

3. This section is based on a comprehensive assessment of the critical incident technique in D. D. Gremler, "The Critical Incident Technique in Service Research," *Journal of Service Research* 7 (August 2004), pp. 65–89.

4. Ibid.

5. E. E. Lueke and T. W. Suther III, "Market-Driven Quality: A Market Research and Product Requirements Methodology," *IBM Technical Report*, June 1991.

6. Jake McCaul, quoted in S. Yaffe, "Going Deep: Getting to Know Customers Better Than They Know Themselves Means Asking Different Questions Differently," *Strategy Magazine*, February 2005, p. 9.

7. Susan Bardwell, quoted in S. Yaffe, p. 9.

8. See V. A. Zeithaml and A. Parasuraman, *Service Quality*, MSI Relevant Knowledge Series (Cambridge, MA: Marketing Science Institute, 2004) for a complete review of this research, including the many publications by the original authors of SERVQUAL and the extensions by other authors.

9. E. Day, "Researchers Must Enter Consumer's World," *Marketing News*, August 17, 1998, p. 17.

10. G. Khermouch, "Consumers in the Mist," *BusinessWeek*, February 26, 2001, pp. 92–93.

11. Ibid., p. 92.

12. For examples, see S. J. Grove and R. P. Fiske, "Observational Data Collection Methods for Services Marketing: An Overview," *Journal of the Academy of Marketing Science* 20 (Summer 1992), pp. 117–214.

13. P. R. Magnusson, J. Mathing, and P. Kristensson, "Managing User Involvement in Service Innovation: Experiments with Innovating End Users," *Journal of Service Research* 6 (November 2003), pp. 111–24.

14. V. A. Zeithaml, A. Parasuraman, and L. L. Berry, Delivering Quality Service: *Balancing Customer Perceptions and Expectations* (New York: Free Press, 1990), p. 28.

15. A. Parasuraman, V. A. Zeithaml, and L. L. Berry, "Moving Forward in Service Quality Research," *Marketing Science Institute Report No. 94-114*, September 1994.

16. R. Johnson, "A Strategy for Service—Disney Style," *Journal of Business Strategy*, September/October 1991, pp. 38–43.

17. "Multiple Measures Give FedEx Its 'Good' Data," *The Service Edge*, June 1991, p. 6.
18. Natalia Williams, "Much Accomplishment," *Strategy Magazine*, November 2005, p. 37.
19. T. J. Peters and N. Austin, *A Passion for Excellence* (New York: Random House, 1985), p. 16.
20. L. D'Innocenzo, *Strategy Magazine*, November 2005, p. 14.
21. "Baldridge Winner Co-convenes Quality Summit," *Executive Report on Customer Satisfaction*, October 30, 1992.
22. M. J. Bitner, B. Booms, and L. Mohr, "Critical Service Encounters: The Employee's Viewpoint," *Journal of Marketing* 58 (October 1994), pp. 95–106.
23. S. Koepp, "Make That Sale, Mr. Sam," *Time*, May 18, 1987.
24. Ibid.
25. Zeithaml, Parasuraman, and Berry, *Delivering Quality Service*, p. 64.

Chapter

7

Building Customer Relationships

Provider Gap 1

THIS CHAPTER'S OBJECTIVES ARE TO

1. Explain relationship marketing, its goals, and the benefits of long-term relationships for firms and customers.

2. Explain why and how to estimate customer relationship value.

3. Introduce the concept of customer profitability segments as a strategy for focusing relationship marketing efforts.

4. Present relationship development strategies—including quality core service, switching barriers, and relationship bonds.

5. Identify challenges in relationship development, including the somewhat controversial idea that "the customer is not always right."

REALITY TELEVISION HAS BEGUN BUILDING RELATIONSHIPS WITH VIEWERS

Gone are the days when individuals had only a handful of television channels from which to choose to satisfy their at-home entertainment needs. Today, with a variety of different media options, including several hundred television channels readily accessible, it is becoming increasingly difficult for show creators and networks to create and retain loyal viewers. That is, it was—until reality television made its debut in North America just a few years ago.

These shows have been able to quickly acquire millions of viewers. Discussion of their content has replaced news topics and other traditional programming in many "water cooler conversations" across the continent. These shows seem to offer something for everyone in a variety of genres. There are game shows such as *Survivor*, *Fear Factor*, and *The Amazing Race*; makeover programs such as *Extreme Makeover* and *The Biggest Loser*; and talent competitions such as *American Idol* (www.americanidol.com), *Canadian Idol* (www.idol.ctv.ca), *Nashville Star* (www.usanetwork.com/series/nashvillestar), and *Rock Star Supernova* (www.rockstar.msn.com). As will be discussed in Chapter 7, simply acquiring customers (or viewers) does not a relationship make; but it is a necessary first step.

Among reality shows, the talent genre as a whole seems to have taken its relationship-building efforts with viewers to the next level. On the *American Idol* model, the *Canadian Idol* franchise and shows like it have begun allowing greater levels of interactivity with their audiences in several ways. First, the shows allow viewers to voice their opinion in a very tangible way—they can vote for contestants and influence the show's outcome. Also, most programming of this kind engages in cross-promotion with wireless companies, and all have created online communities with many interesting relationship programs to make the TV experience more personal. Some sites provide access to chat rooms; one *Nashville Star* judge sought and answered viewer questions on the show's site; *Rock Star* contestants regularly post entries in online journals; and *Canadian Idols* blog regularly, and have even designed their own T-shirts sold through the site.

By maintaining greater contact with viewers and monitoring audience feedback, show producers can begin to close Provider Gap 1—Not Knowing What Customers Expect—and increase their focus on viewer retention.

Source: Canadian Idol is a trademark of 19 TV Limited and FremantleMedia North America Inc. (www.fremantlemedia.com). Logo used with permisssion from FremantleMedia North America, Inc.

As noted at the beginning of Chapter 6, closing Provider Gap 1—Not Knowing What Customers Expect—is easier for companies who focus on keeping their customers and building long-term relationships with them. However, many companies fail to understand customers accurately, because they fail to focus on customer relationships. They tend to fixate on acquiring new customers rather than viewing customers as assets that they need to nurture and retain. By concentrating on new customers, firms can fall into the traps of short-term promotions, price discounts, or catchy ads that bring customers in but are not enough to bring them back. By adopting a relationship philosophy, on the other hand, companies begin to understand customers over time and in great depth, and are better able to meet their changing needs and expectations. In so doing, they can help to ensure Provider Gap 1 is kept as small as possible.

RELATIONSHIP MARKETING

> There has been a shift from a transactions to a relationship focus in marketing. Customers become partners and the firm must make long-term commitments to maintaining those relationships with quality, service, and innovation.[1]

Relationship marketing essentially represents a paradigm shift within marketing—away from an acquisitions/transaction focus toward a retention/relationship focus.[2] Relationship marketing is a philosophy of doing business that focuses on *keeping and improving* relationships with current customers rather than on acquiring new customers. This philosophy assumes that many customers prefer to have an ongoing relationship with one organization than to switch continually among providers in their search for value. Building on this assumption and the fact that it is usually much cheaper to keep a current customer than to attract a new one, successful marketers are working on effective strategies for retaining customers.

It has been suggested that firms frequently focus on attracting customers (the "first act") but then pay little attention to what they should do to keep them (the "second act").[3] Ideas expressed in an interview with James L. Schorr, then executive vice-president of marketing at Holiday Inns, illustrate this point.[4] In the interview he stated that he was famous at Holiday Inns for what is called the "bucket theory of marketing." By this he meant that marketing can be thought of as a big bucket: it is what the sales, advertising, and promotion programs do that pours business into the top of the bucket. As long as these programs are effective, the bucket stays full. However, "There's only one problem," he said, "there's a hole in the bucket." When the business is running well and the hotel is delivering on its promises, the hole is small and few customers are leaving. When the operation is weak and customers are not satisfied with what they get, however, people start falling out of the bucket through the holes faster than they can be poured in through the top.

The bucket theory illustrates why a relationship strategy that focuses on plugging the holes in the bucket makes so much sense. Historically, marketers have been more concerned with acquisition of customers, so a shift to a relationship strategy often represents changes in mindset, organizational culture, and employee reward systems. For example, the sales incentive systems in many organizations are set up to reward bringing in new customers. There are often fewer (or no) rewards for retaining current accounts. Thus, even when people see the logic of customer retention, the existing organizational systems may not support its implementation.

The Evolution of Customer Relationships

Firms' relationships with their customers, like other social relationships, tend to evolve over time. Scholars have suggested that marketing exchange relationships between providers and customers often have the potential to evolve from strangers to acquaintances to friends to partners. Exhibit 7.1 illustrates different issues at each successive level of the relationship.[5]

Customers as Strangers

Strangers are those customers who are not aware of or, perhaps, those who have not yet had any transactions (interactions) with a firm. Consequently, the firm's primary goal with these potential customers ("strangers") is to initiate communication with them in order to *attract* them and *acquire* their business.

 EXHIBIT 7.1

A Typology of Exchange Relationships

Customers As ...	Strangers	Acquaintances	Friends	Partners
Product offering	Attractive relative to competative offerings or alternative purchases.	Parity product as a form of industry standard.	Differentiated product adapted to specific market segments.	Customized product and dedicated resources adapted to an individual customer or organization.
Source of competitive advantage	Attractiveness	Satisfaction	Satisfaction + trust	Satisfaction + trust + commitment
Buying activity	Interest, exploration, and trial.	Satisfaction facilitates and reinforces buying activity and reduces need to search for market information.	Trust in firm is needed to continue the buying activity without perfect information.	Commitment in the form of information sharing and idiosyncratic investments is needed to achieve customized product and to adjust product continuously to changing needs and situations.
Focus of selling	Awareness of firm's offerings (encouraging trial) facilitates initial selling.	Familiarity and general knowledge of customer (identification) facilitates selling.	Specific knowledge of customer's connection to segment need and situation facilitates selling.	Specific knowledge of customer's need and situation and idiosyncratic investments facilitates selling.
Relationship time horizon	None: Buyer may have had no previous interactions with or knowledge of the firm.	Short: Generally short because the buyer can often switch firms without much effort or cost.	Medium: Generally longer than aquaintance relationships because trust in a differentiated position takes a longer time to build and imitate.	Long: Generally long because it takes time to build and replace interconnected activities and to develop a detailed knowledge of a customer's needs and the unique resources of a supplier to commit resources to the relationship.

continued

Customers As ...	Strangers	Acquaintances	Friends	Partners
Sustainability of competitive advantage	Low: Generally low, as firm must continually find ways to be attractive, in terms of the value offered, in order to induce trial.	Low: Generally low, but competitors can vary in how they build unique value into selling and serving even if the product is a form of industry standard.	Medium: Generally medium but depends on competitors' ability to understand heterogeneity of customer needs and situations and the ability to transform this knowledge into meaningful, differentiated products.	High: Generally high but depends on how unique and effective the interconnected activities between customer and supplier are organized.
Primary relationship marketing goal	*Acquire* customer's business.	*Satisfy* customer's needs and wants.	*Retain* customer's business.	*Enhance* relationship with customer.

Source: Adapted from M. D. Johnson and F. Seines, "Customer Portfolio Management: Toward a Dynamic Theory of Exchange Relationships," *Journal of Marketing* 68 (April 2004), p. 5. Reprinted by permission of the American Marketing Association.

Customers as Acquaintances

Once customer awareness and trial are achieved, familiarity is established and the customer and the firm become acquaintances, creating the basis for an exchange relationship. A primary goal for the firm at this stage of the relationship is *satisfying* the customer. In the acquaintance stage, firms are generally concerned about providing a value proposition to customers that is comparable with that of competitors. An acquaintanceship is effective as long as the customer is relatively satisfied with what is being received. With repetitive interactions, the customer gains experience and becomes more familiar with the firm. These encounters can help reduce uncertainty about the benefits expected in the exchange and, therefore, increase the attractiveness of the company relative to the competition. Repetitive interactions improve the firm's knowledge of the customer, helping to facilitate marketing, sales, and service efforts. Thus, an acquaintance relationship facilitates transactions primarily through the reduction of the customer's perceived risk and the provider's costs.

Customers as Friends

As a customer continues to make purchases from a firm, the firm begins to acquire specific knowledge of the customer's needs, allowing it to create an offering that directly addresses the customer's situation. The provision of a unique offering, and thus differential value, transforms the exchange relationship from acquaintance to friendship. This transition from acquaintanceship to friendship, particularly in service exchange relationships, requires the development of trust.[6] As discussed in an earlier chapter, customers may not be able to assess a service outcome prior to purchase and consumption, and for those services high in credence qualities, customers may not be able to discern service performance even after experiencing it. Therefore, customers must trust the provider to do what is promised. As customers become friends they not only become familiar with the company but also come to trust that it provides superior value.

A primary goal for firms at the friendship stage of the relationship is customer *retention*. Given their likelihood of past satisfying experiences and repeated purchases, these customers ("friends") are more likely to appreciate the firm's product offerings and are more open to other related services. A firm's potential to develop sustainable competitive advantage through friends should be higher than for acquaintances, because the offering is more unique (and more difficult for competition to imitate) and the customer comes to trust that uniqueness.[7]

Customers as Partners

As a customer continues to interact with a firm, the level of trust often deepens and the customer may receive more customized product offerings and interactions. The trust developed in the friendship stage is a necessary but not sufficient condition for a customer–firm partnership to develop.[8] That is, the creation of trust leads to (ideally) the creation of commitment—and that is the condition necessary for customers to extend the time perspective of a relationship.[9] The deepening of trust and the establishment of commitment reduce the customer's need to solve problems in the traditional sense of "finding a better alternative." Thus, in order to move the relationship into a partner relationship, a firm must use customer knowledge and information systems to deliver highly personalized and customized offerings.

At the partnership stage, the firm is concerned with *enhancing* the relationship. Customers are more likely to stay in the relationship if they feel that the company understands their changing needs and is willing to invest in the relationship by constantly improving and evolving its product and service mix. By enhancing these relationships, the firm expects such customers to be less likely to be lured away by competitors and more likely to buy additional products and services from the company over time. These loyal customers not only provide a solid base for the organization, they may represent growth potential. A bank chequing account customer becomes a better customer when she sets up a savings account, takes out a loan, and/or uses the financial advising services of the bank. And a corporate account becomes a better customer when it chooses to do 75 percent of its business with a particular supplier rather than splitting the business equally among three suppliers. In recent years, in fact, many companies have aspired to be the "exclusive supplier" of a particular product or service for their customers. Over time these enhanced relationships can increase market share and profits for the organization. Our Technology Spotlight features Ritz-Carlton, which is successfully using information technology to enhance relationships with its customers.

The Goal of Relationship Marketing

The discussion of the evolution of customer relationships demonstrates how a firm's relationship with its customers might be enhanced as customers move further along this relationship continuum. As the relationship value of a customer increases, the provider is more likely to pursue a closer relationship. Thus, the primary goal of relationship marketing is *to build and maintain a base of committed customers who are profitable for the organization.* Figure 7.1 graphically illustrates the goals of relationship marketing. The overriding goal is to move customers up the ladder (i.e., along the relationship continuum) from the point at which they are strangers that need to be attracted through to the point at which they are highly valued, long-term customers whose relationship with the firm has been enhanced. From a customer's problem-solving perspective, the formation of satisfaction, trust, and commitment corresponds to being an acquaintance, friend, and partner, respectively. From a firm's resource-allocation perspective, the delivery of differential value corresponds to the extent of its desire to create an acquaintance, friend, or partner relationship with the customer. The AIC print ad shown in Figure 7.2 shows how one firm tries to communicate the need for a long-term relationship.

Benefits for Customers and Firms

Both parties in the customer–firm relationship can benefit from customer retention. That is, it is not only in the best interest of the organization to build and maintain a loyal customer base, but customers themselves also benefit from long-term associations.

Benefits for Customers

Assuming they have a choice, customers will remain loyal to a firm when they receive greater value relative to what they expect from competing firms. *Value* represents a tradeoff for the consumer between the "give" and the "get" components. Consumers are more likely to stay in a relationship when the gets (quality, satisfaction, specific

FIGURE 7.1

Customer goals of relationship marketing: acquiring customers, satisfying customers, retaining customers, and enhancing customers.

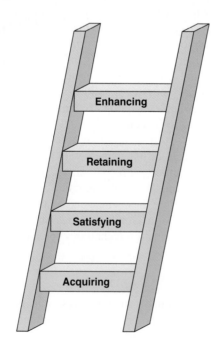

FIGURE 7.2

AIC's way of showing that a long-term relationship is best.

Source: Reprinted with permission of AIC Limited.

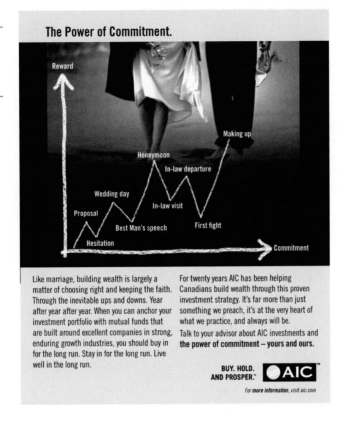

benefits) exceed the gives (monetary and nonmonetary costs). When firms can consistently deliver value from the customer's point of view, clearly the customer benefits and has an incentive to stay in the relationship. As noted in our Technology Spotlight, customers can't afford to forget about renewing important medical prescriptions. Being reminded can be a real help.

Beyond the specific inherent benefits of receiving service value, customers also benefit in other ways from long-term associations with firms. Sometimes these relationship benefits keep customers loyal to a firm more than the attributes of the core service. Research has uncovered specific types of relational benefits that customers experience in long-term service relationships including confidence benefits, social benefits, and special treatment benefits.[10]

Confidence Benefits   Confidence benefits comprise feelings of trust or confidence in the provider along with a sense of reduced anxiety in knowing what to expect. Across all the services studied in the research just cited, confidence benefits were the most important to customers.

Human nature is such that most consumers would prefer not to change service providers, particularly when there is a considerable investment in the relationship. The costs of switching are frequently high in terms of dollar costs and associated psychological and time-related costs. Most customers have many competing demands on their time and money and are continually searching for ways to balance and simplify decision making to improve the quality of their lives. When they can maintain a relationship with a service provider, they free up time for other concerns and priorities.

Technology Spotlight

Customer Information Systems Help Enhance the Customer Relationship

The potential of today's customer information systems far exceeds any traditional marketing information system that has gone before. These new systems differ from the old in their scale (thousands of bits of information on tens of millions of customers), the depth of information that can be captured on each individual or household, and the ways in which the information can be used. In many cases, access to this type of information about individual customers allows the organization to customize to the individual level what previously would have been undifferentiated services.

For example, The Ritz-Carlton Hotel Company L.L.C. (www.ritzcarlton.com) targets its services to industry executives, meeting and corporate travel planners, and affluent travellers. Although there are many dimensions to the company's success, one of the keys is the quality of its customer database. By training each employee to note the likes and dislikes of regular guests and to enter this information immediately into the customer's file, employees at any Ritz-Carlton Hotel are able to personalize services to the Ritz-Carlton's 240,000 repeat customers. The employees can know in advance the guest's preferences and be prepared to provide individualized service even before the guest's arrival. For example, if a guest prefers a feather pillow, wants extra brown sugar with her oatmeal, or always orders a glass of sherry before retiring, this information can be entered into the database and these needs anticipated—often much to the guest's surprise.

Other examples abound. Dentist offices send reminders or make phone calls to patients when it is time to make an appointment for regular cleanings. The technology required is very simple, but the firm must still have made the commitment to deploy it.

In the Canadian retail sector, a growing concern among health care workers is the ongoing tendency for people to quit taking their medication. For conditions such as blood pressure, anxiety, cholesterol, or asthma, symptoms can eventually disappear. However, that often means the condition is merely under control, not cured. When patients stop taking their prescriptions, sometimes a visit to the emergency room is the result. A technologically simple, yet effective, way to reduce their risk of non-adherence is for pharmacies to set up a database and automatically fill soon-to-expire prescriptions. They then call the patient to advise them that their prescription is ready. This way, everyone benefits.

Welcome
TO
THE RITZ-CARLTON
How may we be of Assistance?

The Ritz-Carlton provides the finest personal service and facilities throughout the world. The atmosphere is warm and relaxed and the ambience embraces the uniqueness of the local culture. The variety of services offered will enable you to create your own experience.

Social Benefits Over time, customers develop a sense of familiarity and even a social relationship with their service providers. These ties make it less likely that they will switch, even if they learn about a competitor that might have better quality or a lower price. This customer's description of her hair stylist illustrates the concept of social benefits: "I like him. . . . He's really funny and always has lots of good jokes. He's kind of like a friend now. . . . It's more fun to deal with somebody that you're used to. You enjoy doing business with them."

In some long-term customer–firm relationships, a service provider may actually become part of the consumer's social support system.[11] Hairdressers, as in the example just cited, often serve as personal confidants.

These types of personal relationships can develop for business-to-business customers as well as for end consumers of services. The social support benefits resulting from these relationships are important to the consumer's quality of life above and beyond the technical benefits of the service provided. Many times the close personal and professional relationships that develop between service providers and clients are the basis for the customer's loyalty. The flip side of this customer benefit is the risk to the firm of losing customers when a valued employee leaves the firm and takes customers with him or her.[12] We're probably all familiar with advertisements for hair stylists or automobile salespeople inviting former friends and clients to visit them at their new locations following a change in employers.

Special Treatment Benefits   Special treatment includes getting the benefit of the doubt, being given a special deal or price, or getting preferential treatment as exemplified by the following quote from the research:

> I think you get special treatment [when you have established a relationship]. My pediatrician allowed me to use the back door to the office so my daughter could avoid contact with other sick children. Other times I have been in a hurry and they take me right back.

Interestingly, special treatment benefits are less important than the other types of benefits received in service relationships.

Benefits for Firms

The benefits to organizations of developing a loyal customer are numerous. In addition to the economic benefits, a variety of customer behaviour benefits and human resource management benefits are also often received.

Economic Benefits   Research based on information contained in the Compustat and Compact Disclosure databases reveals that over the long run, relationship-oriented service firms achieve higher overall returns than do transaction-oriented firms.[13] These bottom-line benefits come from a variety of sources, including increased revenues over time from the customer, reduced marketing and administrative costs, and the ability to maintain margins without reducing prices.

One of the most commonly cited economic benefits of customer retention is increased purchases over time, as illustrated in Figure 7.3. The figure summarizes studies showing that customers generally spent more each year with a particular relationship partner than they did in the preceding period.[14] As customers get to know a firm, they give more of their business to the firm.

Another economic benefit is lower costs. Some estimates suggest that repeat purchases by established customers require as much as 90 percent less marketing expenditure.[15] Many startup costs are associated with attracting new customers, including advertising and other promotion costs, the operating costs of setting up new accounts, and time costs of getting to know the customers. Sometimes these initial costs can outweigh the revenue expected from the new customers in the short term, so it is to the firm's advantage to cultivate long-term relationships. In Chapter 18 we will provide more specifics on the financial impact of customer retention.

Customer Behaviour Benefits   The contribution that loyal customers make to a service business can go well beyond their direct financial impact on the firm.[16] The first benefit that a firm receives from long-term customers is free word-of-mouth advertising. When a product is difficult to evaluate and when risk is involved in the decision to buy it—as is the case with many services—consumers often look to

FIGURE 7.3

Profit Generated by a Customer over Time

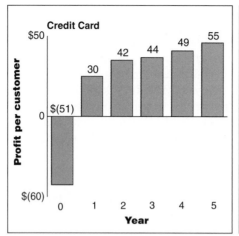

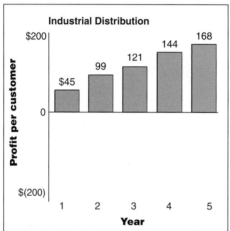

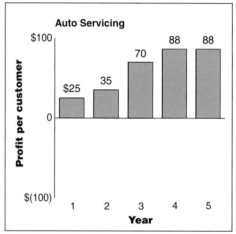

others for advice on which providers to consider. Satisfied, loyal customers are likely to provide a firm with strong word-of-mouth endorsements. This form of advertising can be more effective than any paid advertising that the firm might use, and it has the added benefit of reducing the costs of attracting new customers. Imagine, for instance, that you and your friends are planning an outdoor adventure vacation to British Columbia. Wouldn't you feel better about your decision of which tour operator to use if a close friend gave a glowing recommendation for a particular firm? Now, if you were that firm, wouldn't it be worth a little extra effort to ensure your former customers always gave glowing recommendations?

In addition to word-of-mouth communication, there is a second consumer behaviour benefit sometimes labelled customer voluntary performance;[17] in a restaurant, such behaviour might include reporting messy restrooms to an employee or picking up trash in the parking lot. Such behaviours support the firm's ability to deliver quality services. Third, for some services loyal customers may provide social benefits to other customers in the form of friendships or encouragement. At a physical therapy clinic, for example, a patient recovering from knee surgery is likely to think more highly of the clinic when fellow patients provide encouragement and emotional support during the rehabilitation process. That is precisely what happens at Shouldice, a famous Canadian hospital specializing in hernia operations (discussed in Chapter 11). Finally, loyal customers may serve as mentors and, because of their experience with the provider, help other customers understand the explicitly or implicitly stated rules of conduct.[18]

Human Resource Management Benefits   Loyal customers may also provide a firm with human resource management benefits. First, loyal customers may be able to contribute to the co-production of the service by assisting in service delivery; often the more experienced customers can make the service employees' job easier. For example, a regular patient of a medical service provider is likely to know how the system works; she would know to bring her medication with her on a visit, to plan on paying by cheque (having previously learned that the office cannot process credit cards), and to schedule an annual mammogram without waiting for her doctor to prompt her. A second benefit relates to one of the benefits for customers that we have already discussed. We noted that loyal customers receive social benefits as a result of being in a relationship with a firm; employees who regularly interact with the same customers may also receive similar social benefits.[19] A third benefit of customer retention is employee retention. It is easier for a firm to retain employees when it has a stable base of satisfied customers. People like to work for companies whose customers are happy and loyal. Their jobs are more satisfying, and they are able to spend more of their time fostering relationships than scrambling for new customers. In turn, customers are more satisfied and become even better customers—a positive upward spiral. Because employees stay with the firm longer, service quality improves and costs of turnover are reduced, adding further to profits.

RELATIONSHIP VALUE OF CUSTOMERS

Relationship value of a customer is a concept or calculation that looks at customers from the point of view of their lifetime revenue and/or profitability contributions to a company. This type of calculation is obviously needed when companies start thinking of building long-term relationships with their customers. Just what is the potential financial value of those long-term relationships? And what are the financial implications of *losing* a customer? Here we will only summarize the factors that influence a customer's relationship value. In Chapter 18 we provide more detail on lifetime value financial calculations.

Factors That Influence Relationship Value

The lifetime or relationship value of a customer is influenced by the length of an average "lifetime," the average revenues generated per relevant time period over the lifetime, sales of additional products and services over time, referrals generated by the customer over time, and costs associated with serving the customer. *Lifetime value* sometimes refers to lifetime revenue stream only; but most often when costs are considered, lifetime value truly means "lifetime profitability."

Estimating Customer Lifetime Value

If companies knew how much it really costs to lose a customer, they would be able to accurately evaluate investments designed to retain customers. One way of documenting the dollar value of loyal customers is to estimate the increased value or profits that accrue for each additional customer who remains loyal to the company rather than defecting to the competition. This is what Bain & Co. has done for a number of industries, as shown in Figure 7.4.[20] The figure shows the percentage of increase in

FIGURE 7.4

Profit Impact of
5 Percent Increase in
Retention Rate

Source: Reprinted with
permission of the American
Marketing Association. From
F. F. Reichheld, "Loyalty and
the Renaissance of Marketing,"
Marketing Management 2, no.
4 (1994), p. 15.

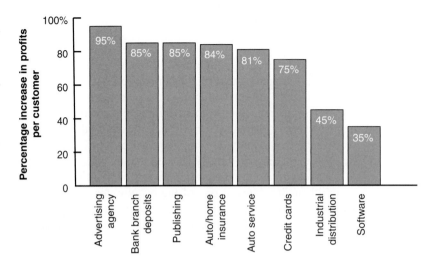

total firm profits when the retention or loyalty rate rises by 5 percentage points. The
increases are dramatic, ranging from 35 to 95 percent. These increases were calculated
by comparing the net present values of the profit streams for the average customer life
at current retention rates with the net present values of the profit streams for the average customer life at 5 percent higher retention rates.[21]

Linking Customer Relationship Value to Firm Value

The emphasis on estimating the relationship value of customers has increased substantially in the past decade. Part of this emphasis has resulted from an increased appreciation of the economic benefits that firms accrue with the retention of loyal customers.
Interestingly, recent research suggests that customer retention has a large impact on
firm value and that relationship value calculations can also provide a useful proxy for
assessing the value of a firm.[22] That is, a firm's market value can be roughly determined
by carefully calculating customer lifetime value. The approach is straightforward:
estimate the relationship value of a customer, forecast the future growth of the number
of customers, and use these figures to determine the value of a company's current and
future base. To the extent that the customer base forms a large part of a company's overall value, such a calculation can provide an estimate of a firm's value—a particularly
useful figure for young, high-growth firms for which traditional financial methods (e.g.,
discounted cash flow) do not work well.

CUSTOMER PROFITABILITY SEGMENTS

Companies may want to treat all customers with excellent service, but they generally
find that customers differ in their relationship value and that it may be neither practical
nor profitable to meet (and certainly not to exceed) *all* customers' expectations.[23] FedEx
Corporation, for example, has categorized its customers internally as the good, the bad,
and the ugly—based on their profitability. Rather than treating all its customers the
same, the company pays particular attention to enhancing their relationships with the
good, tries to move the bad to the good, and discourages the ugly.[24] Other companies
also try to identify segments—or, more appropriately, tiers of customers—that differ in
current and/or future profitability to a firm. This approach goes beyond usage or volume
segmentation, because it tracks costs and revenues for segments of customers, thereby

capturing their financial worth to companies. After identifying profitability bands, the firm offers services and service levels in line with the identified segments. Building a high-loyalty customer base of the right customers increases profits. At MBNA Canada, a leading financial services firm, a 5 percent jump in retention increased the company profits 60 percent by the fifth year.[25]

Profitability Tiers—The Customer Pyramid

Although some people may view the FedEx grouping of customers into "the good, the bad, and the ugly" as negative, descriptive labels of the tiers can be very useful internally. Labels are especially valuable if they help the company keep track of which customers are profitable.

Virtually all firms are aware that their customers differ in profitability, in particular, that a minority of their customers accounts for the highest proportion of sales or profit. This finding has often been called the "80/20 rule"—20 percent of customers produce 80 percent of sales or profit.

In this version of tiering, 20 percent of the customers constitute the top tier, those who can be identified as the most profitable in the company. The rest are indistinguishable from each other but differ from the top tier in profitability. Most companies realize that there are differences among customers within this tier but do not possess the data or capabilities to analyze the distinctions. The 80/20 two-tier scheme assumes that consumers within the two tiers are similar, just as conventional market segmentation schemes typically assume that consumers within segments are similar.

However, more than two tiers are likely and can be used if the company has sufficient data to analyze customer tiers more precisely. Different systems and labels can be helpful. One useful four-tier system, shown in Figure 7.5, includes the following:

1. The *platinum tier* describes the company's most profitable customers, typically those who are heavy users of the product, are not overly price-sensitive, are willing to invest in and try new offerings, and are committed customers of the firm. Closing Provider Gap 1 is most critical for this group. Unfortunately, many firms don't know who those customers are and therefore can't focus attention on them.

2. The *gold tier* differs from the platinum tier in that profitability levels are not as high, perhaps because the customers want price discounts that limit margins or are not as loyal. They may be heavy users who minimize risk by working with multiple vendors rather than just the focal company.

3. The *iron tier* contains essential customers who provide the volume needed to utilize the firm's capacity, but their spending levels, loyalty, and profitability are not substantial enough for special treatment.

4. The *lead tier* consists of customers who are costing the company money. They demand more attention than they are due given their spending and profitability and are sometimes problem customers—complaining about the firm to others and tying up the firm's resources.

Examples of effective use of the customer pyramid approach exist in a number of business contexts. Financial services firms are leading the way, perhaps because of the vast amounts of data already housed in those firms. Bank of Montreal has managed to classify approximately one-third of its more than 5 million customers as profitable and

FIGURE 7.5

The Customer
Pyramid

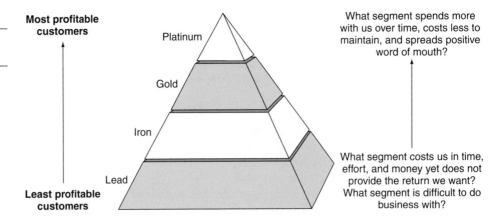

plans to continue focus on these clients. Similarly, Royal Bank, using CRM technology, has segmented a group of customers it refers to as the Growth Market. Its commitment to better serve such core customers required revamping whole departments.[26]

Once a system has been established for categorizing customers, the multiple levels can be identified, motivated, served, and expected to deliver differential levels of profit. Companies improve their opportunities for profit when they increase shares of purchases by customers who either have the greatest need for the services or show the greatest loyalty to a single provider. By strengthening relationships with the loyal customers, increasing sales with existing customers, and increasing the profitability on each sale opportunity, companies thereby increase the potential of each customer.

The Customer's View of Profitability Tiers

Whereas profitability tiers make sense from the company's point of view, customers don't appreciate being categorized into a less desirable segment.[27] For example, at some companies the top clients have their own individual account representative whom they can contact personally. The next tier of clients may be handled by representatives who each have 100 clients. Meanwhile, the majority of clients are served by an 800 number, an automated voice response system, or referral to a website. Customers are aware of this unequal treatment, and many resist and resent it.

Therefore, it is increasingly important that firms communicate with customers so they understand the level of service they can expect and what they would need to do to get better service. The most significant issues result when customers do not understand, believe they have been singled out for poor service, or feel that the system is unfair.

The ability to segment customers narrowly based on profitability implications also raises questions of privacy for customers. In order to know who is profitable and who is not, companies must collect large amounts of individualized data on consumers. Many consumers today resent what they perceive as an intrusion into their lives, especially when it results in differential treatment that they perceive is unfair.

Making Business Decisions Using Profitability Tiers

Prudent business managers are well aware that past customer purchase behaviour, although useful in making predictions, can be misleading.[28] What a customer spends today, or has spent in the past, may not necessarily be reflective of what he or she will do (or be worth) in the future. Banks serving university and college students know this well—a typical such student generally has minimal financial services needs (i.e., a chequing account) and tends to not have a high level of deposits. However, within a few years that student may embark on a professional career, start a family, and/or purchase a house, and thus require several financial services and become a very profitable bank customer. Generally speaking, a firm would like to keep its consistent big spenders and lose the erratic small spenders. But all too often a firm also has two other groups they must consider: erratic big spenders and consistent small spenders. So, in some situations in which consistent cash flow is a concern, it may be helpful to a firm to have a portfolio of customers that includes steady customers, even if they have a history of being less profitable. Some service providers have actually been quite successful in targeting customers who were previously considered to be unworthy of another firm's marketing efforts.[29] For example, brokerage firms such as The Cash Store provide small short-term loans for clients, many of whom may not qualify for financing through a more traditional lending institution. Firms, therefore, need to be cautious in blindly applying customer value calculations without thinking carefully about the implications.

RELATIONSHIP DEVELOPMENT STRATEGIES

To this point in the chapter, we have focused on the rationale for relationship marketing and the benefits (to both firms and customers) of the development of strong exchange relationships. In this section we examine factors that influence the development of strong customer relationships, including the customer's overall evaluation of a firm's offering, bonds created with customers by the firm, and barriers that the customer faces in leaving a relationship. These factors, illustrated in Figure 7.6, provide the rationale for specific strategies that firms use to keep their current customers.

FIGURE 7.6

Relationship Development Model

Source: Adapted from D. D. Gremler and S. W. Brown, "Service Loyalty: Antecedents, Components, and Outcomes," in *1998 AMA Winter Educators' Conference: Marketing Theory and Applications,* Vol. 9, D. Grewal and C. Pechmann, eds. (Chicago: American Marketing Association,) pp. 165–166.

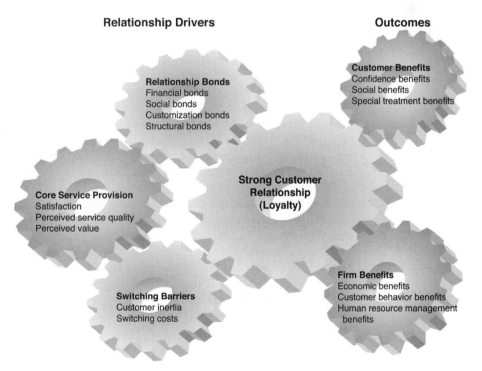

Core Service Provision

Retention strategies will have little long-term success unless the firm has a solid base of customer satisfaction on which to build. The firm does not necessarily have to be the very best among its competitors. It must be competitive, however, and frequently better than that. All the retention strategies that we describe in this section are built on the assumption of competitive quality and value being offered. Clearly, a firm needs to begin the relationship development process by providing good core service that, at minimum, meets customer expectations; it does no good to design relationship strategies for inferior services.

Switching Barriers

When considering a switch in service providers, a customer may face a number of barriers that make it difficult to leave one service provider and begin a relationship with another. Literature suggests that switching barriers influence consumers' decisions to exit from relationships with firms and, therefore, help to facilitate customer retention.[30] This might be called the "negative reinforcement" model.

Customer Inertia

One reason that customers commit to developing relationships with firms is that a certain amount of effort may be required to change firms. Sometimes consumers simplistically state that "it's just not worth it" to switch providers. Inertia may even explain why some dissatisfied customers stay with a provider. In discussing why people remain in relationships (in general) that they no longer find satisfying, scholars suggest that people may stay because breaking the relationship would require them to restructure their life—to develop new habits of living, to refashion old friendships, and to find new ones.[31] In other words, people do not like to change their behaviour.

Switching Costs

In many instances, customers develop loyalty to an organization in part because of costs involved in changing to and purchasing from a different firm. These costs, both real and perceived, monetary and nonmonetary, are termed *switching costs.* Switching costs include investments of time, money, or effort—such as setup costs, search costs, learning costs, and contractual costs—that make it challenging for the customer to move to another provider.[32] To illustrate, a patient may incur *setup costs* such as paying for a complete physical when changing doctors or for new X-rays when switching dentists. Because services often have characteristics that make them difficult to evaluate—including intangibility, nonstandardization, and inseparability of production and consumption as well as high experience and credence qualities—high *search costs* may be required to obtain suitable information about alternative services. *Learning costs* are those costs associated with learning the idiosyncrasies of how to use a product or service; in many situations, a customer who wishes to switch firms may need to accumulate new user skills or customer know-how. *Contractual costs* arise when the customer is required to pay a penalty to switch providers (e.g., prepayment charges for customer-initiated switching of mortgage companies or mobile telephone services), making it financially difficult, if not impossible, for the customer to initiate an early termination of the relationship.

In order to retain customers, some firms even increase switching costs. Therefore, to attract new customers, a service provider should consider implementing strategies designed to *lower* the switching costs of customers not currently using the provider.

FIGURE 7.7

What if banks really listened to their customers?

Source: © Graham Harrop

For example, providers might complete the customer's required paperwork themselves.

Banks, for example, might offer both automatic deposits and automatic payments. IBM, which provides banking services to large Canadian firms, learned that account opening is both intensive and repetitive. They are now actively trying to help banks simplify the process. This will make it easier for people to switch to IBM's customers. (Figure 7.7 provides a humorous look at what might happen if banks really listened to their customers.)

Relationship Bonds

Relationship bonds attempt to give customers reasons to *want to be loyal*—as opposed to feeling they *might as well* or *have to be loyal*.[33] We call this the positive reinforcement model of customer retention.

Recall that Provider Gap 1—Not Knowing What Customers Expect—is magnified when service providers focus on generating transactions and acquiring new customers instead of fostering relationships with existing customers. Hence, assuming a company has a clearly defined position in the market and has chosen its customer segments carefully, that company can use different relationship strategies to reduce Gap 1. As is depicted in Figure 7.8, these relationship strategies can be grouped into four categories according to the type of relationship bonds the company is pursuing—financial bonds, social bonds, customization bonds, and structural bonds.

Level 1—Financial Bonds

Financial bonds, the first and weakest level of relationship bond, provide some type of economic incentive for a customer to continue a relationship with a company, such as the guarantee of stable prices or discounts or reward miles associated with frequent

FIGURE 7.8

Levels of
Relationship
Strategies

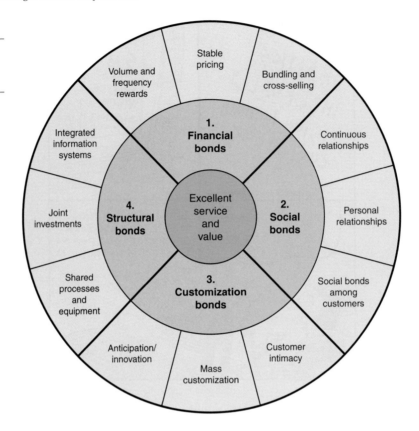

shopper or loyalty cards. They are the weakest level because they are easily imitated by competitors.[34]

Level 2—Social Bonds

Social bonds, the level-two strategies, provide additional attraction for customers. Retention marketers enhance relationships previously based on financial bonds with social and interpersonal relationships. Many service providers use strategies to create social bonds with clients. Lawyers, teachers, and hairdressers, when referring to their clients by name and who bring personal details into conversations, are using these level-two strategies.

Sometimes relationships are formed with the organization because of the social bonds that develop *among customers* rather than between customers and the provider of the service. Such bonds are often formed in health clubs, country clubs, educational settings, and other service environments where customers interact with each other. Over time the social relationships they have with other customers are important factors that keep them from switching to another organization. One company that has built a significant strategy around customer-to-customer bonds is Harley Davidson, with its local Harley Owners Groups, or HOGs. HOGs are involved in local rallies, tours, and parties as well as in national HOG events organized by the company. Through the HOGs, Harley customers come to know each other and develop a sense of community around their common interest—motorcycle riding—as illustrated in Figure 7.9.

Social bonds alone may not tie the customer permanently to the firm, but they are much more difficult for competitors to imitate than price incentives. In the absence of

FIGURE 7.9

Harley Davidson riders develop customer-to-customer bonds through Harley Owners Group (HOG) activities.

Source: EyeWire Collection/ Getty Images.

strong reasons to shift to another provider, interpersonal bonds can encourage customers to stay in a relationship.[35] In combination with financial incentives, social bonding strategies may be very effective.

Level 3—Customization Bonds

Customization bonds, or level-three strategies, may have commonalities with level-one and level-two strategies, but they are stronger still. These types of relationships are often established by companies that have intimate knowledge of customers and personalized services to meet their needs. Even large companies with many clients can develop one-to-one relationships with sophisticated technology solutions as indicated in our Global Feature.

Level 4—Structural Bonds

Structural bonds are the strongest, because they are the most difficult to imitate. This type of bond is often realized in business-to-business relationships where companies become structurally tied to each other (frequently with technology) but also exhibit customization, social, and financial bonds. Structural bonds are created by providing services to the client that are frequently designed right into the service delivery, and are characterized by some type of integration between the organizations.

An example of structural bonds can be seen in the long competitive battle between UPS and Federal Express (now known as FedEx).[36] In the mid-1990s, both firms attempted to tie their clients closer to them by providing them with free computers—Federal Express's PowerShips and UPS's MaxiShips—that stored addresses and shipping data, printed mailing labels, and helped track packages. By tying into one of the systems, a company saved time overall and could better track daily shipping records. As technology has continued to advance, the two companies have tied their customers to them through the Web and now through wireless technology, as shown in the UPS ad in Figure 7.10.

But there is also a potential downside to this arrangement from the customer's perspective. Customers may fear that tying themselves too closely to one provider may not allow them to take advantage of potential price savings from other providers in the future.

FIGURE 7.10

UPS uses technology
to build ties to
customers.

Source: Courtesy of UPS;
Photo by William Howard ©
The Martin Agency.

RELATIONSHIP CHALLENGES

Given the many benefits of long-term customer relationships, it would seem that a company would not want to refuse or terminate a relationship with any customer. Yet situations arise in which either the firm, the customer, or both want to end (or have to end) their relationship. The final section of this chapter discusses situations in which the firm might actually consider ending the relationship and how that might occur. In the next chapter we discuss situations in which the customer decides to terminate the relationship and switch providers.

The Customer Is *Not* Always Right

The assumption that all customers are good customers is very compatible with the belief that "The customer is always right," an almost sacrosanct tenet of business. However, the preceding section on profitability tiers reminded us that *not* all customers are good customers. To close Gap 1, it is as important to know what unprofitable customers want and expect as it is to know what profitable customers want and expect. If these expectations can't be met profitably—and the reason is not simply that the firm lacks the will to raise the level of its game—the firm must find ways to reallocate its scarce resources.

Why are many customers unprofitable? Some of the time, in our opinion, it is because the firm hasn't given these customers sufficient reason to be loyal. The service simply isn't good enough. But sometimes the reasons lie elsewhere. It may be, for

Global Feature

Developing Loyal Customers at Boots The Chemists

Boots The Chemists is one of the best-known and trusted brands in the United Kingdom and is the United Kingdom's leading health and beauty retailer. The company was founded in 1887, spanning three centuries of successful operations. Currently offering its products through 1,400 retail stores in the United Kingdom, numerous satellite stores within other retail outlets in the United States, Europe, Asia, and New Zealand, and an online store at www.boots.com, the company is deservedly called the "Chemist to the Nation." On its website, the Boots Company states that it intends to become the global leader in well-being products and services and is expanding globally through Boots Retail International.

A foundation for Boots's success in recent years is its increased focus on the customer and a desire to develop customer loyalty through a number of retention and relationship strategies. At the heart of the company's loyalty strategy is its Advantage Card, started in 1997. The Advantage Card is right now the world's largest smart card loyalty scheme, with close to 14 million members. Over 50 percent of Boots's current sales are now linked to the card. The card offers a number of benefits to customers and has helped the company increase sales, but more than that, it has been the foundation for building greater loyalty among Boots's best customers.

Using the card for purchases, Boots's customers receive 4 points for every pound spent. These points can be redeemed for selected products, aimed to treat customers to something special rather than simply to offer discounts off purchases. In fact the card is *not* about discounts; rather, it is about treating oneself. Customers can use their points to treat themselves to a simple lunch or to a full day of pampering at a spa. From a financial perspective, the company has seen increasing average transaction values among higher-spending customers. Boots managers say that they have increased loyalty and spending from people who were already good and profitable customers—a clear win for the company.

A number of initiatives are tied to the Advantage Card, taking it beyond a pure points reward program from the customer's perspective. For example, Boots now mails a first-class health and beauty magazine to the top spending 3 million Advantage Card holders. The magazine is Britain's biggest health and beauty magazine; it is not viewed as a "Boots" magazine but rather as a health and beauty magazine sent by Boots. Cardholders also have access to additional benefits and discounts using interactive kiosks in over 380 stores. The card can be used for purchases at the online store through the www.boots.com site that was launched jointly with Granada Media in 2001. Many products are offered on the site that are not available in Boots stores. In addition, the site provides access to an online magazine, answers to questions, a chat room, and other features and services. A credit card version of the Advantage Card was launched in 2001. And Boots joined with the Department of Health to enable Advantage Card holders to register with the National Health Service Organ Donor program and to carry an Advantage Card featuring the program's logo.

continued

Source: Newscast.

Global Feature

Developing Loyal Customers at Boots The Chemists—continued

From the company's perspective as well, the card is much more than a reward program. Data generated through the card is used to understand customers and to anticipate and identify individual needs in health and beauty care products. In fact, the goals with the Advantage Card program back in 1997 were to gain customer insight; build a database that would allow the company to tailor offerings to individual customers' needs; develop incremental sales by building customer loyalty; and use the customer knowledge to develop and introduce new products and services. A great deal of planning and testing went into developing the program, and this planning paid off in customer loyalty. Buy-in from the company's 60,000 staff members also aided in the rapid success of the program. All associates were signed up as members six months before the launch of the card. After experiencing the benefits of the card firsthand, they became enthusiastic advocates, encouraging customers to sign up.

Through the program, Boots has learned that the more broadly customers buy, in more categories over time, the more they increase visits to Boots stores. The result has been customization of product and service offerings and more sales and greater loyalty from its best customers.

Sources: Frederick Newell, *Loyalty.com,* New York: McGraw-Hill, 2000, Chapter 24, pp. 239–45; www.boots-plc.com, 2002; www.wellbeing.com, 2002.

example, that the customers simply represent the wrong segment, are unprofitable in the long run, or are too difficult to deal with.

The Wrong Segment

A company cannot target its services to all customers; some segments will be more appropriate than others. It would not be beneficial to either the company or the customer for a company to establish a relationship with a customer whose needs the company cannot meet. For example, a school offering only a lockstep, daytime MBA program in downtown Montreal would not encourage full-time working people to apply for its program, nor would a law firm based in Ottawa that specializes in government issues establish a relationship with individuals seeking advice on divorce. These examples seem obvious. Yet firms frequently do give in to the temptation to make a sale by agreeing to serve a customer who would be better served by someone else.

Similarly, it would not be wise to forge relationships simultaneously with incompatible market segments. In many service businesses (such as restaurants, hotels, tour package operators, entertainment, and education), customers experience the service together and can influence each other's perceptions about value received. Thus, to maximize service to core segments, an organization may choose to turn away marginally profitable segments that would be incompatible. For example, a conference hotel may find that mixing executives in town for a serious educational program with students in town for a regional track meet may not be wise. If the executive group is a key long-term customer, the hotel may choose to pass up the sports group in the interest of retaining the executives.

Not Profitable in the Long Term

In the absence of ethical or legal mandates, organizations will prefer *not* to have long-term relationships with unprofitable customers. Some segments of customers will not be profitable for the company even if their needs can be met by the services offered. Some examples of this situation are when there are not enough customers in the segment to make it profitable to develop a marketing approach, when the segment cannot afford to pay the cost of the service, or when the projected revenue flows from the segment would not cover the costs incurred to originate and maintain the business. For example, in the banking industry it has been estimated that 40 to 70 percent of customers served in a typical bank are not profitable in the sense that the costs of serving these customers exceed the revenues generated.[37]

At the individual customer level, it may not be profitable for a firm to engage in a relationship with a particular customer who has bad credit or who is a poor risk for some other reason. Retailers, banks, mortgage companies, and credit card companies routinely refuse to do business with individuals whose credit histories are unreliable. Although the short-term sale may be beneficial, the long-term risk of nonpayment makes the relationship unwise from the company's point of view. Similarly, some car rental companies check into the driving records of customers and reject bad-risk drivers.[38] This practice, while controversial, is logical from the car rental companies' point of view because they can cut back on insurance costs and accident claims (thus reducing rental costs for good drivers) by not doing business with accident-prone drivers.

Beyond the monetary costs associated with serving the wrong customers, there can be substantial time investments in some customers that, if actually computed, would make them unprofitable for the organization. Everyone has had the experience of waiting in a bank, a retail store, or even an education setting while a particularly demanding customer seems to use more than his share of the service provider's time. The dollar value of the time spent with a specific customer is typically not computed or calculated into the price of the service.

In a business-to-business relationship, the variability in time commitment to customers is even more apparent. Some customers may use considerable resources of the supplier organization through inordinate numbers of phone calls, excessive requests for information, and other time-consuming activities. In the legal profession, clients are billed for every hour of the firm's time that they use in this way because time is essentially the only resource the firm has. Yet in other service businesses, all clients essentially pay the same regardless of the time demands they place on the organization.

Difficult Customers

Managers have repeated the dictum "The customer is always right" so often that you would expect it to be accepted by every employee in every service organization. So why isn't it? Perhaps because it simply is not true. The customer is not always right. No matter how frequently it is said, repeating that mantra does not make it become reality, and service employees know it.

In many situations, firms have service encounters that fail because of *dysfunctional customers*. Dysfunctional customer behaviour refers to actions by customers who intentionally, or perhaps unintentionally, act in a manner that in some way disrupts otherwise functional service encounters.[39] Such customers have been described as "customers from hell," "problem customers," or "jay customers." One of us was awakened during a recent hotel stay at 4 a.m. by drunk customers who were arguing with each other in a room above; management eventually called the police and asked them to escort the customers off the property. An Enterprise Rent-A-Car customer demanded that she not be charged for any of the two weeks that she had a car because, near the end of the rental period, she found a small stain in the back seat.[40] These customers often have the objective of gaining faster, superior, or perhaps free service, but their behaviour is considered dysfunctional from the perspective of the service provider and perhaps fellow customers.

Dysfunctional customer behaviour can affect employees, other customers, and the organization. Research suggests that exposure to dysfunctional customer behaviour can have psychological, emotional, behavioural, and physical effects on employees.[41] For example, customer-contact employees who are exposed to rude, threatening, obstructive, aggressive, or disruptive behaviour by customers often have their mood or temper negatively affected as well as their motivation and morale. Such customers are difficult to work with and often create stress for employees. (See Figure 7.11 for one example.) Dysfunctional customers can also have an impact on other customers. Such behaviour can spoil the service experience for other customers, or become contagious, particularly if it includes vociferous or illegitimate complaining. Finally, dysfunctional customer behaviour can create both direct costs and indirect costs for the organization. Direct costs of such behaviour can include the expense of restoring damaged property, increased insurance premiums, property loss by theft, costs incurred in compensating customers affected by the dysfunctional behaviour of others, and the costs incurred through illegitimate claims by dysfunctional customers. Additionally, indirect costs might include increased workloads for staff required to deal with dysfunctional behaviour as well as increased costs for attracting and retaining appropriate personnel and, perhaps, for absenteeism payments.

Although often these difficult customers will be accommodated and employees can be trained to recognize and deal with them appropriately, at times the best choice may be to not maintain the relationship at all—especially at the business-to-business level, where long-term costs to the firm can be substantial. Take, for example, the view of some of Bay Street's major ad agencies. "Some ad agencies say some accounts are so difficult to work with that they simply cannot—or will not—service them."[42] Difficult clients paralyze an ad agency for a variety of reasons. Some ask that a particular ad campaign work for all their diverse constituencies at the same time, which in some cases may be next to impossible. Others require so much up-front work and ad testing

FIGURE 7.11

Some customers may be difficult, if not impossible, to serve.

Source: Masterfile.

before selecting an agency that the work is essentially done for free by those agencies not selected. Other clients are stingy, require dozens of storyboards before settling on a concept, or require a lot of direct, frequently disruptive, involvement in the production process. As a result, agencies have become more wary of chasing every client that comes along. "As in a marriage, all agencies and all clients don't work well together."[43]

Ending Business Relationships

Managers should not only know how to establish a relationship but also how to end one. A company may *not* want to continue in a relationship with every customer. However, gracefully exiting a relationship may not be easy. Customers may end up feeling disappointed, confused, or hurt if a firm attempts to terminate the relationship.

Relationship Endings

Relationships end in different ways—depending on the type of relationship in place.[44] In some situations, a relationship is established for a certain purpose and dissolves when it has served its purpose. For example, a house painting service may be engaged while painting the house exterior, but both parties understand that the end of the relationship is predetermined—the end occurs when the house has been painted. Sometimes a relationship has a natural ending. Piano lessons for children often cease as the child gets older and develops interests in other musical areas. Or an ending may occur because the customer is not fulfilling his or her obligations. For example, a bank may choose to end the relationship with a customer who regularly has insufficient funds in the chequing account. Whatever the reason for ending the relationship, firms should clearly communicate their reasons for wanting (or needing) to terminate it so that customers understand what is occurring and why.

Should Firms Fire Their Customers?

A logical conclusion to be drawn from the discussion of the challenges firms face in customer relationships is that perhaps firms should seek to get rid of those customers who are not right for the company. More and more companies are making these types of decisions in the belief that troublesome customers are usually less profitable and less loyal and that it may be counterproductive to attempt to retain their business.[45] Another reason for "firing" a customer is the negative effect that these customers can have on employee quality of life and morale.

One company came to this conclusion when a client, the CEO of an Internet startup company, paged one of its employees at her home on the West Coast at 4 a.m. and asked her to order a limousine for him in New York City.[46] This incident was enough to push the employee over the edge and cause her boss to agree that the company should fire this client. It did so by directly telling him that the relationship was not working out and to take his business elsewhere.

Although it may sound like a good idea, firing customers is not that simple and needs to be done in a way that avoids negative publicity or negative word of mouth. Sometimes raising prices or charging for services that previously had been given away for free can move unprofitable customers out of the company. Helping a client find a new supplier who can better meet its needs is another way to gracefully exit a nonproductive relationship. If the customer has become too demanding, the relationship may be salvaged by negotiating expectations or finding more efficient ways to serve the client. If not, both parties may find an agreeable way to end the relationship.

One of the key benefits to paying attention to Provider Gap 1 is that firms will develop a better appreciation for what their customers expect. When this is tied to recognition that not all customers are profitable, it is possible to assess what expectations *un*profitable customers have. If these expectations can't be met without excessive cost, firms must transition their business to a greater focus on those customers whose expectations they *can* satisfy. Going forward, firms must also attempt to identify what aspects of their strategy may have inadvertently attracted the wrong segments.

SUMMARY

In this chapter we focused on the rationale for, benefits of, and strategies for developing long-term relationships with customers. It should be obvious by now that organizations that focus only on acquiring new customers may well fail to understand their current customers; thus, while a company may be bringing customers in through the front door, equal or greater numbers may be exiting. Estimates of lifetime relationship value accentuate the importance of retaining current customers.

The particular strategy that an organization uses to retain its current customers can and should be customized to fit the industry, the culture, and the customer needs of the organization. However, in general, customer relationships are driven by a variety of factors that influence the development of strong customer relationships, including (1) the customer's overall evaluation of the quality of a firm's core service offering, (2) the switching barriers that the customer faces in leaving a relationship, and (3) the relationship bonds developed with that customer by the firm. By developing strong relationships with customers and by focusing on factors that influence customer relationships, the organization will accurately understand customer expectations over time and consequently will narrow Provider Gap1.

The chapter concluded with a discussion of the challenges that firms face in developing relationships with customers. Although long-term customer relationships are critical and can be very profitable, firms should not attempt to build relationships with just any customer. In other words, the customer is *not* always right. Indeed, in some situations it may be best for firms to discontinue relationships with some customers—for the sake of the customer, the firm, or both.

⟼ Discussion Questions

1. Discuss how relationship marketing or retention marketing is different from the traditional emphasis in marketing.
2. Describe how a firm's relationships with customers may evolve over time. For each level of relationship discussed in the chapter, identify a firm with which you have that level of relationship and discuss how its marketing efforts differ from other firms.
3. Think about a service organization that retains you as a loyal customer. Why are you loyal to this provider? What are the benefits to you of staying loyal and not switching to another provider? What would it take for you to switch?
4. With regard to the same service organization, what are the benefits to the organization of keeping you as a customer? Calculate your "lifetime value" to the organization.

5. Describe the logic behind "customer profitability segmentation" from the company's point of view. Also discuss what customers may think of the practice.

6. Describe the various switching barriers discussed in the text. What switching barriers might you face in switching banks? Mobile telephone service providers? Universities?

7. Describe the four levels of retention strategies, and give examples of each type. Again, think of a service organization to which you are loyal. Can you describe the reason(s) you are loyal in terms of the different levels? In other words, what ties you to the organization?

8. Have you ever worked as a front-line service employee? Can you remember having to deal with difficult or "problem" customers? Discuss how you handled such situations. As a manager of front-line employees, how would you help your employees deal with difficult customers?

Exercises

1. Interview the manager of a local service organization. Discuss with the manager the target market(s) for the service. Estimate the lifetime value of a customer in one or more of the target segments. To do this estimate, you will need to get as much information from the manager as you can. If the manager cannot answer your questions, make some assumptions.

2. In small groups in class, debate the question "Is the customer always right?" In other words, are there times when the customer may be the wrong customer for the organization?

3. Design a customer appreciation program for the organization with whom you currently work. Why would you have such a program, and to whom would it be directed toward?

4. Choose a specific company context (your class project company, the company you work for, or a company in an industry you are familiar with). Calculate the lifetime value of a customer for this company. You will need to make assumptions to do this calculation, so make your assumptions clear. Using ideas and concepts from this chapter, describe a relationship marketing strategy to increase the number of lifetime customers for this firm.

Notes

1. F. E. Webster Jr., "The Changing Role of Marketing in the Corporation," *Journal of Marketing,* October 1992, pp. 1–17.

2. For discussions of relationship marketing and its influence on the marketing of services, consumer goods, strategic alliances, distribution channels, and buyer–seller interactions, see *Journal of the Academy of Marketing Science* 23, Special Issue on Relationship Marketing (Fall 1995). Some of the early roots of this paradigm shift can be found in C. Gronroos, *Service Management and Marketing* (New York: Lexington Books, 1990) and E. Gummesson, "The New Marketing—Developing Long-Term Interactive Relationships," *Long Range Planning* 20 (1987), pp. 10–20. For current thinking and excellent reviews of relationship

marketing across a spectrum of topics, see J. N. Sheth, *Handbook of Relationship Marketing* (Thousand Oaks, CA: Sage Publications, 2000).

3. L. L. Berry and A. Parasuraman, *Marketing Services* (New York: Free Press, 1991), chap. 8.

4. G. Knisely, "Comparing Marketing Management in Package Goods and Service Organizations," a series of interviews appearing in *Advertising Age,* January 15, February 19, March 19, and May 14, 1979.

5. This discussion is based on M. D. Johnson and F. Selnes, "Customer Portfolio Management: Toward a Dynamic Theory of Exchange Relationships," *Journal of Marketing* 68 (April 2004), pp. 1–17.

6. R. M. Morgan and S. D. Hunt, "The Commitment-Trust Theory of Relationship Marketing," *Journal of Marketing* 58 (July 1994), pp. 20–38; N. Bendapudi and L. L. Berry, "Customers' Motivations for Maintaining Relationships with Service Providers," *Journal of Retailing* 73 (Spring 1997), pp. 15–37.

7. Johnson and Selnes, "Customer Portfolio Management."

8. Ibid.

9. See also D. Siredeshmukh, J. Singh, and B. Sabol, "Customer Trust, Value, and Loyalty in Relational Exchanges," *Journal of Marketing* 66 (January 2002), pp. 15–37.

10. The three types of relational benefits discussed in this section are drawn from K. P. Gwinner, D. D. Gremler, and M. J. Bitner, "Relational Benefits in Service Industries: The Customer's Perspective," *Journal of the Academy of Marketing Science* 26 (Spring 1998), pp. 101–14.

11. See M. B. Adelman, A. Ahuvia, and C. Goodwin, "Beyond Smiling: Social Support and Service Quality," in *Service Quality: New Directions in Theory and Practice,* ed. R. T. Rust and R. L. Oliver (Thousand Oaks, CA: Sage Publications, 1994), pp. 139–72; and C. Goodwin, "Private Roles in Public Encounters: Communal Relationships in Service Exchanges," unpublished manuscript, University of Manitoba, 1993.

12. N. Bendapudi and R. P. Leone, "How to Lose Your Star Performer Without Losing Customers, Too," *Harvard Business Review,* November 2001, pp. 104–15.

13. P. Kumar, "The Impact of Long-Term Client Relationships on the Performance of Business Service Firms," *Journal of Service Research* 2 (August 1999), pp. 4–18.

14. F. F. Reichheld and W. E. Sasser Jr., "Zero Defections: Quality Comes to Services," *Harvard Business Review,* September/October 1990, pp. 105–11; and F. F. Reichheld, *The Loyalty Effect* (Boston: Harvard Business School Press, 1996).

15. R. Dhar and R. Glazer, "Hedging Customers," *Harvard Business Review* 81 (May 2003), pp. 86–92.

16. D. D. Gremler and S. W. Brown, "The Loyalty Ripple Effect: Appreciating the Full Value of Customers," *International Journal of Service Industry Management* 10, no. 3 (1999), pp. 271–91.

17. L. A. Bettencourt, "Customer Voluntary Performance: Customers as Partners in Service Delivery," *Journal of Retailing* 73 (Fall 1997), pp. 383–406.

18. S. J. Grove and R. P. Fisk, "The Impact of Other Customers on Service Experiences: A Critical Incident Examination of 'Getting Along,'" *Journal of Retailing* 73 (Spring 1997), pp. 63–85.

19. L. L. Price, E. J. Arnould, and A. Hausman, "Commercial Friendships: Service Provider–Client Relationship Dynamics," in *Frontiers in Services,* ed. R. T. Rust and R. L. Oliver (Nashville: Vanderbilt University, 1996).

20. Reichheld and Sasser, "Zero Defections."

21. Additional frameworks for calculating lifetime customer value that include a variety of other variables can be found in W. J. Reinartz and V. Kumar, "The Impact of Customer Relationship Characteristics on Profitable Lifetime Duration," *Journal of Marketing* 67 (January 2003), pp. 77–99; Dhar and Glazer, "Hedging Customers"; H. K. Stahl, K. Matzler, and H. H. Hinterhuber, "Linking Customer Lifetime Value with Shareholder Value," *Industrial Marketing Management* 32, no. 4 (2003), pp. 267–79.

22. S. Gupta, D. R. Helmann, and J. A. Stuart, "Valuing Customers," *Journal of Marketing Research* 41 (February 2004), pp. 7–18.

23. For more on customer profitability segments and related strategies, see V. A. Zeithaml, R. T. Rust, and K. N. Lemon, "The Customer Pyramid: Creating and Serving Profitable Customers," *California Management Review* 43 (Summer 2001), pp. 118–42.

24. R. Brooks, "Alienating Customers Isn't Always a Bad Idea, Many Firms Discover," *The Wall Street Journal*, January 7, 1999, p. A1.

25. F. Reichheld, "Loyalty-Based Management," *Harvard Business Review,* March/April 1993, pp. 64–74.

26. L. Young, "Cutting Through All the Hype About CRM: A Handful of Pioneers Such as the Bank of Montreal Are Turning CRM into More Than Just a Buzzword," *Marketing Magazine*, February 12, 2001, p. 15.

27. D. Brady, "Why Service Stinks," *BusinessWeek,* October 23, 2000, pp. 118–28.

28. Dhar and Glazer, "Hedging Customers."

29. D. Rosenblum, D. Tomlinson, and L. Scott, "Bottom-Feeding for Blockbuster Businesses," *Harvard Business Review* 81 (March 2003), pp. 52–59.

30. See T. A. Burnham, J. K. Frels, and V. Mahajan, "Consumer Switching Costs: A Typology, Antecedents, and Consequences," *Journal of the Academy of Marketing Science* 32 (Spring 2003), pp. 109–26; F. Selnes, "An Examination of the Effect of Product Performance on Brand Reputation, Satisfaction, and Loyalty," *European Journal of Marketing* 27, no. 9 (2003), 19–35; P. Klemperer, "The Competitiveness of Markets with Switching Costs," *Rand Journal of Economics* 18 (Spring 1987), pp. 138–50.

31. T. L. Huston and R. L. Burgess, "Social Exchange in Developing Relationships: An Overview," in *Social Exchange in Developing Relationships*, ed. R. L. Burgess and T. L. Huston (New York: Academic Press, 1979), pp. 3–28; L. White and V. Yanamandram, "Why Customers Stay: Reasons and Consequences of Inertia in Financial Services," *Managing Service Quality* 14, nos. 2/3 (2004), pp. 183–94.

32. See J. P. Guiltinan, "A Classification of Switching Costs with Implications for Relationship Marketing," in *Marketing Theory and Practice*, ed. Terry L. Childers et al. (Chicago: American Marketing Association, 1989), pp. 216–20; Klemperer, "The Competitiveness of Markets with Switching Costs"; C. Fornell, "A National Customer Satisfaction Barometer: The Swedish Experience," *Journal of Marketing* 56 (January 1992), pp. 6–21; P. G. Patterson and T. Smith, "A

Cross-Cultural Study of Switching Barriers and Propensity to Stay with Service Providers," *Journal of Retailing* 79 (Summer 2003), pp. 107–20.

33. See Bendapudi and Berry, "Customers' Motivations for Maintaining Relationships with Service Providers"; H. S. Bansal, P. G. Irving, and S. F. Taylor, "A Three-Component Model of Customer Commitment to Service Providers," *Journal of the Academy of Marketing Science* 32 (Summer 2004), pp. 234–50.

34. For more information on cautions to be considered in implementing rewards strategies, see L. O'Brien and C. Jones, "Do Rewards Really Create Loyalty?" *Harvard Business Review,* May/June 1995, pp. 75–82; and G. R. Dowling and M. Uncles, "Do Customer Loyalty Programs Really Work?" *Sloan Management Review,* Summer 1997, pp. 71–82.

35. D. D. Gremler and S. W. Brown, "Service Loyalty: Its Nature, Importance, and Implications," in *Advancing Service Quality: A Global Perspective*, ed. Bo Edvardsson et al. (Jamaica, NY: International Service Quality Association, 1996), pp. 171–80; H. Hansen, K. Sandvik, and F. Selnes, "Direct and Indirect Effects of Commitment to a Service Employee on the Intention to Stay," *Journal of Service Research* 5 (May 2003), pp. 356–68.

36. L. M. Grossman, "Federal Express, UPS Face Off on Computers," *The Wall Street Journal,* September 17, 1993, p. B1.

37. R. Brooks, "Alienating Customers Isn't Always a Bad Idea." P. Carroll and S. Rose, "Revisiting Customer Retention," *Journal of Retail Banking* 15, no. 1 (1993), pp. 5–13.

38. J. Dahl, "Rental Counters Reject Drivers Without Good Records," *The Wall Street Journal,* October 23, 1992, p. B1.

39. See L. C. Harris and K. L. Reynolds, "The Consequences of Dysfunctional Customer Behavior," *Journal of Service Research* 6 (November 2003), p. 145 for cites; also, see A. A. Grandey, D. N. Dickter, and H. P. Sin, "The Customer Is *Not* Always Right: Customer Aggression and Emotion Regulation of Service Employees," *Journal of Organizational Behavior* 25 (2004), pp. 397–418.

40. K. Ohnezeit, recruiting supervisor for Enterprise Rent-A-Car, personal communication, February 12, 2004.

41. See Harris and Reynolds, "The Consequences of Dysfunctional Customer Behavior."

42. L. Bird, "The Clients That Exasperate Madison Avenue," *The Wall Street Journal,* November 2, 1993, p. B1.

43. Ibid.

44. For a detailed discussion on relationship ending, see A. Halinen and J. Tähtinen, "A Process Theory of Relationship Ending," *International Journal of Service Industry Management* 13, no. 2 (2002), 163–80.

45. M. Schrage, "Fire Your Customers," *The Wall Street Journal,* March 16, 1992, p. A8.

46. S. Shellenbarger, "More Firms, Siding with Employees, Bid Bad Clients Farewell," *The Wall Street Journal,* February 16, 2000, p. B1.

Chapter

8

Service Recovery

Provider Gap 1

1. Illustrate the importance of recovering from service failures.

2. Discuss consumer complaints and why people do and do not complain.

3. Discuss what customers expect and the kind of responses they want when they do complain.

4. Present strategies for effective service recovery, together with examples of what does and does not work.

5. Discuss service guarantees—what they are, the benefits of guarantees, and when to use them—as a particular type of service recovery strategy.

TORONTO MAPLE LEAFS SPORTS AND ENTERTAINMENT—EMPLOYEE EMPOWERMENT PREVENTS OUTRAGED FANS

Toronto Maple Leafs Sports and Entertainment manage the fan experience at the Air Canada Centre (www.theaircanadacentre.com) for Leafs hockey games, Raptors basketball games, and also any of the many concerts that take place in the venue. And, with Toronto Maple Leafs ticket holders being 97 percent season-pass customers, retaining the loyalty of such valued patrons requires not only being able to meet clients' basic expectations for clean facilities and friendly service, but also being able to prevent fan outrage by quickly recovering when service does falter. Director of Client Services

Chris Gibbs therefore instils in his employees the importance of three rules for service recovery: "Recover quickly, recover effectively, and improve the situation."

In order to quickly and effectively recover and improve a poor situation at the Air Canada Centre, employees must be empowered to act. Ushers are therefore responsible for their own areas. When a fan spills a drink, for instance, the usher quickly replaces the item and has the area cleaned. For larger concerns, like a patron requiring relocation, the customer service department may need to be contacted to find an available location. Finally, senior staff sometimes need to take action to remedy larger situations, as was the case at a Julio Iglesias concert. When many attendees experienced poor sound quality and complained, the entire section was given complimentary tickets to the next Julio concert.

Gibbs has also managed to defuse other potentially damaging situations by using a problem to create an opportunity to delight the customer and build goodwill. Consider, for example, the situation when three visiting Israeli patrons missed a Raptors game due to miscalculating the time change from their home. It would have been easy to politely explain to these fans that there was nothing that could (or would) be done because the Centre was not at fault. Instead, Gibbs and his employees functioned as travel agents for the group, rescheduling their flights, finding a cheap hotel, and providing complimentary tickets to the next home game.

By first taking care to meet customers' basic expectations, empowering employees to act quickly and responsibly to diffuse negative experiences, and leading by example in service recovery efforts, Toronto Maple Leafs Sports and Entertainment are well positioned to build and maintain stronger relationships with their clientele.[1]

Source: www.theaircanadacentre.com.

The preceding two chapters have given you grounding in understanding customers through research as well as through knowing them as individuals and developing strong relationships with them. These strategies are designed to help minimize Provider Gap 1—Not Knowing What Customers Expect. But, in all service contexts—whether customer service, consumer services, or business-to-business services—service failure is inevitable. This is true even for the best of firms with the best of intentions, even for those with world-class service systems. To continue closing Provider Gap 1, firms must also know what their customers expect when service failures occur, and must implement effective strategies for service recovery.

THE IMPACT OF SERVICE FAILURE AND RECOVERY

Service recovery refers to the actions taken by an organization in response to a service failure. Failures occur for all kinds of reasons—the service may be unavailable when promised, it may be delivered late or too slowly, the outcome may be incorrect or poorly executed, or employees may be rude or uncaring.[2] All these types of failures bring about negative feelings and responses from customers. Left unfixed, they can result in customers leaving, telling other customers about their negative experiences, and even challenging the organization through consumer rights organizations or legal channels.

Service Recovery Effects

Research has shown that resolving customer problems effectively has a strong impact on customer satisfaction, loyalty, word of mouth communication, and bottom-line performance.[3] That is, customers who experience service failures but who are ultimately satisfied based on recovery efforts by the firm, will be more loyal than those whose problems are not resolved. That loyalty translates into profitability, as you learned in Chapter 7. Data from the Technical Assistance Research Program (TARP) verifies this relationship, as shown in Figure 8.1.[4] Customers who complain and have their problems resolved quickly are much more likely to repurchase than those whose complaints are not resolved. Those who never complain are *least* likely to repurchase.

Hampton Inn Hotels directly realized the benefits of effective service recovery through their service guarantee. They achieved $11 million in additional annual revenue and the highest customer retention rate in their industry after implementing the 100 percent customer satisfaction guarantee shown in Figure 8.2.[5] The guarantee reimburses customers who experience service failures in their hotels—and is part of an overall service recovery and customer retention strategy.

An effective service recovery strategy has multiple potential impacts. It can increase customer satisfaction and loyalty and generate positive word of mouth communication. A well-designed, well-documented service recovery strategy also provides information that can be used to improve service as part of a continuous improvement effort. By making adjustments to service processes, systems, and

FIGURE 8.1

Unhappy Customers'
Repurchase
Intentions

Source: Adapted from data reported by the Technical Assistance Research Program.

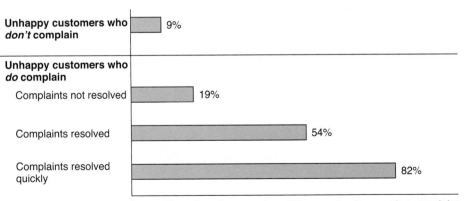

Percentage of customers who will buy again after a major complaint (over $100 losses)

FIGURE 8.2

The 100 Percent
Hampton Inn Hotels
Guarantee

Source: Courtesy of Hampton
Inn® Hotels.

outcomes based on previous service recovery experiences, companies increase the likelihood of "doing it right the first time." In turn, this reduces costs of failures and increases initial customer satisfaction.

An interesting example of a very visible service recovery is provided by Canadian Imperial Bank of Commerce (CIBC). See Figure 8.3. The bank went to a lot of trouble to recover from a service failure that might have gone completely unnoticed. The cost of producing, mailing, and processing the cheques was certainly much more than would have been incurred had they simply credited the affected accounts. But it communicated that the CIBC took the error seriously and could be trusted to do the right thing.

Unfortunately, many firms do not employ effective recovery strategies. A recent study suggests that 50 percent of customers who experienced a serious problem received no response from the firm.[6] There are tremendous downsides to having weak service recovery strategies. Poor recovery following a bad service experience can lead to customers who are so dissatisfied that they become "terrorists," actively pursuing

FIGURE 8.3

CIBC's High-Profile
Service Recovery

Source: Reprinted by
permission of CIBC.

Re: Personal overdraft protection service reimbursement

We recently discovered an error in the amount we charged to some customers on their overdraft protection service. The amounts involved are quite small: we estimate the average amount per account to be $3.46. We have corrected this error and are working diligently to reimburse customers as promptly as possible.

Our records indicate that your account was not affected by this error in the period after May 1998. However, as an expression of good faith, we are also reimbursing you a proportional share of the total estimated amount our customers were overcharged for the pre-1998 period. We are doing this as part of our effort to make things right and to ensure that CIBC does not retain any of the money it received in error.

Accordingly, please find enclosed a cheque payable to you in the amount of $3.46. This amount includes interest calculated at the rate of 10% per year.

Please accept my apologies for this error. Should you have any questions, you can call us at 1-877-757-1535.

We appreciate your business and look forward to serving you in the future.

Yours truly

Robert Cummings
Senior Vice President
CIBC Mortgages & Lending

CIBC

Canadian Imperial Bank of Commerce
Main Branch-Commerce Court
Toronto ON M5L 1G9

Date JUNE 10, 2004

Cheque Number

Account Number

PAY THE SUM OF   THREE 46/100**********************

Amount $3.46

To

Cdn. Dollars $

Payable through Canadian Imperial Bank of Commerce.

Authorized Signature

VOID

Complainers Spread the Word

Doubletree Inns

When Web consultants Tom F. and Shane A. experienced poor service at a Doubletree Inn while on a business trip (not at one of the Canadian locations), they decided to create a PowerPoint presentation to vent their frustrations and chronicle their "shabby treatment." The men sent the presentation, not only to two managers at the hotel, but also to two clients and Shane's mother-in-law, encouraging these three latter people to "share it with a few of your friends." Within a month the presentation, titled "Yours is a Very Bad Hotel," had been circulated around the globe. As a result, the two men got more than 9,000 email messages from six continents, and there were stories about their experience in publications such as the *Wall Street Journal* and *Forbes*.

Just what had prompted the pair to react in this way? Well, upon arriving at their hotel with a confirmation and credit card guarantee for late arrival, they had discovered the hotel was overbooked and that their rooms had already been given away. Tom, a frequent business traveller and a Hilton Honors Gold VIP, understood the situation to be fairly common, but he and his companion did expect at least an apology and prompt resolution. Instead

---

Yours is a Very Bad Hotel

A graphic complaint prepared for:

J___ C___
General Manager

L___ R___
Front Desk Manager

DoubleTree Club Hotel
2828 Southwest Freeway

---

they received "insolence and insults," and were given two smoking rooms in a "dump" of a hotel several kilometres away and farther from the downtown area where they needed to be.

Finally, after all the publicity generated by the circulation of their presentation, Hilton offered a free two-night stay at any Hilton hotel and informed Tom and Shane of actions taken to improve employee training and overbooking policies. The men declined the free hotel and requested instead that a $1,000 charitable donation be made to a local organization.

Citizens Bank

Another example of a disgruntled customer generating quite a bit of media attention in Canada is Don Rogers. The retired Kingston-area gentleman, after discovering that his bank was outsourcing some of its credit card processing to the United States, decided to pay his $230 Visa bill in 985 instalments, sometimes only pennies at a time. Upset that U.S. authorities could technically access his personal information under the *Patriot Act*, Rogers asked Vancouver-based Citizens Bank to abandon the practice. His request being refused, Rogers thought it necessary to find a way to get the company's attention and perhaps eventually achieve the results he desired. To date, his "creative solution" has generated stories in the *Globe and Mail* and on *CTV News*, has garnered him a one-on-one conversation with the Citizens Bank CEO and privacy officer, has jammed the bank's system, has forced employees to process some payments manually, and has created a 35-page Visa statement—but the bank still has not changed its Visa processing company and there is no indication that they intend to do so.

Sources: L. Bly, "Online Complaint About Bad Hotel Service Scores Bull's-Eye," *USA Today*, January 4, 2002, p. D6; S. Stewart, "Irate Client Pays Visa Pennies," *Globe and Mail*, November 23, 2005, p. A11.

---

opportunities to openly criticize the company.[7] When customers experience a service failure, they talk about it to others no matter what the outcome. That recent study also found that customers who were satisfied with a firm's recovery efforts talked to an average of seven people, whereas those customers who were dissatisfied with the response talked to an average of 25 people.[8] With the ability to share such stories on the Internet, the potential reach of such dissatisfied customers is even greater. (See Exhibit 8.1 about the two dissatisfied Doubletree Inn customers.) Further, repeated service failures can aggravate employees. The costs in employee morale and even lost employees is an often overlooked cost of not having effective service recovery.

The Recovery Paradox

Some businesses have customers who are initially dissatisfied with a service and then experience excellent service recovery, seemingly leading them to be more satisfied after they experience a service failure than they otherwise would have been![9] To illustrate, consider a hotel customer who arrives to check in and finds that no room is available. In an effort to recover, the front desk person immediately upgrades this guest to a better room at the original price. The customer, thrilled with this compensation, reports that she is even more impressed with the hotel than before, and vows to be loyal into the future. Although such extreme instances are relatively rare, this idea—that an initially disappointed customer who has experienced good service recovery might be even more satisfied and loyal as a result—has been labelled the *recovery paradox.*

So, should a firm "screw up" so that it can "fix the problem" superbly? If doing so would actually lead to more satisfied customers, is this strategy worth pursuing? First, as we indicated earlier in this chapter, a vast majority of customers do not complain when they experience a problem. The possibility of a recovery exists only in situations in which the firm is aware of a problem and is able to recover well; if customers do not make the firm aware of the failure—and most do not—dissatisfaction is most likely to be the result. Second, it is expensive to fix mistakes; re-creating a service may be quite costly. Third, it is ludicrous to encourage service failures—after all, reliability ("doing it right the first time") is the most critical determinant of service quality. Finally, although the recovery paradox suggests that a customer *may* end up more satisfied after experiencing excellent recovery, there is certainly *no* guarantee that the customer actually *will* end up more satisfied. The recovery paradox is highly dependent on the context and situation; although one customer may find it easy to forgive a restaurant who provides him with a gift certificate for a later date for having lost his dinner reservation, another customer who had planned to propose marriage to his date over dinner may not be so happy with the same recovery scenario.

The intrigue stimulated by the recovery paradox has led to empirical research specifically on this issue. Although anecdotal evidence provides limited support for the recovery paradox, research seems to indicate that this phenomenon is not pervasive. In one study, researchers found that only the very highest levels of customers' service recovery ratings resulted in increased satisfaction and loyalty.[10] This research suggests that customers weigh their most recent experiences heavily in their determination of whether to buy again. If the most recent experience is negative, feelings about the company decrease and repurchase intentions diminish significantly. A second study found that overall satisfaction was consistently lower for those customers who experienced a service failure than for those who experienced no failure, no matter what the recovery effort.[11] An explanation for why no recovery paradox occurred is suggested by the magnitude of the service failure in this study—a three-hour airplane flight delay. Perhaps this type of failure may be too much to be overcome by any recovery effort. However, in this study, strong service recovery was able to mitigate, if not reverse, the effects of the failure by reducing overall dissatisfaction. Finally, a rather recent study suggests that the recovery paradox phenomenon *may* only exist after *one* service failure; however, if a customer experiences a *second* service failure, the likelihood of the customer's evaluation of the service being greater after the second failure is minimal.[12]

Given the mixed opinions on the extent to which the recovery paradox exists, "doing it right the first time" is still the best and safest strategy in the long run. However, when a failure does occur, every effort should be made to mitigate its negative effects. If the failure can be fully overcome, if the failure is less critical, or if the recovery effort is clearly superlative, it may be possible to observe the recovery paradox.

HOW CUSTOMERS RESPOND TO SERVICE FAILURES

Customers who experience service failures can respond in a variety of ways, as illustrated in Figure 8.4.[13] Research suggests that a variety of negative emotions follow service failure, including anger, discontent, disappointment, self-pity, and anxiety.[14] These initial negative responses affect how customers evaluate the service recovery and their ultimate decision to return or not.[15]

Many customers are passive about their dissatisfaction, simply saying or doing nothing. As we have pointed out, customers who do not complain are least likely to return. For companies, customer passivity in the face of dissatisfaction is a threat to future success. If dissatisfied customers don't complain, the company won't learn about their failure and will be less likely to correct it. For that reason, complaints have sometimes been referred to as "gifts." And although there are times when the firm receiving such a "gift" might prefer it otherwise (as in Exhibit 8.1), companies that are sincerely committed to meeting customer expectations are better off knowing what it is they are doing wrong and thus minimizing Gap 1.

Why People Do (and Do Not) Complain

Some customers are more likely to complain than others for a variety of reasons. These consumers believe that positive consequences may occur, that there are social benefits to complaining, and that their personal norms support complaining behaviour. They believe they should and will be provided compensation for the service failure. They also believe that in cases of service failure, someone should make good. In some

FIGURE 8.4 Customer Complaint Actions Following Service Failure

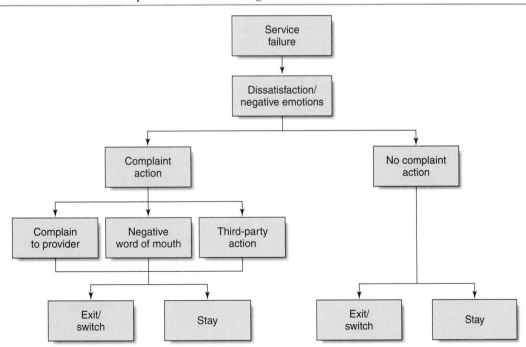

FIGURE 8.5

Sometimes customers don't complain because it doesn't seem "worth it."

Source: © Graham Harrop.

cases they feel a social obligation to complain—to help others avoid similar situations or to punish the service provider. A very small number of consumers even have "complaining personalities"—they just like to complain or cause trouble!

Consumers who are unlikely to take any action believe the opposite. They see complaining as a waste of time. (See Figure 8.5 for another angle on this!) Sometimes they do not know how to complain—they do not understand that avenues are open to them to voice their complaints. In some cases noncomplainers may engage in "emotion-focused coping" to deal with their negative experiences. This type of coping involves self-blame, denial, and possibly seeking social support.[16] They may feel that the failure was somehow their fault and that they do not deserve redress.

Personal relevance of the failure can also influence whether people complain.[17] The situation at Doubletree Inn, which is described in Exhibit 8.1, illustrates a failure that had been considered especially important to two customers. Consumers are also more likely to complain about services that are expensive, high-risk, and ego-involving (like vacation packages, airline travel, and medical services) than they are about less expensive, frequently purchased services (fast-food drive-through service, a cab ride, a call to a customer service help line). These latter services are simply not important enough to warrant the time to complain. Unfortunately, even though the experience may not be important to the consumer at the moment, a dissatisfying encounter can still drive him or her to a competitor next time the service is needed.

Types of Customer Complaint Actions

If customers initiate actions following service failure, the action can be of various types. A dissatisfied customer can choose to complain on the spot to the service provider, giving the company the opportunity to respond immediately. This reaction is often the best-case scenario for the company because it has a second chance right at that moment to satisfy the customer. Customers who do not complain immediately may choose to complain later to the provider by phone, in writing, or via the Internet. Again, the company has a chance to recover.

Some customers choose not to complain directly to the provider but rather spread negative word of mouth to friends and coworkers. This negative word of mouth can be extremely detrimental, because it can reinforce the customer's feelings of negativism and spread that negative impression to others as well. Further, the company has no chance to recover. In recent years, customers have taken to complaining via the Internet. A variety of websites[18] have been created to facilitate customer complaints and have provided customers with the possibility of spreading negative word-of-mouth

FIGURE 8.6

The Government of Canada has instituted a process for people to complain.

Source: Reproduced with the permission of the Minister of Public Works and Government Services, 2006.

communication to a much broader audience. Some customers become so dissatisfied with a product or service failure that they construct websites targeting the firm's current and prospective customers. On these sites,[19] angry customers convey their grievances against the firm in ways designed to convince other consumers of the firm's incompetence and evil.[20]

Finally, customers may choose to complain to third parties such as the Better Business Bureau, to consumer affairs arms of the government, to a licensing authority, to a professional association, or potentially to a private attorney. The Government of Canada has even instituted a process for people to complain (see Figure 8.6).

Types of Complainers

Research suggests that people can be grouped into categories according to how they respond to failures. Four categories of response types were identified in a study that focused on grocery stores, automotive repair services, medical care, and banking and financial services[21]: *passives, voicers, irates,* and *activists.*

Passives

This group of customers is least likely to take any action. They are unlikely to say anything to the provider, less likely than others to spread negative word of mouth, and unlikely to complain to a third party. They often doubt the effectiveness of complaining. Sometimes their personal values or norms argue against complaining. These customers tend to feel less alienated from the marketplace than irates and activists.

Voicers

These customers actively complain to the service provider, but they are less likely to spread negative word of mouth, to switch patronage, or to go to third parties with their complaints. *These customers should be viewed as the service provider's best friends!* They actively complain and thus give the company a second chance. As with the passives, these customers are less alienated from the marketplace than those in the next two groups. They tend to believe complaining has social benefits. They believe that the consequences of complaining can be very positive, and they believe less in other types of complaining such as spreading word of mouth or talking to third parties. Their personal norms are consistent with complaining. Don Rogers, the Kingston, Ontario man who wanted Citizens Bank to change its policies as described in Exhibit 8.1, is clearly a "voicer."

Irates

These consumers are more likely than others to engage in negative word-of-mouth communication and to switch providers. They are about average in their propensity to complain to the provider. They are unlikely to complain to third parties. They tend to feel somewhat alienated from the marketplace. As their label suggests, they are more angry with the provider, although they do believe that complaining to the provider can have social benefits. They are less likely to give the service provider a second chance and instead will switch to a competitor, spreading the word to friends and relatives along the way.

Activists

These consumers are most likely to complain: they will complain to the provider, they will tell others, and they are more likely to complain to third parties. Complaining fits with their personal norms. As with the irates, these consumers are more alienated from the marketplace than the other groups. They have a very optimistic sense of the potential positive consequences of all types of complaining. In extreme cases these consumers can become "terrorists," as in the Starbucks Coffee case described at the end of this text.

CUSTOMERS' RECOVERY EXPECTATIONS

When they take the time and effort to complain, customers generally have high expectations. Our "Story of a Service Hero," Exhibit 8.2, epitomizes this kind of service recovery.

Understanding and Accountability

In many service failure situations, customers are not looking for extreme actions from the firm; however, they want to understand what happened and for firms to be accountable.[22] One study identified the seven most common "remedies" that customers seek when they experience a serious problem[23]; three remedies were to have the service fixed, to be reimbursed all their money, or to be reimbursed part of their money. Interestingly, however, the other four remedies—including an apology, an explanation, assurance that the problem would not be repeated, and an opportunity for the customer to vent—cost the firm very little.

These four nonmonetary remedies consist primarily of providing employees the opportunity to communicate with customers. Customers expect an apology when things go wrong; they also want to know what the company is going to do to ensure that the problem does not recur.[24]

Demonstrating an understanding of customer concerns requires cultural sensitivity, too. One of us recently took two flights to Paris, the first with Air Canada and the second with Air France. Both airlines lost our luggage, but the respective recovery efforts were a bit different. Air Canada provided the usual toothpaste, comb, shaving gel, etc.; Air France provided all this plus one additional item—a condom.

Fair Treatment

Customers also want justice and fairness in handling their complaints. Service recovery experts Steve Brown and Steve Tax have documented three specific types of justice that customers are looking for following their complaints: *outcome fairness,*

Story of a Service Hero

A good recovery can turn angry, frustrated customers into loyal ones. It can, in fact, create more goodwill than if things had gone smoothly in the first place. Consider how Club Med–Cancun, part of the Paris-based Club Mediterranèe, recovered from a service nightmare and won the loyalty of one group of vacationers.

The vacationers had nothing but trouble getting from New York to their Mexican destination. The flight took off 6 hours late, made two unexpected stops, and circled 30 minutes before it could land. Because of all the delays and mishaps, the plane was en route for 10 hours more than planned and ran out of food and drinks. It finally arrived at two o'clock in the morning, with a landing so rough that oxygen masks and luggage dropped from overhead. By the time the plane pulled up to the gate, the soured passengers were faint with hunger and convinced that their vacation was ruined before it had even started. One lawyer on board was already collecting names and addresses for a class-action lawsuit.

Silvio de Bortoli, the general manager of the Cancun resort and a legend throughout the organization for his ability to satisfy customers, got word of the horrendous flight and immediately created an antidote. He took half the staff to the airport, where they laid out a table of snacks and drinks and set up a stereo system to play lively music. As the guests filed through the gate, they received personal greetings, help with their bags, a sympathetic ear, and a chauffeured ride to the resort. Waiting for them at Club Med was a lavish banquet, complete with mariachi band and champagne. Moreover, the staff had rallied other guests to wake up and greet the newcomers, and the partying continued until sunrise. Many guests said it was the most fun they'd had since college.

In the end, the vacationers had a better experience than if their flight from New York had gone like clockwork. Although the company probably couldn't measure it, Club Mediterranèe won market share that night. After all, the battle for market share is won not by analyzing demographic trends, ratings points, and other global measures, but rather by pleasing customers one at a time.

Source: Reprinted by permission of *Harvard Business Review.* An excerpt from C. W. L. Hart, J. L. Heskett, and W. E. Sasser, Jr., "The Profitable Art of Service Recovery," *Harvard Business Review,* July/August 1990, pp. 148, 149. © 1990 by the Harvard Business School Publishing Corporation. All rights reserved.

procedural fairness, and *interactional fairness.*[25] Outcome fairness concerns the results that customers receive from their complaints; procedural fairness refers to the policies, rules, and timeliness of the complaint process; and interactional fairness focuses on the interpersonal treatment received during the complaint process.[26] Exhibit 8.3 shows examples of each type of fairness taken from Brown and Tax's study of consumers who reported on their experiences with complaint resolution.

Outcome Fairness

Customers expect outcomes, or compensation, that match the level of their dissatisfaction. This compensation can take the form of actual monetary compensation, an apology, future free services, reduced charges, repairs, and/or replacements. Customers expect equity in the exchange—that is, they want to feel that the company has "paid" for its mistakes in a manner at least equal to what the customer has suffered. The company's "punishment should fit the crime." Outcome fairness is especially important in settings in which customers have particularly negative emotional responses to the service failure; in such situations recovery efforts should focus on improving the outcome from the customer's point of view.[27]

In the Club Med example in Exhibit 8.2, customers were compensated in a variety of ways. These guests had suffered a lot and the compensation definitely was adequate. Note that in this case the service failure was not even Club Med's fault.

On the other hand, customers can be uncomfortable if they are overly compensated. Early in its experience with service guarantees, Domino's Pizza offered not to charge

Fairness Themes in Service Recovery

	Fair	Unfair
Outcome fairness: The results that customers receive from complaints	"The waitress agreed that there was a problem. She took the sandwiches back to the kitchen and had them replaced. We were also given a free drink." "They were very thorough with my complaint. One week later I received a coupon for a free oil change and an apology from the shop owner."	"Their refusal to refund our money or make up for the inconvenience and cold food was inexcusable." "If I wanted a refund, I had to go back to the store the next day. It's a 20-minute drive; the refund was barely worth the trouble." "All I wanted was for the ticket agent to apologize for doubting my story. I never got the apology."
Procedural fairness: The policies, rules, and timeliness of the complaint process	"The hotel manager said that it didn't matter to her who was at fault, she would take responsibility for the problem immediately." "The sales manager called me back one week after my complaint to check if the problem was taken care of to my satisfaction."	"They should have assisted me with the problem instead of giving me a phone number to call. No one returned my calls, and I never had a chance to speak to a real person." "I had to tell my problem to too many people. I had to become irate in order to talk with the manager, who was apparently the only one who could provide a solution."
Interactional fairness: The interpersonal treatment received during the complaint process	"The loan officer was very courteous, knowledgeable, and considerate—he kept me informed about the progress of the complaint." "The teller explained that they had a power outage that morning so things were delayed. He went through a lot of files [effort] so that I would not have to come back the next day."	"The person who handled my complaint about the faulty air conditioner repair wasn't going to do anything about it and didn't seem to care." "The receptionist was very rude; she made it seem like the doctor's time was important but mine was not."

for the pizza if the driver arrived after the 30-minute guaranteed delivery time. Many customers were not comfortable asking for this level of compensation, especially if the driver was only a few minutes late. In this case "the punishment was greater than the crime."

Procedural Fairness

In addition to fair compensation, customers expect fairness in terms of policies, rules, and timeliness of the complaint process. They want easy access to the complaint process, and they want things handled quickly, preferably by the first person they contact. They appreciate companies that can be adaptable in their procedures so that the recovery effort can match their individual circumstances. In some cases, particularly in business-to-business services, companies actually ask the customer, "What can we do to compensate you for our failure?" Many times what the customer asks for is actually less than the company might have expected.

Fair procedures are characterized by clarity, speed, and absence of hassles. Unfair procedures are those that customers perceive as slow, prolonged, and inconvenient. Customers also feel it is unfair if they have to prove their case—when the assumption seems to be they are wrong or lying until they can prove otherwise.

In the Club Med case in Exhibit 8.2, the recovery happened as quickly as possible when the passengers landed in Mexico. And the vacationers had no more hassles once they were on the ground.

Interactional Fairness

Above and beyond their expectations of fair compensation and hassle-free, quick procedures, customers expect to be treated politely, with care and honesty. This form of fairness can dominate the others if customers feel the company and its employees have uncaring attitudes and have done little to try to resolve the problem. This type of behaviour on the part of employees may seem strange—why would they treat customers rudely or in an uncaring manner under these circumstances? Often it is due to lack of training and empowerment—a frustrated front-line employee who has no authority to compensate the customer may easily respond in an aloof or uncaring manner, especially if the customer is angry and/or rude.

In the Club Med case in Exhibit 8.2, Silvio de Bortoli and his staff were gracious, caring, and upbeat when they greeted the long-delayed passengers. They personally met them at the airport even though it was late at night. They even involved other guests already staying at the resort to greet the new arrivals.

⟶ SWITCHING VS. STAYING FOLLOWING SERVICE RECOVERY

Whether customers switch to a new provider following service failure will depend on a number of factors. The more serious the failure, the more likely the customer is to switch no matter what the recovery effort.[28]

The nature of the customer's relationship with the firm may also influence whether the customer stays or switches providers. Research suggests that customers who have "true relationships" with their service providers are more forgiving and less likely to switch than those who have a "first-time encounter" relationship.[29]

Other research reveals that the individual customer's attitude toward switching will strongly influence whether he or she ultimately stays with the provider and that this attitude toward switching will be even more influential than basic satisfaction with the service.[30] This research suggests that certain customers will have a greater propensity to switch service providers no matter how their service failure situations are handled. Research in an online service context showed that the profile of an "online service switcher" is a person who was influenced to subscribe to the service through positive word of mouth; who used the service less; who was less satisfied and less involved with the service; who had a lower income and education level; and who also had a lower propensity for taking risks.[31]

Finally, the decision to switch may not occur immediately following poor service recovery. That is, service switching can be viewed as a process resulting from a series of critical service encounters over time rather than one specific moment in time.[32] This

FIGURE 8.7

Causes Behind Service Switching

Source: Reprinted with permission of the American Marketing Association. From S. Keaveney, "Customer Switching Behavior in Service Industries: An Exploratory Study," *Journal of Marketing* 59 (April 1995), pp. 71–82.

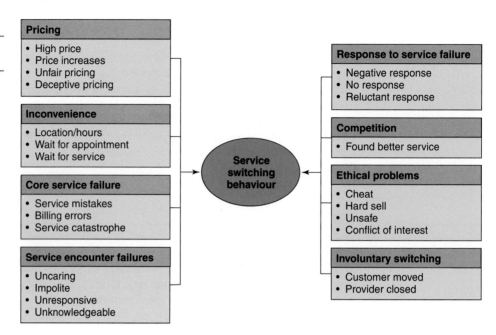

process orientation suggests that companies could potentially track customer interactions and predict the likelihood of defection based on a series of events, intervening earlier in the process to head off the customer's decision to switch.

Another study identified eight broad themes underlying the decision to defect.[33] These themes (pricing, inconvenience, core service failure, service encounter failure, response to service failure, competition, ethical problems, and involuntary switching) are shown in Figure 8.7. As these findings suggest, service failure can cause customers to switch companies. To minimize the impact of service failure, excellent service recovery is needed. In the next section we discuss several service recovery strategies that attempt to keep dissatisfied customers from defecting.

SERVICE RECOVERY STRATEGIES

Many companies have learned the importance of providing excellent recovery for disappointed customers. In this section we examine their strategies and share examples of benchmark companies and what they are doing. It will become clear that excellent service recovery is really a combination of a variety of strategies that need to work together, as illustrated in Figure 8.8. We discuss each of the strategies shown in the figure, starting with the basic "Do it right the first time."

Make the Service Fail-Safe—Do It Right the First Time!

The first rule of service quality is to do it right the first time. In this way recovery is unnecessary, customers get what they expect, and the costs of redoing the service and compensating for errors can be avoided.[34]

Dick Chase, noted service operations expert, suggests that services adopt the notion of *poka yokes* to improve service reliability.[35] Poka yokes are automatic warnings or controls in place to ensure that mistakes are not made; essentially they are quality control mechanisms, typically used on assembly lines. Chase suggests that poka yokes can be devised in service settings to "mistakeproof" the service. In a

FIGURE 8.8

Service Recovery
Strategies

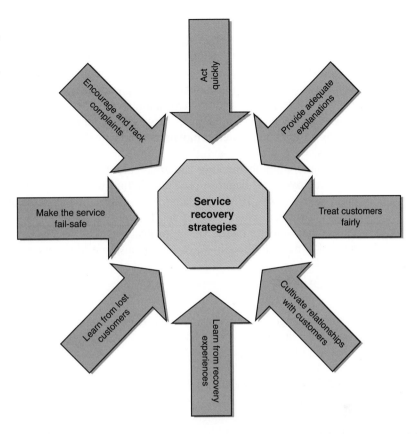

hospital setting, poka yokes ensure that procedures are followed to avoid potentially life-threatening mistakes. For example, trays for surgical instruments have indentations for specific instruments, and each instrument is nested in its appropriate spot. In this way surgeons and their staff know that all instruments are in their places prior to closing the patient's incision.[36]

Similarly, poka yokes can be devised to ensure that the tangibles associated with the service are clean and well maintained and that documents are accurate and up to date. Poka yokes can also be implemented for employee behaviours (checklists, role-playing and practice, reminder signs) and even for ensuring that customers perform effectively. Many of the strategies we discuss in Parts 4 and 5 of the text ("Aligning Service Design and Standards" and "Delivering and Performing Service") are aimed at ensuring service reliability and can be viewed as applications of the basic fail-safe notion of poka yokes.

Even more fundamentally, it is important for a firm to create a culture of zero defections to ensure doing it right the first time.[37] Within a zero-defections culture, everyone understands the importance of reliability. Employees and managers aim to satisfy every customer and look for ways to improve service. Employees in a zero-defections culture fully understand and appreciate the "relationship value of a customer" concept presented in Chapter 7. Thus they are motivated to provide quality service *every time* and to *every customer.*

Encourage and Track Complaints

Even in a zero-defections organization, failures occur. A critical component of a service recovery strategy is thus to encourage and track complaints.

Firms can utilize a number of ways to encourage and track complaints. Customer research can be designed for this purpose through satisfaction surveys, critical incidents studies, and lost customer research, as discussed in Chapter 6. Toll-free call centres, email, and pagers are now used to facilitate, encourage, and track complaints. Software applications in a number of companies also allow complaints to be analyzed, sorted, responded to, and tracked automatically.[38] Our Technology Spotlight shows how a world-class airline, British Airways, encourages, facilitates, and employs technology to track customer complaints as a critical component of its service recovery process.

In some cases technology can anticipate problems and complaints, allowing service employees to diagnose problems before the customer recognizes they exist. At companies such as IBM and Caterpillar, information systems are being implemented to anticipate equipment failures and to send out an electronic alert to the local field technician with the nature of the problem as well as which parts and tools will be needed to make the repair—a repair the customer does not yet know is needed.[39]

Act Quickly

Complaining customers want quick responses.[40] Thus, if the company welcomes, even encourages, complaints, it must be prepared to act on them quickly. Immediate response requires not only systems and procedures that allow quick action but also empowered employees.

Take Care of Problems on the Front Line

Customers want the persons who hear their complaints to solve their problems whether a complaint is registered in person, over the phone, or via the Internet. The Ritz-Carlton, for example, insists that the first person to hear a complaint from a customer "owns" that complaint until the employee is sure it is resolved. If a maintenance employee hears a complaint from a customer while the employee is in the middle of fixing a light in the hotel corridor, he owns that complaint and must be sure that it is handled appropriately before returning to his work.

Finally, if your company knows of a service failure and wants to be proactive, you can always take out an ad in the local paper. That's exactly what the Halifax *Chronicle Herald* did when they were having service delays. (It certainly makes it easier when you don't have to pay for the ad!) "Thank you for your understanding" said the ad, addressed "To Our Valued Readers," explaining that the delays were due to modernization at one of their printing plants.

Empower Employees

Employees must be trained and empowered to solve problems as they occur. A problem not solved can quickly escalate. Take, for example, the true story of a corporate vice-president who sent an email to his bank to register a complaint while he was attempting a transaction through its Internet banking service. The email was never answered. The customer then sent an email directly to the president of the bank. That one was never answered either. Ultimately the customer withdrew his approximately $70,000 account because his complaint was not handled in a timely manner. In this case the technology was not effectively linked to other systems, nor ultimately to employees. The Internet access encouraged the complaint, but the response never occurred.

Global Feature

September 11, 2001: Rebuilding a Firm—Service Recovery in the Wake of Disaster

"As I watched TV on September 11, 2001, I was struck with horror along with the rest of the world at the sight of the World Trade Center towers in New York City collapsing. My immediate thoughts that morning were, as for many, of friends and loved ones who worked in those towers, wondering where they were and if they were all right. In my case, it was a friend of over 30 years who worked in the North Tower of the World Trade Center, on the 55th floor, in a law firm where he is a partner. Other friends and I immediately started to think of ways to reach him, and eventually one of us did, that afternoon. He was safe."

M.J.B.

The story of how Sidley Austin Brown & Wood was able to rebuild itself and serve its clients and employees was reported in *The New York Times* the following Sunday, September 16. The remarkable story is the ultimate example of service recovery in its most monumental proportions. All but one of the firm's 600 employees who worked in the WTC survived the disaster, and they were back in business, able to serve their clients, within six days.

Sidley Austin Brown & Wood is the fourth-largest law firm in the United States, employing 1,325 attorneys and serving large corporate, financial, and government clients. The firm is the result of a merger in 2001 of two firms with long histories—Sidley & Austin was founded in 1866 in Chicago, Brown & Wood in 1914 in New York. The firm has primary offices in New York and Chicago and additional offices in San Francisco, Los Angeles, Washington (DC), Seattle, Dallas, Shanghai, Tokyo, Hong Kong, Beijing, Singapore, and London.

How did the firm achieve its remarkable recovery following September 11? Some of it had to do with careful planning as a result of surviving the WTC bombing in 1993. A lot of it had to do with courageous, focused employees as well as cooperative,

helpful suppliers and understanding clients. We can capture here only a tiny bit of what happened.

The first and highest priority of the firm was, of course, its employees and their safety. All 13 offices of the firm around the world were shut down the day following the collapse of the Towers, and three centres of activity were established to deal with the aftermath. Once it was learned that most employees were accounted for and out of the building, the firm's administrators and managing partners focused on reestablishing the New York office and began assessing what it needed to do to serve its employees and its corporate and government clients.

Within three hours of the disaster, a partner in the firm had secured leases on four additional floors of a building in midtown New York where the firm already had some space. The cost of the space was not discussed, and a firm that was due to move into the space agreed to delay its move to give the space to Sidley, at least temporarily. By the end of the day, others had arranged for the delivery of 800 desks, 300 computers, and hundreds of cell phones. Contractors were hired that day to string cable and reestablish the firm's computer network. Normal rules of business were bypassed as suppliers and even competitors offered to help. Nightly backups of the firm's entire electronic network enabled everything up to the night before the attacks to be restored. The backup tapes were stored in New Jersey by two independent firms and needed to be shipped immediately to Chicago so they could be restored and readied for use. Because no planes were flying for several days, these companies offered to have their own employees drive the tapes to Chicago from New Jersey.

On September 12 a letter to "our colleagues, clients, and friends" appeared on the firm's website to assure clients of the progress being made to serve

continued

Global Feature

September 11, 2001: Rebuilding a Firm—Service Recovery in the Wake of Disaster—*continued*

them without interruption, ending with the following statement: "We will not let down our predecessors, or our current colleagues, clients, and friends. From this tragedy, we have the opportunity to build something stronger and more energized than ever before, and we intend to do so. Thank you for your thoughts and prayers. We will keep you informed." The firm was back in business, serving its clients, in its new midtown offices on September 17.

During and following all the hectic efforts to reopen the firm for business, people remained a primary concern. Once the safety of employees, friends, and loved ones was assured, the firm turned to providing counselling, to ensuring that employees' pay was not interrupted, to bringing people together to see each other and share their feelings, and to ensuring the security of the workplace. Heroic stories of employee actions and sad accounts of the things they felt and saw in those days in September have become part of the fabric and culture of the firm. Six hundred of its employees worked in the WTC and were displaced on that day in September. All but one of those employees survived the disaster.

Sources: J. Schwartz, "Up from the Ashes, One Firm Rebuilds," *The New York Times*, September 16, 2001, sec. 3, p. 1. For a follow-up story see John Schwartz, "Rebuilding a Day at a Time: Law Firm Pushes Two Steps Forward for Every Step Back," *The New York Times*, December 14, 2001, p. C1. See also: "Our Test," a personal account of the events surrounding September 11, 2001, by Thomas Cole, chairperson of the executive committee of Sidley Austin Brown & Wood, at www.sidley.com, news and events; accessed November 15, 2004; Sidley Austin Brown & Wood website; www.sidley.com.

Sometimes employees can even anticipate problems before they arise and surprise customers with a solution. For example, flight attendants on a flight severely delayed because of weather anticipated everyone's hunger, particularly the young children's. Once in flight, they announced to the harried travellers, "Thank you for your extreme patience in waiting with us. Now that we're on our way, we'd like to offer you complimentary beverages and dinner. Because we have a number of very hungry children on board, we'd like to serve them first, if that's OK with all of you." The passengers nodded and applauded their efforts, knowing that hungry, crying children could make the situation even worse. The flight attendants had anticipated a problem and solved it before it escalated.

Service employees have a specific and real need for recovery training. Because customers demand that service recovery take place on the spot and quickly, front-line employees need the skills, authority, and incentives to engage in effective recovery. Effective recovery skills include hearing the customer's problems, taking initiative, identifying solutions, improvising, and perhaps bending the rules from time to time.

Not only do employees need the authority to act (usually within certain defined limits), but they also should not be punished for taking action. In fact, incentives should exist that encourage employees to exercise their recovery authority. At the Ritz-Carlton, employees are authorized to spend $2,000 on behalf of the customer to solve a problem. This amount of money is rarely needed, but knowing that they have it encourages employees to be responsive without fear of retribution.

Allow Customers to Solve Their Own Problems

Another way problems or complaints can be handled quickly is by building systems that allow customers to actually solve their own service needs and fix their own problems. Typically this is acheived through technology that the customers directly interface with, and that provides them with instant answers. FedEx uses this in its package tracking services, for example.

Provide Adequate Explanations

In many service failures, customers try to understand why the failure occurred. Research suggests that when the firm's ability to provide an adequate *outcome* is not successful, further dissatisfaction can be reduced if an adequate *explanation* is provided to the customer.[41] In order for an explanation to be perceived as adequate, it must possess two primary characteristics. First, the explanation must be appropriate; relevant facts and pertinent information are important in helping the customer understand what occurred. Second, how the explanation is delivered can also reduce customer dissatisfaction. This includes the personal characteristics of the explanation givers, including their credibility and sincerity. Part of the frustration of the Doubletree Inn customers mentioned in Exhibit 8.1 was the result of not receiving an adequate explanation from the hotel.

Treat Customers Fairly

In responding quickly, it is also critical to treat each customer fairly. In the section "Customers' Recovery Expectations," we discussed results of research that focused on fairness in service recovery. Here we remind you that fair treatment is an essential component of an effective service recovery strategy.

Cultivate Relationships with Customers

A benefit of relationship marketing is that if the firm fails in service delivery, customers who have a strong relationship with the firm are more forgiving and more open to service recovery efforts. Research suggests that strong customer–firm relationships can help shield the firm from the negative effects of failures on customer satisfaction.[42] To illustrate, one study demonstrated that the presence of rapport between customers and employees provided several service recovery benefits, including increased post-failure satisfaction, increased loyalty intentions, and decreased negative word-of-mouth communication.[43] Another study found that customers who expect the relationship to continue also tend to have lower service recovery expectations and may demand less immediate compensation for a failure, because they consider the balance of equity across a longer time horizon.[44] Thus, cultivation of strong customer relationships can provide an important buffer to service firms when failures occur.

Learn from Recovery Experiences

"Problem-resolution situations are more than just opportunities to fix flawed services and strengthen ties with customers. They are also a valuable—but frequently ignored or underutilized—source of diagnostic, prescriptive information for improving customer service."[45] By conducting root-cause analysis, firms can identify the sources of problems and modify processes, sometimes eliminating almost completely the need for recovery.

Technology Spotlight

British Airways—Complaint Handling Model Pays Off

Ads for British Airways (BA) reinforce the company's branding strategy as the "World's Favourite Airline." Indeed, British Airways is a favourite among world travellers—but it was not always so. The success in turning BA around from a bureaucratic institution that regarded itself as doing the public a favour by allowing them to fly on its planes to a customer-responsive, world-class service provider can be attributed to its CEO at the time, Sir Colin Marshall. Marshall (currently chair of the board) was brought in to head up a major change for BA in the 1980s—and he did. His legacy has sustained and further propelled the airline to its current level of success.

A big part of this success was achieved in new ways of listening to customers and new approaches to dealing with customer complaints. One of the first things Marshall did was to install video booths at Heathrow airport so that upset customers could immediately go to the video booth while still at the airport and complain directly to him. In addition to this type of innovative action, Marshall instituted a series of systems and training changes to encourage and be responsive to customer complaints. To quote him directly, "I ardently believe that customer complaints are precious opportunities to hold on to customers who otherwise might take their business elsewhere and to learn about problems that need to be fixed."

Initially BA did research to understand the effect that dissatisfied or defecting customers had on the business. It learned that 50 percent of the dissatisfied customers who did *not* tell BA about their problems left the airline for a competitor. However, of those who *did* tell the company of their problems, 87 percent remained loyal to BA. It quickly became obvious that complaints should be encouraged! Considering that an average business class passenger has a lifetime value of $150,000, encouraging complaints and retaining their business was obviously critical.

Source: Newscast.

BA responded by building a model for "Making Customers into Champions." Goals of the new system were to (1) use customer feedback more effectively to improve quality; (2) strive to prevent future service problems through teamwork; (3) compensate customers on their terms, not the company's; and (4) practise customer retention, not adjudication. The bottom-line objective: to prevent customer defections.

To accomplish this objective, BA set up a four-step process to guide development of its technical and human delivery systems. This process was based on knowledge of how customers would like their complaints handled. The first step in the process was to *apologize and own the customer's problem*—not to search for someone to blame but rather to become the customer's advocate. The second essential was to *respond quickly*—taking absolutely no longer than 72 hours, and preferably providing an immediate solution. The third step was to *assure the customer that the problem is being fixed*. Finally, as much as possible, *handle complaints by phone*. BA found that customers with problems were delighted to speak personally to a customer service representative who could solve their problems.

To facilitate the process just described required major investments in systems and people. First, BA

continued

Technology Spotlight

British Airways—Complaint Handling Model Pays Off—continued

invested in a computer system called Caress that eliminated all paper by scanning or manually entering all customer information relevant to a complaint into a customer complaint database. A particular customer's information was thus easily accessed, and the data could be analyzed for patterns as well. The process for dealing with a complaint was also shortened by eliminating a number of unnecessary and redundant steps: the number of steps required to deal with a complaint was reduced from 13 to 3. Further, customer service representatives were given the tools and authority—they were empowered—to use whatever resources were needed to retain the customer's business. New training on listening skills, how to handle anger, and how to negotiate win-win solutions were put in place for customer service representatives. Finally, customers were encouraged to complain. Prior to the new initiatives, BA knew that only about 10 percent of its customers ever communicated with the airline directly—whether for good or bad reasons. The airline thus worked hard to get customers to complain and provide input by establishing 12 different "listening posts" or ways of communicating, including postage-paid cards, customer forums, surveys, and a "Fly with Me" program, in

which customer service representatives flew with customers to experience and hear their responses firsthand.

Not only did BA use the information and systems it developed to directly retain dissatisfied customers, it also built systems to use the data and information to improve systems for the future. It used the information to design out common failure patterns and to design early-warning mechanisms to alert the company to potential future failures.

BA found that all its efforts toward complaint management paid off. For every £1 spent in customer retention efforts, BA found it had a £2 return. BA continues to take great pride in delivering the highest levels of customer service. In January 2000 the company unveiled £600,000,000 worth of new customer service initiatives to be rolled out over the following two years.

Sources: J. Barlow and C. Moller, *A Complaint Is a Gift* (San Francisco: Berrett-Koehler Publishers, 1996), pp. 16–18; C. R. Weiser, "Championing the Customer," *Harvard Business Review,* November/December 1995, pp. 113–15; S. E. Prokesch, "Competing on Service: An Interview with British Airways' Sir Colin Marshall," *Harvard Business Review,* November/December 1995, pp. 101–16; and www.britishairways.com, 2002.

At Ritz-Carlton Hotels, all employees carry service recovery forms called "instant action forms" with them at all times so that they can immediately record service failures and suggest actions to address them. In turn, the employees report to management these sources of service failure and the remedies. This information is then entered into the customer database and analyzed for patterns and systemic service issues that need to be fixed. If common themes are observed across a number of failure situations, changes are made to service processes or attributes. In addition, the information is entered into the customer's personal data file so when that customer stays at the Ritz-Carlton again (no matter what hotel), employees can be aware of the previous experience, ensuring that it does not happen again for that particular customer.

Learn from Lost Customers

Another key component of an effective service recovery strategy is to learn from the customers who decide to leave. Formal market research to discover the reasons customers have left can assist in preventing failures in the future. This type of research is difficult, even painful for companies. No one really likes to examine their failures. Yet such examination is essential for preventing the same mistakes.[46]

As presented in Chapter 6, lost customer research is most effectively obtained by depth interviews, administered by interviewers who truly understand the business. It may be best to have this type of research done by senior people in the company, particularly in business-to-business contexts in which customers are large and the impact of even one lost customer is great. The type of depth analysis often requires a series of "why" questions or "tell me more about that" questions to get at the actual, core reason for the customer's defection.[47]

In conducting this kind of research, a firm must focus on important or profitable customers who have left—not just everyone who has left the company. An insurance company in Australia once began this type of research to learn about their lost customers, only to find that the customers they were losing tended to be their least profitable customers anyway. They quickly determined that research on how to keep these *un*profitable customers would not be a good investment!

SERVICE GUARANTEES

A guarantee is a particular type of recovery tool. Guarantees have only recently been used for services. Traditionally, people believed that services could not be guaranteed given their intangible and variable nature. With a product, the customer is guaranteed that it will perform as promised and if not, that it can be returned. With services, it is generally not possible to take returns or to "undo" what has been performed. The skepticism about service guarantees is being dispelled, however, as more and more companies find they can guarantee their services and that there are tremendous benefits to doing so.

FIGURE 8.9 Corus Radio offers Canadians a performance guarantee.

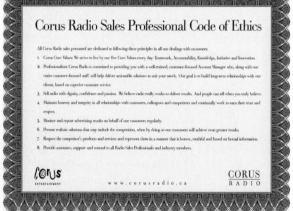

Source: Corus Entertainment Inc., 2005.

Companies are finding that effective service guarantees can complement the company's service recovery strategy—serving as one tool to help accomplish the service recovery strategies depicted in Figure 8.8. The Hampton Inn Hotels guarantee shown in Figure 8.3 is an example of such an effective guarantee. The Corus Radio guarantee depicted in Figure 8.9 is another.

Benefits of Service Guarantees

"Service organizations, in particular, are beginning to recognize that guarantees can serve not only as a marketing tool but as a means for defining, cultivating, and maintaining quality throughout an organization."[48] The benefits to the company of an effective service guarantee are numerous:[49]

- *A good guarantee forces the company to focus on its customers.* To develop a meaningful guarantee, the company must know what is important to its customers—what they expect and value. In many cases "satisfaction" is guaranteed, but in order for the guarantee to work effectively, the company must clearly understand what satisfaction means for its customers (what they value and expect).

- *An effective guarantee sets clear standards for the organization.* It prompts the company to clearly define what it expects of its employees and to communicate that expectation to them. The guarantee gives employees service-oriented goals that can quickly align employee behaviors around customer strategies. For example, Pizza Hut's guarantee that "If you're not satisfied with your pizza, let our restaurant know. We'll make it right or give you your money back" lets employees know exactly what they should do if a customer complains. It is also clear to employees that making it right for the customer is an important company goal.

- *A good guarantee generates immediate and relevant feedback from customers.* It provides an incentive for customers to complain and thereby provides more representative feedback to the company than simply relying on the relatively few customers who typically voice their concerns. The guarantee communicates to customers that they have the right to complain.

- *When the guarantee is invoked there is an instant opportunity to recover,* thus satisfying the customer and helping retain loyalty.

- *Information generated through the guarantee can be tracked and integrated into continuous improvement efforts.* A feedback link between customers and service operations decisions can be strengthened through the guarantee.

- *Studies of the impact of service guarantees suggest that employee morale and loyalty can be enhanced as a result.* A guarantee generates pride among employees. Through feedback from the guarantee, improvements can be made in the service that benefit customers and, indirectly, employees.

- *For customers, the guarantee reduces their sense of risk* and builds confidence in the organization. Because services are intangible and often highly personal or ego-involving, customers seek information and cues that will help reduce their sense of uncertainty. Guarantees have been shown to reduce risk and increase positive evaluation of the service prior to purchase.[50]

The bottom line for the company is that an effective guarantee can affect profitability through building customer awareness and loyalty, through positive word of mouth, and through reduction in costs as service improvements are made and service recovery expenses are reduced. Indirectly, the guarantee can reduce costs of employee turnover through creating a more positive service culture.

Types of Service Guarantees

Satisfaction vs. Service Attribute Guarantees

Service guarantees can be *unconditional satisfaction guarantees* or *service attribute guarantees*. Hampton Inn Hotels' guarantee is an unconditional satisfaction guarantee. In another context, Bain & Company, a management consulting firm, has offered some clients an unconditional guarantee for its services.[51] If clients are unhappy, they do not pay for the services. Lands' End, a catalogue retailer, has abbreviated its guarantee to "Guaranteed. Period."

In other cases, firms offer guarantees of particular aspects of the service that are important to customers. FedEx guarantees package delivery by a certain time. In introducing a new seat design in first class, British Airways advertised "Comfort guaranteed or you get 25,000 miles." McDonald's advertised a guarantee that stated "Hot Food; Fast, Friendly Delivery; Double-Check Drive-Thru Accuracy…We'll make it right, or your next meal is on us." In all these cases, the companies have guaranteed elements of the service that they know are important to customers.

Another type of service guarantee, a *combined guarantee,* combines the wide scope of the total satisfaction guarantee with specific attribute performance standards. Research suggests that this type of guarantee can be more effective than either of the other two types.[52]

External vs. Internal Guarantees

Interestingly, guarantees do not have to be only for external customers. Some companies are finding that internal service guarantees—one part of the organization guaranteeing its services to others—are effective ways of aligning internal service operations. At one direct-mail firm, the sales force guarantees to give the production department all the specifications needed to provide service to the external customer, or the offending salesperson will take the production department to lunch, sing a song at their next department meeting, or personally input all the specs into the computer.[53]

Characteristics of Effective Guarantees

No matter what the type of guarantee, certain characteristics make some guarantees more effective than others. Characteristics of effective guarantees are shown in Exhibit 8.4. But companies shouldn't expect the development of a guarantee to happen overnight. Travelocity.com recently launched its "Travelocity Service Guarantee." According to one of the company's VPs who worked on it, "It's taken a year of planning and a [huge] investment to be able to get the infrastructure in place to stand behind our guarantee. To do it correctly, you can't do it overnight."[54]

When to Use (or Not Use) a Guarantee

Service guarantees are not appropriate for every company and certainly not in every service situation. Before putting a guarantee strategy in place, a firm needs to address a number of important questions (see Exhibit 8.5). A guarantee is probably *not* the right strategy when:

> EXHIBIT 8.4

Characteristics of an Effective Service Guarantee

UNCONDITIONAL
- The guarantee should make its promise unconditionally—no strings attached.

MEANINGFUL
- The firm should guarantee elements of the service that are important to the customer.
- The payout should cover fully the customer's dissatisfaction.

EASY TO UNDERSTAND AND COMMUNICATE
- Customers need to understand what to expect.
- Employees need to understand what to do.

EASY TO INVOKE AND COLLECT
- The firm should eliminate hoops or red tape in the way of accessing or collecting on the guarantee.

Source: C. W. L. Hart, "The Power of Unconditional Guarantees," *Harvard Business Review,* July/August 1988, pp. 54–62.

- *Existing service quality in the company is poor.* Before instituting a guarantee, the company should fix any significant quality problems. Otherwise the costs of implementing the guarantee might easily outweigh any benefits.

- *A guarantee does not fit the company's image.* Research suggests that the benefits of offering a guarantee for a high-end hotel like the Four Seasons may be significantly less than the benefits that a hotel of lesser quality would enjoy.[55]

- *Service quality is truly uncontrollable.* Uncontrollable service quality is often merely an excuse for not employing a guarantee. However, there are situations in which service quality is truly uncontrollable. For example, it would not be a good practice for a training organization to guarantee that all participants would pass a certification exam on completion of the training course if passing depends too much on the participants' own effort. The company might, however, guarantee satisfaction with the training or certain aspects of the training process.

- *Potential exists for customer abuse of the guarantee.* Fear of opportunistic customer behaviour, including customer cheating or fraudulent invocation of service guarantees, is a common reason that firms hesitate to offer guarantees.[56] In general, however, customer abuse of service guarantees is fairly minimal and not at all widespread.[57]

- *Costs of the guarantee outweigh the benefits.* As with any quality investment, the company will want to carefully calculate expected costs (payouts for failures and costs of making improvements) against anticipated benefits (customer loyalty, quality improvements, attraction of new customers, word-of-mouth advertising).

- *Customers perceive no risk in the service.* If there is no risk, a guarantee will likely produce little benefit for the company other than perhaps some promotional value.[58]

- *Customers perceive little variability in service quality between competitors.* Unless industries exhibit extreme variability in quality between competitors, a guarantee will yield little benefit.[59]

Questions to Consider in Implementing a Service Guarantee

DECIDING WHO DECIDES

- Is there a guarantee champion in the company?
- Is senior management committed to a guarantee?
- Is the guarantee design a team effort?
- Are customers providing input?

WHEN DOES A GUARANTEE MAKE SENSE?

- How high are quality standards?
- Can we afford a guarantee?
- How high is customer risk?
- Are competitors offering a guarantee?
- Is the company's culture compatible with a guarantee?

WHAT TYPE OF GUARANTEE SHOULD WE OFFER?

- Should we offer an unconditional guarantee or a specific-outcome one?

- Is our service measurable?
- What should our specific guarantee be about?
- What are the uncontrollables?
- Is the company particularly susceptible to unreasonable triggerings?
- What should the payout be?
- Will a refund send the wrong message?
- Could a full refund make customers feel guilty?
- Is the guarantee easy to invoke?

Source: A. L. Ostrom and C. W. L. Hart, "Service Guarantees: Research and Practice," in *Handbook of Services Marketing and Management,* ed. D. Iacobucci and T. Swartz (Thousand Oaks, CA: Sage Publications, 2000). © 2000 by Sage Publications. Reprinted by permission of Sage Publications.

SUMMARY

Part 3 of this text (Chapters 6, 7, and 8) focused on the critical importance of understanding customer expectations as well as many of the strategies firms use to accomplish this goal. Part of understanding customer expectations is being prepared for and knowing what to do when things go wrong or when the service fails. In this chapter we focused on service recovery, the actions taken by an organization in response to a service failure.

You learned in this chapter the importance of an effective service recovery strategy for retaining customers and increasing positive word of mouth communication. Another major benefit of an effective service recovery strategy is that the information it provides can be useful for service improvement. The potential downsides of poor service recovery are tremendous—negative word of mouth, lost customers, and declining business when quality issues are not addressed.

In this chapter you learned how customers respond to service failures and why some complain while others do not. You learned that customers expect to be treated fairly when they complain—not just in terms of the actual outcome or compensation they receive, but also in terms of the procedures that are used and how they are treated interpersonally. We pointed out in this chapter that there is tremendous room for improvement in service recovery effectiveness across firms and industries.

The second half of the chapter focused on specific strategies that firms are using for service recovery: (1) making the service fail-safe, or doing it right the first time, (2) encouraging and tracking complaints, (3) acting quickly, (4) providing adequate explanations, (5) treating customers fairly, (6) cultivating relationships with customers, (7) learning from recovery experiences, and (8) learning from lost customers. The chapter ended with a discussion of service guarantees as a tool used by many firms to build a foundation for service recovery. You learned the benefits of service guarantees, the elements of a good guarantee, and the pros and cons of using guarantees under various circumstances.

Discussion Questions

1. Why is it important for a service firm to have a strong recovery strategy? Think of a time when you received less-than-desirable service from a particular service organization. Was any effort made to recover? What should/could have been done differently? Do you still buy services from the organization? Why or why not? Did you tell others about your experience?

2. Discuss the benefits to a company of having an effective service recovery strategy. Describe an instance in which you experienced (or delivered as an employee) an effective service recovery. In what ways did the company benefit in this particular situation?

3. Explain the recovery paradox, and discuss its implications for a service firm manager.

4. Discuss the types of actions that customers can take in response to a service failure. What type of complainer are you? Why? As a manager, would you want to encourage your customers to be voicers? If so, how?

5. Review Exhibits 8.1 and 8.2. What would you have done if you were on the management team at Doubletree Inn, Ctizens Bank, or Club Med?

6. Explain the logic behind these two quotes: "A complaint is a gift" and "The customer who complains is your friend."

7. Choose a firm you are familiar with. Describe how you would design an ideal service recovery strategy for that organization.

8. What are the benefits to the company of an effective service guarantee? Should every service organization have one?

9. Describe three service guarantees that are currently offered by companies or organizations in addition to the ones already described in the chapter. (Examples are readily available on the Internet.) Are your examples good guarantees or poor guarantees based on the criteria presented in this chapter?

Exercises

1. Write a letter of complaint (or voice your complaint in person) to a service organization from which you have experienced less-than-desirable service. What do you expect the organization to do to recover? (Later, report to the class the results of your complaint, whether you were satisfied with the recovery, what could/should have been done differently, and whether you will continue using the service.)

2. Interview five people about their service recovery experiences. What happened, and what did they expect the firm to do? Were they treated fairly according to the definition of recovery fairness presented in the chapter? Will they return to the company in the future?

3. Interview a manager about service recovery strategies used in his or her firm. Use the strategies shown in Figure 8.8 to frame your questions.

4. Visit Cisco Systems' website (www.cisco.com). Consider what the company is currently doing to help its customers solve their own problems. Compare what Cisco is doing with the self-service efforts of another service provider of your choice.

5. Choose a service you are familiar with. Explain the service offered and develop a good service guarantee for it. Discuss why your guarantee is a good one, and list the benefits to the company of implementing it.

⊢⟶ Notes

1. As quoted in F. Van Bennekom, "A Sporting Service Recovery," Great Brook site, 2005, www.greatbrook.com/complaint_handling.htm, accessed September 30, 2006.

2. For research that shows different types of service failures, see M. J. Bitner, B. H. Booms, and M. S. Tetreault, "The Service Encounter: Diagnosing Favorable and Unfavorable Incidents," *Journal of Marketing* 54 (January 1990), pp. 71–84; and S. M. Keaveney, "Customer Switching Behavior in Service Industries: An Exploratory Study," *Journal of Marketing* 59 (April 1995), pp. 71–82.

3. For research on important outcomes associated with service recovery, see S. S. Tax, S. W. Brown, and M. Chandrashekaran, "Customer Evaluations of Service Complaint Experiences: Implications for Relationship Marketing," *Journal of Marketing* 62 (April 1998), pp. 60–76; S. S. Tax and S. W. Brown, "Recovering and Learning from Service Failure," *Sloan Management Review,* Fall 1998, pp. 75–88; A. K. Smith and R. N. Bolton, "An Experimental Investigation of Customer Reactions to Service Failure and Recovery Encounters," *Journal of Service Research* 1 (August 1998), pp. 65–81; S. W. Kelley, K. D. Hoffman, and M. A. Davis, "A Typology of Retail Failures and Recoveries," *Journal of Retailing* 69 (Winter 1993), pp. 429–52; R. N. Bolton, "A Dynamic Model of the Customer's Relationship with a Continuous Service Provider: The Role of Satisfaction," *Marketing Science* 17, no. 1 (1998), pp. 45–65; A. K. Smith and R. N. Bolton, "The Effect of Customers' Emotional Responses to Service Failures on Their Recovery Effort Evaluations and Satisfaction Judgments," *Journal of the Academy of Marketing Science,* 30 (Winter 2002), pp. 5–23.

4. Technical Assistance Research Program, "Consumer Complaint Handling in America: An Update Study" (Washington, DC: Department of Consumer Affairs, 1986).

5. B. Ettorre, "Phenomenal Promises That Mean Business," *Management Review,* March 1994, pp. 18–23.

6. M. Granier, J. Kemp, and A. Lawes, "Customer Complaint Handling—The Multimillion Pound Sinkhole: A Case of Customer Rage Unassuaged," study conducted by the Customer Care Alliance, 2004.

7. Tax and Brown, "Recovering and Learning from Service Failure."

8. Granier, Kemp, and Lawes, "Customer Complaint Handling—The Multimillion Pound Sinkhole."

9. See C. W. Hart, J. L. Heskett, and W. E. Sasser Jr., "The Profitable Art of Service

Recovery," *Harvard Business Review* 68 (July/August 1990), pp. 148–56; M. A. McCollough and S. G. Bharadwaj, "The Recovery Paradox: An Examination of Consumer Satisfaction in Relation to Disconfirmation, Service Quality, and Attribution Based Theories," in *Marketing Theory and Applications,* ed. C. T. Allen et al. (Chicago: American Marketing Association, 1992), p. 119.

10. Smith and Bolton, "An Experimental Investigation of Customer Reactions to Service Failure and Recovery Encounters."

11. M. A. McCullough, L. L. Berry, and M. S. Yadav, "An Empirical Investigation of Customer Satisfaction After Service Failure and Recovery," *Journal of Service Research,* 3 (November 2000), pp. 121–37.

12. J. G. Maxham III and R. G. Netemeyer, "A Longitudinal Study of Complaining Customers' Evaluations of Multiple Service Failures and Recovery Efforts," *Journal of Marketing* 66 (October 2002), pp. 57–71.

13. For research foundations on typologies of customer responses to failures, see R. L. Day and E. L. Landon Jr., "Towards a Theory of Consumer Complaining Behavior," in *Consumer and Industrial Buying Behavior,* ed. A. Woodside, J. Sheth, and P. Bennett (Amsterdam: North-Holland Publishing Company, 1977); J. Singh, "Consumer Complaint Intentions and Behavior: Definitional and Taxonomical Issues," *Journal of Marketing* 52 (January 1988), pp. 93–107; and J. Singh, "Voice, Exit, and Negative Word of mouth Behaviors: An Investigation Across Three Service Categories," *Journal of the Academy of Marketing Science* 18 (Winter 1990), pp. 1–15.

14. Smith and Bolton, "The Effect of Customers' Emotional Responses to Service Failures."

15. Ibid.

16. N. Stephens and K. P. Gwinner, "Why Don't Some People Complain? A Cognitive–Emotive Process Model of Consumer Complaining Behavior," *Journal of the Academy of Marketing Science* 26 (Spring 1998), pp. 172–89.

17. Ibid.

18. T. Hennig-Thurau, K. P. Gwinner, G. Walsh, and D. D. Gremler, "Electronic Word of mouth via Consumer-Opinion Platforms: What Motivates Consumers to Articulate Themselves on the Internet?" *Journal of Interactive Marketing* 18 (Winter 2004), pp. 38–52.

19. Many such websites exist; examples include www.untied.com (for United Airlines experiences), www.starbucked.com (for Starbucks), and www.walmart sucks.org (for Wal-Mart).

20. J. C. Ward and A. L. Ostrom, "Online Complaining via Customer-Created Web Sites: A Protest Framing Perspective," working paper, W. P. Carey School of Business, Arizona State University, 2004.

21. J. Singh, " A Typology of Consumer Dissatisfaction Response Styles," *Journal of Retailing* 66 (Spring 1990), pp. 57–99.

22. J. R. McColl-Kennedy and B. A. Sparks, "Application of Fairness Theory to Service Failures and Service Recovery," *Journal of Service Research* 5 (February 2003), pp. 251–66; M. Davidow, "Organizational Responses to Customer Complaints: What Works and What Doesn't," *Journal of Service Research* 5 (February 2003), pp. 225–50.

23. Granier, Kemp, and Lawes, "Customer Complaint Handling—The Multimillion Pound Sinkhole."

24. Davidow, "Organizational Responses to Customer Complaints."

25. See Tax, Brown, and Chandrashekaran, "Customer Evaluations of Service Complaint Experiences"; Tax and Brown, "Recovering and Learning from Service Failure."

26. Tax and Brown, "Recovering and Learning from Service Failure."

27. Smith and Bolton, "The Effect of Customers' Emotional Responses to Service Failures."

28. McCullough, Berry, and Yadav, "An Empirical Investigation of Customer Satisfaction After Service Failure and Recovery."

29. A. S. Mattila, "The Impact of Relationship Type on Customer Loyalty in a Context of Service Failures," *Journal of Service Research* 4 (November 2001), pp. 91–101; see also R. L. Hess Jr., S. Ganesan, and N. M. Klein, "Service Failure and Recovery: The Impact of Relationship Factors on Customer Satisfaction," *Journal of the Academy of Marketing Science* 31 (Spring 2003), pp. 127–45; R. Priluck, "Relationship Marketing Can Mitigate Product and Service Failures," *Journal of Services Marketing* 17, no. 1 (2003), pp. 37–52.

30. H. S. Bansal and S. F. Taylor, "The Service Provider Switching Model (SPSM)," *Journal of Service Research* 2 (November 1999), pp. 200–218.

31. S. M. Keaveney and M. Parthasarathy, "Customer Switching Behavior in Online Services: An Exploratory Study of the Role of Selected Attitudinal, Behavioral, and Demographic Factors," *Journal of the Academy of Marketing Science* 29, no. 4 (2001), pp. 374–90.

32. I. Roos, "Switching Processes in Customer Relationships," *Journal of Service Research* 2 (August 1999), pp. 68–85.

33. Keaveney, "Customer Switching Behavior in Service Industries."

34. A. Parasuraman, V. A. Zeithaml, and L. L. Berry, "SERVQUAL: A Multiple-Item Scale for Measuring Consumer Perceptions of Service Quality," *Journal of Retailing* 64 (Spring 1988), pp. 64–79.

35. R. B. Chase and D. M. Stewart, "Make Your Service Fail-Safe," *Sloan Management Review,* Spring 1994, pp. 35–44.

36. Ibid.

37. F. R. Reichheld and W. E. Sasser Jr., "Zero Defections: Quality Comes to Services," *Harvard Business Review,* September/October 1990, pp. 105–7.

38. L. M. Fisher, "Here Comes Front-Office Automation," *Strategy and Business* 13 (Fourth Quarter, 1999), pp. 53–65; and R. A. Shaffer, "Handling Customer Service on the Web," *Fortune,* March 1, 1999, pp. 204, 208.

39. S. W. Brown, "Service Recovery Through IT," *Marketing Management,* Fall 1997, pp. 25–27.

40. Davidow, "Organizational Responses to Customer Complaints."

41. J. Dunning, A. Pecotich, and A. O'Cass, "What Happens When Things Go Wrong? Retail Sales Explanations and Their Effects," *Psychology and Marketing* 21, no. 7 (2004), pp. 553–72; McColl-Kennedy and Sparks, "Application of Fairness Theory to Service Failures and Service Recovery"; Davidow, "Organizational Responses to Customer Complaints."

42. Hess, Ganesan, and Klein, "Service Failure and Recovery"; Priluck, "Relationship Marketing Can Mitigate Product and Service Failures."

43. T. DeWitt and M. K. Brady, "Rethinking Service Recovery Strategies: The Effect of Rapport on Consumer Responses to Service Failure," *Journal of Service Research* 6 (November 2003), pp. 193–207.

44. Hess, Ganesan, and Klein, "Service Failure and Recovery."

45. L. L. Berry and A. Parasuraman, *Marketing Services* (New York: Free Press, 1991), p. 52.

46. F. F. Reichheld, "Learning from Customer Defections," *Harvard Business Review,* March/April 1996, pp. 56–69.

47. Ibid.

48. A. L. Ostrom and C. W. L. Hart, "Service Guarantees: Research and Practice," in *Handbook of Services Marketing and Management,* ed. D. Iacobucci and T. Swartz (Thousand Oaks, CA: Sage Publications, 2000), pp. 299–316.

49. See ibid.; C. W. L. Hart, "The Power of Unconditional Guarantees," *Harvard Business Review,* July/August 1988, pp. 54–62; and C. W. L. Hart, *Extraordinary Guarantees* (New York: AMACOM, 1993).

50. A. L. Ostrom and D. Iacobucci, "The Effect of Guarantees on Consumers' Evaluation of Services," *Journal of Services Marketing* 12, no. 5 (1998), pp. 362–78; S. B. Lidén and P. Skålén, "The Effect of Service Guarantees on Service Recovery," *International Journal of Service Industry Management* 14, no. 1 (2003), pp.-36–58.

51. Ostrom and Hart, "Service Guarantees."

52. J. Wirtz and D. Kum, "Designing Service Guarantees: Is Full Satisfaction the Best You Can Guarantee?" *Journal of Services Marketing* 15, no. 4 (2001), pp. 282–99.

53. Example cited in Ostrom and Hart, "Service Guarantees."

54. As quoted in *Strategy Magazine*, November 2005, p. 15.

55. J. Wirtz, D. Kum, and K. S. Lee, "Should a Firm with a Reputation for Outstanding Service Quality Offer a Service Guarantee?" *Journal of Services Marketing* 14, no. 6 (2000), pp. 502–12.

56. J. Wirtz, "Development of a Service Guarantee Model," *Asia Pacific Journal of Management* 15 (April 1998), pp. 51–75; Wirtz and Kim, "Consumer Cheating on Service Guarantees," *Journal of the Academy of Marketing Science* 32 (Spring 2004), pp. 159–75.

57. Wirtz, "Development of a Service Guarantee Model."

58. Ostrom and Iacobucci, "The Effect of Guarantees."

59. Wirtz, "Development of a Service Guarantee Model."

PART 4

Aligning Service Design and Standards

III

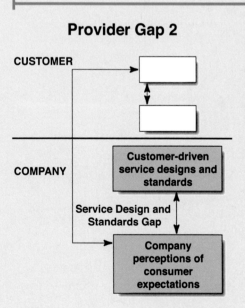

Provider Gap 2

CUSTOMER

COMPANY

Customer-driven service designs and standards

Service Design and Standards Gap

Company perceptions of consumer expectations

Meeting customer expectations of service requires not only understanding what the expectations are, but also taking action on that knowledge. Action takes several forms: designing services based on customer requirements, setting service standards to ensure that employees perform as customers expect, and providing physical evidence that creates the appropriate cues and ambience for service. When action does not take place, there is a gap—a service design and standards gap—as shown in the accompanying figure. Having the wrong standards—or no standards at all—can make Provider Gap 2 very large. Once Gap 1 is closed, we can be confident that management knows what customers expect. Management must then *do* something with this knowledge. In this section you will learn to identify the causes of Gap 2 as well as effective strategies for closing this gap.

Chapter 9 describes the tools that are most effective in service development and design, especially a tool called service blueprinting. Chapter 10 helps you differentiate between company-defined standards and customer-defined standards and to recognize how they can be developed. Chapter 11 explores the strategic importance of physical evidence, the variety of roles it plays, and strategies for effectively designing physical evidence and the servicescape to meet customer expectations.

Chapter

9

Service Development and Design

Provider Gap 2

1. Describe the challenges inherent in service design.

2. Present the stages and unique elements of the new service development process.

3. Demonstrate the value of service blueprinting and how to develop and read service blueprints.

4. Present lessons learned in choosing and implementing high-performance service innovations.

SATELLITE RADIO—AN INNOVATIVE NEW SERVICE IN CANADA

Have you ever considered starting your own service business? What type of service would it be? What would you do first? Assuming you understood your market and had a good feel for potential customers' needs and expectations, how would you go about designing the service to meet those needs? If you were starting a business to manufacture a new product, you would most likely begin by designing and building a prototype of your new product. But how could you do this for a service?

These are the kinds of questions that satellite radio broadcasters XM Radio Canada (www.xmradio.ca) and Sirius Radio (www.siriuscanada.ca) probably asked before launching their services in Canada in 2005. While the technology itself is not particularly new, satellite radio service availability in

Source: Courtesy of XM Satellite Radio.

Canada is. After gaining regulatory approval by the CRTC, satellite radio was able to launch in the Canadian market in November 2005 and is expected to have 3.5 million subscribers by 2015.

Whereas traditional radio has been locally based and paid for by commercials, with varied reception quality, satellite radio is global and commercial-free (paid for by subscription fees), and offers consistent sound quality comparable to that of a CD. But convincing customers to pay for something that has always been free may be a challenge. John Bitove, CEO of XM Canada satellite radio service, does not see it that way. As he states, it is all about communicating the superiority of the service: "Did you ever think you'd pay for TV when you used to get five channels over the air for free? Did you ever think you'd pay for bottled water? In both cases you pay. Why? You want better choice, you want better quality, and that's what satellite radio is all about." The service offering, then, must be carefully designed so that customers feel as though satellite radio is a better alternative or at least complementary to traditional, free radio.

Even if broadcasters convince listeners to pay for this new service because of its superiority, the services offered will likely continue to evolve as satellite radio companies seek to expand their business. For instance, at the time of writing, satellite service has only been available in Canada for six months, but already changes are being made and new services added in response to customer demand. Realizing that listeners were seeking local content, satellite stations introduced a new service—local weather and traffic information broadcasts in urban areas.[1]

To learn more about satellite radio in Canada, visit the Canadian Radio-television and Telecommunications Commission website (www.crtc.gc.ca).

So what causes new products and services such as those offered by Sirius Radio to fail or succeed? If you decide to start your own business, what can you do to protect yourself as much as possible from failure?

A study of 11,000 new products launched by 77 manufacturing, service, and consumer products companies found that only 56 percent of new offerings are still on the market five years later.[2] Failures can be traced to a number of causes: no unique benefits offered, insufficient demand, unrealistic goals for the new product/service, poor fit between the new service and others within the organization's portfolio, poor location, insufficient financial backing, or failure to take the necessary time to develop and introduce the product.[3] An analysis of over 60 studies on new product and service success showed that the dominant and most reliable predictors of success for new introductions relate to *product/service characteristics* (product meeting customer needs, product advantage over competing products, technological sophistication); *strategy characteristics* (dedicated human resources to support the initiative, dedicated R&D focused on the new product initiative); *process characteristics* (marketing, predevelopment, technological, and launch proficiencies); and *marketplace characteristics* (market potential).[4]

Unfortunately, many good service ideas fail because of development, design, and specification flaws, topics that are emphasized in this chapter. As you can imagine, developing brand-new services presents a wonderful opportunity to design in appropriate customer driver standards of service at the very beginning of the process. This attention to design helps to significantly reduce the size of Gap 2.

CHALLENGES OF SERVICE DESIGN

Because services are largely intangible and process-oriented (such as a hospital stay, a golf lesson, or an NHL hockey game), they are difficult to describe and communicate. When services are delivered over a long period—a week's resort vacation, a six-month consulting engagement, ten weeks on a Weight Watchers program—their complexity increases, and they become even more difficult to define and describe. Further, because services are delivered by employees to customers, they are variable. Rarely are two services experienced in the same way. These characteristics of services are the challenge involved in designing services.

Because services cannot be touched, examined, or tried out, people frequently resort to words in their efforts to describe them. Lynn Shostack, a pioneer in developing design concepts for services, has pointed out four risks of attempting to describe services in words alone.[5] The first risk is *oversimplification*. Shostack points out that "to say that 'portfolio management' means 'buying and selling stocks' is like describing the space shuttle as 'something that flies.' Some people will picture a bird, some a helicopter, and some an angel" (p. 76). Words are simply inadequate to describe a complex service system.

The second risk is *incompleteness*. In describing services, people (employees, managers, customers) tend to omit details or elements of the service with which they are not familiar. A person might do a fairly credible job of describing how a discount stock brokerage service takes orders from customers. But would that person be able to describe fully how the monthly statements are created, how the interactive computer system works, and how these two elements of the service are integrated into the order-taking process?

The third risk is *subjectivity*. Any one person describing a service in words will be biased by personal experiences and degree of exposure to the service. There is a natural (and mistaken) tendency to assume that because all people have gone to a fast-food restaurant, they all understand what that service is. Persons working in different functional areas of the same service organization (a marketing person, an operations person, a finance person) are likely to describe the service very differently as well, biased by their own functional blinders.

A final risk of describing services using words alone is *biased interpretation*. No two people will define "responsive," "quick," or "flexible" in exactly the same way. For example, a supervisor or manager may suggest to a front-line service employee that the employee should try to be more flexible or responsive in providing service to the customer. Unless the term "flexibility" is further defined, the employee is likely to interpret the word differently from the manager.

All these risks become very apparent in the new service development process, when organizations may be attempting to design services never before experienced by customers. It is critical that all involved (managers, front-line employees, and behind-the-scenes support staff) be working with the same concepts of the new service, based on customer needs and expectations. For a service that already exists, any attempt to improve it will also suffer unless everyone has a shared vision of the service and associated issues.

In the following sections of this chapter, we present approaches for new service development and design to address these unique challenges.

NEW SERVICE DEVELOPMENT

Research suggests that products that are designed and introduced via the steps in a structured planning framework have a greater likelihood of ultimate success than those not developed within a framework.[6] The fact that services are intangible makes it even more imperative for a new service development system to have four basic characteristics. (1) It must be objective, not subjective. (2) It must be precise, not vague. (3) It must be fact-driven, not opinion-driven. (4) It must be methodological, not philosophical.[7] Although the process of developing new services should be structured and should follow a set of defined stages, it should not become overly rigid or bureaucratized. Such structure taken to an extreme can result in a rigid approach that could waste time and/or allow competitors to get out in front. Thus, common sense must dictate when flexibility and speed will override the structure.

Often new services are introduced on the basis of managers' and employees' subjective opinions, rather than on objective designs incorporating data about customer perceptions, market needs, and feasibility. A new service design process may be imprecise in defining the nature of the service concept because the people involved believe either that intangible processes cannot be defined precisely or that "everyone knows what we mean." Neither of these explanations or defences for imprecision is justifiable, as we illustrate in this chapter's model for new service development.[8]

FIGURE 9.1

Madame Zoe has just developed a new service, but perhaps her subjective impressions are better than those of most managers!

Source: By permission of Dave Coverly and Creators Syndicate Inc.

Because services are produced and consumed simultaneously and often involve interaction between employees and customers, it is also critical that the new service development involve both employees and customers. Employees frequently *are* the service, or at least they perform the service, and thus their involvement can be very beneficial. Contact employees are close to customers and can identify customer needs for new services. Involving employees in the process also increases the likelihood of success because employees can identify the organizational issues that need to be addressed to support the delivery of the service to customers.[9] For example, in order to have operations, IT, and marketing work better together, many organizations, including Bell Canada, Travelocity.com, VIA Rail, and AIR MILES, are putting the customer at the centre of their organizations and using this customer focus to understand each "moment of truth" the customer experiences during their experience with the brand. Bell Canada, for instance, is working on a program called "simplicity certification," designed to ensure that Bell extensively reviews all new and modified services before they go to market. This includes looking at how each step of the new service looks and feels from the customer's point of view.

Because customers often actively participate in service delivery, they too should be involved in the development process. Marriott Corporation is well known for involving guests in the design of its hotel rooms. Bank of America has also been very successful with developing new service innovations in branch banking by relying on results of a series of experiments in its Atlanta branches.[10] The experiments are designed to more rigorously test, in real time and with real customers, new service innovations that the bank is considering (see the Global Feature later in this chapter for details about Bank of America's experiments). In this way the bank gains actual customer feedback as well as employee reactions to new service ideas.

TYPES OF NEW SERVICES

As we describe the new service development process, remember that not all new services are "new" to the same degree. New service options can run the gamut from major innovations to minor style changes:[11]

- *Major or radical innovations* are new services for markets as yet undefined. Past examples include the first broadcast television services and FedEx's introduction of nationwide, overnight small package delivery. Our Technology Spotlight features eBay, a company that epitomizes radical service innovations.

- *Startup businesses* consist of new services for a market that is already served by existing products that meet the same generic needs. An example is online banking for financial transactions, and door-to-door airport shuttle services that compete with traditional taxi and limousine services.

- *New services for the currently served market* offer existing customers a service not previously available from the company (although it may be available from other companies). Examples include airlines offering fax, phone, and Internet service during flights.

- *Service line extensions* represent augmentations of the existing service line, such as a restaurant adding new menu items and a university adding new courses or degrees.

- *Service improvements* are the most common service innovation. Changes in features of services that are already offered might involve faster execution of an existing service process or extended hours of service.

Technology Spotlight

eBay: A Radical Service Innovation

When eBay (www.ebay.ca) was founded, it was not much more than an online flea market for individuals seeking to buy and sell old or unique items to other individuals. The original eBay concept was to provide the online service needed to facilitate these basic, simple trades among buyers and sellers. In the intervening years, the company has grown into a powerhouse of Internet retailing, payment solutions, and communications, with over 180 million users worldwide and $44 billion in annual trade. Meg Whitman, the company's now-famous CEO, describes eBay as a "dynamic self-regulating economy."

Clearly, eBay is a radical service innovation. Nothing like it existed before, and its limits and bounds are yet unknown. From basic trading services, the company has evolved to a complex self-regulating system that is completely dependent on its community of members. Services offered by eBay now include PayPal, an online payment system, education classes for prospective sellers, and a developer's program for members who want to create their own software solutions for making eBay transactions more efficient and effective. Going far beyond its original focus on individual members, eBay has introduced important services for small businesses to help address issues such as improving cash flow, hiring, and shipping. eBay offers employment services through Monster.com, integrated shipping solutions through Canada Post, and cost-effective online payment through PayPal. More than 430,000 small business sellers are trading through eBay, and the number of business-related items for sale on eBay doubled to one million in just one year.

One of the most important aspects of eBay's success is its member community and the support and services they provide to each other. The company encourages open communication among members through discussion and chat boards that are actively used. These member-facilitated services and communications can be viewed as new service innovations in their own right. There are even "neighbourhood watch" groups that ensure that everyone in the community learns and follows the etiquette and behaviour norms that govern the community. Through an ongoing feedback system, members rate each other in terms of reliability and quality; this system provides a "self-policing" orientation for the community. (As the community has

Source: www.ebay.com.

grown, more formalized fraud protection and policing services have been initiated by the company as well.) Extending the community aspect further, some members even interact with each other offline, going so far as to vacation together and buy special items for one another. One group even spent vacation time doing home repairs for an eBay member in need. eBay has become a part of many people's lives around the world.

Strategically, one of the most important elements of eBay's success has been its unrelenting devotion to its members and its willingness to listen. Being innovative in developing new services is dependent on listening to customers. One of eBay's most cherished institutions, according to Whitman, is the Voice of the Customer program. eBay regularly brings in groups of customers to ask them how they work and how eBay can change to make things better. At least twice a week the company holds hour-long teleconferences to poll members on new features or policies. eBay's listening ear encourages constant complaints and suggestions to the company. And unlike many companies, eBay responds. Change is constant on eBay's site and in its service features—almost to a fault, say some users. According to the company's senior vice-president of international operations, "Some of the terms you learn in business school—drive, force, commit—don't apply … we're over here listening, adapting, enabling." The result is that eBay users feel like owners, and their voices have shaped the company, its practices, the site itself, and the community norms.

eBay is a growing, dynamic community that has evolved from a radical service innovation made possible through technology. Undoubtedly it will continue to evolve and play an important role in the world of retail and business trade.

Sources: R. D. Hof, "The eBay Economy," *BusinessWeek,* August 25, 2003, pp. 124–28; www.ebay.com, 2004; D. McDonald, "Meet eBay's New Postman," *Business 2.0,* September 2004, pp. 52–54; www.ebay.com, 2006.

- *Style changes* represent the most modest service innovations, although they are often highly visible and can have significant effects on customer perceptions, emotions, and attitudes. Changing the colour scheme of a restaurant, revising the logo for an organization, or painting aircraft a different colour all represent style changes. These innovations are similar to how packaging changes are used for consumer products.

STAGES IN NEW SERVICE DEVELOPMENT

In this section we focus on the actual steps to be followed in new service development. Much of this section has direct parallels in the new product development process for manufactured goods. Because of the inherent characteristics of services, however, the development process for new services requires adaptations.[12] Figure 9.2 shows the basic principles and steps in new service development. Although these steps may be similar to those for manufactured goods, their implementation is significantly different.[13] The challenges typically lie in defining the concept in the early stages of the development process and again at the prototype development stage. Partly because of these challenges, service firms are generally less likely to carry out a structured development process than are their manufacturing counterparts.[14]

An underlying assumption of new product development process models is that new product ideas can be dropped at any stage of the process if they do not satisfy the criteria for success at that particular stage.[15] Figure 9.2 shows the checkpoints (represented by stop signs) that separate critical stages of the development process. The checkpoints specify requirements that a new service must meet before it can proceed to the next stage of development.

FIGURE 9.2

New Service
Development Process

Sources: Booz-Allen & Hamilton, Inc., *New Product Management for the 1980s* (New York: Booz-Allen & Hamilton, 1982); M. J. Bowers, "An Exploration into New Service Development: Organization, Process, and Structure," doctoral dissertation, Texas A&M University, 1985; A. Khurana and S. R. Rosenthal, "Integrating the Fuzzy Front End of New Product Development," *Sloan Management Review,* Winter 1997, pp. 103–20; and R. G. Cooper, *Winning at New Products,* 3rd ed. (Cambridge, MA: Perseus Publishing, 2001).

Front-end planning

- **Business strategy development or review**

- **New service strategy development**

- **Idea generation**
  - Screen ideas against new service strategy **STOP**

- **Concept development and evaluation**
  - Test concept with customers and employees **STOP**

- **Business analysis**
  - Test for profitability and feasibility **STOP**

Implementation

- **Service development and testing**
  - Conduct service prototype test **STOP**

- **Market testing**
  - Test service and other marketing mix elements **STOP**

- **Commercialization**

- **Postintroduction evaluation**

New service development is rarely a linear process. Many companies are finding that to speed up new service development, some steps can be worked on simultaneously, and in some instances a step may even be skipped. The overlapping of steps and simultaneous development of various pieces of the process has been referred to as "flexible product development." This type of flexible, speedy process is particularly important in technology industries, in which products and services evolve extremely quickly. In these environments, computer technology lets companies monitor customer opinions and needs during development and change the final offering right up until it is launched. Often, the next version of the service is in planning stages at the same time that the current version is being launched.[16] Even if the stages are handled simultaneously, however, the important checkpoints noted in the figure must be assessed to maximize chances of success.

The process shown in Figure 9.2 is divided into two sections: front-end planning and implementation. The front end determines what service concepts will be developed, whereas the back end executes or implements the service concept. When asked where the greatest weaknesses in product and service innovation occur, managers typically report problems with the "fuzzy front end."[17] The front end is called "fuzzy" because of its relative abstractness, which is even more apparent with intangible and variable services than with manufactured products.

SERVICE BLUEPRINTING

A stumbling block in developing new services (and in improving existing services) is the difficulty of describing and depicting the service at the concept development, service development, and market test stages. One of the keys to matching service specifications to customer expectations is the ability to describe critical service steps objectively and to depict them so that employees, customers, and managers alike know what the service is, can see their role in its delivery, and understand all the steps and flows involved in the service process. In this section of the chapter we look in depth at service blueprinting, a useful tool for designing and specifying intangible service processes.[18]

What Is a Service Blueprint?

The manufacturing and construction industries have a long tradition of engineering and design. Can you imagine a house being built without detailed specifications? Can you imagine a car, a computer, or even a simple product like a child's toy or a shampoo being produced without concrete and detailed plans, written specifications, and engineering drawings? Yet services commonly lack concrete specifications. A service, even a complex one, might be introduced without any formal, objective depiction of the process.

A service blueprint is a picture or map that accurately portrays the service system so that the different people involved in providing it can understand and deal with it objectively regardless of their roles or their individual points of view. Blueprints are particularly useful at the design stage of service development. A service blueprint visually displays the service by simultaneously depicting the process of service delivery, the points of customer contact, the roles of customers and employees, and the visible elements of the service (see Figure 9.3). It provides a way to break a service down into its logical components and to depict the steps or tasks in the process, the means by which the tasks are executed, and the evidence of service as the customer experiences it.

Global Feature

New Service Experiments at Bank of America

Through a series of mergers and acquisitions over the last three decades, Bank of America has become one of the largest banks in the United States, operating in 21 states and serving approximately 27 million households and 2 million businesses. In recent years, the opportunities for further growth by acquisition have become limited, and the bank has turned to other strategies for growth—particularly growth through new and improved services.

One major initiative at the Bank of America is its Innovation and Development (I&D) Team, a corporate unit charged with pioneering new services and service delivery approaches aimed at strengthening customer relationships and improving efficiencies. Instead of focusing on growth by acquisition, this group focuses on organic growth of the company through attracting more customers and fulfilling more of their needs. Recognizing that it did not have a formal new service development process in place, the bank looked to traditional and well-established prototype testing procedures in the manufacturing sector for guidance. Although these models were very helpful, bank strategists realized that they would need to fine-tune these formal research and development approaches to fit the intangible, simultaneous nature of service processes. Live experimentation was the approach that the bank chose to use in testing its new ideas.

To accomplish its objectives, the I&D team has created an "innovation market" in Atlanta, Georgia, where it has set up a series of experiments to test innovative services and approaches to branch banking. These "live experiments" are conducted in actual bank branches with real customers. The first step was to reconfigure the 20 Atlanta branches into three alternative branch models. The first model is an "express centre" that is efficient, modern, and quick—and focused on getting customers in and out efficiently. Express centres are housed in modern facilities that reinforce the concept. The second model is a "financial centre," spacious and relaxed, in which trained staff and advanced technologies offer high-end, sophisticated banking services such as stock trading and portfolio management. The rest of the banks in the innovation market were configured as "traditional centres," with familiar decor and conventional banking services.

Once the test branches were reconfigured, the I&D team followed a structured process to come up with experimental services and service improvements worthy of testing. Every potential idea was entered into a spreadsheet called an "idea portfolio" that included a description of the idea, the process or problem it addressed, and the customer segment affected by the idea. The I&D team then categorized and prioritized the ideas on the basis of projected impact on customers and the fit with the bank's strategy.

More than 200 new ideas were generated, and 40 of them had been tested through formal experiments. For example, one experiment tested whether the presence of TV monitors set to CNN in the bank could reduce the perceived waiting time of patrons. Once the I&D team determined that the presence of TV monitors might indeed reduce waiting time perceptions and thus increase customer satisfaction, the bank proceeded to evaluate the costs and benefits of installing TVs in all branches over a certain size. They also continued with testing of placement of monitors within the branches as well as the effects of programming beyond CNN.

By introducing formal idea-generation processes and live experimentation into its innovation process, Bank of America and its customers have benefited. Within the innovation market, customer satisfaction has significantly improved and the experimental branches have drawn in new customers. In the process, the bank has also learned many lessons and overcome many of the challenges inherent in developing new services. Experimenting with real people (employees and customers) in actual service delivery settings is much different than running a highly controlled prototype test of a product in a laboratory. Bank of America's experience illustrates clearly that product testing approaches that are second nature to manufacturers and IT developers require adaptation and refinement in a services setting.

Source: S. Thomke, "R&D Comes to Services: Bank of America's Pathbreaking Experiments," *Harvard Business Review,* April 2003, pp. 70–79.

FIGURE 9.3

Service Blueprinting

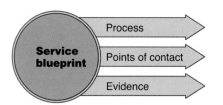

Service blueprinting
A tool for simultaneously depicting the service process, the points of customer contact, and the evidence of service from the customer's point of view.

Blueprinting has its origins in a variety of fields and techniques, including logistics, industrial engineering, decision theory, and computer systems analysis—all of which deal with the definition and explanation of processes.[19] Because services are "experiences" rather than objects, blueprinting is a particularly useful tool for describing them.

Blueprint Components

The key components of service blueprints are shown in Figure 9.4.[20] They are customer actions, "onstage" contact employee actions, "backstage" contact employee actions, and support processes. The conventions for drawing service blueprints are not rigidly defined, and thus the particular symbols used, the number of horizontal lines in the blueprint, and the particular labels for each part of the blueprint may vary somewhat depending on what you read and the complexity of the blueprint being described. These variations are not a problem as long as you keep in mind the purpose of the blueprint and view it simply as a useful tool rather than as a set of rigid rules for designing services.

The *customer actions* area encompasses the steps, choices, activities, and interactions that the customer performs in the process of purchasing, consuming, and evaluating the service. The total customer experience is apparent in this area of the blueprint. In a legal services example, the customer actions might include a decision to contact an attorney, phone calls to the attorney, face-to-face meetings, receipt of documents, and receipt of a bill.

FIGURE 9.4

Service Blueprint Components

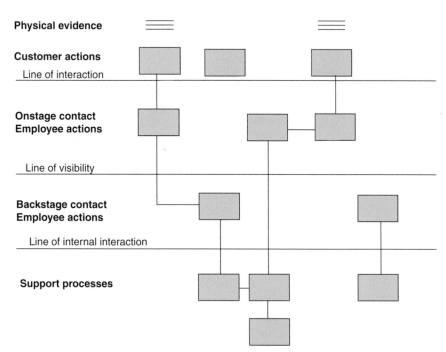

Parallelling the customer actions are two areas of contact employee actions. The steps and activities that the contact employee performs that are visible to the customer are the *onstage contact employee actions.* In the legal services setting, the actions of the attorney (the contact employee) that are visible to the client are, for example, the initial interview, intermediate meetings, and final delivery of legal documents.

Employee actions that occur behind the scenes to support the onstage activities are the *backstage contact employee actions.* In the example, anything the attorney does behind the scenes to prepare for the meetings or to prepare the final documents will appear in this section of the blueprint, together with phone call contacts the customer has with the attorney or other front-line staff in the firm. All *non-visible* contact employee actions are shown in this area of the blueprint.

The *support processes* section of the blueprint covers the internal services, steps, and interactions that take place to support the contact employees in delivering the service. Again, in our legal example, any service support activities such as legal research by staff, preparation of documents, and secretarial support to set up meetings will be shown in the support processes area of the blueprint.

At the very top of the blueprint you see the *physical evidence* of the service. Typically, above each point of contact the actual physical evidence of the service is listed. In the legal example, the physical evidence of the face-to-face meeting with the attorney would be such items as office decor, written documents, lawyer's clothing, and so forth.

The four key action areas are separated by three horizontal lines. First is the *line of interaction,* representing direct interactions between the customer and the organization. Anytime a vertical line crosses the horizontal line of interaction, a direct contact between the customer and the organization, or a service encounter, has occurred. The next horizontal line is the critically important *line of visibility.* This line separates all service activities that are visible to the customer from those that are not visible. In reading blueprints it is obvious whether the consumer is provided with much visible evidence of the service simply by analyzing how much of the service occurs above the line of visibility. This line also separates what the contact employees do onstage from what they do backstage. For example, in a medical examination situation, the doctor would perform the actual exam and answer the patient's questions above the line of visibility, or onstage, whereas she might read the patient's chart in advance and dictate notes following the exam below the line of visibility, or backstage. The third line is the *line of internal interaction,* which separates contact employee activities from those of other service support activities and people. Vertical lines cutting across the line of internal interaction represent internal service encounters.

One of the most significant differences between service blueprints and other process flow diagrams is the inclusion of customers and their views of the service process. In fact, in designing effective service blueprints it is recommended that the diagramming start with the customer's view of the process and work backward into the delivery system. The boxes shown within each action area depict steps performed or experienced by the actors at that level.

Service Blueprint Examples

Figures 9.5 and 9.6 show service blueprints for two different services: express mail delivery and an overnight hotel stay.[21] These blueprints are deliberately kept very simple, showing only the most basic steps in the services. Complex diagrams might be developed for each step, and the internal processes might be much more fully

FIGURE 9.5   Blueprint for Express Mail Delivery Service

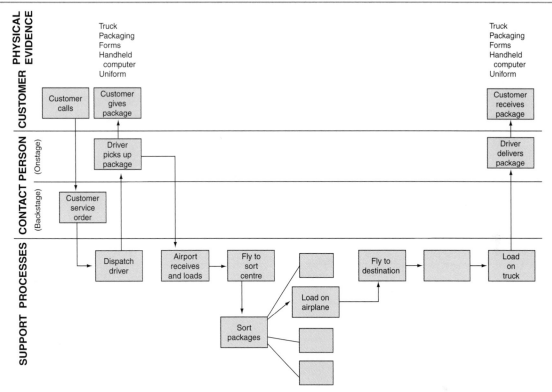

developed. In addition to the four action areas separated by the three horizontal lines, these blueprints also show the physical evidence of the service from the customer's point of view.

Examine the express mail delivery blueprint in Figure 9.5. It is clear that from the customer's point of view there are only three steps in the service process: the phone call, the package pickup, and the package delivery. The process is relatively standardized; the people who perform the service are the phone-order-taker and the delivery person; and the physical evidence is the document package, the transmittal forms, the truck, and the handheld computer. In some cases the customer may also engage the online or phone-based package tracking system. The complex process that occurs behind the line of visibility is of little interest or concern to the customer. However, for the three visible-to-the-customer steps to proceed effectively, invisible internal services are needed. What these steps are and the fact that they support the delivery of the service to the external customer are apparent from the blueprint.

Any of the steps in the blueprint might be exploded into a detailed blueprint if needed for a particular purpose. For example, if the delivery company learned that the "unload and sort" step was taking too long and causing unacceptable delays in delivery, that step could be blueprinted in much greater detail to isolate the problems.

In the case of the overnight hotel stay depicted in Figure 9.6, the customer obviously is more involved in the service than he is in the express mail service. The guest

FIGURE 9.6   Blueprint for Overnight Hotel Stay Service

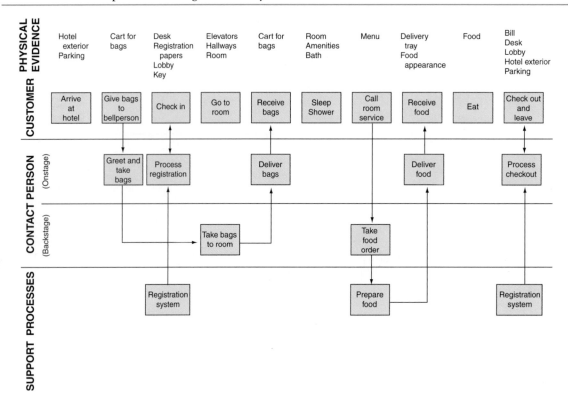

first checks in, then goes to the hotel room where a variety of steps take place (receiving bags, sleeping, showering, eating breakfast, and so on), and finally checks out. Imagine how much more complex this process could be and how many more interactions might occur if the service blueprint depicted a week-long vacation at the hotel, or even a three-day business conference. The service blueprint makes clear also (by reading across the line of interaction) those employees with whom the guest interacts and thus provide evidence of the service to the customer. Several interactions occur with a variety of hotel employees including the bellperson, the front desk clerk, the food service order-taker, and the food delivery person. Each step in the customer action area is also associated with various forms of physical evidence, from the hotel parking area and hotel exterior and interior to the forms used at guest registration, the lobby, the room, and the food. The hotel facility itself is critical in communicating the image of the hotel company, in providing satisfaction for the guest through the manner in which the hotel room is designed and maintained, and in facilitating the actions and interactions of both the guest and the employees of the hotel. In the hotel case, the process is relatively complex (although again somewhat standardized), the people providing the service are a variety of front-line employees, and the physical evidence includes everything from the guest registration form to the design of the lobby and room to the uniforms worn by front-line employees.

FIGURE 9.7

The Belfry Theatre in Victoria is a case study in designing service performance as theatre.

Source: Belfry Theatre/Photo by T. Gregg Eligh/Photo manipulation by Liam Regan.

Designing Service Performance as Theatre

An interesting extension to the work on service blueprinting comes from the research of F. Ian Stuart and Stephen Tax. According to Stuart and Tax, "Insights into managing services constantly evolve, but one fundamental principle remains: Services are performances. Despite this, most service firms still focus on delivering intangible products. ... An alternate view is for firms to consider designing and staging memorable personal experiences for their customers or, simply stated, designing performances" (p. 8).[22]

To learn more about how to design performances, the researchers turned to the Belfry Theatre in Victoria, British Columbia (see Figure 9.7). Using a case study methodology, they identified a number of key lessons that staging a play can teach firms about designing service performances:[23]

- Place extensive reliance on integrating mechanisms.

- Seek improvement through continuous experimentation.

- Share responsibilities.

- Continuously strive for authenticity.

- Seek total role immersion.

- See the Director as Facilitator.

Theatres have, after all, mastered the art of staging a performance, opening on time, and, usually, opening at peak performance levels. Lighting, sound, scripts, props, and actors interact to deliver performances that have been endlessly rehearsed. Think of the design work that went into Mirvish Productions' recent staging of *The Lord of the Rings* in Toronto. The play took four years of development, six months of rehearsal, and seven weeks of previews. Clearly, theatre productions have much to

FIGURE 9.8

The Toronto premiere of *The Lord of the Rings* took four years of development and six months of rehearsals.

Source: CP/Aaron Harris.

teach us about the rigour and commitment needed to stage memorable performances (see Figure 9.8).

Blueprints for Technology-Delivered Self-Service

To this point all our discussion of service blueprints has related to services that are delivered in person, services in which employees interact directly with customers at some point in the process. But what about technology-delivered services like self-service websites (Expedia's travel information site, Cisco Systems' customer self-service site) and interactive kiosks (ATMs, airline self-check in machines)? Can service blueprinting be used effectively to design these types of services? Certainly it can, but the lines of demarcation change, and some blueprint labels may need to be adapted.

If no employees are involved in the service (except when there is a problem or the service does not function as planned), the contact person areas of the blueprint are not needed. Instead, the area above the line of visibility can be used to illustrate the interface between the customer and the computer website or the physical interaction with the kiosk. This area can be relabelled onstage technology. The backstage contact person actions area would be irrelevant in this case.

If the service involves a combination of human and technology interfaces, as with airline computerized check-in, the onstage area can be cut into two distinct spaces divided by an additional horizontal line. In the airline computerized check-in example, the human contact with the airline employee who takes the bags and checks identification would be shown in one area and the technology interactions with the check-in computer kiosk would be shown in the second area, both above the line of visibility.

Reading and Using Service Blueprints

A service blueprint can be read in a variety of ways, depending on the purpose. If the purpose is to understand the customer's view of the process or the customer experience, the blueprint can be read from left to right, tracking the events in the customer action area. Questions that might be asked include these: How is the service initiated

Benefits of Service Blueprinting

1. Provides an overview so employees can relate "what I do" to the service viewed as an integrated whole, thus reinforcing a customer-oriented focus among employees.

2. Identifies fail points—that is, weak links of the chain of service activities, which can be the target of continuous quality improvement.

3. Line of interaction between external customers and employees illuminates the customer's role and demonstrates where the customer experiences quality, thus contributing to informed service design.

4. Line of visibility promotes a conscious decision on what customers should see and which employees will be in contact with customers, thus facilitating rational service design.

5. Line of internal interaction clarifies interfaces across departmental lines, with their inherent interdependencies, thus strengthening continuous quality improvement.

6. Stimulates strategic discussions by illuminating the elements and connections that constitute the service. Those who participate in strategic sessions tend to exaggerate the significance of their own special function and perspective unless a common ground for an integrated view of the service is provided.

7. Provides a basis for identifying and assessing cost, revenue, and capital invested in each element of the service.

8. Constitutes a rational basis for both external and internal marketing. For example, the service map [blueprint] makes it easier for an advertising agency or an in-house promotion team to overview a service and select essential messages for communication.

9. Facilitates a top-down, bottom-up approach to quality improvement. It enables managers to identify, channel, and support quality improvement efforts of grass-roots employees working on both front-line and support teams. Employee work teams can create service maps [blueprints] and thus more clearly apply and communicate their experience and suggestions for improvements.

Source: Reprinted with permission from E. Gummesson and J. Kingman-Brundage, "Service Design and Quality: Applying Service Blueprinting and Service Mapping to Railroad Services," in *Quality Management in Services,* ed. P. Kunst and J. Lemmink (Assen/Maastricht, Netherlands: Van Gorcum, 1991).

by the customer? What choices does the customer make? Is the customer highly involved in creating the service, or are few actions required of the customer? What is the physical evidence of the service from the customer's point of view? Is the evidence consistent with the organization's strategy and positioning?

If the purpose is to understand contact employees' roles, the blueprint can also be read horizontally but this time focusing on the activities directly above and below the line of visibility. Questions that might be asked include these: How rational, efficient, and effective is the process? Who interacts with customers, when, and how often? Is one person responsible for the customer, or is the customer passed off from one contact employee to another? One hospital, recognizing that its patients were passed from one employee to another with little or no individual attention, reorganized itself so that each patient was assigned to a "care pair" (usually a nurse and an assistant) who served the patient's needs from check-in to discharge. The result was a reduction in operating costs of greater than 9 percent, along with higher patient satisfaction.[24]

If the purpose is to understand the integration of the various elements of the service process, or to identify where particular employees fit into the bigger picture, the blueprint can be analyzed vertically. In this analysis, it becomes clear what tasks and which employees are essential in the delivery of service to the customer. The linkages from internal actions deep within the organization to front-line effects on the customer can also be seen in the blueprint. Questions that might be asked include: What actions are being performed backstage to support critical customer interaction points? What are the associated support actions? How are handoffs from one employee to another taking place?

If the purpose is service redesign, the blueprint can be looked at as a whole to assess the complexity of the process, how it might be changed, and how changes from the customer's point of view would impact the contact employee and other internal processes, and vice versa. Blueprints can also be used to assess the overall efficiency and productivity of the service system and to evaluate how potential changes will impact the system.[25] The blueprint can also be analyzed to determine likely failure points or bottlenecks in the process. When such points are discovered, a firm can introduce measures to track failures, or that part of the blueprint can be exploded so that the firm can focus in much greater detail on that piece of the system.

A blueprinting application in the design of a new rapid train service in Sweden illustrated a number of benefits (see Exhibit 9.1).[26] Clearly, one of the greatest benefits of blueprinting is education.[27] When people begin to develop a blueprint, it quickly becomes apparent what is actually known about the service. Sometimes the shared knowledge is minimal. Biases and prejudices are made explicit, and agreements and compromises must be reached. The process itself promotes cross-functional integration and understanding. In the attempt to visualize the entire service system, people are forced to consider the service in new and more comprehensive ways.

Building a Blueprint

Recall that many of the benefits and purposes of building a blueprint evolve from the process of doing it. Thus the final product is not necessarily the only goal. Through the process of developing the blueprint, many intermediate goals can be achieved: clarification of the concept, development of a shared service vision, recognition of complexities and intricacies of the service that are not initially apparent, and delineation of roles and responsibilities, to name a few. The development of the blueprint needs to involve a variety of functional representatives as well as information from customers. Drawing or building a blueprint is not a task that should be assigned to one person or one functional area. Figure 9.9 identifies the basic steps in building a blueprint. Exhibit 9.2 provides answers to frequently asked questions about service blueprints.

Step 1: Identify the Service Process to Be Blueprinted

Blueprints can be developed at a variety of levels, and there needs to be agreement on the starting point. For example, the express mail delivery blueprint shown in Figure 9.5 is at the basic service concept level. Little detail is shown, and variations based on market segment or specific services are not shown. Specific blueprints might be developed for two-day express mail, large accounts, Internet-facilitated services, and/or storefront dropoff centres. Each of these blueprints would share some features with the concept blueprint but would also include unique features. Or if the "sort packages" and "loading" elements of the process were found to be problem areas or bottlenecks

FIGURE 9.9

Building a Service Blueprint

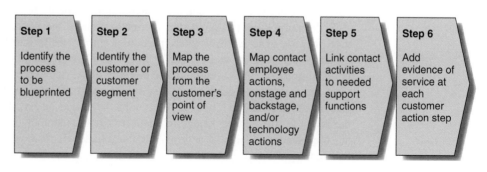

Step 1	Step 2	Step 3	Step 4	Step 5	Step 6
Identify the process to be blueprinted	Identify the customer or customer segment	Map the process from the customer's point of view	Map contact employee actions, onstage and backstage, and/or technology actions	Link contact activities to needed support functions	Add evidence of service at each customer action step

Frequently Asked Questions About Service Blueprinting

What process should be blueprinted?
What process to map depends on the team or organization's objectives. If these are not clearly defined, then identifying the process can present a challenge. Questions to ask: Why are we blueprinting the service? What is our objective? Where does the service process begin and end? Are we focusing on the entire service, a component of the service, or a period of time?

Can multiple market segments be included on one blueprint?
Generally the answer to this question is no. Assuming that market segments require different service processes or attributes, the blueprint for one segment may look very different from the blueprint for another. Only at a very high level (sometimes called a *concept blueprint*) might it be relevant to map multiple segments simultaneously.

Who should "draw" the blueprint?
A blueprint is a team effort. It should not be assigned as an individual task, certainly not in the development stages. All relevant parties should be involved or represented in the development effort. The task might include employees across multiple functions in the organization (marketing, operations, human resources, facilities design) as well as customers in some cases.

Should the actual or desired service process be blueprinted?
If a new service is being designed, then clearly it is important to start with the desired service process. However, in cases of service improvement or service redesign, it is very important to map (at least at a conceptual level) the actual service process first. Once the group knows how the service is actually functioning, then the blueprint can be modified or used as a base for changes and improvements.

Should exceptions or recovery processes be incorporated within the blueprint?
It may be possible to map relatively simple, commonly occurring recovery processes onto a blueprint, assuming there are not a lot of these. However, this process can quickly become complex and cause the blueprint to be confusing or unreadable. Often a better strategy is to indicate common fail points on the blueprint and, if needed, develop sub-blueprints for the service recovery processes.

What is the appropriate level of detail?
The answer to this question depends again on the objective or purpose for doing the blueprint in the first place. If it is to be used primarily to communicate the general nature of the service, then a concept blueprint with few details is best. If it is being used to focus on diagnosing and improving the service process, then more detail is needed. Because some people are more detail oriented than others, this particular question will always arise and needs to be resolved in any team blueprinting effort.

What symbols should be used?
At this point in time, there is not a lexicon of blueprinting symbols that is commonly used or accepted across companies. What is most important is that the symbols be defined, be kept relatively simple, and be used consistently by the team and across the organization if blueprints are being shared internally.

Should time or dollar costs be included on the blueprint?
Blueprints are very versatile. If reducing the time taken for various parts of the service process is an objective of the blueprinting effort, then time can definitely be included. The same is true for dollar costs or anything else that is relevant as an objective. However, it is not advisable to put such information on the blueprint unless it is of central concern.

---

that were slowing service to customers, a detailed blueprint of the subprocesses at work in those two steps might be developed. A firm can identify the process to be mapped once it has determined the underlying purpose for building the blueprint.

Step 2: Identify the Customer or Customer Segment Experiencing the Service

A common rationale for market segmentation is that each segment's needs are different and therefore will require variations in the service or product features. Thus, blueprints are most useful when developed for a particular customer or customer segment, assuming that the service process varies across segments. At a very abstract or conceptual level it may be possible to combine customer segments on one blueprint. However, once almost any level of detail is reached, separate blueprints should be developed to avoid confusion and maximize their usefulness.

Step 3: Map the Service Process from the Customer's Point of View

Step 3 involves charting the choices and actions that the customer performs or experiences in purchasing, consuming, and evaluating the service. Identifying the service from the customer's point of view first will help avoid focusing on processes and steps that have no customer impact. This step forces agreement on who the customer is (sometimes no small task) and may involve considerable research to determine exactly how the customer experiences the service. In mapping the Margaret River Masters surfing event in Australia, researchers used a team of participant observers who involved themselves in the event while recording details about each stage and encounter in the total experience. These detailed observations, combined with customer surveys, allowed the researchers to identify the important actions and activities of this unique event from a customer's point of view. The blueprint was then used to identify points for improvement in this competitive event that attracts the world's best surfers.[28]

Sometimes the beginning and ending of the service from the customer's point of view may not be obvious. For example, research in a hair-cutting context revealed that customers viewed the process as beginning with the phone call to the salon and setting the appointment, whereas the hair stylists did not typically view the making of appointments as part of the service process.[29] Similarly, in a mammography screening service, patients viewed driving to the clinic, parking, and locating the screening office as part of the service experience. If the blueprint is being developed for an existing service, it may be helpful at this point in the process to videotape or photograph the service process from the customer's point of view. Often managers and others who are not on the front lines do not actually know what the customers are experiencing.

Step 4: Map Contact Employee Actions, Both Onstage and Backstage, and/or Technology Actions

First the lines of interaction and visibility are drawn, and then the process from the customer contact person's point of view is mapped, distinguishing visible or onstage activities from invisible backstage activities. For existing services this step involves questioning front-line operations employees to learn what they do and which activities are performed in full view of the customer as against which activities are carried out behind the scenes.

For technology-delivered services or those that combine technology and human delivery, the required actions of the technology interface will be mapped above the line of visibility as well. If no employees are involved in the service, the area can be relabelled "onstage technology actions." If both human and technology interactions are involved, an additional horizontal line can separate "onstage contact employee actions" from "onstage technology actions." Using the additional line will facilitate reading and interpretation of the service blueprint.

Step 5: Link Contact Activities to Needed Support Functions

The line of internal interaction can then be drawn and linkages from contact activities to internal support functions can be identified. In this process, the direct and indirect impact of internal actions on customers becomes apparent. Internal service processes take on added importance when viewed in connection with their link to the customer. Alternatively, certain steps in the process may be viewed as unnecessary if there is no clear link to the customer's experience or to an essential internal support service.

Step 6: Add Evidence of Service at Each Customer Action Step

Finally, the evidence of service can be added to the blueprint to illustrate what the customer sees and receives as tangible evidence of the service at each step in the customer experience. A photographic blueprint, including photos, slides, or video of the process, can be very useful at this stage to aid in analyzing the impact of tangible evidence and its consistency with the overall strategy and service positioning.

QUALITY FUNCTION DEPLOYMENT

In addition to service blueprinting, another approach that can be used to develop a service architecture is *quality function deployment (QFD)*. QFD has been defined as "a system for translating customer requirements into appropriate company requirements at every stage, from research through production design and development to manufacture; distribution; installation; and marketing, sales, and services."[30] Because QFD is used as a means of integrating marketing and engineering personnel in the development process, it has more applications in manufacturing than in services. Its ideas are also applicable to services, however. QFD is implemented via what is known as the "house of quality," which links customer requirements to design characteristics of the product or service.[31] These are then linked to internal processes such as product planning, process planning, production planning, and parts deployment. The house of quality is a diagrammatic representation of the service, its attributes, the customers' requirements, and the company's capabilities.

For services, the concept of service quality deployment has been suggested as a means of adapting QFD tools for service development and design.[32] The resulting house of service quality (see Figure 9.10 for an example) comprises three distinct sections: customer quality criteria (what customers perceive), service company facets (how these criteria are created by the firm), and the relationship grid (how the two are related). This matrix is extended to include quantitative information so that relative importance of relationships among different functions of the firm can be highlighted.

Figure 9.10 provides an example of QFD applied to Village Volvo, a Volvo service garage, to create a house of service quality.[33] The following paragraphs explain elements of the house of service quality shown in Figure 9.10:

1. *Customer expectations.* On the far left of the house are listed the customers' expectations of Village Volvo's customer service. In this case the customers' expectations correspond to the five service quality dimensions presented in Chapter 5.

2. *Importance of expectations.* Next to each expectation (on the chimney of the house) is listed the importance of that particular attribute to customers on a scale from 1 to 9, with 9 being the most important. These importance weights are determined by customer research.

3. *Controllable elements of service.* The columns of the house represent the elements of service that the company has control over, such as training, capacity, equipment, attitude, and information.

4. *Relationships among elements.* The relationships among the elements of service are shown in the roof of the house. The relationships among elements can be strong, medium, or weak. For example, the relationship between training and attitude is strong, whereas the relationship between training and capacity is weak.

FIGURE 9.10

House of Service
Quality for Village
Volvo

Source: Reprinted from
J. A. Fitzsimmons and M.
J. Fitzsimmons, *Service
Management,* 3rd ed. (New
York: Irwin McGraw-Hill,
2000), p. 58. © 2000 by The
McGraw-Hill Companies, Inc.
Reprinted by permission of
The McGraw-Hill Companies.

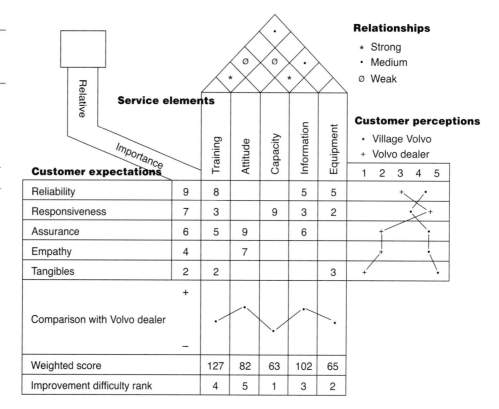

Customer expectations	Relative Importance	Training	Attitude	Capacity	Information	Equipment	Customer perceptions 1 2 3 4 5
Reliability	9	8			5	5	
Responsiveness	7	3		9	3	2	
Assurance	6	5	9		6		
Empathy	4		7				
Tangibles	2	2				3	
Comparison with Volvo dealer							
Weighted score		127	82	63	102	65	
Improvement difficulty rank		4	5	1	3	2	

Relationships
* ★ Strong
* • Medium
* ⊘ Weak

Customer perceptions
* • Village Volvo
* + Volvo dealer

5. *Association between expectations and service elements.* In the body of the matrix are
   numbers representing the strength of the relationship between each expectation and
   the related service element. The numbers reflect (from the service team's perspective)
   how various elements affect the company's ability to satisfy the particular customer
   expectation. A 0 suggests no effect, whereas a 9 suggest a very strong effect.

6. *Overall importance of service elements for meeting customer expectations.* The
   weighted score on the floor of the house represents the total points for each element,
   calculated by multiplying the importance weights by the element association ratings
   and adding all the scores for each element together. For example, Training =
   $(9)(8) + (7)(3) + (6)(5) + (4)(0) + (2)(2) = 127$. These scores should be treated
   relatively, however, and not as absolutes, because they are based on some subjectivity and judgment.

7. *Difficulty rankings.* In the basement of the house are listed the difficulty rankings
   assigned to each element in terms of how difficult it would be to make improvements in that element, with the ranking of 1 being the most difficult.

8. *Competitive assessment.* Two areas of the house suggest some comparisons of
   Village Volvo with the competing Volvo dealership. On the right are shown comparisons of the two on the dimensions of service quality. Just above the floor of the
   house are shown relative ratings comparing Village Volvo with the Volvo dealership on the elements of service.

The completed house of service quality in Figure 9.10 can be used to make preliminary service design decisions based on the relative importance of various attributes

to customers, Village Volvo's relative competitive position, the weighting of the elements in terms of their contribution overall to customer satisfaction, and the difficulty of implementing change. In this example it would appear that training would be a good investment because it has the strongest weight, is rated relatively weak with respect to competition, and is relatively less difficult to change.

HIGH-PERFORMANCE SERVICE INNOVATIONS

To this point in the chapter, we have discussed approaches and tools for developing and designing new services. A dilemma in most companies is that there are too many new ideas from which to choose.

In this section we summarize some of what has been learned about successful new services in terms of measures of success, key success drivers, and the importance of integrating new services.

Choose the Right Projects

Success with new services is going to be determined by two things: choosing the right projects and doing the projects right.[34] Researchers confirm that following the new service development process discussed earlier in the chapter and illustrated in Figure 9.2 will help with both these goals.[35]

Another concept, *portfolio management for new products,* is very useful in helping companies choose the right projects in the first place.[36] Using this approach, companies manage their product portfolio like they manage their financial portfolio. Methods for portfolio management include financial models, scoring models and checklists, mapping approaches, and behavioural approaches.[37]

Integrate New Services

Because of the nature of services—they are processes, typically delivered at least in part by people, consumed and produced simultaneously—any new service introduction will affect the existing systems and services. Unlike when a manufacturer adds a new product to its production facility, new service introductions are frequently visible to customers and may even require their participation. Explicit recognition of these potential impacts, and planning for the integration of people, processes, and physical evidence, will facilitate success.[38]

Consider Multiple Measures of Success

In predicting the success of a new service, multiple performance measures may be considered.[39] First, and most commonly used, is near-term *financial performance* including revenue growth, profitability, market share, and return on investment (ROI). In other cases, *relationship enhancement* may be a more appropriate measure of success. This measurement might include (1) the new service's effect on customer loyalty, (2) image enhancement, and (3) the effect on the success of other products and services. Or success may be measured in terms of *market development*—the degree to which the new service opens up new markets or new customer segments. Successful projects will lead to increases in one, or perhaps more than one, of these measures.

Learn from Major Successes

In investing in new products and services, most companies are looking for big winners rather than modest improvements.[40] In a study of financial services, the following factors were found to distinguish major successes from moderate or small successes:[41]

- *Market synergy.* A strong fit exists between the new service and the company's marketing resources.

- *Market-driven new product process.* The company has a well-planned and executed new service development process.

- *Effective marketing communications.* The company has an effective strategy for establishing a unique positioning and distinct brand image.

- *Customer service.* The most successful new financial products were linked to excellent customer service support.

- *Managerial and financial synergy.* A strong fit exists between the new project and the company's management and financial expertise and resources.

- *Launch preparation.* The company provides extensive training and preparation of front-line personnel to support the product prior to launch.

- *Product responsiveness.* Major successes are new services that truly offer improvements from the customers' point of view—better than competition, responsive to a new need, or offering greater flexibility.

- *Product advantage.* Major successes are better than alternatives in terms of benefits, quality, and distinct branding.

- *Innovative technology.* Technology is instrumental in providing a superior product, or it provides innovation for the delivery system, or the company uses hardware and software to develop significant new offerings. (This factor is particularly important for market development.)

Maintain Some Flexibility

New service success depends on (1) market-driven, customer-focused new product processes; (2) emphasis on planning for and executing the launch; (3) integration of services within existing processes (including staff training); and (4) strong marketing communications, both external and internal. Yet firms must be cautioned about being too rigid in the new service development approach. Steps in the development process should be allowed some flexibility, and there will no doubt be overlapping processes. Initial service development, for example, can be occurring simultaneously with additional gathering of customer information. Because services, particularly business-to-business services, are often very complex, some creativity and "out of order" decisions will be needed. There must be some elements of improvisation, anarchy, and internal competition in the development of new services. "Consequently, the innovation and adoption of new services must be both a planned process and a happening!"[42]

SUMMARY

Service providers must effectively match customer expectations to new service innovations and actual service process designs. However, because of the very nature of services—their intangibility and variability specifically—the design and development of service offerings are complex and challenging. Many services are only vaguely defined before their introduction to the marketplace. This chapter has outlined some of the challenges involved in designing services and some strategies for effectively overcoming the challenges.

Through adaptations of the new product development process that is commonplace in goods production and manufacturing companies, service providers can begin to not only make their offerings more explicit but also avoid failures. The new service development process presented in the chapter includes nine stages, beginning with the development of a business and new service strategy and ending with postintroduction evaluation of the new service. Between these initial and ending stages are a number of steps and checkpoints designed to maximize the likelihood of new service success. Carrying out the stages requires the inclusion of customers, contact employees, and anyone else who will affect or be affected by the new service. Because successful new service introduction is often highly dependent on service employees (often they are the service), integration of employees at each stage is critical.

Service blueprinting is a particularly useful tool in the new service development process. A blueprint can make a complex and intangible service concrete through its visual depiction of all the steps, actors, processes, and physical evidence of the service. The key feature of service blueprints is their focus on the customer—the customer's experience is documented first and is kept fully in view as the other features of the blueprint are developed. This chapter has provided the basic tools needed to build, use, and evaluate service blueprints. Quality function deployment (QFD) was introduced as another tool for linking customer requirements to internal elements of service design.

The final section of the chapter summarized some of the key factors driving successful new service innovations, including the need for portfolio planning and integration of new services with existing processes and systems. The need to consider multiple measures of success was highlighted as well as the importance of maintaining flexibility in the new service development process.

Discussion Questions

1. Why is it challenging to design and develop services?
2. What are the risks of attempting to describe services in words alone?
3. Compare and contrast the blueprints in Figures 9.5 and 9.6.
4. How might a service blueprint be used for marketing, human resource, and operations decisions? Focus on one of the blueprint examples shown in the text as a context for your answer.
5. Assume that you are a multiproduct service company that wants to grow through adding new services. Describe a logical process you might use to introduce a new service to the marketplace. What steps in the process might be most difficult and why? How might you incorporate service blueprinting into the process?
6. Explain the house of service quality that is shown in Figure 9.10. Based on the information in that figure for Village Volvo, what might you do to improve service if you were the manager of that organization?

Exercises

1. Think of a new service you would like to develop if you were an entrepreneur. How would you go about it? Describe what you would do and where you would get your information.

2. Find a new and interesting service in your local area, or a service offered on your campus. Document the service process via a service blueprint. To do this exercise, you will probably need to interview one of the service employees. After you have documented the existing service, use blueprinting concepts to redesign the service or change it in some way.

3. Choose a service you are familiar with and document the customer action steps through a photographic blueprint. What is the "evidence of service" from your point of view as a customer?

4. Develop a service blueprint for a technology-delivered service (such as an Internet-based travel service). Compare and contrast this blueprint to one for the same service delivered via more traditional channels (such as a personal travel agent).

5. Interview customers and employees of a service of your choice. Construct a basic house of service quality. What would you recommend to the manager of the service based on your analysis?

6. Compare two services on the Internet. Discuss the design of each in terms of whether it meets your expectations. How could the design or the service process be changed? Which one is most effective, and why?

⟼ Notes

1. A. Holloway, "Star Power?" *Canadian Business*, December 26, 2005–January 15, 2006, p. 84; A. Holloway, "Radio Waves," *Canadian Business*, December 26, 2005–January 15, 2006, p. 51; A. Holloway, "Sound Bytes," *Canadian Business*, February 13–26, 2006, p. 52; J. Klepko, "Satellite Radio," *Professional Sound*, February 2006, p. 38; Canadian Satellite Radio site, www.cdnsatrad.com.

2. "Flops, Too Many New Products Fail. Here's Why—and How to Do Better," cover story, *BusinessWeek*, August 16, 1993, pp. 76–82.

3. Ibid.; R. G. Cooper, *Winning at New Products,* 3rd ed. (Cambridge, MA: Perseus Publishing, 2001); R. G. Cooper and S. J. Edgett, *Product Development for the Service Sector* (Cambridge, MA: Perseus Books, 1999); C. M. Froehle, A. V. Roth, R. B. Chase, and C. A. Voss, "Antecedents of New Service Development Effectiveness," *Journal of Service Research* 3 (August 2000), pp. 3–17.

4. D. H. Henard and D. M. Szymanski, "Why Some New Products Are More Successful Than Others," *Journal of Marketing Research,* August 2001, pp. 362–75.

5. G. L. Shostack, "Understanding Services Through Blueprinting," in *Advances in Services Marketing and Management,* vol. 1, ed. T. A. Swartz, D. E. Bowen, and S. W. Brown (Greenwich, CT: JAI Press, 1992), pp. 75–90.

6. Cooper, *Winning at New Products;* Cooper and Edgett, *Product Development for the Service Sector;* Henard and Szymanski, "Why Some New Products Are More Successful Than Others."

7. G. L. Shostack, "Service Design in the Operating Environment," in *Developing New Services,* ed. W. R. George and C. Marshall (Chicago: American Marketing Association, 1984), pp. 27–43.

8. For excellent reviews of research and issues in new services development, see *Journal of Operations Management* 20 (2002), Special Issue on New Issues and Opportunities in Service Design Research; A. Johne and C. Story, "New Service Development: A Review of the Literature and Annotated Bibliography," *European*

Journal of Marketing 32, nos. 3–4 (1998), pp. 184–251; B. Edvardsson, A. Gustafsson, M. D. Johnson, and B. Sanden, *New Service Development and Innovation in the New Economy* (Lund, Sweden: Studentlitteratur AB, 2000).

9. B. Schneider and D. E. Bowen, "New Services Design, Development and Implementation and the Employee," in George and Marshall, *Developing New Services,* pp. 82–101.

10. S. Thomke, "R&D Comes to Services: Bank of America's Pathbreaking Experiments," *Harvard Business Review,* April 2003, pp. 70–79.

11. Adapted from D. F. Heany, "Degrees of Product Innovation," *Journal of Business Strategy,* Spring 1983, pp. 3–14, appearing in C. H. Lovelock, "Developing and Implementing New Services," in George and Marshall, *Developing New Services,* pp. 44–64.

12. For a discussion of these adaptations and related research issues, see M. V. Tatikonda and V. A. Zeithaml, "Managing the New Service Development Process: Synthesis of Multidisciplinary Literature and Directions for Future Research," in *New Directions in Supply Chain Management: Technology, Strategy, and Implementation,* ed. T. Boone and R. Ganeshan (New York: AMACOM, 2002), pp. 200–236; B. Edvardsson et al., *New Service Development and Innovation in the New Economy.*

13. The steps shown in Figure 9.2 and discussed in the text are based primarily on the model developed by M. J. Bowers, "An Exploration into New Service Development: Organization, Process, and Structure," doctoral dissertation, Texas A&M University, 1985. Bowers' model is adapted from Booz-Allen & Hamilton, Inc., *New Product Management for the 1980s* (New York: Booz-Allen & Hamilton, 1982).

14. A. Griffin, "PDMA Research on New Product Development Practices: Updating Trends and Benchmarking Best Practices," *Journal of Product Innovation Management* 14 (1997), pp. 429–58; Thomke, "R&D Comes to Services."

15. R. G. Cooper, "Stage Gate Systems for New Product Success," *Marketing Management* 1, no. 4 (1992), pp. 20–29.

16. M. Iansiti and A. MacCormack, "Developing Products on Internet Time," *Harvard Business Review,* September/October 1997, pp. 108–17.

17. A. Khurana and S. R. Rosenthal, "Integrating the Fuzzy Front End of New Product Development," *Sloan Management Review,* Winter 1997, pp. 103–20.

18. The service blueprinting section of the chapter draws from the pioneering works in this area: G. L. Shostack, "Designing Services That Deliver," *Harvard Business Review,* January/February 1984, pp. 133–39; G. L. Shostack, "Service Positioning Through Structural Change," *Journal of Marketing* 51 (January 1987), pp. 34–43; J. Kingman-Brundage, "The ABC's of Service System Blueprinting," in *Designing a Winning Service Strategy,* ed. M. J. Bitner and L. A. Crosby (Chicago: American Marketing Association, 1989), pp. 30–33.

19. Shostack, "Understanding Services Through Blueprinting," pp. 75–90.

20. These key components are drawn from Kingman-Brundage, "The ABC's."

21. The text explaining Figures 9.5 and 9.6 relies on M. J. Bitner, "Managing the Evidence of Service," in *The Service Quality Handbook,* ed. E. E. Scheuing and W. F. Christopher (New York: American Management Association, 1993), pp. 358–70.

22. Stephen S. Tax and F. Ian Stuart, "Designing Service Performances," *Marketing Management* 10, no. 2 (July/August 2001) pp. 8–9.

23. F. Ian Stuart and Stephen Tax, "Toward an Integrative Approach to Designing Service Experiences: Lessons Learned from the Theatre," *Journal of Operations Management* 22 (2004), pp. 609–627.

24. "Hospital, Heal Thyself," *BusinessWeek,* August 27, 1990, pp. 66–68.

25. S. Flieb and M. Kleinaltenkamp, "Blueprinting the Service Company: Managing Service Processes Efficiently," *Journal of Business Research* 57 (2004), pp. 392–404.

26. E. Gummesson and J. Kingman-Brundage, "Service Design and Quality: Applying Service Blueprinting and Service Mapping to Railroad Services," in *Quality Management in Services,* ed. P. Kunst and J. Lemmink (Assen/Maastricht, Netherlands: Van Gorcum, 1991).

27. Shostack, "Understanding Services Through Blueprinting."

28. D. Getz, M. O'Neill, and J. Carlsen, "Service Quality Evaluation at Events Through Service Mapping," *Journal of Travel Research* 39 (May 2001), pp. 380–90.

29. A. R. Hubbert, A. Garcia Sehorn, and S. W. Brown, "Service Expectations: The Consumer vs. the Provider," *International Journal of Service Industry Management* 6, no. 1 (1995), pp. 6–21.

30. American Supplier Institute, 1987, as quoted in R. S. Behara and R. B. Chase, "Service Quality Deployment: Quality Service by Design," in *Perspectives in Operations Management: Essays in Honor of Elwood Buffa,* ed. R. V. Sarin (Norwell, MA: Kluwer Academic Publisher, 1993).

31. J. R. Hauser and D. Clausing, "The House of Quality," *Harvard Business Review,* May/June 1988, pp. 63–73.

32. Behara and Chase, "Service Quality Deployment." See also F. I. Stuart and S. S. Tax, "Planning for Service Quality: An Integrative Approach," *International Journal of Service Industry Management* 7, no. 4 (1996), pp. 58–77.

33. J. A. Fitzsimmons and M. J. Fitzsimmons, *Service Management,* 4th ed. (New York: McGraw-Hill/Irwin, 2004), pp. 144–46.

34. R. G. Cooper, S. J. Edgett, and E. J. Kleinschmidt, *Portfolio Management for New Products* (Reading, MA: Addison-Wesley, 1998).

35. Froehle et al., "Antecedents of New Service Development Effectiveness"; Henard and Szymanski, "Why Some New Products Are More Successful Than Others"; Edvardsson et al., *New Service Development and Innovation in the New Economy.*

36. Cooper et al., *Portfolio Management for New Products.*

37. See ibid. for an excellent discussion and coverage of multiple methods for managing product and service portfolios.

38. S. S. Tax and I. Stuart, "Designing and Implementing New Services: The Challenges of Integrating Service Systems," *Journal of Retailing* 73 (Spring 1977), pp. 105–34.

39. R. G. Cooper, C. J. Easingwood, S. Edgett, E. J. Kleinschmidt, and C. Storey, "What Distinguishes the Top Performing New Products in Financial Services," *Journal of Product Innovation Management* 11(1994), pp. 281–99.

40. For information on success and failure of new services, see Cooper et al., "What Distinguishes the Top Performing New Products"; Ulrike de Brentani, "New Industrial Service Development: Scenarios for Success and Failure," *Journal of Business Research* 32 (1995), pp. 93–103; C. R. Martin Jr. and D. A. Horne,

"Services Innovation: Successful Versus Unsuccessful Firms," *International Journal of Service Industry Management* 4, no. 1 (1993), pp. 49–65; B. Edvardsson, L. Haglund, and J. Mattsson, "Analysis, Planning, Improvisation, and Control in the Development of New Services," *International Journal of Service Industry Management* 6, no. 2 (1995), pp. 24–35; Froehle et al., "Antecedents of New Service Development Effectiveness"; Henard and Szymanski, "Why Some New Products Are More Successful Than Others"; Cooper and Edgett, *Product Development for the Service Sector.*

41. Cooper et al., "What Distinguishes the Top Performing New Products in Financial Services."

42. Edvardsson, Haglund, and Mattsson, "Analysis, Planning, Improvisation, and Control," p. 34.

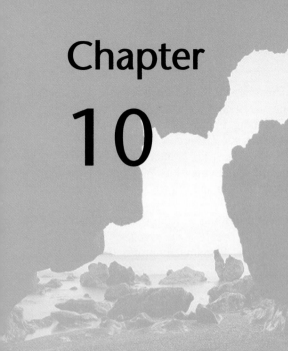

Chapter 10

Customer-Defined Service Standards

Provider Gap 2

> ## THIS CHAPTER'S OBJECTIVES ARE TO
>
> 1. Demonstrate how customer-defined service standards can help firms close Gap 2—Not Having the Right Service Quality Standards
>
> 2. Distinguish between company-defined and customer-defined service standards.
>
> 3. Differentiate among one-time service fixes and "hard" and "soft" customer-defined standards.
>
> 4. Explain the critical role of the service encounter sequence in developing customer-defined standards.
>
> 5. Illustrate how to translate customer expectations into behaviours and actions that are definable, repeatable, and actionable.
>
> 6. Explain the process of developing customer-defined service standards.
>
> 7. Emphasize the importance of service performance indexes in implementing strategy for service delivery.

FedEx Sets Standards Through SQI

Marketing research data are not the only numbers that FedEx (www. fedex.com) tracks to run its business. The company, which began delivery to Canada more than 25 years ago, drives its operations with the aid of the most comprehensive, customer-defined index of service standards and measures in the world. FedEx's service quality indicator (SQI) was designed as "unforgiving internal performance measurement" to ensure that the company delivered to its goal of "100 percent customer satisfaction after every interaction and transaction and 100 percent service performance on every package handled."[1] The development and implementation of SQI led to a U.S.-based Malcolm Baldrige National Quality Award.

What makes this service index different from those of other companies is its foundation in customer feedback. Since the 1980s, FedEx has documented customer complaints and used the information to improve internal processes. Its composite listing of the 12 most common customer complaints, called the "Hierarchy of Horrors," included wrong-day delivery, right-day late delivery, pickup not made, lost package, customer misinformed by FedEx, billing and paperwork mistakes, employee performance failures, and damaged packages. Although this list was useful, it fell short of giving management the ability to anticipate and eliminate customer complaints before they occurred.

The company developed the 12-item statistical SQI to be a more "comprehensive, pro-active, customer-oriented measure of customer satisfaction and service quality."[2] The SQI consists of the following components and weighting (based on relative importance of each component to customers):

Indicator	Weight
Right-day late deliveries	1
Wrong-day late deliveries	5
Traces not answered	1
Complaints reopened	5
Missing proofs of delivery	1
Invoice adjustments	1
Missed pickups	10
Damaged packages	10
Lost packages	10
Aircraft delay minutes	5
Overgoods	5
Abandoned calls	1

Another distinguishing feature of the SQI is its reporting in terms of *numbers* of errors rather than percentages. Management of the company strongly believes that percentages distance the company from the consumer: to report 1 percent of packages late diminished the reality of 20,000 unhappy customers (1% of the approximately 2 million packages shipped a day). The service quality indicator report is disseminated weekly to everyone in the company. On receipt of the report, root causes of service failures are investigated. With a senior officer assigned to each component, and with bonuses for everyone in the company tied to performance on the SQI, the company drives continuously closer to its goal of 100 percent satisfaction with every transaction.[3]

As we saw in Chapters 6, 7, and 8, understanding customer requirements is the first step in delivering high service quality. Once managers accurately understand what customers expect, they face a second critical challenge: using this knowledge to set service quality standards for the organization. Service companies experience difficulty in setting standards partly because doing so requires that the marketing and operations departments within a company work together. In most service companies, integrating the work of the marketing function and the operations function (appropriately called *functional integration*) is not a typical approach; more frequently these two functions operate separately. The reason that operations and marketing must work hard to achieve better integration has its roots in how firms have evolved. Until recently, marketing wasn't even a function in many service firms. Consider Canada Post. Its operations staff were responsible for "getting the job done." That job might be delivering the mail, shipping parcels, providing forwarding addresses, and so forth. Metrics for these activities were based on efficiency, speed, accuracy, and cost. When Canada Post realized that they must do more to compete with firms like FedEx, they added marketing staff, trained their clerks, and tried to become customer-responsive. These first steps were, however, relatively superficial, because the firm still had not changed the way it did business and measured itself.

To this day, many formerly operationally driven companies continue to find it hard to change the way they run their businesses. It is only gradually, and with significant difficulty, that many service firms are actually integrating concern for their customers into their business.

But although closing Gap 2 is taking a while, progress is being made. Customer standards are replacing or being added to company standards—marketing is slowly integrating with operations.

FACTORS NECESSARY FOR APPROPRIATE SERVICE STANDARDS

Standardization of Service Behaviours and Actions

The translation of customer expectations into specific service standards depends on the degree to which tasks can be standardized (Figure 10.1). Some managers believe that services cannot be standardized—that customization is essential. Managers also may feel that standardizing tasks is inconsistent with employee empowerment—that employees will feel controlled by the company if tasks are standardized. Further, they feel that services are too intangible to be measured. This view leads to vague and loose standard setting with little or no measurement or feedback.

In reality, many service tasks are routine (such as those needed for opening chequing accounts or spraying lawns for pests), and for these, specific rules and standards can be fairly easily established. Employees may welcome knowing how to perform actions most efficiently: it frees them to use their ingenuity in the more personal aspects of their jobs.

According to one observer, standardization of service can take three forms: (1) substitution of technology for personal contact (2) improvement in work methods, and (3) combinations of these two methods.[4] Examples of technology substitution include automatic teller machines and automatic car washes. Improvements in work methods are illustrated by restaurant salad bars.

Standardization, whether accomplished by technology or by improvements in work processes, reduces Gap 2. Standardization does not mean that service is performed in a rigid, mechanical way. Customer-defined standardization ensures that the most critical

FIGURE 10.1

Federal Express has standardized service behaviours and actions, resulting in superior employee performance.

elements of a service are performed as expected by customers, not that every action in a service is executed in a uniform manner. Using customer-defined standardization can, in fact, allow for and be compatible with employee empowerment. For instance, companies such as Amex Bank of Canada, in using customer priorities rather than company priorities, have no set standard for the amount of time an employee spends on the telephone with a customer. Instead, they have standards that focus on making the customer satisfied and comfortable, allowing telephone representatives to use their own judgment about the time limits.

Formal Service Targets and Goals

Successful companies are noted for establishing formal standards to guide employees. These companies have an accurate sense of how well they are performing—how long it takes to conduct transactions, how frequently service fails, how quickly they settle customer complaints—and strive to improve by defining goals that lead them to meet or exceed customer expectations.

One type of formal goal setting that is relevant in service businesses involves specific targets for individual behaviours. As an example, consider the behaviour "calls the customer back quickly," an action that signals responsiveness in contact employees. If the service goal for employee behaviour is stated in such a general term as "call the customer back quickly," the standard provides little direction. Different employees will interpret this vague objective in their own way: some may call the customer back in 10 minutes whereas others may wait two to four days. And the firm itself will not be able to determine when or if individual employees meet the goal because its expression is not measurable—one could justify virtually any amount of time as "quickly." On the other hand, if the individual employee's service goal is to call each customer back within four hours, employees have a specific, unambiguous guideline about how quickly they should execute the action (four hours). If you have ever done a performance review at your workplace, you will immediately recognize the importance of having specific metrics. Vague standards lead to many misunderstandings.

Another type of formal goal setting involves the overall department or company. For example, a department might set as its overall goal "to call the customer back within four hours 97 percent of the time" and collect data over a month's or year's time to evaluate the extent to which it meets the target.

Customer- Not Company-Defined Standards

Virtually all companies possess service standards that are *company-defined*—they are established to reach internal company goals for productivity, efficiency, cost, or technical quality. A current company-defined standard that does not meet customer expectations is the common practice of voice-activated telephone support systems that do not allow consumers to speak to humans. Because these systems save companies money many organizations have switched to them. To close Gap 2, standards set by companies must be based on customer requirements and expectations rather than just on internal company goals. In this chapter we make the case that *company-defined* standards are not typically successful in driving behaviours that close Provider Gap 2. Instead, a company must set *customer-defined standards:* operational standards based on pivotal customer requirements that are visible to and measured by customers. These standards are deliberately chosen to match customer expectations and to be calibrated the way the customer views and expresses them. Because these goals are essential to the provision of excellent service, the rest of this chapter focuses on customer-defined standards.

Knowing customer requirements, priorities, and expectation levels can be both effective and efficient. Anchoring service standards on customers can save money by identifying what the customer values, thus eliminating activities and features that the customer either does not notice or will not pay for.

On the other hand, many firms create standards and policies to suit their own needs that are so counter to the wishes of customers that the companies endanger their customer relationships. When the hotel industry was booming, many hotels initiated policies penalizing late arrivals and early departures as well as imposing minimum-stay requirements. Some began to charge guests $50 when they stayed fewer days than agreed to at check-in. B&Bs often kept guests' one-night deposits unless they cancelled at least three days prior to arrival. And then, of course, there is the famous *Seinfeld* episode in which George is charged for missing his appointment with Elaine's friend, the masseuse! Businesses defend these policies on the basis of self-protection, but they are clearly not customer-oriented.

Although customer-defined standards need not conflict with productivity and efficiency, they are not developed for these reasons. Rather, they are anchored in and steered by customer perceptual measures of service quality or satisfaction. The service standards that evolve from a customer perspective are likely to be different from company-defined service standards.

Virtually all organizations have lists of actions that they measure regularly, most of which fall into the category of company-defined standards. As noted earlier, often these standards deal with activities or actions that reflect the history of the business rather than the reality of the needs of current customers.

➡ TYPES OF CUSTOMER-DEFINED SERVICE STANDARDS

The type of standards that close Provider Gap 2 are *customer-defined standards:* operational measures based on customer requirements that are visible to customers rather than on company concerns such as productivity or efficiency. Two major types of customer-defined service standards can be distinguished: "hard" and "soft." These standards will be discussed in the following two sections.

Hard Customer-Defined Standards

All the FedEx standards that comprise the SQI fall into the category of hard standards and measures: *things that can be counted, timed, or observed through audits.* A series of 35 studies across numerous industries from the Arthur D. Little management consulting firm found that the most frequently cited customer complaint was late product and service delivery (44%), followed by product and service quality mistakes (31%).[5]

Reliability is the single most important concern of service customers. One of the best examples of customer-defined hard standards in the Internet context is the set of summary metrics that Dell Computer uses for fulfilment.[6] They include:

- *Ship to target (SSTT)*—the percentage of orders delivered on time with complete accuracy

- *Initial field incident rate (IFIR)*—the frequency of customer problems

- *On-time first-time fix (OTFTF)*—the percentage of problems fixed on the first visit by a service representative arriving at the time promised

Dell tracks its performance to these standards and rewards employees on the basis of their "met promises" or reliability, which is often higher than 98 percent.

When it comes to providing service across cultures and continents, service providers need to recognize that customer-defined service standards often need to be adapted. In Canada we expect waiters to bring the cheque promptly. In fact, if we do not receive it shortly after the last course, and without our asking for it, we evaluate the service as slow and nonresponsive. In Spain, however, customers consider it rude for the waiter to bring the bill to the table without being asked to do so. They feel rushed, a state they dislike during meals.

Hard service standards for responsiveness are set to ensure the speed or promptness with which companies deliver products (within two working days), handle complaints (by sundown each day), answer questions (within two hours), answer the telephone (see the Technology Spotlight), and arrive for repair calls (within 30 minutes of the estimated time). In addition to standard setting that specifies levels of response, companies must have well-staffed customer service departments.

FIGURE 10.2

Reliability—"getting it done right"—is the most important dimension of service quality.

Source: By permission of Dave Coverly and Creators Syndicate, Inc.

Responsiveness perceptions diminish when customers wait to get through to the company by telephone, are put on hold, or are dumped into a phone mail system.

The Global Feature in this chapter provides some real examples of these hard customer-defined standards, along with some soft customer-defined standards, which will be discussed next.

Soft Customer-Defined Standards

Not all customer priorities can be counted, timed, or observed through audits. As Albert Einstein once said, "Not everything that counts can be counted, and not everything that can be counted, counts." In contrast to hard measures, soft measures are those that must be documented using perceptual data. We call these standards *soft standards and measures,* because they are opinion-based and cannot be directly observed. They must be collected by talking to customers, employees, or others. Soft standards provide direction, guidance, and feedback to employees in ways to achieve customer satisfaction and can be quantified by measuring customer perceptions and beliefs.

Mini Maid Services, a firm that franchises home and office janitorial services, successfully built a business by developing a repertoire of 22 customer-defined soft standards for daily cleaning chores. The company sends out crews of four who perform these 22 tasks in an average time of 55 minutes for a fee ranging from approximately $45 to $55. These standards are considered soft because they are measured by follow-up trailer calls that survey customer perceptions.

One-Time Fixes

When customer research is undertaken to find out what aspects of service need to be changed, requirements can sometimes be met using one-time fixes. One-time fixes are *technology, policy, or procedure changes that, when instituted, address customer requirements.* We include one-time fixes in our discussion of standards because organizations with multiple outlets often must clearly define these standards to ensure consistency. As an example, Hampton Inns' new "Make It Hampton" program requires that all inns institute 60 new product and service standards, many of which are one-time fixes. These include providing lap desks in rooms, outdoor planter gardens to hide trash containers, red-carpet welcome mats, and new lobby artwork and music that celebrates travel.[7] Performance standards do not typically need to be developed for these dissatisfiers, because the one-time change in technology, policy, or procedures accomplishes the desired change.

Examples of successful one-time fixes include Hertz and other rental car companies' express check-in and GM Saturn's one-price policy for automobiles. In each of these examples, customers expressed a desire to be served in ways different from the past. Hertz's customers had clearly indicated their frustration at waiting in long lines. Saturn customers disliked haggling over car prices in dealer showrooms.

Whereas most companies in these industries decided for various reasons not to address these customer requirements, Hertz and Saturn each responded with one-time fixes that virtually revolutionized the service quality delivered by their companies. Hertz used technology to create Express Checkout, a one-time fix that also resulted in productivity improvements and cost reductions. The company also pioneered a similar one-time fix for hotel Express Check-In, again in response to customers' expressed desires. Saturn countered industry tradition and offered customers a one-price policy that eliminated the haggling characteristics of automobile dealerships.

Technology Spotlight

The Power of a Good Telephone Responsiveness Standard

Customer-defined service standards resulted for all United States public service agencies after a 1993 National Performance Review, when all government agencies that dealt directly with the public were required to survey customers and establish service standards on the basis of the feedback. By 1998 more than 4,000 customer service standards had been created by 570 agencies. One of the most successful came from the Social Security Administration (SSA) and illustrates a customer-defined hard standard relating to a technology issue that all customers face in dealing with public and private companies alike: telephone responsiveness.

The SSA knew that access—getting through to the agency on its 800 number—was the single biggest driver of customer satisfaction and public perception of the agency's competency. Unfortunately, customers more often than not repeatedly encountered busy signals on the 60 million calls they placed to the SSA's high-volume 800 number. The National Performance Review suggested to the agency that its service standard ought to be that everyone who called its 800 number would get through on the first try: 100 percent access! The SSA balked, recognizing that its telephone technology, limited employee resources, and wide fluctuations in demand would prevent the standard from being met.

The agency ultimately settled on a more reasonable standard: 95 percent of all callers would be served

Source: Royalty-Free/CORBIS.

within five minutes. This standard became a very clear and focused goal that "everybody knew and everybody was shooting for," according to an SSA manager. Early measurements indicated less-than-stellar performance; in 1995 only 73.5 percent of callers got through in five minutes.

What followed was an impressive effort of technology, people, and measurement. According to an expert, "SSA endured tremendous expense, dislocation, pain—and even failure—to meet its standard." First, SSA officials developed a new phone system with AT&T (www.att.sbc.com) that involved a sophisticated call-routing approach. Second, the organization trained virtually all technical people who held jobs other than in teleservices in those skills so that they could be shifted during peak hours to help with the volume. Third, the agency restricted leave for teleservice representatives at peak time, increased the use of overtime, and worked with employees to change processes and rules to improve performance.

The low point in performance to the standard was during the transition to the new system. In November 1995 only 57.2 percent of callers got through within five minutes. Even worse was that on the first day back to work in January 1996, the AT&T 800-number system crashed, leading to even more busy signals. By February, after AT&T fixed the system and the organization got used to its changes, performance improved significantly. The five-minute access rate was 92.1 percent in February, 95.9 percent in November, and above 95 percent ever since.

The SSA standard was successful because it was specific, measurable, and meaningful to customers. Because its results were documented and publicized both within and outside the agency, both employees and management were accountable for performance. Unlike many of the vague, meaningless standards that resulted from the National Performance Review's work with government agencies, this one was a winner.

Source: D. Osborne, "Higher Standards," *Government Executive,* July 2000, pp. 63–71.

Global Feature

Distinguishing Hard and Soft Customer-Defined Standards

Even though Canadians do not have access to Cingular Wireless, you have likely seen some of their television commercials. The spring 2006 advertising campaign that had the company promoting itself as the wireless network with "the fewest dropped calls" serves as a good illustration of a hard customer-defined standard.

In an industry that had been competing on price, wireless carriers are now moving to a more service-oriented differentiation strategy. Thinking that consumers care more about calls getting through than their cost, Cingular Wireless appears to have adopted a hard customer-defined standard to differentiate itself from the competition. Its assertion that it has the fewest dropped calls is specific, measurable, and seemingly meaningful to customers.

Not to be left out, competitors Sprint and Verizon were touting similar claims: that they were each the most reliable wireless carrier. However, these competitors' advertising did not point to hard standards. The difference was that Sprint's ads declared it was "America's most reliable wireless" without pointing to specific, measurable attributes, and Verizon's only implied the reliability of their network by asking, "Can you hear me now?"

Table 10.1 presents some more North American examples of some hard and soft customer-defined standards.

Sources: B. Mohl, "The Fewest Dropped Calls," *The Boston Globe*, April 23, 2006, available www.boston.com/business/articles/2006/04/23/the_fewest_dropped_calls, accessed October 1, 2006; "The Ritz-Carlton Basics," flyer distributed by The Ritz-Carlton Hotel Company L.L.C. to all employees.

One-time fixes are often accomplished by technology. Technology can simplify and improve customer service, particularly when it frees company personnel by handling routine, repetitive tasks and transactions. Effective use of information databases is illustrated in this example from Pizza Hut:

> Pizza Hut centralized and computerized its home delivery operations. Rather than having the separate tasks of order taking, baking, and delivery all in the same location, the company developed a system that works more effectively for both the company and the customer. Operators in a customer service center (not a bakery) take requests for pizza. Working from a database that shows past orders, trained operators take an average of 17 seconds to verify directions to a caller's home and enter his or her request. Operators then route the orders to the closest bake shops, which are strategically located throughout cities to ensure fast deliveries. Cooks in the satellite bake shops prepare pizzas on instructions sent to bake shop printers from order-takers' computers. Drivers aim to complete their deliveries within a half hour of a customer's call, and usually succeed.[8]

One-time fixes also deal with the aspects of service that go beyond human performance: rules and policies, operating hours, product quality, and price. "Poka yokes," discussed in Chapter Eight, are also excellent illustrations of one-time fixes. Recall that poka yokes include, for instance, trays for surgical instruments that include indentations for each specific instrument to ensure that surgeons know all instruments are back in their proper place prior to closing a patient's incision.

TABLE 10.1   Examples of Hard and Soft Customer-Defined Standards

Hard Customer-Defined Standards		
Company	**Customer Priorities**	**Customer-Defined Standards**
FedEx	On-time delivery	Number of packages right day late Number of packages wrong day late Number of missed pickups
Dell Computer	On-time delivery Computer works properly	Ship to target Initial field incident rate Missing wrong and damaged rate Service delivery on time first-time fix
LensCrafters	Quick turnaround on eyeglasses	Glasses ready in one hour
Honeywell Home and Building Division	Fast delivery On-time delivery Order accuracy	Orders entered first day received Orders delivered when promised Order 100% accurate
Texas Instruments Defense Systems	Compliance with commitments More personal contact	On-time delivery Product compliance to requirements Increased number of personal visits
Soft Customer-Defined Standards		
General Electric	Interpersonal skills of operators: • Tone of voice • Problem solving • Summarizing actions • Closing	Taking ownership of the call; following through with promises made; being courteous and knowledgeable; understanding the customer's question or request
The Ritz-Carlton Hotel Company L.L.C.	Being treated with respect	"Gold Standards" • Uniforms are to be immaculate. • Wear proper and safe footwear. • Wear name tag. • Adhere to grooming standards. • Notify supervisor immediately of hazards. • Use proper telephone etiquette. • Ask the caller, "May I place you on hold?" • Do not screen calls. • Eliminate call transfers when possible.
L. L. Bean	Calming human voice; minimal customer anxiety	Tone of voice; other tasks (e.g., arranging gift boxes) not done while on the telephone with customers
American Express	Resolution of problems Treatment Courtesy of representative	Resolve problem at first contact (no transfers, other calls, or multiple contacts); communicate and give adequate instructions; take all the time necessary. Listen; do everything possible to help; be appropriately reassuring (open and honest). Put card member at ease; be patient in explaining billing process; display sincere interest in helping card member; listen attentively; address card member by name; thank card member at end of call.

DEVELOPMENT OF CUSTOMER-DEFINED SERVICE STANDARDS

Basing Standards on the Service Encounter Sequence

Performance requirements are rarely the same across all parts of a company; instead, they are associated with particular service processes and encounters.

A customer's overall service quality evaluation is the accumulation of evaluations of multiple service experiences. Service encounters are the component pieces needed to establish service standards in a company. Therefore, one of the first steps in establishing customer-defined standards is to delineate the service encounter sequence. Identifying the sequence can be done by listing the sequential steps and activities that the customer experiences in receiving the service. Alternatively, service blueprints (see Chapter 9) can be used to identify the sequence by noting all the customers' activities across the top of the blueprint. Vertical lines from customer activities into the lower levels of the blueprint signal the points at which service encounters take place. Standards that meet customer expectations can then be established.

Because many services have multiple encounters, companies and researchers have examined whether some encounters (e.g., the first or the last) are more important than others. The Marriott Corporation identified the encounters that occur in the first 10 minutes of a hotel stay as the most critical, leading the hospitality company to focus on hotel front desk experiences (such as Express Check-In) when making improvements. Although service practice and management literature have emphasized strong starts, recent research indicates that strong finishes in the final event of the encounter have a greater impact on overall satisfaction. Further, the research shows that consistent performance throughout the encounter—widely believed to produce the most favourable evaluations—is not as effective as a pattern of improving performance that culminates in a strong finish.[9] An implication of this research for hotels is that managers should focus on the "back end" of the hotel experience—checkout, parking, bellperson services—to leave a strong final impression.

Expressing Customer Requirements as Specific Behaviours and Actions

Effective service standards are defined in very specific ways that enable employees to understand what they are being asked to deliver. At best, these standards are set and measured in terms of specific responses of human behaviours and actions.

Figure 10.3 shows different levels of abstraction/concreteness for standards in a service firm, arrayed from top (most abstract) to bottom (most concrete and specific). At the very abstract level are customer requirements that are too general to be useful to employees: customers want satisfaction, value, and relationships. One level under these very general requirements are abstract dimensions of service quality already discussed in this text, such as reliability, responsiveness, empathy, assurance, and tangibles. One level further are attributes more specific in describing requirements. If we dig still deeper beneath the attribute level, we get to specific behaviours and actions that are at the right level of specificity for setting standards.

A real-world example of the difference in requirements across these levels will illustrate their practical significance. In a traditional measurement system for a major company's training division, only one aspect of the instructor was included in its class evaluation: ability of instructor. During qualitative research relating to the attributes that satisfy students, three somewhat more specific requirements were elicited: (1) instructor's style, (2) instructor's expertise, and (3) instructor's management of class.

FIGURE 10.3 What Customers Expect: Getting to Actionable Steps

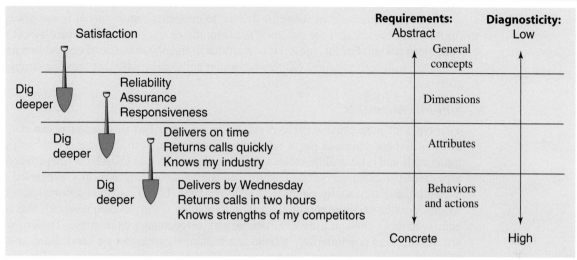

Although the articulation of the three attributes was more helpful to instructors than the broad "ability of instructor," management found that the attributes were still too broad to help instructors wanting to improve their course delivery. When the company invested in a customer-defined standards project, the resulting measurement system was far more useful in diagnosing student requirements, because the research focused on *specific behaviours and actions* of instructors that met student requirements. Instead of a single broad requirement or three general attributes, the requirements of students were articulated in 14 specific behaviours and actions that related to the instructor and 11 specific behaviours and actions that related to the course content. These behaviours and actions were clearly more diagnostic for communicating what was good and bad in the courses. An additional benefit of this approach was that feedback on behaviours and actions was less personal than feedback on traits or personal characteristics. It was also easier for employees of the company to make changes that related to behaviours rather than to personality traits.

Measuring Behaviours and Actions

Hard Measurements

Hard measurements consist of counts that provide feedback about the performance of a service standard. To demonstrate, here are some of the actual hard measurements for components of the FedEx SQI:

- *Missing proofs of delivery*—the number of invoices that do not include proof-of-delivery paperwork

- *Overgoods*—lost and found packages that lack, or have lost, identifying labels for the sender and the addressee and are sent to the Overgoods Department

- *Wrong-day late deliveries*—number of packages delivered after the commitment date

- *Traces*—the number of "proof of performance" requests from customers that cannot be answered through data contained in the computer system[10]

In these and other hard measurements, the actual gauge involves a count of the number and type of actions or behaviours that are correct or incorrect. Somewhere in the operation system these actions and behaviours are tabulated, frequently through information technology.

The appropriate hard measure to deliver to customer requirements is not always intuitive or obvious, and the potential for counting or tracking an irrelevant aspect of operations is high. For this reason it is desirable to link the measure of operational performance with soft measures (surveys or trailer calls) to be sure that they are strongly correlated.

Soft Measurements

Two types of perceptual measurement that were described in Chapter 6 can document customers' opinions about whether performance met the standards established: trailer calls and relationship surveys. Relationship and SERVQUAL surveys cover all aspects of the customer's relationship with the company, are typically expressed in attributes, and are usually completed once per year. Trailer calls are associated with specific service encounters, are short (approximately six or seven questions), and are administered as close in time to a specific service encounter as possible. Trailer calls are administered continuously, whenever a customer experiences a service encounter of the type being considered, and they provide data on a continuous basis. The company must decide on a survey strategy combining relationship surveys and trailer calls to provide soft measurement feedback.

Adapting Standards Globally or Locally

How do companies adjust for cultural or local differences in service standards if they recognize that these geographic differences are related to varying customer expectations? Companies with worldwide brands have much to lose if their service standards vary too much across countries, and therefore they must find ways to achieve universally high quality while still allowing for local differences.

As one of the world's leading operators of luxury hotels and resorts, the Four Seasons Hotel manages 63 properties in 29 countries, and successfully accomplishes this goal by balancing universal services standards with standards that vary by country.[11] The company, world-famous for its service, owes at least some of its success to its seven "service culture standards" expected of *all* staff *all* over the world at *all* times. The seven standards, which form the acrostic SERVICE, are:

1. **Smile:** Employees will actively greet guests, smile, and speak clearly in a friendly manner.

2. **Eye:** Employees will make eye contact, even in passing, with an acknowledgment.

3. **Recognition:** All staff will create a sense of recognition by using the guest's name, when known, in a natural and discreet manner.

4. **Voice:** Staff will speak to guests in an attentive, natural, and courteous manner, avoiding pretension and in a clear voice.

5. **Informed:** All guest contact staff will be well informed about their hotel, their product, will take ownership of simple requests, and will not refer guests elsewhere.

6. **Clean:** Staff will always appear clean, crisp, well-groomed, and well-fitted.

7. **Everyone:** Everyone, everywhere, all the time, show their care for our guests.

In addition to these culture standards that are expected of all staff all over the world, the hotel has 270 core standards that apply to different aspects of service provision

FIGURE 10.4

The Four Seasons in Toronto standardizes a long list of in-room service activities to ensure consistency.

Source: Tibor Kolley/The Globe and Mail.

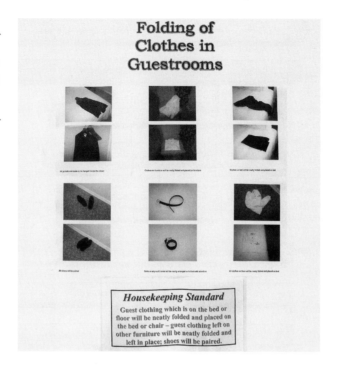

(examples include "the staff will be aware of arriving vehicles and will move toward them, opening doors within 30 seconds" and "unanswered guest room phones will be picked up within 5 rings, or 20 seconds"). Exceptions to these 270 standards are allowed if they make local or cultural sense. For example, in North America, coffee pots are left on tables at breakfast; in many parts of Europe, including France, customers perceive this practice as a lack of service and servers personally refill coffee cups as needed. Standards for uniforms and decor differ across cultures, but minimum expectations must be met everywhere.

Developing Customer-Defined Standards

Figure 10.5 shows the general process for setting customer-defined service standards.

Step 1: Identify Existing or Desired Service Encounter Sequence

The first step involves delineating the service encounter sequence. A service blueprint may be used to identify the service encounter sequence. Ideally, the company would be open to discovering customers' desired service encounter sequences, exploring the ways customers want to do business with the firm.

Step 2: Translate Customer Expectations into Behaviours and Actions for Each Service Encounter

The input to step 2 is existing research on customer expectations. In this step, abstract customer requirements and expectations must be translated into concrete, specific behaviours and actions associated with each service encounter. Abstract requirements (like reliability) can call for a different behaviour or action in each service encounter, and these differences must be probed. Eliciting these behaviours and actions is likely to require additional qualitative research because in most service companies, marketing information has not been collected for this purpose.

FIGURE 10.5

Process for Setting
Customer-Defined
Standards

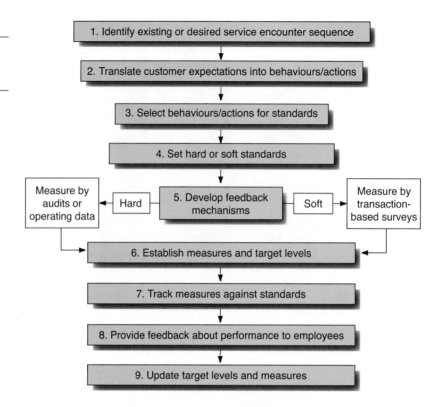

Information on behaviours and actions must be gathered and interpreted by an objective source such as a research firm or an inside department with no stake in the ultimate decisions. If the information is filtered through company managers or front-line people with an internal bias, the outcome would be company-defined rather than customer-defined standards. When this happens, Gap 2 usually gets wider.

Research techniques discussed in Chapter 6 that are relevant for eliciting behaviours and actions include in-depth interviewing of customers, focus group interviews, and other forms of research such as partnering.

Step 3: Select Behaviours and Actions for Standards

This stage involves prioritizing the behaviours and actions, of which there will be many, into those for which customer-defined standards will be established. The following are the most important criteria for creation of the standards:

1. *The standards are based on behaviours and actions that are very important to customers.* Customers have many requirements for the products and services that companies provide. Customer-defined standards need to focus on what is *very important* to customers.

2. *The standards cover performance that needs to be improved or maintained.* The company gets the highest leverage or biggest impact from focusing on behaviours and actions that need to be improved. Figure 10.6 shows an importance/performance matrix for a computer manufacturer. It combines the importance and performance criteria and indicates them by the shading in the cell in the matrix where behaviours and actions should be selected to meet those criteria.

3. *The standards cover behaviours and actions employees can improve.* Employees perform according to standards consistently only if they understand, accept, and

FIGURE 10.6

Importance/
Performance Matrix:
Delivery, Installing,
Performing

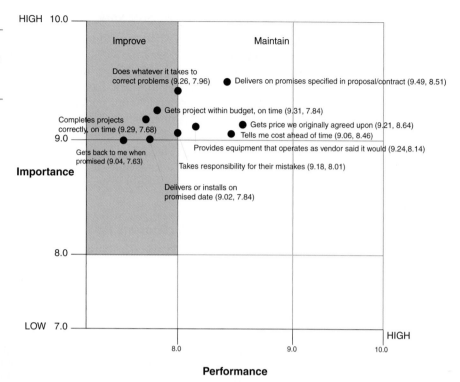

have control over the behaviours and actions specified in the standards. Holding contact people to standards that they cannot control (such as product quality or time lag in introduction of new products) does not result in improvement. For this reason, service standards should cover controllable aspects of employees' jobs.

4. *The standards are accepted by employees.* Employees will perform to standards consistently only if they understand and accept the standards. Imposing standards on unwilling employees often leads to resistance, resentment, absenteeism, even turnover. Many companies establish standards for the amount of time it should take (rather than for the time it does take) for each service job and gradually cut back on the time to reduce labour costs. This practice inevitably leads to increasing tensions among employees. In these situations, managers, financial personnel, and union employees can work together to determine new standards for the tasks.

5. *The standards are predictive rather than reactive.* Customer-defined standards should not be established on the basis of complaints or other forms of reactive feedback. Reactive feedback deals with past concerns of customers rather than with current and future customer expectations. Rather than waiting for dissatisfied customers to complain, the company should actively seek both positive and negative perceptions of customers in advance of complaints.

6. *The standards are challenging but realistic.* A large number of studies on goal setting show that highest performance levels are obtained when standards are challenging but realistic. If standards are not challenging, employees get little reinforcement for mastering them. On the other hand, unrealistically high standards leave an employee feeling dissatisfied with performance and frustrated by not being able to attain the goal.

Step 4: Decide Whether Hard or Soft Standards Are Appropriate

The next step involves deciding whether hard or soft standards should be used to capture the behaviour and action. One of the biggest mistakes companies make in this step is to choose a hard standard hastily. Companies are accustomed to operational measures and have a bias toward them. However, unless the hard standard adequately captures the expected behaviour and action, it is not customer-defined. The best way to decide whether a hard standard is appropriate is to first establish a soft standard by means of trailer calls and then determine over time which operational aspect most correlates to this soft measure. Figure 10.7 shows the linkage between speed of complaint handling (a hard measure) and satisfaction (a soft measure); the figure illustrates that satisfaction strongly depends on the number of hours it takes to resolve a complaint.

Step 5: Develop Feedback Mechanisms for Measurement to Standards

Once companies have determined whether hard or soft standards are appropriate and which specific standards best capture customer requirements, they must develop feedback mechanisms that adequately capture the standards. Hard standards typically involve mechanical counts or technology-enabled measurement of time or errors. Soft standards require perceptual measurements through the use of trailer surveys or employee monitoring. Employee monitoring is illustrated by the practice of supervisors listening in on employee calls. You may have experienced this when you called customer service numbers for many organizations and noticed that the voice prompts tell you that calls may be monitored for quality purposes. The purpose of this monitoring is to provide feedback on employee performance to the standards set by the organization to meet customer needs. One critical aspect of developing feedback mechanisms is ensuring that performance captures the process from the customer's view rather than the company's perspective. A supervisor monitoring an employee's handling of a customer service call, for example, should focus not so much on how quickly the employee gets the customer off the phone as on how adequately he or she handles the customer's request.

FIGURE 10.7

Linkage Between Soft and Hard Measures for Speed of Complaint Handling

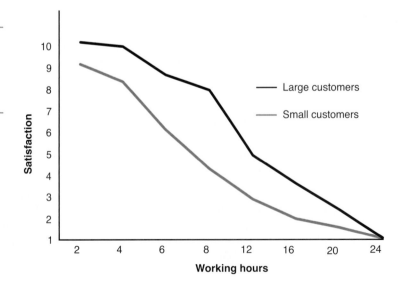

Step 6: Establish Measures and Target Levels

The next step requires that companies establish target levels for the standards. Without this step the company lacks a way to quantify whether the standards have been met. When the service consists of repetitive processes, companies can relate levels of customer satisfaction with actual performance of a behaviour or task. Consider, for example, a study to determine the standard for customers' wait time in a line. The information needed includes customer perceptions of their wait in line (soft perceptual measure) and the amount of time they actually stand in line (hard operations measure). The joint collection of these data over many transactions provides evidence of the sensitivity of customers to different wait times.

An airline conducted precisely this study by having a flight attendant intercept customers as they approached the ticket counter. As each customer entered the line, the attendant stamped the entry time on a ticket (using a machine like those in parking lots) and handed the customer the stamped ticket. As the customer exited the line at the end of the transaction, the flight attendant restamped the ticket with the exit time and asked the customer three or four questions about perceptions of the wait in line and satisfaction with the transaction. Aggregating the individual customer data provided a graph that allowed the company to evaluate the impact on perceptions of various levels of line waits.

Step 7: Track Measures Against Standards

Roger Milliken, former head of Milliken Industries, is reported to have said, "In God we trust, all others bring data." Successful service businesses, such as FedEx and Walt Disney, have careful and comprehensive fact-based systems about their operations. One company that has recently made a very significant commitment to fact-based decision making is the TD Bank Financial Group. Following the merger between TD and Canada Trust, they had their hands full combining products and services, systems, branches, and of course management and staff. Naturally, such a process can lead to customer service problems. To address these, TD Canada Trust implemented a Customer Problem Resolution Process. Employees were invited to identify obstacles to customer service and customers were regularly surveyed to track progress.[12]

Since the quality movement of the 1980s, many techniques have been developed to track measures against standards. W. Edwards Deming, one of the most influential leaders of the quality movement, developed an approach called the P-D-C-A cycle (Plan-Do-Check-Act) that is applied to processes to measure and continuously improve their performance. Joseph Juran, another founder of the quality movement, was one of the first to apply statistical methods to improvement, leading to the widespread use of statistical process control as a way to measure performance to standards.

Step 8: Provide Feedback About Performance to Employees

FedEx communicates the performance on its service quality indicator daily so that everyone in the company knows how the company is performing. When problems occur, they can be identified and corrected. The SQI measurement gives everyone in the company immediate feedback on activity that is strongly related to customer perceptions. In a general sense, data and facts need to be analyzed and distributed to support evaluation and decision making at multiple levels within the company. The data also must be deployed quickly enough that the people who need it to make decisions about service or processes can do so. Responsibility for meeting service requirements must also be communicated throughout the organization. All parts of the organization must be measuring their services to internal customers and, ultimately, measuring how that performance relates to external customer requirements.[13]

Step 9: Periodically Update Target Levels and Measures

The final step involves revising the target levels, measures, and even customer requirements regularly enough to keep up with customer expectations.

Developing Service Performance Indexes

One outcome from following the process for developing customer-defined standards is a service performance index. *Service performance indexes* are comprehensive composites of the most critical performance standards. Development of an index begins by identifying the set of customer-defined standards that the company will use to drive behaviour. Not all service performance indexes contain customer-defined standards, but the best ones, like FedEx's SQI, are based on them. Most companies build these indexes by (1) understanding the most important requirements of the customer, (2) linking these requirements to tangible and measurable aspects of service provision, and (3) using the feedback from these indexes to identify and improve service problems. The most progressive companies also use the feedback for reward and recognition systems within the company. Here are a few examples of service performance indexes in some companies.

TD Bank Financial Group

As part of its ongoing desire to improve service, TD Canada Trust has created its Customer Service Index (CSI). In 2005, TD surveyed approximately 400,000 customers. Categories tracked included treating customers in a respectful manner, processing transactions quickly and accurately, handling customer requests, giving customers individual attention, and greeting customers pleasantly. In the same year, TD Canada Trust was rewarded for its efforts with the Contact Centre Industry Service Quality of Excellence Award. It also placed first among Canada's major banks in the national Synovate Survey on eight of eleven categories including "overall quality of service." According to their Corporate Social Responsibility Report, "Our customers are why we exist so paying attention to what counts to them is the overarching focus that propels our business" (p. 36).[14]

The Ritz-Carlton Hotel Company L.L.C.

The Ritz-Carlton has created a Service Quality Indicator that is patterned on FedEx's SQI (discussed in this chapter's opening). The Ritz's SQI spells out the 12 most serious defects that can occur in the operation of a hotel and weights them by their seriousness. The defects and points associated with them include:

1. Missing guest preferences (10 points)
2. Unresolved difficulties (50 points)
3. Inadequate guestroom housekeeping (1 point)
4. Abandoned reservation calls (5 points)
5. Guestroom changes (5 points)
6. Inoperable guestroom equipment (5 points)
7. Unready guestroom (10 points)
8. Inappropriate hotel appearance (5 points)

9. Meeting event difficulties (5 points)

10. Inadequate food/beverage (1 point)

11. Missing/damaged guest property/accidents (50 points)

12. Invoice adjustment (3 points)

The hotel calculates the SQI by multiplying the total number of occurrences by their points, totals the points, and divides by the number of working days to get an average daily point value. This value is communicated daily to employees.[15]

Among the issues that companies must tackle when developing service performance indexes are (1) the number of components to be contained, (2) what overall or summary measures will be included, (3) whether the index should be weighted or unweighted (to put greater emphasis on the performance of the attributes considered most important to customers), and (4) whether all parts of the business (departments, sectors, or business units) will be held to the same performance measures. One of the most important goals of an index is to simply and clearly communicate business performance in operational and perceptual terms. Companies must develop the rigour in these measurement areas that they have in financial performance.

Recently, subscribers to Aliant (Atlantic Canada's major telecommunications firm) received an insert in their monthly statements. This insert reported on a CRTC-mandated set of customer-driven measures that all Canadian telecommunications firms had to track to avoid a monetary penalty. Go to the CRTC website at www.crtc. gc.ca/ENG/publications/reports/8660/8660.htm to find out how companies in your part of the country performed.

SUMMARY

This chapter discussed the discrepancy between company perceptions of customer expectations and the standards they set to deliver to these expectations. Among the major causes for Provider Gap 2 are inadequate standardization of service behaviours and actions, absence of formal processes for setting service quality goals, and lack of customer-defined standards. These problems were discussed and detailed, along with strategies to close the gap.

Customer-defined standards are at the heart of delivery of service that customers expect: they are the link between customers' expressed expectations and company actions to deliver to those expectations. Creating these service standards is not a common practice in many firms. Doing so requires that companies' marketing and operations departments work together by using marketing research as input for operations. Unless the operations standards are defined by customer priorities, they are not likely to have an impact on customer perceptions of service.

⟼ Discussion Questions

1. How does the service measurement that we describe in this chapter differ from the service measurement in Chapter 6? Which of the two types do you think is most important? Why?

2. In what types of service industries are standards most difficult to develop? Why? Recommend three standards that might be developed in one of the firms from the industries you specify. How would employees react to these standards? How could you gain buy-in for them?

3. Given the need for customer-defined service standards, do firms need company-defined standards at all? Could all standards in a company be customer-defined? Why or why not? What functional departments in a firm would object to having all standards customer-defined?

4. What is the difference between hard and soft standards? Which do you think would be more readily accepted by employees? By management? Why?

5. Consider the university or school you currently attend. What are examples of hard standards, soft standards, and one-time fixes that would address student requirements? Does the school currently use these standards for delivery of service to students? Why or why not? Do you think your reasons would apply to private-sector companies as well? To public or nonprofit companies?

6. Think of a service that you currently use, then map out the service encounter sequence for that service. What is your most important requirement in each interaction? Document these requirements, and make certain that they are expressed at the concrete level of behaviours and actions.

7. Which of the service performance indexes described at the end of this chapter is the most effective? Why? What distinguishes the one you selected from the others? How would you improve each of the others?

Exercises

1. Select a local service firm. Visit the firm and ascertain the service measurements that the company tracks. What hard measures does it monitor? Soft measures? On the basis of what you find, develop a service performance index.

2. Choose one of the peripheral services (such as computer, library, placement) provided by your school. What hard standards would it be useful to track to meet student expectations? What soft standards? What one-time fixes would improve service?

3. Think of a service company you have worked for or know about. Using Figure 10.3, write in customer requirements at each of the levels. How far down in the chart can you describe requirements? Is that far enough?

4. Look at three websites from which you can order products (such as Amazon.ca or LLBean.com). What are the companies' delivery promises? What types of standards might they set for these promises? Are these customer- or company-defined standards?

Notes

1. "Taking the Measure of Quality," *Service Savvy*, March 1992, p. 3.
2. Ibid.
3. Speech by Federal Express Manager in Baltimore, Maryland, June 1993.
4. T. Levitt, "Industrialization of Service," *Harvard Business Review*, September/October 1976, pp. 63–74.
5. "Fast, Reliable Delivery Processes Are Cheered by Time-Sensitive Customers," *The Service Edge* 4, no. 3 (1993): 1.

6. F. Reichhold, "e-Loyalty," *Harvard Business Review*, July/August 2000, pp. 105–13.

7. J. Weinstein, "Redesigning the Box," *Hotels* 38, no. 3 (2004), p. 7.

8. "Fast, Reliable Delivery Processes," p. 21.

9. D. E. Hansen and P. J. Danaher, "Inconsistent Performance During the Service Encounter: What's a Good Start Worth?" *Journal of Service Research* 1 (February 1999), pp. 227–35.

10. "Taking the Measure of Quality," p. 3.

11. This discussion about the Four Seasons is based on R. Hallowell, D. Bowen, and C. Knoop, "Four Seasons Goes to Paris," *Academy of Management Executive* 16, no. 4 (2002), pp. 7–24.

12. *TDBFG Corporate Social Responsibility Report*, 2003, pp. 28, 29.

13. "Taking the Measure of Quality," p. 3.

14. *TDBFG Corporate Social Responsibility Report*, 2004, p. 36; *TDBFG Annual Report*, 2005.

15. 1999 Application Summary for The Ritz-Carlton Hotel Company L.L.C., Malcolm Baldrige National Quality Award, 2000.

Chapter 11

Physical Evidence and the Servicescape

Provider Gap 2

THIS CHAPTER'S OBJECTIVES ARE TO

➤ 1. Demonstrate how physical evidence can help firms close Provider Gap 2—Not Having the Right Service Quality Standards.

➤ 2. Explain the profound impact of physical evidence, particularly the servicescape, on customer perceptions and experiences.

➤ 3. Illustrate differences in types of servicescapes, the roles played by the servicescape, and the implications for strategy.

➤ 4. Explain *why* the servicescape affects customer and employee behaviour, using a framework based in marketing, organizational behaviour, and environmental psychology.

➤ 5. Present elements of an effective physical evidence strategy.

USING PHYSICAL EVIDENCE TO POSITION A NEW SERVICE

When Speedi-Lube first opened its doors, it was one of the first 10-minute oil and lubrication services ever introduced. Now there are thousands of such outlets, but then the concept was totally new. The idea was to offer an alternative to corner gas stations for basic car lubrication service, quickly (within 10 minutes), with no appointment necessary. Because the concept was unknown to consumers at the time, the owners of Speedi-Lube needed to communicate and position the service clearly so that consumers would form accurate expectations. And because car maintenance is highly intangible and consumers often do not understand what is actually done to their cars, the owners relied heavily on tangible physical evidence to communicate the concept before, during, and after the sale.

To communicate an image of fast, efficient service, Speedi-Lube relied on straightforward, to-the-point advertising using clean, crisp letters. For example, a large billboard read in large blue and white letters: SPEEDI-LUBE, 10-MINUTE OIL CHANGE, NO APPOINTMENT, OPEN 7 DAYS, 9 TO 6. The very buildings in which the service was performed communicated the efficiency theme clearly. In fact, the exteriors of some of the first Speedi-Lube facilities had the look of a fast-food restaurant, not inconsistent with the intended image of speed, efficiency, and predictability. Entrance and exit signs were clearly displayed so that customers coming to Speedi-Lube for the first time would know exactly where to drive their cars.

On driving into the service bay the customer was greeted with additional physical evidence that clearly differentiated Speedi-Lube from its competitors at that time. The service bay was very neat and brightly painted, with a professional-appearing service counter in the bay where the customer filled out paperwork to get the service. Service personnel in professional uniforms helped with the paperwork, and the customer was invited to wait in a clean and functional waiting area where coffee and magazines were provided. (Alternatively, customers were welcome to stay in the service area to observe the work on their cars.) On one of the waiting room walls was displayed a large schematic that showed the underside of an automobile and identified all the lubrication points and exactly what was being done to the car (Figure 11.1). This form of evidence informed customers and gave them confidence in what was being done.

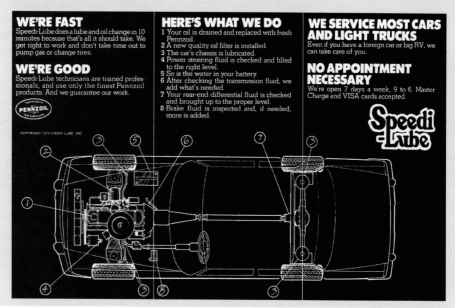

On completion, the customer was given a checklist itemizing the lubrication services provided. As a finishing touch, the employee would then lubricate the door locks on the car to indicate that nothing had been overlooked. Three months later Speedi-Lube would send a reminder suggesting that it was time for another oil change.

It is difficult to imagine a time when 10-minute oil and lubrication services did not exist. Yet when Speedi-Lube was established, the quick oil change concept was totally new. Speedi-Lube was dealing with both a totally new concept and an industry in which services are generally high in credence attributes. The company used physical evidence very effectively to communicate the new concept and to make elements of the process itself very concrete. The schematic on the waiting room wall detailing what the service entailed, as well as the checklist showing exactly what had been done, were ways the company tried to make credence attributes more tangible. Even today, when quick oil and lubrication services are the norm, companies like Mr. Lube (www.mrlube.com) and Jiffy Lube (www.jiffylube.com) have websites that carefully explain all that is involved in the service they provide.

In this chapter we explore the importance of physical evidence for communicating service quality attributes, setting customer expectations, and creating the service experience. In Chapter 1, when we introduced the expanded marketing mix for services, we defined physical evidence as *the environment in which the service is delivered and in which the firm and the customer interact, and any tangible commodities that facilitate performance or communication of the service.* The first part of this definition encompasses the actual physical facility in which the service is performed, delivered, and consumed; throughout this chapter the physical facility is referred to as the *servicescape.*[1]

Physical evidence is particularly important for communicating about credence services (such as auto repair), but it is also important for services such as hotels, hospitals, and theme parks that are dominated by experience attributes. In this chapter we present many examples of how physical evidence communicates with customers and how it can play a role in creating the service experience, in satisfying customers, and in enhancing customers' perceptions of quality.

➡ PHYSICAL EVIDENCE

What Is Physical Evidence?

Because services are intangible, customers often rely on tangible cues, or physical evidence, to evaluate the service before its purchase and to assess their satisfaction with the service during and after consumption. Effective design of physical, tangible evidence is important for closing Gap 2. Just as customers have expectations for how long they must wait in line, they also have expectations for the physical evidence that firms use. These expectations must be identified by management and translated into appropriate standards that guide the development and maintenance of the actual servicescape itself.

FIGURE 11.2

Many aspects of "physical evidence" are used in today's servicescape.

Source: By permission of Dave Coverly and Creators Syndicate, Inc.

General elements of physical evidence are shown in Table 11.1. They include all aspects of the organization's physical facility (the servicescape) as well as other forms of tangible communication. Elements of the servicescape that affect customers include both exterior attributes (such as signage, parking, and the landscape) and interior attributes (such as design, layout, equipment, and decor). Note that Web pages and virtual servicescapes conveyed over the Internet are more recent forms of physical evidence that companies can use to communicate about the service experience, making services more tangible for customers both before and after purchase (see our Technology Spotlight).

Physical evidence examples from different service contexts are given in Table 11.2. It is apparent that some services (like hospitals, resorts, and child care) rely heavily on physical evidence to communicate and create customer experiences. Others (insurance, express mail) provide limited physical evidence for customers. All the elements of evidence listed for each service communicate something about the service to consumers.

TABLE 11.1

Elements of Physical Evidence

Servicescape	Other Tangibles
Facility exterior:	Business cards
Exterior design	Stationery
Signage	Billing statements
Parking	Reports
Landscape	Employee dress
Surrounding environment	Uniforms
Facility interior:	Brochures
Interior design	Web pages
Equipment	Virtual servicescape
Signage	
Layout	
Air quality/temperature	

Technology Spotlight

Virtual Servicescapes: Experiencing Services on the Internet

Web pages and virtual service tours allow customers to preview service experiences through the Internet and see tangible evidence of the service without actually being there. This medium offers firms tremendous potential to communicate experiential aspects of their services in ways that were previously very difficult, if not impossible. Here we present several examples, across different industries.

TRAVEL

Travellers can now preview destinations, view hotels and their rooms, tour natural environments, and "experience" entertainment venues before booking their trips or even deciding where to travel. Before booking a trip to Great Britain, travellers can preview websites that show hotels, bed and breakfast inns, and other lodging all over the country. The exterior of the facilities as well as actual rooms can be examined in selecting accommodations. Likewise, before planning a trip to the CN Tower (www.cntower.ca), visitors can plan their excursion in detail using the information provided on the site, and view the attraction's electronic brochure for great images of the servicescape. When using the Vancouver airport, travellers can access maps of the area online ahead of time at www.yvr.com. This feature is particularly helpful to international travellers, who may need to make quick transfers and do not have time to make mistakes navigating a large foreign airport. Before the Internet, this kind of servicescape knowledge, available at a moment's notice, would have been impossible.

UNIQUE RETAIL EXPERIENCES

Many of today's unique retail experiences can be conveyed effectively via the Internet to give customers a preview of what they can expect. A great example is Build-A-Bear Workshop, where children "from 3 to 103" can create their own teddy bears and other furry friends during their visits to the store. The experience itself is memorable and fun, and the servicescape of the stores is a big part of creating the experience. For a preview of how it works and what the stores look like, the website of Build-A-Bear Workshops (www.buildabear.com) includes a step-by-step "virtual visit" that shows the various stations in the store and what happens at each

Source: CN TOWER
CANADA'S WONDER OF THE WORLD
LA TOUR CN
NOTRE MERVEILLE DU MONDE

one. In creating a furry friend, consumers go through the following steps: Choose Me; Hear Me; Stuff Me; Stitch Me; Fluff Me; Name Me; Dress Me; Take Me Home®. The virtual visit on the website shows each stage sequentially, detailing the activities at each step and providing a colourful photo that gives a real sense of the store environment and the emotions of its patrons. Build-A-Bear Workshop began operations in 1997 and operates 170 of its stores, primarily in major mall locations, throughout Canada and the United States.

HIGHER EDUCATION

One of the most significant decisions that young people and their families make is the decision of what college or university to attend. For students lucky enough to have the means and intellectual abilities, the choices can be endless. The physical environment of the university —the campus itself as well as specific facilities—can play a major role in students' choices as well as their actual experiences. Some schools now offer virtual tours of their campuses online that allow students to preview the physical environment in advance. Saint Francis Xavier University in Antigonish, Nova Scotia has a tour on their site that allows students to view an interactive map of all buildings on campus, so they can get their bearings before arriving (www.stfx.ca/campus/virtual-tour/virtualcampus tour_content.html). Clicking on one

continued

Technology Spotlight

Virtual Servicescapes: Experiencing Services on the Internet—continued

of the buildings activates a window with photos, a written description, and in some instances 360-degree views of the area or interior.

Internet technology clearly provides tremendous opportunities for firms to communicate about their services. Tangible images on the Web create expectations for customers that set standards for service delivery, and it is critical that the actual services live up to these expectations. Images and virtual service tours presented on the Internet also need to support the positioning of the service brand and be consistent with other marketing messages.

TABLE 11.2

Examples of Physical Evidence from the Customer's Point of View

Service	Physical Evidence	
	Servicescape	**Other Tangibles**
Insurance	Not applicable	Policy itself Billing statements Periodic updates Company brochure Letters/cards Website
Hospital	Building exterior Parking Signs Waiting areas Admissions office Patient care room Medical equipment Recovery room	Uniforms Reports/stationery Billing statements Website
Airline	Airline gate area Airplane exterior Airplane interior (decor, seats, air quality)	Tickets Food Uniforms Website
Express mail	Not applicable	Packaging Trucks Uniforms Computers Website
Sporting event	Parking Stadium exterior Ticketing area Entrance Seating Restrooms Concession areas Playing field	Signs Tickets Programs Uniforms Website

How Does Physical Evidence Affect the Customer Experience?

Physical evidence, particularly the servicescape, can have a profound effect on the customer experience. This is true whether the experience is mundane (e.g., a bus or subway ride), personally meaningful (e.g., a church wedding experience, or a birthing room at a hospital), or spectacular (e.g., a week-long travel adventure).

As marketers and corporate strategists begin to pay more attention to experiences, they have recognized the impact of physical space and tangibles in creating those experiences. Lewis Carbone, a leading consultant on experience management, has developed an entire lexicon and management process around the basic idea of "experience engineering" through "clue management."[2] *Clue management* refers to the process of clearly identifying and managing *all* the various clues that customers use to form their impressions and feelings about the company. Included in this set of clues are what Carbone refers to as *mechanics clues,* or the physical and tangible clues that we focus on in this chapter. Other writers and consultants who focus on managing customer experiences also zero in on the importance of tangible evidence and physical facilities in shaping those experiences.[3]

TYPES OF SERVICESCAPES

This chapter relies heavily on ideas and concepts from environmental psychology, a field that encompasses the study of human beings and their relationships with built (man-made), natural, and social environments.[4] Table 11.3 is a framework for categorizing service organizations on two dimensions that impact the management of the servicescape. Organizations that share a cell in the matrix will face similar issues and decisions regarding their physical spaces.

Servicescape Usage

First, organizations differ in terms of *whom* the servicescape will actually affect. At one extreme is the *self-service* environment, in which the customer performs most of the activities. Examples of self-service environments include ATMs, movie theatres, express mail dropoff facilities, and online Internet services. In these primarily self-service environments the organization can plan the servicescape to focus exclusively on marketing goals such as attracting the right market segment and creating the desired service experience.

At the other extreme is the *remote service,* which has little or no customer involvement with the servicescape. Telecommunications, utilities, financial consultants, editorial, and mail-order services are examples of services that can be provided without the customer ever seeing the service facility. In fact, the facility may even be in a different country. In remote services, the facility can be set up to keep employees motivated and to facilitate productivity, teamwork, and operational efficiency without any consideration of customers because they will never need to see the servicescape.

In Table 11.3, *interpersonal services* represent situations in which both customers and employees are present in the servicescape. Examples abound, such as hotels, restaurants, hospitals, educational settings, and banks. In these situations the servicescape must be planned to attract, satisfy, and facilitate the activities of both customers and employees simultaneously. Special attention must also be given to how the servicescape affects the nature and quality of the social interactions between and among customers and employees.

TABLE 11.3

Typology of Service Organizations Based on Variations in Form and Use of the Servicescape

Servicescape Usage	Complexity of the Servicescape	
	Elaborate	**Lean**
Self-service (customer only)	Golf course eBay	ATM Car wash Simple Internet services Express mail dropoff
Interpersonal services (both customer and employee)	Hotel Restaurant Health clinic Hospital Bank Airline School	Dry cleaner Retail cart Hair salon
Remote service (employee only)	Telephone company Insurance company Utility Many professional services	Telephone mail-order desk Automated voice messaging services

Source: M. J. Bitner, "Servicescapes: The Impact of Physical Surroundings on Customers and Employees," *Journal of Marketing* 56 (April 1992), pp. 57–71. Reprinted with permission of the American Marketing Association.

Servicescape Complexity

The horizontal dimension of Table 11.3 suggests another factor that will influence servicescape management. Some service environments are very simple, with few elements, few spaces, and few pieces of equipment. Such environments are termed *lean*. Shopping mall information kiosks and FedEx dropoff facilities would be considered lean environments, because both provide service from one simple structure. For lean servicescapes, design decisions are relatively straightforward.

Very complicated servicescapes are termed *elaborate* environments. An example is a hospital with its many floors and rooms, sophisticated equipment, and complex variability performed within the physical facility. A patient's hospital room can be designed to enhance patient comfort and satisfaction while simultaneously facilitating employee productivity. To illustrate, Shouldice Hospital outside Toronto has a very unique servicescape that plays a critical role in actually helping patients recover from their surgery (see Exhibit 11.2). Similarly, when the Mayo Clinic opened its hospital in Scottsdale, Arizona, the organization painstakingly considered the interrelated goals, needs, and feelings of its employees, doctors, patients, and visitors in designing its distinctive servicescape (see the Global Feature later in this chapter).

STRATEGIC ROLES OF THE SERVICESCAPE

Within the cells of the typology, the servicescape can play many strategic roles simultaneously. An examination of the variety of roles and how they interact makes clear how strategically important it is to provide appropriate physical evidence of the service. In fact, the servicescape is frequently one of *the* most important elements used in positioning a service organization.

Package

Similarly to a tangible product's package, the servicescape and other elements of physical evidence essentially "wrap" the service and convey to consumers an external image of what is "inside." Product packages are designed to portray a particular image as well as to evoke a particular sensory or emotional reaction. The physical setting of a service does the same thing through the interaction of many complex stimuli. The servicescape is the outward appearance of the organization and thus can be critical in forming initial impressions or setting up customer expectations—it is a visual metaphor for the intangible service. This packaging role is particularly important in creating expectations for new customers and for newly established service organizations that are trying to build a particular image (as noted in the chapter's opening vignette on Speedi-Lube). The packaging role extends to the appearance of contact personnel through their uniforms or dress and other elements of their outward appearance.[5] If you have ever had a chance to visit one of the Hard Rock Cafés, you will immediately grasp the packaging role performed by the exterior and interior elements, especially the extensive use of rock-and-roll memorabilia.

Interestingly, the same care given to package design in product marketing is often not provided for services, even though the service package serves a variety of important roles. There are many exceptions, however. FedEx, for example, embarked on a major overhaul of its image by rethinking and redesigning all its tangibles—everything from its drop boxes to its service centres to the bags carried by its couriers.[6] The idea was to convey a consistent look and feel of "Things are simple here," and "Here, give us your package; we'll take care of everything."

Facilitator

The servicescape can also serve as a facilitator in aiding the performances of persons in the environment. How the setting is designed can enhance or inhibit the efficient

FIGURE 11.3

The interiors of Hard Rock Cafés (like this one in Toronto) play strong packaging (and differentiating) roles within the servicescape.

Source: © Hard Rock Café International.

flow of activities in the service setting. A well-designed, functional facility can make the service a pleasure to experience from the customer's point of view and a pleasure to perform from the employee's. On the other hand, poor and inefficient design may frustrate both customers and employees. For example, an international air traveller who finds himself in a poorly designed airport with few signs, poor ventilation, and few places to sit or eat will find the experience quite dissatisfying, and employees who work there will probably be unmotivated as well. The same traveller will appreciate seats on the airplane that are conducive to work and sleep. The seating itself, part of the physical surroundings of the service, has been improved over the years to better facilitate travellers' needs to sleep. In fact, the competition for better seat design continues as a major point of contention among the international airline carriers, and the results have translated into greater customer satisfaction for business travellers.[7] British Airways has even seen its market share increase on some routes as a direct result of its award-winning Club-World seat.[8] All these examples emphasize the facilitator role of the servicescape.

Socializer

The design of the servicescape aids in the socialization of both employees and customers in the sense that it helps convey expected roles, behaviours, and relationships. For example, a new employee in a professional services firm would come to understand her position in the hierarchy partially through noting her office assignment, the quality of her office furnishings, and her location relative to others in the organization.

The design of the facility can also suggest to customers what their role is relative to employees, what parts of the servicescape they are welcome in and which are for employees only, how they should behave while in the environment, and what types of interactions are encouraged. For example, consider a Club Med vacation environment that is set up to facilitate customer–customer interactions as well as guest interactions with Club Med staff. The organization also recognizes the need for privacy, providing areas that encourage solitary activities.

Differentiator

The design of the physical facility can differentiate a firm from its competitors and signal the market segment that the service is intended for. In shopping malls the signage, colours used in decor and displays, and type of music wafting from a store signal the intended market segment. Ryanair.com, based in Ireland, is the answer to most students' dreams. Cheap, safe flights all over Europe—some even for *free* (see Figure 11.4). Ryanair competes aggressively in the discount air travel business—a vital and healthy sector in Europe—and it uses its website as a key element of its overall physical evidence. It only takes a quick look at the site to recognize the differentiating role played by Ryanair's servicescape. Through a combination of out-of-the-way airports, municipal incentives, and an incredibly low cost structure that includes using its website for all ticketing, Ryanair competes on price, and every element of its servicescape reinforces this positioning.

In another context, the servicescape has been used as a major point of differentiation for PETsMART in the introduction of its innovative PETsHotel concept.[9] The hotels, which offer overnight care as well as day care for pets, are designed very differently from typical kennels or veterinary facilities. They feature a lobby area, colourful play areas, comfortable sleeping rooms, television, a "bone booth" for calling in, and another amenities that give the facilities a more residential, homelike appeal than traditional kennels have.

FIGURE 11.4

Ryanair.com
uses its website
as a key element
of its strategic
positioning as a
discount airline.

Source: Ryanair Ltd.

FRAMEWORK FOR UNDERSTANDING SERVICESCAPE EFFECTS ON BEHAVIOUR

Although it is useful from a strategic point of view to think about the multiple roles of the servicescape and how they interact, making actual decisions about servicescape design requires an understanding of why the effects occur and how to manage them. The next sections of the chapter present a model of environment and behaviour relationships in service settings.

The Underlying Framework

The framework for understanding servicescape effects on behaviour follows from basic *stimulus–organism–response* theory. In the framework the multidimensional environment is the *stimulus,* consumers and employees are the *organisms* that respond to the stimuli, and behaviours directed at the environment are the *responses.* The assumptions are that dimensions of the servicescape will impact customers and employees and that they will behave in certain ways depending on their internal reactions to the servicescape (Figure 11.5).

Our discussion of the framework will begin on the right side of the model with *behaviours.* Next we will explain and develop the *internal responses* portion of the model. Finally we will turn to the dimensions of the *environment* and the holistic perception of the environment.

FIGURE 11.5   A Framework for Understanding Environment–User Relationships in Service Organizations

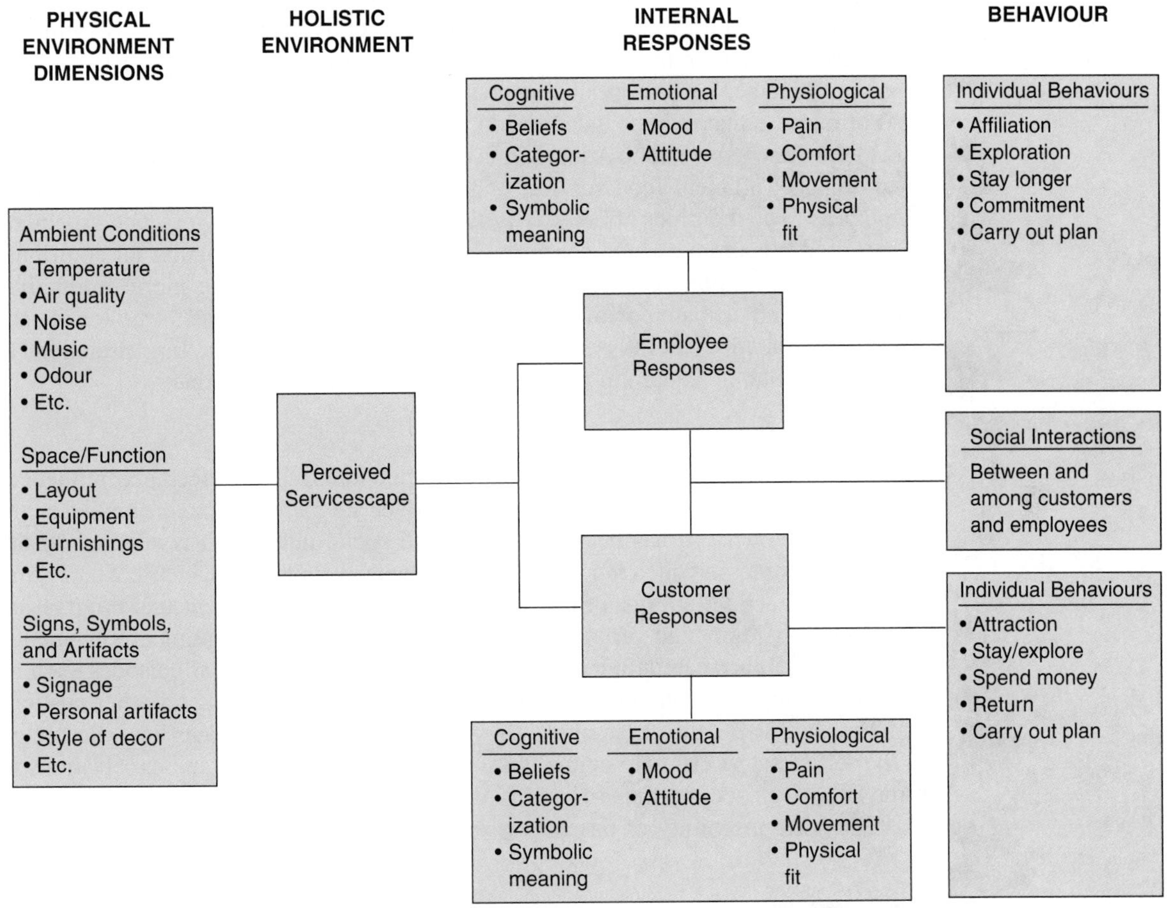

PHYSICAL ENVIRONMENT DIMENSIONS	HOLISTIC ENVIRONMENT	INTERNAL RESPONSES			BEHAVIOUR

Cognitive
- Beliefs
- Categorization
- Symbolic meaning

Emotional
- Mood
- Attitude

Physiological
- Pain
- Comfort
- Movement
- Physical fit

Individual Behaviours
- Affiliation
- Exploration
- Stay longer
- Commitment
- Carry out plan

Ambient Conditions
- Temperature
- Air quality
- Noise
- Music
- Odour
- Etc.

Space/Function
- Layout
- Equipment
- Furnishings
- Etc.

Signs, Symbols, and Artifacts
- Signage
- Personal artifacts
- Style of decor
- Etc.

Perceived Servicescape

Employee Responses

Social Interactions
Between and among customers and employees

Customer Responses

Individual Behaviours
- Attraction
- Stay/explore
- Spend money
- Return
- Carry out plan

Cognitive
- Beliefs
- Categorization
- Symbolic meaning

Emotional
- Mood
- Attitude

Physiological
- Pain
- Comfort
- Movement
- Physical fit

Source: Adapted from M. J. Bitner, "Servicescapes: The Impact of Physical Surroundings on Customers and Employees," *Journal of Marketing* 56 (April 1992), pp. 57–71. Reprinted with permission of the American Marketing Association.

Behaviours in the Servicescape

That human behaviour is influenced by the physical setting in which it occurs is essentially a truism. Interestingly, however, until the 1960s psychologists largely ignored the effects of physical setting in their attempts to predict and explain behaviour. Since that time, a large and steadily growing body of literature within the field of environmental psychology has addressed the relationships between human beings and their built environments. Recent marketing focus on the customer experience has also drawn attention to the effects of physical spaces and design on customer behaviour.[10]

Individual Behaviours

Environmental psychologists suggest that individuals react to places with two general, and opposite, forms of behaviour: approach and avoidance. Approach behaviours include all positive behaviours that might be directed at a particular place, such as desire to stay, explore, work, and affiliate.[11] Avoidance behaviours reflect the opposite. In a study of consumers in retail environments, researchers found that approach behaviours (including shopping enjoyment, returning, attraction and friendliness toward others, spending money, time spent browsing, and exploration of the store) were influenced by perceptions of the environment.[12]

In addition to attracting or deterring entry, the servicescape can actually influence the degree of success that consumers and employees experience in executing their plans once inside. Each individual comes to a particular service organization with a goal or purpose that may be aided or hindered by the setting. The enjoyment of visitors to the Vancouver Public Aquarium is enhanced by adequate, easy-access parking; clear signage; efficient food service; and clean restrooms. The ability of the VPA's employees to do their jobs effectively is also influenced by the servicescape. Adequate space, proper equipment, and comfortable temperature and air quality all contribute to employees' comfort and job satisfaction, causing them to be more productive, stay longer, and affiliate positively with coworkers. The same is also true for the sea life! Without a very carefully controlled servicescape, the sea-dwelling attractions at Vancouver's Public Aquarium wouldn't be able to do their job, either.

Social Interactions

In addition to its effects on their individual behaviours, the servicescape influences the nature and quality of customer and employee interactions, most directly in interpersonal services. It has been stated that "all social interaction is affected by the physical container in which it occurs."[13] The "physical container" can affect the nature of social interaction in terms of the duration of interaction and the actual progression of events. Environmental variables such as physical proximity, seating arrangements, size, and flexibility can define the possibilities and limits of social episodes such as those occurring between customers and employees, or customers and other customers. The Carnival Cruise Line photo shown in Figure 11.6 illustrates how the design of the servicescape can help define the social rules, conventions, and expectations in force in a given setting, thus serving to define the nature of social interaction.[14] The close physical proximity of passengers on the sunbathing deck will in and of itself

FIGURE 11.6

Social interactions are defined partially by the configuration of the servicescape.

Source: Carnival Cruise Lines.

prescribe certain patterns of behaviour. This vacation is not designed for a recluse! Some researchers have implied that recurring social behaviour patterns are associated with particular physical settings and that when people encounter typical settings, their social behaviours can be predicted.[15]

Examples of how environments shape social interactions—and how these interactions in turn influence the environment—are abundant.[16] Even casual observation of Canada's world-renowned Shouldice Hospital demonstrates a unique service strategy—so unique that a recent *Globe and Mail* story was titled "Hernia Hospital Teaches Harvard About Service." The service strategy is based, at least in part, on cultivating very important social interactions both between patients and between patients and staff (see Exhibit 11.1).

Internal Responses to the Servicescape

Employees and customers respond to dimensions of their physical surroundings cognitively, emotionally, and physiologically, and those responses are what influence their behaviours in the environment. In other words, the perceived servicescape does not directly *cause* people to behave in certain ways. Although the internal responses are discussed *independently* here, they are clearly *interdependent*: a person's beliefs about a place, a cognitive response, may well influence the person's emotional response, and vice versa. For example, patients who come into a dentist's office that is designed to calm and sooth their anxieties (emotional responses) may believe as a result that the dentist is caring and competent (cognitive responses).

Environment and Cognition

The perceived servicescape can have an effect on people's beliefs about a place and their beliefs about the people and products found in that place. In a sense the servicescape can be viewed as a form of nonverbal communication, imparting meaning through what is called "object language."[17] For example, in a consumer study, variations in descriptions of store atmospheres were found to alter beliefs about a product (perfume) sold in the store.[18] Another study showed that a travel agent's office decor affected customer attributions and beliefs about the travel agent's behaviour.[19] Travel agents whose facilities were more organized and professional were viewed more positively than were those whose facilities were disorganized and unprofessional.

In other cases, perceptions of the servicescape may simply help people distinguish a firm by influencing how it is categorized. The overall perception of the servicescape enables the consumer or employee to categorize the firm mentally. Research shows that in the restaurant industry a particular configuration of environmental cues suggests "fast food," whereas another configuration suggests "elegant sit-down restaurant."[20] In such situations, environmental cues serve as a shortcut device that enables customers to categorize and distinguish types of restaurants.

Environment and Emotion

In addition to influencing beliefs, the perceived servicescape can directly elicit emotional responses that, in turn, influence behaviours. Just being in a particular place can make a person feel happy, whereas being in another place may make that person feel sad. The colours, decor, music, and other elements of the atmosphere can have an unexplainable and sometimes very subconscious effect on the moods of people in the place.

MEC (Mountain Equipment Co-op) provides an example of emotional connection through architectural design and the servicescape. MEC stores typically bring the

EXHIBIT 11.1

Shouldice Hospital

Shouldice Hospital is renowned for its treatment of hernias—a condition many of the readers of this textbook may not have experienced given that the condition primarily affects middle-aged or older men. But although you may not have had any personal need for its service, you may still find their strategy very interesting. Shouldice boasts a 99 percent success rate, which is much better than that of any other hospital. And it knows its success rate, because it contacts as many as 130,000 patients a year.

The service strategy used at Shouldice (which won't be completely detailed here, because users of this textbook have access to the full case study) is heavily dependent upon its servicescape—not just the quality of its surgeons and nurses. You will recall from earlier

Source: Photo courtesy of Shouldice Hospital Limited.

chapters that in many services, customers themselves play a key role in service outcomes. That is certainly true in health care. At Shouldice, it is critical that patients begin to walk as soon as possible after their surgery to ensure successful recovery. It is also critical to their mental well-being that they avoid unnecessary anxiety. The servicescape used by the hospital helps to achieve both of these outcomes. Hence, in the language of our conceptual model in Figure 11.4, the Shouldice encourages important individual and social interactions.

According to Daryl Urquhart, Shouldice's director of business development, the strategy is to increase surgical success rates by facilitating patient activities that get patients to undertake much of their own diagnosis and postoperative care, as well as helping to create their own patient communities:

- Stays are 3–4 days in duration, in contrast to the traditional hectic schedules in hospitals that need to discharge patients as soon as possible. During this time, patients get to know each other and form instant support groups that permit them to compare experiences and therefore reduce anxiety.

- All rooms have two beds; no private rooms are allowed. This not only maximizes the usefulness of the space and thus increases overall capacity, but also ensures that each patient has a "buddy," serving the important servicescape role of socializing.

- Phones and TVs are not permitted in the rooms, only in common areas. This accomplishes two objectives. First, it encourages patients to get up and walk around. Second, it encourages interaction with other patients. Because a lot of attention is given to having to walk around, even the stairs have been designed with lower-than-normal risers to facilitate walking.

- All meals are taken in common dining rooms—not patient rooms. Patients must therefore walk to dinner, and when they get there, they must sit with each other—all tables seat six.

Shouldice therefore has a very focused service strategy, and its servicescape is a critical element in achieving its overall service goals. Interestingly, the hospital's fame is further enhanced by its widespread citation as a case study. As noted earlier, it is the subject of a Harvard Business School case and ranks as Harvard's fourth all-time bestselling case with 259,000 cases sold and annual sales of about 20,000 or more.

Sources: Gordon Pitts, "Hernia Hospital Teaches Harvard About Service," *Globe and Mail*, January 9, 2006; Ben McConnell and Jackie Huba, "Creating Surgical Communities: A Surgical Approach," *MarketingProfs*, March 11, 2003; conversations between the authors and Daryl Urquhart.

outdoors in with skylights, exposed beams, green roofs, climbing walls, tents assembled for trial, and walkways made of dirt and gravel to test hiking shoes (see Figure 11.7). Customers' approach response is further strengthened by the organization's building philosophy that fits with their mission of "striving for environmental leadership." MEC's Winnipeg store, for example, was built using 97 percent recycled material and consumes less energy, reduces greenhouse emissions, saves water, and supports sustainability by using solar panels, rain-catching cisterns, and composting toilets. MEC's new Ottawa store was the first retail building in Canada to comply with Canada's C2000 Green Building Standard. All aspects of MEC's servicescape reinforce the organization's environmental philosophy.

Environmental psychologists have researched people's emotional responses to physical settings.[21] They have concluded that any environment, whether natural or engineered, will elicit emotions that can be captured by two basic dimensions: (1) pleasure/displeasure and (2) degree of arousal (amount of stimulation or excitement). Servicescapes that are both pleasant and arousing would be termed *exciting,* whereas those that are pleasant and nonarousing, or sleepy, would be termed *relaxing.* Unpleasant servicescapes that are arousing would be called *distressing,* whereas unpleasant, sleepy servicescapes would be *gloomy.* These basic emotional responses to environments can be used to begin predicting the expected behaviours of consumers and employees who find themselves in a particular type of place.

Environment and Physiology

The perceived servicescape may also affect people in purely physiological ways. It is well known that the comfort of seating in a restaurant influences how long people stay. The hard seats in a fast-food restaurant cause most people to leave within a predictable period of time, whereas the soft, cozy chairs in some Starbucks coffee shops have the opposite effect, encouraging people to stay. Similarly, environmental design and related physiological responses affect whether employees can perform their job functions well.

FIGURE 11.7

MEC stores explicitly align their physical evidence with their core business philosophy so that the servicescape reinforces the business model.

Source: Courtesy of Mountain Equipment Co-op.

A vast amount of research in engineering and design has addressed human physiological responses to ambient conditions as well as physiological responses to equipment design.[22] Such research fits under the rubric of *human factors design* or *ergonomics.* Human factors research systematically applies relevant information about human capabilities and limitations to the design of items and procedures that people use. For example, Choice Hotels International targeted empty-nester couples and senior citizens in the redesign of many of the rooms in its Rodeway and EconoLodge brands. A significant percentage of the rooms in these hotels were converted to senior-friendly suites with brighter lighting, larger-button telephones and TV remotes, and grab bars in the showers.[23] Wall switches have lights so they can be found easily at night. To help people with arthritis, doors have lever handles instead of knobs so that every door and every drawer in the room can be opened with a fist rather than requiring hand and wrist dexterity.

Variations in Individual Responses

In general, people respond to the environment in the ways just described—cognitively, emotionally, physiologically—and their responses influence how they behave in the environment. However, the response will not be the same for every individual, every time. Personality differences as well as temporary conditions such as moods or the purpose for being there can cause variations in how people respond to the servicescape.[24]

One personality trait that has been shown to affect how people respond to environments is *arousal seeking.* In a related vein, it has been suggested that some people are better *screeners* of environmental stimuli than others.[25] Screeners of stimuli would be able to experience a high level of stimulation but not be affected by it. Nonscreeners would be highly affected and might exhibit extreme responses even to low levels of stimulation.

The particular purpose for being in a servicescape can also affect a person's response to it. A person who is on an airplane for a one-hour flight will likely be less affected by the atmosphere on the plane than a traveller who is embarking on a 10-hour overseas flight. Similarly, a day-surgery hospital patient will likely be less sensitive and demanding of the hospital environment than would a patient who is spending two weeks in the hospital.

Temporary mood states can also cause people to respond differently to environmental stimuli. A person who is feeling frustrated and fatigued after a long day at work is likely to be affected differently by a highly arousing restaurant than the same person would be after a relaxing three-day weekend.

Environmental Dimensions of the Servicescape

The preceding sections have described customer and employee behaviours in the servicescape and the three primary responses—cognitive, emotional, and physiological—that lead to those behaviours. In this section we turn to the complex mix of environmental features that influence these responses and behaviours (the left portion of Figure 11.4). In Figure 11.4 and in the discussion that follows here, the hundreds of potential elements have been categorized into three composite dimensions: *ambient conditions*; *spatial layout and functionality*; and *signs, symbols, and artifacts.* The Global Feature here illustrates how the Mayo Clinic took into consideration all these dimensions in designing its hospital to accommodate patients, doctors, employees, and visitors.

Although we discuss the three dimensions separately, environmental psychology explains that people respond to their environments holistically. That is, it is the total

Global Feature

Mayo Clinic Hospital Designs a Servicescape for All Users

In 1998 Mayo opened the Mayo Clinic Hospital in Scottsdale, Arizona, the first hospital planned, designed, and built by Mayo Clinic. Located on an 85-hectare site, the hospital houses 178 hospital rooms on five floors. More than 275 physicians, 3,500 support staff, and 300 volunteers serve patients from across the United States and 80 other countries at the facility.

What is unique about this hospital facility is the care that was taken in its design to serve the needs of patients, doctors, staff, and visitors. The hospital is designed as a "healing environment" focused on patient needs, and focus groups were held with all constituents to determine how the hospital should be designed to facilitate this overall goal. A quotation from the Mayo brothers (founders of the clinic) captures the underlying belief that supported the design of the hospital: "The best interest of the patient is the only interest to be considered." To focus on the best interests of the patient also requires acknowledgment of the needs of the care providers and the patient's family and friend support system. All these interests were clearly considered in the design of the hospital.

A FIVE-STOREY ATRIUM LOW-STRESS ENTRY

As patients and others enter the Mayo Hospital, they encounter a five-storey enclosed atrium, reminiscent of a luxury hotel lobby. A grand piano sits in the lobby, and volunteers play beautiful, relaxing music throughout the day. An abundance of plants and glass gives the lobby a natural feel and provides a welcoming atmosphere. On entering, visitors see the elevator bank directly in front of them across the atrium, so there is no stress in figuring out where to go.

ALL PATIENT AND VISITOR SERVICES ARE TOGETHER

All services needed by patients and their families (information desk, cafeteria, chapel, patient admissions, gift shop) are located around the atrium, easily visible and

Source: Photo courtesy of Mayo Clinic Scottsdale.

accessible. A sense of peace and quiet permeates the lobby—all by deliberate design to reduce stress and promote caring and wellness. There is no confusion here and very little of the atmosphere of a typical hospital entry.

ROOMS ARE DESIGNED AROUND PATIENT NEEDS AND FEELINGS

On disembarking the elevators to go to patient rooms, people again sense relaxation and peace in the environment. As the doors open, patients and guests face a five-storey wall of paned glass with views out to the desert and mountains that ring the hospital site. As one progresses left or right down well-marked corridors to the patient rooms, the atmosphere becomes even quieter. Rooms (all of them private) are arranged in 12-bed pods surrounding a nursing station. Nurses are within 20 steps of any patient room. Nurses and other attendants use cell phones—there is no paging system with constant announcements, as in many hospitals.

The rooms themselves have interesting features, some designed by patients. For example, rooms contain a multi-shelf display area on which patients can put cards, flowers, and other personal items. Fold-out, cushioned bed-chairs are in each room so family members can

continued

Global Feature

Mayo Clinic Hospital Designs a Servicescape for all Users—continued

nap or even spend the night with their loved ones. The rooms are arranged with consideration to what patients see from the beds, where they spend the most time. For example, special attention is paid to the ceilings, which patients view while flat on their backs; all rooms have windows; and a whiteboard on the wall at the foot of each bed displays important information that patients want to know (like the name of the nurse on duty, the date, the room phone number, and other information).

DEPARTMENTS THAT WORK TOGETHER ARE ADJACENT

Another interesting design feature in this hospital is that departments that work together are housed very close

to each other to facilitate communication and to reduce walking time between areas. This important feature allows caregivers to spend more time with patients and also lessens employee fatigue.

It is clear that the design of the Mayo Hospital takes into account the critical importance of the servicescape in facilitating Mayo's primary goal: patient healing. All parties' voices were heard, and the place itself provides an environment that promotes well-being for patients, visitors, doctors, nurses, and other staff.

Sources: *Teamwork at Mayo: An Experiment in Cooperative Individualism* (Rochester, MN: Mayo Press, 1998); www.mayo.edu; www.mayoclinic.org; author's personal tour of the Mayo Clinic Hospital in Scottsdale.

configuration of stimuli that determines their reactions to a place. Hence, though the dimensions of the environment are defined independently in the following sections, it is important to recognize that they are perceived by employees and customers as a holistic pattern of interdependent stimuli. The holistic response is shown in Figure 11.4 as the "perceived servicescape."

Ambient Conditions

Ambient conditions include background characteristics of the environment such as temperature, lighting, noise, music, scent, and colour. All these factors can profoundly affect how people feel, think, and respond to a particular service establishment. For example, a number of studies have documented the effects of music on consumers' perceptions of products, their perceptions of how long they have waited for service, and the amount of money they spend.[26] When there is music, shoppers tend to perceive that they spend less time shopping and in line than when there is no music. Slower music tempos at lower volumes tend to make people shop more leisurely, and in some cases, they spend more. At Hard Rock Cafés like the ones in Montreal, Toronto, and Vancouver, the music is intended to reinforce the entire service concept as well as putting guests in the mood to buy souvenirs before leaving. Shoppers also spend more time when the music "fits" the product or matches their musical tastes. Other studies have similarly shown the effects of scent on consumer responses.[27] Scent in bakeries, coffee shops, and tobacco shops, for example, can be used to draw people in, and pleasant scents can increase lingering time. The presence of a scent can reduce perceptions of time spent and improve store evaluations.

Ambient conditions have a greater effect when the customer or employee spends considerable time in the servicescape. The impact of temperature, music, odours, and colours builds over time. Another instance in which ambient conditions will be particularly influential is when they conflict with what the customer or employee expects.

Spatial Layout and Functionality

Because service environments exist to fulfil specific purposes or needs, spatial layout and functionality of the physical surroundings are particularly important. *Spatial layout* refers to the ways in which machinery, equipment, and furnishings are arranged, the size and shape of those items, and the spatial relationships among them. *Functionality* refers to the ability of the same items to facilitate the accomplishment of customer and employee goals. Previous examples in this chapter illustrate the layout and functionality dimensions of the servicescape—for example the Carnival ad in Figure 11.6, and the design of the Shouldice Hospital (Exhibit 11.1).

The spatial layout and functionality of the environment are particularly important for customers in self-service environments, where they must perform the service on their own and cannot rely on employees to assist them. Thus the functionality of an ATM machine and of self-serve restaurants, gasoline pumps, and Internet shopping are critical to success and customer satisfaction.

The importance of facility layout is particularly apparent in retail, hospitality, and leisure settings, where research shows it can influence customer satisfaction, store performance, and consumer search behaviour.[28]

Signs, Symbols, and Artifacts

Many items in the physical environment serve as explicit or implicit signals that communicate about the place to its users. Signs displayed on the exterior and interior of a structure are examples of explicit communicators. They can be used as labels (name of company, name of department, and so on), for directional purposes (entrances, exits), and to communicate rules of behaviour (no smoking, children must be accompanied by an adult). Adequate signs have even been shown to reduce perceived crowding and stress.

Other environmental symbols and artifacts may communicate less directly than signs, giving implicit cues to users about the meaning of the place and norms and expectations for behaviour in the place. Quality construction materials, artwork, certificates and photographs, floor coverings, and personal objects displayed in the environment can all communicate symbolic meaning and create an overall aesthetic impression. Restaurant managers in Canada, for example, know that white tablecloths and subdued lighting symbolically convey full service and relatively high prices, whereas counter service, plastic furnishings, and bright lighting symbolize the opposite. In Canadian office environments, certain cues such as desk size and placement symbolize status and may be used to reinforce professional image.[29]

Signs, symbols, and artifacts are particularly important in forming first impressions and for communicating service concepts. When customers are unfamiliar with a particular service establishment, they look for environmental cues to help them categorize the place and form their expectations. A study of dentists' offices found that consumers use the environment, in particular its style of decoration and level of quality, as a cue to the competence and manner of the service provider.[30] Another interesting study explored the roles of ethnicity and sexual orientation on consumers' interpretation of symbols within consumption environments. Specifically, the study found that people of Jewish descent observe particular symbols in places that encourage them to feel at home and approach those places.[31] The same study found that homosexuals were also drawn to environments that included particular symbols and artifacts that they identified with. In the presence of other symbols, these groups felt unwelcome or even discriminated against.

GUIDELINES FOR PHYSICAL EVIDENCE STRATEGY

To this point in the chapter we have presented models for understanding the effects of the physical facility or servicescape. In this section we suggest some general guidelines for an effective physical evidence strategy.[32]

Recognize the Strategic Impact of Physical Evidence

Physical evidence can play a prominent role in determining service quality expectations and perceptions. For some organizations, just acknowledging the impact of physical evidence is a major first step. After this step they can take advantage of the potential of physical evidence and plan strategically.

For an evidence strategy to be effective, it must be linked clearly to the organization's overall goals and vision. Thus planners must know what those goals are and then determine how the physical evidence strategy can support them. At minimum, the basic service concept must be defined, the target markets (both internal and external) identified, and the firm's broad vision of its future known. Because many evidence decisions are relatively permanent and costly (particularly servicescape decisions), they must be planned and executed deliberately.

Blueprint the Physical Evidence of Service

The next step is to map the service. Everyone should be able to see the service process and the existing elements of physical evidence. An effective way to depict service evidence is through the service blueprint. (Service blueprinting was presented in detail in Chapter 9.) Although service blueprints clearly have multiple purposes, they can be particularly useful in visually capturing physical evidence opportunities. People, process, and physical evidence can all be seen in the blueprint. Firms can read the actions involved in service delivery, the complexity of the process, the points of human interaction that provide evidence opportunities, and the tangible representations present at each step. To make the blueprint even more useful, photographs or videotape of the process can be added to develop a photographic blueprint that provides a vivid picture of physical evidence from the customer's point of view.

Clarify Strategic Roles of the Servicescape

Early in the chapter we discussed the varying roles played by the servicescape and how firms could locate themselves in the typology shown in Table 11.3 to begin to identify their roles. For example, a child care company would locate itself in the "elaborate, interpersonal" cell of the matrix and quickly see that its servicescape decisions would be relatively complex and that the servicescape strategy (1) would have to consider the needs of both the children and the service providers and (2) could impact marketing, organizational behaviour, and consumer satisfaction goals.

Sometimes the servicescape may have no role in service delivery or marketing from the customer's point of view, such as in telecommunications services or utilities. Clarifying the roles played by the servicescape in a particular situation will aid in identifying opportunities and deciding who needs to be consulted in making facility design decisions. Clarifying the strategic role of the servicescape also forces recognition of the importance of the servicescape in creating customer experiences.

Assess and Identify Physical Evidence Opportunities

Once the current forms of evidence and the roles of the servicescape are understood, possible changes and improvements can be identified. One question to ask is: Are there missed opportunities to provide service evidence? The service blueprint of an insurance or utility service may show that little, if any, evidence of service is ever provided to the customer. A strategy might then be developed to provide more evidence of service to show customers exactly what they are paying for. Speedi-Lube, our opening example, effectively used this approach in providing multiple forms of evidence to make car maintenance service more tangible to the consumer.

Or it may be discovered that the evidence provided is sending messages that do not enhance the firm's image or goals or that do not match customer expectations. For example, a restaurant might find that its high-price menu cues are not consistent with the design of the restaurant, which suggests "family dining" to its intended market segment. Either the pricing or the facility design would need to be changed, depending on the restaurant's overall strategy.

Another set of questions addresses whether the current physical evidence of service suits the needs and preferences of the target market. To begin answering such questions, the framework for understanding environment–user relationships (Figure 11.5) and the research approaches suggested in this chapter could be employed. And finally, does the evidence strategy take into account the needs (sometimes incompatible) of both customers and employees? This question is particularly relevant in making decisions regarding the servicescape.

Be Prepared to Update and Modernize the Evidence

Some aspects of the evidence, particularly the servicescape, require frequent or at least periodic updating and modernizing. Even if the vision, goals, and objectives of the company do not change, time itself takes a toll on physical evidence, necessitating change and modernization. Clearly, an element of fashion is involved, and over time different colours, designs, and styles may come to communicate different messages. Organizations obviously understand this concept when it comes to advertising strategy, but sometimes they overlook other elements of physical evidence.

Work Cross-Functionally

In presenting itself to the consumer, a service firm is concerned with communicating a desired image, with sending consistent and compatible messages through all forms of evidence, and with providing the type of service evidence the target customers want and can understand. Frequently, however, physical evidence decisions are made over time and by various functions within the organization. For example, decisions regarding employee uniforms may be made by the human resources area, servicescape design decisions may be made by the facilities management group, process design decisions are most frequently made by operations managers, and advertising and pricing decisions may be made by the marketing department. Thus it is not surprising that the physical evidence of service may at times be less than consistent. Service blueprinting can be a valuable tool for communicating within the firm, identifying existing service evidence, and providing a springboard for changing or providing new forms of physical evidence.

A multifunction team approach to physical evidence strategy is often necessary, particularly for making decisions about the servicescape. It has been said that "Facility planning and management … is a problem-solving activity that lies on the boundaries between architecture, interior space planning and product design, organizational [and consumer] behavior, planning and environmental psychology."[33]

SUMMARY

In this chapter we explored the roles of physical evidence in forming customer and employee perceptions and shaping customer experiences. Because services are intangible and because they are often produced and consumed at the same time, they can be difficult to comprehend or evaluate before their purchase. The physical evidence of the service thus serves as a primary cue for setting customer expectations before purchase. These tangible cues, particularly the servicescape, also influence customers' responses as they experience the service. Because customers and employees often interact in the servicescape, the physical surroundings also influence employees and the nature of employee–customer interactions.

The chapter focused primarily on the servicescape—the physical surroundings or the physical facility where the service is produced, delivered, and consumed. We presented a typology of servicescapes that illustrated their range of complexity and usage. By locating itself in the appropriate cell of the typology, an organization can quickly see who needs to be consulted regarding servicescape decisions, what objectives might be achieved through careful design of the facility, and how complex the decisions are likely to be. General strategic roles of the servicescape were also described. The servicescape can serve as a package (a "visual metaphor" for the service itself), a facilitator in aiding the accomplishment of customer and employee goals, a socializer in prescribing behaviours in the environment, and a differentiator to distinguish the organization from its competitors.

With this grounding in the importance of physical evidence, in particular the servicescape, we presented a general framework for understanding servicescape effects on employee and customer behaviours. The servicescape can affect the approach and avoidance behaviours of individual customers and employees as well as their social interactions. These behavioural responses come about because the physical environment influences (1) people's beliefs or cognitions about the service organization, (2) their feelings or emotions in response to the place, and (3) their actual physiological reactions while in the physical facility. The chapter also pointed out that individuals may respond differently to the servicescape depending on their personality traits, the mood they are in, or the goals they are trying to accomplish.

Three categories of environmental dimensions capture the complex nature of the servicescape: ambient conditions; spatial layout and functionality; and signs, symbols, and artifacts. These dimensions affect people's beliefs, emotions, and physical responses, causing them to behave in certain ways while in the servicescape.

Given the importance of physical evidence and its potentially powerful influence on both customers and employees, it is important for firms to think strategically about the management of the tangible evidence of service. The impact of physical evidence and design decisions needs to be researched and planned as part of the marketing strategy. The chapter concluded with specific guidelines for physical evidence strategy. If physical evidence is researched, planned, and implemented effectively, key problems leading to service quality shortcomings can be avoided. Through careful thinking about physical evidence decisions, an organization can avoid miscommunicating to customers via incompatible or inconsistent evidence or overpromising and raising customer expectations unrealistically. Beyond its role in helping avoid these negative outcomes, an effective physical evidence strategy can play a critically important role in communicating to customers and in guiding them in understanding the firm's offerings and setting up accurate expectations. During the service experience, physical evidence plays a major role in creating memorable outcomes and emotional connections with customers.

Discussion Questions

1. What is physical evidence, and why have we devoted an entire chapter to it in a marketing text?

2. Describe and give an example of how servicescapes play each of the following strategic roles: package, facilitator, socializer, and differentiator.

3. Imagine that you own an independent copying and printing shop (similar to Kinko's). In which cell would you locate your business in the typology of servicescapes shown in Table 11.3? What are the implications for designing your physical facility?

4. How can an effective physical evidence strategy help close Provider Gap 2? Explain.

5. Why are both customers and employees included in the framework for understanding servicescape effects on behaviour (Figure 11.5)? What types of behaviours are influenced by the servicescape according to the framework? Think of examples.

6. Using your own experiences, give examples of times when you have been affected cognitively, emotionally, and physiologically by elements of the servicescape (in any service context).

7. Why is everyone not affected in exactly the same way by the servicescape?

8. Describe the physical environment of your favourite restaurant in terms of the three categories of servicescape dimensions: ambient conditions; spatial layout and functionality; and signs, symbols, and artifacts.

9. Imagine that you are serving as a consultant to a local health club. How would you advise the health club to begin the process of developing an effective physical evidence strategy?

Exercises

1. Choose two very different firms (different market segments or service levels) in the same industry. Observe both establishments. Describe the service "package" in both cases. How does the package help distinguish the two firms? Do you believe that the package sets accurate expectations for what the firm delivers? Is either firm overpromising through the manner in which its servicescape (or other types of physical evidence) communicates with customers?

2. Think of a particular service organization (it can be a class project company, the company you work for, or some other organization) for which you believe physical evidence is particularly important in communicating with and satisfying customers. Prepare the text of a presentation you would give to the manager of that organization to convince him or her of the importance of physical evidence in the organization's marketing strategy.

3. Create a photographic blueprint for a service of your choice.

4. Choose a service organization and collect all forms of physical evidence that the organization uses to communicate with its customers. If customers see the firm's facility, also take a photo of the servicescape. Analyze the evidence in terms of compatibility, consistency, and whether it overpromises or underpromises what the firm can deliver.

5. Visit the websites of several service providers. Does the physical evidence of the website portray an image consistent with other forms of evidence provided by the organizations?

Notes

1. The term *servicescape* used throughout this chapter, and much of the content of this chapter, are based, with permission, on M. J. Bitner, "Servicescapes: The Impact of Physical Surroundings on Customers and Employees," *Journal of Marketing* 56 (April 1992), pp. 57–71. For recent contributions to this topic, see *Servicescapes: The Concept of Place in Contemporary Markets,* ed. J. F. Sherry Jr. (Chicago: NTC/Contemporary Publishing Company, 1998); and M. J. Bitner, "The Servicescape," in *Handbook of Services Marketing and Management,* ed. T. A. Swartz and D. Iacobucci (Thousand Oaks, CA: Sage Publications, 2000), pp. 37–50.

2. L. P. Carbone, *Clued In: How to Keep Customers Coming Back Again and Again* (Upper Saddle River, NJ: Prentice Hall, 2004). See also L. L. Berry and N. Bendapudi, "Clueing In Customers," *Harvard Business Review,* February 2003, pp. 100–106.

3. J. H. Gilmore and B. J. Pine II, "The Experience Is the Marketing," *Strategic Horizons,* 2002; B. J. Pine II and J. H. Gilmore, *The Experience Economy: Work Is Theater and Every Business Is a Stage* (Boston: Harvard Business School Press, 1999); B. H. Schmitt, *Experiential Marketing* (New York: The Free Press, 1999).

4. For reviews of environmental psychology, see D. Stokols and I. Altman, *Handbook of Environmental Psychology* (New York: John Wiley, 1987); S. Saegert and G. H. Winkel, "Environmental Psychology," *Annual Review of Psychology* 41 (1990), pp. 441–77; and E. Sundstrom, P. A. Bell, P. L. Busby, and C. Asmus, "Environmental Psychology 1989–1994," *Annual Review of Psychology* 47 (1996), pp. 485–512.

5. See M. R. Solomon, "Dressing for the Part: The Role of Costume in the Staging of the Servicescape," in Sherry, *Servicescapes: The Concept of Space in Contemporary Markets*; and A. Rafaeli, "Dress and Behavior of Customer Contact Employees: A Framework for Analysis," in *Advances in Services Marketing and Management,* vol. 2, ed. T. A. Swartz, D. E. Bowen, and S. W. Brown (Greenwich, CT: JAI Press, 1993), pp. 175–212.

6. S. Casey, "Federal Expressive," *eCompanyNow,* May 2001, pp. 45–48.

7. D. Michaels, "Business-Class Warfare: Rival Airlines Scramble to Beat BA's Reclining Bed Seats," *The Wall Street Journal,* March 16, 2001, p. B1.

8. Ibid.; and British Airways website, www.britishairways.com.

9. www.petsmart.com, 2004.

10. Carbone, *Clued In*; Berry and Bendapudi, "Clueing In Customers"; Gilmore and Pine, "The Experience Is the Marketing"; Pine and Gilmore, *The Experience Economy*; Schmitt, *Experiential Marketing.*

11. A. Mehrabian and J. A. Russell, *An Approach to Environmental Psychology* (Cambridge, MA: Massachusetts Institute of Technology, 1974).

12. R. Donovan and J. Rossiter, "Store Atmosphere: An Environmental Psychology Approach," *Journal of Retailing* 58 (Spring 1982), pp. 34–57.

13. D. J. Bennett and J. D. Bennett, "Making the Scene," in *Social Psychology Through Symbolic Interactionism,* ed. G. Stone and H. Farberman (Waltham, MA: Ginn-Blaisdell, 1970), pp. 190–96.

14. J. P. Forgas, *Social Episodes* (London: Academic Press, 1979).

15. R. G. Barker, *Ecological Psychology* (Stanford, CA: Stanford University Press, 1968).

16. For a number of excellent papers on this topic spanning a range from toy stores to bridal salons to cyber marketpaces to Japanese retail environments and others, see Sherry, *Servicescapes: The Concept of Place in Contemporary Markets.*

17. A. Rapoport, *The Meaning of the Built Environment* (Beverly Hills, CA: Sage Publications, 1982); R. G. Golledge, "Environmental Cognition," in Stokols and Altman, *Handbook of Environmental Psychology,* vol. 1, pp. 131–74.

18. M. P. Gardner and G. Siomkos, "Toward a Methodology for Assessing Effects of In-store Atmospherics," in *Advances in Consumer Research,* vol. 13, ed. R. J. Lutz (Ann Arbor, MI: Association for Consumer Research, 1986), pp. 27–31.

19. M. J. Bitner, "Evaluating Service Encounters: The Effects of Physical Surroundings and Employee Responses," *Journal of Marketing* 54 (April 1990), pp. 69–82.

20. J. C. Ward, M. J. Bitner, and J. Barnes, "Measuring the Prototypicality and Meaning of Retail Environments," *Journal of Retailing* 68 (Summer 1992), pp. 194–220.

21. See, for example, Mehrabian and Russell, *An Approach to Environmental Psychology;* J. A. Russell and U. F. Lanius, "Adaptation Level and the Affective Appraisal of Environments," *Journal of Environmental Psychology* 4, no. 2 (1984), pp. 199–235; J. A. Russell and G. Pratt, "A Description of the Affective Quality Attributed to Environments," *Journal of Personality and Social Psychology* 38, no. 2 (1980), pp. 311–22; J. A. Russell and J. Snodgrass, "Emotion and the Environment," in Stokols and Altman, *Handbook of Environmental Psychology,* vol. 1, pp. 245–81; J. A. Russell, L. M. Ward, and G. Pratt, "Affective Quality Attributed to Environments," *Environment and Behavior* 13 (May 1981), pp. 259–88.

22. See, for example, M. S. Sanders and E. J. McCormick, *Human Factors in Engineering and Design,* 7th ed. (New York: McGraw-Hill, 1993); and D. J. Osborne, *Ergonomics at Work,* 2nd ed. (New York: John Wiley, 1987).

23. "Empty Nests, Full Pockets," *Brandweek,* September 23, 1996, pp. 36ff; and "Lodging Chain to Give Older Guests a Choice," *The Wall Street Journal,* February 19, 1993, p. B1.

24. Mehrabian and Russell, *An Approach to Environmental Psychology;* Russell and Snodgrass, "Emotion and the Environment."

25. A. Mehrabian, "Individual Differences in Stimulus Screening and Arousability," *Journal of Personality* 45, no. 2 (1977), pp. 237–50.

26. For recent research documenting the effects of music on consumers, see J. Baker, D. Grewal, and A. Parasuraman, "The Influence of Store Environment on Quality Inferences and Store Image," *Journal of the Academy of Marketing Science* 22 (Fall 1994), pp. 328–39; J. C. Chebat, C. Gelinas-Chebat, and P. Filliatrault, "Interactive Effects of Musical and Visual Cues on Time Perception: An Application to Waiting Lines in Banks," *Perceptual and Motor Skills*

77 (1993), pp. 995–1020; L. Dube, J. C. Chebat, and S. Morin, "The Effects of Background Music on Consumers' Desire to Affiliate in Buyer–Seller Interactions," *Psychology and Marketing* 12, no. 4 (1995), pp. 305–19; J. D. Herrington and L. M. Capella, "Effects of Music in Service Environments: A Field Study," *Journal of Services Marketing* 10, no. 2 (1996), pp. 26–41; J. D. Herrington and L. M. Capella, "Practical Applications of Music in Service Settings," *Journal of Services Marketing* 8, no. 3 (1994), pp. 50–65; M. K. Hui, L. Dube, and J. C. Chebat, "The Impact of Music on Consumers' Reactions to Waiting for Services," *Journal of Retailing* 73 (Spring 1997), pp. 87–104; A. S. Matila and J. Wirtz, "Congruency of Scent and Music as a Driver of In-store Evaluations and Behavior," *Journal of Retailing* 77 (Summer 2001), pp. 273–89; L. Dube and S. Morin, "Background Music Pleasure and Store Evaluation: Intensity Effects and Psychological Mechanisms," *Journal of Business Research* 54 (November 2001), pp. 107–13; J. Bakec, A. Parasuraman, D. Grewal, and G. B. Voss, "The Influence of Multiple Store Environment Cues as Perceived Merchandise Value and Patronage Intentions," *Journal of Marketing* 66 (April 2002), pp. 120–41.

27. For recent research documenting the effects of scent on consumer responses, see D. J. Mitchell, B. E. Kahn, and S. C. Knasko, "There's Something in the Air: Effects of Congruent and Incongruent Ambient Odor on Consumer Decision Making," *Journal of Consumer Research* 22 (September 1995), pp. 229–38; and E. R. Spangenberg, A. E. Crowley, and P. W. Henderson, "Improving the Store Environment: Do Olfactory Cues Affect Evaluations and Behaviors?" *Journal of Marketing* 60 (April 1996), pp. 67–80.

28. See J. M. Sulek, M. R. Lind, and A. S. Marucheck, "The Impact of a Customer Service Intervention and Facility Design on Firm Performance," *Management Science* 41, no. 11 (1995), pp. 1763–73; P. A. Titus and P. B. Everett, "Consumer Wayfinding Tasks, Strategies, and Errors: An Exploratory Field Study," *Psychology and Marketing* 13, no. 3 (1996), pp. 265–90; C. Yoo, J. Park, and D. J. MacInnis, "Effects of Store Characteristics and In-store Emotional Experiences on Store Attitude," *Journal of Business Research* 42 (1998), pp. 253–63; K. L. Wakefield and J. G. Blodgett, "The Effect of the Servicescape on Customers' Behavioral Intentions in Leisure Service Settings," *Journal of Services Marketing* 10, no. 6 (1996), pp. 45–61.

29. T. R. V. Davis, "The Influence of the Physical Environment in Offices," *Academy of Management Review* 9, no. 2 (1984), pp. 271–83.

30. J. C. Ward and J. P. Eaton, "Service Environments: The Effect of Quality and Decorative Style on Emotions, Expectations, and Attributions," in *Proceedings of the American Marketing Association Summer Educators' Conference,* ed. R. Achrol and A. Mitchell (Chicago: American Marketing Association 1994), pp. 333–34.

31. M. S. Rosenbaum, "The Symbolic Servicescape: Your Kind Is Welcomed Here," *Journal of Consumer Behaviour* 4, no. 4, pp. 257–67.

32. This section is adapted from M. J. Bitner, "Managing the Evidence of Service," in *The Service Quality Handbook,* ed. E. E. Scheuing and W. F. Christopher (New York: AMACOM, 1993), pp. 358–70.

33. F. D. Becker, *Workspace* (New York: Praeger, 1981).

PART 5

Delivering and Performing Service

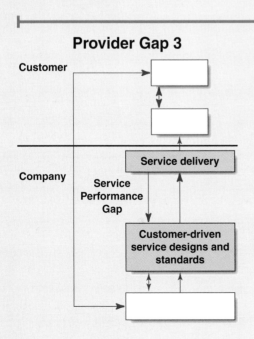

Provider Gap 3

Customer

Company

Service Performance Gap

Service delivery

Customer-driven service designs and standards

In the Gaps model of service quality, Provider Gap 3 (the Service Performance Gap) is the discrepancy between customer-driven service standards and actual service delivery (see the figure here). Even when guidelines exist for performing service well and treating customers correctly, high-quality service performance is not a certainty. Part 5 deals with all the ways in which companies ensure that services are performed according to customer-defined designs and standards.

In Chapter 12, we focus on the key roles that employees play in service delivery and strategies that ensure they are effective in their roles. Issues of particular concern include employees who feel in conflict between customers and company management, the wrong employees, inadequate technology, inappropriate compensation and recognition, and lack of empowerment and teamwork.

In Chapter 13, we discuss the variability caused by customers. If customers do not perform appropriately—if they do not follow instructions or if they disturb other customers receiving service at the same time—service quality is jeopardized. Effective service organizations acknowledge the role of customer variability and develop strategies to teach customers to perform their roles appropriately.

Chapter 14 describes service delivery through intermediaries such as retailers, franchisees, agents and brokers, and electronic channels. Although some service companies have control over the delivery channel, many service companies depend on other organizations to provide service to the end customer. For this reason, firms must develop ways to either control or motivate these intermediaries to meet company goals and deliver consistent quality service.

Chapter 15 emphasizes the need to synchronize demand and capacity in service organizations in order to deliver consistent, high-quality service. Service organizations often face situations of over- or underdemand because they lack inventories to smooth demand. Marketing strategies for managing demand, such as price changes, advertising, promotion, and alternative service offerings, can help this challenge.

Chapter 12

Employees' Roles in Service Delivery

Closing Provider Gap 3

THIS CHAPTER'S OBJECTIVES ARE TO

1. Demonstrate the importance of creating a service culture in which providing excellent service to both internal and external customers is a way of life.

2. Illustrate the critical importance of service employees in creating customer satisfaction and service quality.

3. Identify the challenges inherent in boundary-spanning roles.

4. Provide examples of strategies for creating customer-oriented service delivery through hiring the right people, developing employees to deliver service quality, providing needed support systems, and retaining the best service employees.

THE GREAT PLACE TO WORK INSTITUTE CANADA—RECOGNITION FOR EMPLOYEE INVESTMENT

Source: Courtesy of the Great Place to Work Institute® Canada.

It is often said that human capital, or an organization's employees, are a firm's most important assets. Particularly in services, front-line employees are the face of the company and directly impact customer satisfaction (as suggested by Figure 12.1). Leonard Berry, a noted service expert, has documented that investments in employee success are key drivers in business success. However, when faced with financial challenges, employee initiatives are often viewed as "extras" and seen as an opportunity to cut costs. But these investments in employees—from recruiting, to training, to compensating, and to creating, developing, and sustaining the overall organizational culture—often provide great returns. Keeping happy employees reduces the costs associated with turnover and can increase productivity.

So how does a firm maintain happy employees? Often compensation packages and employee perks are used as a measure. And, while these items are still important, a relatively new indicator developed by the Great Place to Work Institute Canada (www.greatplacetowork.ca) involves calculating what is referred to as a Trust Index. This appraisal is different from the more common measures, because it results from employee surveys (not just company records) and is meant to represent what employees say they really want in an employer—trust.

The Great Place to Work Institute has been surveying employees and ranking the best places to work since 1998. In 2005 alone, 500,000 employees from 28 different countries provided feedback. And, in the fall of that year, the Institute released its first results, naming 30 organizations as Canada's Best Places to Work. Take a look at some of the interesting employee investments being made by some of the companies on the Canadian list:

- Information technology consulting firm Sapient Canada offers employees negotiable sabbatical leaves.

- TD Bank Financial Group, in addition to offering the standard competitive salaries and stock options, also makes a significant investment in employee volunteerism.

- SaskTel, the telecommunications Crown corporation for Saskatchewan, takes employees to sweat-lodge ceremonies and on "medicine walks."

- Banff Caribou Properties Ltd., which owns seven hotels in the Banff area, offers employees a type of interest-free loan for a mortgage on a home in Banff.

- Globalive Communications Corp. offers all employees expert individual career coaching sessions.

- Saint Elizabeth Health Care, a not-for-profit organization making millions of in-home health visits in Markham, Ontario, has created a virtual meeting place for nurses with the moniker "School of Thought" to encourage sharing of ideas.

As the Great Place to Work Institute Canada indicates through its research, investment in employees is all about creating and

FIGURE 12.1

Service employees directly impact customers' satisfaction.

Source: John A. Rizzo/Getty Images.

sustaining a culture. And it is from this culture that effective or ineffective service performance emanates. Investing in employees, therefore, can be instrumental in minimizing Provider Gap 3—the service performance gap.[1]

In this chapter we focus on service employees and human resource practices that facilitate delivery of quality services. The assumption is that even when customer expectations are well understood (Gap 1) and services have been designed and specified to conform to those expectations (Gap 2), there may still be discontinuities in service quality when the service is not delivered as specified. These discontinuities are labelled Gap 3—the service performance gap—in the service quality framework. Because employees frequently deliver or perform the service, human resource issues are a major cause of this gap. By focusing on the critical role of service employees and by developing strategies that will lead to effective customer-oriented service, organizations can begin to close the service delivery gap.

The failure to deliver services as designed and specified can result from a number of employee and human performance factors: ineffective recruitment of service-oriented employees; role ambiguity and role conflict among contact employees; poor employee–technology–job fit; inappropriate evaluation and compensation systems; and lack of empowerment, perceived control, and teamwork. Prior to examining these factors and strategies for overcoming them, we begin the chapter with a discussion of service culture and its influence on employee behaviour.

→ SERVICE CULTURE

Before addressing the role of the employee in service delivery, we should look at the bigger picture. The behaviour of employees in an organization will be heavily influenced by the culture of an organization, or the pervasive norms and values that shape individual and group behaviour. *Corporate culture* has been defined as "the pattern of shared values and beliefs that give the members of an organization meaning, and provide them with the rules for behavior in the organization."[2] *Culture* has been defined more informally as "the way we do things around here."

Piglet in *Winnie the Pooh* might refer to culture as one of those things we sense "in an underneath sort of way." To understand at a personal level what corporate culture is, think of different places you have worked or organizations you have been a member of, such as churches, fraternities, schools, or associations. Your behaviour and the behaviours of others were no doubt influenced by the underlying values, norms, and culture of the organization. Even when you first interview for a new job, you can begin to get a sense of the culture through talking to a number of employees and observing behaviour. Once you are on the job, your formal training as well as informal observation of behaviour will work together to give you a better picture of the organization's culture.

Experts have suggested that a customer-oriented, service-oriented organization will have at its heart a *service culture*, defined as "a culture where an appreciation for good service exists, and where giving good service to internal as well as ultimate, external customers is considered a natural way of life and one of the most important norms by everyone."[3] This very rich definition has many implications for employee behaviours. First, a service culture exists if there is an "appreciation for good service." This phrase does not mean that the company has an advertising campaign that stresses the importance of service, but in that "underneath sort of way" people know that good service is appreciated and valued. A second important point in this definition is that good service is given to internal as well as external customers.[4] It is not enough to promise excellent service to final customers; all people within the organization deserve the same kind of service. Finally, in a service culture good service is "a way of life" and it comes naturally because it is an important norm of the organization.

Service culture has been linked to competitive advantage in companies.[5] Why is it so important? No realistic amount of supervision would allow a firm to exercise sufficient control over *all* employee behaviour. In many service settings, employees interact with customers with no management present. In such instances, the firm must rely on its service culture to influence employee thoughts, feelings, and behaviours.

THE CRITICAL IMPORTANCE OF SERVICE EMPLOYEES

This text is subtitled *Integrating Customer Focus Across the Firm*. Achieving this integration has many implications. Michel Bon, CEO of France Telecom, identifies one of these implications:

> If you sincerely believe that "The customer is king," the second most important person in this kingdom must be the one who has a direct interaction on a daily basis with the one who is king.[6]

People—front-line employees and those supporting them from behind the scenes—are critical to the success of any service organization. The importance of people in the marketing of services is captured in the *people* element of the services marketing mix, which we described in Chapter 1 *as all the human actors who play a part in service delivery and thus influence the buyer's perceptions; namely, the firm's personnel, the customer, and other customers in the service environment*. As we also learned in Chapter 1, services are often produced and consumed simultaneously unlike in most product-based firms where goods may be produced by employees who rarely, if ever, come face-to-face with their customers. Services are also highly intangible. These two characteristics—simultaneity of production and consumption and intangibility—increase the significance of front-line staff. Hence, the key focus in this chapter is on customer-contact employees, because in services:

- They *are* the service.

- They *are* the organization in the customer's eyes.

- They *are* the brand.

- They *are* marketers.

In many cases, the contact employee *is the service*—there is nothing else. For example, in most personal and professional services (like haircutting, physical trainers, child care, cleaning/maintenance, counselling, and legal services) the contact employee provides the entire service singlehandedly. The offering *is* the employee.

Even if the contact employee doesn't perform the service entirely, he or she may still *personify the firm in the customer's eyes*. All the employees of a law firm or health clinic—from the professionals who provide the service to the receptionists and office staff—represent the firm to the client, and everything these individuals do or say can influence perceptions of the organization. Even off-duty employees, such as flight attendants, reflect on the organizations they represent. The Disney Corporation insists that its employees maintain "onstage" attitudes and behaviours whenever they are in front of the public and that they relax these behaviours only when they are truly behind the scenes or "backstage" in underground tunnels where guests cannot see them in their off-duty times.

Service employees *are the brand*. A VanCity financial advisor, a Canadian Tire sales associate, a WestJet Airlines flight attendant—in each case, the primary image that a customer has of the firm is formed by the interactions the customer has with the employees of that firm. A customer sees VanCity Credit Union as a good provider of financial services if the employees she interacts with are knowledgeable, understanding, and concerned about her financial situation and goals. According to WestJet, "The driver for our brand is our people."[7] For WestJet (see Figure 12.2), where 86 percent of employees are also shareholders, the link between the brand and the employee is very strong. "What our people drive is the experience that our guests receive."[8]

Even in a nonservice setting, Audi, an automobile manufacturer, recognizes the importance of its employees in representing and reinforcing the brand image of the company. As a result, Audi recruits service personnel at all levels whose psychological traits parallel and support the Audi image.[9] For example, Audi looks to hire employees who are not afraid to develop a personal relationship with customers. At Audi the brand image is not just built and maintained by the cars themselves and the advertising: it is a function of the people who work at Audi.

Because contact employees represent the organization and can directly influence customer satisfaction, they *perform the role of marketers*. They physically embody the product and are walking billboards from a promotional standpoint. Some service employees may also perform more traditional selling roles. For example, bank CSRs are often called on to cross-sell bank products, a departure from the traditional teller role of operations function only. Whether acknowledged or not, whether actively selling or not, service employees perform marketing functions. They can perform these functions well, to the organization's advantage, or poorly, to the organization's detriment.

FIGURE 12.2

WestJet: "The driver for our brand is our people."

Source: Courtesy of WestJet.

According to VanCity Credit Union in Vancouver, "We can have the best products in the world, but if everyone on the front line was deadpan, we wouldn't sell or keep much business."[10] In this chapter we examine frameworks, tools, and strategies for ensuring that service employees perform their marketing functions well.

The Services Triangle

Services marketing is about promises—promises made and promises kept to customers. A strategic framework known as the *services triangle* (illustrated in Figure 12.3) visually reinforces the importance of people in the ability of firms to keep their promises and succeed in building customer relationships.[11] The triangle shows the three interlinked groups that work together to develop, promote, and deliver services. These key players are labelled on the points of the triangle: the *company* (or SBU or department or "management"); the *customers*; and the *providers*. Providers can be the firm's employees, subcontractors, or outsourced entities who actually deliver the company's services. Between these three points on the triangle, three types of marketing must be successfully carried out for a service to succeed: external marketing, interactive marketing, and internal marketing.

On the right side of the triangle are the *external marketing* efforts that the firm engages in to set up its customers' expectations and make promises to customers. Anything or anyone that communicates to the customer before service delivery can be viewed as part of this external marketing function. But external marketing is just the beginning: promises made must be kept. On the bottom of the triangle is what has been termed *interactive marketing* or *real-time marketing*. Here is where promises are kept or broken by the firm's employees, subcontractors, or agents. People are critical at this juncture. If promises are not kept, customers become dissatisfied and eventually leave. The left side of the triangle suggests the critical role played by *internal marketing*. Management engages in these activities to aid the providers in their ability to deliver on the service promise: recruiting, training, motivating, rewarding, and providing equipment and technology. Unless service employees are able *and* willing to deliver on the promises made, the firm will not be successful, and the services triangle will collapse.

All three sides of the triangle are essential to complete the whole, and the sides of the triangle should be aligned. That is, what is promised through external marketing should be the same as what is delivered; and the enabling activities inside the organization should be aligned with what is expected of service providers. Strategies for aligning

FIGURE 12.3

The Services Marketing Triangle

Source: Adapted from M. J. Bitner, "Building Service Relationships: It's All About Promises," *Journal of the Academy of Marketing Science* 23, no. 4 (1995), pp. 246–51; C. Gronroos, *Service Management and Marketing* (Lexington, MA: Lexington Books, 1990); and P. Kotler, *Marketing Management: Analysis, Planning, Implementation, and Control*, 8th ed. (Englewood Cliffs, NJ: Prentice Hall, 1994), p. 470.

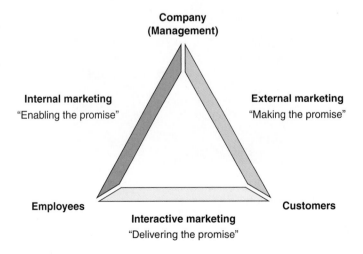

FIGURE 12.4

By targeting customers and employees in this ad, TD Canada Trust engages in external and internal marketing at the same time.

Source: Photographer: Paul Weeks/Westside Studio.

the triangle, particularly the strategies associated with internal marketing and with interactive marketing, are the subject of this part of our text. Strategies associated with external marketing, "Making the Promise," are covered in Part 6.

TD Canada Trust's recent full-page newspaper advertisement demonstrates key aspects of the Services Marketing Triangle. (See Figure 12.4.)

Employee Satisfaction, Customer Satisfaction, and Profits

Satisfied employees make for satisfied customers (and satisfied customers can, in turn, reinforce employees' sense of satisfaction in their jobs). Some researchers have even gone so far as to suggest that unless service employees are happy in their jobs, customer satisfaction will be difficult to achieve.[12]

Through their research with customers and employees, Benjamin Schneider and David Bowen have shown that both a *climate for service* and *a climate for employee well-being* are highly correlated with overall service quality.[13] That is, both service climate and human resource management experiences that *employees* have within their organizations are reflected in how *customers* experience the service. In a similar vein, Sears found customer satisfaction to be strongly related to employee turnover. In its stores with the highest customer satisfaction, employee turnover was 54 percent, whereas in stores with the lowest customer satisfaction, turnover was 83 percent.[14] Other research suggests that employees who feel they are treated fairly by their organizations will treat customers better, resulting in greater customer satisfaction.[15]

The underlying logic connecting employee satisfaction and loyalty to customer satisfaction and loyalty and ultimately profits is illustrated by the service profit chain shown in Figure 12.5.[16] In earlier chapters we focused on customer satisfaction and retention; here we focus on employee issues. The service profit chain suggests that there are critical linkages among internal service quality; employee satisfaction/productivity; the value of services provided to the customer; and ultimately customer satisfaction, retention, and profits.

Service profit chain researchers are careful to point out that the model does not suggest causality. That is, employee satisfaction does not *cause* customer satisfaction;

FIGURE 12.5 The Service Profit Chain

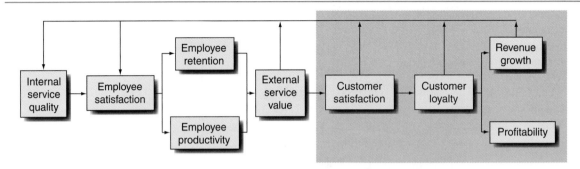

rather the two are interrelated and feed off each other. The model does imply that companies that exhibit high levels of success on the elements of the model will be more successful and profitable than those that do not. This finding is borne out in other research, which reports that companies that manage people right will outperform by 30 to 40 percent companies that do not.[17]

The Effect of Employee Behaviours on Service Quality Dimensions

Customers' perceptions of service quality will be impacted by the customer-oriented behaviours of employees.[18] In fact, all of the five dimensions of service quality (reliability, responsiveness, assurance, empathy, and tangibles) can be influenced directly by service employees.

Delivering the service as promised—*reliability*—is often totally within the control of front-line employees. Even in the case of automated services (such as ATMs), behind-the-scenes employees are critical for making sure all the systems are working properly. When errors are made, employees are essential for setting things right and determining the best course of action for service recovery.

Front-line employees directly influence customer perceptions of *responsiveness* through their personal willingness to help and their promptness in serving customers. Consider the range of responses you receive from different retail store clerks when you need help finding a particular item of clothing. One employee may ignore your presence, whereas another offers to help you search and calls other stores to locate the item.

The *assurance* dimension of service quality is highly dependent on employees' ability to communicate their credibility and to inspire trust and confidence. The reputation of the organization will help, but in the end, individual employees confirm and build trust or detract from its reputation and ultimately destroy trust. For startup or relatively unknown organizations, credibility, trust, and confidence will be tied totally to employee actions.

It is difficult to imagine how an organization would deliver "caring, individualized attention" to customers independently of its employees. *Empathy* implies that employees will pay attention, listen, adapt, and be flexible in delivering what individual customers need.[19] For example, when employees are customer-oriented, have good rapport with customers, and exhibit perceptive and attentive listening skills, customers will evaluate the service more highly and be more likely to return.[20]

Employee appearance and dress are important aspects of the tangibles dimension of quality, along with many other factors that are independent of service employees (the service facility, decor, brochures, signage, and so on).

BOUNDARY-SPANNING ROLES

Our focus in this chapter is on front-line service employees who interact directly with customers. The front-line service employees are referred to as *boundary spanners* because they operate at the organization's boundary. Boundary spanners provide a link between the external customer and the internal operations of the organization. They serve a critical function in understanding, filtering, and interpreting information and resources to and from the organization.

Who are these boundary spanners? What types of people and positions make up critical boundary-spanning roles? Their skills and experience cover the full spectrum of jobs and careers. In industries such as fast food, hotels, telecommunication, and retail, the boundary spanners are the least-skilled, lowest-paid employees in the organization. They are order-takers, front-desk employees, telephone operators, store clerks, truck drivers, and delivery people. In other industries, boundary spanners are well-paid, highly educated professionals—for example, doctors, lawyers, accountants, consultants, architects, and teachers.

No matter what the level of skill or pay, boundary-spanning positions are often high-stress jobs. In addition to mental and physical skills, these positions require extraordinary levels of emotional labour, frequently demand an ability to handle interpersonal and interorganizational conflict, and call on the employee to make real-time tradeoffs between quality and productivity on the job. These stresses and tradeoffs can result in failure to deliver services as specified, which widens Gap 3.

Emotional Labour

The term *emotional labour* was coined by Arlie Hochschild to refer to the labour that goes beyond the physical or mental skills needed to deliver quality service.[21] It means delivering smiles, making eye contact, showing sincere interest, and engaging in friendly conversation with people who are essentially strangers and who may or may not ever be seen again. Friendliness, courtesy, empathy, and responsiveness directed toward customers all require huge amounts of emotional labour from the front-line employees who shoulder this responsibility for the organization. Emotional labour draws on people's feelings (often requiring them to suppress their true feelings) to be effective in their jobs. A front-line service employee who is having a bad day or is not feeling just right is still expected to put on the face of the organization when dealing with customers. One of the clearest examples of emotional labour is the story (probably apocryphal) of the flight attendant who was approached by a businessman who said, "Let's have a smile." "Okay," she replied, "I'll tell you what, first you smile and then I'll smile, okay?" He smiled. "Good," she said. "Now hold that for 15 hours," and walked away.[22]

Many of the strategies we will discuss later in the chapter can help organizations and employees deal with the realities of emotional labour on the job. For the organization, such strategies include carefully selecting people who can handle emotional stress, training them in needed skills (like listening and problem solving), and teaching or giving them coping abilities and strategies (via job rotation, scheduled breaks, teamwork, or other techniques).[23] Exhibit 12.1 describes additional emotional labour strategies that service firms employ.

Strategies for Managing Emotional Labour

Customer contact employees in service positions are often required to display (or, conversely, to withhold display of) a variety of emotions. Such employees are increasingly being required to invest personal identity and expression into their work in many situations. The following description suggests how the experience of the service employee, even in the most routine of occupations, is markedly different from that of the traditional manufacturing worker:

> The assembly-line worker could openly hate his job, despise his supervisor, and even dislike his co-workers, and while this might be an unpleasant state of affairs, if he [completes] his assigned tasks efficiently, his attitude [is] his own problem. For the service worker, inhabiting the job means, at the very least, pretending to like it, and, at most, actually bringing his whole self into the job, liking it, and genuinely caring about the people with whom he interacts.*

Emotional labour occurs more often when the job requires frequent contact and long durations of voice contact or face-to-face contact with customers. These employees often need emotional management to deal with such situations. Later in this chapter we suggest many strategies for organizations to create an environment that helps employees deal with the realities of emotional labour on the job. Here we present some specific strategies that some firms are using to more directly support employee efforts to manage their emotions in the face of demanding, obnoxious, or unruly customers.

SCREENING FOR EMOTIONAL LABOUR ABILITIES

Making sure job candidates are aware of the emotional labour requirements of the job via realistic job previews is a good first step in finding the right person to fill the position. For instance, an organization in Saskatoon that provides services to those with mental or physical disabilities requires a special type of employee comfortable with the unique emotional demands of such a vocation. Potential job applicants might therefore read about the job demands on the organization's website. Other organizations put prospective employees through simulated customer contact exercises to see the kind of friendliness and warmth they naturally communicate. Such practices help in identifying employees whose

values, background, and personalities match the job's emotional labour requirements.

TEACHING EMOTIONAL MANAGEMENT SKILLS AND APPROPRIATE BEHAVIOURS

The customer is always right. Well, at least that is what most service employees are taught. So when customers are not courteous or empathetic, employees may find it understandably challenging to suppress their true feelings. The emotional labour required in these instances amounts to acting. Arlie Hochschild has classified such behaviour as *surface acting*, in which employees pretend to feel emotions that are not really present and, in doing so, deliberately and consciously create an outward appearance in order to deceive others; and *deep acting*, in which employees attempt to experience the real feelings they must express to the customer, including the active invocation of "thoughts, images, and memories to induce the associated emotion."** Hair salon stylists and airline flight attendants are often encouraged to engage in deep-acting strategies such as imagining that the client is a friend or that the passenger is a frightened little child flying for the first time. Often, in order to persuade clients to buy hair products or colour their hair, stylists have to moderate their language or behaviour; they may use deep acting to justify these behaviours to themselves. Companies may also train employees in how to avoid absorbing a customer's bad mood, perhaps by having employees spend hours role-playing to suppress their natural reaction to return negative customer emotions with their own negative emotions.

ALLOWING EMPLOYEES TO VENT

Employees who must exert emotional labour often need to have an outlet to let off steam. Allowing employees to vent lets them get rid of their frustrations. If such venting is done in a group setting, it can provide emotional support and encouragement as well as allowing employees to see that others are experiencing the same problems and that they are not alone. If part of the work day (or week) is explicitly set aside to allow employees to share their frustrations, it delivers a message to employees that the company is aware of and acknowledges the emotional contribution that they have made. Ritz-Carlton, Wal-Mart, and other companies

continued

regularly set aside time for such venting. In addition to the cathartic benefit this experience can provide, other employees may reveal coping strategies that they have found useful.

PUTTING MANAGEMENT ON THE FRONT LINE

Customer contact employees often feel that management does not truly understand or appreciate the emotional labour they must expend. Managers should regularly be required to interact with customers. This is not lost on Canada's best employers. Hewitt Associates' Best Employers in Canada 2006 study found that the leaders in those companies making the list were more likely to "roll up their sleeves and work alongside employees to get the job done" than in other organizations.*** In addition to understanding what the issues are, managers are truly able to empathize with employees. Managers who do so not only have an appreciation for the emotional labour requirements of their employees, but they are also in a better position to serve as role models and mentors in using emotional management skills.

GIVING EMPLOYEES A BREAK

In situations in which an employee has just handled a particularly tough customer, especially if the employee has frequent and long durations of voice or face-to-face contact with customers, a particularly helpful strategy is to allow the employee a short break to regroup. Many companies with toll-free call centres rotate employees into different positions throughout the day so that they do not spend the entire time on the telephone with customers. Customer contact employees can be reenergized and refreshed after spending a little time away from the situation, even if they take only a few minutes to finish paperwork or complete some other job responsibility.

*Quoted from C. L. Macdonald and C. Sirianni, *Working in the Service Society* (Philadelphia: Temple University Press, 1996), p. 4.

**Quoted from B. F. Ashforth and R. H. Humphrey, "Emotional Labor in Service Roles: The Influence of Identity," *Academy of Management Review* 18 (1993), p. 93.

***Quoted from Hewitt Associates, "Hewitt Associates Announce 50 Best Employers in Canada," http://was4.hewitt.com/hewitt/resource/newsroom/pressrel/2005/12-23-05_eng.htm, accessed June 7, 2006.

Sources: J. Solomon, "Trying to Be Nice Is No Labor of Love," *The Wall Street Journal*, November 29, 1990, p. B1; A. Hochschild, *The Managed Heart: Commercialization of Human Feeling* (Berkeley: University of California Press, 1983); B. F. Ashforth and R. H. Humphrey, "Emotional Labor in Service Roles: The Influence of Identity," *Academy of Management Review* 18 (1993), pp. 88–115; S. D. Pugh, "Service with a Smile: Emotional Contagion in the Service Encounter," *Academy of Management Journal* 44, no. 5 (2001), pp. 1018–27; A. A. Grandey, "When 'The Show Must Go On': Surface Acting and Deep Acting as Determinants of Emotional Exhaustion and Peer-Rated Service Delivery," *Academy of Management Journal* 46, no. 1 (2003), pp. 86–96; C. Salter, "And Now the Hard Part," *Fast Company* 82 (May 2004), pp. 66–74; and Hewitt Associates, "Hewitt Associates Announce 50 Best Employers in Canada," http://was4.hewitt.com/hewitt/resource/newsroom/pressrel/2005/12-23-05_eng.htm, accessed June 7, 2006.

Sources of Conflict

Front-line employees often face interpersonal and interorganizational conflicts on the job. Their frustration and confusion can, if left unattended, lead to stress, job dissatisfaction, a diminished ability to serve customers, and burnout.[24] Because they represent the customer to the organization and often need to manage a number of customers simultaneously, front-line employees inevitably have to deal with conflicts, including person/role conflicts, organization/client conflicts, and interclient conflicts, as suggested by Figure 12.6 and discussed in the next sections.[25]

Person/Role Conflicts

In some situations, boundary spanners feel conflicts between what they are asked to do and their own personalities, orientations, or values. In a society such as Canada, where equality is highly valued, service workers may feel role conflict when they are required to subordinate their feelings or beliefs, as when they are asked to live by the motto "The customer is always right—even when wrong." Sometimes there

Technology Spotlight

The High Price of Work Extension Technology

The goal of many companies has been achieving a real-time enterprise in which employees can access company information and be accessible to clients and employers continuously. The belief is that by employing work extension technologies (WET) such as email, laptops, cell phones, and PDAs, people will work more efficiently and be more productive. And some companies are thrilled with the results. As Derek Smith, a partner with the global law firm of Paul, Hastings, Janofsky & Walker puts it, "Technology has changed and enabled us to serve our clients better. One of the things we try to do at Paul Hastings is equip our attorneys so that wherever or whenever they are, they can access their clients."*

Source: © Comstock/Punchstock.

However, while using work extension technologies might be a common trend in many organizations, Carleton University's Linda Duxbury's study of workplace culture and workload indicates that the mental health of employees is declining and that technology

is an underlying cause. In particular, part of Duxbury's study examines WET users. And, while the study shows that the majority of technology users say technology has increased their productivity and interest in work, more than 60 percent experience more stress, and 70 percent have increased workloads. Further, those who were classified as frequent WET users worked more hours, had more job stress and stress in general, had a higher intent to turn over, had higher burnout, and had lower job and life satisfaction than employees using WET less frequently.

Duxbury's study points up a real area of concern. Creating an effective culture and thereby maintaining satisfied employees has been identified as a goal of many companies cited throughout this chapter, but employees who are high users of WET may be quite stressed and unhappy. And this will have a real and significant cost to organizations. Health Canada estimates that mental health disorders in the workplace cost Canadian companies approximately $16 billion, or 14 percent of net income nationally.

*Quoted in J. Zipperer, "The Real-Time Enterprise," *Internet World*, March 2003, p. 22.

Sources: J. Zipperer, "The Real-Time Enterprise," *Internet World*, March 2003, p. 22; L. Duxbury, "Understanding How Culture and Workload Influence Employee Engagement and Performance ... and Doing Something About It," conference proceedings from the Canadian Institute's (www.canadianinstitute.com); "Winning HR Practices of the Best Employers in Canada," April 25–26, 2006; National Quality Institute, "Think Health: A Knowledge Economy Places a Premium on Mental Performance and Innovation," advertising supplement appearing in *Canadian Business*.

is a conflict between role requirements and the self-image or self-esteem of the employee. An Israeli service expert tells an example from that culture:

> In Israel, for instance, most buses are operated by one man, the driver, who is also responsible for selling tickets. No trays are installed in buses for the transferring of bus fare from passenger to driver, and the money is transferred directly. Bus drivers often complain about the humiliating experience of having to stretch out their hands like beggars in order to collect the fare. Another typical case in Israeli buses is when money changes hands and a coin falls down accidentally onto the bus floor. The question, who will bend down to lift the coin, the driver or the passenger, clearly reflects the driver's role conflict.[26]

Whoever stoops to pick up the coin is indicating subservient status.

Person/role conflict also arises when employees are required to wear specific clothing or change some aspect of their appearance to conform to the job requirements. A young lawyer, just out of school, may feel an internal conflict with his new role when his employer requires him to cut his long hair and trade his casual clothes for a three-piece suit. Many university and college students will likely empathize with some young people who feel embarrassed about having to wear hair nets or the wait staff uniforms required by their jobs at fast-food restaurants.

Organization/Client Conflict

A more common type of conflict for front-line service employees is the conflict between their two bosses, the organization and the individual customer. Service employees are typically rewarded for following certain standards, rules, and procedures. Ideally these rules and standards are customer-based, as described in Chapter 10. When they are not, or when a customer makes excessive demands, the employee has to choose whether to follow the rules or satisfy the demands. The conflict is greatest when the employee believes the organization is wrong in its policies and must decide whether to accommodate the client and risk losing a job, or to follow the policies. These conflicts are especially severe when service employees depend directly on the customer for income. For example, employees who depend on tips or commissions are likely to face greater levels of organization/client conflict because they have even greater incentives to identify with the customer. As one management consultant noted, "You can inhale and you can exhale but its very hard to do both at the same time."[27]

Interclient Conflict

Sometimes conflict occurs for boundary spanners when incompatible expectations and requirements arise from two or more customers. This situation occurs most often when the service provider is serving customers in turn (a bank teller, a ticketing agent, a doctor) or is serving many customers simultaneously (teachers, entertainers).

When serving customers in turn, the provider may satisfy one customer by spending additional time, customizing the service, and being very flexible in meeting the customer's needs. Meanwhile, waiting customers are becoming dissatisfied because their needs are not being met in a timely way. Beyond the timing issue, different clients may prefer different modes of service delivery. Having to serve one client who prefers personal recognition and a degree of familiarity in the presence of another client who is all business and would prefer little interaction can also create conflict for the employee.

When serving many customers at the same time, employees often find it difficult to simultaneously serve the full range of needs of a group of customers. This type of conflict is readily apparent in any college classroom in which the instructor must meet a multitude of expectations and different preferences for formats and style.

Quality/Productivity Tradeoffs

Front-line service workers are asked to be both effective and efficient: they are expected to deliver satisfying service to customers and at the same time to be cost-effective and productive in what they do. A checker at a grocery store is expected to know his customers and to be polite and courteous, yet also to process the groceries accurately and move people through the line quickly. An architectural draftsperson is expected to create quality drawings, yet to produce a required quantity of drawings in a given period of time. These essential tradeoffs between quality and quantity and between maximum effectiveness and efficiency put real-time demands and pressures on service employees. Until recently, companies like Bell Canada, AIR MILES, and Travelocity.com measured call centre staff on how long a call lasted. The shorter the call, the better.

Research suggests that these tradeoffs are more difficult for service businesses than for manufacturing and packaged goods businesses and that pursuing goals of customer satisfaction and productivity simultaneously is particularly challenging in situations in which service employees are required to customize service offerings to meet customer needs.[28]

Jagdip Singh, a noted services researcher, has studied productivity and quality as two types of performance inherent in frontline service jobs.[29] He explains the difficult tradeoffs that employees face and has developed ways to measure these two types of performance together with a theoretical model to predict the causes and consequences of these tradeoffs. He finds that quality of job performance is particularly susceptible to burnout and job stress. He also finds that internal support from understanding managers and control over the job tasks can help employees in making quality and productivity tradeoffs, avoiding burnout, and maintaining their performance. Technology is being used to an ever-greater degree to balance the quality/quantity tradeoff to increase productivity of service workers and at the same time free them to provide higher-quality service for the customer.

⟼ STRATEGIES FOR DELIVERING SERVICE QUALITY THROUGH PEOPLE

A complex combination of strategies is needed to ensure that service employees are willing and able to deliver quality services and that they stay motivated to perform in customer-oriented, service-minded ways. These strategies for enabling service promises are often referred to as *internal marketing*, as shown on the left side of Figure 12.3.[30] Even during slow economic times, the importance of attracting, developing, and retaining good people in knowledge- and service-based industries cannot be over-emphasized, as *Fast Company* magazine suggested:

> When it comes to building great companies, the most urgent business challenge is finding and keeping great people. Sure a Web strategy is important, and the stock market is scary, but still the best companies know that people are the foundation of greatness.[31]

By approaching human resource decisions and strategies from the point of view that the primary goal is to motivate and enable employees to deliver customer-oriented promises successfully, an organization will move toward delivering service quality through its people. The strategies presented here are organized around four basic themes. To build a customer-oriented, service-minded workforce, an organization must (1) hire the right people, (2) develop people to deliver service quality, (3) provide the needed support systems, and (4) retain the best people. Within each of these basic strategies are a number of specific substrategies for accomplishing the goal, as shown in Figure 12.6.

Hire the Right People

To effectively deliver service quality, considerable attention should be focused on hiring and recruiting service personnel. Such attention is contrary to traditional practices in many service industries, where service personnel are the lowest on the corporate ladder and work for minimum wage. At the other end of the spectrum, in the professional services, the most important recruiting criteria are typically technical training, certifications, and expertise. However, many organizations are now looking above and

FIGURE 12.6

Human Resource Strategies for Delivering Service Quality Through People

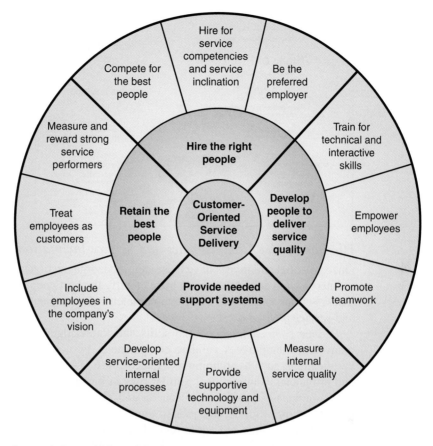

beyond the technical qualifications of applicants to assess their customer and service orientation as well. Figure 12.6 shows a number of ways to go about hiring the right people. One company trying to carve out a niche for itself by assisting in the recruitment and retention process focuses on overcoming the negative consequences related to employee theft ("shrinkage") when the wrong person is hired (see Figure 12.7).

Compete for the Best People

To get the best people, an organization needs to identify them and compete with other organizations to hire them. Leonard Berry and A. Parasuraman refer to this approach as "competing for talent market share."[32] They suggest that firms act as marketers in their pursuit of the best employees, just as they use their marketing expertise to compete for customers. Firms that think of recruiting as a marketing activity will address issues of market (employee) segmentation, product (job) design, and promotion of job availability in ways that attract potential long-term employees. According to Anthony Meehan, president of Mediacorp Canada, Inc., the firm that creates the annual list of Canada's 100 Best Employers, recruiters are now starting to call themselves "talent acquisition specialists."[33] Doing so recognizes the importance of the function and helps elevate the role to the strategic importance it deserves.[34] The Vancouver tech firm Business Objects recently created a position called "talent brand manager." One of the key tasks of the new position is to make Business Objects—which is based in San Jose and Paris but which has the majority of its employees in Vancouver—an "employer of choice."[35] VanCity Credit Union also competes for staff, as is shown in their recent ad (Figure 12.8), by exploiting their award as Canada's Best Employer.

FIGURE 12.7

One of HiringSmart's primary appeals to employers is based on screening for dishonest employees.

Source: Courtesy of HiringSmart/blindSpot Business Consulting Inc.

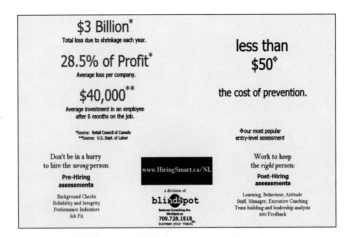

Hire for Service Competencies and Service Inclination

Once potential employees have been identified, organizations need to be conscientious in interviewing and screening to truly identify the best people from the pool of candidates. Service employees need two complementary capacities: *service competencies* and *service inclination*.[36]

Service competencies are the skills and knowledge necessary to do the job. In many cases, employees validate competencies by achieving particular degrees and certifications, such as attaining a CA, CGA, or CMA and passing the relevant national and provincial examinations. Similar rites of passage are required of doctors, airline pilots, university professors, teachers, and many other job seekers before they are ever interviewed for service jobs in their fields. In other cases, service competencies may not be diploma- or degree-related but may instead relate to basic intelligence or physical requirements. A retail clerk, for example, must possess basic math skills and the potential to operate a cash register. The Canadian Retail Institute (CRI) is working hard to foster an industry-based certification program for retail staff.

Given the multidimensional nature of service quality, service employees should be screened for more than their service competencies. They must also be screened for *service inclination*—their interest in doing service-related work—which is reflected in their attitudes toward service and orientation toward serving customers. Self-selection suggests that most service jobs will draw applicants with some level of service inclination and that most employees in service organizations are inclined toward service. However, some employees clearly have a greater service inclination than others. Research has shown that service effectiveness is correlated with service-oriented personality characteristics such as helpfulness, thoughtfulness, and sociability.[37] An

FIGURE 12.8

VanCity Credit Union competes for staff who want more from their work.

Source: Photographer: Anton Franko Ad Agency: TWBA Vancouver.

FIGURE 12.9

The Employee's
Perspective on the
Job Interview

Source: Dan Piraro. King
Features Syndicate.

ideal selection process for service employees assesses both service competencies and service inclination, resulting in employee hires who are high on both dimensions.[38]

In addition to traditional employment interviews, many firms use innovative approaches to assessing service inclination and other personal characteristics that fit the organization's needs. Southwest Airlines in the United States as well as Canada's WestJet Airlines look for people who are compassionate and who have common sense, a sense of humour, a "can do" attitude, and an egalitarian sense of themselves ("we" rather than "me"). One way Southwest assesses these service inclinations is by interviewing potential flight attendants in groups to see how they interact with each other. Pilots are also interviewed in groups to assess their teamwork skills, a critical factor above and beyond the essential technical skills they are required to possess.[39]

In many cases a component of the selection process will include a form of work simulation that allows employees to demonstrate how they would actually perform on the job. A simulation may take the form of role-playing or a series of exercises that parallel the demands of the actual job. In addition to being a good way to assess potential employee abilities, simulations can give the potential hire a better view of what the job is actually like. Those candidates who do not like what they experience can back out of the applicant pool before being hired and then finding out the job is not what they had expected.

Be the Preferred Employer

One way to attract the best people is to be known as the preferred employer in a particular industry or in a particular location. Rosenbluth International, recently aquired by American Express Corporate Travel, enjoys a reputation as a preferred employer. With 56 offices in 15 countries around the world, the company provides corporate travel management for its clients. The company's former president, Hal Rosenbluth, has gone so far as to say, "We don't believe that the customer can come first unless our people come first. If our people don't come first, then they're not free to focus on our clients; they're worrying about other kinds of things."[40]

Other strategies that support a goal of being the preferred employer include extensive training, career and advancement opportunities, excellent internal support, attractive incentives, and quality goods and services that employees are proud to be associated with. SAS Institute (Canada) Inc., ranked as one of Canada's Top 100 Employers of 2005, has a number of benefits that make it easy to see why it is a preferred employer despite the fact it does not offer stock options or notably high salaries common in the software industry. Instead, the company offers a variety of perks that focus on corporate culture, health, and the family. Among the benefits afforded SAS employees are access to nearby child care, above-average health coverage including fitness membership and equipment subsidies, flexible work hours, a company-wide, paid shutdown between Christmas and New Year's, free snacks, and several company-sponsored social events annually. Perhaps the most unique feature of the benefit package at SAS Institute (Canada) is the $100 social allowance paid to each employee to be used for socializing with department members.

Employees who work for SAS are, for the most part, professional or technical and well paid. In a very different industry, dominated by lower-paid workers, Marriott International has a stated company goal of being the "preferred employer" in its industry. Marriott uses employee stock options, a social services referral network, day care, welfare-to-work training classes, and English and reading classes to be the preferred employer in the highly competitive hospitality industry.[41] Both SAS Institute and Marriott International are consistently rated among Fortune's list of the top 100 companies to work for, with rankings of 8 and 84, respectively, as recently as 2004.[42]

Develop People to Deliver Service Quality

To grow and maintain a workforce that is customer-oriented and focused on delivering quality, an organization must develop its employees to deliver service quality. That is, once it has hired the right employees, the organization must train and work with these individuals to ensure service performance.

Train for Technical and Interactive Skills

To provide quality service, employees need ongoing training in the necessary technical skills and knowledge and in process or interactive skills.[43] Examples of technical skills and knowledge are working with accounting systems in hotels, POS procedures in a retail store, and underwriting procedures in an insurance company. Most service organizations are relatively effective at training employees in technical skills. These skills may be taught through formal education, as is the case at McDonald's Hamburger University, which trains McDonald's managers from all over the world. Additionally, technical skills are often taught through on-the-job training, as when education students work with experienced teachers in internship programs or when telephone service trainees listen in on the conversations of experienced employees. Recently, companies are increasing their use of information technology to train employees in the technical skills and knowledge needed on the job.

Service employees also need training in interactive skills that allow them to provide courteous, caring, responsive, and empathetic service. The Global Feature here explains how the Tokyo Imperial Hotel in Japan effectively combines service employee training in both the technical and interactive skills needed to provide quality service.

Successful companies invest heavily in training and make sure that the training fits their business goals and strategies. For example, at the Ritz-Carlton, all employees go through extensive initial training and are given pocket-sized, laminated credo cards to carry in their wallets. The credo card specifies the three steps of service, Ritz-Carlton's well-known motto "We Are Ladies and Gentlemen Serving Ladies and Gentlemen," and the credo itself. Further, employees in every hotel attend a brief staff meeting every day to review one of Ritz-Carlton's "Gold Standards: The 20 Basics" so as to continually reinforce earlier training.

Empower Employees

Many organizations have discovered that to be truly responsive to customer needs, front-line providers need to be empowered to accommodate customer requests and to recover on the spot when things go wrong. *Empowerment* means giving employees

Global Feature

Training at Tokyo's Imperial Hotel

Tokyo's Imperial Hotel (www.imperialhotel.co.jp) provides an excellent example of training for both knowledge and skills as well as interactive service quality. The hotel's "Capability Development Program" consists of training in "occupational abilities and knowledge" (technical skills) as well as "service manners training" (interactive skills). The first type of training involves on-the-job apprenticing, rotations through all the major departments within the hotel, visitations and inspection tours of comparable hotels in other countries, and focused study tours (e.g., Imperial Hotel's senior waiters and sommeliers might tour famous wineries in California and France every three years). In addition, employees get specialized skills training through independent educational organizations on needed topics ranging from management strategy decision making to food hygiene to presentation know-how.

The "service manners training" focuses on the etiquette and psychology of guest contact and attitudes of service. Proper etiquette is taught via role playing and videotaping (to critique appearance, mannerisms, and personal idiosyncrasies). The way the staff should appear to hotel guests is stressed and demonstrated, with emphasis placed on cleanliness, a sense of understated elegance, and good taste. Guest psychology is discussed, emphasizing the following main points:

1. Imperial Hotel patrons, given the rank and reputation of the hotel, expect that you will consider them your most important priority, the centre of your attention.

2. Guests do not want to suffer losses of any kind while in the hotel.

3. Guests expect to be received in a warm, welcoming fashion.

4. A guest does not want to be extended a level of treatment that is in any way inferior to that provided to other guests of the hotel.

5. Guests wish to experience an appropriate feeling of prestige or superiority, purely by virtue of their using what is commonly evaluated as a deluxe enterprise.

6. Guests enjoy feeling possessive about the hotel's facilities and services, and expect exclusive attention.

Finally, the basic principles of nonverbal communication and body language are discussed. Demonstrations and detailed explanations of appropriate behaviours are given, covering such points as facial expressions, appearance, and posture when standing; pleasing, attractive ways of talking and carriage; proper posture; and courtesy when escorting guests within the hotel premises. Because the bow is used regardless of the national origin of the guest, considerable time is spent on the intricacies of proper bowing. A bow of welcome involves a 15-degree angle, a bow of gratitude is 30 degrees, and a bow of apology is a full 45 degrees from the normal straight standing position. The remainder of the service manners training concentrates on the complexities of the Japanese language and the appropriate applications for hotel service. Trainees are instructed in some 25 common daily expressions, learning their politest forms as well as the English equivalents.

Ongoing training and service improvement programs at all levels are part of the hotel's total operations strategy.

Source: *Service Quality Handbook* by Scheuing, Ebert © 1993 by AM MGMT ASSN/AMACOM (A). Reproduced with permission of AM MGMT ASSN/AMACOM (B) in the format textbook via Copyright Clearance Center.

the desire, skills, tools, and authority to serve the customer. Although the key to empowerment is giving employees authority to make decisions on the customer's behalf, authority alone is not enough. Employees need the knowledge and tools to be able to make these decisions, and they need incentives that encourage them to make the right decisions. Organizations do not succeed in empowering their employees if they simply tell them, "You now have the authority to do whatever it takes to satisfy the customer." First, employees often do not believe this statement. Second, employees often do not know what it means to "do whatever it takes" if they have not been given the tools needed to make such decisions.

Research suggests positive benefits to empowering front-line service workers. Some of these benefits include reduction in job-related stress, improved job satisfaction, greater adaptability, and better outcomes for customers.[44] But such success does not come easily. In fact, some experts have concluded that few organizations have truly taken advantage of, or properly implemented, successful empowerment strategies.[45] Nor is empowerment the answer for all organizations. Exhibit 12.2 enumerates both the costs and benefits of empowerment as documented by David Bowen and Edward Lawler, experts on this subject.[46] They suggest that organizations well suited to empowerment strategies are ones in which (1) the business strategy is one of differentiation and customization, (2) customers are long-term relationship customers, (3) technology is nonroutine or complex, (4) the business environment is unpredictable, and (5) managers and employees have high growth and social needs and strong interpersonal skills.

Hewlett Packard (HP) is, according to Bowen and Lawler's criteria, well suited to using an empowerment strategy. HP is a differentiator; seeks long-term customer relationships; uses complex technologies; competes in an uncertain environment; and employs people who have high growth needs. It is no surprise then, that HP Canada would run the kind of employment ad shown in Figure 12.10.

FIGURE 12.10

HP stresses employee empowerment in their recruiting ads for boundary spanners.

Source: Courtesy of HP, Canada.

EXHIBIT 12.2

Potential Costs and Benefits of Empowerment

BENEFITS

- *Quicker online responses to customer needs during service delivery.* Employees who are allowed to make decisions on behalf of the customer can make decisions more quickly, bypassing what in the past might have meant a long chain of command, or at least a discussion with an immediate supervisor.

- *Quicker online responses to dissatisfied customers during service recovery.* When failures occur in the delivery system, customers hope for an immediate recovery effort on the part of the organization. Empowered employees can recover on the spot, and a dissatisfied customer can potentially be turned into a satisfied, even loyal one.

- *Employees feel better about their jobs and themselves.* Giving employees control and authority to make decisions makes them feel responsible and gives them ownership for the customer's satisfaction. Decades of job design research suggest that when employees have a sense of control and of doing meaningful work, they are more satisfied. The result is lower turnover and less absenteeism.

- *Employees will interact with customers with more warmth and enthusiasm.* Employees feel better about themselves and their work, and these attitudes will spill over into their feelings about customers and will be reflected in their interactions.

- *Empowered employees are a great source of service ideas.* When employees are empowered, they feel responsible for the service outcome and they will be excellent sources of ideas about new services or how to improve current offerings.

- *Great word-of-mouth advertising from customers.* Empowered employees do special and unique things that customers will remember and tell their friends, family, and associates about.

COSTS

- *A potentially greater dollar investment in selection and training.* To find employees who will work well in an empowered environment requires creative, potentially more costly selection procedures. Training will also be more expensive in general because employees need more knowledge about the company, its products, and how to work in flexible ways with customers.

- *Higher labour costs.* The organization may not be able to use as many part-time or seasonal employees, and it may need to pay more for asking employees to assume responsibility.

- *Potentially slower or inconsistent service delivery.* If empowered employees spend more time with all, or even some, customers, then service overall may take longer and may annoy customers who are waiting. Empowerment also means that customers will get what they need or request. When decisions regarding customer satisfaction are left to the discretion of employees, there may be inconsistency in the level of service delivered.

- *May violate customers' perceptions of fair play.* Customers may perceive that sticking to procedures with every customer is fair. Thus, if they see that customers are receiving different levels of service or that employees are cutting special deals with some customers, they may believe that the organization is not fair.

- *Employees may "give away the store" or make bad decisions.* Many people fear that empowered employees will make costly decisions that the organization cannot afford. Although this situation can happen, good training and appropriate guidelines will help.

Source: Reprinted from "The Empowerment of Service Workers: What, Why, How, and When," by D. E. Bowen and E. E. Lawler, *Sloan Management Review*, Spring 1992, pp. 31–39, by permission of the publisher. Copyright 1992 by Massachusetts Institute of Technology. All rights reserved.

Promote Teamwork

The nature of many service jobs suggests that customer satisfaction will be enhanced when employees work as teams. Because service jobs are frequently frustrating, demanding, and challenging, a teamwork environment will help alleviate some of the stresses and strains. Employees who feel supported and feel that they have a team backing them up will be better able to maintain their enthusiasm and provide quality service.[47] "An interactive community of coworkers who help each other, commiserate, and achieve together is a powerful antidote to service burnout,"[48] and, we would add, an important ingredient for service quality. By promoting teamwork, an organization can enhance the employees' *abilities* to deliver excellent service while the camaraderie and support enhance their *inclination* to be excellent service providers. This view is shared by Robert Meggy, CEO of one of *BC Magazine*'s Best Employers. According to Meggy, it is important for staff to get along with each other. When they do, they communicate better and get their work done more smoothly. As well, Meggy notes that staff who don't socialize with each other usually leave the company sooner. Other firms on Canada's Top 100 Employers list put similar stress on employee cohesion. VanCity, for example, hosts recognition nights, picnics, and skating and costume parties, and has softball, dragonboat, and kayak teams.[49]

One way of promoting teamwork is to encourage the attitude that "everyone has a customer." That is, even when employees are not directly responsible for or in direct interaction with the final customer, they need to know whom they serve directly and how the role they play in the total service picture is essential to the final delivery of quality service. If each employee can see how he or she is somehow integral in delivering quality to the final customer and if each employee knows whom to support to make service quality a reality, teamwork will be enhanced. Service blueprints, described in Chapter 9, can serve as useful tools to illustrate for employees their integral roles in delivering service quality to the ultimate customer.

Team goals and rewards also promote teamwork. When a firm rewards teams of individuals rather than basing all rewards on individual achievements and performance, team efforts and team spirit are encouraged.

Provide Needed Support Systems

Service workers require internal support systems that are aligned with their need to be customer-focused. This point cannot be overemphasized. In fact, without customer-focused internal support and customer-oriented systems, it is nearly impossible for employees to deliver quality service no matter how much they want to. For example, a bank teller who is rewarded for customer satisfaction as well as for accuracy in bank transactions needs easy access to up-to-date customer records, a well-staffed branch (so that he or she is not constantly facing a long line of impatient customers), and supportive customer-oriented supervisors and back-office staff. Researchers have found that internal support from supervisors, teammates, and other departments as well as evaluations of technology used on the job were all strongly related to employee satisfaction and ability to serve customers.[50] The following sections suggest strategies for ensuring customer-oriented internal support.

Measure Internal Service Quality

One way to encourage supportive internal service relationships is to measure and reward internal service. By first acknowledging that everyone in the organization has a customer and then measuring customer perceptions of internal service quality, an organization can begin to develop an internal quality culture. Internal customer service audits can be used to implement a culture of internal service quality. Through the audit, internal organizations identify their customers, determine their needs, measure how well they are doing, and make improvements. The process parallels market research practices used for external customers. Exhibit 12.3 outlines the steps in an internal service audit.

One risk of measuring and focusing on internal service quality and internal customers is that people can sometimes get so wrapped up in meeting the needs of internal customers that they forget they are in business to serve the ultimate, external

Steps in Conducting an Internal Customer Service Audit

1. *Define your customer.*
   a. List all the people or departments in the organization who need help from you or your department in any way. This list may include specific departments, particular staff people, the CEO, certain executives, or the board of directors.
   b. Prioritize the names on the list, placing the people or departments that rely on you the most at the top.

2. *Identify your contribution.*
   a. For each of these customers, specify the primary need you think they have to which you can contribute. Talk to your internal customers about what problems they are trying to solve and think about how you can help.

3. *Define service quality.*
   a. What are the critical moments of truth that really define the department–internal customer interface from your customer's point of view? Blueprint the process, and list the moments of truth.
   b. For each major internal customer, design a customer report card (based on customer input) and a set of evaluation criteria for your department's service package, as seen through the eyes of that customer. The criteria might include such dimensions as timeliness, reliability, and cost.

4. *Validate your criteria.*
   a. Talk to your customers. Allow them to revise, as necessary, how you saw their needs and the criteria they used in assessing your performance. This dialogue itself can go a long way toward building internal service teamwork.

5. *Measure service quality.*
   a. Evaluate your service (using internal measures and/or customer surveys) against the quality criteria you established in talking to your customers. See how you score. Identify opportunities for improvement. Set up a process and timetable for following through.

6. *Develop a mission statement based on what you contribute.*
   a. Consider drafting a brief, meaningful service mission statement for your operation. Be certain to frame it in terms of the value you *contribute,* not what you *do.* For example, the mission of the HR department should not be "to deliver training" (the action); it would be "to create competent people" (the contribution).

Source: Reprinted from K. Albrecht, *At America's Service* (Homewood, IL: Dow-Jones-Irwin, 1988), pp. 139–42, as discussed in B. Schneider and D. E. Bowen, *Winning at the Service Game* (Boston: The Harvard Business School Press, 1995), pp. 231–32. © 1988 by Dow-Jones-Irwin. Reprinted by permission of The McGraw-Hill Companies.

customers.[51] In measuring internal service quality, therefore, it is important to constantly draw the linkages between what is being delivered internally and how it supports the delivery of the final service to customers. Service blueprinting, introduced in Chapter 9, can help to illustrate these critical linkages.

Provide Supportive Technology and Equipment

When employees do not have the right equipment or their equipment fails them, they can be easily frustrated in their desire to deliver quality service. To do their jobs effectively and efficiently, service employees need the right equipment and technology. Our Technology Spotlight earlier in this chapter highlights the role of front-office automation in providing technology support for employees.

Having the right technology and equipment can extend into strategies regarding workplace and workstation design. For example, in designing their corporate headquarters' offices, Scandinavian Airline Systems identified particular service-oriented goals that it wished to achieve, among them teamwork and open, frequent communication among managers. An office environment was designed with open spaces (to encourage meetings) and internal windows in offices (to encourage frequent interactions). In this way the work space facilitated the internal service orientation.

Develop Service-Oriented Internal Processes

To best support service personnel in their delivery of quality service on the front line, an organization's internal processes should be designed with customer value and customer satisfaction in mind. In other words, internal procedures must support quality service performance. In many companies internal processes are driven by bureaucratic rules, tradition, cost efficiencies, or the needs of internal employees. Providing service- and customer-oriented internal processes can therefore imply a need for total redesign of systems. This kind of wholesale redesign of systems and processes has become known as "process reengineering." Although developing service-oriented internal processes through reengineering sounds sensible, it is probably one of the most difficult strategies to implement, especially in organizations that are steeped in tradition.

Retain the Best People

An organization that *hires* the *right* people, *trains* them to deliver service quality, and *provides* the needed *support* must also work to *retain* them. Employee turnover, especially when the best service employees are the ones leaving, can be very detrimental to customer satisfaction, employee morale, and overall service quality. And, just as they do with customers, some firms spend a lot of time attracting employees but then tend to take them for granted (or even worse), causing these good employees to search for job alternatives. Although all the strategies depicted earlier in Figure 12.6 will support the retention of the best employees, here we will focus on some strategies that are particularly aimed at this goal.

Include Employees in the Company's Vision

For employees to remain motivated and interested in sticking with the organization and supporting its goals, they need to share an understanding of the organization's vision. People who deliver service day in and day out need to understand how their work fits into the big picture of the organization and its goals. They will be motivated to some extent by their paycheques and other benefits, but the best employees will be attracted away to other opportunities if they are not committed to the vision of the organization. And they cannot be committed to the vision if that vision is kept secret from them. What this strategy means in practice is that the vision is communicated to employees frequently and that it is communicated by top managers, often by the CEO.[52] Respected CEOs such as Howard Schulz of Starbucks, Fred Smith of FedEx, Bill Marriott of Marriott International, Dave Mowat of VanCity, and Clive Beddow of WestJet are known for communicating their visions clearly and often to employees.

Tom Siebel, the founder of Siebel Systems, which became the industry leader in CRM software applications before being acquired by Oracle, is another good example. He communicated clearly, through words and actions, that the company's mission was "customer first," no matter what the situation. He believed in putting customers ahead of technology and discipline ahead of inspiration; and he upheld these strong messages through his own actions—at every fork in the road, the decision rule was "customer first." In fact, he turned down lucrative business accounts if he felt that they would take away from current customer needs or that the company was not ready to provide 100 percent satisfaction to the customers. This type of action sent a strong message to employees, reinforcing the company vision.[53] When the vision and direction are clear and motivating, employees are more likely to remain with the company through the inevitable rough spots along the path to the vision.

Treat Employees as Customers

If employees feel valued and their needs are taken care of, they are more likely to stay with the organization. An extreme example of this view is provided by a quotation from Hal Rosenbluth:

> As I watched people knocking themselves out for Rosenbluth … I suddenly realized that it was my responsibility to make their lives more pleasant. In simple terms, that meant giving people the right working environment, the right tools, and the right leadership. It meant eliminating fear, frustration, bureaucracy, and politics. Of course, it meant decent compensation—and bonuses when the company did well—but it also meant helping people develop as human beings.[54]

Many companies have adopted the idea that employees are also customers of the organization and that basic marketing strategies can be directed at them.[55] The products that the organization has to offer its employees are a job (with assorted benefits) and quality of work life. To determine whether the job and work-life needs of employees are being met, organizations conduct periodic internal marketing research to assess employee satisfaction and needs. For example, within American Express Travel Related Services, the Travelers Check Group (TCG) had a goal of "Becoming the Best Place to Work" by treating employees as customers.[56]

On the basis of the research, TCG launched a number of initiatives to benefit employees: an expanded employee assistance program; child care resource and referral service; adoption assistance; health care and dependent care reimbursement plans; family leave; family sick days; flexible returns; sabbaticals; improved part-time employee benefits; flexible benefits; and workplace flexibility initiatives including job-sharing, flexplace, and flextime scheduling. What American Express and many other companies are finding is that to ensure employee satisfaction, productivity, and retention, companies are getting more and more involved in the private lives and family support of their workers.[57] And employees appreciate such efforts; American Express is regularly included in *Fortune*'s list of "Top 100 Companies to Work For"—making it every year between 2000 and 2004!

In addition to basic internal research, organizations can apply other marketing strategies to their management of employees. For example, segmentation of the employee population is apparent in many of the flexible benefit plans and career path choices now available to employees. Organizations that are set up to meet the needs of specific segments and to adjust as people proceed through their lives will benefit from increased employee loyalty. Advertising and other forms of communication directed at employees can also increase their sense of value and enhance their commitment to the organization.[58]

Measure and Reward Strong Service Performers

If a company wants the strongest service performers to stay with the organization, it must reward and promote them. This strategy may seem obvious, but often the reward systems in organizations are not set up to reward service excellence. Reward systems may value productivity, sales, or some other dimension that can potentially work *against* good service. Even those service workers who are intrinsically motivated to deliver high service quality will become discouraged at some point and start looking elsewhere if their efforts are not recognized and rewarded.

Reward systems need to be linked to the organization's vision and to outcomes that are truly important. For instance, if customer satisfaction and retention are viewed as critical outcomes, service behaviours that increase those outcomes need to be recognized and rewarded. At Siebel Systems all employees—the salespeople, the service people, the engineers, the product marketers, and everyone else—received incentive compensation based on the company's customer satisfaction scores. For salespeople the bulk of their incentive compensation was paid only *after* the company knew the level of customer satisfaction—four quarters after the sales contract was signed.[59] At Intel, the "Vender of Choice" (VOC) customer retention measure is incorporated into all employees' incentive systems. The measure itself, along with all the analyses and service improvement initiatives that are behind it, is intended to align employee behaviour around retaining customers.

Companies with a goal of customer satisfaction in every service encounter often need to adjust the criteria by which employee performance is judged. Some companies will have to shift from a total emphasis on productivity data and hard numbers to other means of assessment. Ongoing "true moments" surveys can be used whereby customers are called and asked to assess the level of service they received from the particular employee they interacted with over the phone. These measurements (multiple customers for each employee each quarter) are then integrated into the employee's performance evaluation and rewarded. Such measurement systems are challenging to effectively implement. The measures must be appropriate, the sampling of customers must be performed fairly, and the employees must buy in to the validity of the results.

Aligning reward systems with customer outcomes can be challenging. Reward systems are usually well entrenched, and employees have learned over time how they need to perform within the old structures. Change is difficult both for the managers who may still believe in the old systems and for employees who are not sure what they need to do to succeed under the new rules. In many organizations, however, reward and incentive systems are still not matched with customer satisfaction and loyalty goals.[60]

Taking the argument one step further, some leading-edge Canadian companies are also tying management compensation to employee satisfaction. From a services marketing perspective, this makes sense. According to Towers Perrin, one of Canada's largest HR consultancies, although measuring employee engagement is becoming common, only a few firms have made the leap to tying management compensation to it. But because higher employee engagement levels mean higher retention, its worth paying for.[61]

In developing new systems and structures to recognize customer focus and customer and employee satisfaction, organizations have turned to a variety of rewards. Traditional approaches such as higher pay, promotions, and one-time monetary awards or prizes can be linked to service performance. In some organizations employees are encouraged to recognize each other by personally giving a "peer award" to an employee they believe has excelled in providing service to the customer. Other types of rewards include special organizational and team celebrations for achieving improved customer satisfaction or for attaining customer retention goals. In most service organizations it is not only the major accomplishments but the daily perseverance and attention to detail that move the organization forward, so recognition of the "small wins" is also important.

In many situations, a customer's relationship is with a specific employee and may be stronger with the *employee* than with the firm. If this employee leaves the firm and is no longer available to the customer, the firm's relationship with the customer may be jeopardized.[62] Clearly a firm should make great efforts to retain such employees; however, in spite of the firm's best efforts, some good employees are going to leave. If the firm is not successful at retaining a key customer contact employee, what can it do to reduce the impact on the customer? Employees could be rotated occasionally in order to ensure that the customer has exposure to and is comfortable with more than one employee. Firms might also form teams of employees who are responsible for interacting with each customer. In both cases, the idea is that the customer would have multiple contacts with several employees in the organization, thus reducing the firm's vulnerability to losing the customer should any one employee leave. Emphasis should also be placed on creating a positive firm image in the minds of its customers and in so doing convey that *all* its employees are capable.[63]

SUMMARY

Because many services are delivered by people in real time, closing the service performance gap is heavily dependent on human resource strategies. The successful execution of such strategies begins with the development and nurturing of a true service culture in which "an appreciation for good service exists, and where giving good service to internal as well as ultimate, external customers is considered a natural way of life and one of the most important norms by everyone."[64]

Often, service employees are the service, and in all cases they represent the organization in customers' eyes. They affect service quality perceptions to a large degree through their influence on the five dimensions of service quality: reliability, responsiveness, empathy, assurance, and tangibles. It is essential to match what the customer wants and needs with service employees' abilities to deliver.

In this chapter we focused on service employees to provide you with an understanding of the critical nature of their roles and appreciation of the inherent stresses and conflicts they face. You learned that front-line service jobs demand significant investments of emotional labour and that employees confront a variety of on-the-job conflicts. Sometimes service employees are personally uncomfortable with the roles they are asked to play; other times the requirements of the organization may conflict with client expectations, and employees must resolve the dilemma on the spot. Sometimes there are conflicting needs among customers who are being served in turn (such as in a bank teller line) or among customers being served simultaneously (as in a college classroom). At other times a frontline employee may be faced with a decision about whether to satisfy a customer or meet productivity targets (such as a call centre employee who must keep the average length of each call to a minimum regardless of the needs of the caller).

Grounded in this understanding of the importance of service employees and the nature of their roles in the organization, you learned strategies for integrating appropriate human resource practices into service firms. The strategies are aimed at allowing employees to effectively satisfy customers as well as be efficient and productive in their jobs. The strategies were organized around four major human resource goals in service organizations: to hire the right people, to develop people to deliver service quality, to provide needed support systems, and to retain the best people. A company that works toward implementing these strategies is well on its way to delivering service quality through its people, thereby diminishing Provider Gap 3.

Discussion Questions

1. Define *service culture*. Why is service culture so important? Can a manufacturing firm have a service culture? Why or why not?

2. Why are service employees critical to the success of any service organization? Why do we include an entire chapter on service employees in a marketing course?

3. What is emotional labour? How can it be differentiated from physical or mental labour?

4. Reflect on your own role as a front-line service provider, whether in a current job or in any full- or part-time service job you have had in the past. Did you experience the kinds of conflicts described in the boundary-spanning roles section of the chapter? Be prepared with some concrete examples for class discussion.

5. Select a service provider (your dentist, doctor, lawyer, hair stylist) with whom you are familiar, and discuss ways this person could positively influence the five dimensions of service quality in the context of delivering his or her services. Do the same for yourself (if you are currently a service provider).

6. Describe the four basic human resource strategy themes and why each plays an important role in building a customer-oriented organization.

7. What is the difference between technical and interactive service skills? Provide examples (preferably from your own work context or from another context with which you are familiar). Why do service employees need training in both?

8. Is empowerment always the best approach for effective service delivery? Why is employee empowerment so controversial?

Exercises

1. Visit the websites of companies with known world-class service cultures (such as Ritz-Carlton, FedEx, or TD Bank Financial Group). How does the information conveyed on the website reinforce the company's service culture?

2. Review the section of the chapter on boundary-spanning roles. Interview at least two front-line service personnel regarding the stresses they experience in their jobs. How do the examples they provide relate to the sources of conflict and tradeoffs described in the text?

3. Assume that you are the manager of a crew of front-line customer-service employees in a credit card company. Assume that these employees work over the phone and that they deal primarily with customer requests, questions, and complaints. In this specific context,
   a. Define what is meant by *boundary-spanning roles,* and discuss the basic purposes or functions performed by participants in these roles.
   b. Discuss two of the potential conflicts that your employees may face on the basis of their roles as boundary spanners.
   c. Discuss how you, as their supervisor, might deal with these conflicts based on what you have learned.

4. Choose one or more of the human resource strategy themes (hire the right people, develop people to deliver service quality, provide needed support systems, retain

the best people). Interview a manager in a service organization of your choice regarding his or her current practices within the theme you have chosen. Describe the current practices and recommend any appropriate changes for improving them.

⟼ Notes

1. L. L. Berry, *Discovering the Soul of Service* (New York: The Free Press, 1999); A. Wahl, "The Best Workplaces in Canada," *Canadian Business*, April 10–23, 2006; L. Bogomolny, P. Evans, A. Holloway, Z. Olijnyk, E. Pooley, and A. Wahl, "Best Workplaces 2006: The List," *Canadian Business*, April 10–23, 2006; A. Wahl, Z. Olijnyk, P. Evans, A. Holloway, and E. Pooley, "Best Workplaces 2006: Lessons from Some of the Best," *Canadian Business*, April 10–23, 2006.
2. S. M. Davis, *Managing Corporate Culture* (Cambridge, MA: Ballinger, 1985).
3. C. Gronroos, *Service Management and Marketing* (Lexington, MA: Lexington Books, 1990), p. 244.
4. See K. N. Kennedy, F. G. Lassk, and J. R. Goolsby, "Customer Mind-Set of Employees Throughout the Organization," *Journal of the Academy of Marketing Science*, 30 (Spring 2002), pp. 159–71.
5. R. Hallowell, D. Bowen, and C. Knoop, "Four Seasons Goes to Paris," *Academy of Management Executive* 16, no. 4 (2002), pp. 7–24; J. L. Heskett, L. A. Schlesinger, and E.W. Sasser Jr., *The Service Profit Chain* (New York: The Free Press, 1997); B. Schneider and D. E. Bowen, *Winning the Service Game* (Boston: Harvard Business School Press, 1995).
6. Quoted in D. Stauffer, "The Art of Delivering Great Customer Service," *Harvard Management Update* 4, no. 9 (September 1999), pp. 1–3.
7. Natalia Williams, "Travel & Tourism: Why It's (Still) Good to be WestJet," *Strategy* (Toronto, ON), November 2005, p. 243.
8. Ibid.
9. J. Garrett, "The Human Side of Brand: Why Audi Hires Workers with the Same Traits as Its Luxury Cars," *Gallup Management Journal*, Summer 2001, pp. 4–5.
10. Katherine Macklem, "Canada's Top 100 Employers: No. 1, VanCity Confidential," *Maclean's* 117, nos. 41/42 (October 11, 2004), p. 22.
11. The conceptualization of the services triangle presented in Figure 12.3 and the related text discussion are based on M. J. Bitner, "Building Service Relationships: It's All About Promises," *Journal of the Academy of Marketing Science* 23 (Fall 1995), pp. 246–51; P. Kotler, *Marketing Management: Analysis, Planning, Implementation, and Control*, 8th ed. (Englewood Cliffs, NJ: Prentice Hall, 1994); and Gronroos, *Service Management and Marketing*.
12. See, for example, H. Rosenbluth, "Tales from a Nonconformist Company," *Harvard Business Review*, July/August 1991, pp. 26–36; and L. A. Schlesinger and J. L. Heskett, "The Service-Driven Service Company," *Harvard Business Review*, September/October 1991, pp. 71–81.
13. B. Schneider and D. E. Bowen, "The Service Organization: Human Resources Management Is Crucial," *Organizational Dynamics* 21 (Spring 1993), pp. 39–52.
14. Ibid.
15. D. E. Bowen, S. W. Gilliland, and R. Folger, "How Being Fair with Employees Spills over to Customers," *Organizational Dynamics* 27 (Winter 1999), pp. 7–23.

16. See J. L. Heskett, T. O. Jones, G. W. Loveman, W. E. Sasser Jr., and L. A. Schlesinger, "Putting the Service–Profit Chain to Work," *Harvard Business Review*, March/April 1994, pp. 164–74; G. W. Loveman, "Employee Satisfaction, Customer Loyalty, and Financial Performance," *Journal of Service Research* 1 (August 1998), pp. 18–31; A. Rucci, S. P. Kirn, and R. T. Quinn, "The Employee–Customer Profit Chain at Sears," *Harvard Business Review*, January/February 1998, pp. 82–97; and R. Hallowell and L. L. Schlesinger, "The Service–Profit Chain," in *The Handbook for Services Marketing and Management*, ed. T. A. Swartz and D. Iacobucci (Thousand Oaks, CA: Sage Publications, 2000), pp. 203–22.

17. J. Pfeffer, *The Human Equation* (Boston: Harvard Business School Press, 1998); and A. M. Webber, "Danger: Toxic Company," Fast Company, November 1998, pp. 152–62.

18. M. K. Brady and J. J. Cronin Jr., "Customer Orientation: Effects on Customer Service Perceptions and Outcome Behaviors," *Journal of Service Research* 3 (February 2001), pp. 241–51.

19. L. A. Bettencourt and K. Gwinner, "Customization of the Service Experience: The Role of the Frontline Employee," *International Journal of Service Industry Management* 7, no. 2 (1996), pp. 3–20.

20. For research on the influence of front-line employee behaviours on customers, see D. D. Gremler and K. P. Gwinner, "Customer–Employee Rapport in Service Relationships," *Journal of Service Research* 3 (August 2000), pp. 82–104; K. de Ruyter and M. G. M. Wetzels, "The Impact of Perceived Listening Behavior in Voice-to-Voice Service Encounters," *Journal of Service Research* 2 (February 2000), pp. 276–84; Tom J. Brown, John C. Mowen, D. Todd Donavan, and Jane W. Licata, "The Customer Orientation of Service Workers: Personality Trait Effects of Self- and Supervisor Performance Ratings," *Journal of Marketing Research* 39 (February 2002), pp. 110–19.

21. A. Hochschild, *The Managed Heart: Commercialization of Human Feeling* (Berkeley: University of California Press, 1983).

22. A. Hochschild, "Emotional Labor in the Friendly Skies," *Psychology Today*, June 1982, pp. 13–15.

23. For additional discussion on emotional labour strategies, see R. Leidner, "Emotional Labor in Service Work," *Annals of the American Academy of Political and Social Science* 561, no. 1 (1999), pp. 81–95.

24. M. D. Hartline and O. C. Ferrell, "The Management of Customer-Contact Service Employees: An Empirical Investigation," *Journal of Marketing* 60 (October 1996), pp. 52–70; J. Singh, J. R. Goolsby, and G. K. Rhoads, "Burnout and Customer Service Representatives," *Journal of Marketing Research* 31 (November 1994), pp. 558–69; L. A. Bettencourt and S. W. Brown, "Role Stressors and Customer-Oriented Boundary-Spanning Behaviors in Service Organizations," *Journal of the Academy of Marketing Science* 31 (Fall 2003), pp. 394–408.

25. B. Shamir, "Between Service and Servility: Role Conflict in Subordinate Service Roles," *Human Relations* 33, no. 10 (1980), pp. 741–56.

26. Ibid., pp. 744–45.

27. Randal Craig as quoted by Suzanne Wintrob, "Do You Have Multiple Boss Syndrome?" *Globe and Mail*, October 7, 2005, p. C7, available www.workopolis. com/servlet/Content/fasttrack/20051007/CAMULTI07?section=HomePage, accessed October 1, 2006.

28. E. W. Anderson, C. Fornell, and R. T. Rust, "Customer Satisfaction, Productivity, and Profitability: Differences Between Goods and Services," *Marketing Science* 16, no. 2 (1997), pp. 129–45.

29. J. Singh, "Performance Productivity and Quality of Frontline Employees in Service Organizations," *Journal of Marketing* 64 (April 2000), pp. 15–34.

30. For discussions of internal marketing, see L. L. Berry and A. Parasuraman, "Marketing to Employees," ch. 9 in *Marketing Services* (New York: The Free Press, 1991); C. Gronroos, "Managing Internal Marketing: A Prerequisite for Successful External Marketing," ch. 10 in *Service Management and Marketing* (Lexington, MA: Lexington Books, 1990).

31. B. Breen and A. Muoio, "PeoplePalooza 2001," *Fast Company*, January 2001, cover and feature article.

32. Berry and Parasuraman, "Marketing to Employees," p. 153.

33. Katherine Macklem, "Showing the Love," *Maclean's*, October 17, 2005.

34. K. J. Dunham, "The Jungle: Focus on Recruitment, Pay, and Getting Ahead," *The Wall Street Journal*, April 10, 2001, p. B14.

35. Macklem, "Showing the Love."

36. This section on hiring for service competencies and service inclination draws from work by B. Schneider and colleagues, specifically B. Schneider and D. Schechter, "Development of a Personnel Selection System for Service Jobs," in *Service Quality: Multidisciplinary and Multinational Perspectives*, ed. S. W. Brown, E. Gummesson, B. Edvardsson, and B. Gustavsson (Lexington, MA: Lexington Books, 1991), pp. 217–36.

37. J. Hogan, R. Hogan, and C. M. Busch, "How to Measure Service Orientation," *Journal of Applied Psychology* 69, no. 1 (1984), pp. 167–73. See also Brown et al., "The Customer Orientation of Service Workers" and D. T. Donovan, T. J. Brown, and J. C. Mowen, "Internal Benefits of Service-Worker Customer Orientation: Job Satisfaction, Commitment, and Organizational Citizenship Behaviors," *Journal of Marketing* 68 (January 2004), pp. 128–46.

38. For a detailed description of a model selection system for telephone sales and service people, see Schneider and Schechter, "Development of a Personnel Selection System."

39. For additional information on Southwest Airlines hiring practices, see C. Mitchell, "Selling the Brand Inside," *Harvard Business Review* 80 (January 2002), pp. 99–105.

40. R. Levering and M. Moskowitz, *The 100 Best Companies to Work For in America* (New York: Penguin Group, 1994), p. 457.

41. "Low Wage Lessons: How Marriott Keeps Good Help Even at $7.40 an Hour," *BusinessWeek*, cover story, November 11, 1996, pp. 108–16.

42. R. Levering and M. Moskowitz, "The 100 Best Companies to Work For," *Fortune*, January 12, 2004, pp. 56–80.

43. R. Normann, "Getting People to Grow," *Service Management* (New York: John Wiley, 1984), pp. 44–50.

44. J. C. Chebat and P. Kollias, "The Impact of Empowerment on Customer Contact Employees' Roles in Service Organizations," *Journal of Service Research* 3 (August 2000), pp. 66–81.

45. C. Argyris, "Empowerment: The Emperor's New Clothes," *Harvard Business Review* 76 (May/June 1998), pp. 98–105.

46. D. E. Bowen and E. E. Lawler III, "The Empowerment of Service Workers: What, Why, How, and When," *Sloan Management Review*, Spring 1992, pp. 31–39.

47. J. H. Gittell, "Relationships Between Service Providers and Their Impact on Customers," *Journal of Service Research* 4 (May 2002), pp. 299–311.

48. Berry and Parasuraman, "Marketing to Employees," p. 162.

49. Macklem, "Showing the Love."

50. A. Sergeant and S. Frenkel, "When Do Customer-Contact Employees Satisfy Customers?" *Journal of Service Research* 3 (August 2000), pp. 18–34.

51. Schneider and Bowen, *Winning the Service Game*, pp. 230–34.

52. O. Gadiesh and J. L. Gilbert, "Transforming Corner-Office Strategy into Front-line Action," *Harvard Business Review*, May 2001, pp. 73–79.

53. B. Fryer, "High Tech the Old Fashioned Way," *Harvard Business Review*, March 2001, pp. 119–25; C. Hawn, "The Man Who Sees Around Corners," *Forbes*, January 21, 2002, pp. 72–78.

54. H. Rosenbluth, "Tales from a Nonconformist Company," *Harvard Business Review*, July/August 1991, p. 33.

55. L. L. Berry, "The Employee as Customer," *Journal of Retail Banking* 3 (March 1981), pp. 33–40.

56. C. Hegge-Kleiser, "American Express Travel-Related Services: A Human Resources Approach to Managing Quality," in *Managing Quality in America's Most Admired Companies*, ed. J. W. Spechler (San Francisco: Berrett-Koehler Publishers, 1993), pp. 205–12.

57. "Balancing Work and Family," *BusinessWeek*, cover story, September 16, 1996, pp. 74–84.

58. M. C. Gilly and M. Wolfinbarger, "Advertising's Internal Audience," *Journal of Marketing* 62 (January 1998), pp. 69–88.

59. Fryer, "High Tech the Old-Fashioned Way."

60. See Schneider and Bowen, Winning the Service Game, ch. 6, for an excellent discussion of the complexities and issues involved in creating effective reward systems for service employees.

61. Macklem, "Showing the Love."

62. N. Bendapudi and R. P. Leone, "Managing Business-to-Business Customer Relationships Following Key Contact Employee Turnover in a Vendor Firm," *Journal of Marketing* 66 (April 2002), pp. 83–101.

63. Ibid.

64. Gronroos, *Service Management and Marketing*, p. 244.

Chapter

13

Customers' Roles in Service Delivery

Closing Provider Gap 3

THIS CHAPTER'S OBJECTIVES ARE TO

→ 1. Illustrate the importance of customers in successful service delivery and cocreation of service experiences.

→ 2. Discuss the variety of roles that service customers play: productive resources for the organization; contributors to quality and satisfaction; competitors.

→ 3. Explain strategies for involving service customers effectively to increase both quality and productivity.

CURVES INTERNATIONAL—HELPING CLIENTS GET THE MOST FROM THE SERVICE

When service providers require the customer to actively participate in the service delivery and outcomes, as with many health clubs, it may become particularly difficult to ensure company standards and customer expectations are met. Curves International (www.curves.com), the world's largest and fastest-growing fitness franchise, seems to have an appropriate strategy. The company, which has grown to more than 9,500 locations and four million members worldwide since its opening in 1992, has a number of initiatives that ensure its entirely female customer-base are aware of their roles and responsibilities.

Curves' success requires that customers be successful and that their expectations be met in their quest for fitness and/or weight loss. But how does an international company that relies on both franchisees and millions of individual members for service delivery achieve such a goal? And how can such a company expect to be successful when those millions of individual members become wholly responsible for the service outcome? A closer look at Curves indicates that the company's successful model involves setting reasonable expectations, having well-defined customer roles, and providing motivation and support to fulfil the required roles and reach expectations.

Even before a woman purchases a Curves membership, potential customers viewing any of the company's promotional material should have reasonable expectations of the service. Instead of using perfectly sculpted models in their ads, Curves showcases real-looking women. Members also set reasonable expectations. Every month, a member's body measurements are recorded and individuals can set realistic goals for weight loss.

When a woman buys a Curves membership, the role responsibilities are clear. New members are guided through the 30-minute strength and cardio workout by staff and taught proper technique at that time. After the initiation, members understand how to use the hydraulic weight machines, but also recognize that to be successful they must commit to work out the recommended three times per week.

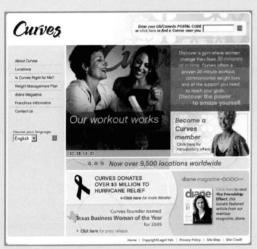

Source: Curves International, Inc.

Finally, the motivation and support offered at the corporate level and from franchisees and fellow members is an important part of Curves strategy to have customers successfully manage the service delivery. To this end, the company publishes success stories online and in their magazine, *diane*. And individual gym owners also run their own promotions and offer incentives to help clients reach their goals and ensure satisfaction. At Christine Flemming's Curves in Pictou, Nova Scotia, for example, clients get one ballot entered into a monthly draw for each week they work out the recommended three times. This location also has a wall of accomplishment where individuals' names and success measures are posted on stars that cover the wall.[1]

In this chapter we examine the unique roles played by customers in service delivery situations. Service customers are often present in the "factory" (the place the service is produced and/or consumed), interacting with employees and with other customers. For example, in a classroom or training situation, students (the customers) are sitting in the factory interacting with the instructor and other students as they consume and co-create the educational services. Because they are present during service production, customers can contribute to or detract from the successful delivery of the service and to their own satisfaction. In a manufacturing context, rarely does the production facility contend with customer presence on the factory floor, nor does it rely on the customer's immediate real-time input to manufacture the product. As our opening vignette illustrates, service customers can actually produce the service themselves and to some extent are responsible for their own satisfaction. Using Curves' facilities, equipment, and workout approach, customers co-create value for themselves.

Because customers are participants in service production and delivery, they can contribute to the widening of Gap 3. That is, customers themselves can influence whether the delivered service meets customer-defined specifications. Sometimes customers contribute to Gap 3 because they lack understanding of their roles and exactly what they should do in a given situation, particularly if the customer is confronting a service concept for the first time. Customers using Curves for the first time need detailed, but simple, instructions to help them understand how to use the service effectively and get the greatest value.

At other times customers may understand their roles but be unwilling or unable to perform for some reason. In a health club context, members may understand that to get into good physical shape they must follow the workout guidelines set up by the trainers. If work schedule or illness keeps members from living up to their part of the guidelines, the service will not be successful because of customer inaction. In a different service situation, customers may choose not to perform the roles defined for them because they are not rewarded in any way for contributing their effort. When service customers are enticed through price reductions, greater convenience, or some other tangible benefit, they are more likely to perform their roles willingly, as in the case of our opening vignette about Curves.

Finally, Gap 3 may be widened not through actions or inactions on the part of the customer, but because of what *other* customers do. Other customers who are in the service factory either receiving the service simultaneously (passengers on an Air Canada flight) or waiting their turn to receive the service sequentially (bank customers waiting in line or Canada's Wonderland customers waiting for one of the rides) can influence whether the service is effectively and efficiently delivered.

This chapter focuses on the roles of customers in service delivery and cocreation of service experiences as well as strategies to effectively manage them.

→ THE IMPORTANCE OF CUSTOMERS IN SERVICE DELIVERY

Customer participation at some level is inevitable in service delivery and cocreation. Services are actions or performances, typically produced and consumed simultaneously. In many situations employees, customers, and even others in the service environment interact to produce the ultimate service outcome. Because they participate, customers are indispensable to the production process of service organizations, and they can actually control or contribute to their own satisfaction.[2]

The importance of customers in successful service delivery is obvious if service performances are looked at as a form of drama. The drama metaphor for services (discussed in Chapter 3) suggests the reciprocal, interactive roles of employees (actors) and customers (audience) in creating the service experience. The service actors and audience are surrounded by the service setting or the servicescape (discussed in Chapter 11). The drama metaphor argues that the development and maintenance of an interaction (a service experience) relies on the audience's input as well as the actors' presentation. Through this metaphor, service performances or service delivery situations are viewed

as tenuous, fragile processes that can be influenced by behaviours of customers as well
as by employees.[3] Service performance results from actions and interactions among
individuals in both groups.

Consider the services provided by a cruise ship company. The actors (ship's personnel) provide the service through interactions with their audience (the passengers) and among each other. The audience also produces elements of the service through interactions with the actors and other audience members. Both actors and audience are surrounded by an elaborate setting (the cruise ship itself) that provides a context to facilitate the service performance. The drama metaphor provides a compelling frame of reference for recognizing the interdependent roles of actors and audience in service delivery.[4]

Recognition of the role of customers is also reflected in the definition of the *people* element of the services marketing mix given in Chapter 1: *all human actors who play a part in service delivery and thus influence the buyer's perceptions; namely, the firm's personnel, the customer, and other customers in the service environment.* Chapter 12 examined the role of employees in delivering the service. In this chapter we focus on the customer receiving the service and on fellow customers in the service environment.

Customer Receiving the Service

Because the customer participates in the delivery process, he or she can contribute to narrowing or widening Gap 3 through behaviours that are appropriate or inappropriate, productive or unproductive. Even in a relatively simple service such as retail mail order, customers' actions and preparation can have an effect on service delivery. Customers who are unprepared in terms of what they want to order can soak up the customer service representative's time as they seek advice. Similarly, shoppers who are not prepared with their credit card numbers can put the representative on hold while they search for their cards or retrieve them from another room or their cars. Meanwhile, other customers and calls are left unattended, causing longer wait times and potential dissatisfaction.

The level of customer participation—low, medium, high—varies across services, as shown in Table 13.1. In some cases, all that is required is the customer's physical

TABLE 13.1   Levels of Customer Participation Across Different Services

Low: **Consumer Presence Required During Service Delivery**	*Moderate:* **Consumer Inputs Required for Service Creation**	*High:* **Customer Co-creates the Service Product**
Products are standardized.	Client inputs (information, materials) customize a standard service.	Active client participation guides the customized service.
Service is provided regardless of any individual purchase.	Provision of service requires customer purchase.	Service cannot be created apart from the customer's purchase and active participation.
Payment may be the only required customer input.	Customer inputs are necessary for an adequate outcome, but the service firm provides the service.	Customer inputs are mandatory and co-create the outcome.
End Consumer Examples		
Airline travel	Haircut	University classes
Motel stay	Annual physical exam	Personal training
Fast-food restaurant	Full-service restaurant	Weight reduction program
		Major illness or surgery
Business-to-Business Customer Examples		
Uniform cleaning service	Agency-created advertising campaign	Management consulting
Pest control	Payroll service	Executive management seminar
Interior greenery maintenance service	Freight transportation	Installation of computer network

Source: Adapted from A. R. Hubbert, "Customer Co-creation of Service Outcomes: Effects of Locus of Causality Attributions," doctoral dissertation, Arizona State University, Tempe, Arizona, 1995.

presence (*low level of participation*), with the employees of the firm doing all the service production work, as in the example of a symphony concert. Symphony-goers must be present to receive the entertainment service, but little else is required once they are seated. In other situations, consumer inputs are required to aid the service organization in creating the service (*moderate level of participation*). Inputs can include *information*, effort, or *physical possessions*. All three of these are required for a CA to prepare a client's tax return effectively: information in the form of tax history, marital status, and number of dependents; effort in putting the information together in a useful fashion; and physical possessions such as receipts and past tax returns. In some situations, customers are truly co-creators of the service (*high level of participation*). For these services, customers have mandatory production roles that, if not fulfilled, will affect the nature of the service outcome. In a complex or long-term business-to-business consulting engagement, the client can be involved in activities such as identification of issues, shared problem solving, ongoing communication, provision of equipment and work space, and implementation of solutions.[5] Facilitating this type of positive customer participation can help ensure a successful outcome, as described in Exhibit 13.1.

Table 13.1 provides several examples of each level of participation for both consumer and business-to-business services. The effectiveness of customer involvement at all the levels will impact organizational productivity and, ultimately, quality and customer satisfaction.

Client Coproduction in Business-to-Business Services

What do firms like IBM, McKinsey, Accenture, and neoIT have in common? All can be described as knowledge-intensive business services (KIBS) whose value-added activities provide their business clients with highly customized services (e.g., technical engineering, consulting, software development, business process outsourcing). To develop and deliver optimal service solutions, KIBS rely on inputs and cooperation from their clients as integral coproducers of the services. The KIBS provider needs accurate and detailed information from the client, access to people and resources, and cooperation in terms of deadlines and contingencies that inevitably arise.

Depth interviews and research conducted with clients of employees of an IT services provider ("TechCo") identified a number of *client* characteristics that can enhance the quality of the client's participation and the ultimate service outcome in these types of KIBS relationships. The characteristics are listed here with an illustrative quote from or about one of TechCo's clients, using disguised names. Clients who display these types of coproduction behaviors will contribute to the success of their projects and are likely to get better outcomes and be more satisfied.

- **Communication openness:** The client is forthcoming and honest in sharing pertinent information for project success.

  PharmCo actually did the up-front work to understand what it is we have to do, when we have to do it, and how it fits into our overall scheme of things . . . We [spent] the first days doing nothing but teaching them about what we're trying to accomplish.—TechCo, about PharmCo Client

- **Shared problem solving:** The client takes individual initiative and shared responsibility for developing solutions to problems that arise in the relationship.

  I think, as a customer, I have a responsibility to bring some critical thinking to what they've brought to the table. Not just to accept it . . . [You need to be able to say,] "I don't know if that's going to work for our environment" or technically, "Why did you do that?" So a lot of it's just asking questions and saying, "Why are we doing it that way? Is that the best way to do it?"—GovCo Client

- **Tolerance:** The client responds in an understanding and patient manner in the face of minor project encumbrances.

  That certainly was our goal—not to have roadblocks, not to have problems . . . And even at that, it took us longer than

we had hoped. Again, not anybody's fault, it's just one of those things. It's a process, and sometimes those processes take a little longer than you initially had planned for.—EduCo Client

- **Accommodation:** The client demonstrates a willingness to accommodate the desires, approaches, and expert judgment of the service provider.

  [If we saw something that didn't fit with our goals,] we'd call them and ask them . . . If they could do it, they would simply say, "Oh, you bet, no problem" . . . If it was something that we really couldn't monkey with too much, they'd come out and say, "No, you probably don't want to change that because of this reason and that reason" and we'd say, "Okay, that's fine" and we'd go on to the next one. —EduCo Client

- **Advocacy:** The client firm provides a vocal advocate and salesperson for the project.

  [The scope of the project] was cumbersome. Had we not had involvement and not had a group of people who had ownership, who really wanted to succeed, we might have been inclined to say . . . "I don't really care how this turns out because the boss told me I need to do it. I don't care if it's ugly because I'm never going to use it." So, I think it was a combination of things. One is having people who have a vested interest in making sure it worked and knew why they were doing it and [second] continuous involvement.—AgCo Client

- **Involvement in project governance:** The client takes an active role in monitoring project progress toward the stated goal.

  We would have our meetings and we'd set these action items. We would say when they're supposed to be done, and we would set the next meeting before we ended that meeting so everybody knew what their expectations were. —DonorCo Client

- **Personal dedication:** The client demonstrates a sense of personal obligation for project success by performing individual responsibilities in a conscientious manner.

  I think that was one of the things that I probably did right— was staying that involved. But it was hard, from my perspective, because it took time away from other things that I had to do. But I think I brought some things to the project that, if I hadn't been as involved, I don't know that we would have had as successful an implementation of the three systems as I think we did.—GovCo Client

continued

The challenge for KIBS firms is to develop processes, systems, and practices that will ensure that clients engage in these ways. The research suggests that these positive co-production behaviors will be most likely when KIBS provider firms engage in (1) *client selectivity* (carefully screening clients in advance to ensure a good fit between provider and client); (2) *client training, education, and socialization* (making clients feel that they are part of the team by kicking off the relationship with a cooperative spirit, perhaps including events and expectations-setting workshops); and (3) *project leadership and client performance evaluation* (selecting the right project leaders on both sides and evaluating both on their relationship management skills as well as technical capabilities).

This research illustrates the importance of business clients as coproducers of the service and the value to both provider and client that can result from quality coproduction behaviors and associated business practices.

Source: © 2002, by The Regents of the University of California. Reprinted from the *California Management Review*, 44, no. 4 by permission of the Regents.

Fellow Customers

In many service contexts, customers receive the service simultaneously with other customers or must wait their turn while other customers are being served. In both cases, "fellow customers" are present in the service environment and can affect the nature of the service outcome or process. Fellow customers can either *enhance* or *detract* from customer satisfaction and perceptions of quality.[6]

Some of the ways fellow customers can negatively affect the service experience are by exhibiting disruptive behaviours, causing delays, excessively crowding, and manifesting incompatible needs. In restaurants, hotels, airplanes, and other environments in which customers are cheek to jowl as they receive the service, crying babies, smoking patrons, and loud, unruly groups can be disruptive and detract from the experiences of their fellow customers. The customer is disappointed through no direct fault of the provider. In other cases, overly demanding customers (even customers with legitimate problems) can cause a delay for others while their needs are met. This occurrence is common in banks, post offices, and customer service counters in retail stores. Overcrowding or overuse of a service can also affect the nature of the customer's experience. Visiting Old Montreal or Quebec City during celebrations for St-Jean-Baptiste Day on June 24 is a very different experience from visiting the same area at other times of the year. Similarly, the quality of telecommunication services can suffer on special holidays such as Christmas and Mother's Day when large numbers of customers all try to use the service at once.

Finally, customers who are being served simultaneously but who have incompatible needs can negatively affect each other. This situation can occur in restaurants, classrooms, hospitals, and any service establishment in which multiple segments are served simultaneously. In a study of critical service encounters occurring in tourist attractions, researchers found that customers negatively affected each other when they failed to follow either explicit or implicit "rules of conduct." Customers reported such negative behaviours as pushing, shoving, smoking, drinking alcohol, being verbally abusive, or cutting in line. Other times, dissatisfaction resulted when other customers were impersonal, rude, unfriendly, or even spiteful.[7]

We can offer just as many examples of other customers enhancing satisfaction and quality for their fellow customers as detracting from them. Sometimes the mere presence of other customers enhances the experience, for example, at sporting events, in

FIGURE 13.2

Social interactions with others can influence health club members' satisfaction with the service.

Source: JupiterImages.

movie theatres, and in other entertainment venues. The presence of other patrons is essential for true enjoyment of these experiences. In other situations, fellow customers provide a positive social dimension to the service experience. At health clubs, churches, and student pubs such as AJ's Hangar in Kingston, Ontario, other customers provide opportunities to socialize and build friendships, as suggested in Figure 13.2.

In some situations, customers may actually help each other achieve service goals and outcomes. The success of the Weight Watchers organization, for example, depends significantly on the camaraderie and support that group members provide each other. The study of tourist attractions mentioned earlier found that customers increased the satisfaction of others by having friendly conversations while waiting in line, by taking photos, by assisting with children, and by returning dropped or lost items.[8] An ethnographic study that observed hundreds of hours of customer interactions among travellers on the U.K. rail system found that customers often helped each other by (1) providing important service-related information (e.g., schedules, interesting features en route) that can reduce trip-related anxiety; (2) engaging in enjoyable conversation, thus making the trip more pleasant; and (3) serving as someone to complain to when mishaps and service failures occurred.[9]

Customers helping each other is not limited to consumer services. An interesting example occurs at networking giant Cisco. By giving business customers open access to its information and systems through its online self-service, Cisco enables customers to engage in dialogue with each other, helping themselves and other customers who may be experiencing similar challenges.

CUSTOMERS' ROLES

The following sections examine in more detail three major roles played by customers in service delivery: customers as productive resources; customers as contributors to quality and satisfaction; and customers as competitors.

Customers as Productive Resources

Service customers have been referred to as "partial employees" of the organization—human resources who contribute to the organization's productive capacity.[10] Some management experts have suggested that the organization's boundaries be expanded to consider the customer as part of the service system. In other words, if customers contribute effort, time, or other resources to the service production process, they should be considered as part of the organization. (Later in the chapter we devote a section to defining customers' jobs and strategies for managing them effectively.)

Customer inputs can affect the organization's productivity through both the quality of what they contribute and the resulting quality and quantity of output generated. In a business-to-business services context (see Exhibit 13.1), the contributions of the client can enhance the overall productivity of the firm in both quality and quantity of service.[11] In a very different context, discount airlines such as Jazz or WestJet depend on customers to perform critical service roles for themselves, thus increasing the overall productivity of the airline. Passengers are asked to carry their own bags when transferring to other airlines, get their own food, and seat themselves.

Customer participation in service production raises a number of issues for organizations. Because customers can influence both the quality and quantity of production, some experts believe the delivery system should be isolated as much as possible from customer inputs in order to reduce the uncertainty they can bring into the production process. This view sees customers as a major source of uncertainty—in the timing of their demands and the uncontrollability of their attitudes and actions. The logical conclusion is that any service activities that do not require customer contact or involvement should be performed away from customers: The less direct contact there is between the customer and the service production system, the greater the potential for the system to operate at peak efficiency.[12]

Other experts believe that services can be delivered most efficiently if customers are truly viewed as partial employees and their coproduction roles are designed to maximize their contributions to the service creation process. The logic behind this view is that organizational productivity can be increased if customers learn to perform service-related activities they currently are not doing or are educated to perform more effectively the tasks they are already doing.[13]

For example, when self-service gasoline stations first came into being, fewer employees were needed and the productivity of gas stations improved. Now many gas stations offer customers the option of paying for their gas at the pump and leaving the station without dealing directly with a cashier. Similarly, the introduction of many automated airline services such as baggage check-in and self-ticketing are intended to speed up the process for customers while freeing employees for other tasks.[14] Organizational productivity is increased by using customers as a resource to perform tasks previously completed by employees. One prominent goal with online customer service is to increase organizational productivity by using the customer as a partial employee, performing his or her own service.

Although organizations derive obvious productivity benefits by involving customers as coproducers, customers do not always like or accept their new roles, especially when they perceive the purpose to be bottom-line cost savings for the company. If customers see no clear benefit to being involved in coproduction (e.g., lower prices, quicker access, better quality outcome), then they are likely to resent and resist their coproduction roles.

Customers as Contributors to Service Quality and Satisfaction

Another role customers can play in services is that of contributor to their own satisfaction. Customers may care little that they have increased the productivity of the organization through their participation, but they likely care a great deal about whether their needs are fulfilled. Effective customer participation can increase the likelihood that needs are met and that the benefits the customer seeks are actually attained. Think of services such as health care, education, personal fitness, and weight loss, in which the service outcome is highly dependent on customer participation. In these services, unless the customers perform their roles effectively, the desired service outcomes are not possible.

Research has shown that in education, active participation by students—as opposed to passive listening—increases learning (the desired service outcome) significantly.[15] The same is true in health care; patient compliance, in terms of taking prescribed medications or changing diet or other habits, can be critical to whether patients regain their health (the desired service outcome).[16] In both these examples, the customers contribute directly to the quality of the outcome and to their own satisfaction with the service. In a business-to-business context, Allied Van Lines and others in the moving industry have found that in many situations customers cause their own *dissatisfaction* with the service by failing to pack shipments appropriately, resulting in breakage or delays while items are repacked.

Research suggests that customers who believe they have done their part are more satisfied with the service. In a study of the banking industry, bank customers were asked to rate themselves (on a scale from "strongly agree" to "strongly disagree") on questions related to their contributions to service delivery, as follows:

What They Did—Outcome Quality of Customer Inputs

- I clearly explained what I wanted the bank employee to do.
- I gave the bank employee proper information.
- I tried to cooperate with the bank employee.
- I understand the procedures associated with this service.

How They Did It—Interaction Quality of Customer Inputs

- I was friendly to the bank employee.
- I have a good relationship with the bank employee.
- I was courteous to the bank employee.
- Receiving this service was a pleasant experience.

Results of the study indicated that the customers' perceptions of both what they did and how they did it were significantly related to customers' satisfaction with the service they received from the bank.[17] That is, those customers who responded more positively to the questions listed above were also more satisfied with the bank. Research in another context showed that customers' perceptions of service quality increased with greater levels of participation. Specifically, customers (in this case members of a YMCA) who participated more in the club gave the club higher ratings on aspects of service quality than did those who participated less.[18]

Customers contribute to quality service delivery when they ask questions, take responsibility for their own satisfaction, and complain when there is a service failure. Customers who take responsibility and providers who encourage their customers to become their partners in identifying and satisfying their own needs will together produce higher levels of service quality. Our Global Feature shows how Sweden's IKEA, the world's largest retailer of home furnishings, has creatively engaged its customers in a new role: "IKEA wants its customers to understand that their role is not to *consume* value but to *create* it."[19]

Global Feature

At Sweden's IKEA, Customers Create Value for Themselves

IKEA (www.ikea.com) of Sweden has managed to transform itself from a small mail-order furniture company in the 1950s into the world's largest retailer of home furnishings. In 2006, two hundred thirty-five stores in thirty-four countries around the world generated $20.9 billion (CAD) in revenue. The company sells simple Scandinavian design furnishings, charging 25 to 50 percent less than its competitors.

A key to IKEA's success is the company's relationship with its customers. IKEA has drawn the customer into its production system: "If customers agree to take on certain key tasks traditionally done by manufacturers and retailers—the assembly of products and their delivery to customers' homes—then IKEA promises to deliver well-designed products at substantially lower prices." In effect IKEA's customers become essential contributors to value—they create value for themselves through participating in the manufacturing, design, and delivery processes.

IKEA has made being part of the value creation process an easy, fun, and pleasant experience for customers. The company's stores are a pleasure to shop in. The stores are set up with "inspirational displays," including realistic room settings and real-life homes that allow customers to get comfortable with the furnishings, try them out, and visualize the possibilities in their own homes. To make shopping easy, free strollers and supervised child care are provided as well as wheelchairs for those who need them.

When customers enter the store they are given catalogues, tape measures, pens, and notepaper to use as they shop, allowing them to perform functions commonly done by sales and service staff. After payment, customers take their purchases to their cars on carts; if necessary they can rent or buy a roof rack to carry larger purchases. Thus customers also provide furniture loading and delivery services for themselves. At home, IKEA customers then take on the role of manufacturer in assembling the new furnishings following carefully written, simple, and direct instructions.

IKEA prints catalogues in 17 different languages, making its products and instructions for their use accessible worldwide. In addition to tailoring its catalogues, another key to IKEA's successful global expansion has been the company's policy of allowing each store to tailor its mix according to the local market needs and budgets. For example, in its Chinese stores, layouts reflect the design of many Chinese apartments. Because many of the apartments have balconies, the stores have a selection of balcony furnishings and displays. And because Chinese kitchens are generally small, few kitchen items and furnishings are shown. Even IKEA's famous "do it yourself" (DIY) assembly concept has also been adapted to some extent in China. Because fewer people have cars and therefore use public transportation, IKEA has more extensive delivery service in China than in most countries. And because labour is cheaper in China, many customers choose to have their furniture assembled for them rather than doing it themselves. Although IKEA has not abandoned its DIY strategy, it has been somewhat more flexible in China to suit customer realities in that country.

IKEA's success is attributable in part to recognizing that customers can be part of the business system, performing roles they have never performed before. The company's flexible implementation of this idea through clearly defining customers' new roles and making it fun to perform these roles is the genius of its strategy. Through the process, customers cocreate their own experiences and contribute to their own satisfaction.

Sources: R. Normann and R. Ramirez, "From Value Chain to Value Constellation: Designing Interactive Strategy," *Harvard Business Review,* July/August 1993, pp. 65–77; B. Edvardsson and B. Enquist, "The IKEA Saga: How Service Culture Drives Service Strategy," *The Service Industries Journal* 22 (October 2002), pp. 153–86; P. M. Miller, "IKEA with Chinese Characteristics," *The China Business Review* (July/August 2004), pp. 36–38; www.ikea.com, 2006.

In addition to contributing to their own satisfaction by improving the quality of service delivered to them, some customers simply enjoy participating in service delivery. These customers find the act of participating to be intrinsically attractive.[20] They enjoy using the Internet to attain airline tickets, or doing all their banking via ATMs and automated phone systems, or pumping their own gas. Often customers who like self-service in one setting are predisposed to serving themselves in other settings as well.

Interestingly, because service customers must participate in service delivery, they frequently blame themselves (at least partially) when things go wrong. Why did it take so long to reach an accurate diagnosis of my health problem? Why was the service contract for our company's cafeteria food full of errors? Why was the room we reserved for our meeting unavailable when we arrived? If customers believe they are partially (or totally) to blame for the failure, they may be less dissatisfied with the service provider than when they believe the provider is responsible.[21] A recent series of studies suggests the existence of this "self-serving bias." That is, when services go better than expected, customers who have participated tend to take credit for the outcome and are less satisfied with the firm than are those customers who have not participated. However, when the outcome is worse than expected, customers who have chosen to participate in service production are less dissatisfied with the service than are those who choose not to participate—presumably because the participating customers have taken on some of the blame themselves.[22]

Customers as Competitors

A final role played by service customers is that of potential competitor. If self-service customers can be viewed as resources of the firm, or as "partial employees," they could in some cases partially perform the service or perform the entire service for themselves and not need the provider at all. Thus customers in a sense are competitors of the companies that supply the service. Whether to produce a service for themselves (*internal exchange*)—for example, child care, home maintenance, car repair—or have someone else provide the service for them (*external exchange*) is a common dilemma for consumers.[23]

Similar internal versus external exchange decisions are made by organizations. Firms frequently choose to outsource service activities such as payroll, data processing, research, accounting, maintenance, and facilities management. They find that it is better to focus on their core businesses and leave these support services to others with greater expertise. Alternatively, a firm may decide to stop purchasing services externally and bring the service production process in-house.

Whether a household or a firm chooses to produce a particular service for itself depends on a variety of factors. A proposed model of internal/external exchange suggests that such decisions depend on the following:[24]

- *Expertise capacity.* The likelihood of producing the service internally is increased if the household or firm possesses the specific skills and knowledge needed to produce it. Having the expertise will not necessarily result in internal service production, however, because other factors (available resources and time) will also influence the decision. (For firms, making the decision to outsource is often based on recognizing that although they may have the expertise, someone else can do it better.)

- *Resource capacity.* To decide to produce a service internally, the household or firm must have the needed resources including people, space, money, equipment, and materials. If the resources are not available internally, external exchange is more likely.

- *Time capacity.* Time is a critical factor in internal/external exchange decisions. Households and firms with adequate time capacity are more likely to produce services internally than are groups with time constraints.

- *Economic rewards.* The economic advantages or disadvantages of a particular exchange decision will be influential in choosing between internal and external options. The actual monetary costs of the two options will sway the decision.

- *Psychic rewards.* Rewards of a noneconomic nature have a potentially strong influence on exchange decisions. Psychic rewards include the degree of satisfaction, enjoyment, gratification, or happiness that is associated with the external or internal exchange.

- *Trust.* In this context *trust* means the degree of confidence or certainty the household or firm has in the various exchange options. The decision will depend to some extent on the level of self-trust in producing the service versus trust of others.

- *Control.* The household or firm's desire for control over the process and outcome of the exchange will also influence the internal/external choice. Entities that desire and can implement a high degree of control over the task are more likely to engage in internal exchange.

The important thing to remember from this section is that in many service scenarios customers can choose to produce the service themselves. Thus, in addition to recognizing that customers can be productive resources and cocreators of quality and value, organizations also need to recognize the customer's role as a potential competitor.

SELF-SERVICE TECHNOLOGIES—THE ULTIMATE IN CUSTOMER PARTICIPATION

Self-service technologies (SSTs) are services produced entirely by the customer without any direct involvement or interaction with the firm's employees. As such SSTs represent the ultimate form of customer participation along a continuum from services that are produced entirely by the firm to those that are produced entirely by the customer. At one end of the continuum, the gas station attendant does everything from pumping the gas to taking payment. On the other end, the customer does everything; in between are various forms and levels of customer participation. Many service delivery options, across industries, might be laid out on this type of continuum from total customer production through total firm production.

A Proliferation of New SSTs

Advances in technology, particularly the Internet, have allowed the introduction of a wide range of self-service technologies. These technologies have proliferated as companies see the potential cost savings and efficiencies that can be achieved, potential sales growth, increased customer satisfaction, and competitive advantage.

The rapid proliferation of new SSTs is occurring for several reasons.[25] Many times firms are tempted by the cost savings that they anticipate by shifting customers to technology-based, automated systems and away from expensive personal service. If cost savings is the only reason for introducing an SST and if customers see no apparent benefits, the SST is likely to fail. Customers quickly see through this strategy and are not likely to adopt the SST if they have alternative options for service. Other times, firms introduce new SSTs based on customer demand. More and more, customers are expecting to find access to information, services, and delivery options online. When they do not find what they want from a particular firm online, they are likely to choose a competitor. Thus, customer demand in some industries is forcing firms to develop and offer their services via technology. Other companies are developing SSTs in order to open up new geographic, socioeconomic, and lifestyle markets that were not available to them through traditional channels.

Customer Usage of SSTs

Some SSTs—ATMs, pay-at-the-pump gas, Internet information search—have been very successful, embraced by customers for the benefits they provide in terms of convenience, accessibility, and ease of use.[26] Benefits to firms, including cost savings and revenue growth, can also result for those SSTs that succeed. Others—airline ticket kiosks, online hotel bookings, grocery self-scanning—have been less quickly embraced by customers.

Failure results when customers see no personal benefit in the new technology or when they do not have the ability to use it or know what they are supposed to do. Often, adopting a new SST requires customers to change their traditional behaviours significantly, and many are reluctant to make those changes. Research looking at customer adoption of SSTs found that "customer readiness" was a major factor in determining whether customers would even try a new self-service option.[27] Customer readiness results from a combination of personal motivation (What's in it for me?), ability (Do I have the ability to use this SST?), and role clarity (Do I understand what I am supposed to do?). Other times customers see no value in using the technology when compared to the alternative interpersonal mode of delivery; or the SSTs may be so poorly designed that customers may prefer not to use them, as we noted in the Technology Spotlight in Chapter 3.[28]

The red-hot economy in western Canada during 2006 caused severe labour shortages, and nowhere was this more evident than in the retail and service sectors. Fort McMurray grocery stores, for example, couldn't find and keep staff despite paying twice the provincial average for wages. As a result, self-scanning technologies were more rapidly deployed by Canada Safeway, Loblaws, and Wal-Mart. Whereas the usual payback period for these units due to decreased employee costs might often be 12 to 18 months, in Fort McMurray's overheated employment market self-scanning units had payback periods of as little as six months. So even if customers were initially reluctant, self-scanning was far preferable to waiting in long lines caused by staffing shortages.

Success with SSTs

Throughout the text we have highlighted some of the most successful self-service technologies such as eBay and Amazon. These companies have been successful because they offer clear benefits to customers, the benefits are well understood and appreciated compared to the alternative delivery modes, and the technology is user-friendly and reliable. In addition, customers understand their roles and have the capability to use the technology.

From a strategic perspective, research suggests that as firms move into SSTs as a mode of delivery, these questions are important to ask:[29]

- What is our strategy? What do we hope to achieve through the SST (cost savings, revenue growth, competitive advantage)?

- What are the benefits to customers of producing the service on their own through the SST? Do they know and understand these benefits?

- How can customers be motivated to try the SST? Do they understand their role? Do they have the capability to perform this role?

- How "technology-ready" are our customers?[30] Are some segments of customers more ready to use the technology than others?

- How can customers be involved in the design of the service technology system and processes so that they will be more likely to adopt and use the SST?

- What forms of customer education will be needed to encourage adoption? Will other incentives be needed?

- How will inevitable SST failures be handled to regain customer confidence?

STRATEGIES FOR ENHANCING CUSTOMER PARTICIPATION

The level and the nature of customer participation in the service process are strategic decisions that can impact an organization's productivity, its positioning relative to competitors, its service quality, and its customers' satisfaction. In the following sections we will examine the strategies captured in Figure 13.3 for involving customers effectively in the service delivery process. The overall goals of a customer participation strategy will typically be to increase organizational productivity and customer satisfaction while simultaneously decreasing uncertainty due to unpredictable customer actions.

Define Customers' Jobs

In developing strategies for addressing customer involvement in service delivery, the organization first determines what type of participation it wants from customers, thus beginning to define the customer's "job." Identifying the current level of customer

FIGURE 13.3

Strategies for Enhancing Customer Participation

Source: Adapted from M. L. Meuter and M. J. Bitner, "Self-Service Technologies: Extending Service Frameworks and Identifying Issues for Research," in *Marketing Theory and Applications*, ed. D. Grewal and C. Pechmann (American Marketing Association Winter Educators' Conference, 1998), pp. 12–19. Reprinted by permission of the American Marketing Association.

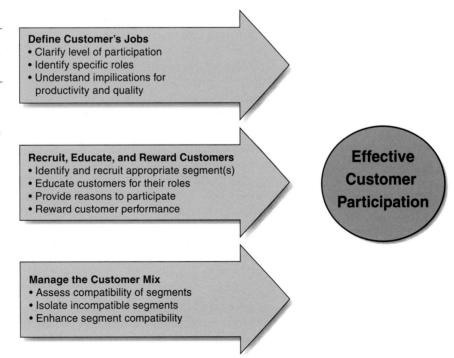

participation can serve as a starting point. Customers' roles may be partially predetermined by the nature of the service, as suggested in Table 13.1. The service may require only the customer's presence (a concert, airline travel), or it may require moderate levels of input from the customer in the form of effort or information (a haircut, tax preparation), or it may require the customer to actually cocreate the service outcome (fitness training, consulting self-service offerings).

The organization may decide that it is satisfied with the existing level of participation it requires from customers but wants to make the participation more effective. For example, Credential Direct has always positioned itself as a company whose customers are highly involved in their personal investment decisions. Over time this position has been implemented in different ways. Advances in technology have allowed Credential Direct to solidify its position as a leading investment company for independent investors in Canada.

Alternatively, the organization may choose to increase the level of customer participation, which may reposition the service in the customers' eyes. Experts have suggested that higher levels of customer participation are strategically advisable when service production and delivery are inseparable; marketing benefits (cross-selling, building loyalty) can be enhanced by on-site contact with the customer; and customers can supplement for the labour and information provided by employees.[31]

In health care, researchers and providers are working on ways to gain more active customer participation in treatment decisions. The Internet and other technology advances have helped propel customers into this role in taking responsibility for their own health and well-being, as illustrated in our Technology Spotlight.

Finally, the organization may decide it wants to reduce customer participation due to all the uncertainties it causes. In such situations the strategy may be to isolate all but the essential tasks, keeping customers away from the service facility and employees as much as possible.[32] Mail order is an extreme example of this form of service. Customers are in contact with the organization via telephone or the Internet, never see the organization's facility, and have limited employee interactions. The customer's role is thus extremely limited and can interfere very little with the service delivery process.

Once the desired level of participation is clear, the organization can define more specifically what the customer's "job" entails.[33] The customer's "job description" will vary with the type of service and the organization's desired position within its industry. The job might entail helping oneself, helping others, or promoting the company.

Helping Oneself

In many cases the organization may decide to increase the level of customer involvement in service delivery through active participation, as shown in Figure 13.4. In such situations the customer becomes a productive resource, performing aspects of the service heretofore performed by employees or others. Many of the examples presented in this chapter are illustrations of customers "helping themselves." The result may be increased productivity for the firm and/or increased value, quality, and satisfaction for the customer.

Helping Others

Sometimes the customer may be called on to help others who are experiencing the service. A child at a day care centre might be appointed "buddy of the day" to help a new child acclimate into the environment. Long-time residents of retirement communities

Technology Spotlight

Technology Facilitates Customer Participation in Health Care

Customer participation is facilitated by technology in many industries. For example, in education, technology allows students to interact with each other and their professors via e-mail and discussion boards. In real estate, technology allows buyers to preview homes and develop lists of places they would like to visit without having to rely totally on a real estate agent to find all available properties. And in high-technology industries, business customers often interact with each other on the Web, helping each other solve problems, answering each other's questions, and so forth. All these examples show how technology—particularly the Internet—has facilitated customer participation and increased customer satisfaction.

Nowhere is this result more apparent than in health care. There is probably no greater, higher-participation service context than health care, where the customer must participate and where the provider and customer clearly cocreate the service. Patient participation is required at multiple levels. To achieve optimal health outcomes, patients must

• Provide accurate information about symptoms and health background.

• Answer detailed questions.

• Help to decide on a course of treatment.

• Carry out the prescribed regimen leading to recovery.

Technology is clearly influencing how customers perform these roles, and is in some sense shifting the power of information into their hands. Thousands of Internet sites provide some type of health-related information. Some sites belong to health care providers such as Shouldice Hospital (www.shouldice.com) and the IWK Health Centre (www.iwk.nshealth.ca). Others, such as WebMD (www.webmd.com), are operated totally online without affiliation to a specific health care provider. Some respected sites are sponsored by government entities such as Health Canada (www.hc-sc.gc.ca). These sites provide information to visitors and have begun to transform patients into active participants who can become better educated about health, well-being, and prevention, and engage in self-diagnosis.

The Canadian and provincial governments are now recognizing the value of more patient involvement in health care, and have increased their funding of such initiatives accordingly. With a health care system often said to be in crisis, and armed with a Healthcare in Canada Survey that indicated 90 percent of Canadians supported "the development of information systems that would make it easier to access and share information,"* the federal government has pledged more than $1.2 billion to various national electronic health projects. Canada Health Infoway (www.infoway-inforoute.ca), the largest national undertaking of this kind, is an independent, not-for-profit organization that, through various projects, is expected to deliver increased coordination of health information nationally.

Source: Reprinted by permission of Canada Health Infoway.

At the provincial level, a number of health organizations are using the Web to provide patients with information about wait times so they can take more control of their health care provision. It is no secret that wait times for various procedures have been increasing, and doctor shortages are often cited as the problem. But provincial governments have realized that wait times vary within provinces, and that the Internet can be a valuable tool in creating more balance. For instance,

continued

Technology Spotlight

Technology Facilitates Customer Participation in Health Care—continued

wait times for angioplasty in Sudbury are usually about 13 days, but a Toronto suburban hospital has wait times of only two days for the same procedure. By creating publicly accessible provincially-based websites with this information, patients now have the opportunity to decide to travel to areas within their home province with shorter wait times. The expectation is that many patients will decide to travel, decreasing wait times generally and removing some of the pressure from the system entirely.

*Quoted from S. Schirdewahn, "Public Speaking: How Canadians View the Role of ICTs in the Health Sector," *Healthcare Information Management and Communications Canada* XVI, no. 3 (October 2002), available www.hc-sc.gc.

ca/hcs-sss/alt_formats/iacb-dgiac/pdf/pubs/2002-publi-opin-speak/2002-publi-opin-speak_e.pdf, accessed October 2, 2006.

Sources: B. Assadi, "Information and Communications Technologies in the Canadian Health Care System: An Analysis of Federally Funded ICT-Related Projects" (Ottawa: Office of Health and the Information Highway, Health Canada, June 2003), available www.hc-sc.gc.ca/hcs-sss/pubs/ehealth-esante/2003-ict-tic-analys-proj/index_e.html, accessed October 2, 2006; S. Schirdewahn, "Public Speaking: How Canadians View the Role of ICTs in the Health Sector," *Healthcare Information Management and Communications Canada* XVI, no. 3 (October 2002), available www.hc-sc.gc. ca/hcs-sss/alt_formats/iacb-dgiac/pdf/pubs/2002-publi-opin-speak/2002-publi-opin-speak_e.pdf, accessed October 2, 2006; and J. Geddes, "Bypassing Your Doctor," *Maclean's,* October 12, 2005.

often assume comparable roles to welcome new residents. Many universities have established mentoring programs, particularly for students from minority groups, in which experienced students with similar backgrounds help newcomers adjust and learn the system. Many membership organizations (like health clubs, churches, and social organizations) also rely heavily, although often informally, on current members

FIGURE 13.4

Customers help produce the service for themselves by scanning their own groceries.

Source: The McGraw-Hill Companies, Inc./Andrew Resek, Photographer.

to help orient new members and make them feel welcome. In engaging in these types of roles, customers are again performing productive functions for the organization, increasing customer satisfaction and retention. Acting as a mentor or facilitator can have very positive effects on the person performing the role and is likely to increase his or her loyalty as well.

Promoting the Company

In some cases the customer's job may include a sales or promotional element. As you know from previous chapters, service customers rely heavily on word-of-mouth endorsements in deciding which providers to try. They are more comfortable getting a recommendation from someone who has actually experienced the service than from advertising alone. A positive recommendation from a friend, relative, colleague, or even an acquaintance can pave the way for a positive service experience. Many service organizations have been very imaginative in getting their current customers to work as promoters or salespeople, as shown in Exhibit 13.2.

At Shouldice Hospital, where customer participation in service delivery is essential (see Figure 13.5, which contains a form prospective patients fill out), word of mouth is key. It has been estimated that fully 49 percent of new patients come by way of referrals from former patients.

FIGURE 13.5 **Shouldice Hospital Self-Examination Questionnaire**

THIS CHART IS FOR EXPLANATION ONLY

Ordinary hernias are mostly either at the navel ("belly-button") - or just above it

or down in the groin area on either side

An "inclsional hernia" is one that bulges through the scar of any other surgical operation that has failed to hold - wherever it may be.

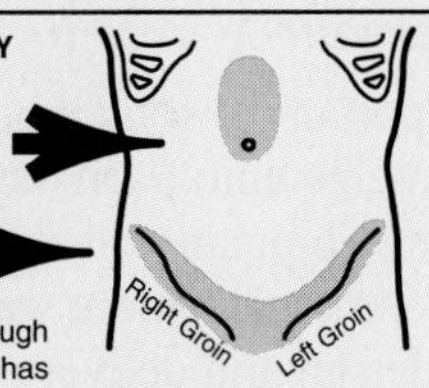

THIS IS YOUR CHART – PLEASE MARK IT!

(MARK THE POSITION OF EACH HERNIA YOU WANT REPAIRED WITH AN "X")

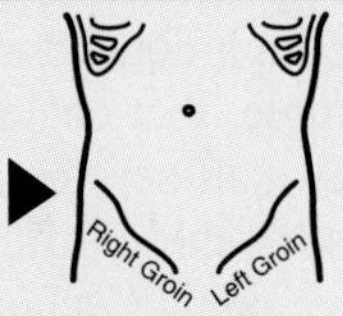

APPROXIMATE SIZE . . .
Walnut (or less) ☐ ☐
Hen's Egg or Lemon ☐ ☐
Grapefruit (or more) ☐ ☐

ESSENTIAL EXTRA INFORMATION

Use only the sections that apply to your hernias and put a ✓ in each box that seems appropriate.

NAVEL AREA (AND JUST ABOVE NAVEL) ONLY Yes No
Is this navel (bellybutton) hernia your FIRST one? ☐ ☐

If it's NOT your first, how many repair attempts so far? ☐

GROIN HERNIAS ONLY RIGHT GROIN LEFT GROIN
Yes No Yes No
Is this your FIRST GROIN HERNIA ON THIS SIDE? ☐ ☐ ☐ ☐

How many hernia operations in this groin already? Right ☐ Left ☐

DATE OF LAST OPERATION ☐

INCISIONAL HERNIAS ONLY (the ones bulging through previous operation scars)
Was the original operation for your Appendix? ☐ . or Gallbladder? ☐ .
or Stomach? ☐ . or Prostate? ☐ . or Hysterectomy? ☐ . or Other? ....
....
How many attempts to repair the hernia have been made so far? ☐

PLEASE BE ACCURATE: Misleading figures, when checked on a admission day, could mean postponement of your operation till your weight is suitable.

HEIGHT ....ft ....ins. WEIGHT ....lbs. Nude or just pyjamas Recent gain? .... lbs. Recent loss? .... lbs.

Waist (muscles relaxed) .... ins. Chest (not expanded) .... ins.

GENERAL HEALTH

Age ....years Is your health now GOOD ☐ . FAIR ☐ . or POOR ☐

Please mention briefly any severe past illness — such as a "heart attack" or a "stroke", for example, from which you have now recovered (and its approximate date) ....
....

We need to know about other present conditions, even though your admission is NOT likely to be refused because of them.

Please tick ☐u any condition for which you are having regular treatment:

Blood Pressure ☐
Excess body fluids ☐
Chest pain ("angina") ☐
Irregular Heartbeat ☐
Diabetes ☐
Asthma & Bronchitis ☐
Ulcers ☐
Anticoagulants (to delay blood-clotting or to "thin the blood") ☐
Other ....

Name of any prescribed pills, tablets or capsules you take regularly: –

Did you remember to MARK AN "X" on your body chart to show us where each of your hernias is located?

Source: Courtesy of Shouldice Hospital Ltd.

Organizations often encourage their customers to help promote their services through word of mouth. Here we share a variety of examples from different industry contexts:

A dental practice encourages referrals by sending flowers, candy, or tickets to a local sports event to its patients whose names appear frequently in their "who referred you?" database.

A bowling alley holds a drawing for its regular patrons. The person whose name is drawn is given a party at the bowling alley to which he or she can invite friends for free bowling. This effectively creates a "word-of-mouth champion" who brings new people into the establishment.

A chiropractor gives a free next exam to people who refer new patients. Patients who make referrals have their names listed on a board in the office waiting area.

To increase membership, a credit union published a member referral coupon in its newsletter. Those who referred new members were then given $5.

A credit card that gives customers frequent flyer points every time they use their credit cards offers 10,000 free miles to those who solicit a new credit card customer.

A nightclub holds regular drawings (using business cards left by its patrons). Those whose names are drawn get a free party (no entry charge) for as many of their friends as they want to invite.

An express contact lens company asks patrons to list friends' names on a card. For each friend who buys, the original patron gets $15 or free contact lenses.

Individual Differences: Not Everyone Wants to Participate

In defining customers' jobs it is important to remember that not everyone will want to participate.[34] Some customer segments enjoy self-service, whereas others prefer to have the service performed for them. Companies that provide education and training services to organizations know that some customers want to be involved. Other companies want to hand over the entire design and delivery to the consulting organization. Despite all the customer service and purchase options now available via the Internet, many customers still prefer human, high-contact service delivery rather than self-service. Research has shown, for example, that customers with a high "need for human interaction" are less likely to try new self-service options offered via the Internet and automated phone systems.[35] Because of these differences in preferences, most companies find they need to provide service delivery choices for different market segments.

Often an organization can customize its services to fit the needs of these different segments—those who want to participate and those who prefer little involvement. Banks typically customize their services by offering both automated self-service options and high-touch, human delivery options. At other times, organizations such as Charles Schwab or IKEA (see the Global Feature) can effectively position themselves to specifically serve segments of customers who want a high level of participation.

Recruit, Educate, and Reward Customers

Once the customer's role is clearly defined, the organization can think in terms of facilitating that role. In a sense, the customer becomes a "partial employee" of the organization at some level, and strategies for managing customer behaviour in service production and delivery can mimic to some degree the efforts aimed at service employees discussed in Chapter 12. As with employees, customer participation in service production and delivery will be facilitated when (1) customers understand their roles and how they are expected to perform, (2) customers are able to perform as expected, and (3) customers receive valued rewards for performing as expected.[36] Through these

EXHIBIT 13.3

Weight Watchers Educates and Orients New Members

When new members first join Weight Watchers, one of the largest and most successful commercial weight loss organizations in the world, they are thoroughly educated regarding the program and their responsibilities. For example, when a new member attends her first meeting at a local chapter of Weight Watchers, she watches a video that tells about the program and reviews how the food plan works. New members are also given a booklet called "Welcome to Weight Watchers" that covers various introductory topics.

In addition to the video, the booklet, and a discussion of all topics led by the group leader, the new member also receives a "Program Planner and Tracker." This form is used by the member to record daily food selections and physical activity. Weight Watchers knows that its business can succeed only if members do their part in following the weight loss plan. Through the orientation, the booklets, and the food and activity forms, the organization clearly defines the member's responsibilities and makes the plan as easy as possible to follow.

means, the organization will also reduce the inherent uncertainty associated with the unpredictable quality and timing of customer participation.

Recruit the Right Customers

Before the company begins the process of educating and socializing customers for their roles, it must attract the right customers to fill those roles. The expected roles and responsibilities of customers should be clearly communicated in advertising, personal selling, and other company messages. By previewing their roles and what is required of them in the service process, customers can self-select into (or out of) the relationship. Self-selection should result in enhanced perceptions of service quality from the customer's point of view and reduced uncertainty for the organization.

To illustrate, a child care centre that requires parent participation on the site at least one-half day per week needs to communicate that expectation before it enrols any child in its program. For some families, this level of participation will not be possible or desirable, thus precluding them from enrolling in the centre. The expected level of participation needs to be communicated clearly in order to attract customers who are ready and willing to perform their roles. In a sense this situation is similar to a manufacturing firm exercising control over the quality of inputs into the production process.[37]

Educate and Train Customers to Perform Effectively

Customers need to be educated, or in essence "socialized," so that they can perform their roles effectively. Through the socialization process, service customers gain an appreciation of specific organizational values, develop the abilities necessary to function within a specific context, understand what is expected of them, and acquire the skills and knowledge to interact with employees and other customers.[38] Customer education programs can take the form of formal orientation programs, written literature provided to customers, directional cues and signage in the service environment, and information obtained from employees and other customers.

Many services offer "customer orientation" programs to assist customers in understanding their roles and what to expect from the process before experiencing it. When customers begin the Weight Watchers program, their first group meeting includes a thorough orientation to the program and their responsibilities, as described in Exhibit 13.3. In a mammography screening context, research has found that orientation and formal education of customers can relieve customer fears and perceptions of risk and ultimately increase customer satisfaction (see Exhibit 13.4).

Realistic Service Previews Reduce Customer Anxiety and Improve Satisfaction

Research in a mammography screening context found that if potential patients are oriented through a realistic preview of the process, patient anxiety is reduced and ultimate satisfaction is increased. Researchers conducted a study that involved 134 women who had never experienced a mammogram and who had little knowledge about the procedure. Half the women were given a realistic preview of the process, and the others received no preview. The preview consisted of written information about mammography, including sections on how the procedure works, instructions to follow before mammography, what happens during mammography, after the examination, the role of mammography, and some common misconceptions. The realistic preview also included a seven-minute videotape illustrating the entire procedure. The written materials and the videotape helped to both dispel overly pessimistic expectations and guard against overly positive ideas the potential patients may have had.

After the preview (or no preview), women in the experiment answered questions that assessed the accuracy of their expectations, their sense of control, and their level of anxiety relative to mammography. The women then read one of three versions of an actual mammography experience and were asked to imagine themselves as the woman in the story. One version of the story followed the realistic preview exactly; another version included several blunders on the part of the fictitious provider; and the final version enhanced the service experience, making it even better than the realistic preview. After reading the story and imagining that the events had actually happened to them, the women responded to questions regarding their satisfaction with the mammography screening process.

Results of the study showed that those women who had been oriented through the realistic preview did indeed have more realistic and accurate expectations for the mammography experience than did those who had no preview. Second, the women who saw the preview reported significantly less anxiety and significantly greater perceptions of control over the process than did women who had no preview. Finally, across all the different scenarios, women who received the preview were more satisfied with the actual service experience. The realistic preview thus affected potential mammography patients' preservice feelings (anxiety and control) as well as their satisfaction with the service.

Source: W. T. Faranda, "Customer Participation in Service Production: An Empirical Assessment of the Influence of Realistic Service Previews," doctoral dissertation, Arizona State University, Tempe, Arizona, 1994.

Customer education can also be partially accomplished through written literature and customer handbooks. Many hospitals have developed patient handbooks, very similar in appearance to employee handbooks, to describe what the patient should do in preparation for arrival at the hospital, what will happen when he or she arrives, and policies regarding visiting hours and billing procedures. The handbook may even describe the roles and responsibilities of family members.

Although formal training and written information are usually provided in advance of the service experience, other strategies can continue customer socialization during the experience itself. On site, customers require two kinds of orientation: *place orientation* (Where am I? How do I get from here to there?) and *function orientation* (How does this organization work? What am I supposed to do?).[39] Signage, the layout of the service facility, and other orientation aids can help customers answer these questions, allowing them to perform their roles more effectively. Orientation aids can also take the form of rules that define customer behaviour for safety (airlines, health clubs), appropriate dress (restaurants, entertainment venues), and noise levels (hotels, classrooms, theatres).

Customers may also be socialized to their expected roles through information provided by employees and by observing other customers. It has been said that when McDonald's first went to England, the British customers were not accustomed to busing their own trays. They quickly learned, however, by observing the customers that McDonald's had hired to "demonstrate" appropriate busing behaviour. These customers were paid to sit in the restaurants and at predictable intervals carry a dirty tray over to the trash can and dispose of it.

Reward Customers for Their Contributions

Customers are more likely to perform their roles effectively, or to participate actively, if they are rewarded for doing so. Rewards are likely to come in the form of increased control over the delivery process, time savings, monetary savings, and psychological or physical benefits. ATM customers who perform banking services for themselves are also rewarded through greater access to the bank, in terms of both locations and times. In some situations, ATM customers are also rewarded because they avoid fees that are assessed for interpersonal transactions with tellers. In health care contexts, patients who perform their roles effectively are likely to be rewarded with better health or quicker recovery. For a long time airlines have offered price discounts for passengers who ordered tickets online, providing a monetary incentive for customer participation.

Customers may not realize the benefits or rewards of effective participation unless the organization makes the benefits apparent to them. In other words, the organization needs to clarify the performance-contingent benefits that can accrue to customers just as it defines these types of benefits to employees. The organization also should recognize that not all customers are motivated by the same types of rewards. Some may value the increased access and time savings they can gain by performing their service roles effectively. Others may value the monetary savings. Still others may be looking for greater personal control over the service outcome.

Avoid Negative Outcomes of Inappropriate Customer Participation

If customers are not effectively socialized, the organization runs the risk that inappropriate customer behaviours will result in negative outcomes for customers, employees, and the organization itself:[40]

1. Customers who do not understand the service system or the process of delivery may slow down the service process and negatively affect their own as well as other customers' outcomes. In a rental car context, customers who do not understand the reservation process can slow the flow for employees and other customers.

2. If customers do not perform their roles effectively, it may not be possible for employees to provide the levels of technical and process quality promised by the organization. For example, in a management consulting practice, clients who do not provide the information and cooperation needed by the consultants will likely receive inferior service.

3. If customers are frustrated because of their own inadequacies and incompetencies, employees are likely to suffer emotionally and be less able to deliver quality service. For example, if customers routinely enter the service delivery process with little knowledge of how the system works and their role in it, they are likely to take out their frustrations on frontline employees. This negative impact on individual employees can take its toll on the organization in the form of turnover and decreased motivation to serve.

Besides customers who simply misunderstand their roles or perform them ineffectively, there are also customers who are intentionally disruptive. Lovelock and Wirtz have grouped these into six broad categories: the thief; the rulebreaker; the belligerent; the family feuders; the vandal; and the deadbeat.[41] You've no doubt seen some of these

FIGURE 13.6

Swedish supermodel Mazena Kamizela arrives at a Newfoundland courtroom after an air-rage incident in which she assaulted crew members.

Source: CP/Amy Patey.

types yourself and can appreciate the kinds of problems they pose for service providers and fellow service customers alike. As we discussed in Chapter 7, not all customers are good customers. David Maister notes that the key to success is getting *better* business, not just *more* business.[42] For that reason, when the preceding strategies don't work, firms should fire customers who intentionally misbehave (see Figure 13.6).

Manage the Customer Mix

Because customers frequently interact with each other in the process of service delivery and consumption, another important strategic objective is the effective management of the mix of customers who simultaneously experience the service. If a restaurant chooses to serve two segments during the dinner hour that are incompatible with each other—for example, single college students who want to party and families with small children who want quiet—it may find that the two groups do not merge well. Of course it is possible to manage these segments so that they do not interact with each other by seating them in separate sections or by attracting the two segments at different times of day.

The process of managing multiple and sometimes conflicting segments is known as *compatibility management*, broadly defined as "a process of first attracting homogeneous consumers to the service environment, then actively managing both the physical environment and customer-to-customer encounters in such a way as to enhance satisfying encounters and minimize dissatisfying encounters."[43] Compatibility management will be critically important for some businesses (such as health clubs, public transportation, and hospitals) and less important for others. Table 13.2 lists seven interrelated characteristics of service businesses that will increase the importance of compatibility management.

To manage multiple (and sometimes conflicting) segments, organizations rely on a variety of strategies. Attracting maximally homogeneous groups of customers through careful positioning and segmentation strategies is one approach. This strategy is used by the Ritz-Carlton Hotel, for which upscale travellers are the primary target segment. However, even in that context there can be potential conflicts—for example, when the hotel is simultaneously hosting a large business convention and serving individual leisure travellers. A second strategy is often used in such cases. Compatible customers are grouped together physically so that the segments are less likely to interact directly with each other. The Ritz-Carlton keeps meetings and large group events separated from the areas of the hotel used by individual businesspeople.

Other strategies for enhancing customer compatibility include customer "codes of conduct" such as the regulation of smoking behaviour and dress codes. Clearly such codes of conduct may vary from one service establishment to another. Finally, training employees to observe customer-to-customer interactions and to be sensitive to potential conflicts is another strategy for increasing compatibility among segments. Employees can also be trained to recognize opportunities to foster positive encounters among customers in certain types of service environments.

TABLE 13.2 Characteristics of Service That Increase the Importance of Compatible Segments

Characteristic	Explanation	Examples
Customers are in close physical proximity to each other.	Customers will more often notice each other and be influenced by each other's behaviour when they are in close physical proximity.	Airplane flights Entertainment events Sports events
Verbal interaction takes place among customers.	Conversation (or lack thereof) can be a component of both satisfying and dissatisfying encounters with fellow patrons.	Full-service restaurants Cocktail lounges Educational settings
Customers are engaged in numerous and varied activities.	When a service facility supports varied activities all going on at the same time, the activities themselves may not be compatible.	Libraries Health clubs Resort hotels
The service environment attracts a heterogeneous customer mix.	Many service environments, particularly those open to the public, will attract a variety of customer segments.	Public parks Public transportation Open-enrolment colleges
The core service is compatibility.	The core service is to arrange and nurture compatible relationships between customers.	Big Brothers/Big Sisters Weight loss group programs Mental health support groups
Customers must occasionally wait for the service.	Waiting in line for service can be monotonous or anxiety-producing. The boredom or stress can be magnified or lessened by other customers, depending on their compatibility.	Medical clinics Tourist attractions Restaurants
Customers are expected to share time, space, or service utensils with each other.	The need to share space, time, and other service factors is common in many services but may become a problem if segments are not comfortable with sharing with each other or if the need to share is intensified because of capacity constraints.	Golf courses Hospitals Retirement communities Airplanes

Source: Adapted from C. I. Martin and C. A. Pranter, "Compatibility Management: Customer-to-Customer Relationships in Service Environments," *Journal of Services Marketing* 3, no. 3 (Summer 1989), pp. 5–15. Reprinted with the permission of MCB University Press.

SUMMARY

This chapter focused on the role of customers in service creation and delivery. The customer receiving the service and the fellow customers in the service environment can all potentially cause a widening of Provider Gap 3 if they fail to perform their roles effectively. A number of reasons why customers may widen the service delivery gap were suggested: customers lack understanding of their roles; customers are unwilling or unable to perform their roles; customers are not rewarded for good performance; other customers interfere; or market segments are incompatible.

Managing customers in the process of service delivery is a critical challenge for service firms. Whereas manufacturers are not concerned with customer participation in the manufacturing process, service managers constantly face this issue because their customers are often present and active partners in service production. As participants in service creation, production, and delivery, customers can perform three primary roles, discussed and illustrated in the chapter: *productive resources* for the organization, *contributors* to service quality and satisfaction, and *competitors* in performing the service for themselves.

Through understanding the importance of customers in service delivery and identifying the roles played by the customer in a particular context, managers can develop strategies to enhance customer participation. Strategies discussed in the text include defining the customers' roles and jobs, recruiting customers who match the customer profile in terms of desired level of participation, educating customers so they can perform their roles effectively, rewarding customers for their contributions, and managing the customer mix to enhance the experiences of all segments. By implementing these strategies, organizations should see a reduction in Gap 3 due to effective, efficient customer contributions to service delivery

Discussion Questions

1. Using your own personal examples, discuss the general importance of customers in the successful creation and delivery of service experiences.

2. Why might customer actions and attitudes cause Provider Gap 3 to occur? Use your own examples to illustrate your understanding.

3. Using Table 13.1, think of specific services you have experienced that fall within each of the three levels of customer participation: low, medium, high. Describe specifically what you did as a customer in each case. How did your involvement vary across the three types of service situations?

4. Describe a time when your satisfaction in a particular situation was *increased* because of something another customer did. Could (or does) the organization do anything to ensure that this experience happens routinely? What does it do? Should it try to make this situation a routine occurrence?

5. Describe a time when your satisfaction in a particular situation was *decreased* because of something another customer did. Could the organization have done anything to manage this situation more effectively? What?

6. Discuss the customer's role as a *productive resource* for the firm. Describe a time when you played this role. What did you do and how did you feel? Did the firm help you perform your role effectively? How?

7. Discuss the customer's role as a *contributor to service quality and satisfaction.* Describe a time when you played this role. What did you do and how did you feel? Did the firm help you perform your role effectively? How?

8. Discuss the customer's role as a potential *competitor*. Describe a time when you chose to provide a service for yourself rather than pay someone to provide the service for you. Why did you decide to perform the service yourself? What could have changed your mind, causing you to contract with someone else to provide the service?

Exercises

1. Visit a service establishment where customers can influence each other (such as a theme park, entertainment establishment, resort, shopping mall, restaurant, airline, school, or hospital). Observe (or interview) customers and record cases of positive and negative customer influence. Discuss how you would manage the situation to increase overall customer satisfaction.
2. Interview someone regarding his or her decision to outsource a service—for example, legal services, payroll, or maintenance in a company; or cleaning, child care, or pet care in a household. Use the criteria for internal versus external exchange described in the text to analyze the decision to outsource.
3. Think of a service in which a high level of customer participation is necessary for the service to be successful (health club, weight loss, educational setting, health care, golf lessons, or the like). Interview a service provider in such an organization to find out what strategies the provider uses to encourage effective customer participation.
4. Visit a service setting in which multiple types of customer segments use the service at the same time (such as a theatre, golf course, resort, or theme park). Observe (or interview the manager about) the organization's strategies to manage these segments effectively. Would you do anything differently if you were in charge?
5. Visit iPrint's website (www.iprint.com). Compare its printing service process to that of similar onsite services offered by Kinko's. Compare and contrast the customer's role in each situation.

Notes

1. Curves International site, www.curves.com.
2. See B. Schneider and D. E. Bowen, *Winning the Service Game* (Boston: Harvard Business School Press, 1995), ch. 4; L. A. Bettencourt, "Customer Voluntary Performance: Customers as Partners in Service Delivery, *Journal of Retailing* 73, no. 3 (1997), pp. 383–406; P. K. Mills and J. H. Morris, "Clients as 'Partial' Employees: Role Development in Client Participation," *Academy of Management Review* 11, no. 4 (1986), pp. 726–35; C. H. Lovelock and R. F. Young, "Look to Customers to Increase Productivity," *Harvard Business Review*, Summer 1979, pp. 9–20; A. R. Rodie and S. S. Kleine, "Customer Participation in Services Production and Delivery," in *Handbook of Services Marketing and Management*, ed. T. A. Swartz and D. Iacobucci (Thousand Oaks, CA: Sage Publications, 2000), pp. 111–26; C. K. Prahalad and V. Ramaswamy, "Co-opting Customer Competence," *Harvard Business Review*, January/February 2000, p. 7; N. Bendapudi and R. P.

Leone, "Psychological Implications of Customer Participation in Co-production," *Journal of Marketing* 67 (January 2003), pp. 14–28.

3. S. J. Grove, R. P. Fisk, and M. J. Bitner, "Dramatizing the Service Experience: A Managerial Approach," in *Advances in Services Marketing and Management*, ed. T. A. Swartz, D. E. Bowen, and S. W. Brown, vol. 1 (Greenwich, CT: JAI Press, 1992), pp. 91–122.

4. For an interesting view of work and business as theater, see B. Joseph Pine II and J. H. Gilmore, *The Experience Economy: Work Is Theatre and Every Business a Stage* (Boston: Harvard Business School Press, 1999).

5. L. A. Bettencourt, S. W. Brown, A. L. Ostrom, and R. I. Roundtree, "Client Co-production in Knowledge-Intensive Business Services," *California Management Review* 44 (Summer 2002), pp. 100–28.

6. See S. J. Grove and R. P. Fisk, "The Impact of Other Customers on Service Experiences: A Critical Incident Examination of 'Getting Along,'" *Journal of Retailing* 73, no. 1 (1997), pp. 63–85; C. I. Martin and C. A. Pranter, "Compatibility Management: Customer-to-Customer Relationships in Service Environments," *Journal of Services Marketing* 3 (Summer 1989), pp. 5–15.

7. Grove and Fisk, "The Impact of Other Customers on Service Experiences."

8. Ibid.

9. K. Harris and S. Baron, "Consumer-to-Consumer Conversations in Service Settings," *Journal of Service Research* 6 (February 2004), pp. 287–303.

10. See P. K. Mills, R. B. Chase, and N. Margulies, "Motivating the Client/Employee System as a Service Production Strategy," *Academy of Management Review* 8, no. 2 (1983), pp. 301–10; D. E. Bowen, "Managing Customers as Human Resources in Service Organizations," *Human Resource Management* 25, no. 3 (1986), pp. 371–83; and Mills and Morris, "Clients as 'Partial' Employees."

11. Bettencourt et al., "Client Co-production in Knowledge-Intensive Business Services."

12. R. B. Chase, "Where Does the Customer Fit in a Service Operation?" *Harvard Business Review*, November/December 1978, pp. 137–42.

13. Mills, Chase, and Margulies, "Motivating the Client/Employee System."

14. Marilyn Adams, "Tech Takes Bigger Role in Air Services," *USA Today*, July 18, 2001, p. 1.

15. See D. W. Johnson, R. T. Johnson, and K. A. Smith, *Active Learning: Cooperation in the College Classroom* (Edina, MN: Interaction Book Company, 1991).

16. S. Dellande, M. C. Gilly, and J. L. Graham, "Gaining Compliance and Losing Weight: The Role of the Service Provider in Health Care Services," *Journal of Marketing* 68 (July 2004), pp. 78–91.

17. S. W. Kelley, S. J. Skinner, and J. H. Donnelly Jr., "Organizational Socialization of Service Customers," *Journal of Business Research* 25 (1992), pp. 197–214.

18. C. Claycomb, C. A. Lengnick-Hall, and L. W. Inks, "The Customer as a Productive Resource: A Pilot Study and Strategic Implications," *Journal of Business Strategies* 18 (Spring 2001), pp. 47–69.

19. R. Normann and R. Ramirez, "From Value Chain to Value Constellation: Designing Interactive Strategy," *Harvard Business Review*, July/August 1993, pp. 65–77; www.ikea.com, 2002.

20. J. E. G. Bateson, "The Self-Service Customer—Empirical Findings," in *Emerging Perspectives in Services Marketing*, ed. L. L. Berry, G. L. Shostack, and G. D. Upah (Chicago: American Marketing Association, 1983), pp. 50–53.

21. V. S. Folkes, "Recent Attribution Research in Consumer Behavior: A Review and New Directions," *Journal of Consumer Research* 14 (March 1988), pp. 548–65; and M. J. Bitner, "Evaluating Service Encounters: The Effects of Physical Surroundings and Employee Responses," *Journal of Marketing* 54 (April 1990), pp.-69–82.

22. Bendapudi and Leone, "Psychological Implications of Customer Participation in Co-production."

23. R. F. Lusch, S. W. Brown, and G. J. Brunswick, "A General Framework for Explaining Internal vs. External Exchange," *Journal of the Academy of Marketing Science* 10 (Spring 1992), pp. 119–34.

24. Ibid.

25. See M. J. Bitner, A. L. Ostrom, and M. L. Meuter, "Implementing Successful Self-Service Technologies," *Academy of Management Executive* 16 (November 2002), pp. 96–109.

26. See P. Dabholkar, "Consumer Evaluations of New Technology-Based Self-Service Options: An Investigation of Alternative Models of Service Quality," *International Journal of Research in Marketing* 13 (1), pp. 29–51; F. Davis, "User Acceptance of Information Technology: System Characteristics, User Perceptions and Behavioral Impact," *International Journal of Man–Machine Studies* 38 (1993), pp. 475–87; L. M. Bobbitt and P. A. Dabholkar, "Integrating Attitudinal Theories to Understand and Predict Use of Technology-Based Self-Service," *International Journal of Service Industry Management* 12, no. 5 (2001), pp. 423–50; J. M. Curran, M. L. Meuter, and C. F. Surprenant, "Intentions to Use Self-Service Technologies: A Confluence of Multiple Attitudes," *Journal of Service Research* 5, no. 3 (2003), pp. 209–24.

27. M. L. Meuter, M. J. Bitner, A. L. Ostrom, and S. W. Brown, "Choosing Among Alternative Service Delivery Modes: An Investigation of Customer Trial of Self-Service Technologies," *Journal of Marketing* 69, no. 2 (April 2005), pp. 61–83.

28. M. L. Meuter, A. L. Ostrom, R. I. Roundtree, and M. J. Bitner, "Self-Service Technologies: Understanding Customer Satisfaction with Technology-Based Service Encounters," *Journal of Marketing* 64 (July 2000), pp. 50–64.

29. Meuter et al., "Choosing Among Alternative Service Delivery Modes"; see also Y. Moon and F. X. Frei, "Exploding the Self-Service Myth," *Harvard Business Review*, May/June 2000; M. J. Bitner, A. L. Ostrom, and M. L. Meuter, "Implementing Successful Self-Service Technologies."

30. A. Parasuraman and C. L. Colby, *Techno-Ready Marketing: How and Why Your Customers Adopt Technology* (New York: The Free Press, 2001).

31. Bowen, "Managing Customers as Human Resources."

32. Chase, "Where Does the Customer Fit in a Service Operation?"

33. See Schneider and Bowen, *Winning the Service Game,* ch. 4. The four job descriptions in this section are adapted from M. R. Bowers, C. L. Martin, and A. Luker, "Trading Places, Employees as Customers, Customers as Employees," *Journal of Services Marketing* 4 (Spring 1990), pp. 56–69.

34. Bateson, "The Self-Service Customer."

35. Meuter et al., "Choosing Among Alternative Service Delivery Modes."

36. Bowen, "Managing Customers as Human Resources"; and Schneider and Bowen, *Winning the Service Game*, ch. 4; Meuter et al., "Choosing Among Alternative Service Delivery Modes"; Dellande et al., "Gaining Compliance and Losing Weight."

37. C. Goodwin and R. Radford, "Models of Service Delivery: An Integrative Perspective," in *Advances in Services Marketing and Management*, ed. T. A. Swartz, D. E. Bowen, and S. W. Brown, pp. 231–52.

38. S. W. Kelley, J. H. Donnelly Jr., and S. J. Skinner, "Customer Participation in Service Production and Delivery," *Journal of Retailing* 66 (Fall 1990), pp. 315–35; and Schneider and Bowen, *Winning the Service Game*, ch. 4.

39. Bowen, "Managing Customers as Human Resources."

40. Ibid.; see also L. C. Harris and K. L. Reynolds, "The Consequences of Dysfunctional Customer Behavior," *Journal of Service Research* 6 (November 2003), pp. 144–61.

41. Christopher Lovelock and Joachim Wirtz, *Services Marketing: People, Technology, Strategy*, 5th ed. (Upper Saddle River, NJ: Pearson Prentice Hall, 2004).

42. David H. Maister, *True Professionalism* (New York: The Free Press, 1997).

43. Martin and Pranter, "Compatibility Management."

Chapter

14

Delivering Service Through Intermediaries and Electronic Channels

Closing Provider Gap 3

THIS CHAPTER'S OBJECTIVES ARE TO

    1. Identify the primary channels through which services are delivered to end customers.

    2. Provide examples of each of the key service intermediaries.

    3. View delivery of service from two perspectives—the service provider and the service deliverer.

    4. Discuss the benefits and challenges of each method of service delivery.

    5. Outline the strategies that are used to manage service delivery through intermediaries.

DISTANCE LEARNING: DELIVERING EDUCATION ELECTRONICALLY

Distance learning is education that is accessible at a time, place, location, and pace that is convenient to the user. It can come in many forms: over phone lines, on CD-ROM, over the Internet, or through a video camera. It can be an instructor in Halifax videoconferencing with managers in Ottawa, Winnipeg, and Vancouver on the fundamentals of risk analysis. It can be an engineer taking a motor repair certification course online at home. It can be a lineman on a laptop during his lunch break brushing up on the latest pole maintenance techniques via CD-ROM. It can be a customer learning about the features of a product online before making a purchase. Distance learning breaks down the boundaries of the classroom and makes education more accessible than ever.[1]

The concept of distance learning, although not new, has evolved in technology and scope. At its best, distance learning involves a rich interactive environment with multimedia including slides, video, text, email, chat rooms, and two-way communication. The most effective environments also involve some ability to interact with the professor. In fact, an expert in distance learning found that successful programs had in common one factor: a minimum of 30 percent airtime dedicated to student interaction in which the learner is actively asking questions, talking with experts in the field, working in small groups, or putting answers into the keypad.[2]

Perhaps the widest application of distance learning is on-the-job training, but its role in universities and colleges is escalating. Although there is no concrete data about distance education enrolment in Canada, it has been estimated that approximately one in every nine university students participates in some form of distributed learning.[3] Currently outpacing growth in on-campus enrolment, distance education enrolment is expected to continue to rise, as a recent poll conducted by Ipsos Reid indicates.[4]

With the increased interest in distance education, a variety of credible resources are available to potential students interested in learning more about the institutions offering such services and the types of programs and courses available. Distance Ed Canada (www.distanceedcanada.ca), for instance, has a searchable database of programs from more than 30 different schools. Industry Canada's Campus Connection (www.campusconnection.net) is a portal providing information on more than 2,700 online courses offered by 75 participating Canadian colleges and universities.

Most notable among Canadian institutions offering distance education is Athabasca University (www.athabascau.ca). Athabasca, created by the Government of Alberta in 1970, is Canada's leading distance and online university serving approximately 35,000 students every year.[5] The university's service delivery model is intended to reduce the barriers of time, space, past educational experience, and level of income, making a university education more accessible. "Athabasca University's programs are predominantly available through individualized study where the student decides the pace and study schedule. All materials and a collect-call link with a tutor are included in the fees. Seminar and teleconference delivery modes are also provided. A growing number of programs and courses are offered online or with online enhancements, including Athabasca University's online Executive MBA program, which is offered through a highly collaborative online learning platform."[6]

Source: Courtesy of Athabasca University.

Whether distance education is as effective as more traditional educational experiences is difficult to say. Some limited research indicates that it is, but there are critics as well. Until more research is conducted, it does appear that the distance education revolution will continue, but many prognosticators expect it to completely alter the way learning is achieved. According to one expert:

> Education will change from a place-centered enterprise to "education where you need it." A decade from now, it wouldn't surprise me if the majority of education took place in people's homes, in people's offices, on the production line, wherever it is needed.[7]

Although experts tend to agree that great value exists in an on-campus educational experience, the truth is that for much of the world's population on-campus education is not a realistic alternative.

Except for situations such as distance learning, where electronic channels can distribute services, providers and consumers come into direct contact in service provision. Because of the inseparability of production and consumption in service, providers must be present when customers receive service or find ways to involve others in distribution. Involving others can be problematic. Unless the distributor is able to perform the service as well as the service principal would, the value of the offering decreases and the reputation of the original service may be damaged. Chapter 12 pointed out the challenges of controlling encounters within service organizations themselves, but most service (and many manufacturing) companies face an even more formidable task: attaining service excellence and consistency when intermediaries represent them to customers.

Two distinct services marketers are involved in delivering service through intermediaries: the *service principal*, or originator, and the *service deliverer*, or intermediary. In this chapter, we examine the issues surrounding distribution of services from both perspectives and provide tools and frameworks to help ensure a close alignment between the service principals and their intermediaries so that Provider Gap 3 (the service performance gap) does not occur.

SERVICE DISTRIBUTION

Direct Delivery of Service

As we have indicated throughout this textbook, services are generally intangible and experiential in nature. Thus, service distribution does not typically involve moving items through a chain of firms that begins with a manufacturer and ends with a consumer, as is the case for goods distribution. That is, in contrast to channels for goods, channels for services are often *direct*—with the creator of the service (i.e., the service principal) selling directly to and interacting directly with the customer. Examples include air travel (CanJet), health care (Princess Margaret Hospital), and consulting services (IBM Global Services). In general, because services cannot be produced, warehoused, and then retailed, as goods can, many channels available to goods producers are not feasible for service firms. Thus, many of the primary functions that distribution channels serve—inventorying, securing, and taking title to goods—have no meaning in services, allowing the service principal to deliver the service directly to the customer.

Delivery of Service Through Intermediaries

Even though many of the functions that intermediaries provide for goods manufacturers are not relevant for service firms, intermediaries often deliver services and perform several important functions for service principals. First, they may coproduce the service, fulfilling service principals' promises to customers. Franchise services such as haircutting, key making, and dry cleaning are produced by the intermediary (the franchisee) using a process developed by the service principal. Service intermediaries also make services locally available, providing time and place convenience for the customer. Because they represent multiple service principals, such intermediaries as travel and insurance agents provide a retailing function for customers, gathering together in one place a variety of choices. And in many financial or professional services, intermediaries function as the glue between the brand or company name and the customer by building the trusting relationship required in these complex and expert offerings.

The primary types of intermediaries used in service delivery are franchisees, agents, brokers, and electronic channels. *Franchisees* are service outlets licensed by a principal to deliver a unique service concept it has created or popularized. Examples include fast-food chains (McDonald's, Pizza Delight), video stores (Blockbuster), automobile repair services (Canadian Tire Auto Centre, Midas), and hotels (Holiday Inn, Best Western). *Agents and brokers* are representatives who distribute and sell the services of one or more service suppliers. Examples include insurance (Meloche-Monnex), financial services (Investors Group), and travel services (Carson Wagonlit). *Electronic channels* include all forms of service provision through television, telephone, interactive multimedia, and computers. Many financial and information services are currently distributed through electronic media: banking, bill paying, education.

Goods retailers, by the way, are service organizations themselves; they are intermediaries for goods and perhaps services. Manufacturing companies depend on retailers to represent, explain, promote, and ensure their products—all of which are presale services. Manufacturers also need retailers to return, exchange, support, and service products—all of which are postsale services. These roles are increasingly critical as products become more complex, technical, and expensive. For example, camera and computer firms rely on retailers carrying their products to understand and communicate highly technical information so that customers choose products that fit their needs. A retailer that leads the customer to the wrong product choice or that inadequately instructs the customer on how to use the product creates service problems that strongly influence the manufacturer's reputation.

Service principals depend on their intermediaries to deliver service to their specifications. Service intermediaries determine how the customer evaluates the quality of the company. When a Pizza Delight franchisee does not cook a pizza long enough, the customer's perception of the company—and of other Pizza Delight franchisees—is tarnished. When someone other than the service principal is critical to the fulfillment of quality service, a firm must develop ways to either control or motivate these intermediaries to meet company goals and standards. In the sections that follow, we discuss both direct delivery of service by the service principal and indirect delivery of the service through intermediaries.

DIRECT OR COMPANY-OWNED CHANNELS

Although we call this chapter "Delivering Service Through Intermediaries and Electronic Channels," it is important to acknowledge that many services are distributed directly from provider to customer. Some of these are local services—doctors, dry cleaners, and hairstylists—whose area of distribution is limited. Others are national chains with multiple outlets but are considered direct channels because the provider owns all the outlets. Starbucks, the popular chain of coffee shops, is an example of a service provider that doesn't franchise within its home country. Exhibit 14.1, which describes some of the reasons for the success of the chain, illustrates the general benefits of company-owned outlets: control, consistency, and maintenance of image.

Perhaps the major benefit of distributing through company-owned channels is that the company has complete *control* over the outlets. One of the most critical implications of this type of control is that the owner can maintain consistency in service provision. Standards can be established and will be carried out as planned because the company itself monitors and rewards proper execution of the service. Control over hiring, firing, and motivating employees is also a benefit of company-owned channels. As demonstrated in Exhibit 14.1, one of the keys to Starbucks' success is hiring the right baristas, or coffee makers, something the company is far more likely to do than a franchisee.

Not having enough control over the operating practices of its franchisees is one of the reasons Domino's Pizza experienced difficulty when it tried to reduce the number of automobile accidents involving its delivery drivers. Domino's famous "30 minutes or your pizza is free" service guarantee helped drive tremendous revenue growth for the chain, but the need for speed is believed to have caused overenthusiastic franchisees to create an unsafe working environment—especially as related to deliveries. Domino's ability to alter its driver hiring and training processes was hampered by the fact that many of its stores were franchised.

A final benefit of company-owned channels is that the company owns the customer relationship. In service industries in which workers have individual relationships with customers, a major concern is whether the loyalty the customer feels is for the company or for the employee. It is well known, for example, that most people are loyal to individual hairstylists and will follow them from one place of business to another. Therefore, one of the important issues in service delivery is who owns the customer relationship—the store or the employee. With company-owned channels, the company owns the store and therefore has more control over the customer relationship.

However, several disadvantages exist with company-owned channels. First, the company must bear all the financial risk. When expanding, the firm must find all the capital, sometimes using it for store proliferation rather than for other uses (such as advertising, service quality, or new service development) that would be more profitable. Second, large companies are rarely experts in local markets—they know their businesses but not all markets. This disadvantage is especially evident when companies expand into other cultures. Partnering or joint-venturing is almost always preferred to company-owned channels in these situations. Starbucks International's expansion has occurred with "strategic partners" in each new country—including Canada—not franchises. To date, more than 600 stores have been opened in Canada, the majority (266) in British Columbia (see the Global Feature later in this chapter).[8]

Starbucks Shows Success of Company-Owned Service Channels

One of the biggest marketing success stories of the last decade is Starbucks Coffee Company, although it has been in business for more than 35 years. Twenty-five years ago, its owner began to think of coffee not as something to retail in a store but instead as something to experience in a coffeehouse. At that point, he created the Starbucks that we know today, the Starbucks that perfectly replicates the same café latte in stores around the globe. Consistency of service and product are two of the most important reasons that Starbucks has grown to more than 7,000 U.S. and 550 Canadian locations and expanded internationally, and annually reports profit growth of more than 50 percent a year. (Even a world-class service provider such as Starbucks can have a "bad day," as we saw in Chapter 8!) Starbucks owns more than 4,000 of the stores and maintains control over all that takes place in those stores. Here are some of the efforts it undertakes to ensure that the Starbucks experience is always the same, always positive.

EMPLOYEE TRAINING: LEARNING TO BE A BARISTA

All employees are called partners, and those who prepare coffee are called "baristas," the Italian name for one who prepares and serves coffee. As many as 400 to 500 employees per month nationally are carefully trained to "call" ("triple-tall nonfat mocha"), make drinks, clean espresso machines, and deliver quality customer service. Baristas are taught "coffee knowledge," so that among other things they know how everything tastes, and "customer service," so that they can explain the Italian drink names to customers.

ENSURING PRODUCT QUALITY

"Retail skills" are another portion of the training. Employees are taught such specifics as how to wipe oil from the coffee bin, open a giant bag of beans, and clean the milk wand on the espresso machine, all of which ensures that the coffee drinks taste just right. Another part, "brewing the perfect cup at home," helps baristas teach customers how to use the espresso machines and coffee they buy at Starbucks to replicate the product they get in the coffeehouse.

SERVICE STANDARDS

No pot of Starbucks coffee sits on a burner for more than 20 minutes. An espresso machine with unused coffee must be purged regularly. And no one goes home at night until everything is completed, cleaned, and polished according to the service standards in the manual. Using such standards ensures that both service and quality are maintained.

Source: Reprinted with permission of Starbucks Coffee Company.

STAR SKILLS

To hire, keep, and motivate the very best employees, Starbucks has three guidelines for on-the-job interpersonal relations: (1) maintain and enhance self-esteem, (2) listen and acknowledge, and (3) ask for help. These and other human resources practices, including higher-than-average pay, health insurance, and stock options, lower barista turnover to 60 percent compared with 140 percent for hourly workers in the fast-food business in general.

STARBUCKS AND THE INTERNET

Starbucks had high hopes for the Internet, given that its shops tend to attract young, affluent, tech-savvy customers, 70 percent of whom are Internet users. However, it overestimated its ability to transition offline success to the online environment. Several of its online initiatives failed, including Starbucks X, which was a quasi-separate division built around the Internet, and its online retail store, which once sold coffee beans, mugs, and brewing machines. Now, customers who wish to purchase Starbucks products must physically visit a store; no purchases can be made via the Internet. Starbucks originally refused to offer Internet connections in the coffee shops themselves, not wanting to create dimly lit cybercafés with people hunched over machines. The company has since changed its stance and has

continued

EXHIBIT 14.1

—*continued*

partnered with T-Mobile to create Wireless HotSpot Stores. As we go to press, Starbucks provides high-speed wireless Internet connections in about 40 percent of its stores.

LICENSE SITES

If you have any doubt about whether all these steps pay off in terms of quality product and service, check out Starbucks at airports or on the turnpike. You will notice a difference. While the company does not franchise domestically, it does license sites to companies with contracts from public agencies to run those facilities. No highly trained baristas work at these outlets, and no service quality standards are enforced in them. The result is a less consistent, less pleasant, and less flavourful experience.

Sources: J. Reese, "Starbucks: Inside the Coffee Cult," *Fortune,* December 9, 1996, pp. 190–200; G. Anders, "Starbucks Brews a New Strategy," *Fast Company,* August 2001, pp. 144–46; "Starbucks Keeps Pace," *Beverage Industry,* October 2001, p. 11; www.starbucks.com.

When two or more service companies want to offer a service and neither has the full financial capability or expertise, they often undertake service partnerships. The benefit is that risk and effort are shared, but the disadvantage is that control and returns are also distributed among the partners. Several areas in which partnerships are common are telecommunications, high-technology services, Internet-based services, and entrepreneurial services. Service partnerships also proliferate when companies expand beyond their country boundaries—typically one partner provides the business format and the other provides knowledge of the local market.

FRANCHISING

Franchising is the most common type of distribution in services, with franchisers licensing their brand names, business processes or formats, unique products, services, or reputations in return for fees and royalties. Nearly half of all new retail businesses in Canada are franchised. With more than 1,200 franchisors, 76,000 franchisees, and 1,000,000 jobs in this sector, Canada is the second-most-developed franchised market in the world.[9] Franchising works well with services that can be standardized and duplicated through the delivery process, service policies, warranties, guarantees, promotion, and branding. Mr. Lube, H&R Block, Best Western Hotels, and Boston Pizza are examples of companies that are ideal for franchise operations. At its best, franchising is a relationship or partnership in which the service provider—the franchiser—develops and optimizes a service format that it licenses for delivery by other parties—the franchisees. There are benefits and disadvantages for both the franchiser and the franchisee in this relationship (see Table 14.1).

The Franchiser's Perspective

A franchiser typically begins by developing a business concept that is unique in some way. Perhaps it is a fast-food concept (such as Tim Hortons or Subway) with unique cooking or delivery processes. Perhaps it is a health and fitness centre (such as Curves) with established formats for marketing to customers, pricing, and hiring employees. Or maybe it is a video store (such as Blockbuster) with unique store environments,

TABLE 14.1

Benefits and
Challenges in
Franchising

Benefits	Challenges
For Franchisers	
Leveraged business format for greater expansion and revenues	Difficulty in maintaining and motivating franchisees
Consistency in outlets	Highly publicized disputes and conflict
Knowledge of local markets	Inconsistent quality
Shared financial risk and more working capital	Control of customer relationship by intermediary
For Franchisees	
An established business format	Encroachment
National or regional brand marketing	Disappointing profits and revenues
Minimized risk of starting a business	Lack of perceived control over operations
	High fees

employee training, purchasing, and computer systems. A franchiser typically expands business through this method because it expects the following benefits:

- *A leveraged business format for greater expansion and revenues.* Most franchisers want wider distribution—and increased revenues, market share, brand name recognition, and economies of scale—for their concepts and practices than they can support in company outlets.

- *Consistency in outlets.* When franchisers have strong contracts and unique formats, they can require that service be delivered according to their specifications. This chapter's Global Feature, for example, shows how Starbucks is maintaining consistency across cultures and countries through franchising.

- *Knowledge of local markets.* National chains are unlikely to understand local markets as well as the businesspeople who live in the geographic areas. With franchising, the company obtains a connection to the local market.

- *Shared financial risk and more working capital.* Franchisees must contribute their own capital for equipment and personnel, thereby bearing part of the risk of doing business.

Franchising is not without its challenges, however. Most franchisers encounter the following disadvantages:

- *Difficulty in maintaining and motivating franchisees.* Motivating independent operators to price, promote, deliver, and hire according to standards the principal establishes is a difficult job, particularly when business is down.

- *Highly publicized disputes between franchisees and franchisers.* Franchisees are organizing and hiring lobbyists and lawyers to gain more economic clout. Subway, one of Canada's leading franchises, had many conflicts. In response, franchisees organized their own organization, the North American Association of Subway

Franchisees (NAASF) in 1998. The NAASF has been instrumental in improving goal congruence between the franchisor and its franchisees, and improving overall performance for both parties.

- *Inconsistent quality.* Although some franchisees deliver the service in the manner in which the franchiser intended, other franchisees do not perform the service as well as desired. This inconsistency can undermine the company's image, reputation, and brand name.

- *Customer relationships controlled by the franchisee rather than the franchiser.* The closer a company is to the customer, the better able it is to listen to that customer's concerns and ideas. When franchisees are involved, a relationship forms between the customer and the franchisee rather than between the customer and the franchiser. All customer information, including demographics, purchase history, and preferences, is in the hands of the intermediary rather than the principal.

The Franchisee's Perspective

From the perspective of the franchisee, one of the main benefits of franchising is obtaining an established business format on which to base a business, something one expert has defined as an "entrepreneur in a prepackaged box, a super-efficient distributor of services and goods through a decentralized web."[10] A second benefit is receiving national or regional brand marketing. Franchisees obtain advertising and other marketing expertise as well as an established reputation. Finally, franchising minimizes the risks of starting a business. It is estimated that while 30 to 35 percent of all small businesses fail every year, only 5 percent of all franchises fail.[11]

Disadvantages for franchisees also exist. One of the most problematic is *encroachment*—the opening of new units near existing ones without compensation to the existing franchisee. When encroachment occurs, potential revenues are diminished

FIGURE 14.1

The Canadian Franchise Association (CFA) publishes a directory of franchises that includes valuable information and advice.

Source: Courtesy of Canadian Franchise Association.

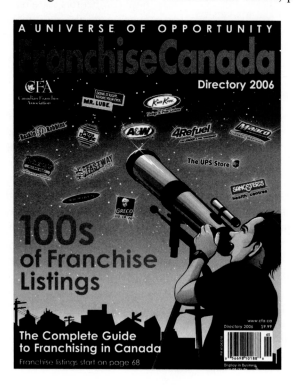

Global Feature

Starbucks Goes Global

> Even in [China's] Forbidden City—where emperors and empresses, concubines and eunuchs, palanquins and peons roamed for five centuries—there could not have been a more striking contraposition in the only store I found in the palace interior: a Starbucks!
>
> —Michael Shermer in *Scientific American*

Starbucks, the Seattle-based coffee chain, has grown into one of the most recognizable brands globally, operating more than 11,000 outlets in Canada, the United States, and 35 countries worldwide. The coffee giant began its expansion as a company-owned service organization in 1987 when it opened 16 locations including an outlet in Vancouver, British Columbia. When the company decided to expand outside North America, management realized that its best route was not to own but instead to franchise or form other types of alliances with organizations within each country. This approach would allow Starbucks to understand the individual markets better and would limit the capital investment necessary to expand. In an unusual twist, the company began its expansion in Asia rather than in Europe. In every country Starbucks has entered, it has met with different scenarios and challenges, as is illustrated by its experiences in Japan and China. Interestingly, some of the company's Canadian expansion required the company to use a licensing format.

JAPAN

Joining with Sazaby, a Japanese retailer and restaurateur, Starbucks opened more than a dozen stores in Japan beginning in 1997. The company chose Japan as its first expansion outside North America because it is the third-largest coffee-consuming country in the world. Possibly the most compelling result of the announcement of the entry of Starbucks was intense fear on the part of existing coffee-bar owners in Japan. Even though Starbucks was introducing a mere dozen outlets, the owners of the mega-chains were filled with anxiety. A manager of Doutor Coffee Company, Japan's number one coffee-bar chain (453 shops at the time), exclaimed, "They're a big threat and could take customers away from us." Many coffee bars imitated Starbucks in design and started offering "Seattle coffee." Executives such as Seiji Homma, president of Pronto Corporation (94 stores), travelled to the United States to gather intelligence from more than 20 Starbucks locations on the West Coast. He, like others, worried that the Japanese outlets lacked the sophistication of Starbucks, the ability to "(package) the store: (mesh) such elements as store design, package design, and other merchandising techniques into a compelling entity." Starbucks had so successfully created and distributed its service in the United States that the Japanese were afraid they could not compete. But as Starbucks opened more stores (it now has more than 500 in Japan), the Japanese competitors were ready. Rather than entering quietly and gaining a toehold before having to compete, Starbucks was targeted before it opened its first Japanese store.

CHINA

After selling Starbucks coffee to Beijing hotels for four years, the company decided to open franchise outlets there in 1998. Challenges abounded. "There (was) of course, the challenge of persuading members of a tea-drinking nation to switch to java. But more immediate has been the challenge of establishing local managers to run shops that can convey the spirit of Seattle in Beijing." The problem was hiring, motivating, and training both baristas who could deliver the consistent service and coffee drinks that made the chain so successful in the United States and managers who would uphold the high standards of the company. The company approached the hiring problem for managers by targeting young people who had experience in running successful North American–style restaurants such as the Hard Rock Café. They recruited baristas

continued

Global Feature

Starbucks Goes Global—continued

through job fairs and ads and focused on aspects such as career and personal development as well as the "cool" factor of being associated with the pop culture scene in Seattle. Starbucks dealt with the motivation issue by sending the best manager recruits to Seattle for three months to absorb the culture and lifestyle of Starbucks and the West Coast. The structured training, as it turns out, helped motivate and keep employees, because they felt confident in the company. The informality and culture of listening at Starbucks also help because they inculcate trust in employees and thereby generate loyalty.

Starbucks' first outlet in China opened in January 1999 at the China World Trade Centre in Beijing. The company now has more than 200 outlets, mainly in Beijing and Shanghai. According to David Sun, president of Beijing Mei Da Coffee Company, which owns the Starbucks franchise for northern China, expansion is going well: "When we first started, people didn't know who we were and it was rough finding sites. Now landlords are coming to us."

CANADA

When Starbucks considered opening stores in the Montreal area, the firm realized that it was dealing with an area unique enough to require firsthand knowledge. Rather than open its own shops, the company decided to license Interaction Restaurants to lead the firm into Montreal.

Moving the firm into the Montreal culture while maintaining the Starbucks identity was a concern. Starbucks wanted to maintain the essence of its image, so it was very careful about the company it chose to become its ambassador. Starbucks had dealt with different cultures—such as the U.S. Hispanic community, Japan, and China—but there were important differences in Quebec. One involves the language, which is mandated by government and is a very emotional issue. In 2000, three coffee shops

belonging to Canadian-owned Second Cup Ltd., a rival of Starbucks, were bombed by an anti-English group because the company retained its English name. To prevent such problems yet remain consistent, Starbucks agreed to be called Café Starbucks Coffee, which combines French and English. Over time, the Starbucks brand became recognizable and accepted in Quebec. Today, there are 18 stores in Montreal.

Perhaps a larger issue was that Montreal residents had a firmly entrenched, sophisticated coffee culture with a history of small coffee shops and Van Houtte (the dominant firm in the market) serving dark, rich coffee. Unlike in the United States, where Starbucks popularized the latte and the coffee tradition that went with it, "[t]here already is a café paradigm there, so Starbucks [did not] have quite the free rein to invent café culture in Quebec." Fortunately, Starbucks' darkly roasted taste was consistent with the preferences in Montreal. Even so, the firm created a special blend called Melange Mont-Royal to recognize the new market and acknowledge that it was special.

The Canadian outlets are also different in that they contain a kitchen for preparing sandwiches and simple meals and an oven for breads and muffins. Freshly prepared food is not typical of Starbucks, and it will be an interesting experiment to see if the outlets can operate the kitchens as efficiently as they do their coffee machines.

Sources: N. Shirouzu, "Japan's Staid Coffee Bars Wake Up and Smell the Starbucks," *The Wall Street Journal,* July 25, 1996, pp. B1ff; J. Lee-Young, "Starbucks' Expansion in China Is Slated; Coffee-Shop Managers Face Cultural Challenges," *The Wall Street Journal,* October 5, 1998, pp. A27Lff; "Business: Coffee with Your Tea? Starbucks in China," *The Economist,* October 6, 2001, p. 62; Z. Olijnyk, "Latte, s'il Vous Plait," *Canadian Business,* September 3, 2001, pp. 50–52; M. Shermer, "Starbucks in the Forbidden City," *Scientific American,* July 2001, pp. 34–35; Starbucks annual reports, 2003, 2005; www.starbucks.com.

and competition is increased. Another frequent disadvantage involves disappointing profits and revenues: "Most people think of franchising as some kind of bonanza … the reality is you get a solid operation, work damn hard, and if you're making $40,000 a year after four years, that's good."[12] Other disadvantages include lack of perceived control over operations and high fees. Many of these problems are due to overpromising by the franchiser, but others are caused by unrealistic expectations about what will be achieved in a franchise agreement.

AGENTS AND BROKERS

An *agent* is an intermediary who acts on behalf of a service principal (such as a real estate agent) or a customer and is authorized to make agreements between the principal and the customer. Some agents, called selling agents, work with the principal and have contractual authority to sell a principal's output (such as travel, insurance, or financial services), usually because the principal lacks the resources or desire to do so. Other agents, called purchasing agents, often have long-term relationships with buyers and help them in evaluating and making purchases. Such agents are frequently hired by companies and individuals to find art, antiques, and rare jewellery. A *broker* is an intermediary who brings buyers and sellers together while assisting in negotiation. Brokers are paid by the party who hired them, rarely become involved in financing or assuming risk, and are not long-term representatives of buyers or sellers. The most familiar examples are real estate brokers, insurance brokers, and security brokers.

Agents and brokers do not take title to services but instead deliver the rights to them. They have legal authority to market services as well as to perform other marketing functions on behalf of producers. The benefits and challenges in using agents and brokers are summarized in Table 14.2.

Benefits of Agents and Brokers

The travel industry provides an example of both agents and brokers. Three main categories of travel intermediaries exist: tour packagers, retail travel agents, and specialty channellers (including incentive travel firms, meeting and convention planners, hotel representatives, association executives, and corporate travel offices). Industry convention terms the travel companies as brokers and the individuals who work for them as agents or sales associates. We use this industry to illustrate some of the benefits and challenges of delivering service through agents and brokers. This traditional industry is changing rapidly because of electronic channels, and we illustrate these new entrants and their impact later in the chapter.

TABLE 14.2

Benefits and Challenges in Distributing Services Through Agents and Brokers

Benefits	Challenges
Reduced selling and distribution costs	Loss of control over pricing
Intermediary's possession of special skills and knowledge	Representation of multiple service principals
Wide representation	
Knowledge of local markets	
Customer choice	

Reduced Selling and Distribution Costs

If an airline or resort hotel needed to contact every potential traveller to promote its offerings, costs would be exorbitant. Because most travel services are transactional rather than long term, travellers would need to expend tremendous effort to find services that meet their needs. Travel agents and brokers accomplish the intermediary role by assembling information from travel suppliers and offering it to travellers.

Possession of Special Skills and Knowledge

Agents and brokers have special knowledge and skills in their areas. For example, retail travel agents know the industry well and know how to access the information they do not possess, often through reference materials and online services. Tour packagers have a more specialized role—they assemble, promote, and price bundles of travel services from travel suppliers, then offer these bundles either to travellers themselves or to retail travel agents. Specialty channelers have even more specialized roles. Some work in corporate travel offices to lend their skills to an entire corporation; others are business meeting and convention planners who act almost as tour packagers for whole companies or associations; and some are incentive travel firms that focus on travel recognition programs in corporations or associations.

Wide Representation

Because agents and brokers are paid by commission rather than by salary, there is little risk or disadvantage to the service principal in extending the service offerings to a wide geography. Thus companies have representatives in many places, far more than if fixed costs such as buildings, equipment, and salaries were required.

Knowledge of Local Markets

Another key benefit of agents and brokers is that they become experts in the local markets they serve. They know or learn the unique needs of different markets, including international markets. They understand what their clients' preferences are and how to adapt the principal's services to match the needs of clients. This benefit is particularly needed and appreciated when clients are dispersed internationally. Knowing the culture and taboos of a country is critical for successful selling. Most companies find that obtaining local representation by experts with this knowledge is necessary.

Customer Choice

Travel and insurance agents provide a retailing service for customers—they represent the services of multiple suppliers. If a traveller needed to visit six or eight different travel agencies, each of which carried the services of a single supplier, imagine the effort a customer would need to make to plan a trip! Similarly, independent insurance agents have the right to sell a wide variety of insurance, which allows them to offer customers a choice. These types of agents also are able to compare prices across suppliers and get the best prices for their clients.

Challenges of Delivering Service Through Agents and Brokers

Loss of Control over Pricing

As representatives of service principals and experts on customer markets, agents and brokers are typically empowered to negotiate price, configure services, and otherwise alter the marketing of a principal's service. This issue could be particularly important—and possibly detrimental—when a service provider depends on a particular (high) price to convey a level of service quality. If the price can be changed, it might drop to a level that undermines the quality image. In addition, the agent often has the flexibility to give different prices to different customers. As long as the customers are geographically dispersed, this variation will not create a problem for the service principal; however, if buyers compare prices and realize they are being given different prices, they may perceive the service principal as unfair or unethical.

Representation of Multiple Service Principals

When independent agents represent multiple suppliers, they offer customer choice. From the perspective of the service principal, however, customer choice means that the agent represents—and in many cases advocates—a competitive service offering. This is the same challenge a manufacturer confronts when distributing products in a retail store. Only in rare cases are its products the only ones in a given category on the retail floor. In a service context, consider the use of independent insurance agents. These agents carry a range of insurance products from different companies, serving as a surrogate service retail store for customers. When they find a customer who needs insurance, they sell from their portfolio the offerings that best match the customer's requirements.

⊢ ⟶ ELECTRONIC CHANNELS

Electronic channels are the only service distributors that do not require direct human interaction. What they do require is some predesigned service (almost always information, education, or entertainment) and an electronic vehicle to deliver it. The consumer and business services that are made possible through these vehicles include movies on demand, interactive news and music, banking and financial services, multimedia libraries and databases, distance learning, desktop videoconferencing, remote health services, and interactive, network-based games.

The more a service relies on technology and/or equipment for service production and the less it relies on face-to-face contact with service providers, the less the service is characterized by inseparability and nonstandardization. As you will see in the following section, using electronic channels overcomes some of the problems associated with service inseparability and allows a form of standardization not previously possible in most services. Table 14.3 summarizes the benefits and challenges of electronic distribution.

FIGURE 14.2

A tongue-in-cheek look at the delivery of a psychiatric service through an electronic channel.

Hello, and welcome to the gethuman psychiatric hotline.

- If you are obsessive-compulsive, please press 1 repeatedly.
- If you are co-dependent, please ask someone to press 2.
- If you have multiple personalities, please press 3, 4, 5, and 6.
- If you are paranoid-delusional, we know who you are and what you want. Stay on the line so we can trace the call.
- If you are schizophrenic, listen carefully and a little voice will tell you what number to press.
- If you are manic-depressive, it doesn't matter which number you press. No one will answer.

TABLE 14.3

Benefits and
Challenges
in Electronic
Distribution of
Services

Benefits	Challenges
Consistent delivery for standardized services	Price competition
Low cost	Inability to customize with highly standardized services
Customer convenience	Lack of consistency due to customer involvement
Wide distribution	
Customer choice and ability to customize	Changes in consumer behaviour
	Security concerns
Quick customer feedback	Competition from widening geographies

Benefits of Electronic Channels

Consistent Delivery for Standardized Services

Electronic channels such as television and telecommunication do not alter the service, as channels with human interaction tend to do. Unlike delivery from a personal provider, electronic delivery does not interpret the service and execute it according to that interpretation. Its delivery is likely to be the same in all transmissions.

Distribution of television programming from networks through affiliate television and radio stations illustrates standardized electronic distribution. Networks create and finance programming including shows, news, and sports and distribute them through local stations in return for fees and advertising dollars. In most cases, the local stations deliver what is fed to them through the networks. Local stations can elect not to carry a particular show because of low ratings or lack of fit with the local market. They can also refuse to carry advertising spots that are judged in bad taste or too controversial. Except for these situations, which are not common, what is distributed through electronic channels is what the service creator sends.

Low Cost

Electronic media offer more efficient means of delivery than does interpersonal distribution. For example, the cost of reaching buyers using a direct sales force has been estimated to exceed $150 per interaction, whereas the use of electronic media such as television or radio often costs less than $30 per *thousand* interactions. Critics could rightly claim that the personal sales interaction is more powerful and effective, but with interactive media service, advertisers are able to gain some of the credibility benefits of personal interaction (such as being able to answer individual questions or tailor the service for individuals).

Customer Convenience

With electronic channels, customers are able to access a firm's services when and where they want. "Retailers still tell customers, You have to come to us. But online consumers are saying, No way—*you* have to come to *us*. My place, my time is the new mantra of consumers everywhere."[13] Just as catalogue shopping freed working women from the perceived drudgeries of having to go to the mall—and fattened the purses of forward-thinking companies that recognized an underserved market—e-commerce is changing the way people shop. Many mail-order companies still limit their hours of availability, a real mistake if they are going to match the customer convenience of being able to order online 24 hours a day, seven days a week. For the marketer, electronic channels allow access to a large group of customers who would otherwise be unavailable to them because of busy schedules that do not allow them to shop in other ways.

Wide Distribution

Electronic channels do more than allow the service provider to interact with a large number of consumers. They also allow the service provider to interact (often simultaneously) with a large number of intermediaries. The costs and effort to inform, select, and motivate nonelectronic channels are higher than the costs to accomplish the same activities with electronic channels. Many franchisers have found that prospecting through the Internet provides better-qualified franchisees than the traditional methods of mainstream advertising and trade shows. Seattle-based World Inspection Network, a franchiser of home inspection operators, increased its franchisee pool fivefold using evaluation and prequalification on the Internet.[14]

Customer Choice and Ability to Customize

Consider the options available in movies and videos to customers who use video-on-demand services. Just as Dell Computer allows customers to configure entire products to their own particular needs and desires, the Internet allows many companies to design services from the beginning. Individuals who want to renovate their kitchen may now go to many Internet sites, specify their requirements, and order what they wish. Whether the supplier is a large retailer such as Home Depot or a small startup company, customers get exactly what they want.

Quick Customer Feedback

Rapid customer feedback is without doubt one of the major strengths of e-commerce. Companies can find out immediately what customers think of services and can gain far higher participation from customers in surveys. With quick customer feedback, changes can be made rapidly to service assortments, problems can be addressed immediately, and the learning cycles of companies can speed up dramatically.

Challenges in Distributing Services Through Electronic Channels

Price Competition

One of the traditional differences between goods and services has been the difficulty of directly comparing features and prices of services with each other. Whereas goods can typically be compared in retail settings, few retail settings exist that offer services from multiple sources. The Internet has changed all that. Services such as Travelocity.com and Priceline.com make it simple for customers to compare prices for a wide variety of services. Priceline.com allows customers to name their price for a service such as an airline ticket, wait until Priceline.com finds an airline willing to accept it, then purchase the ticket. Never has the customer had such ability to bid on prices for services. In Chapter 17 we describe another type of price competition spawned by the Internet: the Internet auction as presented by such companies as eBay, which sells millions of products and services in more than 1,000 categories.

Inability to Customize with Highly Standardized Electronic Services

Some of you have learned college or university basics through video-transmitted courses. If you consider what you missed in learning that way compared with learning directly from a professor, you will understand this challenge. In mass sections, you cannot interact directly with the professor, ask questions, raise points for clarification, or experience the connection that you receive in person. In electronic classes—as in videoconferences that are springing up in many businesses—the quality of the service can also be impeded by the way the audience reacts (or does not react) in those situations. People talk among themselves, leave, laugh, and criticize, among other behaviours.

Lack of Consistency Because of Customer Involvement

Although electronic channels are very effective in minimizing the inconsistency from employees or providers of service, customer variability still presents a problem. Many times customers use the technology themselves to produce the service and this can lead to errors or frustration unless the technology is highly user-friendly. Maneuvering online can sometimes be overwhelming, and not all websites are easy to use. Furthermore, many customers may not have computers and, even if they do, may be reluctant to use this medium.

Changes in Consumer Behaviour

A consumer purchasing a service through electronic channels engages in very different behaviour than one entering a retail store and talking to a salesperson. Considerable changes—in the willingness to search for information, in the willingness to perform some aspects of the services themselves, in the acceptance of different levels of service—are necessary when customers use electronic channels. Behaviour change is difficult, even for a consumer wanting to make a change; therefore, marketers wishing to motivate consumers to alter long-established patterns will be challenged.

Security Concerns

One issue confronting marketers using electronic channels is concern about the security of information, particularly health and financial information. Many customers are still hesitant about giving credit-card numbers on the Internet. These problems can undermine consumers' trust in the Internet as a safe place to do business. Companies doing business through the Internet must continually devise ways to protect their systems from penetration, vandalism, eavesdropping, and impersonation.[15] With penetration, intruders steal passwords and exploit unprotected modems and connections, actually taking over the sites. With vandalism, hackers crash corporate and other computers. To combat these problems, firewalls and other software scan for unusual activity. With eavesdropping, hackers snoop on information as it passes through multiple computers to the Internet. The typical solution is encryption software that scrambles electronic mail and other data to make it unintelligible to eavesdroppers. Finally, with impersonation, criminals steal consumers' identities in order to buy goods and services. A form of encryption technology is often used to deal with this problem, and special service companies confirm signature holders.[16]

Competition from Widening Geographies

Historically, many services were somewhat protected from competition because customers had limited choice among the providers they could physically drive to. Banks, for example, supplied all local customers with chequing accounts, savings accounts, and mortgages. In fact, it used to be said that because services could not be transported they were limited in their scope. Not any longer—and not with electronic channels. Through the Internet, many services, including financial services, can be purchased from service providers far from the local area. See this chapter's Technology Spotlight for several examples.

COMMON ISSUES INVOLVING INTERMEDIARIES

Key problems with intermediaries include conflict over objectives and performance, difficulty controlling quality and consistency across outlets, tension between empowerment and control, and channel ambiguity.

Channel Conflict over Objectives and Performance

The parties involved in delivering services do not always agree about how the channel should operate. Channel conflict can occur between the service provider and the service intermediary, among intermediaries in a given area, and between different types of channels used by a service provider (such as when a service principal has its own outlets as well as franchised outlets). The conflict most often centres on the parties having different goals, competing roles and rights, and conflicting views of the way the channel is performing. Sometimes the conflict occurs because the service principal and its intermediaries are too dependent on each other.

Recently, Air Canada decided to bypass travel agents when offering their Tango (lowest-priced) fares. Instead, these fares were made available only to consumers who visited the company's website. According to Air Canada, the technology of existing global distribution channels did not lend itself to new pricing strategies such as Go Discount—a lower-priced fare that can be obtained when passengers meet certain conditions such as travelling with no checked luggage.[17]

By cutting out its intermediaries in this way, Air Canada was able to reduce its prices, drive traffic to its website, and exercise more control. The strategy brings risks too, though. According to one estimate, Air Canada might lose as much as $245 million per year in revenue if travel agents and their global distribution systems (Sabre Holdings) "de-preference" Air Canada's remaining, higher-margin fares. The risk is further magnified when one considers that WestJet Airlines had earlier in the year decided to *boost* the commission it paid to its travel agents from 9 to 12 percent for the month of September. As you can see, these two service firms are taking very different approaches to their distribution channels.[18]

Difficulty Controlling Quality and Consistency Across Outlets

One of the biggest difficulties for both principals and their intermediaries involves the inconsistency and lack of uniform quality that result when multiple outlets deliver services. When shoddy performance occurs, even at a single outlet, the service principal suffers because the entire brand and reputation are jeopardized, and other intermediaries endure negative attributions to their outlets. The problem is particularly acute in highly specialized services such as management consulting or architecture, in which execution of the complex offering may be difficult to deliver to the standards of the principal.

Tension Between Empowerment and Control

McDonald's and other successful service businesses were founded on the principle of performance consistency. Both they and their intermediaries have attained profits and longevity because the company controls virtually every aspect of their intermediaries'

Technology Spotlight

Electronic Channels in Action

The possibilities for selling and servicing on the Internet and other electronic channels are virtually limitless. Some baseball teams let you see the view of the field from any seat before you buy your ticket. At Lands' End you can create an onscreen model with your figure, then try clothes on the model to find out how they will look on you. Progressive real estate firms let you tour homes as if you were walking through them. Some interesting and innovative applications of the Internet and other electronic channels are illustrated here.

ONLINE TRAVEL

Online travel has been one of the biggest success stories in electronic channels. A recent survey by Jupiter Research now estimates the online travel industry at approximately $77 billion, with future growth anticipated. The Internet has been an extremely effective channel for travel for three key reasons:

1. Prices are more competitive than offline prices, and the technology can conjure up literally thousands of providers in an instant.

2. Online travel companies have no inventory costs and therefore low cost of goods sold.

3. Sites obtain significant advertising revenue due to focused clientele, with advertisers knowing that all users are potential buyers of their travel services.

One of the most successful, profitable online travel sites is Travelocity.ca. Like other online travel sites, it sells airline tickets, hotel rooms, and car rentals directly to consumers, avoiding travel agents. It has been one of the top online travel sites since its inception in 1996 by Sabre Holdings. In 2005 it had record revenues of $2.5 billion. The site earned the loyalty of its users by being very customer-focused in an industry that is all too often technology-focused. Using focus groups and surveys to assess site design and ease of use, the company created excellent customer service, carefully detailed explanations, and guarantees of its credit card security and privacy policies. The company has a special help desk that focuses on taking credit card numbers over the telephone for those afraid to input them online. The site

Source: © 1996–2006 Travelocity.com LP. All rights reserved. Travelocity.ca and the Stars Design are trademarks of Travelocity.com LP.

also offers instantaneous quotes and the ability to track prices to cities that customers plan to visit.

BILL PAYING ONLINE

In recent years many financial institutions have provided an online banking mechanism for customers to pay bills via the Internet. Once customers have made arrangements with their bank and supplied information about each of the companies that send them bills, customers can make payments to those companies using the Internet. This process is generally triggered when customers receive a bill (or bills). Then, accessing their bank account through the Internet, customers identify the company (or companies) to which they owe money and click through a couple of screens and options to initiate payments.

TelPay (www.telpay.ca), a privately held Canadian bill payment company based in Winnipeg, can take the process of customer online bill payment further with their TelPay for You service. Whereas most financial institutions will allow you to make payments to a select list of payees, TelPay will allow you to arrange funds transfers to anyone. Customers set up their list of payees and

continued

Technology Spotlight

Electronic Channels in Action—continued

indicate the payment amount and date. Funds are then transferred the next business day. TelPay for Business offers businesses the ability to pay 100 percent of their suppliers and employees electronically. Businesses can also receive, view, and pay electronically presented bills. The payment system integrates with a user's accounting system. TelPay for Financial Services provides online bill payment functionality to more than 250 financial institutions (primarily credit unions and caisses-populaires) in Canada.

Source: Courtesy of TelPay.

OPPORTUNITIES TO DESIGN YOUR OWN SPORTS GEAR

Companies that mass-market consumer items such as packaged goods have been challenged to use the Internet as a channel to increase loyalty and create customer excitement. Nike.com found success when the company launched an Internet service allowing its U.S. website shoppers to create personalized shoes. Users can select shoes, colour them to fit their tastes, and then emblazon their own names on the shoes. Canadian customers have the opportunity to customize hockey goal equipment at www.nikebauer.com. Customers customize colours,

stitching, and logos and then save their designs online and order their equipment via email or in-store. These initiatives are just one step toward far greater custom services on the Web, including using the Internet to custom-fit shoes to unique foot sizes.

REMOTE COMPUTER ACCESS

Our mobile society has created a desire by many people to have access to a specific computer without being in the same physical location. For example, many companies are allowing (and, in some cases, encouraging) employees to work outside the office. However, in order to work effectively, these employees often need access to the same computer resources they would expect if they were in their office. GoToMyPC.com provides a service that allows access to a host computer from any other computer connected to the Internet. Travellers, telecommuters, or anyone desiring to access their computer from a location other than where it is physically located simply need to install GoToMyPC software on a select (host) computer and leave that computer running and connected to the Internet. These customers then log onto the GoToMyPC website with any remote computer, laptop, or handheld device that has access to the Internet, and they can connect directly to that host computer. This service provides a window on the customer's remote computer that looks just like the video screen on the host computer; once connected, the service allows customers to work as if they were sitting in front of their (host) computer. Any files that the customer has access to from the host computer can be transferred to the remote computer; any software programs on the host computer can be run; and, documents on the host computer can be printed on any printer connected to the remote computer. In using an electronic channel to deliver its service, GoToMyPC provides time savings and convenience to its customers.

Sources: Danny Kucharsky, "World Wide Vacations," *Marketing Magazine*, June 12, 2006, available www.marketingmag.ca, accessed October 2, 2006; D. Coleman, "Internet Success Stories: Travelocity," Australia.internet.com, November 12, 2001, p. 1; Travelocity company websites, www.travelocity.ca and www.travelocity.com; www.telpay.ca; www.nikebauer.ca.

businesses. McDonald's, for example, is famous for its demanding and rigid service standards (such as "Turn, never flip, hamburgers on the grill"), carefully specified supplies, and performance monitoring. The strategy makes sense: unless an intermediary delivers service exactly the same way the successful company outlets provide it, the service may not be as desirable to customers. From the principal's point of view, its name and reputation are on the line in each outlet, making careful control a necessity.

Control, however, can have negative ramifications within intermediaries. Many service franchisees, for example, are entrepreneurial by nature and select service franchising because they can own and operate their own businesses. If they are to deliver according to consistent standards, their independent ideas must be integrated into and often subsumed by the practices and policies of the service principal. In these situations they often feel like automatons with less freedom than they have anticipated as owners of their own businesses.

Channel Ambiguity

When control is not the chosen strategy, doubt exists about the roles of the company and the intermediary. Who will undertake market research to identify customer requirements, the company or an intermediary? Who owns the results and in what way are they to be used? Who determines the standards for service delivery, the franchiser or the franchisee? Who should train a dealer's customer service representatives, the company or the dealer? In these and other situations, the roles of the principal and its intermediaries are unclear, leading to confusion and conflict.

STRATEGIES FOR EFFECTIVE SERVICE DELIVERY THROUGH INTERMEDIARIES

Service principals, of course, want to manage their service intermediaries to improve service performance, solidify their images, and increase profits and revenues. The principal has a variety of choices, which range from strict contractual and measurement control to partnering with intermediaries in a joint effort to improve service to the customer. One of the biggest issues a principal faces is whether to view intermediaries as extensions of its company, as customers, or as partners. We discuss three categories of intermediary management strategies: control strategies, empowerment strategies, and partnering strategies.

Control Strategies

In the control strategies category, the service principal believes that intermediaries will perform best when it creates standards both for revenues and service performance, measures results, and compensates or rewards on the basis of performance level. To use these strategies the principal must be the most powerful participant in the channel, possessing unique services with strong consumer demand or loyalty, or other forms of economic power.

Measurement

Some franchisers maintain control of the service quality delivered by their franchisees by ongoing measurement programs that feed data back to the principal. Virtually all automobile dealers' sales and service performance is monitored regularly by the manufacturer, which creates the measurement program, administers it, and maintains control of the information. The company surveys customers at key points in the service encounter sequence: after sale, 30 days out, 90 days out, and after a year. The manufacturer designs the survey instruments (some of them with the assistance of dealer councils) and obtains the customer feedback directly. On the basis of this information, the manufacturer rewards and recognizes both individuals and dealerships that perform well and might punish those that perform poorly. The obvious advantage to this approach is that the manufacturer retains control; however, the trust and goodwill between manufacturers and dealers can easily be eroded if dealers feel that the measurement is used to control and punish.

Review

Some franchisers control through terminations, nonrenewals, quotas, and restrictive supplier sources. Expansion and encroachment are two of the tactics being used today. Another means by which franchisers exert control over franchisees is through quotas and sales goals, typically by offering price breaks after a certain volume is attained.

Empowerment Strategies

Empowerment strategies—in which the service principal allows greater flexibility to intermediaries on the belief that their talents are best revealed in participation rather than acquiescence—are useful when the service principal is new or lacks sufficient power to govern the channel using control strategies. In empowerment strategies, the principal provides information, research, or processes to help intermediaries perform well in service.

Help the Intermediary Develop Customer-Oriented Service Processes

Individual intermediaries rarely have the funds to sponsor their own customer research studies or training programs. One way for a company to improve intermediary performance is to conduct research or standard-setting studies relating to service performance, then provide the results as a service to intermediaries. As an example, H&R Block amassed its customer information and codified it in a set of 10 "Ultimate Client Service" standards, which were displayed in each office. The standards, which tend to change over time, have included:

- No client will wait more than 30 minutes in the waiting area.

- Phone calls will be answered by the fourth ring, and no caller will be on hold for more than one minute.

- Every tax preparation client will receive a thorough interview to determine the client's lowest legal tax liability.

- Accurately prepared and checked returns will be delivered in four days or fewer.

Rather than administer this customer program from the home office, which could cause it to be perceived as a measurement "hammer," the company asks each franchisee to devise a way to measure the standards in its own offices, then report this information to H&R Block.

Provide Needed Support Systems

After Ford Motor Company conducted customer research and identified six sales standards and six service standards that address the most important customer expectations, it found that dealers and service centres did not know how to implement, measure, and improve service with these standards. For example, one sales standard specified that customers be approached within the first minute they enter the dealership and be offered help when and if the customer needs it. Although dealers could see that this standard was desirable, they did not immediately know how to make it happen. Ford stepped in and provided the research and process support to help the dealers. As another form of support, the company created national advertising featuring dealers discussing the quality care standards.

In airlines and hotels as well as other travel and ticketing services, the service principal's reservation system is an important support system. Holiday Inn, for instance, has a franchise service delivery system that adds value to the Holiday Inn franchise and differentiates it from competitors.

Develop Intermediaries to Deliver Service Quality

Service originators can invest in training or other forms of development to improve the skills and knowledge of intermediaries and their employees. Prudential Real Estate Associates, a national franchiser of real estate brokers, engaged in a companywide program of service excellence. To teach sales associates (real estate agents) about what buyers and sellers expect, the company first conducted focus group interviews with end customers, then created a half-day training program to communicate what the research revealed. To teach brokers (the companies that employ the sales associates), the company created a highly successful operations review that examined the operational and financial aspects of the brokers, assessed their levels of effectiveness, then communicated individually with each broker about the specific issues that needed to be addressed and the approaches that would be successful in improving performance.

Change to a Cooperative Management Structure

Companies such as Taco Bell use the technique of empowerment to manage and motivate franchisees. They develop worker teams in their outlets to hire, discipline, and handle financial tasks such as deposits and audits. Taco Bell deliberately reduced levels of management (regional managers used to oversee five stores; now they oversee fifty) and reported improvements in revenue, employee morale, and profits.

Partnering Strategies

The group of strategies with the highest potential for effectiveness involves partnering with intermediaries to learn together about end customers, set specifications, improve delivery, and communicate honestly. This approach capitalizes on the skills and strengths of both principal and intermediary and engenders a sense of trust that improves the relationship.

Alignment of Goals

One of the most successful approaches to partnering involves aligning company and intermediary goals early in the process. Both the service principal and the intermediary have individual goals that they strive to achieve. If channel members can see that they benefit the ultimate consumer of services and in the process optimize their own revenues and profit, they begin the relationship with a target in mind.

Consultation and Cooperation

A strategy of consultation and cooperation is not as dramatic as setting joint goals, but it does result in intermediaries participating in decisions. In this approach, which can involve virtually any issue from compensation to service quality to the service environment, the principal makes a point of consulting intermediaries and asking for their opinions and views before establishing policy. The approach makes the franchisees feel that they have some control over the way they do business and also generates a steady stream of improvement ideas. Taco John's, one of the largest Mexican fast-food chains, is known for its cooperative relationships with franchisees.

SUMMARY

This chapter discussed the benefits and challenges of delivering service through intermediaries. Service intermediaries perform many important functions for the service principal—coproducing the service, making services locally available, and functioning as the link between the principal and the customer. The focus in service distribution is on identifying ways to bring the customer and principal or its representatives together.

In contrast to channels for products, channels for services are almost always direct, if not to the customer then to the intermediary that sells to the customer. Many of the primary functions that distribution channels serve—inventorying, securing, and taking title to goods—have no meaning in services because of services' intangibility. Because services cannot be owned, most have no titles or rights that can be passed along a delivery channel. Because services are intangible and perishable, inventories cannot exist, making warehousing dispensable. In general, because services cannot be produced, warehoused, and then retailed as goods can, many channels available to goods producers are not feasible for service firms.

Four forms of distribution in service were described in the chapter: franchisees, agents/brokers, and direct and electronic channels. The benefits and challenges of each type of intermediary were discussed, and examples of firms successful in delivering services through each type were detailed. Discussion centred on strategies that can be used by service principals to improve management of intermediaries.

⟼ Discussion Questions

1. In what specific ways does the distribution of services differ from the distribution of goods?
2. Identify other service firms that are company owned and see whether the services they provide are more consistent than ones provided by the franchisees mentioned in this chapter.
3. List five services that could be distributed on the Internet that are not mentioned in this chapter. Why are these particular services appropriate for electronic distribution? Choose two that you particularly advocate. How would you address the challenges to electronic media discussed in this chapter?
4. List services that are sold through selling agents. Why is the use of agents the chosen method of distribution for these services? Could any be distributed in the other ways described in this chapter?
5. What are the main differences between agents and brokers?
6. What types of services are bought through purchasing agents? What qualifies a purchasing agent to represent a buyer in these transactions? Why do buyers themselves not engage in the purchase, rather than hiring someone to do so?

7. Which of the reasons for channel conflict described in this chapter is the most problematic? Why? Based on the chapter, and in particular the strategies discussed at the end of the chapter, what can be done to address the problem you selected? Rank the possible strategies from most effective to least effective.

8. Which of the three categories of strategies for effective service delivery through intermediaries do you believe is most successful? Why? Why are the other two categories less successful?

Exercises

1. Develop a brief franchising plan for a service concept or idea that you believe could be successful.

2. Visit a franchisee and discuss the pros and cons of the arrangement from his or her perspective. How closely does this list of benefits and challenges fit the one provided in this chapter? What would you add to the chapter's list to reflect the experience of the franchisee you interviewed?

3. Select a service industry with which you are familiar. How do service principals in that industry distribute their services? Develop possible approaches to manage intermediaries using the three categories of strategies in the last section of this chapter. Which approach do you believe would be most effective? Why? Which approaches are currently used by service principals in the industry?

4. On the Internet, locate three services that you believe are interesting. What benefits does buying on the Internet have over buying those services elsewhere?

Notes

1. P. Mangan, "What Is Distance Learning?" *Management Quarterly*, Fall 2001, pp. 30–35.

2. A. E. Hancock, "The Evolving Terrain of Distance Learning," *Satellite Communications*, March 1999, pp. 24ff.

3. R. Hirshhorn, "Assessing the Economic Impact of Copyright Reform in the Area of Technology-Enhanced Learning," report prepared for Marketplace Framework Policy Branch, Industry Canada (Ottawa: Industry Canada, 2004), http://strat egis.ic.gc.ca/epic/internet/inippd-dppi.nsf/vwapj/hirshhorn_final_e.pdf/$FILE/ hirshhorn_final_e.pdf, accessed October 1, 2006.

4. Ibid.

5. Athabasca University, www.athabascau.ca/aboutau, accessed June 12, 2006.

6. Ibid.

7. R. Cwiklik, "Pieces of the Puzzle—A Different Course: For Many People, College Will No Longer Be a Specific Place, or a Specific Time," *The Wall Street Journal*, November 6, 1998, p. R31.

8. "Frequently Asked Questions," Starbucks site, www.starbucks.com/aboutus/ ICMSfaq.asp, accessed October 1, 2006.

9. Franchise.com, "Research/FAQ: Canadian Franchises," www.franchise.com/en/ ca/template/buyer,ResearchCenter.vm/display/2833, accessed October 1, 2006.

10. A. E. Serwer, "Trouble in Franchise Nation," *Fortune*, March 6, 1995, pp. 115–129.

11. Franchise.com, "Research/FAQ: New Franchise Success Rate," www.franchise. com/en/us/template/buyer,ResearchCenter.vm/display/542, accessed October 1, 2006.

12. Serwer, "Trouble in Franchise Nation," p. 116.

13. G. Hamel and J. Sampler, "The e-Corporation," *Fortune*, December 7, 1998, pp. 80–92.

14. C. A. Laurie, "Franchisers Meet Challenges of Growth, Change," *Franchising World*, March/April 1999, pp. 11–14.

15. D. Clark, "Safety First," *The Wall Street Journal*, December 7, 1998, p. R14.

16. Ibid.

17. James Stevenson, "Air Canada Angers Travel Group by Pulling Cheap Fares off Distribution System," *Canadian Press NewsWire*, May 17, 2006.

18. Chris Sorenson, "WestJet Tries to Bring Travel Agents on Side: Offers Higher Commission During September," *National Post*, August 31, 2005, p. FP6.

Chapter

15

Managing Demand and Capacity

Closing Provider Gap 3

THIS CHAPTER'S OBJECTIVES ARE TO

1. Explain the underlying issue for capacity-constrained services: lack of inventory capability.

2. Present the implications of time, labour, equipment, and facilities constraints combined with variations in demand patterns.

3. Lay out strategies for matching supply and demand through (a) shifting demand to match capacity or (b) adjusting capacity to meet demand.

4. Demonstrate the benefits and risks of yield management strategies in forging a balance among capacity utilization, pricing, market segmentation, and financial return.

5. Provide strategies for managing waiting lines for times when capacity and demand cannot be aligned.

How to Fill 1,590 Rooms 365 Days of the Year

The Delta Chelsea Hotel (www.deltahotels.com), located in the heart of downtown Toronto, is Canada's largest hotel. It has 1,590 rooms, three restaurants, three lounges, two pools, a health club, and spacious meeting and conference facilities.[1] These restaurants and meeting facilities are available to guests 365 days and nights of the year. Yet natural demand for them can vary widely. Since the hotel is located in Canada's top tourist destination,[2] demand for rooms is understandably high during the peak tourist season, between June and October. But though Toronto has one of the milder climates in Canada, the winter months are still cold, with

temperatures getting as low as –10 degrees Celsius. Consequently, tourism declines in the winter. Because the hotel caters to business travellers and business meetings, demand has a weekly cycle in addition to the seasonal fluctuations. Business travellers do not stay over weekends. Thus, demand for rooms from the hotel's primary market segment drops on Friday and Saturday nights.

To balance demand and capacity throughout the year, the Delta Chelsea targets more than just business travellers. Group business (primarily business conferences) is pursued throughout the year to fill the lower demand periods. A variety of special events, sports, weddings, and getaway packages are offered year-round to increase weekend demand for rooms. And promotions that encourage more local clientele or are run in conjunction with local attractions or events like "Shop 'N Stay" can help round out demand during the traditionally slower times of the year. The Shop 'N Stay package features exclusive discounts to some of Toronto's best shopping and entertainment venues, all just steps away from the comfort of a hotel room. This package includes accommodation as well as special offers from well-known retailers such as the Eaton Centre, The Shoe Company, Sam the Record Man, and The Bay, Queen Street. Area attractions such as the Royal Ontario Museum, the Art Gallery of Ontario, Olympic Spirit, and CanStage are also offering reduced rates on admission and ticket prices. Of note now as well is their Gas Up and Go promotion: with gasoline prices continuing to rise, people generally travel less, so the Gas Up and Go initiative includes gasoline rebates.

Most downtown hotels in urban areas face the same weekly demand fluctuations that the Delta Chelsea deals with, and many have found a partial solution by catering to families and children on the weekends.[3] For many dual-career couples, weekend getaways are a primary form of relaxation and vacation. The downtown hotels cater to these couples and families by offering discounted room rates, child-oriented activities and amenities, and an environment in which families feel comfortable. The Delta Chelsea has recently been dubbed "The Entertainment Hotel" for its ability to combine a variety of entertainment options with a hotel stay, including many activities for children. The hotel boasts being home to Toronto's only indoor water slide, which happens to be four storeys tall. Families also like the fact that the hotel has Camp Chelsea available on weekends, whereby children can partake in a variety of activities supervised by hotel staff while parents are free to enjoy other aspects of Toronto life.

Source: Courtesy of Delta Chelsea Hotel.

For the Delta Chelsea in Toronto, managing demand and utilizing the hotel's fixed capacity of rooms, restaurants, and meeting facilities can be a seasonal, weekly, and even daily challenge. Although the hotel industry epitomizes the challenges of demand and capacity management, many service providers face similar problems. For some businesses, demand is predictable, as for a tax accountant. For others, such as management or technology consultants, demand may be less predictable, fluctuating according to customer needs and business cycles. Sometimes firms experience too much demand for the existing capacity and sometimes capacity sits idle.

Overuse or underuse of a service can directly contribute to Gap 3—failure to deliver what was designed and specified. For example, when demand for services exceeds maximum capacity, the quality of service may drop because staff and facilities are overtaxed. And some customers may be turned away, not receiving the service at all. During periods of slow demand it may be necessary to reduce prices or cut service amenities, changing the makeup of the clientele and the nature of the service and thus running the risk of not delivering what customers expect.[4]

In this chapter we focus on the challenges of matching supply and demand in capacity-constrained services. Gap 3 can occur when organizations fail to smooth the peaks and valleys of demand, overuse their capacities, attract an inappropriate customer mix in their efforts to build demand, or rely too much on price in smoothing demand. The chapter gives you an understanding of these issues and strategies for addressing them. The effective use of capacity is frequently a key success factor for service organizations.

⟼ THE UNDERLYING ISSUE: LACK OF INVENTORY CAPABILITY

The fundamental issue underlying supply and demand management in services is the lack of inventory capability. Unlike manufacturing firms, service firms cannot build up inventories during periods of slow demand to use later when demand increases. This lack of inventory capability is due to the perishability of services and their simultaneous production and consumption. An airline seat that is not sold on a given flight cannot be resold the following day. The productive capacity of that seat has perished. Similarly, an hour of a lawyer's billable time cannot be saved from one day to the next. Services also cannot be transported from one place to another or transferred from person to person. Thus the Delta's services cannot be moved to an alternative location in the winter months.

The lack of inventory capability combined with fluctuating demand leads to a variety of potential outcomes, as illustrated in Figure 15.1.[5] The horizontal lines in the figure indicate service capacity, and the curved line indicates customer demand for the service. In many services, capacity is fixed; thus capacity can be designated by a flat horizontal line over a certain time period. Demand for service frequently fluctuates, however, as indicated by the curved line. The topmost horizontal line in the figure represents maximum capacity. For example, in our opening vignette, the horizontal line would represent the Delta's maximum number of rooms, or it could represent the approximately 10,000 seats in the Halifax Metro Centre. The rooms and the seats remain constant, but demand for them fluctuates. The band between the second and third horizontal lines represents optimum capacity—the best use of the capacity from the perspective of both customers and the company (the difference between optimal and maximum capacity utilization is discussed later in the chapter).

FIGURE 15.1 Variations in Demand Relative to Capacity

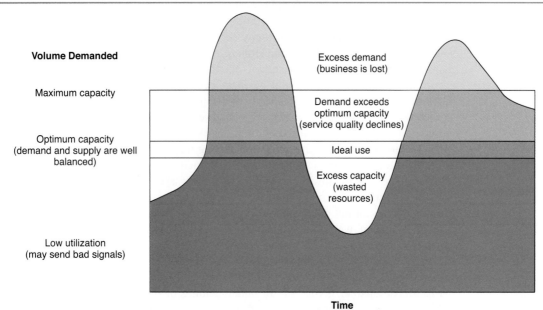

Source: Reprinted from C. Lovelock, "Getting the Most out of Your Productive Capacity," *Product Plus* (Boston: McGraw Hill, 1994), ch. 16, p. 241. © 1994 by The McGraw-Hill Companies, Inc. Reprinted by permission of The McGraw-Hill Companies.

The areas in the middle of the figure are labelled to represent four basic scenarios that can result from different combinations of capacity and demand:

1. *Excess demand.* The level of demand exceeds maximum capacity. In this situation some customers will be turned away, resulting in lost business opportunities. For the customers who do receive the service, its quality may not match what was promised because of crowding or overtaxing of staff and facilities.

2. *Demand exceeds optimum capacity.* No one is being turned away, but the quality of service may still suffer because of overuse, crowding, or staff being pushed beyond their abilities to deliver consistent quality.

3. *Demand and supply are balanced at the level of optimum capacity.* Staff and facilities are occupied at an ideal level. No one is overworked, facilities can be maintained, and customers are receiving quality service without undesirable delays.

4. *Excess capacity.* Demand is below optimum capacity. Productive resources in the form of labour, equipment, and facilities are underutilized, resulting in lost productivity and lower profits. Customers may receive excellent quality on an individual level because they have the full use of the facilities, no waiting, and complete attention from the staff. If, however, service quality depends on the presence of other customers, customers may be disappointed or may worry that they have chosen an inferior service provider.

Not all firms will be challenged equally in terms of managing supply and demand. The seriousness of the problem will depend on the *extent of demand fluctuations over time,* and the *extent to which supply is constrained* (Table 15.1).[6] Some types of organizations will experience wide fluctuations in demand (telecommunications,

TABLE 15.1

Demand versus
Supply

Extent to Which Supply Is Constrained	Extent of Demand Fluctuations over Time	
	Wide 1	**Narrow** 2
Peak demand can usually be met without a major delay	Electricity Natural gas Hospital maternity unit Police and fire emergencies	Insurance Legal services Banking Laundry and dry cleaning
	4	3
Peak demand regularly exceeds capacity.	Accounting and tax preparation Passenger transportation Hotels Restaurants Hospital emergency rooms	Services similar to those in 2 that have insufficient capacity for their base level of business

Source: C. H. Lovelock, "Classifying Services to Gain Strategic Marketing Insights," *Journal of Marketing* 47 (Summer 1983), p. 17. Reprinted by permission from the American Marketing Association.

hospitals, transportation, restaurants), whereas others will have narrower fluctuations (insurance, laundry, banking). For some, peak demand can usually be met even when demand fluctuates (electricity, natural gas), but for others peak demand may frequently exceed capacity (hospital emergency rooms, restaurants, hotels). Those firms with wide variations in demand (cells 1 and 4 in the table), and particularly those with wide fluctuations in demand that regularly exceed capacity (cell 4), will find the issues and strategies in this chapter particularly important to their success. Those firms that find themselves in cell 3 need a "one-time-fix" to expand their capacity to match regular patterns of excessive demand. The example industries in the table are provided to illustrate where *most* firms in those industries would likely be classified. In reality, an individual firm from any industry could find itself in any of the four cells, depending on its immediate circumstances.

To identify effective strategies for managing supply and demand fluctuations, an organization needs a clear understanding of the constraints on its capacity and the underlying demand patterns.

⟶ CAPACITY CONSTRAINTS

Later in the chapter, we present some creative ways to expand and contract capacity in the short and long term, but for our discussion now, you can assume that service capacity is fixed. Depending on the type of service, critical fixed-capacity factors can be time, labour, equipment, facilities, or (in many cases) a combination of these.

Time, Labour, Equipment, Facilities

For some service businesses, the primary constraint on service production is *time.* For example, a lawyer, a consultant, a hairdresser, a plumber, and a psychological counselor all primarily sell their time. If their time is not used productively, profits are lost. If there is excess demand, time cannot be created to satisfy it. From the point of view of the individual service provider, time is the constraint.

From the point of view of a firm that employs a large number of service providers, *labour* or staffing levels can be the primary capacity constraint. A law firm, a university department, a consulting firm, a tax accounting firm, and a repair and maintenance contractor may all face the reality that at certain times demand for their organizations' services cannot be met because the staff is already operating at peak capacity. However, it does not always make sense (nor may it be possible in a competitive labour market) to hire additional service providers if low demand is a reality at other times.

In other cases, *equipment* may be the critical constraint. For trucking or air-freight delivery services, the trucks or airplanes needed to service demand may be the capacity limitation. During the Christmas holidays, Purolator, Canada Post, and other delivery service providers face this issue. Health clubs also deal with this limitation, particularly at certain times of the day (before work, during lunch hours, after work) and in certain months of the year. For network service providers, bandwidth, servers, and switches represent their perishable capacity.

Finally, many firms face restrictions brought about by their limited *facilities*. Hotels have only a certain number of rooms to sell, airlines are limited by the number of seats on the aircraft, educational institutions are constrained by the number of rooms and the number of seats in each classroom, and restaurant capacity is restricted to the number of tables and seats available.

Understanding the primary capacity constraint, or the combination of factors that restricts capacity, is a first step in designing strategies to deal with supply and demand issues (Table 15.2).

TABLE 15.2

Constraints on Capacity

Nature of the Constraint	Type of Service*
Time	Legal
	Consulting
	Accounting
	Medical
Labour	Law firm
	Accounting firm
	Consulting firm
	Health clinic
Equipment	Delivery services
	Telecommunications
	Network services
	Utilities
	Health club
Facilities	Hotels
	Restaurants
	Hospitals
	Airlines
	Schools
	Theatres
	Churches

*The examples illustrate the most common capacity constraint for each type of service. In reality, any of the service organizations listed can be operating under multiple constraints. For example, a law firm may be operating under constrained labour capacity (too few attorneys) and facilities constraints (not enough office space) at the same time.

Optimal vs. Maximum Use of Capacity

To fully understand capacity issues, it is important to know the difference between optimal and maximum use of capacity. As suggested in Figure 15.1, optimum and maximum capacity may not be the same. Using capacity at an optimum level means that resources are fully employed but not overused and that customers are receiving quality service in a timely manner. Maximum capacity, on the other hand, represents the absolute limit of service availability. In the case of a football game, optimum and maximum capacity may be the same. The entertainment value of the game is enhanced for customers when every single seat is filled, and obviously the profitability for the team is greatest under these circumstances (Figure 15.2). On the other hand, in a university classroom it is usually not desirable for students or faculty to have every seat filled. In this case, optimal use of capacity is less than the maximum. In some cases, maximum use of capacity may result in excessive waiting by customers, as in a popular restaurant. From the perspective of customer satisfaction, optimum use of the capacity will be less than maximum use.

In the case of equipment or facilities constraints, the maximum capacity at any given time is obvious. There are only a certain number of weight machines in the health club, a certain number of seats in the airplane, and a limited amount of space in a cargo carrier. In the case of a bottling plant, when maximum capacity on the assembly line is exceeded, bottles begin to break and the system shuts down. Thus it is relatively easy to observe the effects of exceeding maximum equipment capacity.

When the limitation is people's time or labour, maximum capacity is harder to specify because people are in a sense more flexible than facilities and equipment. When an individual service provider's maximum capacity has been exceeded, the result is likely to cause decreased service quality, customer dissatisfaction, and employee burnout and turnover, but these outcomes may not be immediately observable even

FIGURE 15.2

For sports and other entertainment venues, maximal and optimal capacity use are close to the same.

Source: CP/Larry MacDougal.

to the employee herself. It is often easy for a consulting firm to take on one more assignment, taxing its employees beyond their maximum capacity, or for a clinic to schedule a few more appointments in a day, stretching its staff and physicians beyond their maximum capacity. Given the potential costs in terms of reduced quality and customer and employee dissatisfaction, it is critical for the firm to understand optimum and maximum human capacity limits.

DEMAND PATTERNS

To manage fluctuating demand in a service business, it is necessary to have a clear understanding of demand patterns, why they vary, and the market segments that comprise demand at different points in time.[7] A number of questions need to be answered regarding the predictability and underlying causes of demand.

The Charting of Demand Patterns

First, the organization needs to chart the level of demand over relevant time periods. Organizations that have good computerized customer information systems can chart this information very accurately. Others may need to chart demand patterns more informally. Daily, weekly, and monthly demand levels should be followed, and if seasonality is a suspected problem, graphing should be done for data from at least the past year. In some services, such as restaurants or health care, hourly fluctuations within a day may also be relevant. Sometimes demand patterns are intuitively obvious; in other cases patterns may not reveal themselves until the data are charted.

Predictable Cycles

In looking at the graphic representation of demand levels, is there a predictable cycle daily (variations occur by hours), weekly (variations occur by day), monthly (variations occur by day or week), and/or yearly (variations occur according to months or seasons)? In some cases, predictable patterns may occur at all periods. For example, in the restaurant industry, especially in seasonal tourist locations, demand can vary predictably by month, by week, by day, and by hour.

If a predictable cycle is detected, what are its underlying causes? The Delta in Toronto knows that demand cycles are based on seasonal weather patterns and that weekly variations are based on the workweek (business travellers do not stay at the hotel over the weekend). Tax accountants can predict demand on the basis of when taxes are due. Services catering to children respond to variations in school hours and vacations. Retail services have peak periods at certain holidays and times of the week and day. When predictable patterns exist, generally one or more causes can be identified. A surprising pattern even exists for hospital maternity wards. You might expect that births would always be randomly spread over the course of a week, but it turns out that a full moon occasions a predictable spike in births.

Random Demand Fluctuations

Sometimes the patterns of demand appear to be random—there is no apparent predictable cycle. Yet even in this case, causes can often be identified. For example, day-to-day changes in the weather may affect use of recreational, shopping, or entertainment facilities. Although the weather cannot be predicted far in advance, it may be possible to anticipate demand a day or two ahead. Health-related events also cannot be predicted. Accidents and heart attacks increase demand for hospital services, but the level of demand cannot generally be determined in advance. Natural disasters such as floods, fires, and hurricanes can dramatically increase the need for such services as insurance, telecommunications, and health care. Canada has had its share of floods and hurricanes. Whether we look at flooding in western Canada, the ice storm in Quebec, or Hurricane Juan in Nova Scotia, natural disasters cause unpredicted demand fluctuations.

Our Global Feature illustrates how one company with seemingly random and chaotic demand for its services was able to change its business to serve customers. The feature is also a good example of organizational learning across cultures.

Demand Patterns by Market Segment

An organization that has detailed records on customer transactions may be able to disaggregate demand by market segment, revealing patterns within patterns. Or the analysis may reveal that demand from one segment is predictable whereas demand from another segment is relatively random. For example, for a bank, the visits from its commercial accounts may occur daily at a predictable time, whereas personal account holders may visit the bank at seemingly random intervals. Health clinics often notice that walk-in or "care needed today" patients tend to concentrate their arrivals on Monday, with fewer needing immediate attention on other days of the week. Knowing that this pattern exists, some clinics schedule more future appointments (which they can control) for later days of the week, leaving more of Monday available for same-day appointments and walk-ins.

STRATEGIES FOR MATCHING CAPACITY AND DEMAND

When an organization has a clear grasp of its capacity constraints and an understanding of demand patterns, it is in a good position to develop strategies for matching supply and demand. There are two general approaches for accomplishing this match. The first is to smooth the demand fluctuations themselves by shifting demand to match existing supply. This approach implies that the peaks and valleys of the demand curve (Figure 15.1) will be flattened to match as closely as possible the horizontal optimum capacity line. The second general strategy is to adjust capacity to match fluctuations in demand. This implies moving the horizontal capacity lines shown in Figure 15.1 to match the ups and downs of the demand curve. Each of these two basic strategies is described next with specific examples.

Shifting Demand to Match Capacity

With this strategy an organization seeks to shift customers away from periods in which demand exceeds capacity, perhaps by convincing them to use the service during periods of slow demand. This change may be possible for some customers but not for others. For example, many business travellers are not able to shift their needs for airline, car rental, and hotel services; pleasure travellers, on the other hand, can often shift the timing of their trips. Customers who cannot shift and cannot be accommodated will represent lost business for the firm.

During periods of slow demand, the organization seeks to attract more and/or different customers to utilize its productive capacity. A variety of approaches, detailed

Global Feature

Cemex Creatively Manages Chaotic Demand for Its Services

Imagine a business in which customers' orders are unpredictable, where more than half of all customer orders are changed, often repeatedly and at the last minute, and where the product being delivered is never more than 90 minutes from spoiling. Welcome to the concrete delivery business. Cemex (www.cemex.com), based in Monterrey, Mexico, and founded in 1906, is a highly successful global player in this industry. Having grown substantially through acquisitions, the company now operates in more than 50 countries with more than 50,000 employees and annual sales in excess of $15 billion.

Yet, when two internal consultants examined the business several years ago, they were amazed at the chaos that ruled the industry. Wild weather, unpredictable traffic, spontaneous labour disruptions, and sporadic government inspections of construction sites all combined with ever-changing customer orders to create a sense of chaos and uncontrollability in the business. Combine this chaos with 8,000 grades of concrete available through a half-dozen regional mixing plants, and you have an extremely complex system to manage.

Historically, Cemex had attempted to run the business through controlling its customers to stick with their orders and by imposing fines for changed orders. Efficiency ruled, not customers—in order to conquer the natural randomness of demand and the customers' needs to change orders at the last minute.

The company began searching for new ways to do business. It turned to FedEx and to the 911 emergency dispatch centre in Houston, Texas, for ideas. What it found were organizations that, instead of trying to control demand for their services, had developed people and technology to be flexible in meeting customers' seemingly random demand patterns. Instead of penalizing customers for changing their orders, FedEx does not restrict its customers and, in fact, guarantees delivery at a certain time to any and all locations. This ability to serve customers is made possible by sophisticated information systems that track demand and schedule pickups and deliveries, customer-focused front-line employees, and a customer-centric corporate culture that supports it all. From the 911 centre in Houston, Cemex learned that even seemingly random occurrences such as emergency health needs and accidents occur in sufficient number to allow patterns of demand to be discerned and planned for. In terms of Figure 15.1, what FedEx and the 911 emergency centre did was adjust their capacity to meet the peaks and valleys of customer demand rather than insist that the customers adjust their demand to fit the company's constrained capacity.

The experiences at FedEx and in Houston at the 911 centre were a revelation to Cemex's team. The company went back to Mexico determined to embrace the complexity of its marketplace and to do business on the customers' terms. The company launched a project called Sincronizacion Dinamica de Operaciones: the dynamic synchronization of operations. It unleashed trucks from previous zone assignments, allowing them to roam the city. It outfitted the trucks with transmitters and receivers connected to a GPS system so that locations, direction, and speed of every vehicle could be tracked. It enrolled its drivers in secondary education classes over a period of two years so they would be more service-oriented and able to deal with customers.

Impressed with FedEx's guaranteed service, Cemex worked toward being able to offer "same-day service, with free, unlimited order changes." Now, if a load fails to arrive within 20 minutes of its scheduled delivery time, the buyer gets back 20 pesos per cubic metre—"guarantia 20 × 20"—amounting to roughly 5 percent of the total cost.

Cemex embraced the chaos of its industry instead of trying to adjust and change it. By using technology, people, and systems, it was able to match its capacity

continued

Global Feature

Cemex Creatively Manages Chaotic Demand for Its Service—continued

constraints with its customers' wildly fluctuating demands. And the company came out a winner. Cemex can afford to offer its 20 × 20 guarantee now that its reliability exceeds 98 percent!

Today, the company's focus on the customer is clearly stated in the slogan across the top of its website: "By connecting with customer needs, we deliver value worldwide."

Sources: T. Petzinger Jr., "This Promise Is Set in Concrete," *Fast Company,* April 1999, pp. 216–18. See also T. Petzinger Jr., *The New Pioneers* (New York: Simon & Schuster, Inc., 1999), pp. 91–93. M. Dickerson, "Foundation Rock Solid for Mexico's Cement Giant," *Chicago Tribune,* online edition, May 30, 2006, www.chicagotribune.com, accessed June 1, 2006. Reprinted with the permission of Simon & Schuster, Inc. © 1999 by Thomas Petzinger Jr.; updated with company information from the Cemex website, www.cemex.com, 2004.

in the following sections, can be used to shift or increase demand to match capacity. Frequently a firm uses a combination of approaches. Ideas for how to shift demand during both slow and peak periods are shown in Figure 15.3. Note that providing incentives to customers for usage during non-peak times is a very common practice of WestJet's (Figure 15.4).

Vary the Service Offering

One approach is to change the nature of the service offering, depending on the season of the year, day of the week, or time of day. For example, Whistler Mountain, a ski resort near Vancouver, offers its facilities for executive development and training programs during the summer when skiing is not possible. Accounting firms focus on tax preparation late in the year and until April 30, when taxes are due. During other times of the year they can focus on audits and general tax consulting activities. Airlines even

FIGURE 15.3   Strategies for Shifting Demand to Match Capacity

| DEMAND TOO HIGH | SHIFT DEMAND | DEMAND TOO LOW |

- Use signage to communicate busy days and times.
- Offer incentives to customers for usage during nonpeak times.
- Take care of loyal or "regular" customers first.
- Advertise peak usage times and benefits of nonpeak use.
- Charge full price for the service—no discounts.

- Use sales and advertising to increase business from current market segments.
- Modify the service offering to appeal to new market segments.
- Offer discounts or price reductions.
- Modify hours of operation.
- Bring the service to the customer.

change the configuration of their plane seating to match the demand from different market segments. Some planes may have no first-class section at all. On routes with a large demand for first-class seating, a significant proportion of seats may be placed in first class. Our opening vignette featured ways in which downtown hotels have changed their offerings to appeal to the family market segment on weekends. In all these examples, the service offering and associated benefits are changed to smooth customer demand for the organization's resources.

Care should be exercised in implementing strategies to change the service offering, because such changes may easily imply and require alterations in other marketing mix variables—such as promotion, pricing, and staffing—to match the new offering. Unless these additional mix variables are altered effectively to support the offering, the strategy may not work. Even when done well, the downside of such changes can be a confusion in the organization's image from the customers' perspective, or a loss of strategic focus for the organization and its employees.

Communicate with Customers

Another approach for shifting demand is to communicate with customers, letting them know the times of peak demand so they can choose to use the service at alternative times and avoid crowding or delays. For example, signs in banks and post offices that let customers know their busiest hours and busiest days of the week can serve as a warning, allowing customers to shift their demand to another time if possible. Research in a bank context found that customers who were forewarned about the bank's busiest hours were more satisfied even when they had to wait than were customers who were not forewarned.[8]

In addition to signage that communicates peak demand times to customers, advertising and other forms of promotion can emphasize different service benefits during peak and slow periods. Advertising and sales messages can also remind customers about peak demand times.

Modify Timing and Location of Service Delivery

Some firms adjust their hours and days of service delivery to more directly reflect customer demand. Historically, banks were open only during "bankers' hours" from 10 a.m. to 3 p.m. every weekday. Obviously these hours did not match the times when most people preferred to do their personal banking. Now many banks open early, stay open until 6 p.m., and are often open on Saturdays, better reflecting customer demand patterns. TD Canada Trust in particular has chosen to expand its hours of operation by staying open late—a strategy they have extensively promoted. Online banking has also shifted demand from branches to "anytime, anywhere" websites. Theatres accommodate customer schedules by offering matinees on weekends and holidays when people are free during the day for entertainment. Movie theatres are sometimes rented during weekdays by business groups—an example of varying the service offering during a period of low demand.

Differentiate on Price

A common response during slow demand is to discount the price of the service. This strategy relies on basic economics of supply and demand. To be effective, however, a price differentiation strategy depends on solid understanding of customer price-sensitivity and demand curves. For example, business travellers are far less price-sensitive than families travelling for pleasure. For the Delta Hotel (the subject of our opening vignette), lowering prices during the slow summer months is not likely to increase bookings from business travellers dramatically. However, the lower summer prices attract considerable numbers of families and local guests who want an opportunity to experience a luxury hotel but are not able to afford the rooms during peak season.

The maximum capacity of any hotel, airline, restaurant, or other service establishment could be reached if the price were low enough. But the goal is always to ensure the highest level of capacity utilization without sacrificing profits. We explore this complex relationship among price, market segments, capacity utilization, and profitability later in the chapter in the section on yield management.

Heavy use of price differentiation to smooth demand can be a risky strategy. Over-reliance on price can result in price wars in an industry in which eventually all competitors suffer. Price wars are well known in the airline industry, and total industry profits often suffer as a result of airlines simultaneously trying to attract customers through price discounting. Another risk of relying on price is that customers grow accustomed to the lower price and expect to get the same deal the next time they use the service. If communications with customers are unclear, customers may not understand the reasons for the discounts and will expect to pay the same during peak demand periods. Overuse or exclusive use of price as a strategy for smoothing demand is also risky because of the potential impact on the organization's image, the potential for attracting undesired market segments, and the possibility that higher-paying customers will feel they have been treated unfairly. Recently, residents and business owners in Whistler have begun planning how to discourage an undesirable influx of high school students from Vancouver who show up in droves on the May long weekend. During this time, partying students clash with traditional and full-time residents.

Adjusting Capacity to Meet Demand

A second strategic approach to matching supply and demand focuses on adjusting capacity. The fundamental idea here is to adjust, stretch, and align capacity to match customer demand (rather than working on shifting demand to match capacity, as just

FIGURE 15.5 Strategies for Adjusting Capacity to Match Demand

DEMAND TOO HIGH

ADJUST CAPACITY

DEMAND TOO LOW

- Stretch time, labour, facilities, and equipment.
- Cross-train employees.
- Hire part-time employees.
- Request overtime work from employees.
- Rent or share facilities.
- Rent or share equipment.

- Subcontract or outsource activities.
- Perform maintenance, renovations.
- Schedule vacations.
- Schedule employee training.
- Lay off employees.

described). During periods of peak demand the organization seeks to stretch or expand its capacity as much as possible. During periods of slow demand it tries to shrink capacity so as not to waste resources. General strategies for adjusting the four primary service resources (time, people, equipment, and facilities) are discussed throughout the rest of this section. In Figure 15.5, we summarize specific ideas for adjusting capacity during periods of peak and slow demand. Often, a number of different strategies are used simultaneously.

Stretch Existing Capacity

The existing capacity of service resources can often be expanded temporarily to match demand. In such cases no new resources are added; rather the people, facilities, and equipment are asked to work harder and longer to meet demand.

Stretch Time   It may be possible to extend the hours of service temporarily to accommodate demand. A health clinic might stay open longer during flu season, retailers are open longer hours during the holiday shopping season, and accountants have extended appointment hours (evenings and Saturdays) before tax deadlines.

Stretch Labour   In many service organizations, employees are asked to work longer and harder during periods of peak demand. For example, consulting organizations face extensive peaks and valleys with respect to demand for their services. During peak demand, associates are asked to take on additional projects and work longer hours. And front-line service personnel in banks, tourist attractions, restaurants, and telecommunications companies are asked to serve more customers per hour during busy times than during hours or days when demand is low.

Stretch Facilities   Theatres, restaurants, meeting facilities, and classrooms can sometimes be expanded temporarily by the addition of tables, chairs, or other equipment needed by customers. Or, as in the case of a commuter train, a car that holds a fixed number of people seated comfortably can "expand" by accommodating standing passengers.

Stretch Equipment   Computers, power lines, and maintenance equipment can often be stretched beyond what would be considered the maximum capacity for short periods to accommodate peak demand.

In using these types of "stretch" strategies, the organization needs to recognize the wear and tear on resources and the potential for inferior quality of service that may go with the use. These strategies should thus be used for relatively short periods in order to allow for later maintenance of the facilities and equipment and refreshment of the people who are asked to exceed their usual capacity.

Align Capacity with Demand Fluctuations

This basic strategy is sometimes known as a "chase demand" strategy. By adjusting service resources creatively, organizations can in effect chase the demand curves to match capacity with customer demand patterns. Time, labour, facilities, and equipment are again the focus, this time with an eye toward adjusting the basic mix and use of these resources. Specific actions might include the following.[9]

Use Part-Time Employees In this situation the organization's labour resource is being aligned with demand. Retailers hire part-time employees during the holiday rush. Restaurants often ask employees to work split shifts (work the lunch shift, leave for a few hours, and come back for the dinner rush) during peak mealtime hours.

Outsourcing Firms that find they have a temporary peak in demand for a service that they cannot perform themselves may choose to outsource the entire service.

Rent or Share Facilities or Equipment For some organizations it is best to rent additional equipment or facilities during periods of peak demand. For example, express mail delivery services rent or lease trucks during the peak holiday delivery season. It would not make sense to buy trucks that would sit idle during the rest of the year. Sometimes organizations with complementary demand patterns can share facilities. An example is a church that shares its facilities during the week with a preschool. The school needs the facilities Monday through Friday during the day; the church needs the facilities evenings and on the weekend.

Schedule Downtime During Periods of Low Demand If people, equipment, and facilities are being used at maximum capacity during peak periods, then it is imperative to schedule repair, maintenance, and renovations during off-peak periods. This schedule ensures that the resources are in top condition when they are most needed. Vacations and training are also scheduled during slow demand periods.

Cross-Train Employees If employees are cross-trained, they can shift among tasks, filling in where they are most needed. Cross-training increases the efficiency of the whole system and avoids underutilizing employees in some areas while others are being overtaxed. Many airlines cross-train their employees to move from ticketing to working the gate counters to assisting with baggage if needed. Grocery stores also use this strategy, most employees being able to move as needed from cashiering to stocking shelves to bagging groceries.

Modify or Move Facilities and Equipment Sometimes it is possible to adjust, move, or creatively modify existing capacity to meet demand fluctuations. Hotels utilize this strategy by reconfiguring rooms—two rooms with a locked door between can be rented to two different parties in high demand times or turned into a suite during slow demand. The airline industry offers dramatic examples of this strategy. Using an approach known as "demand-driven dispatch," airlines have begun to experiment with methods that assign airplanes to flight schedules on the basis of fluctuating market needs.[10] The method depends on accurate knowledge of demand and the ability to quickly move airplanes with different seating capacities to flight assignments that match their capacity. The Boeing 777 aircraft is so flexible that it can be reconfigured within hours to vary the number of seats allocated to one, two, or three classes.[11] The plane can thus be quickly modified to match demand from different market segments, essentially molding capacity to fit demand.

Combining Demand and Capacity Strategies

Many firms use multiple strategies, combining marketing-driven demand management approaches with operations-driven capacity management strategies. Figuring out which is the best set of strategies for maximizing capacity utilization, customer satisfaction, and profitability can be challenging, particularly when the service offering is a constellation of offerings within one service setting, for example, theme parks with rides, restaurants, shopping; hotel vacation villages with hotels, shopping, spas, pools, restaurants; or ski resorts with ski slopes, spas, restaurants, and entertainment. Firms face complex problems in trying to balance demand across all the different offerings with an eye to quality and profitability.

YIELD MANAGEMENT: BALANCING CAPACITY UTILIZATION, PRICING, MARKET SEGMENTATION, AND FINANCIAL RETURN

Yield management is a term that has become attached to a variety of methods, some very sophisticated, matching demand and supply in capacity-constrained services. Using yield management models, organizations find the best balance at a particular point in time among the prices charged, the segments sold to, and the capacity used. The goal of yield management is to produce the best possible financial return from a limited available capacity. Specifically, yield management (also referred to as revenue management) has been defined as "the process of allocating the right type of capacity to the right kind of customer at the right price so as to maximize revenue or yield."[12]

Although the implementation of yield management can involve complex mathematical models and computer programs, the underlying effectiveness measure is the ratio of actual revenue to potential revenue for a particular measurement period:

$$\text{Yield} = \frac{\text{Actual revenue}}{\text{Potential revenue}}$$

where

$$\text{Actual revenue} = \text{Actual capacity used} \times \text{Average actual price}$$

$$\text{Potential evenue} = \text{Total capacity} \times \text{Maximum price}$$

The equations indicate that yield is a function of price and capacity used. Recall that capacity constraints can be in the form of time, labour, equipment, or facilities. Yield is essentially a measure of the extent to which an organization's resources (or capacities) are achieving their full revenue-generating potential. Assuming that total capacity and maximum price cannot be changed, yield approaches 1 as actual capacity utilization increases or when a higher actual price can be charged for a given capacity used. For example, in an airline context, a manager could focus on increasing yield by finding ways to bring in more passengers to fill the capacity, or by finding higher-paying passengers to fill a more limited capacity. In reality, expert yield managers work on capacity and pricing issues simultaneously to maximize revenue across different customer segments. Exhibit 15.1 shows simple yield calculations and the inherent tradeoffs for two types of services: hotel and legal.

Simple Yield Calculations: Examples from Hotel and Legal Services

You can do basic yield calculations for any capacity constrained service assuming you know the actual capacity, average price charged for different market segments, and maximum price that could be charged. Ideally, yield will approach the number 1, or 100 percent, where:

Yield = Actual revenue/Potential revenue

In this box we describe yield calculations for two simple examples—a 200-room hotel and a lawyer with a 40-hour work week—under different assumed pricing and usage situations. Although companies use much more complex mathematical models to determine yield, the underlying ideas are the same. The goal is to maximize the revenue-generating capability of the organization's capacity.

200-ROOM HOTEL WITH MAXIMUM ROOM RATE OF $100 PER ROOM PER NIGHT

Potential revenue = $100 × 200 rooms = $20,000 per night

1. Assume: the hotel rents all its rooms at a discounted rate of $50 per night.

   Yield = $50 × 200 rooms/$20,000 = 50%

   At this rate, the hotel is maximizing capacity utilization, but not getting a very good price.

2. Assume: the hotel charges its full rate, but can only rent 40 percent of its rooms at that price, due to price sensitivity.

   Yield = $100 × 80 rooms/$20,000 = 40%

   In this situation the hotel has maximized the per-room price, but the yield is even lower than in the first situation because so few rooms were rented at that relatively high rate.

3. Assume: the hotel charges its full rate of $100 for 40 percent of its rooms and then gives a discount of $50 for the remaining 120 rooms.

Yield = [($100 × 80) + ($50 × 120)]/$20,000 = $14,000/$20,000 = 70%

Clearly, the final alternative, which takes into account price-sensitivity and charges different prices for different rooms or market segments, will result in the highest yield.

40 HOURS OF A LAWYER'S TIME ACROSS A TYPICAL WORK WEEK AT $200 PER HOUR MAXIMUM (PRIVATE CLIENT RATE)

Potential revenue = 40 hours × $200 per hour = $8,000 per week

1. Assume: the lawyer is able to bill out 30 percent of her billable time at $200 per hour.

   Yield = $200 × 12 hours/$8,000 = 30%

   In this case the lawyer has maximized her hourly rate, but has only enough work to occupy 12 billable hours.

2. Assume: the lawyer decides to charge $100 for nonprofit or government clients and is able to bill out all 40 hours at this rate for these types of clients.

   Yield = $100 × 40 hours/$8,000 = 50%

   In this case, although she has worked a full week, yield is still not very good given the relatively low rate per hour.

3. Assume: the lawyer uses a combined strategy in which she works 12 hours for private clients and fills the rest of her time with nonprofit clients at $100 per hour.

   Yield = [($200 × 12) + ($100 × 28)]/$8,000 = $5,200/$8,000 5 65%

   Again, catering to two different market segments with different price-sensitivities, is the best overall strategy in terms of maximizing revenue-generating capacity of the lawyer's time.

Implementing a Yield Management System

Our Technology Spotlight illustrates several examples of how information technology supports effective yield management applications. To implement a yield management system, an organization needs detailed data on past demand patterns by market segment as well as methods of projecting current market demand. The data can be combined through mathematical programming models, threshold analysis, or use of expert systems to project the best allocation of limited capacity at a particular point in time.[13]

Technology Spotlight

Information and Technology Drive Yield Management Systems

Yield management is not a new concept. In fact, the basic idea behind yield management—achieving maximum profits through the most effective use of capacity—has been around forever. It is easy to find examples of capacity-constrained businesses using price to shift demand: theatres that charge different prices for matinees vs. evening performances, inter-city trains with different prices on weekdays than on weekends, ski resorts with cheaper prices for night skiing, and restaurants with "twilight" dinner specials. All these strategies illustrate attempts to smooth the peaks and valleys of demand using price as the primary motivator.

The difference in these basic pricing strategies and more sophisticated yield management approaches currently in use by airlines, car rental companies, hotels, shippers, and others is the reliance of these latter strategies on massive databases, sophisticated mathematical algorithms, and complex analyses. These forms of yield management consider not only price but also market segments, price-sensitivity among segments, timing of demand, and potential profitability of customer segments—all simultaneously. What makes new forms of yield management possible are the technology and systems underlying them. Here we provide a few examples of what some companies and industries have done.

AUSTRIAN AIRLINES

Austrian Airlines (www.uau.com) has been one of the most consistently profitable airlines in Europe. Prior to deregulation of airlines in Europe, Austrian foresaw the need to develop a competitive advantage that would carry it into the deregulated future. The airline invested in a revenue management computer system to build a two-year historical database of booking data that would monitor flights up to 250 days into the future. Using the system, Austrian saw significant improvements in both number of passengers carried and revenue. By being more selective in its discounting practices than were its competitors, Austrian achieved excellent results.

Source: Courtesy of Marriott International Inc.

MARRIOTT HOTELS

The hotel industry has also embraced the concepts of yield management, and Marriott Hotels (www.marriott.com) has been a leader. The systems at Marriott, for example, maximize profits for a hotel across full weeks rather than by day. In their hotels that target business travellers, Marriott has peak days during the middle of the week. Rather than simply sell the hotel out on those nights on a first-come, first-served basis with no discounts, the revenue management system (which is reviewed and revised daily) now projects guest demand both by price and length of stay, providing discounts in some cases to guests who will stay longer, even on a peak demand night. One early test of the system was at the Munich Marriott during Oktoberfest. Typically no discounts would be offered during this peak period. However, the yield management system recommended that the hotel offer some rooms at a discount, but only for those guests who stayed an extended period before or after the peak days. Although the average daily rate was down 11.7 percent for the period, occupancy was up over 20 percent, and overall revenues were up 12.3 percent. Using yield management practices, Marriott Hotels estimates an additional $400 million per year in revenue.

YELLOW TRANSPORTATION

Pricing in the freight industry still seems to be stuck in a regulated mindset in which cost issues dominate, and discounts from class rates are determined by complex formulas. However, companies such as Yellow Transportation (www.myyellow.com, a subsidiary of YRC Worldwide Inc.) are moving toward market-driven models that price services consistently with the value

continued

Technology Spotlight

Information and Technology Drive Yield Management Systems—continued

as perceived by the customer. New pricing structures recognize the customers' and freight providers' desires for simplification, while combining this with sophisticated use of yield management models that take into account the most profitable use of resources. Yield management systems encourage more-rational scheduling of trucks and drivers by considering such subtle factors as equipment type and the skills of a particular driver.

Source: Courtesy of YRC Worldwide.

The systems can match hundreds of drivers with loads in fractions of seconds to make the best dispatch and driver decisions. By analyzing its services, prices, and demand patterns in this way, Yellow has been able to project the success of its Exact Express service, which targets customers who recognize the value of guaranteed, time-definite delivery.

Sources: R. G. Cross, *Revenue Management* (New York: Broadway Books, 1997); N. Templin, "Your Room Costs $250 . . . No! $200 . . . No," *The Wall Street Journal*, May 5, 1999, p. B1; H. Richardson, "Simplify! Simplify! Simplify!," *Transportation and Distribution* 39 (October 1998), pp. 111–17; and C. Salter "On the Road Again," *Fast Company*, January 2002, pp. 50–58.

Allocations of capacity for specific market segments can then be communicated to reservations staff as targets for selling rooms, seats, time, or other limited resources. Sometimes the allocations, once determined, remain fixed. At other times allocations change weekly, or even daily or hourly, in response to new information.

Recent research indicates that traditional yield management approaches are most profitable when (1) a service provider faces different market segments or customers, who arrive or make their reservations at different times and (2) customers who arrive or reserve early are more price-sensitive than those who arrive or reserve late.[14] These criteria exactly fit the situation for airlines and many hotels—industries that have effectively and extensively used yield management techniques to allocate capacity. In other services (entertainment, sports, fashion), those customers willing to pay the higher prices are the ones who buy early rather than late. People who really want to see a particular performance reserve their seats at the earliest possible moment. Discounting for early purchases would reduce profits. In these situations, the price generally starts out high and is reduced later to fill capacity if needed.

Interestingly, some airlines now use both these strategies effectively. They start with discounted seats for customers who are willing to buy early, usually leisure and discretionary travellers. They charge a higher fare for those who want a seat at the last minute, typically the less price-sensitive business travellers whose destinations and schedules are inflexible. However, in some cases a bargain fare can be found at the last minute as well, commonly via Internet sales, to fill seats that would otherwise go unoccupied. Online auctions and services offered by companies like Internet-based Priceline.com serve a purpose in filling capacity at the last minute, often charging much lower fares. (See the Technology Spotlight in Chapter 17 for examples of dynamic pricing via the Internet.)

Challenges and Risks in Using Yield Management

Yield management programs can significantly improve revenues. However, although yield management may appear to be an ideal solution to the problem of matching supply and demand, it is not without risks. By becoming focused on maximizing financial returns through differential capacity allocation and pricing, an organization may encounter these problems:[15]

- *Loss of competitive focus.* Yield management may cause a firm to overfocus on profit maximization and inadvertently neglect aspects of the service that provide long-term competitive success.

- *Customer alienation.* If customers learn that they are paying a higher price for service than someone else, they may perceive the pricing as unfair, particularly if they do not understand the reasons. However, a study done in the restaurant industry found that when customers were informed of different prices being charged by time of day, week, or table location, they generally felt the practice was fair, particularly if the price difference was framed as a discount for less desirable times rather than a premium for peak times or table locations.[16] Customer education is thus essential in an effective yield management program. Customers can be further alienated if they fall victim (and are not compensated adequately) to overbooking practices that are often necessary to make yield management systems work effectively.

- *Employee morale problems.* Yield management systems take much guesswork and judgment in setting prices away from sales and reservations people. Although some employees may appreciate the guidance, others may resent the rules and restrictions on their own discretion.

- *Incompatible incentive and reward systems.* Employees may resent yield management systems that do not match incentive structures. For example, many managers are rewarded on the basis of capacity utilization *or* average rate charged, whereas yield management balances the two factors.

- *Lack of employee training.* Extensive training is required to make a yield management system work. Employees need to understand its purpose, how it works, how they should make decisions, and how the system will affect their jobs.

- *Inappropriate organization of the yield management function.* To be most effective with yield management, an organization must have centralized reservations. Although airlines and some large hotel chains and shipping companies do have such centralization, smaller organizations may have decentralized reservations systems and thus find it difficult to operate a yield management system effectively.

➤ WAITING LINE STRATEGIES: WHEN DEMAND AND CAPACITY CANNOT BE MATCHED

Sometimes it is not possible to manage capacity to match demand, or vice versa. It may be too costly—for example, most health clinics would not find it economically feasible to add additional facilities or physicians to handle peaks in demand during the winter flu season; patients usually simply have to wait to be seen. Sometimes

FIGURE 15.6

Waiting is common
in many service
industries.

Source: Photodisc Green/Getty
Images.

waits may occur when demand backs up because of the variability in length of time for service. For example, even though patients are scheduled by appointments in a physician's office, frequently there is a wait because some patients take longer to serve than the time allotted to them. According to many sources, the misalignment in capacity and demand has reached crisis proportions in the emergency health care context, as is described in Exhibit 15.2.

For most service organizations, waiting customers are a fact of life at some point (see Figure 15.6). Waiting can occur on the telephone (customers put on hold when they call in to ask for information, order something, or make a complaint) and in person (customers waiting in line at the bank, post office, Disneyland, or a physician's office).

In today's fast-paced society, waiting is not something most people tolerate well. As people work longer hours, as individuals have less leisure, and as families have fewer hours together, the pressure on people's time is greater than ever. In this environment, customers are looking for efficient, quick service with no wait. Organizations that make customers wait take the chance that they will lose business or at the very least that customers will be dissatisfied.[17] To deal effectively with the inevitability of waits, organizations can utilize a variety of strategies, described next.

Employ Operational Logic

If customer waits are common, a first step is to analyze the operational processes to remove any inefficiencies. It may be possible to redesign the system to move customers along more quickly.

In introducing its express check-in, Marriott Hotels used an operations-based modification to eliminate much of the waiting previously experienced by its guests. Guests who use a credit card and preregister can avoid waiting in line at the hotel front desk altogether. The guest can make it from the curb outside the hotel to his or her room in as little as three minutes when escorted by a "guest service associate" who checks the

Overflow in the ER: How to Manage Capacity Constraints and Excess Demand in Hospital Emergency Departments

Nowhere is there a more vivid example of demand and capacity issues than in hospital emergency departments (EDs). (*Emergency department* is the preferred term within the medical community for what has traditionally been called the ER.) In a typical ED, rooms are filled, the corridors may be clogged with waiting patients, wait time may be anywhere from 15 minutes to 8 or 10 hours, and ambulances are routinely turned away to seek other hospitals on what is called "reroute" or "diversion." Many experts have referred to these issues as a national crisis in health care. The emergency department is the front door of hospitals and is also the treatment of last resort for many. Why has this overcrowding issue reached national proportions? Many factors come into play, including increased demand and severe capacity constraints.

INCREASED DEMAND FOR SERVICES

Emergency departments are to some extent victims of their own success. Decades of public health campaigns urging people to call 911 in case of medical emergency have been successful in educating people to do just that—and they end up in the ED. Many do indeed have life-threatening emergencies that belong in the ED. Others waiting in the ED are without a family doctor; the ED is their only option, and legally the ED must care for them. Also crowding EDs are patients who cannot get appointments with their doctors in a timely manner, or who learn that it may be their fastest entry into a hospital bed. Patients and their doctors are becoming aware that they can get sophisticated care in the ED relatively quickly. Thus the demand for ED services has increased.

CAPACITY CONSTRAINTS

It is not just an increase in demand that is causing the overcrowding. It is also a shrinkage or unavailability of critical capacity at the same time. Doctors are overbooked in private practices, so patients who don't want to wait turn to the ED. Also, a shortage of specialists who are willing to take patients on call from the ED results in increased waiting times because these patients waiting for specialized care occupy beds in the ED longer than necessary. Another very critical capacity constraint is the number of beds in hospitals. Over the years many hospitals across the country have, for financial reasons, reduced the number of beds available. So ED patients often cannot get beds right away even if they need one, again increasing waiting time for themselves and others. There is a shortage of nurses as well and staffing shortages in housekeeping play a role. A bed may be empty, but until it is cleaned and remade, it

is not available for a waiting patient. In some communities, patients may find that emergency room facilities are simply not available. Some hospitals have actually closed their emergency departments after determining that it is unprofitable to run them at current reimbursement rates. In other areas, population growth is outpacing hospital and ED construction.

To address this complex set of issues, a few changes are being made or considered.

Technology and Systems Improvements

A partial solution is to turn to technology to smooth the process of admitting patients into the ED and to track the availability of hospital beds. Some Web-based systems are used to reroute ambulances to hospitals that have capacity. Other systems help EDs track the availability of rooms in their own hospitals in terms of knowing exactly when a bed is vacant and when it has been cleaned and is available—similar to what hotels have done for decades. Wireless systems for registering patients at bedside and "radar screens" that track everything going on in the ED are other partial solutions. These screens can track patients, staff, carts, and equipment, making the service delivery process more efficient and quicker.

Other hospitals have segmented their patients and have developed parallel "fast track" processes for dealing with minor emergency patients that can account for 30 to 50 percent of total visits. This process can be separated from the major-emergency situations that may require more time and special equipment. Quicker admitting processes, sometimes done on wireless devices, are also being implemented. Instead of having a patient fill out long forms with detailed questions, the quicker process asks just three to four questions initially, saving the longer admitting forms for after treatment.

Yet another innovation is to have staff administer routine tests while the patient is waiting so that the doctor who finally sees the patient has information at hand. This solution also satisfies the patient's need for "something to happen" during the waiting time. Giving patients pagers so they can do something else while waiting is another way that EDs are helping patients cope with the long waits.

Increasing Capacity

Another set of partial solutions relates directly to hospital and staff capacity issues. Some hospitals have already begun adding rooms and other facilities. More urgent care centres are being built to take some of the pressure off EDs. For patients who need to be admitted to the

continued

hospital, however, increasing capacity is not a total solution. The nursing and doctor shortage, one of the most critical problems, is very difficult to solve.

It is obvious that this classic dilemma of matching supply and demand in a service context has multiple, deeply rooted causes when examined in the context of emergency care. The solutions to the issues are also multifaceted—some can be undertaken by individual hospitals, whereas others need to be addressed by the entire health care industry. Some,

however, are societal issues with only long-term solutions. Yet all these issues play out daily in the very immediate environment of hospital emergency departments.

Sources: L. Landro, "ERs Now Turn to Technology to Help Deal with Overcapacity," *The Wall Street Journal,* July 13, 2001, p. B1; J.-Snyder, "Curing the ER," *The Arizona Republic,* December 9, 2001, p. D1+; N. Shute and M. B. Marcus, "Crisis in the ER," *US News & World Report,* September 10, 2001.

guest into the hotel, picks up keys and paperwork from a rack in the lobby, and then escorts the guest directly to the room.[18]

When queues are inevitable, the organization faces the operational decision of what kind of queuing system to use, or how to configure the queue. Queue configuration refers to the number of queues, their locations, their spatial requirement, and their effect on customer behaviour.[19] Several possibilities exist, as shown in Figure 15.7. In the multiple-queue alternative, the customer arrives at the service facility and must decide which queue to join and whether to switch later if the wait appears to be shorter in another line. In the single-queue alternative, fairness of waiting time is ensured in that the first-come, first-served rule applies to everyone; the system can also reduce the average time customers spend waiting overall. However, customers may leave if they perceive that the line is too long or if they have no opportunity to select a particular service provider. The last option shown in Figure 15.7 is the take-a-number option in which arriving customers take a number to indicate line position. Advantages are similar to the single-queue alternative with the additional benefit that customers are able to mill about, browse, and talk to each other. The disadvantage is that customers must be on the alert to hear their numbers when they are called. Recent research suggests that length of the

FIGURE 15.7

Waiting-Line Configurations

Source: J. A. Fitzsimmons and M. J. Fitzsimmons, *Service Management,* 4th ed. (New York: Irwin/McGraw-Hill, 2004), ch. 11, p. 296. © 2004 by The McGraw-Hill Companies, Inc. Reprinted by permission of The McGraw-Hill Companies.

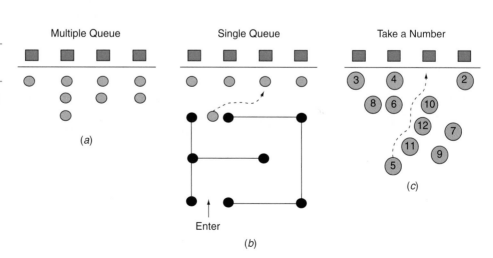

queue and perceived cost of waiting are not the only influences on customers' likelihood of staying in line. In a series of experiments and field tests, researchers showed that the larger the number of customers waiting in line *behind* a consumer, the more likely that consumer is to stay in line and wait for the service.[20]

Many service businesses have become experts at handling queues effectively in terms of minimizing customer dissatisfaction. Some of the benchmarks include Disney, Marriott, and FedEx.

Establish a Reservation Process

When waiting cannot be avoided, a reservation system can help to spread demand. Restaurants, transportation companies, theatres, physicians, and many other service providers use reservation systems to alleviate long waits. The idea behind a reservation system is to guarantee that the service will be available when the customer arrives. Beyond simply reducing waiting time, a reservation system has the added benefit of potentially shifting demand to less desirable time periods. A challenge inherent in reservation systems, however, is what to do about "no-shows." Inevitably there will be customers who reserve a time but do not show up. Some organizations deal with this problem by overbooking their service capacity on the basis of past records of no-show percentages. If the predictions are accurate, overbooking is a good solution. When predictions are inaccurate, however, customers may still have to wait and sometimes may not be served at all, as when airlines overbook the number of seats available on a flight. Victims of overbooking may be compensated for their inconvenience in such cases. To minimize the no-show problem, some organizations (such as hotels, airlines, conferences/training programs, and theatres) charge customers who fail to show up or cancel their reservations within a certain time frame. While overbooking is an intentional strategy for many airlines, WestJet is taking a different approach (see Figure 15.8). By *not* overbooking, they hope to increase average load levels by attracting passengers who don't want to be unpleasantly surprised.

Differentiate Waiting Customers

Not all customers necessarily need to wait the same length of time for service. On the basis of need or customer priority, some organizations differentiate among customers, allowing some to experience shorter waits for service than others. Known as "queue discipline," such differentiation reflects management policies regarding whom to select next for service.[21] The most popular discipline is first-come, first-served.

FIGURE 15.8   WestJet promises not to overbook its flights.

However, other rules may apply. Differentiation can be based on factors such as the following:[22]

- *Importance of the customer.* Frequent customers or customers who spend large amounts with the organization can be given priority in service by providing them with a special waiting area or segregated lines.

- *Urgency of the job.* Those customers with the most urgent need may be served first. This strategy is used in emergency health care. It is also used by maintenance services such as air-conditioning repair that give priority to customers whose air conditioning is not functioning over those who call for routine maintenance.

- *Duration of the service transaction.* In many situations, shorter-service jobs get priority through "express lanes." At other times, when a service provider sees that a transaction is going to require extra time, the customer is referred to a designated provider who deals only with these special-needs customers.

- *Payment of a premium price.* Customers who pay extra (e.g., first class on an airline) are often given priority via separate check-in lines or express systems.

Make Waiting Fun, or at Least Tolerable

Even when they have to wait, customers can be more or less satisfied depending on how the wait is handled by the organization. Of course the actual length of the wait will affect how customers feel about their service experience. But it is not just the actual time spent waiting that has an impact on customer satisfaction—it is how customers feel about the wait and their perceptions during it. The type of wait (e.g., a standard queue versus a wait due to a delay of service) can also influence how customers will react.[23] In a classic article entitled "The Psychology of Waiting Lines," David Maister proposes several principles about waiting, each of which has implications for how organizations can make waiting more pleasurable or at least tolerable.[24]

Unoccupied Time Feels Longer Than Occupied Time

When customers are unoccupied they will likely be bored and will notice the passage of time more than when they have something to do. Providing something for waiting customers to do, particularly if the activity offers a benefit in and of itself or is related in some way to the service, can improve the customer's experience and may benefit the organization as well.[25] Examples include giving customers menus to look at while waiting in a restaurant, providing interesting information to read in a dentist's office, or playing entertaining programs over the phone while customers are on hold. At Macy's in New York, children waiting to see Santa Claus wind their way through displays of dancing teddy bears, elves, and electric trains that become part of the total service adventure.[26]

Preprocess Waits Feel Longer Than In-Process Waits

If wait time is occupied with activities that relate to the upcoming service, customers may perceive that the service has started and they are no longer actually waiting. This in-process activity will make the length of the wait seem shorter and will also benefit the service provider by making the customer better prepared when the service actually does begin. Filling out medical information while waiting to see the physician, reading a menu while waiting to be seated in a restaurant, and watching a videotape of the upcoming service event are all activities that can both educate the customer and reduce perceptions of waiting.

Research in a restaurant context found that customers reacted less negatively to in-process waits than to either preprocess or postprocess waits.[27] Other researchers have found the same for waits due to routine slowness of the process. However, if the wait is due to a service failure, then the in-process wait is viewed more negatively than the preprocess wait.[28] Thus, how customers perceive preprocess, in-process, and postprocess waits may depend to some extent on the cause of the wait.

Anxiety Makes Waits Seem Longer

When customers fear that they have been forgotten or do not know how long they will have to wait, they become anxious, and this anxiety can increase the negative impact of waiting. Anxiety also results when customers are forced to choose in a multiple-line situation and they discover they have chosen the "wrong line." To combat waiting-line anxiety, organizations can provide information on the length of the wait. At its theme parks, Disney uses signs at intervals along the line that let customers know how long the wait will be from that point on. Using a single line also alleviates customer anxiety over having chosen the wrong line. Explanations and reassurances that no one has forgotten them alleviate customer anxiety by taking away their cause for worry.

Uncertain Waits Are Longer Than Known, Finite Waits

Anxiety is intensified when customers do not know how long they will have to wait. Health care providers combat this problem by letting customers know when they check in how far behind the physician is that day. Some patients resolve this uncertainty themselves by calling ahead to ask. Maister provides an interesting example of the role of uncertainty, which he terms the "appointment syndrome." Customers who arrive early for an appointment will wait patiently until the scheduled time, even if they arrive very early. However, once the expected appointment time has passed, customers grow increasingly anxious. Before the appointment time the wait time is known; after that, the length of the wait is not known.

Research in an airline context has suggested that as uncertainty about the wait increases, customers become more angry, and their anger in turn results in greater dissatisfaction.[29] Research also shows that giving customers information on the length of the anticipated wait and/or their relative position in the queue can result in more positive feelings and acceptance of the wait and ultimately more positive evaluation of the service.[30]

Unexplained Waits Are Longer Than Explained Waits

When people understand the causes for waiting, they frequently have greater patience and are less anxious, particularly when the wait is justifiable. An explanation can reduce customer uncertainty and may help customers estimate how long they will be delayed. Customers who do not know the reason for a wait begin to feel powerless and irritated.

Unfair Waits Are Longer Than Equitable Waits

When customers perceive that they are waiting while others who arrived after them have already been served, the apparent inequity will make the wait seem even longer. This situation can easily occur when there is no apparent order in the waiting area and many customers are trying to be served. Queuing systems that work on a first-come, first-served rule are best at combating perceived unfairness. However, other approaches may be required to determine who will be served next. For example, in an emergency medical care situation, the most seriously ill or injured patients would be seen first. When customers understand the priorities and the rules are clearly communicated and enforced, fairness of waiting time should not be an issue.

The More Valuable the Service, the Longer the Customer Will Wait

Customers who have substantial purchases or who are waiting for a high-value service will be more tolerant of long wait times and may even expect to wait longer. For example, in a supermarket, customers who have a full cart of groceries will generally wait longer than customers who have only a few items and expect to be checked through quickly. And diners expect to wait longer for service in an expensive restaurant than they do when eating at a "greasy spoon."

Solo Waits Feel Longer Than Group Waits

People will wait longer when they are in a group than when they are alone because of the distractions provided by other members of the group. People also feel comfort in waiting with a group rather than alone.[31] In some group waiting situations, such as at Disneyland or when patrons are waiting in long lines to purchase concert tickets, customers who are strangers begin to talk to each other and the waiting experience can actually become fun and a part of the total service experience.

SUMMARY

Because service organizations lack the ability to inventory their products, the effective use of capacity can be critical to success. Idle capacity in the form of unused time, labour, facilities, or equipment represents a direct drain on bottom-line profitability. When the capacity represents a major investment (e.g., airplanes, expensive medical imaging equipment, or lawyers and physicians paid on a salary), the losses associated with underuse of capacity are even more accentuated. Overused capacity is also a problem. People, facilities, and equipment can become worn out over time when used beyond optimum capacity constraints. People can quit, facilities become run down, and equipment can break. From the customer's perspective, service quality also deteriorates. Organizations focused on delivering quality service, therefore, have a natural drive to balance capacity utilization and demand at an optimum level in order to meet customer expectations.

This chapter has provided you with an understanding of the underlying issues of managing supply and demand in capacity-constrained services by exploring the lack of inventory capability, the nature of service constraints (time, labour, equipment, facilities), the differences in optimal versus maximum use of capacity, and the causes of fluctuating demand.

Based on grounding in the fundamental issues, the chapter presented a variety of strategies for matching supply and demand. The basic strategies fall under two headings: *demand strategies* (shifting demand to match capacity) and *supply strategies* (adjusting capacity to meet demand). Demand strategies seek to flatten the peaks and valleys of demand to match the flat capacity constraint, whereas supply strategies seek to align, flex, or stretch capacity to match the peaks and valleys of demand. Organizations frequently employ several strategies simultaneously to solve the complex problem of balancing supply and demand.

Yield management was presented as a sophisticated form of supply and demand management that balances capacity utilization, pricing, market segmentation, and financial return. This strategy, long practised by the passenger airline industry, is growing in use by hotel, shipping, car rental, and other capacity-constrained industries in which bookings are made in advance. Essentially, yield management allows organizations to decide on a monthly, weekly, daily, or even hourly basis to whom they want to sell their service capacity at what price.

All strategies for aligning capacity and demand need to be approached with caution. Any one of them is likely to imply changes in multiple marketing mix elements to support the strategy. Such changes, even if done well, carry a risk that the firm will lose focus or inadvertently alter its image in pursuit of increased revenues. Although a different focus or image is not necessarily bad, the potential strategic impact on the total organization should be considered.

In the last section of the chapter, we discussed situations in which it is not possible to align supply and demand. In these unresolved capacity utilization situations, the inevitable result is customer waiting. We described strategies for effectively managing waiting lines, such as employing operational logic, establishing a reservation process, differentiating waiting customers, and making waiting fun or at least tolerable.

Discussion Questions

1. Why do service organizations lack the capability to inventory their services? Compare a car repair and maintenance service with an automobile manufacturer/dealer in terms of inventory capability.

2. Discuss the four scenarios illustrated in Figure 15.1 and presented in the text (excess demand, demand exceeds optimum capacity, demand and supply are balanced, excess capacity) in the context of a professional basketball team selling seats for its games. What are the challenges for management under each scenario?

3. Discuss the four common types of constraints (time, labour, equipment, facilities) facing service businesses and give an example of each (real or hypothetical).

4. How does optimal capacity utilization differ from maximum capacity utilization? Give an example of a situation in which the two might be the same and one in which they are different.

5. Choose a local restaurant or some other type of service with fluctuating demand. What is the likely underlying pattern of demand? What causes the pattern? Is it predictable or random?

6. Describe the two basic strategies for matching supply and demand, and give at least two specific examples of each.

7. What is yield management? Discuss the risks in adopting a yield management strategy.

8. How might yield management apply in the management of the following: a Broadway theatre? A consulting firm? A commuter train?

9. Describe the four basic waiting-line strategies, and give an example of each, preferably based on your own experiences as a consumer.

Exercises

1. Choose a local service organization that is challenged by fixed capacity and fluctuating demand. Interview the marketing manager (or other knowledgeable person) to learn (*a*) in what ways capacity is constrained, (*b*) the basic patterns of

demand, and (*c*) strategies the organization has used to align supply and demand. Write up the answers to these questions, and make your own recommendations regarding other strategies the organization might use.

2. Assume you manage a winter ski resort in Banff or Colorado. *(a)* Explain the underlying pattern of demand fluctuation that is likely to occur at your resort and the challenges it would present to you as a manager. Is the pattern of demand predictable or random? (*b*) Explain and give examples of how you might use both demand-oriented and supply-oriented strategies to smooth the peaks and valleys of demand during peak and slow periods.

3. Choose a local organization in which people have to wait in line for service. Design a waiting-line strategy for the organization.

4. Visit the website of Wells Fargo Bank (www.wellsfargo.com), a leader in online banking. What online services does the bank currently offer? How do these online services help Wells Fargo manage the peaks and valleys of customer demand? How do its strategies to use more ATMs, in-store bank branches, and other, alternative delivery strategies complement the online strategies?

Notes

1 www.deltahotels.com, accessed October 2, 2006.

2. "Toronto's Key Industry Clusters: Tourism," Toronto.ca, www.toronto.ca/economic_profile/tourism.htm, accessed October 2, 2006.

3. J. S. Hirsch, "Vacationing Families Head Downtown to Welcoming Arms of Business Hotels," *The Wall Street Journal,* June 13, 1994, p. B1.

4. Ibid.

5. C. Lovelock, "Getting the Most out of Your Productive Capacity," *Product Plus* (Boston: McGraw-Hill, 1994), ch. 16.

6. C. H. Lovelock, "Classifying Services to Gain Strategic Marketing Insights," *Journal of Marketing* 47 (Summer 1983), pp. 9–20.

7. Portions of this section are based on C. H. Lovelock, "Strategies for Managing Capacity-Constrained Service Organizations," in *Managing Services: Marketing, Operations, and Human Resources,* 2nd ed. (Englewood Cliffs, NJ: Prentice Hall, 1992), pp. 154–68.

8. E. C. Clemmer and B. Schneider, "Toward Understanding and Controlling Customer Dissatisfaction with Waiting During Peak Demand Times," in *Designing a Winning Service Strategy,* ed. M. J. Bitner and L. A. Crosby (Chicago: American Marketing Association, 1989), pp. 87–91.

9. Lovelock, "Getting the Most out of Your Productive Capacity."

10. M. E. Berge and C. A. Hopperstad, "Demand Driven Dispatch: A Method for Dynamic Aircraft Capacity Assignment, Models, and Algorithms," *Operations Research* 41 (January/February 1993), pp. 153–68.

11. Lovelock, "Getting the Most out of Your Productive Capacity."

12. See S. E. Kimes, "Yield Management: A Tool for Capacity-Constrained Service Firms," *Journal of Operations Management* 8 (October 1989), pp. 348–63; S. E. Kimes and R. B. Chase, "The Strategic Levers of Yield Management," *Journal of Service Research* 1 (November 1998), pp. 156–66; S. E. Kimes, "Revenue Management: A Retrospective," *Cornell Hotel and Restaurant Administration Quarterly* 44, no. 5/6 (2003), pp. 131–38.

13. Kimes, "Yield Management."

14. R. Desiraji and S. M. Shugan, "Strategic Service Pricing and Yield Management," *Journal of Marketing* 63 (January 1999), pp. 44–56.

15. Kimes, "Yield Management."

16. S. E. Kimes and J. Wirtz, "Has Revenue Management Become Acceptable? Findings from an International Study on the Perceived Fairness of Rate Fences," *Journal of Service Research* 6 (November 2003), pp. 125–35.

17. For research supporting the relationship between longer waits and decreased satisfaction, quality evaluations, and patronage intentions see Clemmer and Schneider, "Toward Understanding and Controlling Customer Dissatisfaction"; A. Th. H. Pruyn and A. Smidts, "Customer Evaluation of Queues: Three Exploratory Studies," *European Advances in Consumer Research* 1 (1993), pp. 371–82; S. Taylor, "Waiting for Service: The Relationship Between Delays and Evaluations of Service," *Journal of Marketing* 58 (April 1994), pp. 56–69; K. L. Katz, B. M. Larson, and R. C. Larson, "Prescription for the Waiting-in-Line Blues: Entertain, Enlighten, and Engage," *Sloan Management Review,* Winter 1991, pp. 44–53; S. Taylor and J. D. Claxton, "Delays and the Dynamics of Service Evaluations," *Journal of the Academy of Marketing Science* 22 (Summer 1994), pp. 254–64; D. Grewal, J. Baker, M. Levy, and G. B. Voss, "The Effects of Wait Expectations and Store Atmosphere on Patronage Intentions in Service-Intensive Retail Stores," *Journal of Retailing* 79 (Winter 2003), pp. 259–68.

18 R. Henkoff, "Finding, Training, and Keeping the Best Service Workers," *Fortune,* October 3, 1994, pp. 110–22.

19. J. A. Fitzsimmons and M. J. Fitzsimmons, *Service Management*, 3rd ed. (New York: Irwin/McGraw-Hill, 2000), ch. 11.

20. R. Zhou and D. Soman, "Looking Back: Exploring the Psychology of Queuing and the Effect of the Number of People Behind," *Journal of Consumer Research* 29 (March 2003), pp. 517–30.

21. Fitzsimmons and Fitzsimmons, *Service Management,* ch. 11.

22. Lovelock, "Getting the Most out of Your Productive Capacity."

23. For an excellent review of the literature on customer perceptions of and reactions to various aspects of waiting time, see S. Taylor and G. Fullerton, "Waiting for Services: Perceptions Management of the Wait Experience," in *Handbook of Services Marketing and Management,* ed. T. A. Swartz and D. Iacobucci (Thousand Oaks, CA: Sage Publications, 2000), pp. 171–89.

24. D. A. Maister, "The Psychology of Waiting Lines," in *The Service Encounter,* ed. J. A. Czepiel, M. R. Solomon, and C. F. Surprenant (Lexington, MA: Lexington Books, 1985), pp. 113–23.

25. S. Taylor, "The Effects of Filled Waiting Time and Service Provider Control over the Delay on Evaluations of Service," *Journal of the Academy of Marketing Science* 23 (Summer 1995), pp. 38–48.

26. A. Bennett, "Their Business Is on the Line," *The Wall Street Journal,* December 7, 1990, p. B1.

27. L. Dube-Rioux, B. H. Schmitt, and F. Leclerc, "Consumers' Reactions to Waiting: When Delays Affect the Perception of Service Quality," in *Advances in Consumer Research,* vol. 16, ed. T. Srull (Provo, UT: Association for Consumer Research, 1988), pp. 59–63.

28. M. K. Hui, M. V. Thakor, and R. Gill, "The Effect of Delay Type and Service Stage on Consumers' Reactions to Waiting," *Journal of Consumer Research* 24 (March 1998), pp. 469–79.

29. Taylor and Fullerton, "Waiting for Services."

30. M. K. Hui and D. K. Tse, "What to Tell Consumers in Waits of Different Lengths: An Integrative Model of Service Evaluation," *Journal of Marketing* 60 (April 1996), pp. 81–90.

31. J. Baker and M. Cameron, "The Effects of the Service Environment on Affect and Consumer Perception of Waiting Time: An Integrative Review and Research Propositions," *Journal of the Academy of Marketing Science* 24 (Fall 1996), pp. 338–49.

PART

6

Managing Service Promises

The fourth Provider Gap, shown in the figure here, illustrates the difference between service delivery and the service provider's external communications. Promises made by a service company through its media advertising, sales force, and other communications can raise customer expectations that serve as the standard against which customers assess service quality. Broken promises can occur for many reasons: ineffective marketing communications, overpromising in advertising or personal selling, inadequate coordination between operations and marketing, and differences in policies and procedures across service outlets.

In service companies, a fit between communications about service and actual service delivery is necessary. Chapter 16 is devoted to the topic of integrated services marketing communications—careful integration and organization of all of a service marketing organization's external and internal communications

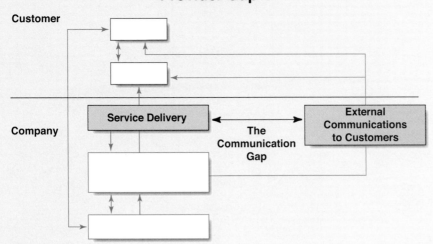

Provider Gap 4

Customer

Company

Service Delivery ←→ External Communications to Customers

The Communication Gap

channels. The chapter describes why this communication is necessary and how companies can do it well. Successful company communications are the responsibility of both marketing and operations: marketing must accurately but persuasively reflect what happens in actual service encounters, and operations must deliver what is promised in advertising. If communications set up unrealistic expectations for customers, the actual encounter will disappoint the customer.

Chapter 17 deals with another issue related to managing promises, the pricing of services. In packaged goods (and even in durable goods), many customers possess enough price knowledge before purchase to be able to judge whether a price is fair or in line with competition. With services, customers often have no internal reference point for prices before purchase and consumption. Techniques for developing prices for services are more complicated than those for pricing tangible goods, and all the approaches for setting prices must be adapted for the special characteristics of services.

In summary, external communications—whether from marketing communications or pricing—can create a larger customer gap by raising expectations about service delivery. In addition to improving service delivery, companies must also manage all communications to customers so that inflated promises do not lead to higher expectations. Companies must also manage the messages conveyed by pricing so that customer expectations are in line with what they perceive that they receive.

Chapter

16

Integrated Services Marketing Communications

Closing Provider Gap 4

THIS CHAPTER'S OBJECTIVES ARE TO

↦ 1. Discuss the key reasons for service communication challenges.

↦ 2. Introduce the concept of integrated service marketing communications.

↦ 3. Present four ways to integrate marketing communications in service organizations.

↦ 4. Present specific strategies for managing promises, managing customer expectations, educating customers, and managing internal communications.

"We Can Explain"—Science World's Integrated Marketing Communications Generate Interest

Think of the last time you visited a museum. Did you consider that experience "fun"? Not likely, though it was probably interesting and worthwhile. Science World, a not-for-profit science museum located in Vancouver, British Columbia, was plagued with just that attitude and sought to change it. Despite having very high awareness, many of Science World's target audiences of 6-to-12-year-olds, their parents, and educators felt it was stodgy and serious. Then, in 2003, advertising agency Rethink stepped in and developed a campaign that changed people's perception and continues to inspire and generate positive results.

The integrated marketing communications strategy that resulted includes some creative outdoor, print, point-of-sale, radio and TV advertisements

Source: Photos care of Science World British Columbia.

with the goal of injecting fun into science. Using the tag line "We can explain," the campaign mentions a variety of little-known science facts to encourage the audience to think about science in an interesting and bizarre way. For example, one TV commercial entitled "Swinger" simply shows a man running wildly around a home furnished in 70s decor swinging a baseball bat and breaking things. The text reads: "The mosquito is the most dangerous animal on earth. We can explain." Another ad on a transit shelter uses black light to illuminate the message "Cat pee glows under black light. We can explain." (More Science World ads can be viewed at its website.)[1]

The Science World website reinforces the message of the campaign. Among other things, it includes information on booking the facility for birthday parties, and has a section where visitors can play science games linked to various exhibits. A video tour of the museum and all the current radio, TV, and out-of-home ads can also be found on the site. Even some of the headlines from Science World's press releases available ("Giant Robot Invades Science World"; "A Toy-tastic Spring Break") communicate the atmosphere of fun.

The organization's sales promotions are linked to its goal of increasing awareness in science and educational activities as well. For instance, in the fall of 2005, membership at Science World also gave members a 10 percent discount at the Greater Vancouver Zoo, and a 20 percent discount at the Vancouver Aquarium Marine Science Centre and the HR MacMillan Space Centre.

Their members' magazine *Currents* also communicates fun and excitement. The Fall 2005 issue is colourful and packed with "Fabulous Factoids," instructions for science activities to try at home, and a variety of features including one about tortoises and another about Vikings, all written in an exciting tone. The question-and-answer presentation of some

topics also serves to reinforce the "Did you know?" feel. Further integrating marketing communications, the magazine also reminds members about the various sales promotions under way and those coming up.

Attendance numbers and the results of attitudinal surveys of members all indicate the success of Science World's integrated communications. In the first year of the campaign, repeat visits increased 10 percent and memberships 20 percent. Member surveys also showed that those becoming members because Science World was "educational and informative" increased 7 percent, and those becoming members because Science World was "fun" increased 15 percent. Attendance continues to climb, with still more members indicating they joined because of the "fun."

A major cause of poorly perceived service is the difference between what a firm promises about a service and what it actually delivers. Customer expectations are shaped by both uncontrollable and company-controlled factors. Although word-of-mouth communication, customer experiences with other service providers, and customer needs are key factors that influence customer expectations, they are rarely controllable by the firm. However, controllable factors such as company advertising, personal selling, and promises made by service personnel also influence customer expectations. In this chapter we focus on these controllable factors. Accurate, coordinated, and appropriate company communication—advertising, personal selling, and online and other messages that do not overpromise or misrepresent—is essential to delivering services that customers perceive as high in quality.

Because company communications about services promise what people do and because what people do cannot be standardized like physical goods produced by machines, the potential for a mismatch between what is communicated and what is delivered (Provider Gap 4) is high. For this reason, whenever Gap 4 is large, it almost always means that Gap 3—the Service Performance Gap—is also large. Ineffective advertising can lead to perceived service failure. By coordinating communication within and outside the organization, companies can minimize the size of Gap 4.

→ THE NEED FOR COORDINATION IN MARKETING COMMUNICATION

Marketing communication is more complex today than it used to be. In the past, customers received marketing information about goods and services from a limited number of sources, usually mass communication sources such as network television and newspapers. With a limited number of sources, marketers could easily convey a uniform brand image and coordinate promises. However, today's consumers of both goods and services receive communications from a far richer variety of advertising vehicles—targeted magazines, websites, direct mail, movie theatre advertising, email solicitation, and a host of sales promotions. Consumers of services receive additional communication from servicescapes, customer service departments, and everyday service encounters with employees. These service interactions add to the variety, volume, and complexity of information that a customer receives. Ensuring that messages from all these company sources are consistent is a major challenge for marketers of services.

Figure 16.1 shows an enhanced version of the services marketing triangle that we presented in Chapter 12, emphasizing that the customer of services is the target of two types of communication. First, external marketing communication includes traditional channels such as advertising, sales promotion, and public relations. Second,

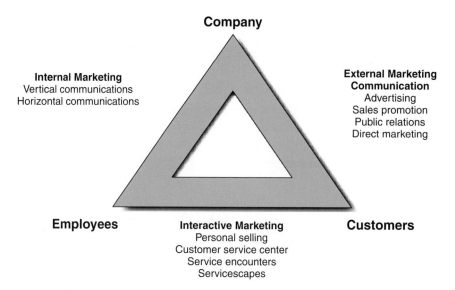

FIGURE 16.1

Communications
and the Services
Marketing Triangle

Source: Philip Kotler,
*Marketing Management:
Analysis, Planning,
Implementation, and Control,*
9th ed., © 1997. Reprinted
by permission of Pearson
Education, Inc., Upper Saddle
River, NJ.

interactive marketing communication involves the messages that employees give to customers through such channels as personal selling, customer service interactions, service encounter interactions, and servicescapes (discussed in Chapter 11). A service company must be sure that these interactive messages are consistent both among themselves and with those sent through external communications. To do so, the third side of the triangle, internal marketing communications, must be managed so that information from the company to employees is accurate, complete, and consistent with what customers are hearing or seeing.

One of Canada's leading grocery chains, Sobeys Canada, recently repositioned its stores to focus more on service, using the tag line "Ready to Serve." In advertisements, cashiers were shown asking customers if they had found everything they were looking for, and when they hadn't the cashier would go and help find it. But with this campaign, Sobeys made explicit and implicit promises that were very difficult for their employees to satisfy. How could the cashiers, many of whom were not even advised of the new campaign, leave the cash register in the middle of scanning an order to go and help a customer find an item? This example indicates that all too often, different parts of the company are responsible for different aspects of communication. The sales department develops and executes sales communication. The marketing department prepares and disseminates advertising. A public relations firm is responsible for publicity. Functional specialists handle sales promotions, direct marketing, and company websites. The human resources department trains front-line employees for service interactions, and still another area is responsible for the customer service department. Rarely is one person responsible for the overall communications strategy in a company, and all too often people responsible for the different communication components do not coordinate their efforts.

Today, however, more companies are adopting the concept of *integrated marketing communications (IMC),* where the company carefully integrates and organizes all of its external communications channels. As a marketing executive explained it,

> Integrated marketing communications build a strong brand identity in the marketplace by tying together and reinforcing all your images and messages. IMC means that all your corporate messages, positioning and images, and identity are coordinated across all venues. It means that your PR materials say the same things as your direct mail campaign, and your advertising has the same "look and feel" as your website.[2]

FIGURE 16.2

Approaches
for Integrating
Services Marketing
Communication

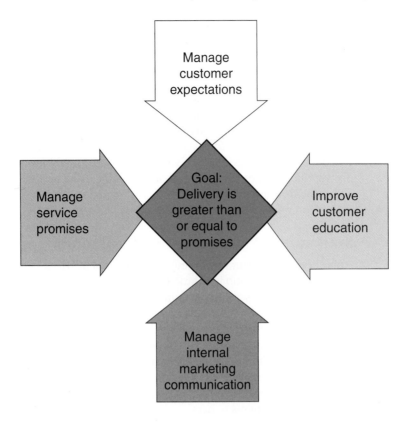

In this chapter we propose that a more complex type of integrated marketing communication is needed for services than for goods. External communications channels must be coordinated, as with physical goods, but both external communications and interactive communication channels must be integrated to create consistent service promises. To do that, internal marketing communications channels must be managed so that employees and the company are in agreement about what is communicated to the customer. As Figure 16.2 shows, this coordination requires both vertical communications—typically called *internal marketing communications*—and horizontal communications across departments and areas of the firm. We call this more complicated version of IMC *integrated services marketing communications (ISMC)*. ISMC requires that everyone involved with communication, and especially everyone in a boundary-spanning role (such as the Sobeys cashiers noted earlier), clearly understand both the company's marketing strategy and its promises to consumers. This is a more complex task than often faces goods manufacturers, and it once again reinforces the notion that effective services marketing requires a cross-functional approach.

KEY REASONS FOR SERVICE COMMUNICATION CHALLENGES

Discrepancies between service delivery and external communications, in the form of exaggerated promises and/or the absence of information about service delivery, can powerfully affect consumer perceptions of service quality. The factors that contribute to these communication problems include (1) inadequate management of service promises, (2) elevated customer expectations, (3) insufficient customer education, and (4) inadequate internal communications. In this chapter, we first describe the challenges stemming from these factors and then detail strategies that firms have found useful in dealing with them.

Inadequate Management of Service Promises

A discrepancy between service delivery and promises occurs when companies fail to manage service promises—the vows made by salespeople, advertising, and service personnel. One of the primary reasons for this discrepancy is that the company lacks the integration needed to make fulfillable promises. Salespeople often sell services without having an exact date of when they will be ready for market. Demand and supply variations make service provision possible at some times, improbable at others, and difficult to predict. The traditional functional structure in many companies also makes communication about promises and delivery difficult.

Inadequate Management of Customer Expectations

Appropriate and accurate communication about services is the responsibility of both marketing and operations. Marketing must accurately (if compellingly) reflect what happens in actual service encounters; operations must deliver what is promised in communications. For example, when a management consulting firm introduces a new offering, the marketing and sales departments must make the offering appealing enough to be viewed as superior to competing services. In promoting and differentiating the service, however, the company cannot afford to raise expectations above the level at which its consultants can consistently perform. If advertising, personal selling, or any other external communication sets up unrealistic expectations, actual encounters will disappoint customers.

Inadequate Customer Education

Differences between service delivery and promises also occur when companies do not sufficiently educate their customers. If customers are unclear about how service will be provided, what their role in delivery involves, and how to evaluate services they have never used before, they will be disappointed. When disappointed, they will often hold the service company, not themselves, responsible. Research by a leading service research firm reveals that one-third of all customer complaints are related to problems caused by customers themselves. These errors or problems in service—even when they are "caused" by the customer—still lead customers to defect. For this reason the firm must assume responsibility for educating customers.

For services high in credence properties—expert services that are difficult for customers to evaluate even after they have received the services—many customers do not know the criteria by which they should judge the service. For high-involvement services, such as long-term medical treatment or purchase of a first home, customers are also unlikely to comprehend and anticipate the service process. First-time home buyers rarely understand the complex set of services (inspection, title services, insurance) and processes (securing a mortgage, offers and counteroffers, escrow) that will be involved in their purchases. Professionals and other providers of high-involvement services often forget that customers are novices who must be educated about each step in the process. They assume that an overview at the beginning of the service will equip the customer. Unfortunately these steps are rarely sufficient, and customers defect because they can neither understand the process nor appreciate the value received from the service.

A final condition under which customer education can be beneficial involves services in which demand and supply are not synchronized, as discussed in Chapter 15. If the customer is not informed about peaks and valleys in demand, service overloads and failures, not to mention underutilized capacity, are likely to result.

Inadequate Internal Marketing Communications

Multiple functions in the organization, such as marketing and operations, must be coordinated to achieve the goal of service provision. Because service advertising and personal selling promise what *people* do, frequent and effective communication across functions—horizontal communication—is critical. If internal communication is poor, perceived service quality is at risk. If company advertising and other promises are developed without input from operations, contact personnel may not be able to deliver service that matches the image portrayed in marketing efforts.

Not all service organizations advertise, but all need coordination or integration across departments to deliver quality service. All need internal communication between the sales force and service providers. Horizontal communication also must occur between the human resource and marketing departments. If marketing and sales personnel who understand customer expectations do not communicate this information to contact employees, the lack of knowledge for these employees will affect the quality of service that they deliver.

A final form of internal coordination central to providing service excellence is consistency in policies across departments and branches. If a service organization operates many outlets under the same name, customers expect similar performance across those outlets. If managers of individual branches or outlets have significant autonomy in policies, customers may not receive the same level of service quality across the branches.

→ FOUR CATEGORIES OF STRATEGIES TO MATCH SERVICE PROMISES WITH DELIVERY

Figure 16.2 shows four categories of strategies to match service delivery with promises: (1) manage service promises, (2) manage customer expectations, (3) improve customer education, and (4) manage internal marketing communication. "Managing service promises" involves coordinating the vows made by all external and interactive marketing sources to ensure that they are consistent and feasible. "Managing customer expectations" incorporates strategies that tell customers that the firm cannot or may not always provide the level of service they expect. "Educating customers" means providing customers with information about the service process or evaluative criteria about important aspects of the service. Finally, "managing internal marketing communication" means transmitting information across organizational boundaries—upward, downward, and across—to align all functions with customer expectations. Strategies in each of these categories are discussed in detail in the following sections.

Manage Service Promises

In manufacturing physical goods, the departments that make promises and those that deliver them can operate independently. Goods can be fully designed and produced and then turned over to marketing for promotion and sale. In services, however, the

FIGURE 16.3

Approaches for
Managing Service
Promises

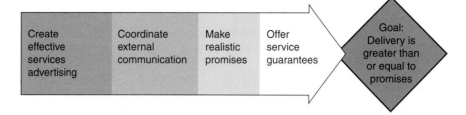

sales and marketing departments make promises about what other employees in the organization will fulfil. Because what employees do cannot be standardized like physical goods produced mechanically, greater coordination and management of promises are required. Successful services advertising and personal selling become the responsibility of both marketing and operations.

Figure 16.3 shows specific strategies that are effective in managing promises.

Create Effective Services Advertising

One of the most critical ways that services promises are communicated is through advertising. Intangibility makes services advertising different from product advertising and difficult for marketers. The *intangible* nature of services creates problems for consumers both before and after purchase. *Before* buying services, consumers have difficulty understanding them and coming up with sets of services to consider.[3] *After* buying services, consumers have trouble evaluating their service experiences. Various authors have suggested strategies to overcome these problems.

- *Use narratives to demonstrate the service experience.* Many services are experiential, and a uniquely effective approach to communicating them involves story-based appeals. Research has concluded that consumers with relatively low familiarity with a service category prefer ads based on stories to ads based on lists of service attributes. Furthermore, the relative advantage of the story is intensified when the novice consumer is in a happy mood rather than a sad one.[4]

- *Present vivid information.* Effective service advertising creates a strong or clear impression on the senses and produces a distinct mental picture. One way to use vivid information is to evoke strong emotion, such as in AT&T's classic "Reach Out and Touch Someone" campaign. Vividness can also be achieved by concrete language and dramatization. The Workers' Compensation Board of Nova Scotia chose a very dramatic approach to increasing awareness about workplace safety among workers under the age of 25. Figure 16.4 shows how they tried to cut through the advertising clutter with a disturbingly vivid dramatization of the risks faced when young workers aren't properly trained (see their website at www. notworthit.ca for more ads and related information about worker safety for young people).

- *Use interactive imagery.* One type of vividness involves what is called *interactive imagery.*[5] Imagery (defined as a mental event that involves the visualization of a concept or relationship) can enhance recall of names and facts about service. Interactive imagery integrates two or more items in some mutual action, resulting in improved recall. Some service organizations effectively integrate their logos or symbols with an expression of what they do. A well-known example is Prudential Financial's rock, whose impression of solidity is meant to carry over to the firm.

FIGURE 16.4

The Workers'
Compensation
Board of Nova
Scotia sought a very
dramatic and vivid
portrayal of the risks
of workplace injury.

Source: Workers'
Compensation Board of Nova
Scotia, 2005.

Two other examples are provided in Figures 16.5 and 16.6. In the United Way ad, note how the "hand" symbolizes some of the many things the organization does. As noted by Yvon Brossard, Vice-President (Creative Group) at Cossette Communication-Marketing, "Such powerful emotion centered on this simple little hand. Advertising as it should always be."[6] A different approach is shown in Figure 16.6. In a themed series of ads, the Certified Management Accountants of Canada highlight their broad range of skills relative to the stereotype of this profession (to see the rest of the campaign on this theme, visit their website at www.cmabranding.com).

FIGURE 16.5   The United Way of Canada effectively uses the symbol of its helping "hand" to illustrate its services in this series of advertisements.

Source: United Way of Lower Mainland. Advertisements created by DDB Canada.

FIGURE 16.6

The CMAs of Canada use interactive imagery in a campaign that stresses their breadth relative to the stereotypical view of accounting.

Source: Reprinted with permission of Certified Management Accountants of Canada (CMA Canada).

• *Focus on the tangibles.*[7] Another way that advertisers can increase the effectiveness of services communications is to feature the tangibles associated with the service, such as showing a bank's marble columns or gold credit card. Showing the tangibles provides clues about the nature and quality of the service. Figure 16.7, which shows an advertisement for Canada's largest online educational institution, Athabasca University in Alberta, is one of many in a campaign that creatively uses the image of a computer mouse and cord. There are few tangibles in education, even fewer in distance education, but the university's use of the mouse is an excellent example of focusing on the tangibles.

FIGURE 16.7

Athabasca University uses a tangible element of its offering as the basis of its advertising approach.

Source: Courtesy of Athabasca University.

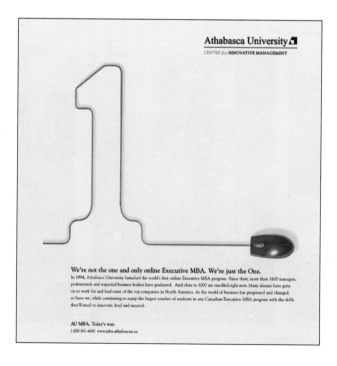

FIGURE 16.8

PetCare Insurance
Brokers use their
association with Don
Cherry to increase
the tangibility of
their service.

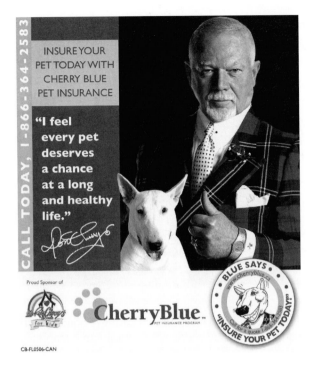

CB-FL0506-CAN

Berry and Clark propose four strategies of tangibilization: association, physical representation, documentation, and visualization.[8] *Association* means linking the service to a tangible person, place, or object. PetCare Insurance Brokers are marketing a new pet insurance program linked to Don Cherry, CBC's colourful hockey commentator. (See Figure 16.8.) The program, called CherryBlue after Cherry's dog, "Blue," has two options: the Red Line, which provides $10,000 in coverage, and the Blue Line, which provides $20,000. Linking the insurance with Don Cherry in this highly customized approach targets pet owners who are also hockey fans and likely to be persuaded by Don Cherry. *Physical representation* means showing tangibles that are directly or indirectly part of the service, such as employees, buildings, or equipment. *Documentation* means featuring objective data and factual information. *Visualization* is a vivid mental picture of a service's benefits or qualities, such as showing people on vacation having fun.

- *Feature service employees in communication.* Customer contact personnel are an important second audience for services advertising.[9] Featuring actual employees doing their jobs or explaining their services in advertising is effective for both the primary audience (customers) and the secondary audience (employees) because it communicates to employees that they are important. Furthermore, when employees who perform a service well are featured in advertising, they become standards for other employees' behaviours. As you know, the vast majority of WestJet's advertisements, many of which have been used as examples already, feature employees. Aliant, one of Canada's smaller telecommunications companies, also recently featured employees, as illustrated in Figure 16.8. Aliant, which recently underwent a nasty strike, are clearly targeting both customers and employees in these ads.

- *Promise what is possible.*[10] Many companies hope to create good service by leading with good advertising, but this strategy can backfire when the actual service does not live up to the promises in advertising. In line with the strategies we discuss in

FIGURE 16.9 Familiprix has generated considerable word of mouth with its TV campaign that ends with the expression, "Ah Ha! Familiprix!"

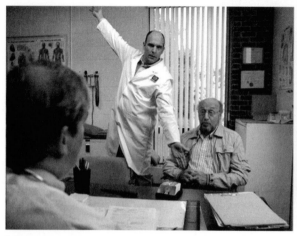 

Source: Courtesy of Familiprix.

the next section, all service communications should promise only what is possible and not attempt to make services more attractive than they actually are.

- *Encourage word-of-mouth communication.* Because services are usually high in experience and credence properties, people frequently turn to others for information rather than to traditional marketing channels. Services advertising and other external messages can generate word-of-mouth communication that extends the investment in paid communication and improves the credibility of the messages. Advertising that generates talk because it is humorous, compelling, or unique can be particularly effective.

  Familiprix, a smaller chain of drugstores in Quebec, has won numerous awards for its innovative TV advertising, which has generated considerable word of mouth according to a case study produced for the CASSIES (a prominent Canadian advertising award show). The advertisements, one of which is provided in storyboard format in Figure 16.9, portray an eccentric pharmacist who is invisible to the hapless people he observes. When the characters suffer a mishap, the pharmacist waves his arms and declares, "Ah Ha! Familiprix!" The campaign achieved significant increases in awareness (from 19% to 37% in the first three weeks it aired); moreover, the expression "Ah Ha! Familiprix" entered common discourse and became used by people who have real-life mishaps similar to those portrayed. (To see more of this word-of-mouth-generating campaign, visit the CASSIES website at www.cassies.ca.)

- *Feature service customers.* One way to generate positive word of mouth is to feature satisfied customers in the communications. Advertising testimonials featuring actual service customers simulate personal communications between people and are thereby a credible way to communicate the benefits of service. A recent award-winning campaign for the United Way (Figure 16.10) provides an excellent illustration of the use of client testimonials. As you can see, it is very believable.

- *Use transformational advertising.*[11] Transformational advertising is image advertising that changes the experience of buying and consuming the product. Most

FIGURE 16.10

The United Way provides an excellent twist on the familiar, and effective, use of client testimonals.

Source: United Way of Greater Toronto.

advertising for vacation destinations is transformational: it invites the consumer to escape into a world that is necessarily subjective and perceptual. This approach involves making the ad vivid or rich in detail, realistic, and rewarding. For examples of very vivid transformational advertising, visit the Gap Adventures website at www.gapadventures.com.

Coordinate External Communication

For any organization, one of the most important yet challenging aspects of managing brand image involves coordinating all the external communication vehicles that send information to customers. These communication vehicles include advertising, websites, sales promotion, public relations, direct marketing, and personal selling.

Advertising is any paid form of nonpersonal presentation and promotion of a company's offerings by an identified sponsor. Because advertising is paid, marketers control the creative appeals, placement, and timing. Internet advertising is becoming a more important and larger portion of companies' advertising budgets (see the Technology Spotlight) and should be synchronized with traditional advertising vehicles. MasterCard's highly successful "Priceless" advertising campaign, which launched in 1997, lists three or four tangible items and their prices followed by a key customer benefit that is "priceless." The campaign is an example of solid synchronization because it is "extraordinarily flexible, and carries a brand message that is not only relevant globally but also adapts well to different media, different payment channels, different markets."[12] The campaign, now seen in 96 countries and 47 languages, has generated strong brand recall and has received many advertising industry awards. You can view some of the numerous TV ads in the "priceless" campaign at MasterCard's website (www.priceless.com/film/nowshowing.html). Every ad in the campaign ends with the slogan (which MasterCard hopes you can finish), "There are some things money can't buy. For everything else, there's ..."

Websites are the company's own online communication to customers. Often a disconnect exists between the look, feel, and content of a company's website and its advertising, usually because different parts of the company (or different advertising

Technology Spotlight

Digital Out-of-Home Advertising

Media fragmentation is making it increasingly difficult to reach target audiences as effectively as in the past. As a result, advertisers are finding new ways of using traditional media to increase interest, excitement, and interactivity. "Out-of-home advertising," which in the past has meant ads that target consumers when they are outside their home, such as billboards, transit ads, or advertisements placed on street furniture, is evolving to incorporate digital technology in the form of video boards.

Customers, marketers, and other parties are embracing this type of advertising. As a Starch Research study conducted in Toronto in December 2005 indicated, more than 80 percent of those polled were aware of the medium, and more than two-thirds viewed it favourably, a majority saying that video boards enliven the areas in which they appear. And, since recall is significantly higher than industry norms when video boards are used and may be more effective given their lower cost, marketers will likely begin relying on this technology more heavily. Interestingly, civic authorities have been developing an interest in it as well.

Perhaps one of the most impressive examples of a video board in Canada is located at Dundas Square in Toronto. In what has been dubbed "Times Square North," screens tower 18 stories above the Eaton Centre entrance and are viewed by upwards of 700,000 people per week.

While interesting examples of the uses and capabilities of such media abound, Tim Hortons (www.timhortons.ca) provides one of the most nationally recognizable.

Before committing to digital video board technology in its stores, Tim Hortons tested only one board at the Dundas Square location. It was used strategically to showcase varying product and price points at different times throughout the day. For instance, video of prepared sandwiches might be broadcast as lunchtime approached, but donuts and coffee might be featured mid-morning. The success of this one board in increasing business for the nearby franchisee resulted in the national rollout of the technology at all stores and drive-thrus. However, while the test results were encouraging, Tim Hortons has no plans to abandon its traditional media. The boards are intended to balance the company's marketing communications strategy by integrating with the current use of television and radio.

The next step in digital out-of-home advertising is to move beyond a soundless video and make the experience truly interactive. Some European companies are using even more innovative technology, replacing posters with holographic imaging. During the promotion for the movie *The Lord of the Rings* in Europe, digital out-of-home ads were played where Gandalf appears and then the message was presented. Nokia pushed the envelope with its downtown Montreal Christmas display, near which people could use their cell phones to change the colour of the lights on a tree. How the more interactive possibilities will play out in the service industry remains to be seen, but it will certainly be interesting to watch.

Source: T. Poulton, "Huge Video Screens Modern Cave Drawings," *Business Edge*, October 27, 2005, www.businessedge.ca/article.cfm/newsID/11007.cfm, accessed October 3, 2006; P. Summerfield, "The Great Outdoor," *Strategy*, April 2006, p. 32.

vendors) are responsible for creating these vehicles. When websites are coordinated in theme, content, and promises—as they are in the Science World advertising in this chapter's opening vignette—a company is better able to match service delivery with promises because the promises themselves are consistent.

Sales promotion includes short-term incentives such as coupons, premiums, discounts, and other activities that stimulate customer purchases and stretch media spending. The fast-food industry, including McDonald's, Burger King, and Wendy's, offers premiums such as action figures that link the chains' offerings to current movies and television shows. A particularly successful joint partnership was the winner of a recent PROMO! Award from the Canadian Association of Promotional Marketing Agencies. AIR MILES partnered with Universal Music to create the Virtual Music Store. AIR MILES collectors could download music from thousands of artists as part of the "AIR MILES Now Means Music" promotion. The Virtual Store received over 400,000 hits with 70,000 redemptions and the campaign ranks as the most successful promotion in AIR MILES history. And of course, no discussion of promotion would be complete without mentioning Canada's most famous, and possibly most successful, sales promotion, Tim Horton's "Rrroll Up the Rim." As iconic as the brand itself, the Rrroll Up the Rim promotion has been running for 20 years and has given away over 150 vehicles since 2001.

Public relations include activities that build a favourable company image with a firm's publics through publicity, relations with the news media, and community events. Richard Branson, founder of Virgin Atlantic Airways (see our Global Feature) is a master at obtaining publicity for his airline. When launching the airline, he claimed, "I knew that the only way of competing with British Airways and the others was to get out there and use myself to promote it."[13] In the years since the airline's launch, his publicity-winning stunts included recording the fastest time across the Atlantic Ocean in a speedboat, flying a hot-air balloon across the Atlantic Ocean and from Japan to Canada, dressing up in everything from a stewardess's uniform to a bikini on Virgin flights, and being photographed in his bath.

Direct marketing involves the use of mail, telephone, fax, email, and other tools to communicate directly with specific consumers to obtain a direct response. American Express is a service company that uses direct marketing extensively and ensures that it integrates well with all other messages, including interactive messages from employees. As the executive vice-president of global advertising at American Express clearly states,

> Service brands are not created solely in advertising. In fact, much of a brand's equity stems from the direct consumer experiences with the brand. We partner with Bronner [Bronner, Slosberg Humphrey, a relationship marketing company] to help us manage consumer experiences with our brand across all products and services—Card, Travel, Financial Services, and Relationship Services—via all direct channels, including phone, Internet, and mail.[14]

Michael Bronner, the founder of the relationship marketing company that American Express uses, emphasizes the need for coordinating external and interactive marketing communications: "The client [such as American Express] may spend millions on network advertising but lose when the customer is working his way through layer upon layer of voice response options on the customer service line."[15]

Personal selling is face-to-face presentation by a representative from the firm to make sales and build customer relationships. One way that personal selling and advertising are integrated in business-to-business companies is through the development of advertising materials that salespeople distribute to customers. This approach not only creates an integrated message to customers but also keeps salespeople fully informed of the promises the company is making.

Make Realistic Promises

The expectations that customers bring to the service affect their evaluations of its quality: the higher the expectation, the higher the delivered service must be to be perceived as high quality. Therefore, promising reliability in advertising is appropriate only when reliability is actually delivered. It is essential for a firm's marketing or sales

Global Feature

Virgin Mobile

> A brand name that is known internationally for innovation, quality and a sense of fun—this is what we have always aspired to with Virgin.
>
> —Richard Branson

Richard Branson, first known for Virgin Records, the legendary record label that signed the Rolling Stones, Janet Jackson, and The Human League, surprised the world in 1984 when he launched an up-start airline called Virgin Atlantic Airways. His vision was to create a high-quality, value-for-the-money airline to challenge the U.K.'s market leader, British Airways. Today his Virgin company (www.virgin.com)—which includes businesses in the entertainment, travel, telecommunications, and lifestyle industries and a presence in the United Kingdom, Europe, the United States, Canada, Asia, Africa, Australia, the Carribbean, and the Middle East—is one of the most diverse brands in the world. Consequently, Virgin companies' marketing communications from all divisions and locations around the globe must work to maintain a cohesive brand image. To prevent any of the subsidiaries from deviating too far from the Virgin brand, all staffers know that communications need to deliver the following brand values:

- Value for Money
- Good Quality
- Brilliant Customer Service
- Innovative
- Competitively Challenging
- Fun

Being a company that values fun and is renowned for pushing the envelope and looking at things differently than many companies, it is no surprise that Virgin's marketing efforts communicate that image as well. For instance, when Virgin Mobile launched in Canada in 2005, the marketing campaign was called "The Catch." In an attempt to make all the troubles with the cell phone industry sound like an STD, Virgin Mobile Canada's coordinated execution involved transit, street posters, and print ads emulating a public health alert, a website (www.curethecatch.ca), Catch Test print inserts, displays, and other traditional media. Within two weeks, "The Catch" had generated 155 million media impressions.

But how is a company to know when it has gone too far in striving to push the envelope? Virgin Mobile Canada (www.virginmobile.ca) has come under fire for a faux pas made as part of a December 2005 Christmas promotion. The idea was that Virgin Mobile had the ability to save people from receiving really bad presents. When an unfortunate gift opening experience was about to occur, the Virgin Mobile angels or reindeer would arrive to fix the situation. The campaign was well integrated in intent. Virgin Mobile had television, print, and transit ads and was also incorporating promotional holiday gift wrap that was distributed at Famous Players theatres across Canada. However, the gift wrap, depicting angels fondling each other, upset several moviegoers. The campaign was intended only for adults, but a third party hired to execute the sample delivery was not adhering to that guideline—making it clear that a truly integrated plan must consider execution.

Sources: Catherine McLean, "Virgin Mobile Blushes over Racy Promotional Wrap," *Globe and Mail*, December 8, 2005; Virgin website, www.virgin.com.

department to understand the actual levels of service delivery (percentage of times the service is provided correctly, or percentage and number of problems that arise) before making promises about reliability. To be appropriate and effective, communications about service quality must accurately reflect what customers will actually receive in service encounters.

Offer Service Guarantees

As discussed in Chapter 8, service guarantees are formal promises made to customers about aspects of the service they will receive. Although many services carry implicit service satisfaction guarantees, the true benefits from them—an increase in the likelihood of a customer choosing or remaining with the company—come only when the customer knows that guarantees exist and trusts that the company will stand behind them.

Manage Customer Expectations

Many service companies find themselves in the position of having to tell customers that service previously provided will be discontinued or available only at a higher price. In the 1990s, service from large computer companies such as IBM typically included salespeople who interacted with customers in person. This level of service attention was deemed necessary. When demand for computers shifted from mainframes to PCs, the personal attention provided by direct salespeople was no longer necessary or cost-effective. Instead of the traditional face-to-face service, the companies shifted to telephone interaction alone, a distinct—and for many customers disappointing—departure from the past.

Service delivery has been cut back in many service industries, but few as dramatically as in the health care industry. Hospital patients now experience far shorter stays, and waiting lines are much longer. According to Bob Bourne, president of the Canadian Orthopaedic Association, Canada now has a "system in which waits for hip and knee replacements are 'probably the longest in the world.'"[16]

How might a company gracefully inform the customer that service will not be as expected? Figure 16.11 summarizes four strategies.

FIGURE 16.11

Approaches for
Managing Customer
Expectations

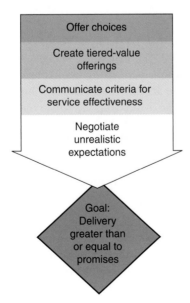

Offer Choices

One way to reset expectations is to give customers options for aspects of service that are meaningful, such as time and cost. This strategy is effective in business-to-business situations, particularly in terms of speed vs. quality. Customers who are time-conscious often want written documents quickly. When asked to provide a 10-page proposal for a project within three days, an architectural firm responded that it could provide either a 2-page proposal in three days or a 10-page proposal in a week. Its customer selected the latter option, recognizing that the deadline could be extended. In most business-to-business services, speed is often essential but threatens performance. If customers understand the tradeoff and are asked to make a choice, they are likely to be more satisfied, because their service expectations for each option become more realistic.

Create Tiered-Value Service Offerings

Product companies are accustomed to offering different versions of their products with prices commensurate with the value customers perceive. Automobiles with different configurations of features carry price tags that match not their cost but instead their perceived value to the customer. This same type of formal bundling and pricing can be accomplished in services, with the extra benefit of managing expectations.

Credit card companies offer tiered-value offerings. American Express, Visa, and MasterCard have multiple levels of credit card services based on the type of service provided: the traditional card offers basic service features, the gold card additional benefits, and the platinum card still more. Two advantages of tiered offerings are (1) the practice puts the burden of choosing the service level on the customer, thereby familiarizing the customer with specific service expectations and (2) the company can identify which customers are willing to pay higher prices for higher service levels.

The opportunity to set expectations accurately is present when the customer makes the decision at the time of purchase when customers can be reminded of the terms of the agreement if they request support that is above the level in the contract.

Communicate the Criteria and Levels of Service Effectiveness

At times companies can establish the criteria by which customers assess service. Consider a business customer who is purchasing market research services for the first time. Because market research is an expert service, it is high in credence properties that are hard for customers to judge. Moreover, the effectiveness of this type of service differs depending on the objectives the client brings to the service. In this situation, a service provider can teach the customer the criteria by which to evaluate the service. The provider that teaches the customer in a credible manner will have an advantage in shaping the evaluation process.

Negotiate Unrealistic Expectations

Sometimes the service customers request for the price they are willing to pay is unrealistic; they know it and the firm knows it. It is, in effect, a starting point for discussion, not the expected end point. In these situations successful service providers present their offerings in terms of value and not price alone. They also negotiate more realistic expectations.

Improve Customer Education

As discussed in Chapter 13, customers must perform their roles properly for many services to be effective. If customers forget to perform their roles, or perform them improperly, disappointment may result. For this reason, communication to customers can take the form of customer education. Figure 16.12 shows several types of customer education approaches that can help match promises with delivery.

Prepare Customers for the Service Process

Customers of management consulting services purchase intangible benefits: marketing effectiveness, motivated workforces, culture change. The very fact that companies purchase these services usually indicates that they do not know how to perform them alone. Many clients will also not know what to look for along the way to judge progress. In management consulting and other complex service situations, the effective provider prepares the customer for the service process and creates structure for the customer. At the beginning of the engagement, the management consulting firm establishes checkpoints throughout the process, at which times progress will be evaluated, and also leads the customer to establish objectives for project completion. Because customers do not know what that progress will look like, the consulting firm takes the lead in setting goals or criteria to be examined at those times.

A similar approach is effective with individual service customers. Do you remember registration at the beginning of your first semester or quarter? You may have required step-by-step—"Next call this telephone number or go to page B"—guidance.

As these examples show, any time a customer is inexperienced or a service process is new or unique, education about what to expect is essential.

Confirm Performance to Standards and Expectations

Service providers sometimes provide service, even explicitly requested service, yet fail to communicate to the customer that it has been accomplished. These providers stop short of getting credit for their actions when they do not reinforce actions with communication about their fulfillment of the request. This situation may occur under one or more of the following conditions:

- The customer cannot evaluate the effectiveness of a service.

- The decision maker in the service purchase is a person different from the users of the service.

- The service is invisible.

- The provider depends on others to perform some of the actions to fulfil customer expectations.

FIGURE 16.12

Approaches for
Improving Customer
Education

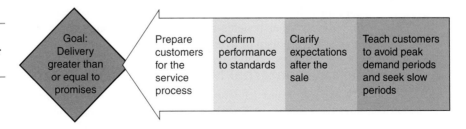

When customers cannot evaluate service effectiveness, usually because they are inexperienced or the service is technical, the provider may fail to communicate specific actions that address client concerns because the actions seem too complex for the customer to comprehend. A personal injury lawyer who aids a client with the medical and financial implications of an accident needs to be able to tell the client in language the client can understand that the lawyer has performed the necessary actions.

When the decision maker in service purchases is different from the users of the service, a wide discrepancy in satisfaction may exist between decision makers and users. An example is in the purchase of information technology products and services in a company. The decision maker—the manager of information technology or someone in a similar position—makes the purchase decisions and understands the service promises. If users are not involved in the purchase process, they may not know what has been promised and may be dissatisfied.

Customers are not always aware of everything done behind the scenes to serve them well. Most services have invisible support processes. For instance, physicians frequently request diagnostic tests to rule out possible causes for illness. When these tests come back negative, doctors may neglect to inform patients. Making customers aware of standards or efforts to improve service that are not readily apparent can improve service quality perceptions.

Clarify Expectations After the Sale

When service involves a hand-off between sales and operations, as it does in most companies, clarifying expectations with customers helps the service delivery arm of the company to align with customer expectations. Salespeople are motivated and compensated to raise customer expectations—at least to the point of making the sale—rather than to communicate realistically what the company can provide. In these situations, service providers can avoid future disappointment by clarifying what was promised as soon as the hand-off is made.

Teach Customers to Avoid Peak Demand Periods and Seek Slow Demand Periods

Few customers want to face delays in receiving services. In the words of two researchers, "At best, waiting takes their time, and at worst, they may experience a range of unpleasant reactions—feeling trapped, tired, bored, angry, or demeaned."[17] In a bank setting, researchers tested three strategies for dealing with customer waits: (1) giving customers prior notice of busy times, (2) having employees apologize for the delays, and (3) assigning all visible employees to serving customers. Only the first strategy focuses on educating customers; the other two involve managing employees. Researchers expected—and confirmed—that customers warned of a wait in line tended to minimize the negative effects of waiting to justify their decision to seek service at peak times. In general, customers given a card listing the branch's busiest and slowest times were more satisfied with the banking service. The other two strategies, apology and all-tellers-serving, showed no effects on satisfaction.[18] Educating customers to avoid peak times benefits both customers (through faster service) and companies (by easing the problem of overdemand).

Manage Internal Marketing Communication

The fourth major category of strategies necessary to match service delivery with promises involves managing internal marketing communications (see Figure 16.13). Internal marketing communications can be both vertical and horizontal. *Vertical*

FIGURE 16.13

Approaches
for Managing
Internal Marketing
Communications

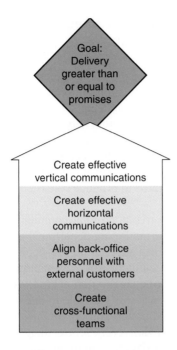

communications are either downward, from management to employees, or upward, from employees to management. *Horizontal communications* are those across functional boundaries in an organization.

Create Effective Vertical Communications

Companies that give customer contact employees adequate information, tools, and skills allow them to perform successful interactive marketing. Some of these skills come through training and other human resource efforts discussed in Chapter 12, but some are provided through downward communication. Among the most important forms of downward communication are company newsletters and magazines, corporate television networks, email, briefings, videotapes and internal promotional campaigns, and recognition programs. One of the keys to successful downward communication is keeping employees informed of everything that is being conveyed to customers through external marketing. Employees should see company advertising before it is aired or published and should be familiar with the website, mailings, and direct selling approaches used. If these vertical communications are not present, both customers and employees suffer—customers will not receive the same messages from employees that they hear in company external marketing, and employees will feel uninformed and not be aware of what their company is doing. Customers come to them asking for services that have been marketed externally but not internally, making the employees feel uninformed, left out, and helpless.[19] Unfortunately, because many service positions are boundary-spanning, entry-level jobs held by part-time staff, not enough companies take the time to notify all staff about new marketing efforts.

Upward communication is also necessary in closing the gap between service promises and service delivery. Employees are at the front line of service, and they know—more than anyone else in the organization—what can and cannot be delivered. They know when service breakdowns are occurring and, very often, why they are happening. Having open communication channels from employees to management can prevent service problems before they occur and minimize them when they do take place.

Create Effective Horizontal Communications

Horizontal communication—communication across functional boundaries in an organization—facilitates coordinated efforts for service delivery. This task is difficult because functions typically differ in goals, philosophies, outlooks, and views of the customer, but the payoff is high. Coordination between marketing and operations can result in communication that accurately reflects service delivery, thus reducing the gap between customer expectations and actual service delivery. Integration of effort between marketing and human resources can improve the ability of each employee to become a better marketer. Coordination between finance and marketing can create prices that accurately reflect the customer's evaluation of a service. In service firms, all these functions need to be integrated to produce consistent messages and to narrow the service gaps.

One important strategy for effective horizontal communications is to open channels of communication between the marketing department and operations personnel. For example, when a company creates advertising that depicts the service encounter, it is essential that the advertising accurately reflect what customers will experience in actual service encounters. Puffery or exaggeration puts service quality perceptions at risk, especially when the firm is consistently unable to deliver to the level of service portrayed in the advertising. Coordination and communication between advertising and service providers are pivotal in delivering service that meets expectations.

Another important strategy for horizontal communications involves opening channels of communication between sales and operations. Mechanisms for achieving this goal can include annual planning meetings, retreats, team meetings, or workshops. Some companies hold "gap workshops" at which employees from both functions meet for a day or two to try to understand the difficulties in matching promises with delivery.[20] Canadian firms that have recently increased their efforts to align brand promises with what actually happens, including Sears and Grand & Toy, report the importance of breaking down the barriers between marketing, logistics, and the supply chain.[21]

Involving the operations staff in face-to-face meetings with external customers is also a strategy that allows operations personnel to more readily understand the salesperson's role. Rather than filtering customers' needs through the sales force, operations employees can witness firsthand the demands of customers. A frequent and desirable result is better service to the internal customer—the salesperson—from the operations staff as they become aware of their own roles in satisfying both external and internal customers.

Align Back-Office and Support Personnel with External Customers Through Interaction or Measurement

As companies become increasingly customer-focused, front-line personnel develop improved skills in discerning what customers require. As they become more knowledgeable about and empathetic toward external customers, they also experience intrinsic rewards for satisfying customers. Back-office or support personnel, who typically do not interact directly with external customers, miss out on this bonding and, as a consequence, fail to gain the skills and rewards associated with it.

Interaction   Companies are creating ways to facilitate the interaction between back-office and support personnel and external customers. Weyerhaeuser, for example, sends employees to customers' plants to better understand their needs. When actual interaction is difficult or impossible, some companies videotape customers during the purchase and consumption process to vividly portray needs and requirements of customers and to show personnel the support that front-line people need to deliver to those expectations.

Measurement   When company measurement systems are established, employees are sometimes judged on the basis of how they perform for the next internal customer in the chain. Although this approach provides feedback in terms of how well the employees are serving the internal customer, it lacks the motivation and reward that come from seeing their efforts affect the end customer. FedEx has aligned internal personnel with the external customer using measurement. As we discussed in Chapter 10, FedEx's service quality indicator (SQI) computes daily the number of companywide service failures. To clearly communicate customer fail points to internal employees, the company created linking measures to trace the causes to each internal department. For example, the company's information technology department affects 8 of the 12 SQI measurements and therefore has submeasures that provide feedback on how the department's work is affecting the SQI.

Create Cross-Functional Teams

Another approach to improving horizontal communications to better serve customers is to involve employees in cross-functional teams to align their jobs with end customer requirements. For example, if a team of telecommunications service representatives is working to improve interaction with customers, back-office people such as computer technicians or training personnel can become part of the team. The team then learns requirements and sets goals for achieving them together, an approach that directly creates communications across the functions.

SUMMARY

Discrepancies between service delivery and external communications have a strong effect on customer perceptions of service quality. In this chapter we discussed the role of and need for integrated services marketing communications in minimizing these discrepancies. We described external, interactive, and internal marketing communications using the service triangle and emphasized the need to coordinate all three forms to deliver service that meets customer expectations. We also discussed the factors that lead to problems in marketing communications and four sets of strategies to deal with them. These strategies include (1) managing service promises, (2) managing customer expectations, (3) improving customer education, and (4) managing internal marketing communications.

Discussion Questions

1. Think of another services company that provides integrated services marketing communications. Is it as comprehensive as Science World's campaign, as described in the opening vignette? Why or why not?

2. Which of the key reasons for Provider Gap 4 discussed in the beginning of this chapter is the easiest to address in a company? Which is the hardest to address? Why?

3. Review the four general strategies for achieving integrated services marketing communications. Would all these strategies be relevant in goods firms? Which

would be most critical in goods firms? Which would be most critical in services firms? Are there any differences between those most critical in goods firms and those most critical in services firms?

4. What are the most effective Internet advertisements you have seen? Why are they effective?

5. Using the section on managing customer expectations, put yourself in the position of your professor, who must reduce the amount of "service" provided to the students in your class. Give an example of each strategy in this context. Which of the strategies would work best with you (the student) in managing your expectations? Why?

6. Why is internal marketing communication so important in service firms? Is it important in product firms?

7. Which form of internal marketing communication—vertical or horizontal—would you invest in if you had to select between them as an organization's CEO? Why?

8. What other strategies can you add to the four offered in the section on customer education? What types of education do you expect from service firms? Give an example of a firm from which you have received adequate education. What firm has not provided you with adequate education?

⟼ Exercises

1. Go to the Science World website referred to in the opening vignette. Explore the site, and make a list of the types of information you can find based on the three categories of marketing communication (external, interactive, internal) discussed in this chapter. What additional useful information do you find on the site?

2. Find five effective service advertisements in newspapers and magazines. According to the criteria given in this chapter, identify why they are effective. Critique them using the list of criteria, and discuss ways they could be improved.

⟼ Notes

1. The primary source is Eve Lazarus, "Fun, with a Bit of Science," *Marketing*, December 13–20, 2004, p. 4. Other sources: Science World 2005 annual report and website, www.scienceworld.ca/general_information/about_science_world/media/advertisements.htm, accessed October 3, 2006; Natalia Williams, "Silver—Rethink Rethink. Rejoice!" *Strategy*, December 2005, p. 45.

2. P. G. Lindell, "You Need Integrated Attitude to Develop IMC," *Marketing News,* May 26, 1997, p. 5.

3. D. Legg and J. Baker, "Advertising Strategies for Service Firms," in *Add Value to Your Service,* ed. C. Suprenant (Chicago: American Marketing Association, 1987), pp. 163–68.

4. A. S. Mattila, "The Role of Narratives in the Advertising of Experiential Services," *Journal of Service Research* 3 (August 2000), pp. 35–45.

5. K. L. Alesandri, "Strategies That Influence Memory for Advertising Communications," in *Information Processing Research in Advertising,* ed. R. J. Harris (Hillsdale, NJ: Erlbaum, 1983).

6. 2004 Extra Awards, Canadian Newspaper Association, Toronto, p. 23.
7. L. L. Berry and T. Clark, "Four Ways to Make Services More Tangible," *Business,* October–December 1986, pp. 53–54.
8. Ibid.
9. W. R. George and L. L. Berry, "Guidelines for the Advertising of Services," *Business Horizons,* May/June 1981, pp. 52–56.
10. Ibid.
11. B. Mittal, "The Advertising of Services: Meeting the Challenge of Intangibility," *Journal of Service Research* 2 (August 1999), pp. 98–116.
12. www.mastercardinternational.com.
13. Pantea Denoyelle and Jean-Claude Larreche, "Virgin Atlantic Airways—Ten Years Later," INSEAD Case, 1995.
14. D. E. Bell and D. M. Leavitt, "Bronner Slosberg Humphrey," *Harvard Business School Case 9-598-136,* 1998, p. 5.
15. Ibid., p. 4.
16. Lisa Priest, "Ruling Opens Door for Canadians to Have Hip Operations in the U.S.," *The Globe and Mail*, October 3, 2005, p. A7.
17. E. C. Clemmer and B. Schneider, "Managing Customer Dissatisfaction with Waiting: Applying Social-Psychological Theory in a Service Setting," in *Advances in Services Marketing and Management,* vol. 2, ed. T. Schwartz, D. E. Bowen, and S. W. Brown (Greenwich, CT: JAI Press, 1993), pp. 213–29.
18. Ibid.
19. L. L. Berry, V. A. Zeithaml, and A. Parasuraman, "Quality Counts in Services, Too," *Business Horizons,* May/June 1985, pp. 44–52.
20. V. A. Zeithaml, A. Parasuraman, and L. L. Berry, *Delivering Quality Service: Balancing Customer Perceptions and Expectations* (New York: The Free Press, 1990), p. 120.
21. Mark Thomas as quoted by Terry Poulton, "Fulfilling Needs," *Strategy*, June 2006, p. 11.

Chapter 17

Pricing of Services

Closing Provider Gap 4

WHAT DO CONSUMERS PAY FOR MUSIC ONLINE?

> Welcome to the post-Napster era of rent-a-tune when music is leased instead of bought, and when every recording, from electric guitars to chamber ensembles, comes with strings attached.[1]

In their heyday, free online music exchange services such as Napster, Fast-Track, and the Dutch firm KaZaA allowed more than 60 million Internet fans to download music free with virtually unrestricted availability of artists and selections. Pirated music, which included the use of these services, was estimated to have drained more than $23 million from the legitimate Canadian music market.[2] These companies were stopped from doing business by the major record companies and their artists, and "pay-for-play"

Source: Courtesy of Puretracks Inc.

services have taken over. Napster initially defined customer expectations for online music services—any time, anywhere, for free. Today many online music services, such as Canadian-owned Puretracks (www.puretracks.com) and Apple Computer's iTunes (www.apple.com/ca/itunes), charge a flat rate per track for downloads. Other services have pricing strategies that are more difficult to compare.

Legitimate digital download music sales account for only 1 percent of the Canadian market, but the competition between service providers is intensifying, particularly since the launch of Apple's iTunes in Canada in November 2004.[3] iTunes, built as an extension of Apple's overwhelmingly successful iPod music player, became immediately successful in the United States when it began offering $0.99 digital music downloads in April 2003, and thus set a standard for industry pricing. Perhaps in anticipation of iTunes' entry into Canada, Canadian-based Puretracks' pricing model mirrored that of the American giant. Today competitors tend to use pricing as part of their strategy to gain customers. Napster, for example, charges a monthly fee of $9.95, after which each download is only $1.19. Puretracks has begun varying prices as well, charging $0.79 for some older indie tracks and for certain promotions while maintaining a premium price of $1.19 for more current, popular songs such as KT Tunstall's "Black Horse & the Cherry Tree." The table here shows several top competitors in the Canadian market along with the prices and benefits they offer.[4]

Which service offers the best deal? As the table shows, service prices are neither straightforward nor consistent. Archambaultzik.ca has some tracks priced more expensively than all competitors and has the smallest catalogue, but the service offers francophone material. On services such as Napster, users obtain an unlimited number of streaming audios and downloads for $9.95 per month but must pay $1.19 for every song they burn to a CD. Users who discontinue their subscription wipe out their downloaded library, so the service is more similar to renting or leasing than owning. And services differ in whether CDs can be burned to play only on home, car, or portable stereos or on portable MP3 players. Only iTunes songs can be downloaded to iPods. Some services, such as Puretracks, offer higher-sound-quality downloads. Companies have added value to their offerings by making it easy to organize tunes into playlists, offering high-resolution album art, giving biographical notes on artists, creating music communities, and providing access to lyrics.

These differences in offerings illustrate an important issue about pricing that will be made clear in this chapter. Price is not only about monetary cost; it also involves time, convenience, and psychic payments. In each of these offerings from online music companies, consumers are constrained in what they receive. How valuable is music if you must sit in front of your computer to hear it? How much is it worth to be able to burn a CD or transfer online music to an MP3 player? Is it enough to rent or license music, or will users want to own it as they have in the past?

INTERNET MUSIC SERVICES:
What You Get, How Much It Costs

Service	Cost	Competitive Advantages	Competitive Disadvantages	Content
Archambaultzik.ca	Songs from $0.99 to $1.39 each	Bilingual site; best francophone selection; visitors can shop for physical product from Archambault's online store simultaneously	Limited catalogue; not iPod-compatible; downloads licensed for Canada only	300,000 tracks
iTunes	$0.99 per song; albums starting at $9.99	iPod-compatible; exclusive tracks; offers music videos; music can be shared with up to 5 Macs and PCs	None	Over one million tracks; 100,000 new tracks from independent artists; 5,000 audio books, 20,000 podcasts, and more than 1,000 music videos
Napster	$9.95 per month; $1.19 per song	Month-by-month subscription; music discovery and sharing through Napster community; Napster custom compilations	Downloads expire if subscription lapses	Over 700,000 tracks
Puretracks	Songs starting at $0.79; albums starting at $9.90	Highest-quality music files available in North America; independent artist mandate; substantial Canadian content; accepts payment via PayStone	Not iPod-compatible	More than one million tracks
Yahoo! Music	$8.99 per month or $83.88 per annum; songs starting at $0.89	Allows sharing of full files among subscription holders using Yahoo! Messenger	Not iPod-compatible; limited to Windows XP users	More than one million tracks

According to one of the leading experts on pricing, most service organizations use a "naive and unsophisticated approach to pricing without regard to underlying shifts in demand, the rate that supply can be expanded, prices of available substitutes, consideration of the price–volume relationship, or the availability of future substitutes."[5] What makes the pricing of services more difficult than pricing of goods? What approaches work well in the context of services?

This chapter builds on three key differences between customer evaluation of pricing for services and goods: (1) customers often have inaccurate or limited reference prices for services, (2) price is a key signal of quality in services, and (3) monetary price is not the only price relevant to service customers. As we demonstrate, these three differences can have a profound impact on the strategies companies use to set and administer prices for services.

The chapter also discusses common pricing structures including (1) cost-based, (2) competition-based, and (3) demand-based pricing. One of the most important aspects of demand-based pricing is perceived value, which must be understood by service providers so that they price in line with offerings and customer expectations. For that reason we also describe how customers define value and discuss pricing strategies in the context of value. You will notice many advertisements by Canadian companies that illustrate the various pricing approaches we describe. In particular, we have featured a number of ads by Air Canada, who have recently introduced a number of important price-based innovations.

But before we begin, it is worth briefly reiterating how pricing relates to our Gaps model. As you know from Chapter 2 and the introduction to Part 6, price sends a signal to an organization's clients. It is what customers give the firm in order to get something in return. Pricing is therefore a key determinant of customer expectations. Having too high (or too low) a price can be caused by Gap 1—Not Knowing What Customers Expect. This may be because the firm has inadequate marketing research, poor upward communication, insufficient relationship focus, or a service recovery process that isn't passing along key information about price perceptions to those in the company who set the prices. If the firm does not know what customers expect to pay or think the service is worth, pricing mistakes will occur.

Price is therefore one of the strongest forms of external communication a firm has under its control. If it is not handled properly, there will be a gap between what a firm does—including its pricing—and what it says. This will lead to an increase in Gap 4—Not Matching Performance to Promises.

In addition, price is the only element of the services marketing mix that generates revenue. All the other elements are cost drivers. Because of this, firms must be careful not only to match their performance to their promises, but also to do so at a profit. It would be a simple matter to offer great service at low prices, for instance. But while this would not lead to an increase in Gap 4, it wouldn't generate a profit, either. Service firms must be able to keep all four gaps closed while maintaining adequate cost control if they are to continue in business. Clearly, pricing plays a big role in a service company's strategy.

THREE KEY WAYS THAT SERVICE PRICES ARE DIFFERENT FOR CONSUMERS

What role does price play in consumer decisions about services? How important is price to potential buyers compared with other factors and service features? Service companies must understand how pricing works, but first they must understand how customers perceive prices and price changes. The three sections that follow describe what we know about the ways that customers perceive services, and each is central to effective pricing.

Customer Knowledge of Service Prices

To what extent do customers use price as a criterion in selecting services? How much do consumers know about the costs of services? Before you answer these questions, take the services pricing quiz in Exhibit 17.1. Were you able to fill in a price for each of the services listed? If you were able to answer the questions from memory, you have internal *reference prices* for the services. A reference price is *a price point in memory for a good or a service,* and can consist of the price last paid, the price most frequently paid, or the average of all prices customers have paid for similar offerings.[6]

To see how accurate your reference prices for services are, you can compare them with the actual price of these services from the providers in your hometown. If you are like many consumers, you feel quite uncertain about your knowledge of the prices of services, and the reference prices you hold in memory for services are not generally as accurate as those you hold for goods. There are many reasons for this difference.

• *Service variability limits knowledge.* Because services are not created on a factory assembly line, service firms have great flexibility in the configurations of services they offer. Firms can conceivably offer an infinite variety of combinations and permutations, leading to complex and complicated pricing structures. As an example, consider how difficult it is to get comparable price quotes when buying life insurance. With the multitude of types (such as whole-life vs. term), features (different deductibles), variations associated with customers (age, health risk, smoking or nonsmoking), few insurance companies offer exactly the same features and the same prices. Only an expert customer, one who knows enough about insurance to completely specify the options across providers, is likely to find prices that are directly comparable.

• *Providers are unwilling to estimate prices.* Another reason customers lack accurate reference prices for services is that many providers are unable or unwilling to estimate price in advance. For example, legal service providers are rarely able to estimate a price in advance. The fundamental reason is that they do not know themselves what the services will involve until they have fully examined the client's situation or until the process of service delivery (such as a trial) unfolds.

• *Individual customer needs vary.* Another factor that results in the inaccuracy of reference prices is that individual customer needs vary. Some hairstylists' service prices vary across customers on the basis of length of hair, type of haircut, and whether a conditioning treatment and style are included. Therefore, if you were to ask a friend what a cut costs from a particular stylist, chances are that your cut from the same stylist may be a different price. Now consider a service purchase as idiosyncratic as braces from a dentist or help from a lawyer. In these and many other services, customer differences in need will play a strong role in the price of the service.

• *Collection of price information is overwhelming in services.* Still another reason customers lack accurate reference prices for services is that customers feel overwhelmed with the information they need to gather. With most goods, retail stores display the products by category to allow customers to compare and contrast the prices of different brands and sizes. Rarely is there a similar display of services in a single outlet. If customers want to compare prices (such as for dry cleaning), they must drive to or call individual outlets. Have a look at Exhibit 17.1 and test your knowledge of service prices with question 1.

Here's one final test about reference prices. Suppose you were having a birthday party and wanted a celebrity—say, INXS, Sheryl Crow, or Shania Twain—to perform. Do you know what celebrities charge for a performance? Steve Einzig, who runs a celebrity-booking firm, reports these going rates for private performances. (www. bookingentertainment.com):[7]

Bette Midler	$750,000 to $1,000,000
Rod Stewart	$500,000
Harry Connick Jr.	$350,000
Chris Rock	$200,000
Lionel Richie	$200,000
Bill Cosby	$150,000

The fact that consumers often possess inaccurate reference prices for services has several important managerial implications. First, promotional pricing may not be as meaningful to consumers who often don't know what price they should *expect* to pay in the first place. Second, promotional pricing may create problems if the promotion—such as $50 for highlights at the salon—is the only price a customer sees; it might become the customer's new reference price, making the regular price of $75 look high. A third implication caused by the absence of accurate reference prices suggests that advertising prices may reduce uncertainty. By featuring its price, the company might overcome the fear of high cost by giving its target audience a reference price.

• *Prices are not visible.* One requirement for the existence of customer reference prices is *price visibility*—the price cannot be hidden or implicit. In many services, particularly financial services, most customers know about only the rate of return and not the costs they pay in the form of fund and insurance fees. American Express Financial Services, the parent company of Amex Bank of Canada, discovered through research that customers knew even less than expected: not only did they not understand *what* they were paying for many of their services, very few consumers understood *how* they pay for financial services in general. Only for financial products in which price was visible—such as with securities and term life insurance—were customers aware of fees. When price was invisible, such as in certificates, whole-life insurance, and annuities, customers did not know how they were charged and what they paid. The company also found that shopping behaviour in the category of financial services was extremely limited. Between 50 and 60 percent of customers bought financial products from the very first person they talked to.[8]

For all the reasons just listed, many customers do not see the price at all until *after* they receive certain services. Of course in situations of urgency, such as in accident or illness, customers must make the decision to purchase without respect to cost. And if cost is not known to the customer before purchase, it cannot be used as a key criterion for purchase, as it often is for goods. Price is likely to be an important criterion in *re-purchase,* however. Furthermore, monetary price in repurchase may be an even more important criterion than in initial purchase.

What Do You Know About the Prices of Services?

1. What do the following services cost in your home-town?

   Dental checkup   _____

   One-month fitness club membership   _____

   Legal help with an impaired driving charge   _____

   Dental braces   _____

   Rental of a video or DVD for one night   _____

   One hour of housecleaning   _____

   Room at the Delta   _____

   Haircut   _____

   Oil change and lube   _____

2. Which of the following would you select if you needed a filling replaced in a tooth?

   a. Dentist A—cost is $50, located 25 kilometres from your home, wait is three weeks for an appointment and 1.5 hours in waiting room

   b. Dentist B—cost is $75, located 25 kilometres from your home, wait is one week for appointment and 0.5 hour in waiting room

   c. Dentist C—cost is $125, located 5 kilometres from your job, wait is one week for appointment and no time in waiting room

   d. Dentist D—cost is $175, located 5 kilometres from your job, wait is one week for appointment and no time in waiting room; nitrous oxide used so no pain is involved

The Role of Nonmonetary Costs

Economists have long recognized that monetary price is not the only sacrifice consumers make to obtain products and services. Demand, therefore, is not just a function of monetary price but is influenced by other costs as well. Nonmonetary costs represent other sources of sacrifice perceived by consumers when buying and using a service. Time costs, search costs, and psychological costs often enter into the evaluation of whether to buy or rebuy a service and may at times be more important concerns than monetary price. Customers will trade money for these other costs.

• *Time costs.* Most services require direct participation of the consumer and thus consume real time: time waiting as well as time when the customer interacts with the service provider. Time becomes a sacrifice made to receive service in multiple ways. First, because service providers cannot completely control the number of customers or the length of time it will take for each customer to be served, customers are likely to expend time waiting to receive the service. As Jerry Seinfeld remarked, we are so conditioned to waiting for service that we aren't even surprised that doctors have "waiting" rooms. And when we've waited in the main waiting room long enough, we get to go into the inner rooms where we get to wait some more. Second, customers often wait for an available appointment from a service provider (in the price quiz, dentist A required a three-week wait whereas dentist D required only one week). Virtually everyone has waited to receive services.

• *Search costs.* Search costs—the effort invested to identify and select among services you desire—are often higher for services than for physical goods. Prices for services are rarely displayed on shelves of service establishments for customers to examine as they shop, so these prices are often known only when a customer has decided to experience the service. As an example, how well did you estimate the costs of an hour of housecleaning in the price quiz? As a student, it is unlikely that you regularly purchase housecleaning, and you probably have not seen the price of an hour of cleaning displayed in any retail store. Another factor that increases search costs is that every service establishment typically offers only one "brand" of a service (with the exception of brokers in insurance or financial services), so a customer must initiate contact with several different companies to get information across sellers. Price comparisons for some services (travel and hotels, for example) has been facilitated through the Internet.

• *Convenience costs.* There are also convenience (or, perhaps more accurately, inconvenience) costs of services. If customers have to travel to a service, they incur a cost, and the cost becomes greater when travel is difficult, as it is for elderly persons. Further, if service hours do not coincide with customers' available time, they must arrange their schedules to correspond to the company's schedule. And if consumers have to expend effort and time to prepare to receive a service (such as removing all food from kitchen cabinets in preparation for an exterminator's spraying), they make additional sacrifices.

• *Psychological costs.* Often the most painful nonmonetary costs are the psychological costs incurred in receiving some services. Fear of not understanding (insurance), fear of rejection (bank loans), fear of outcomes (medical treatment or surgery)—all these fears constitute psychological costs that customers experience as sacrifices when purchasing and using services. New services, even those that create positive change, bring about psychological costs that consumers factor into the purchase of services. Direct deposit, a clear improvement in banking service for the elderly with limited mobility, was viewed with suspicion until the level of comfort improved. And most customers rejected voice mail when it was first developed.

Nonmonetary Cost Priorities

You can assess your own priorities on these nonmonetary cost components—time, effort, search, psychological—by thinking about your answer to question 2 in the price quiz in Exhibit 17.1. If you chose dentist A, you are probably most concerned about monetary costs—you are willing to wait for an appointment and in the waiting room of the dentist's office. If you chose dentist B over dentist A, your time and convenience costs are slightly more important than your monetary costs, because you are willing to pay $25 more to reduce the waiting time. If you chose dentist C, you are much more sensitive to time and convenience costs, including travel time, than to monetary costs—you are willing to pay $125 more than what you would pay for dentist A to avoid the other nonmonetary costs. And if you chose dentist D, you want to minimize psychological costs as well, in this case fear and pain.

Reducing Nonmonetary Costs

The managerial implications of these other sources of sacrifice are compelling. First, a firm may be able to increase monetary price by reducing time and other costs. For example, a services marketer can reduce the perceptions of time and convenience costs when use of the service is embedded in other activities (such as when a convenience store cashes cheques, sells stamps, and serves coffee along with selling products). Second, customers may be willing to pay to avoid the other costs. Many customers willingly pay extra to have items delivered to their home—including restaurant meals—rather than transporting the services and products themselves. Some customers also pay a premium for fast check-in and checkout (as in joining the Hertz #1 club), and to avoid doing the work themselves (such as paying one-and-one-half times the price per litre to avoid having to put gas in a rental car before returning it). If time or other costs are pivotal for a given service, the company's advertising can emphasize these savings rather than monetary savings. The Greater Toronto Airport Authority's (GTAA) Valet Care advertisement (Figure 17.1) makes the case for recognizing the cost of inconvenience, and the monetary value travellers might put on being able to reduce this cost.

Many other services save time, thus actually allowing the customer to "buy" time. Household cleaning services, lawn care, babysitting, interactive cable shopping, personal shopper service, home banking, home delivery of groceries, painting, and carpet cleaning—all these services represent net gains in the discretionary time of consumers and can be marketed that way. Services that allow the customer to buy time are likely to have monetary value for busy consumers.

Price as an Indicator of Service Quality

One of the intriguing aspects of pricing is that buyers are likely to use price as an indicator of both service costs and service quality—price is at once an attraction variable and a repellent.[9] Customers' use of price as an indicator of quality depends on several factors, one of which is the other information available to them. When service cues to quality are readily accessible, when brand names provide evidence of a company's reputation, or when the level of advertising communicates the company's belief in the brand, customers may prefer to use those cues instead of price. In other situations, however, such as when quality is hard to detect or when quality or price varies a great deal within a class of services, consumers may believe that price is the best indicator of quality. Many of these conditions typify situations that face consumers when purchasing services.[10] Another factor that increases the dependence on price as a quality indicator is the risk associated with the service purchase. In high-risk situations, many of which involve credence services such as medical treatment or management consulting, the customer will look to price as a surrogate for quality.

Because customers depend on price as a cue to quality and because price sets expectations of quality, service prices must be determined carefully. In addition to being chosen to cover costs or match competitors, prices must be selected to convey the

FIGURE 17.1

Pearson Airport's Valet Care will reduce travellers' nonmonetary costs in exchange for a fee.

Source: Courtesy of Greater Toronto Airport Authority.

appropriate quality signal. Pricing too low can lead to inaccurate inferences about the quality of the service. Pricing too high can set expectations that may be difficult to match in service delivery.

APPROACHES TO PRICING SERVICES

Rather than repeat what you learned about pricing in your marketing principles class, we want to emphasize in this chapter the way that services prices and pricing differ from both the customer's and the company's perspective. We discuss these differences in the context of the three pricing structures typically used to set prices: (1) cost-based, (2) competition-based, and (3) demand-based pricing. These categories, as shown in Figure 17.2, are the same bases on which goods prices are set, but adaptations must be made in services. The figure shows the three structures interrelating, because companies need to consider each of the three to some extent in setting prices. In the following sections we describe in general each basis for pricing and discuss challenges that occur when the approach is used in services pricing. The figure summarizes those challenges.

Cost-Based Pricing

In cost-based pricing, a company determines expenses from raw materials and labour, adds amounts or percentages for overhead and profit, and thereby arrives at the price. This method is widely used by industries such as utilities, contracting, wholesaling, and advertising. The basic formula for cost-based pricing is

$$Price = Direct\ costs + Overhead\ costs + Profit\ margin$$

Direct costs involve materials and labour that are associated with delivering the service, overhead costs are a share of fixed costs, and the profit margin is a percentage of full costs (direct + overhead).

FIGURE 17.2

Three Basic Marketing Price Structures and Challenges Associated with Their Use for Services

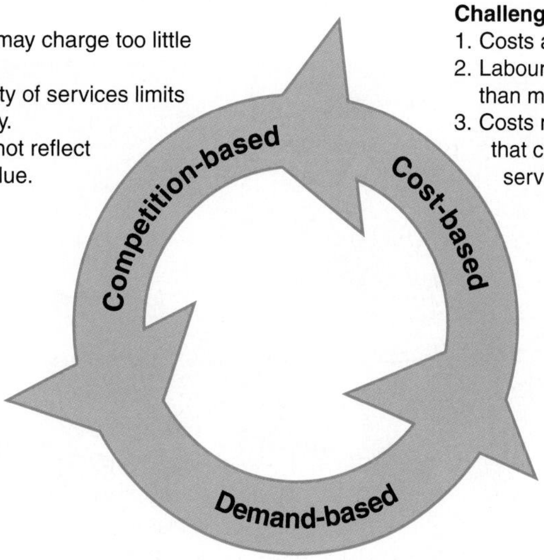

Challenges
1. Small firms may charge too little to be viable.
2. Heterogeneity of services limits comparability.
3. Prices may not reflect customer value.

Challenges
1. Costs are difficult to trace.
2. Labour is more difficult to price than materials.
3. Costs may not equal the value that customers perceive the services are worth.

Challenges
1. Monetary price must be adjusted to reflect the value of nonmonetary costs.
2. Information on service costs is less available to customers; hence, price may not be a central factor.

Special Challenges in Cost-Based Pricing for Services

One of the major difficulties in cost-based pricing involves defining the units in which a service is purchased. Thus the price per unit—a well-understood concept in pricing of manufactured goods—is a vague entity. For this reason many services are sold in terms of input units rather than units of measured output. For example, most professional services (such as consulting, engineering, architecture, psychotherapy, and tutoring) are sold by the hour.

What is unique about services when using cost-based approaches to pricing? First, costs are difficult to trace or calculate in services businesses, particularly where multiple services are provided by the firm.[11] Consider how difficult it must be for a bank to allocate teller time accurately across its chequing, savings, and money market accounts in order to decide what to charge for the services. Or consider how hard it is for an auto insurer to track its customers' mileage and therefore exposure to the risk of having an accident. In this case, though, IBM is using GPS technology to assist insurance companies in delivering an entirely new service, "pay by the kilometre" insurance (see Figure 17.3). Second, a major component of cost is employee time rather than materials, and the value of people's time, particularly nonprofessional time, is not easy to calculate or estimate.

An added difficulty is that actual service costs may underrepresent the value of the service to the customer. A local tailor charges $10 for taking in a seam on a $350 ladies' suit jacket and an equal $10 for taking in a seam on a pair of $14 sweat shorts. The tailor's rationale is that both jobs require the same amount of time. What she neglects to see is that the customer would pay a higher price—and might even be happier about the alterations—for the expensive suit jacket, and that $10 is too high a price for the sweat shorts.

Examples of Cost-Based Pricing Strategies Used in Services

Cost-plus pricing is a commonly used approach in which component costs are calculated and a markup added. In product pricing, this approach is quite simple; in service industries, however, it is complicated because the tracking and identification of costs

FIGURE 17.3

IBM's innovative technology is helping insurers manage risk, and therefore costs, more precisely.

Source: Photographer: Christian Stoll.

are difficult. The approach is typically used in industries in which cost must be estimated in advance, such as construction, engineering, and advertising. In construction, bids are solicited by clients on the basis of the description of the service desired. Using their knowledge of the service (including the raw materials), labour, and margin, the company estimates a price for the finished service. A contingency amount—to cover the possibility that costs may be higher than estimated—is also stated because in large projects specifications can change as the service is provided.

Fee for service is the pricing strategy used by professionals; it represents the cost of the time involved in providing the service. Consultants, psychologists, accountants, and lawyers charge for their services on an hourly basis.

Lawyers and accountants must keep track of the time they spend for a given client, often down to 10-minute increments. For this reason the method has been criticized because it does not promote efficiency and sometimes ignores the expertise of the lawyers. Clients also fear padding of their legal bills, and may audit them. Despite these concerns, the hourly bill dominates the industry, the majority of revenues being billed this way.[12]

Competition-Based Pricing

The competition-based pricing approach focuses on the prices charged by other firms in the same industry or market. Competition-based pricing does not always imply charging the identical rate others charge but rather using others' prices as an anchor for the firm's price. This approach is used predominantly in two situations: (1) when services are standard across providers, such as in the dry cleaning industry, and (2) in oligopolies with a few large service providers, such as in the airline or rental car industry.

Special Challenges in Competition-Based Pricing for Services

Small firms may charge too little and not make margins high enough to remain in business. Many mom-and-pop service establishments—dry cleaning, retail, and tax accounting, among others—cannot deliver services at the low prices charged by chain operations.

Further, the heterogeneity of services across and within providers makes this approach complicated. Bank services illustrate the wide disparity in service prices. Customers buying chequing accounts, money orders, or foreign currency, to name a few services, find that prices are rarely similar across providers. The wide disparity in prices probably reflects the bank's difficulty in determining prices as well as their belief that financial customers do not shop around nor discern the differences (if any) among offerings from different providers. Only in very standardized services where there are few switching barriers (such as dry cleaning) are prices likely to be remembered *and* compared.

Examples of Competition-Based Pricing in Services Industries

Price signalling occurs in markets with a high concentration of sellers. In this type of market, any price offered by one company will be matched by competitors to avoid giving a low-cost seller a distinct advantage. The airline industry exemplifies price signalling in services. When any competitor drops the price of routes, others match the lowered price almost immediately.

Going-rate pricing involves charging the most prevalent price in the market. Rental car pricing is an illustration of this technique (and also an illustration of price signalling, because the rental car market is dominated by a small number of large companies). For years, the prices set by one company (Hertz) have been followed by the other companies. When Hertz instituted a new pricing plan that involved "no mileage charges, ever," other rental car companies imitated the policy. They then had to raise other factors such as base rates, size and type of car, daily or weekly rates, and dropoff charges to continue to make profits. Prices in different geographic markets, even cities, depend on the going rate in that location, and customers often pay different rates in contiguous cities. National toll-free reservation lines may offer better rates than are obtained by calling local rental car companies, because those rates are less influenced by the going rates in a particular area.[13]

The Global Feature in this chapter illustrates some of the practices in pricing that differ across countries.

Demand-Based Pricing

The two approaches to pricing just described are based on the company and its competitors rather than on customers. Neither approach takes into consideration that customers may lack reference prices, may be sensitive to nonmonetary prices, and may judge quality on the basis of price. All these factors can be accounted for in a company's pricing decisions. The third major approach to pricing, *demand-based pricing,* involves setting prices consistent with customer perceptions of value: prices are based on what customers will pay for the services provided.

Special Challenges in Demand-Based Pricing for Services

One of the major ways that pricing of services differs from pricing of goods in demand-based pricing is that nonmonetary costs and benefits must be factored into the calculation of perceived value to the customer. When services require time, inconvenience, and psychological and search costs, the monetary price must be adjusted to compensate. And when services save time, inconvenience, and psychological and search costs, the customer is willing to pay a higher monetary price. The challenge is to determine the value to customers of each of the nonmonetary aspects involved.

Another way services and goods differ with respect to this form of pricing is that information on service costs may be less available to customers, making monetary price not as salient a factor in initial service selection as it is in goods purchasing.

Four Meanings of Perceived Value

One of the most appropriate ways that companies price their services is basing the price on the perceived value of the service to customers. Among the questions a services marketer needs to ask are the following: What do consumers mean by *value?* How can we quantify perceived value in dollars so that we can set appropriate prices for our services? Is the meaning of value similar across consumers and services? How can value perceptions be influenced? To understand demand-based pricing approaches, we must fully understand what value means to customers.

This is not a simple task. When consumers discuss value, they use the term in many different ways and talk about myriad attributes or components. What constitutes value, even in a single service category, appears to be highly personal and idiosyncratic. Customers define value in four ways: (1) Value is low price. (2) Value is whatever I want in a product or service. (3) Value is the quality I get for the price I pay. (4) Value is what I get for what I give (Figure 17.4).[14] Let us take a look at each of these definitions more carefully.

Global Feature

Unique Pricing Around the World

TIPPING

A Cornell University study revealed an interesting fact about tipping: The custom of tipping is more prevalent in countries where citizens value status and prestige than in countries where they do not. Michael Lynn found that the number of service professionals tipped is relatively small in countries where citizens value recognition and esteem less. "Tipping is really a form of conspicuous consumption. We tip more people ... because we value status."

One measure of the differences in tipping is the number of service professionals who are given tips in different countries. The United States leads the list with about 35 different professions. Canada also ranks high on the list with 25 different professions. Other countries that place a high value on recognition and esteem also tip a large number of professionals. These include Spain (29), India (25), and Italy (24). In contrast, in Denmark and Sweden, the number of tipped professionals is under 10, reflecting the lower value placed on recognition and esteem in these countries.

Source: Doug Menuez/Getty Images.

SERVICE FEES

In Europe, Asia, and Latin America, fixed services charges rather than tips are added to customers' bills in restaurants. Except for large parties, this service charge had been an unusual practice in North American restaurants, perhaps for the reason cited in the previous paragraph. However, some U.S. establishments are exchanging tips for service charges in spite of the preference of guests to choose what to tip. The reason is that the IRS has been leaning on restaurants to have their waiters and waitresses report tips. If reported tip income is less than 8 percent of gross receipts, the IRS has now made restaurant owners liable for back taxes on unreported income unless they participate in a program to track their employee's tips. Service personnel do not like the change, partly because they make less money (the restaurant shares the service fee with kitchen personnel) and partly because they do not receive the instant gratification that tips provide. Guests are typically unfavourable as well: "We surveyed our guests and they seem to feel that they have a constitutional right to reward and punish waiters." Canadian guests have maintained such power. Although the Canada Revenue Agency expects earners to report tip income, the agency has not instituted any requirements for restaurants to force compliance on the part of their employees.

PRICELESS

A London restaurant called Just Around the Corner has an extraordinary demand-oriented pricing policy: It lets customers pay whatever they think the meal is worth. The policy has been extremely successful since it was started, with most customers paying more for their meals than the restaurant would charge if it

continued

Global Feature

Unique Pricing Around the World—continued

set the prices. Customers average 25 pounds ($51) for a three-course dinner, but some are especially careful to pay enough. "One night, four American government officials handed over nearly $1,000 for a meal worth less than $200. They asked if they had left enough." The owner, Michael Vasos, claims, "I make more money from this restaurant than from any of my other [four] establishments." He thinks his customers' generosity accounts for the success of the restaurant and its pricing policies, although others state that the fear of embarrassment common to the English prevents patrons from paying too little.

PAY BY THE MINUTE IN TOKYO

Some restaurants in Japan are charging for dinner according to how quickly customers eat. At Dai-ichi Hotel Tokyo Seafort, diners punch a time clock when they start their meals, then pay 25 cents per minute until they clock out. Fast diners—like two young girls who gulped down platefuls of cake in 10 minutes and

paid only $3—can get bargain meals. Perhaps that is why the restaurant is popular among college students! Other franchise restaurants throughout Japan put time limits on their all-you-can-eat buffets. Prices range from $10 an hour to $100 for 90 minutes. During that time, diners can consume unlimited quantities of top-quality sushi or shabu shabu, a Japanese specialty consisting of thin slices of beef cooked in boiling broth. At one restaurant, Mo Mo Paradise in Tokyo, for example, diners can pay $13.50 to eat for 90 minutes or $30 to eat as much as they want for as long as they want.

Sources: Andrea Sachs, "Eat All You Want; Pay by the Minute," *Washington Post*, September 26, 1999, p. H3; © 1999, *The Washington Post*, reprinted with permission. "Study Examines Tipping," *Hotel and Motel Management*, March 17, 1997, p. 14; B. Ortega, "No Tips, Please—Just Pay the Service Fee," *The Wall Street Journal*, September 4, 1998, p.-B1; "Priceless," *People*, February 15, 1999, p. 114; and I. Wall, "It May Be a Dog-Eat-Dog World, But This Restaurant Won't Prove It," *The Wall Street Journal*, December 11, 1998, p. B1.

Value Is Low Price Some consumers equate value with low price, indicating that what they have to give up in terms of money is most salient in their perceptions of value.[15]

Value Is Whatever I Want in a Product or Service Rather than focusing on the money given up, some consumers emphasize the benefits they receive from a service or product as the most important component of value. In the telecommunications industry, for example, business customers strongly value the reliability of the systems and are willing to pay for the safety and confidentiality of the connections.

Value Is the Quality I Get for the Price I Pay Other consumers see value as a tradeoff between the money they give up and the quality they receive.

Value Is What I Get for What I Give Finally, some consumers consider all the benefits they receive as well as all sacrifice components (money, time, effort) when describing value.

FIGURE 17.4

Four Customer
Definitions of Value

Source: N. C. Mohn, "Pricing Research for Decision Making," *Marketing Research: A Magazine of Management and Applications* 7, no. 1 (Winter 1995), pp. 10–19. Reprinted by permission of the American Marketing Association.

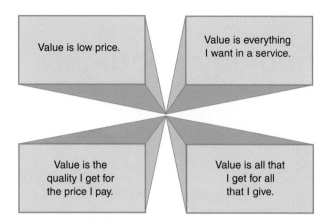

The four consumer expressions of value can be captured in one overall definition consistent with the concept of utility in economics: *Perceived value is the consumer's overall assessment of the utility of a service based on perceptions of what is received and what is given.* Although what is received varies across consumers (some may want volume, others high quality, still others convenience), as does what is given (some are concerned only with money expended, others with time and effort), value represents a tradeoff of the give and get components. Customers will make a purchase decision on the basis of perceived value, not solely to minimize the price paid. These definitions are the first step in identifying the elements that must be quantified in setting prices for services.

Incorporating Perceived Value into Service Pricing

The buyer's perception of total value prompts the willingness to pay a particular price for a service. To translate the customer's value perceptions into an appropriate price for a specific service offering, the marketer must answer a number of questions. What benefits does the service provide? How important is each of these benefits? How much is it worth to the customer to receive a particular benefit from a service? At what price will the service be economically acceptable to potential buyers? In what context is the customer purchasing the service?

The most important thing a company must do—and often a difficult thing—is to estimate the value to customers of the company's services. Value may be perceived differently by consumers because of idiosyncratic tastes, knowledge about the service, buying power, and ability to pay. In this type of pricing, what the consumers value—not what they pay—forms the basis for pricing. *Therefore its effectiveness rests solely on accurately determining what the market perceives the service to be worth.*

When the services are for the end consumer, most often service providers will decide that they cannot afford to give each individual exactly the bundle of attributes he or she values. They will, however, attempt to find one or more bundles that address segments of the market. On the other hand, when services are sold to businesses (or to end customers in the case of high-end services), the company can understand and deliver different bundles to each customer. Exhibit 17.2 presents an illustration of this approach to pricing.

An interesting manifestation of demand-oriented pricing is shown in the Technology Spotlight.

One of the most complex and difficult tasks of services marketers is setting prices internationally. If services marketers price on the basis of perceived value and if

Technology Spotlight

Dynamic Pricing on the Internet Allows Price Adjustments Based on Supply and Demand

When shopping for an airline ticket on the Internet, have you ever found a low-priced ticket that you did not purchase immediately, then returned four hours later to find the same ticket had increased $100 in price? This experience is dynamic pricing in action—the buying and selling of goods in markets in which prices move quickly in response to supply and demand fluctuations. In the case of your airline ticket, chances are that other travellers had purchased tickets at the original low price, reducing the airlines' inventory and allowing the airline to gamble on getting customers to buy the remaining seats at higher prices.

Dynamic pricing is estimated to account for 40 percent of $1.4 trillion in total online transactions in 2004. The approach—often incorporating auctions and other forms of online bidding—is typically used at the end of the supply chain to eliminate surplus inventory or perishable service capacity, as with airline seats. Dynamic pricing has allowed companies to generate significant revenue from excess supply or discontinued products, which they used to turn over to intermediaries. In the past, liquidators would receive unsold services, getting five cents on the dollar in liquidation fees in addition to whatever they could get from reselling the products. Not only did the firm not receive revenue from the sale of the services, but it would also have to pay for liquidation services.

AUCTIONS: EBAY AND 1,500 RIVALS

Online auctions represent dynamic pricing because customers pay what they are willing and they compete with each other on the goods they desire. In 1995, eBay pioneered the Internet auction, but more than 1,500 websites now offer person-to-person online trading. Market leader eBay now offers thousands of new items for auction every day, and reported revenue grew to more than $4.5 billion in 2005, a 39 percent increase over the previous year. Whereas eBay focuses on consumer-to-consumer transactions, uBid.com acts as a consignment house for manufacturers selling directly to customers. uBid, founded in 1997, offers leading manufacturers' merchandise to consumers and businesses at prices lower than wholesale. Most uBid auctions begin at $1 and allow market dynamics to set the price. Interestingly, although uBid.com is an American-based auction and does not directly ship to Canada, the company encourages all international prospective customers to sign up for a U.S. mailing address using Access USA and then continue shopping their auctions.

DUTCH AUCTIONS: KLIK-KLOK.COM, WRHAMBRECHT.COM

Dutch auctions, which originated in Netherlands for selling services such as insurance or perishable items such as tulips, reverse the typical auction in that the prices go down as the auction progresses. Also unlike in typical auctions, in which one of a particular type of product is sold at a given time, in Dutch auctions multiple—albeit limited—quantities of the same services are sold at the same time. The duration of the auction is very short, and the price drops rapidly over this time. At any given time (or price point), a bidder can stop the clock by bidding at the instantaneous price. The bid with time, price, and quantity is then recorded. This bidding continues until all bids have been received. At that point all winning bidders pay the same price, which is the lowest "successful" bid. The catch here is that there is a limited supply of each product. As the clock progresses and the remaining available inventory decreases, the nonbidders (those waiting for the lowest selling price) risk not getting their desired quantities.

REVERSE AUCTIONS: PRICELINE.COM

Reverse auctions are used on the buy side, allowing buyers to see the lowest bid, but not identify the buyer or the seller. The brand or identity of the seller is revealed only if the seller decides to accept the bid offered by the buyer. An advantage for buyers is that they do not need to guess at the price and can receive the same products and services offered elsewhere with static prices at significant discounts. A disadvantage is that although buyers see a rating of the seller, they cannot be sure who the seller is and what the service outcome will be.

Technology Spotlight

Dynamic Pricing on the Internet Allows Price Adjustments Based on Supply and Demand—continued

The brand is eliminated as a communicator of quality. Furthermore, the buyer has to sacrifice control over some aspects of the service that is being consumed. For instance, on Priceline.com, the buyer does not have full control over time of the flights.

GROUP BUYING: ONLINECHOICE.COM, HAPPYMANY.COM

Group buying sites such as HappyMany.com aggregate demand for sellers. This site offers group rates on long distance, Internet, and cell phone services, and has recently introduced group rates on gasoline. The concept behind this form of dynamic pricing is that the greater the number of people who want to buy products, the lower the price will be for everyone. Sellers generally bucket the prices of the product being sold based on the number of buyers. For example, for 0 to 10 buyers, the price for each buyer is $100; for 10 to 20 buyers, the price for each buyer is $95, and so on. Word of mouth is critical, because interested buyers are encouraged to enlist their friends and relatives to get a cheaper price for the whole group. Sellers motivate this action by placing an "Invite Your Friend" icon right next to the service or price information. Advantages of this form of dynamic pricing are that the price decreases as a greater number of people bid and the exact service and its specifications are known to buyers when bidding.

FINDING THE LOWEST PRICE ACROSS INTERNET SITES: BUY.COM CANADA

Buy.com's slogan is "lowest prices on Earth." The Internet allows consumers to do quick price comparisons, and Buy.com wants to make sure its services and products end up being the lowest prices in everyone's search. To deliver on its promises, Buy.com uses software to monitor price changes for products on competing sites. When these price changes occur, the software then recommends price adjustments to Buy.com. The process is automated, but the decision to change prices is made by a manager, usually once a day rather than moment to moment. Buy.com relies on this strategy in highly competitive online categories such as computer software. The

software makes recommendations throughout the day, and decisions are made the next morning. Prices tend to fall more often than they go up.

DINING WITH DYNAMIC PRICING

Flexible, or dynamic, pricing in the restaurant industry involves changing menu prices by hour or time of day to attract diners in nonpeak hours, such as afternoons between 2 p.m. and 6 p.m. or late evenings. Restaurants may use discounts, such as 15 to 30 percent off the total check, to build traffic during off-hours. Typically the restaurants use a "dining aggregator," a site that collects and coordinates information about all restaurants in an area that want to offer dynamic pricing. For example, DinnerBroker.com is a novel dynamic-pricing website representing restaurants in some metropolitan areas of the United States and a few in Canada. The restaurants using DinnerBroker's service use off-peak discount programs to gain incremental business and new customers. DinnerBroker.com has an easy-to-use graphic matrix that allows users to see on one page all participating restaurants and the discounts they offer. The site also enables customers to make online reservations and offers access to prime-time tables. To participate in these services, DinnerBroker.com requires restaurants to pay a subscription of $49 a month and $1 for every off-hour reservation booked and fulfilled by the service.

Sources: Michael Bazeley, "eBay Has Strong Earnings in Quarter," *Knight Ridder Tribune Business News,* October 21, 2004, p. 1; Georgia Perakis, "Third Informs Revenue Management and Pricing Conference," *Journal of Revenue and Pricing Management,* January 2004, p. 388; Vaidyanathan Jayaraman and Tim Baker, "The Internet as an Enabler for Dynamic Pricing of Goods," *IEEE Transactions on Engineering Management,* November 2003, p. 470; Alan J. Liddle, "Using Web for Discounting Clicks with Digital Diners," *Nation's Restaurant News,* May 19, 2003, p. 172; Christopher T. Heun, "Dynamic Pricing Boosts Bottom Line," *Informationweek,* October 29, 2001; Michael Vizard, "With So Very Few Internet Players, Is Dynamic Pricing Good for Our Economy?" *InfoWorld,* March 26, 2001; Michael Vizard, Ed Scannel, and Dan Neel, "Suppliers Toy with Dynamic Pricing," *InfoWorld,* May 14, 2001.

perceived value and willingness to pay differ across countries (which they often do), then service firms may provide essentially the same service but charge different prices in different countries. Here, as in pricing domestically, the challenge is to determine the perceived value not just to different customers but to customers in different parts of the world. Pricing in Europe provides one of the most compelling examples of the pricing challenges that marketers face internationally.

Historically, Europe was considered to be a loosely aligned group of more than 12 separate countries, and a services marketer could have as many different pricing approaches as it had countries in which it offered the services. Although pricing was complex to administer, the marketer had full flexibility in pricing and could seek the profit-maximizing price in each country. The European Community created a single internal market, holding the potential to simplify marketing in the area but also creating grave concerns about pricing. The largest concern is that marketers will be required to offer all services at a single European price—the lowest price offered in any European country—which could dramatically reduce revenues and profits.

PRICING STRATEGIES THAT LINK TO THE FOUR VALUE DEFINITIONS

In this section we describe the approaches to services pricing that are particularly suited to each of the four value definitions.

Pricing Strategies When the Customer Means "Value Is Low Price"

When monetary price is the most important determinant of value to a customer, the company focuses mainly on price. This focus does not mean that the quality level and intrinsic attributes are always irrelevant, just that monetary price dominates in importance. To establish a service price in this definition of value, the marketer must understand to what extent customers know the objective prices of services in this category, how they interpret various prices, and how much is too much of a perceived sacrifice. These factors are best understood when the service provider also knows the relative dollar size of the purchase, the frequency of past price changes, and the range of acceptable prices for the service. Some of the specific pricing approaches appropriate when customers define value as low price include discounting, odd pricing, synchro-pricing, and penetration pricing (Figure 17.5).

Discounting

Service providers offer discounts or price cuts to communicate to price-sensitive buyers that they are receiving value. In Chapter 14, we noted that Air Canada had risked

FIGURE 17.5

Pricing Strategies When the Customer Defines Value as Low Price

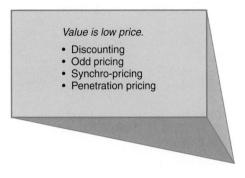

Value is low price.

- Discounting
- Odd pricing
- Synchro-pricing
- Penetration pricing

EXHIBIT 17.2

Pricing for Customer-Perceived Value with Modular Service Pricing and Service Tiering

As described in this chapter, pricing a service in line with what customers perceive it is worth is often difficult. Two approaches that have gained favour in recent years are modular service pricing and service tiering.

MODULAR SERVICE PRICING

One of the reasons that pricing of services is more difficult than pricing of goods is that service units are more variable and difficult to identify than units of goods. Units of goods—automobiles, jeans, litres of milk, and microwaves—are easy to define. Units of service are more difficult in part because they are sold by a variety of units. Information services, for example, are sold by the minute, the web page, the file (as in buying online music), or the search (as in finding and purchasing magazine articles). The services of your doctor are sold by the length and type of the visit, the test performed, the shot given, and the X-rays taken. One approach to dealing with the complexity of pricing services is to develop modular service bundles.

Modular service pricing involves first identifying the basic and value-added services of a provider as components or building blocks for pricing. To create modules, the company first defines the full range of services both that could meet customer needs and for which customers will pay. In the airlines, for example, the base price is set for a seat, but customers will also pay for excess baggage, special ticketing, class of seats, animals, alcoholic beverages, and food. Customers of rental car companies pay by the day but also buy additional services such as liability insurance, collision insurance, dropoff services, and refuelling services.

To create modular pricing, firms need

1. A viable price for each different service

2. The ability to combine prices and services using easy rules

3. Minimum overlap among the service elements so that customers do not pay twice or more for the same service

SERVICE TIERING

Sometimes even good modular pricing can become too complex, and simpler ways to present the company's prices are needed. Service tiering, usually called versioning when applied to the pricing of goods, involves creating a set of prices that corresponds to the price points and value bundles of different customer segments.

In general, service tiers allow customers to quickly and simply match their desires and the price they are willing to pay with an offering from the company. The customer perceives a benefit in choosing one of the tiers because each tier provides a discount over individual services. The company enjoys a benefit because customers typically buy more services when they are sold in tiers than when they are offered individually.

Modular pricing and service tiering allow the company to maximize sales from all parts of a service that the customer desires without having to create unique service bundles for every customer.

Air Canada provides a good illustration of the use of service tiers. Note in the chart shown here how they have grouped their fares into five tiers. Interestingly, they have also added a modular component, so that even if a passenger booked a Tango fare, he or she can, for an additional fee, still change the reservation or get advance seat selection. To further assist passengers in deciding on what fare class to book, Air Canada's website (www.aircanada.com/en/news/oneway/index.html) provides short narratives of options accompanied by photos of the types of people who might choose each. If you read the suggested descriptions for passengers who would choose Tango over Executive Class, for instance, you will see very good illustrations of the "Value Is Low Price" and "Value Is Everything I Want in a Service" points of view, respectively.

Source: Courtesy of Air Canada.

Sources: R. Docters, M. Reopel, J. Sun, and S. Tanny, "Capturing the Unique Value of Services: Why Pricing of Services Is Different," *The Journal of Business Strategy* 25, no. 2 (2004), pp. 23–28.

the ire of its travel agents, the airline's key distribution channel, by removing its lowest fares from the agents' systems. Air Canada has branded these fares GO Discount, and this new fare option provides even lower fares than are available with standard Tango fares. Figure 17.6 shows a recent advertisement Air Canada used to help launch GO Discount, listing the conditions passengers must comply with to qualify for it.

Odd Pricing

Odd pricing is the practice of pricing services just below the exact dollar amount to make buyers perceive that they are getting a lower price. Dry cleaners charge $2.98 for a shirt rather than $3, health clubs have dues priced at $33.90 per month rather than $34, and haircuts are $9.50 rather than $10. Odd prices suggest discounting and bargains and are appealing to customers for whom value means low price.

Synchro-Pricing

Synchro-pricing is the use of price to manage demand for a service by capitalizing on customer sensitivity to prices. Certain services, such as tax preparation, passenger transportation, long-distance telephone, hotels, and theatres, have demand that fluctuates over time as well as constrained supply at peak times. For companies in these and other industries, setting a price that provides a profit over time can be difficult. Pricing can, however, play a role in smoothing demand and synchronizing demand and supply. Time, place, quantity, and incentive differentials have all been used effectively by service firms, as discussed in Chapter 15.

Place differentials are used for services in which customers have a sensitivity to location. The front row at concerts, the 50-yard line in football, centre court in tennis or basketball, oceanside rooms in resort hotels—all these represent place differentials that are meaningful to customers and that therefore command higher prices.

FIGURE 17.6

Air Canada has introduced a new discounted fare option called GO Discount.

Source: Courtesy of Air Canada.

Time differentials involve price variations that depend on when the service is consumed. Examples are cell phone service in the evening and on weekends, and airline tickets that include a Saturday night stay. By offering lower prices for underused time periods, a service company can smooth demand and also gain incremental revenue.

Quantity differentials are usually price decreases given for volume purchasing. This pricing structure allows a service company to predict future demand for its services. Customers who buy a booklet of coupons for a tanning salon or facial, a quantity of tokens for public bridges, or packages of advertising spots on radio or television are all responding to price incentives achieved by committing to future services. Air Canada has recently introduced Canada's first quantity differential for air travel (see Figure 17.7). This innovative pricing approach will likely appeal to tourists and business travellers. For $6,998 (plus GST), consumers can take unlimited flights to more than 100 destinations across North America.[16]

Differentials as incentives are lower prices for new or existing clients in the hope of encouraging them to be regular users or more frequent users. Some professionals—lawyers, dentists, electrologists, and even some physicians—offer free consultations at the front end, usually to overcome fear and uncertainty about high service prices. Other companies stimulate use by offering regular customers discounts or premiums during slow periods.

Penetration Pricing

Penetration pricing is a strategy in which new services are introduced at low prices to stimulate trial and widespread use. The strategy is appropriate when (1) sales volume of the service is very sensitive to price, even in the early stages of introduction; (2) it is possible to achieve economies in unit costs by operating at large volumes; (3) a service faces threats of strong potential competition very soon after introduction; and (4) there is no class of buyers willing to pay a higher price to obtain the service.[17] Penetration pricing can lead to problems when companies

FIGURE 17.7

Air Canada introduced Canada's first-ever subscription to unlimited flights.

Source: Courtesy of Air Canada.

The North America Unlimited Pass:
Fly where you want, when you want, for two whole months.

Only on sale at **aircanada.com** until Sept. 30, 2005.

Enjoy unlimited travel to over 100 cities across North America in October and November. Plus be sure to enter our contest at aircanada.com for your chance to win two passes – and check out our entire family of flight passes at the same time!

You can also ask your travel agent to purchase for you.

AIR CANADA

then select a "regular" increased price. Care must be taken not to penetrate with so low a price that customers feel the regular price is outside the range of acceptable prices.

Pricing Strategies When the Customer Means "Value Is Everything I Want in a Service"

When the customer is concerned principally with the "get" components of a service, monetary price is not of primary concern. The more desirable intrinsic attributes a given service possesses, the more highly valued the service is likely to be and the higher the price the marketer can set. Figure 17.8 shows appropriate pricing strategies.

Prestige Pricing

Prestige pricing is a special form of demand-based pricing by service marketers who offer high-quality or status services. For certain services—restaurants, health clubs, airlines, and hotels—a higher price is charged for the luxury end of the business. Some customers of service companies who use this approach may actually value the high price because it represents prestige or a quality image. Others prefer purchasing at the high end because they are given preference in seating or accommodations and are entitled to other special benefits. In prestige pricing, demand may actually increase as price increases because the costlier service has more value in reflecting quality or prestige.

Care must be taken, though. Whistler Ski Resort (see Figure 17.9) has become known as "a snowy playground for the rich and famous," and this reputation has caused regular travellers to stay away (unless lured by deep discounts in the off-season, which, as we saw in Chapter 15, poses additional problems with segment incompatibility). This reputation as a super-rich resort is due, in part, to $2,000-a-night hotel rooms during the late 90s and illustrates the risks of prestige pricing. In this case, the resort benefited from the strategy during the boom times, but since 9/11 and the increase in value of the Canadian dollar, prestige pricing is no longer working.

Skimming Pricing

Skimming, a strategy in which new services are introduced at high prices with large promotional expenditures, is an effective approach when services are major improvements over past services. In this situation customers are more concerned about obtaining the service than about the cost of the service, allowing service providers to skim the customers most willing to pay the highest prices.

FIGURE 17.8

Pricing Strategies When the Customer Defines Value as Everything Wanted in a Service

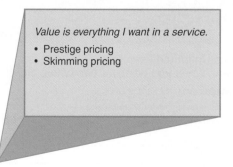

Value is everything I want in a service.

- Prestige pricing
- Skimming pricing

FIGURE 17.9

Whistler no longer wants to be seen as practising prestige pricing and would like to get rid of its image as a resort only for the super-rich.

Source: Lyle Stafford/Photo.

Pricing Strategies When the Customer Means "Value Is the Quality I Get for the Price I Pay"

Some customers primarily consider both quality and monetary price. The task of the marketer is to understand what *quality* means to the customer (or segments of customers) and then to match quality level with price level. Specific strategies are shown in Figure 17.10.

Value Pricing

The widely used term *value pricing* has come to mean "giving more for less." In current usage it involves assembling a bundle of services that are desirable to a wide group of customers and then pricing them lower than they would cost alone. Taco Bell pioneered value pricing with a $0.59 Value Menu. After sales at the chain rose 50 percent in two years to $2.4 billion, McDonald's and Burger King adopted the value pricing practice. WestJet also offers value pricing: a low cost for a bundle of desirable service attributes such as no overbooking, live seat-back TV, and free blankets (in competition with Air Canada who began to charge for their blankets in 2005). See Figure 17.11 for one of WestJet's value pricing advertisements.

FIGURE 17.10

Pricing Strategies When the Customer Defines Value as Quality for the Price Paid

Value is the quality I get for the price I pay.

- Value pricing
- Market segmentation pricing

FIGURE 17.11

WestJet exemplifies a value pricing approach with a "more for less" message.

Source: Courtesy of WestJet.

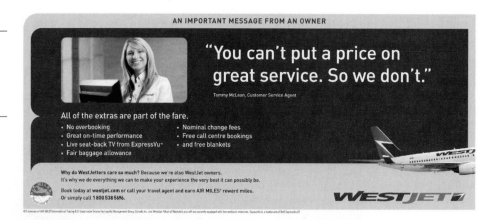

Market Segmentation Pricing

Market segmentation pricing, a service marketer charges different prices to groups of customers, even though there may not be corresponding differences in the costs of providing the service to each of these groups. This form of pricing is based on the premise that segments show different price elasticities of demand and desire different quality levels.

Services marketers often price by *client category.* This may be based on the recognition that some groups find it difficult to pay a recommended price. Health clubs located in university and college communities will typically offer student memberships, recognizing that this segment of customers has limited ability to pay full price. In addition to the lower price, student memberships may also carry with them reduced hours of use, particularly in peak times. The same line of reasoning leads to memberships for "seniors," who are less able to pay full price but are willing to patronize the clubs during daytime hours when most full-price members are working. Sometimes clients may be *able* to pay but not very *willing.* In that case, marketers may also offer price concessions to encourage business. One spa resort whose primary target is women recognizes that men are less likely to stay. It therefore chooses the unique strategy of "Men Stay Free." In so doing, St. Anne's (see Figure 17.12) hopes to get more women during the midweek low demand period by making it possible for a couple to stay for the same price the woman alone would have paid.

FIGURE 17.12

Ste. Anne's targets women by letting their partners stay for free.

Source: Courtesy of Sainte Anne's.

Companies also use market segmentation by *service version,* recognizing that not all segments want the basic level of service at the lowest price. When they can identify a bundle of attributes that are desirable enough for another segment of customers, they can charge a higher price for that bundle. Companies can configure service bundles that reflect price and service points appealing to different groups in the market. Hotels, for example, offer standard rooms at a basic rate but then combine amenities and tangibles related to the room to attract customers willing to pay more for the concierge level, jacuzzis, additional beds, and sitting areas.

Pricing Strategies When the Customer Means "Value Is All That I Get for All That I Give"

Some customers define value as including not just the benefits they receive but also the time, money, and effort they put into a service. Figure 17.13 illustrates the pricing strategies described in this definition of value.

Price Framing

Because many customers do not possess accurate reference prices for services, services marketers are more likely than product marketers to organize price information for customers so they know how to view it. Customers naturally look for price anchors as well as familiar services against which to judge focal services. If they accept the anchors, they view the price and service package favourably.

Price Bundling

Some services are consumed more effectively in conjunction with other services; other services accompany the products they support (such as extended service warranties, training, and expedited delivery). When customers find value in a package of services that are interrelated, price bundling is an appropriate strategy. Bundling, which means pricing and selling services as a group rather than individually, has benefits to both customers and service companies. Customers find that bundling simplifies their purchase and payment, and companies find that the approach stimulates demand for the firm's service line, thereby achieving cost economies for the operations as a whole while increasing net contributions.[18] Bundling also allows the customer to pay less than when purchasing each of the services individually, which contributes to perceptions of value.

The effectiveness of price bundling depends on how well the service firm understands the bundles of value that customers or segments perceive, and on the complementarity of demand for these services. Effectiveness also depends on the right choice of services from the firm's point of view. Because the firm's objective is to increase overall sales, the services selected for bundling should be those with a relatively small

FIGURE 17.13

Pricing Strategies When the Customer Defines Value as All That Is Received for All That Is Given

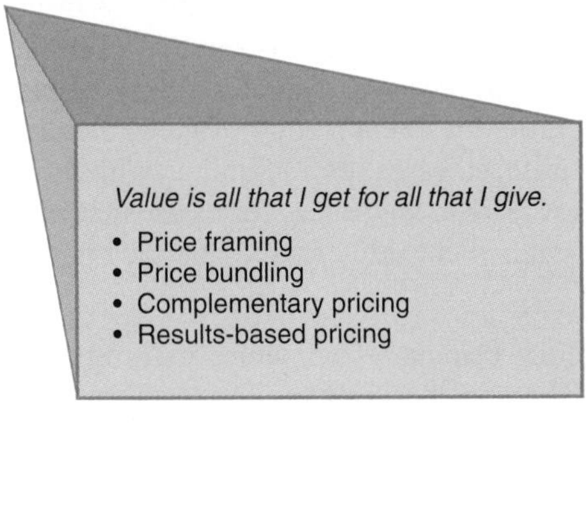

Value is all that I get for all that I give.
- Price framing
- Price bundling
- Complementary pricing
- Results-based pricing

sales volume without the bundling to minimize revenue loss from discounting a service that already has a high sales volume.

Approaches to bundling include mixed bundling and mixed-leader bundling.[19] In *mixed bundling,* the customer can purchase the services individually or as a package, but a price incentive is offered for purchasing the package. As an example, a health club customer may be able to contract for aerobics classes at $10 per month, weight machines at $15, and pool privileges at $15—or the group of three services for $27 (a price incentive of $13 per month).[20] In *mixed-leader bundling,* the price of one service is discounted if the first service is purchased at full price. For example, if cable TV customers buy one premium channel at full price, they can acquire a second premium channel at a reduced monthly rate. The objective is to reduce the price of the higher-volume service to generate an increase in its volume that "pulls" an increase in demand for a lower-volume but higher-contribution margin service.

Complementary Pricing

Services that are highly interrelated can be leveraged by using complementary pricing. This pricing includes three related strategies—captive pricing, two-part pricing, and loss leadership.[21] In *captive pricing* the firm offers a base service or product and then provides the supplies or peripheral services needed to continue using the service. In this situation the company could offload some part of the price for the basic service to the peripherals. For example, cable services often drop the price for installation to a very low level, then compensate by charging enough for the peripheral services to make up for the loss in revenue. With service firms, this strategy is often called *two-part pricing,* because the service price is broken into a fixed fee plus variable usage fees (also found in telephone services, health clubs, and commercial services such as rentals). *Loss leadership* is the term typically used in retail stores when providers place a familiar service on special largely to draw the customer to the store and then reveal other levels of service available at higher prices.

Results-Based Pricing

In service industries in which outcome is very important but uncertainty is high, the most relevant aspect of value is the *result* of the service. In personal injury lawsuits, for example, clients value the settlement they receive at the conclusion of the service. From tax accountants, clients value cost savings. From trade schools, students most value getting a job upon graduation. From Hollywood stars, production companies value high grosses. In these and other situations, an appropriate value-based pricing strategy is to price on the basis of results or outcome of the service.

The most commonly known form of results-based pricing is a practice called *contingency pricing* used by lawyers. Contingency pricing is the major way that personal injury and certain consumer cases are billed; in one study, contingency pricing accounted for 12 percent of commercial law billings.[22] In this approach, lawyers do not receive fees or payment until the case is settled, when they are paid a percentage of the money that the client receives. Therefore, only an outcome in the client's favour is compensated. From the client's point of view, the pricing makes sense in part because most clients in these cases are unfamiliar with and possibly intimidated by law firms. Their biggest fears are high fees for a case that may take years to settle. By using contingency pricing, clients are ensured that they pay no fees until they receive a settlement.

Sealed Bid Contingency Pricing   Companies wishing to gain the most value from their services purchases are increasingly turning to a form of results-based pricing that involves sealed bids guaranteeing results. Consider the challenge of a school district with energy bills so high that money was diverted from its primary mission of educating students. The school board wanted a long-term solution to the problem. The EMS Company, an engineering firm providing services to control and reduce energy use in large buildings, proposed a computer-controlled system that monitored energy use and operated on/off valves for all energy-using systems. The proposal specified a five-year contract with a fixed price of $254,500 per year, with the additional guarantee that the school district would save at least that amount of money every year or EMS would refund the difference.[23]

Although two other firms submitted lower multiyear bids of $190,000 and $215,000 annually, neither bid provided any guarantee for energy savings. EMS was awarded the bid. During the first year, actual calculated savings exceeded $300,000. The use of contingency pricing by EMS removed the risk from the school board's decision and added profits at EMS.[24]

Money-Back Guarantees Many colleges offer one major promise: to get students jobs upon graduation. So many schools commit to this promise—often blatantly in television advertising—that prospective students have come to distrust all promises from these colleges. To give substance to its promise, Brown-MacKenzie College, a for-profit institution, offered a tuition-back guarantee to any graduate who, after due effort, failed to obtain a suitable position within 90 days of program completion. A future-income-dependent payment plan has also been considered by many schools. Under such a plan, a student would receive a full scholarship and, after graduation, pay a fixed percentage of salary for a set period—for example, 5 percent of salary for 20 years.[25]

Commission Many services providers—including real estate agents and advertising agencies—earn their fees through commissions based on a percentage of the selling price. In these and other industries, commission is paid by the supplier rather than the buyer. Advertising agencies are paid 15 percent commission by the print and broadcast

FIGURE 17.14

Summary of Service Pricing Strategies for Four Customer Definitions of Value

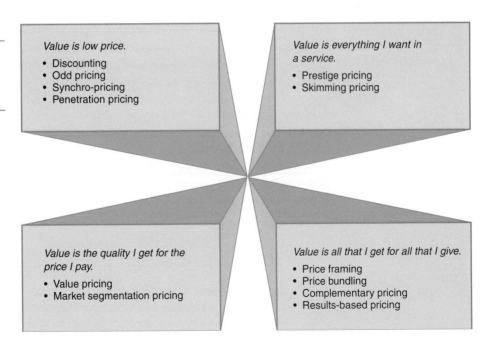

Value is low price.
- Discounting
- Odd pricing
- Synchro-pricing
- Penetration pricing

Value is everything I want in a service.
- Prestige pricing
- Skimming pricing

Value is the quality I get for the price I pay.
- Value pricing
- Market segmentation pricing

Value is all that I get for all that I give.
- Price framing
- Price bundling
- Complementary pricing
- Results-based pricing

media (newspaper, radio, TV, magazines) for the amount of advertising that they place with the media, but agencies are not paid by their clients. Real estate agents are usually paid 6 percent of the selling price of a house.

The commission approach to services pricing is compelling in that agents are compensated most when they find the highest rates and fares. It would seem that agents have an underlying motivation to avoid the lowest fares and rates for their clients.

SUMMARY

This chapter began with three key differences between customer evaluation of pricing for services and goods: (1) customers often have inaccurate or limited reference prices for services, (2) price is a key signal to quality in services, and (3) monetary price is not the only relevant price to service customers. These three differences can have profound impact on the strategies that companies use to set and administer prices for services. The chapter next discussed common pricing structures, including (1) cost-based, (2) competition-based, and (3) demand-based pricing. Central to the discussion were the specific challenges in each of these structures and the services pricing techniques that have emerged in practice.

Finally, the chapter defined customer perceptions of value and suggested appropriate pricing strategies that match each customer definition. Figure 17.14 summarizes these definitions and strategies. The four value definitions include (1) value is low price, (2) value is whatever I want in a product or service, (3) value is the quality I get for the price I pay, and (4) value is all that I get for all that I give.

Discussion Questions

1. Which approach to pricing (cost-based, competition-based, or demand-based) is the most fair to customers? Why?
2. Is it possible to use all three approaches simultaneously when pricing services? If you answer yes, describe a service that is priced this way.
3. For what consumer services do you have reference prices? What makes these services different from others for which you lack reference prices?
4. Name three services you purchase in which price is a signal to quality. Do you believe that there are true differences across services that are priced high and those that are priced low? Why or why not?
5. Describe the nonmonetary costs involved in the following services: getting an automobile loan, belonging to a health club, having allergies diagnosed and treated, attending an executive education class, and getting braces.
6. Consider the specific pricing strategies for each of the four customer value definitions. Which of these strategies could be adapted and used with another value definition?

Exercises

1. List five services for which you have no reference price. Now put yourself in the role of the service providers for two of those services and develop pricing strategies. Be sure to include in your description which of the value definitions you

believe customers will possess and what types of strategies would be appropriate given those definitions.

2. In the next week, find three price lists for services (such as from a restaurant, dry cleaner, or hairstylist). Identify the pricing base and the strategy used in each of them. How effective is each?

3. Consider that you are the owner of a new private college and can prepare a value/price package that is appealing to students. Describe your approach. How does it differ from existing offerings?

4. Go to Priceline.com and get familiar with how the site works.

Notes

1. Peter Lewis, "Pay to Play," *Fortune*, January 7, 2002, pp. 115–17.
2. Canadian Recording Industry Association, "Threat of Piracy to the Legitimate Industry," www.cria.ca/antipiracy.php, accessed October 3, 2006.
3. Larry LeBlanc, "Bell Dialing for Downloads," *Billboard*, March 18, 2006, p. 20.
4. Table compiled from information from company websites and "Archambault Group Launches Archambaultzik.ca, the First French-Language Music Download Site in Canada," January 16, 2004, www.quebecor.com, accessed October 3, 2006; Rob McIntyre, "Canada's Legal Music Download Services," www.music bymailcanada.com/CADOWN.html, accessed October 3, 2006; Fred Goodman, "Will Fans Pay for Music Online?" *Rolling Stone*, January 31, 2002, pp. 17–18; "Bell Canada Acquires Majority Interest in Puretracks, Nation's Premiere Online Digital Music Service," *The Spill*, March 1, 2006, available http://spillmagazine. com/news.htm, accessed October 3, 2006; Larry LeBlanc, "Music Industry Sees Bright Digital Future," *Billboard*, April 2, 2005, p. 44.
5. K. Monroe, "The Pricing of Services," *Handbook of Services Marketing,* ed. C. A. Congram and M. L. Friedman (New York: AMACOM, 1989), pp. 20–31.
6. Ibid.
7. "Rent a Star for the Holidays," *People,* December 15, 2003.
8. M. A. Ernst, "Price Visibility and Its Implications for Financial Services," presentation at the Effective Pricing Strategies for Service Providers Conference, Institute for International Research, Boston, October 1994.
9. Monroe, "The Pricing of Services."
10. V. A. Zeithaml, "The Acquisition, Meaning, and Use of Price Information by Consumers of Professional Services," in *Marketing Theory: Philosophy of Science Perspectives,* ed. R. Bush and S. Hunt (Chicago: American Marketing Association, 1982), pp. 237–41.
11. C. H. Lovelock, "Understanding Costs and Developing Pricing Strategies," *Services Marketing* (New York: Prentice Hall, 1991), pp. 236–46.
12. A. Stevens, "Firms Try More Lucrative Ways of Charging for Legal Services," *The Wall Street Journal,* November 25, 1994, pp. B1ff.
13. C. L. Grossman, "The Driving Forces Behind Rental Car Costs," *USA Today,* October 25, 1994, p. 50.
14. V. A. Zeithaml, "Consumer Perceptions of Price, Quality, and Value: A Means–End Model and Synthesis of Evidence," *Journal of Marketing* 52 (July 1988), pp. 2–22.

15. All comments from these four sections are based on those from Zeithaml, "Consumer Perceptions," pp. 13–14.
16. Sean Monke, *Canada NewsWire*, September 13, 2005, p. 1, quoted in *The Globe and Mail*.
17. Monroe, "The Pricing of Services."
18. Ibid.
19. Ibid.
20. J. P. Guiltinan, "The Price Bundling of Services: A Normative Framework," *Journal of Marketing* 51 (April 1987): 74–85.
21. G. J. Tellis, "Beyond the Many Faces of Price: An Integration of Pricing Strategies," *Journal of Marketing* 50 (October 1986): 146–60.
22. A. Stevens, "Clients Second-Guess Legal Fees," *The Wall Street Journal,* January 6, 1995, pp. B1, B6.
23. Ibid.
24. Ibid.
25. K. Fox, *Service Marketing Newsletter* (Chicago: American Marketing Association, 1984), pp. 1–2.

PART 7

Service and the Bottom Line

‖‖

In this final section of the text, we discuss one of the most important questions about service that managers have been debating over the past 25 years: Is excellent service profitable to an organization? We pull together research and company experience, virtually all of it from the past decade, to answer this question. We present our own model of how the relationship works and show you alternative models that have been used in companies such as Sears. Our model shows how service qualty has offensive effects (gaining new customers) and defensive effects (retaining customers).

We also discuss several important performance models in this chapter. Return on service quality (ROSQ) is a modelling approach that allows a company to gauge the return on investments in different service activities. Customer equity is an extension of the ROSQ approach that compares investments in service with expenditures on other marketing activities. The balanced performance scorecard is an approach that includes multiple company factors including financial, customer, operational, and innovative measures. The balanced performance scorecard allows a company to measure performance from the customer's perspective (Chapter 10), from the employee's perspective (Chapter 12), and from an innovation and new service perspective (Chapter 9). Thus, in Chapter 18 we synthesize the measurement issues that underlie the provision of service and offer a way for companies to demonstrate that service is accountable financially. We also present an approach called strategic performance mapping that helps companies integrate all elements of their balanced scorecards. These models help companies understand more accurately their benefits from investments in service excellence.

Chapter

18

The Financial and Economic Impact of Service

"WHAT RETURN CAN I EXPECT ON SERVICE QUALITY IMPROVEMENTS?"

—A TYPICAL CEO

Consultants who work with companies to improve service quality find that the two most frequently asked questions are:

"How do I know that service quality improvements will be a good investment?"

"Where in the company do I invest money to achieve the highest return?"

For example, a restaurant chain, after conducting consumer research, found that service quality perceptions averaged 85 percent across the chain. The specific items receiving the lowest scores on the survey were appearance of the restaurant's exterior (70 percent), wait time for service

(78 percent), and limited menu (76 percent). The company's CEO wanted to know, first of all, whether making improvements in overall service quality or to any of the specific areas would result in revenues that exceeded their costs. Moreover, he wanted guidance as to which of the service aspects to tackle. He could determine how much each of the initiatives would cost to change, but that was as far as his financial estimates would take him. Clearly, the restaurant's exterior was most in need of change because it was rated lowest; but would it not also be by far the most expensive to change? What could he expect in return for improvements in each service area? Would adjustments in the other two factors be better investments? Which of the three service initiatives would generate noticeable improvements to raise the overall customer perceptions of the restaurant?

Ten years ago, these questions had to be answered on the basis of executive intuition. Today, more rigorous approaches exist to help managers make these decisions about service quality investments. The best-known and most widely respected approach is called return on service quality (ROSQ) and was developed by Roland Rust, Anthony Zahorik, and Tim Keiningham, a team of researchers and consultants.[1] The ROSQ approach is based on the following assumptions:

1. Quality is an investment.

2. Quality efforts must be financially accountable.

3. It is possible to spend too much on quality.

4. Not all quality expenditures are equally valid.

Their approach looks at investments in services as a chain of effects of the following form:

1. A service improvement effort will produce an increased level of customer satisfaction at the process or attribute level. For example, expending money to refurbish the exterior of the restaurants will likely increase customers' satisfaction level from the current low rating of 70 percent.

2. Increased customer satisfaction at the process or attribute level will lead to increased overall customer satisfaction. If satisfaction with the restaurant's exterior goes from 70 to 80 percent, overall service quality ratings may increase from 85 to 90 percent. (Both these percentage changes could be accurately measured the next time surveys are conducted and could even be projected in advance using the ROSQ model.)

3. Higher overall service quality or customer satisfaction will lead to increased behavioural intentions, such as greater repurchase intention and intention to increase usage. Customers who have not yet eaten at the restaurant will be drawn to do so, and many

who currently eat there once a month will consider increasing their patronage.

4. Increased behavioural intentions will lead to behavioural impact, including repurchase or customer retention, positive word of mouth, and increased usage. Intentions about patronizing the restaurant will become reality, resulting in higher revenues and more positive word-of-mouth communications.

5. Behavioural effects will then lead to improved profitability and other financial outcomes. Higher revenues will lead to higher profits for the restaurant, assuming that the original investment in refurbishing the exterior is covered.

The ROSQ methodology can help distinguish among all the company strategies, processes, approaches, and tactics that can be altered. The ROSQ approach is informative because it can be applied in companies to direct their individual strategies. Software has been developed to accompany the approach, and consulting firms work with companies to apply it. No longer do firms like the restaurant discussed here have to depend on intuition alone to guide them in their service quality investments.

In the current era of accountability, companies hunger for tools to monitor the payoff of new investments in service. Many managers still see service quality as costs rather than as contributors to profits, partly because of the difficulty involved in tracing the link between service and financial returns. Determining the financial impact of service parallels the age-old search for the connection between advertising and sales. Service quality's results—like advertising's results—are cumulative, and therefore, evidence of the link may not come immediately or even quickly after investments. And, like advertising, service quality is one of many variables—among them pricing, advertising, efficiency, and image—that simultaneously influence profits. Furthermore, spending on service per se does not guarantee results because strategy and execution must both also be considered.

In recent years, however, researchers and company executives have sought to understand the relationship between service and profits and have found strong evidence to support the relationship. For example, a recent study examined the comparative benefits of revenue expansion and cost reduction on return on quality. The research addressed a common strategic dilemma faced by executives: whether to reduce costs through the use of quality programs such as Six Sigma that focus on efficiencies and cost cutting, or to build revenues through improvements to customer service, customer satisfaction, and customer retention.[2] Using managers' reports as well as secondary data on firm profitability and stock returns, the study investigated whether the highest return on quality was generated from cost cutting, revenue expansion, or a combination of the two approaches. The results suggest that firms that adopt primarily a revenue expansion emphasis perform better and have higher return on quality than firms that emphasize either cost reduction or both revenue expansion and cost reduction together.[3]

Executives are also realizing that the link between service and profits is not simple. Service quality affects many economic factors in a company, some of them leading to profits through variables not traditionally in the domain of marketing. For example, the traditional total quality management approach expresses the financial impact of service quality in lowered costs or increased productivity. These relationships involve operational issues more than marketing issues.

More recently, other evidence has become available examining the relationship between service and profitability. The overall goal of this chapter is to synthesize that recent evidence and to identify relationships between service and profits. This chapter is divided into six sections, parallelling the chapter's objectives. In each section we assess the evidence and identify what is currently known about the topics. The chapter is organized using a conceptual framework linking all the variables in the topics.

SERVICE AND PROFITABILITY: THE DIRECT RELATIONSHIP

Figure 18.1 shows the underlying question at the heart of this chapter. Managers were first interested in this question in the 1980s when service quality emerged as a pivotal competitive strategy. Since that time, a significant amount of research has been conducted into the relationship between service and profit.[4] One study showed the favourable financial impact of complaint recovery systems.[5] Another found a significant and positive relationship between patient satisfaction and hospital profitability. In this study, specific dimensions of hospital service quality, such as billing and discharge processes, explained 17 to 27 percent of hospital earnings, net revenues, and return on assets.[6] Extending the definition of financial performance to include stock returns, another study found a significant positive link between changes in customer quality perceptions and stock return while holding constant the effects of advertising expenditures and return on investment.[7]

Research conducted by Canada's National Quality Institute (NQI) found the following results for Canada Awards for Excellence (CAE) winners:

- 91 percent improvement in employee turnover

- 215 percent increase in cost savings

- 90 percent increase in customer satisfaction

- 59 percent in price savings to client

- 57 percent decrease in injuries

From 1990 to 2005, CAE winners achieved a 143 percent increase in shareholder value. This compares to an overall gain of 88 percent for the TSE 300, a 78 percent gain among companies in the Dow Jones Industrial Average, and a 66 percent gain for the S&P 200.[8]

FIGURE 18.1

The Direct Relationship Between Service and Profits

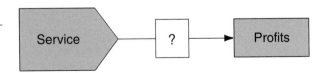

Linking Service to Profits

One way to view the relationship between service and profit has been developed by a group of Harvard professors and is called the "service-profit chain." The professors who created it argue many of the samepoints made in this chapter—that the longer customers stay with companies, the lower the costs to serve them, the higher the volume of purchases they make, the higher the price premium they tolerate, and the greater the positive word-of-mouth communication they engage in. These professors have provided evidence from in-depth studies in multiple companies.

At Sears, for instance, management spent a great deal of time developing a set of total performance indicators (TPI) that showed how well the company was doing:

> We use the TPI at every level of the company, in every store and facility; and nearly every manager has some portion of his or her compensation at risk on the basis of nonfinancial measures . . . . [I]n the course of the last 12 months, employee satisfaction on the Sears TPI has risen by almost 4% and customer satisfaction by 4% ... if our model is correct—and its predictive record is extremely good—that 4% improvement in customer satisfaction translates into more than $200 million in additional revenues in the past 12 months.

At BFI, the international waste management company, research showed that a 1 percent decline in customer defection led to an increase in pre-tax profit of $41 million. BFI worked backward from their customer satisfaction scores in order to further specify its causes—eventually learning that the biggest cause was the dependability of trash pickups. This is consistent with the model we have used in this text, which stresses that the most important dimension of service quality is usually reliability. Once BFI had identified the significance of dependable pickups, they were able to specify what other actions were needed to deliver on their promises.

During the mid-90s, CIBC management faced issues similar to those Sears and BFI faced. Defection rates were high, and there was concern they would go even higher. According to CIBC's analysis, profits were driven by customer behaviour, which was found to be influenced by employee commitment. Employee commitment, in turn, was driven by management style and leadership. When their analysis was complete, the bank's business model showed that a 1 percent increase in any one of their loyalty measures led to an increased profit of $0.60 per customer per month. In addition, they found that a 5 percent increase in employee commitment resulted in a 2 percent increase in customer loyalty.

Sources: J. L. Heskett, W. E. Sasser Jr., and L. A. Schlesinger, *The Service Profit Chain* (New York: The Free Press, 1997); Marc C. Epstein and Robert A. Westbrook, "Linking Actions to Profits in Strategic Decision Making," *MIT Sloan Management Review* 42, no. 3 (Spring 2004), pp. 39–49; an exhibit from A. J. Rucci, S. P. Kirn, and R. T. Quinn, "The Employee-Customer-Profit Chain at Sears," *Harvard Business Review,* January/February 1998, pp. 83–97. © 1998 by the President and Fellows of Harvard College. All rights reserved. Reprinted by permission of *Harvard Business Review.*

Exhibit 18.1 shows how some of these relationships have been examined at Sears, BFI, and CIBC. Although some companies continued to approach the relationship between service and profit at a broad level, others began to focus more specifically on particular elements of the relationship. For example, executives and researchers soon recognized that service quality played a different role in getting new customers than it did in retaining existing customers.

⟼ OFFENSIVE MARKETING EFFECTS OF SERVICE: ATTRACTING MORE AND BETTER CUSTOMERS

Service quality can help companies attract more and better customers to the business through *offensive marketing.*[9] Offensive effects (shown in Figure 18.2) involve market share, reputation, and price premiums. When service is good, a company gains a positive reputation and through that reputation a higher market share and the ability to charge more than its competitors for services. These benefits were documented in a multiyear, multicompany study called PIMS (profit impact of marketing strategy).

FIGURE 18.2

Offensive Marketing
Effects of Service on
Profits

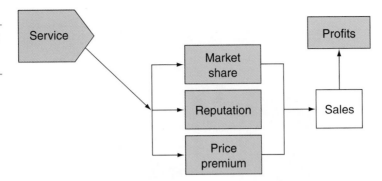

The PIMS research shows that companies offering superior service achieve higher-than-normal market share growth and that service quality influences profits through increased market share and premium prices as well as lowered costs and less rework.[10] The study found that businesses rated in the top fifth of competitors on relative service quality average an 8 percent price premium over their competitors.[11]

To document the impact of service on market share, a group of researchers described their version of the path between quality and market share, claiming that satisfied customers spread positive word of mouth, which leads to the attraction of new customers and then to higher market share. They claim that advertising service excellence without sufficient quality to back up the communications will not increase market share. Further, they confirm that there are time lags in market share effects, making the relationship between quality and market share difficult to discern in the short term.[12]

DEFENSIVE MARKETING EFFECTS OF SERVICE: CUSTOMER RETENTION

When it comes to keeping the customers a firm already has—an approach called *defensive marketing*[13]—researchers and consulting firms have in the last 15 years documented and quantified the financial impact of existing customers. In Chapter 7 we explained that customer defection, or "customer churn," is widespread in service businesses. Customer defection is costly to companies, because new customers must replace lost customers and replacement comes at a high cost. Getting new customers is expensive; it involves advertising, promotion, and sales costs as well as start-up operating expenses. New customers are often unprofitable for a period of time after acquisition. In the insurance industry, for example, the insurer does not typically recover selling costs until the third or fourth year of the relationship. Capturing customers from other companies is also an expensive proposition: A greater degree of service improvement is necessary to make a customer switch from a competitor than to retain a current customer. Selling costs for existing customers are much lower (on average 20 percent lower) than selling to new ones.[14]

In general, the longer a customer remains with the company, the more profitable the relationship is for the organization:

> Served correctly, customers generate increasingly more profits each year they stay with a company. Across a wide range of businesses, the pattern is the same: the longer a company keeps a customer, the more money it stands to make.[15]

FIGURE 18.3

TD Canada Trust offers an attractive incentive to new customers to get them to switch service providers.

Source: Photographer: Paul Weeks/Westside Studio.

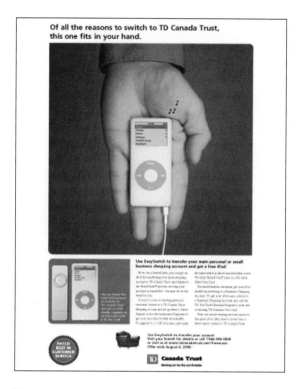

The money a company makes from retention comes from four sources (shown in Figure 18.3): costs, volume of purchases, price premium, and word-of-mouth communication. This section provides research evidence for many of the sources.

Lower Costs

Attracting a new customer can be five times more costly than retaining an existing one. A recent example of the kind of costs needed to acquire new customers in what is typically a "sticky" industry with relatively low levels of churn is provided by TD Canada Trust. Note in Figure 18.4 their strategy of giving free iPods to new customers who transfer their main chequing accounts. Consultants who have focused on these relationships assert that customer defections have a stronger effect on a company's profits than market share, scale, unit costs, and many other factors usually associated with competitive advantage.[16] They also claim that, depending on the industry, companies can increase profits from 25 to 85 percent by retaining just 5 percent more of their customers. A U.S. study conducted on winners of the Malcolm Baldrige National Quality Award found that quality reduced costs: order processing time decreased on average by 12 percent per year, errors and defects fell by 10 percent per year, and cost of quality declined by 9 percent per year.

Consider the following facts about the role of service quality in lowering costs:

- "Our highest quality day was our lowest cost of operations day" (Fred Smith, FedEx).

- "Our costs of not doing things right the first time were from 25 to 30 percent of our-revenue" (David F. Colicchio, regional quality manager, Hewlett-Packard Company).[17]

FIGURE 18.4

Defensive Marketing
Effects of Service on
Profits

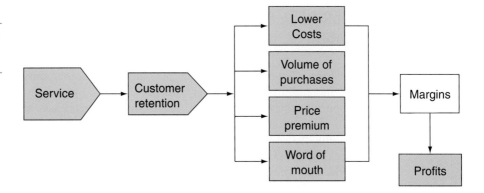

- Profit on services purchased by a 10-year customer is on average three times greater than for a 5-year customer.[18]

- Bain and Company, a consulting organization specializing in retention research, estimates that in the life insurance business, a 5 percent annual increase in customer retention lowers a company's costs per policy by 18 percent.

Volume of Purchases

Customers who are satisfied with a company's services are likely to increase the amount of money they spend with that company or the types of services offered. A customer satisfied with a broker's services, for example, will likely invest more money when it becomes available. Similarly, a customer satisfied with a bank's chequing services is likely to open a savings account with the same bank and to use the bank's loan services as well.

Price Premium

Evidence suggests that a customer who notices and values the services provided by a company will pay a price premium for those services. Graniterock, a winner of the Baldrige Award, has been able to command prices up to 30 percent higher than competitors for its rock (a product that many would claim is a commodity!) because it offers off-hour delivery and 24-hour self-service. In fact, most of the service quality leaders in industry command higher prices than their competitors: Purolator collects more for overnight delivery than Canada Post, Hertz rental cars cost more than Avis cars, and staying at the Ritz-Carlton is more expensive than staying at the Four Seasons.

Word-of-Mouth Communication

In Chapter 3, we described the valuable role of word-of-mouth communications in purchasing service. Because word of mouth is considered more credible than other sources of information, the best type of promotion for a service may well come from other customers who advocate the services provided by the company. Word of mouth brings new customers to the firm, and the financial value of this form of advocacy can be calibrated by the company in terms of the promotional costs it saves as well as the streams of revenues from new customers.

CUSTOMER PERCEPTIONS OF SERVICE AND PURCHASE INTENTIONS

In Chapter 5 we highlighted the links among customer satisfaction, service quality, and increased purchases. Here we provide more research and empirical evidence supporting these relationships. For example, researchers at Xerox offered a compelling insight about the relationship between satisfaction and purchase intentions. Initially, the company focused on satisfied customers, which they identified as those checking either a "4" or a "5" on a five-point satisfaction scale. Careful analysis of the data showed that customers giving Xerox 5s were six times more likely to indicate that they would repurchase Xerox equipment than those giving 4s. This relationship encouraged the company to focus on increasing the 5s rather than the 4s and 5s because of the strong sales and profitability implications.[19] Figure 18.5 shows this relationship.

Evidence also shows that customer satisfaction and service quality perceptions affect consumer intentions to behave in other positive ways—praising the firm, preferring the company over others, increasing volume of purchases, or agreeably paying a price premium. Most of the early evidence looked only at overall benefits in terms of purchase intention rather than examining specific types of behavioural intentions. One study, for example, found a significant association between overall patient satisfaction and intent to choose a hospital again.[20] Another, using information from a Swedish customer satisfaction barometer, found that stated repurchase intention is strongly related to stated satisfaction across virtually all product categories.[21]

More recently, studies have found relationships between service quality and more specific behavioural intentions. One study involving university students found strong links between service quality and other behavioural intentions of strategic importance to a university, including behaviour such as saying positive things about the school, planning to contribute money to the class pledge on graduation, and planning to recommend the school to employers as a place from which to recruit.[22] Another comprehensive study examined a battery of 13 specific behavioural intentions likely to result from perceived service quality. The overall measure was significantly correlated with customer perceptions of service quality.[23]

Individual companies have also monitored the impact of service quality on selected behavioural intentions. Toyota found that intent to repurchase a Toyota automobile increased from a base of 37 to 45 percent with a positive sales experience, from

FIGURE 18.5

The Effects of
Service

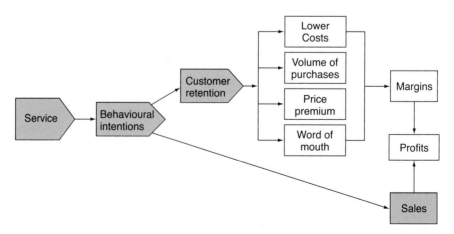

37 to 79 percent with a positive service experience, and from 37 to 91 percent with both positive sales and service experiences.[24] A similar study quantitatively assessed the relationship between level of service quality and willingness to purchase at AT&T. Of AT&T's customers who rated the company's overall quality as excellent, more than 90 percent expressed willingness to purchase from AT&T again. For customers rating the service as good, fair, or poor, the percentages decreased to 60, 17, and 0 percent, respectively. According to these data, willingness to repurchase increased at a steeper rate (by 43 percent) as the service quality rating improved from fair to good than when it went from poor to fair (17 percent) or from good to excellent (30 percent).[25]

Exhibit 18.2 shows a list of the questions that businesses still need to know more about on this topic and the others in this chapter.

THE KEY DRIVERS OF SERVICE QUALITY, CUSTOMER RETENTION, AND PROFITS

Understanding the relationship between overall service quality and profitability is important, but it is perhaps more useful to managers to identify specific drivers of service quality that most relate to profitability (shown in Figure 18.6). Doing so will help firms understand what aspects of service quality to change to influence the relationship, and therefore where to invest resources.

Most evidence for this issue has come from examining the aspects of service (such as empathy, responsiveness, and tangibles) on overall service quality, customer satisfaction, and purchase intentions rather than on financial outcomes such as retention or profitability. As you have discovered in this text, service is multifaceted, consisting of a wide variety of customer-perceived dimensions including reliability, responsiveness, and empathy and resulting from innumerable company strategies such as technology and process improvement. In research exploring the relative importance of service dimensions on overall service quality or customer satisfaction, the bulk of the support confirms that reliability is most critical; but other research has demonstrated the importance of customization and other factors. Because the dimensions and attributes are delivered in many cases with totally different internal strategies, resources must be allocated where they are most needed, and study in this topic could provide direction.

Some companies and researchers have viewed the effect of specific service encounters on overall service quality or customer satisfaction and the effect of specific behaviours within service encounters. As we discussed more fully in Chapters 5 and 8,

FIGURE 18.6

The Key Drivers of Service Quality, Customer Retention, and Profits

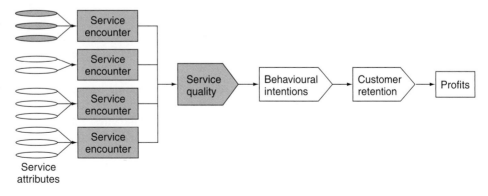

Service attributes

EXHIBIT 18.2

Service Quality and the Economic Worth of Customers: Businesses Still Need to Know More

Topic	Key Research Questions
Service quality and profitability: the direct relationship	1. What methodologies need to be developed to allow companies to capture the effect of service quality on profit? 2. What measures are necessary to examine the relationship in a consistent, valid, and reliable manner? 3. Does the relationship between service quality and profitability vary by industry, country, category of business (e.g., in services companies vs. goods companies, in industrial vs. packaged goods companies), or other variables? 4. What are the moderating factors of the relationship between service quality and profitability? 5. What is the optimal spending level on service in order to affect profitability?
Offensive effects of service quality	1. What is the optimal amount of spending on service quality to obtain offensive effects on reputation? 2. To obtain offensive effect, are expenditures on advertising or service quality itself more effective? 3. In what ways can companies signal high service quality to customers to obtain offensive effects?
Defensive effects of service quality	1. What is a loyal customer? 2. What is the role of service in defensive marketing? 3. How does service compare in effectiveness to other retention strategies such as price? 4. What levels of service provision are needed to retain customers? 5. How can the effects of word-of-mouth communication from retained customers be quantified? 6. What aspects of service are most important for customer retention? 7. How can defection-prone customers be identified?
Perceptions of service quality, behavioural intentions, and profits	1. What is the relationship between customer purchase intentions and initial purchase behaviour in services? 2. What is the relationship between behavioural intentions and repurchase in services? 3. Does the degree of association between service quality and behaviour change at different quality levels?
Identifying the key drivers of service quality, customer retention, and profits	1. What service encounters are most responsible for perceptions of service quality? 2. What are the key drivers in each service encounter? 3. Where should investments be made to affect service quality, purchase, retention, and profits? 4. Are key drivers of service quality the same as key drivers of behavioural intentions, customer retention, and profits?

Marriott Hotels conducted extensive customer research to determine what service elements contribute most to customer loyalty. They found that four of the top five factors came into play in the first 10 minutes of the guest's stay—those that involved the early encounters of arriving, checking in, and entering the hotel rooms. Other companies have found that mistakes or problems that occur in early service encounters are particularly critical, because a failure at early points results in greater risk for dissatisfaction in each ensuing encounter.

COMPANY PERFORMANCE MEASUREMENT: THE BALANCED PERFORMANCE SCORECARD

Traditionally, organizations have measured their performance almost completely on the basis of financial indicators such as profit, sales, and return on investment. This short-term approach leads companies to emphasize financials to the exclusion of other performance indicators. Today's corporate strategists recognize the limitations of evaluating corporate performance on financials alone, contending that these income-based financial figures measure yesterday's decisions rather than indicate future performance. This recognition came when many companies' strong financial records deteriorated because of unnoticed declines in operational processes, quality, or customer satisfaction.[26] In the words of one observer of corporate strategy:

> Financial measures emphasize profitability of inert assets over any other mission of the company. They do not recognize the emerging leverage of the soft stuff—skilled people and employment of information—as the new keys to high performance and near-perfect customer satisfaction. ... If the only mission a measurement system conveys is financial discipline, an organization is directionless.[27]

For this reason, companies began to recognize that *balanced performance scorecards*—strategic measurement systems that captured other areas of performance—were needed. The developers of balanced performance scorecards defined them as follows:

> ... a set of measures that gives top managers a fast but comprehensive view of the business .... [that] complements the financial measures with operational measures of customer satisfaction, internal processes, and the organization's innovation and improvement activities—operational measures that are the drivers of future financial performance.[28]

Having a firm handle on what had been viewed as "soft" measures became the way to help organizations identify customer problems, improve processes, and achieve company objectives.

Balanced performance scorecards have become extremely popular. One recent report indicates that 70 percent of the *Fortune* 1,000 companies have or are experimenting with balanced performance scorecards and more than one-half of the largest companies worldwide use them. Furthermore, according to a report called "Measures That Matter" from Ernst and Young's Center for Business Innovation, investors give nonfinancial measures an average of one-third the weight when making a decision to buy or sell any given stock,[29] strongly demonstrating to companies that investors recognize the value of the new forms of measurement.

As shown in Figure 18.7, the balanced performance scorecard captures three perspectives in addition to the financial perspective: customer, operational, and learning. The balanced scorecard brings together, in a single management report, many of the previously separated elements of a company and forces senior managers to consider all the important measures together. The scorecard has been facilitated by recent developments in enterprise-wide software (discussed in the Technology Spotlight) that allow companies to create, automate, and integrate measurements from all parts of the company.

Methods for measuring financial performance are the most developed and established in corporations, having been created more than 400 years ago. In contrast, efforts to measure market share, quality, innovation, human resources, and customer satisfaction have only recently been created. Companies can improve their performance by developing this discipline in their measurement of all four categories. As noted

FIGURE 18.7 Sample Measurements for the Balanced Scorecard

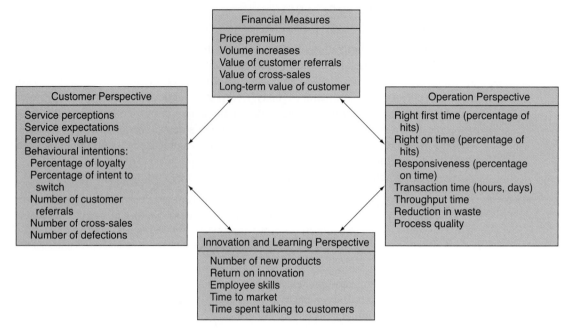

by researchers Marc Epstein and Robert Westbrook, "Much of what has been written about profitability modeling does not take a cross functional approach." A welcome exception to this is represented by Epstein's "Customer Profitability Analysis," recently published by the Society of Management Accountants of Canada (CMAs).[30]

Changes to Financial Measurement

One way that service leaders are changing financial measurement is to calibrate the defensive effect of retaining and losing customers. The monetary value of retaining customers can be projected through the use of average revenues over the lifetimes of customers. The number of customer defections can then be translated into lost revenue to the firm and become a critical company performance standard:

> Ultimately, defections should be a key performance measure for senior management and a fundamental component of incentive systems. Managers should know the company's defection rate, what happens to profits when the rate moves up or down and why defections occur.[31]

Companies can also measure actual increases or decreases in revenue from retention or defection of customers by capturing the value of a loyal customer, including expected cash flows over a customer's lifetime or lifetime customer value (as described in Chapter 7). Other possible financial measures (as shown in Figure 18.7) include the value of price premiums, volume increases, customer referrals, and cross sales.

Customer Perceptual Measures

Customer perceptual measures are leading indicators of financial performance. As we discussed in this chapter, customers who are not happy with the company will defect and will tell others about their dissatisfaction. As we also discussed, perceptual measures

Technology Spotlight

Automating the Balanced Scorecard

A study of the usage of balanced scorecards by North American organizations, sponsored by six organizations that are involved in their preparation and use (AICPA, CAM-I, CMA Canada, IQPC, Targus Corporation, and Hyperion Solutions), examined the factors that make the use of scorecards successful. One of the most important factors was software automation of the scorecards, and the study found that 70 percent of organizations who use balanced scorecards currently use some form of off-the-shelf or in-house software. The use of software allows companies to collect and report information quickly and continuously, removing the time-consuming task of updating data and freeing employees and management to focus on the strategic aspects of the scorecard.

Thirty-six percent of organizations that use software, and virtually all that have been using scorecards for more than five years, use Microsoft Excel spreadsheets, largely because they are easy to use, widely available, inexpensive, and flexible. Spreadsheets are flexible because a template can be created into which multiple parts of

the organization can enter their data. Organizations also tend to add, eliminate, or change measures, and spreadsheets offer the flexibility of adapting. However, users have found that spreadsheets make benchmarking scorecards across performance units difficult because departments can interpret measures differently and can engage in gamesmanship. Spreadsheets are also difficult to maintain because the data are not collected electronically and must be updated by area.

The second-most-popular software is Hyperion's Performance Scorecard, one of the off-the-shelf packages that has been developed by software companies. Hyperion Solutions reports that 88 of the Fortune 100 companies, 66 of the Nikkei top 100, 53 of the Financial Times Europe Top 100, 10 of the top 10 banks and 5 of the top 5 industrial equipment companies use the company's Balanced Performance Scorecard software. These packages have the following advantages over spreadsheet software: better data security, a more focused tool, and more consistent information across the firm. These off-the-shelf programs can extract data from multiple transactional systems and integrate it into one version of the company's financial and operational performance. Therefore, all managers have the same facts and metrics, giving them a common understanding of the factors affecting overall performance.

Organizations use five different ways to communicate scorecard results: paper, email, the Web, LANs, and WANs. The method used by a company tends to be related to organizational size and the use of software. The smallest organizations (fewer than 100 employees)

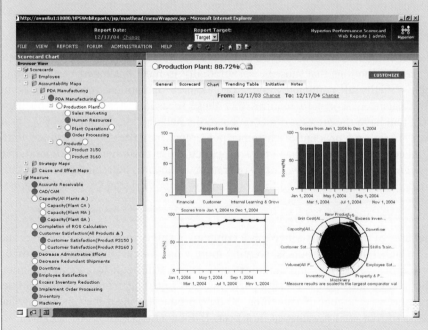

continued

Technology Spotlight

Automating the Balanced Scorecard—continued

typically use paper-based reporting. Medium-sized companies use email and the Web to report the results of spreadsheet software, and companies that use the Web are the most likely to report success. The largest organizations use technologically sophisticated techniques like the Web and LANs, which are easy to use in combination with off-the-shelf software.

The survey showed that the most important feature related to success in using software for balanced scorecards is the ability to provide Web-based reporting. This feature was followed by the ability to drill down to root data, the ability to customize reports, and the ability to link scorecards and roll them up. The system also needs to be able to access data from multiple legacy systems and other data sources and must be flexible enough to easily accommodate future changes to the scorecarding system.

Sources: R. Lawson, W. Stratton, and T. Hatch, "Automating the Balanced Scorecard," *CMA Management* 77, no. 9 (2004), pp. 39–44; www.hyperion.com.

reflect customer beliefs and feelings about the company and its products and services and can predict how the customer will behave in the future. Overall forms of the measurements we discussed in Chapters 5 and 6 (shown in the customer perspective box of Figure 18.7) are measures that can be included in this category. Among the measures that are valuable to track are overall service perceptions and expectations, customer satisfaction, perceptual measures of value, and behavioural intention measures such as loyalty and intent to switch. A company that notices a decline in these numbers should be concerned that the decline will translate into lost dollars for the company.

Operational Measures

Operational measures involve the translation of customer perceptual measures into the standards or actions that must be set internally to meet customers' expectations. Although virtually all companies count or calculate operational measures in some form, the balanced scorecard requires that these measures stem from the business processes that have the greatest effect on customer satisfaction. In other words, these measures are not independent of customer perceptual measures but instead are intricately linked with them. In Chapter 10 we called these customer-linked operational measures *customer-defined standards*—operational standards determined through customer expectations and calibrated the way the customer views and expresses them.

Innovation and Learning

The final area of measurement involves a company's ability to innovate, improve, and learn—by launching new products, creating more value for customers, and improving operating efficiencies. This measurement area is most difficult to capture quantitatively but can be accomplished using performance-to-goal percentages. For example, a company can set a goal of launching 10 new products a year, then measure what percentage of that goal it achieves in a year. If four new products are launched, its percentage for the year is 40 percent, which can then be compared with subsequent years.

The Global Feature shows that implementation of the balanced performance scorecard can vary by culture.

The Balanced Scorecard in Practice

The balanced scorecard has been implemented not only in corporations but also in government and nonprofit organizations. In 2001 the University of Virginia Library (UVL), a system of 11 different libraries with holdings of four million volumes, became the first library in North America to begin using a balanced scorecard to improve its performance.[32]

Lynda White, associate director of management information services at UVL, says that the scorecard is currently used as a management tool to assess the health of the organization, to indicate areas in which it is doing well and other areas that need attention, and to assemble information in a meaningful way. The organization began development of the scorecard by prioritizing the many numbers in the statistics and data that it had collected over the years.

The library's scorecard uses four categories of measures: the user perspective, the internal processes perspective, the financial perspective, and the learning and growth perspective. Each of the four perspectives has four to six measures that tell the organization how well the library is doing in each area. The first two categories, focusing on users and internal processes, were easy for the library to understand and measure. The metrics for user perspective helped the library improve customer service, as White describes:

> We measure how well we do in customer service, what faculty and students think of services and collections, what students think of user instruction, how much special collections is used, how much patrons use new books and electronic resources, how quickly we turn around requests (for searches, recalls, library electronic ordering [LEO] document delivery, interlibrary loan, scanning for e-reserves, new books), how fast and accurately we re-shelve, Web-site usability, renovation of public-service areas, increasing access to digital materials. And of course, measuring the unit cost of various services affects them as taxpayers or donors. It addresses whether we are using their money wisely and efficiently.[33]

According to Jim Self, director of management information services at the library, the other two categories were more difficult. Because UVL, like most libraries, is nonprofit, the financial perspective was the most challenging. In determining what to measure, the scorecard gave the library an opportunity to look at the financial aspects of its operation that had not been emphasized before, such as processing costs incurred in cataloging and acquisitions and transaction costs in reference, circulation, and interlibrary loan.

The organization realized the value of the scorecard when it compared its actual performance to its assumed performance. It found out, for example, that turnaround times for ordering books requested by users were much slower than its promises. It had been promising users that it could get new books for them in one week, but it found that only 17 percent of new books it ordered on request were ready in seven days. Through this comparison and others, the balanced scorecard helped the library look at its priorities, goals, and vision statements, align them with each other, and simplify its priority list. The library's special website (www.lib.virginia.edu/bsc) describes the history, measures, and implementation of the scorecard.

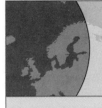

Global Feature

Challenges to Implementation of the Balanced Performance Scorecard in China

As China continues to develop into a world economic power, its organizations are recognizing the value of strategic management concepts to help them formulate and execute effective and competitive strategies. Chinese organizations are now joining the organizations in the world that have adopted the balanced performance scorecard.

Companies in China face many of the same external and internal challenges as Western companies face, including rapidly changing business conditions, increasing competition, and increasing customer expectations. However, many Chinese organizations are unfamiliar with the building blocks needed for strategy development—such as analysis of the business life cycle, SWOT (strengths, weaknesses, opportunities, and threats) analysis, and development of value propositions for target markets. Chinese companies had been successful largely based on entrepreneurship, intuition, or prior market dominance, approaches that have been unsuccessful as competition has intensified.

Consultants and companies that have implemented balanced scorecards in China recognize special challenges:

1. Goal-setting processes are not flexible enough to allow companies to adapt quickly, largely because companies lack the ability to track, analyze, and change goals.

2. Measurement data is either not readily available or is scattered across the organization, with no single system for recording or displaying the information. Enterprise software systems usually have data in the financial and operational areas but lack data in the customer and learning/growth perspectives.

3. Performance appraisal systems in China are particularly susceptible to the problems created by

organizational silos, and managers are compensated based on functional performance.

4. Companies are less likely to have information technology systems to record data for employee evaluations. Therefore, human resource professionals or managers must manually calculate performance scores and bonuses.

Irv Beiman and Yong-Ling Sun of e-Gate Consulting Shanghai, consultants who have applied the balanced performance scorecard to workplaces in China, identify six critical success factors in implementing the scorecard methodology in workplaces: (1) committing and involving top management; (2) overcoming implementation hurdles; (3) overcoming functional silos; (4) establishing linkages to competency development and variable pay; (5) developing infrastructure to communicate the strategy, track performance, and make adjustments based on results; and (6) elevating human resources to the status of a strategic partner to line management. All these criteria are important for a firm in any country to have a successful balanced scorecard, but the challenges in China are harder to overcome, particularly in the area of human resources.

One of the biggest human resource issues is the way that executives, directors, and managers are paid. Variable pay, which creates incentives to aim for common goals, is infrequently used, and compensation is almost always based on individual departments' sales and revenue goals. For example, Chinese sales personnel are almost always paid exclusively for sales volume or revenue. Because of the way they are paid, they do not cooperate with other departments, which results in conflict and tension, particularly with production departments. Consider the experience of a private entrepreneurial company in China. Each department in the firm had developed its own way of approaching work, without coordinating with

continued

Global Feature

Challenges to Implementation of the Balanced Performance Scorecard in China
—continued

other departments. Compensation was based on each department's performance rather than common performance. When faced with increasing pressure from nternational competition in their domestic markets, the firm recognized that it needed to revise its strategy and focus on external customer needs. The company adopted the balanced scorecard methodology and initially found that managers constantly complained about employees in other departments, placing the blame on them. After implementation of the scorecard, managers began working more cooperatively with each other by sharing objectives across departments, improving cross-functional business processes, and fostering teamwork. Measurable improvements in company performance resulted.

Another human resource issue involves performance appraisal, performance management, and job descriptions, which do not always exist in Chinese firms. When they do exist, they are created in each individual department, meaning that each department knows only a piece of the work done by the organization. As a result, training across departments is not connected with a focus on the customer or the firm's overall strategy. In situations in which the balanced performance scorecard approach has been used effectively, the human resource function assumes the responsibility for job descriptions, performance appraisals, variable compensation, and other policies that support strategy execution.

Sources: I. Beiman and Y. L. Sun, "Using the Balanced Scorecard for Strategy Execution in China," *China Staff* 9, no. 8 (2003), pp. 10–14; I. Beiman and Y. Sun, "Implementing a Balanced Scorecard in China: Steps for Success," *China Staff* 9, no. 9 (2003), pp. 11–15. Used with permission.

Strategy Maps to Enhance Balanced Scorecards

The strategy map is a concept that was recently developed to help companies deploy the balanced scorecard more effectively. A strategy map provides a single-page visual representation of a firm's strategy (see Figure 18.8) that links the four perspectives of the balanced scorecard and thereby shows the cause-and-effect relationships among them.[34] Instead of merely showing the four clusters of metrics as separate categories linked by arrows, as shown in the figure, the strategy map shows how the typical 20 to 30 measures in a balanced scorecard are integrated in the creation of a single unified strategy and clearly demonstrates which variables lead, lag, and feed back into other variables. The map also identifies the capabilities of the organization's intangible assets—human capital, information capital, and organization capital—that are required for superior performance.

The essence of the map is that financial outcomes are possible only if targeted customers are satisfied, a complicated process achieved with a set of interrelated capabilities. The mapping process forces managers to identify cause and effect and to clarify the logic of how the company will create value and for whom.[35] As part of the process, companies must identify the customer value proposition and then describe how it will generate sales and loyalty from targeted customers. The company then must link the critical internal processes that are most important to deliver the

FIGURE 18.8 A Strategy Map Helps Companies Align Strategy with Performance

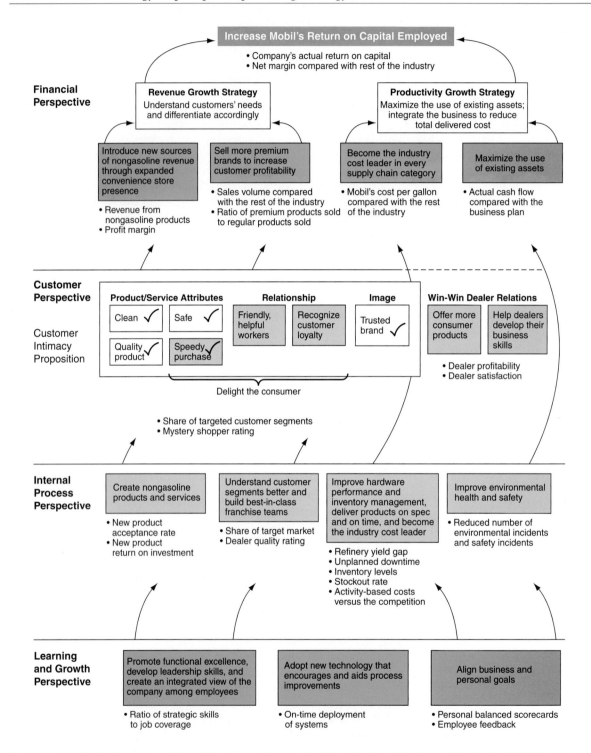

value proposition. Mapping helps identify any of the four categories in which management has not thought through metrics and strategies. Strategies are typically executed through a structure of strategic themes developed during the mapping.

Effective Nonfinancial Performance Measurements

According to field research conducted in 60 companies and survey responses from 297 senior executives, many companies do not identify and act on the correct nonfinancial measures.[36] One example involves a bank that surveyed satisfaction only from customers who physically entered the branches, a policy that caused some branch managers to offer free food and drinks in order to increase their scores. According to the authors of the study, companies make four major mistakes:

1. *Not linking measures to strategy*. Companies can easily identify hundreds of nonfinancial measures to track, but they also need to use analysis that identifies the most important drivers of their strategy. Successful organizations use value driver maps, tools that lay out the cause-and-effect relationships between drivers and strategic success. Figure 18.9 shows the causal model developed by a successful fast-food chain to understand the key drivers of shareholder value. The factors on

FIGURE 18.9

The measures that matter most: A causal model for a fast-food company shows the critical drivers of performance and the concepts that lead to shareholder value.

Source: Christopher D. Ittner and David F. Larcker, "Coming Up Short on Nonfinancial Performance Measurement," *Harvard Business Review,* November 2003, pp. 88–95.

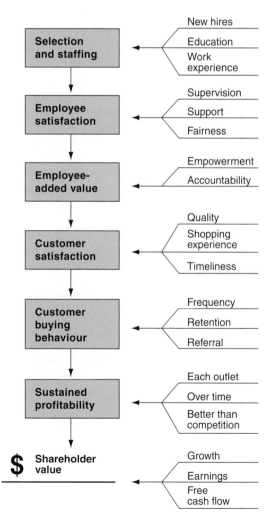

EXHIBIT 18.3

Customer Equity and Return on Marketing: Metrics to Match a Strategic Customer-Centred View of the Firm

Although the marketing concept has articulated a customer-centred viewpoint since the 1960s, marketing theory and practice have become incrementally customer-centred over the past 40 years. For example, marketing has only recently decreased its emphasis on short-term transactions and increased its focus on long-term customer relationships. Much of this refocus stems from the changing nature of the world's leading economies, which have undergone a century-long shift from the goods sector to the service sector.

Because service often tends to be more relationship based, this structural shift in the economy has resulted in more attention to relationships and therefore more attention to customers. This customer-centred viewpoint is starting to be reflected in the concepts and metrics that drive marketing management, including such metrics as customer value and voice of the customer. For example, the concept of brand equity, a fundamentally product-centred concept, is now being challenged by the customer-centred concept of *customer equity*.

Customer equity is the total of the discounted lifetime values summed over all the firm's customers.

In other words, customer equity is obtained by summing up the customer lifetime values of the firm's customers. In fast-moving and dynamic industries that involve customer relationships, products come and go but customers remain. Customers and customer equity may be more central to many firms than brands and brand equity, although current management practices and metrics do not yet fully reflect this shift. The shift from product-centred thinking to customer-centred thinking implies the need for an accompanying shift from product-based metrics to customer-based metrics.

USING CUSTOMER EQUITY IN A STRATEGIC FRAMEWORK

Consider the issues facing a typical marketing manager or marketing-oriented CEO: How do I manage my brand? How will my customers react to changes in service and service quality? Should I raise price? What is the best way to enhance the relationships with my current

customers? Where should I focus my efforts? Determining customer lifetime value, or customer equity, is the first step, but the more important step is to evaluate and test ideas and strategies using lifetime value as the measuring stick. At a very basic level, strategies for building customer relationships can affect five basic factors: retention rate, referrals, increased sales, reduced direct costs, and reduced marketing costs.

Rust, Zeithaml, and Lemon have developed an approach based on customer equity that can help business executives answer their questions. The model that represents this approach is shown in the accompanying figure. In this context, customer equity is a new approach to marketing and corporate strategy that finally puts the customer—and, more importantly, strategies that grow the value of the customer—at the heart of the organization. The researchers identify the drivers of customer equity—value equity, brand equity, and relationship equity—and explain how these drivers work, independently and together, to grow customer equity. Service strategies are prominent in both value equity and relationship equity. Within each of these drivers are specific, incisive actions ("levers") that the firm can take to enhance the firm's overall customer equity.

WHY IS CUSTOMER EQUITY IMPORTANT?

For most firms, customer equity—the total of the discounted lifetime values of all the firm's customers—is certain to be the most important determinant of the long-term value of the firm. Although customer equity will not be responsible for the entire value of the firm (consider, for example, physical assets, intellectual property, research and development competencies, etc.), the firm's current customers provide the most reliable source of future revenues and profits—and provide a focal point for marketing strategy.

Although it may seem obvious that customer equity is key to long-term success, understanding how to grow and manage customer equity is much more complex. Growing customer equity is of utmost importance, and doing it well can lead to significant competitive advantage.

continued

The Customer Equity Model

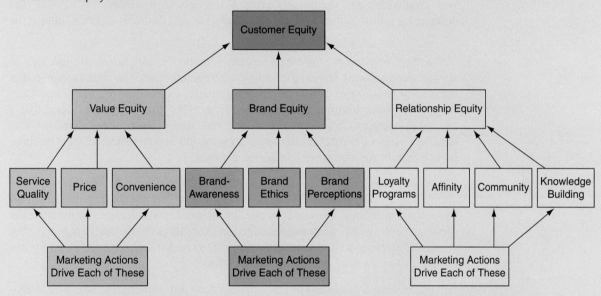

CALCULATING RETURN ON MARKETING USING CUSTOMER EQUITY

At the beginning of this chapter, we told you about an approach called return on quality that was developed to help companies understand where they could get the biggest impact from quality investments. A more general form of that approach is called return on marketing, which enables companies to look at all competing marketing strategy options and trade them off on the basis of projected financial return. This approach allows companies to not just examine the impact of service on financial return but also compare the impact of service with the impact of branding, price changes, and all other marketing strategies. Using the customer equity model, firms can analyze the drivers that have

the greatest impact, compare the drivers' performance with that of competitors' drivers, and project return on investment from improvements in the drivers. The framework enables what-if evaluation of marketing return on investment, which can include such criteria as return on quality, return on advertising, return on loyalty programs, and even return on corporate citizenship, given a particular shift in customer perceptions. This approach enables firms to focus marketing efforts on strategic initiatives that generate the greatest return.

Sources: R. T. Rust, K. N. Lemon, and V. A. Zeithaml, "Return on Marketing: Using Customer Equity to Focus Marketing Strategy," *Journal of Marketing* 68, no. 1 (January 2004), pp. 109; R. Rust, V. Zeithaml, and K. Lemon, *Driving Customer Equity* (New York: The Free Press, 2000).

the right were identified as most important in leading to the concepts on the left, and the sequence of concepts from top to bottom show the relationships among company strategies (such as selection and staffing) and intermediate results (such as employee and customer satisfaction) that result in financial results (such as sustained profitability and shareholder value). The study found that fewer than 30 percent of the firms surveyed used this causal modelling approach.

2. *Not validating the links.* Only 21 percent of companies in the study verify that the nonfinancial measures lead to financial performance. Instead, many firms decide what they are going to measure in each category and never link the categories. Many managers believed that the relationships were self-evident instead of conducting analysis to validate the linkages. Exhibit 18.3 shows one way companies can create this type of linkage. In general, it is critical that companies pull together all their data and examine the relationships among the categories.

3. *Not setting the right performance targets.* Companies sometimes aim too high in setting improvement targets. Targeting 100 percent customer satisfaction might seem to be a desirable goal, but many companies expend far too many resources to gain too little improvement in satisfaction. The study's authors found that a telecommunications company aiming for 100 percent customer satisfaction was wasting resources because customers who were 100 percent satisfied spent no more money than those who were 80 percent satisfied.[37]

4. *Measuring incorrectly.* Companies need to use metrics with statistical validity and reliability. Organizations cannot measure complex phenomenon with one or two simple measures, nor can they use inconsistent methodologies to measure the same concept, such as customer satisfaction. Another problem that companies may encounter is trying to use quantitative metrics to capture qualitative results for important factors such as leadership and innovation.

Creating a balanced scorecard in and of itself does not improve performance. Companies will not reap the benefits of techniques such as the balanced scorecard unless they address these four issues.

SUMMARY

This chapter is divided into six sections, five of which assess the evidence and identify what is currently known about the relationship between service and profitability. The chapter used a conceptual framework to link all the variables in these topics: (1) the direct relationship between service and profits; (2) offensive effects of service quality; (3) defensive effects of service quality; (4) the relationship between service quality and purchase intentions; (5) key drivers of service quality, customer retention, and profits. Considerable progress has been made in the last 10 years in the investigation of service quality, profitability, and the economic worth of customers, but managers are still lacking many of the answers that would help them make informed decisions about service quality investments. The chapter concluded with a discussion of the balanced performance scorecard approach to measuring corporate performance, which offers a strategic approach for measuring all aspects of a company's performance.

Discussion Questions

1. Why has it been difficult for executives to understand the relationship between service improvements and profitability in their companies?
2. What is the ROSQ model, and what is its significance to corporate America?
3. To this day, many companies believe that service is a cost rather than a revenue producer. Why might they hold this view? How would you argue the opposite view?
4. What is the difference between offensive and defensive marketing? How does service affect each of these?
5. What are the main sources of profit in defensive marketing?
6. What are the main sources of profit in offensive marketing?
7. How will the balanced performance scorecard help us understand and document the information presented in this chapter? Which of the five sections that discuss different aspects of the relationship between service quality and profits can it illuminate?

Exercises

1. On the Internet, use a search engine to locate three companies that make balanced scorecard software. What are the software companies' current offerings? How can the software firms help individual companies understand the concepts and relationships discussed in this chapter? Which of the three companies would you select based on the information you locate?
2. Interview a local firm and see what it knows about its key drivers of financial performance. What are the key service drivers of the firm? Does the company know whether these service drivers relate to profit?
3. Select a service industry (such as fast food) or a company (such as McDonald's) that you are familiar with, either as a customer or employee, and create a balanced scorecard. Describe the operational, customer, financial, and learning measures that could be used to capture performance.

Notes

1. R. T. Rust, A. J. Zahorik, and T. L. Keiningham, *Return on Quality* (Chicago: Probus, 1994).
2. R. T. Rust, C. Moorman, and P. R. Dickson, "Getting Return on Quality: Revenue Expansion, Cost Reduction, or Both?" *Journal of Marketing* 66 (October 2002), pp. 7–24.
3. Ibid.
4. J. Matthews and P. Katel, "The Cost of Quality: Faced with Hard Times, Business Sours on Total Quality Management," *Newsweek,* September 7, 1992, pp. 48–49; "The Cracks in Quality," *The Economist* 18 (April 1992), pp. 67–68; *Management Practice, U.S. Companies Improve Performance Through Quality Efforts,* Report No. GAO/NSIAD-91-190 (Washington, DC: U.S. General Accounting Office, 1992).

5. R. Rust, B. Subramanian, and M. Wells, "Making Complaints a Management Tool," *Marketing Management* 3 (1993), pp. 40–45.

6. E. Nelson, R. T. Rust, A. Zahorik, R. L. Rose, P. Batalden, and B. Siemanski, "Do Patient Perceptions of Quality Relate to Hospital Financial Performance?" *Journal of Healthcare Marketing,* December 1992, pp. 1–13.

7. D. A. Aaker and R. Jacobson, "The Financial Information Content of Perceived Quality," *Journal of Marketing* 58 (May 1994), pp. 191–201.

8. National Quality Institute, "Investing in Excellence: A Wise Choice. Celebrating Organizational Excellence in Canada," 2006, available www.nqi.ca/nqistore/product_details.aspx?ID=145, accessed October 3, 2006.

9. C. Fornell and B. Wernerfelt, "Defensive Marketing Strategy by Customer Complaint Management: A Theoretical Analysis," *Journal of Marketing Research* 24 (November 1987), pp. 337–46; see also C. Fornell and B. Wernerfelt, "A Model for Customer Complaint Management," *Marketing Science* 7 (Summer 1988), pp. 271–86.

10. B. Gale, "Monitoring Customer Satisfaction and Market-Perceived Quality," *American Marketing Association Worth Repeating Series,* no. 922CS01 (Chicago: American Marketing Association, 1992).

11. Ibid.

12. R. E. Kordupleski, R. T. Rust, and A. J. Zahorik, "Why Improving Quality Doesn't Improve Quality (or Whatever Happened to Marketing?)," *California Management Review* 35 (1993), pp. 82–95.

13. Fornell and Wernerfelt, "Defensive Marketing Strategy by Customer Complaint Management" and "A Model for Customer Complaint Management."

14. T. J. Peters, *Thriving on Chaos* (New York: Alfred A. Knopf, 1988).

15. F. Reichheld and E. Sasser, "Zero Defections: Quality Comes to Services," *Harvard Business Review,* September/October 1990, p. 106.

16. Ibid., p. 105.

17. D. F. Colicchio, regional quality manager, Hewlett-Packard Company, personal communication.

18. S. Rose, "The Coming Revolution in Credit Cards," *Journal of Retail Banking,* Summer 1990, pp. 17–19.

19. J. L. Heskett, W. E. Sasser, Jr. and L. A. Schlesinger, *The Service Profit Chain* (New York: The Free Press, 1997).

20. A. Woodside, L. Frey, and R. Daly, "Linking Service Quality, Customer Satisfaction and Behavioral Intentions," *Journal of Health Care Marketing* 9 (December 1989), pp. 5–17.

21. E. W. Anderson and M. Sullivan, "The Antecedents and Consequences of Customer Satisfaction for Firms," *Marketing Science* 12 (Spring 1992), pp. 125–43.

22. W. Boulding, R. Staelin, A. Kalra, and V. A. Zeithaml, "Conceptualizing and Testing a Dynamic Process Model of Service Quality," report no. 92-121, Marketing Science Institute, 1992.

23. V. A. Zeithaml, L. L. Berry, and A. Parasuraman, "The Behavioral Consequences of Service Quality," *Journal of Marketing* 60 (April 1996), pp. 31–46.

24. J. P. McLaughlin, "Ensuring Customer Satisfaction Is a Strategic Issue, Not Just an Operational One," presentation at the AIC Customer Satisfaction Measurement Conference, Chicago, December 6–7, 1993.

25. Gale, "Monitoring Customer Satisfaction."

26. R. S. Kaplan and D. P. Norton, "The Balanced Scorecard—Measures That Drive Performance," *Harvard Business Review,* January/February 1992, pp. 71–79.

27. Kaplan and Norton, "The Balanced Scorecard."

28. S. Silk, "Automating the Balance Scorecard," *Management Accounting,* May 1998, pp. 38–42.

29. D. A. Light, "Performance Measurement: Investors' Balance Scorecards," *Harvard Business Review,* November/December 1998, pp. 17–20.

30. Marc C. Epstein and Robert A. Westbrook, "Linking Actions to Profits in Strategic Decision Making," *MIT Sloan Management Review* 42, no. 3 (Spring 2004), pp. 39–49.

31. Reichheld and Sasser, "Zero Defections," p. 111.

32. A. Willis, "Using the Balanced Scorecard at the University of Virginia Library: An Interview with Jim Self and Lynda White," *Library Administration and Management* 18 (2004), pp. 64–67.

33. Ibid., p. 66.

34. R. Kaplan and D. Norton, "Plotting Success with 'Strategy Maps,'" *Optimize,* 2004, pp. 61–65.

35. R. S. Kaplan and D. P. Norton, "How Strategy Maps Frame an Organization's Objectives," *Financial Executive* 20 (2004), pp. 40–45.

36. The material in this section comes from C. D. Ittner and D. F. Larcker, "Coming Up Short on Nonfinancial Performance Measurement," *Harvard Business Review,* November 2003, pp. 88–95.

37. Ibid., p. 92.

Exercises, Mini Cases, and Decision Cases

PART 1 Mini Case 1

⟶ COMPETING STRATEGICALLY THROUGH SERVICE

Firms can compete profitably through services in a variety of different ways. Four of those strategies are described here. Although firms tend to emphasize one or two of these strategies, it may be possible to do more.

Exemplary Out-of-the-Box Customer Service

There are some organizations whose competitive advantage is their reputation for out-of-the-box customer service. WestJet Airlines, Holt Renfrew, and Spence Diamonds are just a few examples. These organizations focus on going out of their way for customers and providing customer service in unique ways. Special services that these companies provide include

- At WestJet (www.westjet.ca), employees are hired and retained for their "West-Jettitude," or ability to demonstrate initiative and exceed customer expectations—such as when a wedding dress was lost and an agent took the bride-to-be to purchase a $2,700 replacement gown with company funds.

- At Holt Renfrew (www.holtrenfrew.com), a concierge will book tickets to local events while customers shop or are pampered in the onsite spa.

- At Spence Diamonds (www.spencediamonds.com), nervous grooms-to-be can take home transitory diamond rings with which to propose and then return with their fiancée to pick out the ring of her dreams.

Innovative, Cutting-Edge Services

Other organizations compete through providing innovative and cutting-edge services—being the first and/or best in their industry or being on the forefront of new inventions, technology, or science. The service does not need to be totally new to be innovative, but the service approach may be unique to the industry. At Shouldice Hospital (www.shouldice.com), in the Toronto suburb of Thornhill, only one kind of operation is performed. But it is performed better than anywhere else in the world. Shouldice (see the case at the end of this book) does hernia surgery—that's all. Its recurrence rate is estimated to be 0.8 percent. Contrast that with an industry-wide recurrence rate of 10 percent and you can see the competitive advantage.

Value-Added, Revenue-Producing Services

A major trend in manufacturing, information technology, retailing, and other nonservice industries in recent years is the introduction of value-added, revenue-producing services. Firms in these industries have recognized that they cannot compete on the sales and margins produced by manufactured products alone. Many firms such as IBM, Hewlett-Packard, GM, and Loblaws have integrated services into their mix of offerings. In some cases, as with IBM, services have actually taken over as the growth engine for the company.

A Service Culture That Differentiates

Finally, a firm can compete by nurturing a service culture that attracts the very best workers, becoming the "employer of choice" in its industry. Marriott Hotels' underlying company philosophy is "Take care of your employees and they will take care of your guests." This philosophy permeates all their brands, from Fairfield Inns to the Ritz Carlton, giving Marriott a worldwide competitive advantage in its industry. You can read more about WestJet's unique culture in Exhibit 1.2 in Chapter 1.

⊢──▶ Exercise

Think of some of your recent service encounters. What kind of out-of-the-box, innovative, or value-added services have you experienced? Have you ever worked for a service organization where culture provided a competitive advantage in the industry? Why do you think some organizations use these strategies and others do not?

Sources: Center for Services Leadership, W. P. Carey School of Business, Arizona State University (www.wpcarey.asu.edu/csl). Reprinted by permission of Mary Jo Bitner, co-author, Center for Services Leadership; www.marriottcanada.com; www.westjet.com.

CONSUMER EXPERIENCES AS CORPORATE STRATEGY

Customer experiences and experience management have become the foundations for important corporate strategies. According to Bernd Schmitt at Columbia University, customer experience management can be defined as the process of strategically managing customers' entire experience with a product—from how they learn about it, to how they consume it, to how they relate to the company that produces it. Firms across industries from airlines to cosmetics and automobiles are developing strategies around providing meaningful customer experiences. Although experience management applies to goods and services, it is particularly relevant for services, given their process nature. Services are experiences. Whether they are managed strategically or not is a choice to be made.

Here are just a few companies that have recognized the value of strategically creating distinctive experiences for their customers. For these companies, "the experience is the marketing," as noted authors James Gilmore and Joseph Pine have said.

Krispy Kreme

What truly can be exciting or fun about buying a doughnut? Sure, they taste great, and people probably shouldn't eat too many, which makes them even more desirable. But why do people flock to Krispy Kreme stores, and why are they willing to wait in long lines to purchase a doughnut? It is not unheard of for people to wait 30 to 40 minutes in the drive-through line to buy doughnuts to take to work. Although it may seem mundane, purchasing a Krispy Kreme doughnut is a true experience. From the "Hot Doughnuts Now" signage to the "doughnut theatre" and free samples, customers connect with Krispy Kreme. Through a large glass window, customers can watch the doughnuts being made. They can see the doughnuts cook for exactly 115 seconds in 365-degree vegetable shortening and then pass through a waterfall of sugar glazing before they trundle along the conveyer to be served. As they come off the line, Krispy Kreme employees hand out free samples to eagerly waiting customers who then proceed to buy more—many more. Despite the fact that carbohydrate-conscious customers are reducing their consumption of high-carb snacks, the experience of a Krispy Kreme outlet will entice many others. The company spends almost nothing on advertising and has no traditional media advertising budget—the experience is truly what sells Krispy Kreme doughnuts—in the United States, at least. Despite providing the same experience to Canadians, Krispy Kreme's Canadian franchisee KremeKo ran into difficulty in this market, and has since been acquired by Krispy Kreme Doughnut Company. It remains to be seen if the company can translate their doughnut experience into financial performance in Canada.

Jack Frost Children's WinterFest

The Jack Frost Children's WinterFest was started in 2005 as an attempt to increase toll-paying traffic across the Confederation Bridge (linking Prince Edward Island with New Brunswick) during slow winter months. This outdoor event, which takes place in Charlottetown and is designed to appeal to families, is the largest winter festival east of Quebec. WinterFest offers visitors the chance to visit a Snow Kingdom,

Source: © Tourism Charlottetown.

"a 1,200-square-foot snow castle made from 180 tonnes of snow and 160 crystal-clear ice blocks, weighing over 300 pounds each," participate in ice-sculpting contests, navigate a 3,600-square-foot snow maze, take sleigh rides, attend concerts featuring children's favourites like Bob the Builder, Batman, and Barbie, and much more. Despite the fact that normal temperatures for mid-February in Charlottetown can be –10 degrees Centigrade and feel much colder with a wind chill, in WinterFest's first year more than 10,000 tickets sold out in advance, and was estimated to generate an economic impact in excess of $720,000. It is not the wonderful weather that brings more than 10,000 people outside in Charlottetown in mid-February, it is the value of the experience.

Business-to-Business Customer Experiences

Although the previous examples have all been consumer companies, business-to-business firms are also recognizing the value of creating experiences. Executive briefing centres, for example, are corporate venues designed to enhance the otherwise mundane customer visit experience for business customers. Customer visits allow business-to-business customers to get to know their suppliers better through personal contact and information provided at the supplier's place of business. To create a memorable experience for its customers, Johnson Controls' flagship centre in Milwaukee simulates for its customers inky, cold darkness on the one hand and arid heat on the other to demonstrate how its technologies can help customers avoid these conditions. And Nortel Networks provides guests with smart cards to activate and guide their experience with Nortel technology at its Executive Briefing Center in North Carolina. The design of the customer experience can be a distinctive corporate advantage and asset for organizations that use it strategically.

Exercise

Think of another example of an organization that uses customer experience as strategy. What are some of the challenges that organization might face with such an approach?

Sources: B. Nussbaum, "The Power of Design," *BusinessWeek*, May 17, 2004, pp. 86–94; J. H. Gilmore and B. J. Pine II, "The Experience Is the Marketing," 2002, Strategic Horizons, LLP; B. H. Schmitt, *Customer Experience Management* (Hoboken, NJ: John Wiley & Sons, 2003); A. Serwer, "The Hole Story: How Krispy Kreme Became the Hottest Brand in America," *Fortune,* July 7, 2003, pp. 52–62; www.krispykreme.com; www.capitalcommission.pe.ca.

CUSTOMER SATISFACTION, LOYALTY, AND SERVICE AS CORPORATE STRATEGIES

CEOs of many highly successful, growth-oriented companies are preoccupied with customer satisfaction, loyalty, and service. They see these corporate objectives as critical challenges but also as the keys to their companies' continued profitable growth. In fact, a recent survey of CEOs identified "customer loyalty and retention" as the leading management issue, ahead of many other critical issues including reducing costs, developing leaders, and increasing innovation. In many firms, these customer goals drive corporate strategies. Measures of improvement in satisfaction and loyalty often are a basis for managers' and employees' incentive compensation, stock performance, growth predictions, and product improvement strategies.

For example, at Enterprise Rent-A-Car (www.enterprise.com), branch managers must meet or exceed corporate customer satisfaction and loyalty averages in order to be eligible for promotion. Clearly this requirement motivates them to develop cross-functional approaches and strategies that will improve satisfaction in their branches. Maritime Life Assurance in Halifax links front-line employee rewards directly with customer satisfaction. Bonuses are paid to employees if customer satisfaction ratings meet or exceed a 90 percent threshold. The reason for the bonuses is twofold as indicated by Steve Christie, Maritime Life's Director of Compensation and Benefits: "We strongly believe that if we can really enforce and educate our people on the importance of customer satisfaction, that's step one. But step two is making sure our staff is satisfied, because happy employees means better customer service."

Because customer satisfaction, loyalty, and service quality are used to predict and reward performance, measuring them accurately and using the measures wisely are critical. A multitude of ways to measure customer satisfaction exist, and all are not equally good for prediction or diagnosis. Some are too complex, others are too simple, and yet others measure the wrong things. One extreme approach was suggested by loyalty expert Frederick Reichheld based on 14 business case studies conducted by his firm. The research promotes *one* customer loyalty question as the best for most industries in terms of predicting repeat customer purchases or referrals. The question is "How likely is it that you would recommend [company X] to a friend or colleague?"

Although this one question may help firms determine where they stand with their customers, it is overly simplistic and doesn't provide the detail that companies need in order to improve. Additional, deeper, and more detailed assessment (as discussed in Chapters 5 and 6) can help firms evaluate potential issues and what improvements may be needed. Improving service and satisfaction most often involves a series of actions related to employees, service operations, and customers. A successful corporate-wide customer satisfaction, loyalty, or service strategy will involve all functional areas that can influence it. It is clearly much more than a marketing, market-research or customer-research program. As it does for Enterprise and Maritime Life, this type of corporate strategy can tie all functions together around the customer.

→ Exercise

Consider the pros and cons of a company financially rewarding employees on the basis of customer satisfaction and loyalty.

Sources: N. Kumar, *Marketing as Strategy: Understanding the CEO's Agenda for Driving Growth and Innovation* (Boston: Harvard Business School Press, 2004); M. D. Johnson and A. Gustafsson, *Improving Customer Satisfaction, Loyalty, and Profit* (San Francisco: Jossey-Bass, 2000); F. F. Reichheld, "The One Number You Need to Grow," *Harvard Business Review,* December 2003, pp. 46–53; C. D. Ittner and D. F. Larcker, "Coming Up Short on Nonfinancial Performance Measurement," *Harvard Business Review,* November 2003, pp. 88–95; G. Loveman, "Diamonds in the Data Mine," *Harvard Business Review,* May 2003, pp. 109–13; and A. Tomlinson, "Maritime Life Assures Employee Rewards," *Canadian HR Reporter,* March 2002, p. 7.

Exercise 1

→ COMPANIES BET ON DATABASE MARKETING RESEARCH

Most of the marketing research approaches introduced in Chapter 6 study patterns of customers in groups. Surveys examine the service quality perceptions of the totality of a firm's customers to get a sense of how they feel as a group. Focus groups identify the needs of important service segments, and lost customer research pinpoints the primary reasons why exiting customers are dissatisfied enough to leave the company. However, an important and powerful form of research—called *database marketing* or *customer relationship management (CRM)*—studies customers one by one to develop profiles on their individual needs, behaviours, and responses to marketing. This approach allows a company to get very close to its customers and to tailor services uniquely to individuals.

Individual customer research is founded on a database, which allows a company to tell customers apart and remember them uniquely. You may be most familiar with this form of data collection in loyalty cards—like Shoppers Optimum—that capture information about your purchases and offer you tailored coupons and specials based on your buying patterns. One of the most familiar examples of using a technology database to remember customers is the Ritz-Carlton's frequent guest registry, which documents preferences of each frequent guest. (Does he or she like a smoking or a nonsmoking room? Feather pillows?) Every time a guest visits, new observations about preferences are entered so that the institution itself comes to "know" each guest.

Casino Nova Scotia

The gambling industry has long recognized that certain customers are better than others and that encouraging the "high rollers" to spend time in one's casinos is a worthwhile and profitable strategy. One of the main ways they encourage increased patronage is "comping"—giving free drinks, hotel rooms, limousines, and sometimes chips to top customers. The strategy has been limited in most casinos to customers who could be identified and followed, making the approach spotty and missing many potential repeat patrons. Casino Nova Scotia in Halifax found a more systematic way to extend the practice to a wider group of customers. The casino developed a customer relationship management system called the Players Club, a loyalty program started several years ago that tracks the names and addresses of repeat visitors along with what slot machines, or table they play, for how long, and how much money they gamble. The company's approach uses a scannable card that any customer can obtain. To earn points toward drinks, rooms, and other benefits, customers allow their cards to be swiped on the casino floor to monitor the sums gambled and time spent at slot machines and card tables. The reaction of gamblers to this kind of intense scrutiny of their habits is still unknown, but Casino Nova Scoita is counting on customers wanting the points enough to agree to be tracked.

To learn more about Casino Nova Scotia and its Players Club, go to www.casino novascotia.com. Click on "Halifax" at the top of the screen, follow the link to Players Club, and scroll to the bottom of the page for a link to a promotional video about the program.

Database marketing has applications in virtually any service in which customers make repeat purchases. Underlying the approach is the necessity for the company to create customer information files that integrate different data sources on individual customers including demographics, segmentation, usage information, customer satisfaction data, and accounting and financial information. Although this approach may raise privacy concerns with some customers and under Canada's new privacy laws, marketing research is enhanced under these conditions. A company no longer needs to depend on the customers' words on a survey about whether they intend to remain customers with a company—it can track their purchases and find out for certain. It no longer needs to guess which demographics are most related to psychographic segmentation information—the company can run an analysis to provide valid and reliable data on the topic.

⟼ Exercise

As a customer, how would you feel knowing the casino had all this information about you? From the casino's perspective, what is the value of CRM? How can CRM initiatives help minimize Provider Gap 1?

Sources: F. Newell, *loyalty.com* (New York: McGraw-Hill, 2000), pp. 232–38; R. Stang, "Loyalty Is The Real Jackpot: Casino Windsor's Relationship with Regular Gamblers Is Its Ace in the Hole," *Marketing Magazine*, March 2, 1998, p. 11; www.casinowindsor.com, 2006; www.hallmark.com, 2004.

⟶ ELICITING COMPLAINTS

Service failures can occur in a variety of ways and at numerous times throughout the service delivery process. However, in many cases it is difficult, if not impossible, for the firm to know that a service failure has occurred unless the customer informs the firm accordingly. Unfortunately, a relatively low percentage of customers (5–10 percent) will actually complain to the firm. Thus, a major challenge facing management is how to get customers to complain when they experience a service failure and/or they are not satisfied with service delivery. What can a firm do to elicit complaints? Here are some issues to consider.

- *Develop the mindset that complaints are good.* Too often the complaining customer is looked on by employees in the organization as the *enemy*—someone to be conquered and subdued. The more prudent approach is to develop the mindset that the complaining customer is the firm's *friend.* Complaints provide valuable feedback to the firm, giving it the opportunity not only to address the service failure for the complaining customer but also to identify problems that other (less vocal) customers may also be experiencing. One scholar suggests that "complainers ought to be treated with the dignity and respect afforded to the highest-priced analysts and consultants." One company puts all customers who have complained on a VIP list. Accepting complaints is truly reflective of firms who are close to their customers.

- *Make complaining easy.* If the firm truly wants to hear from customers who experience poor service, it needs to make it easy for them to share their experiences with the firm. Sometimes customers have no idea whom to speak to if they have a complaint, what the process is, or what will be involved. Complaining should be easy—the last thing customers want when they are dissatisfied is to face a complex, difficult-to-access process for complaining. Customers should know where to go and/or who to talk to when they encounter problems, and they should be made to feel confident that something positive will result from their efforts. Technological advances have made it possible to provide customers with multiple avenues to complain, including toll-free customer call centres, company email addresses, and website feedback forms. The firm should regularly communicate to customers that complaining is easy and that it welcomes and appreciates such feedback.

- *Be an active listener.* Employees should be encouraged and trained to actively listen to customers, particularly to see if they can pick up on any cues to suggest less-than-ideal service. A restaurant customer might respond "Fine" to the waiter's question "How is your meal?" However, the customer's body language and tone of voice, or the amount of food not eaten, might indicate that all is not fine. Some customers may not be assertive in voicing their displeasure, but they may drop clues to suggest that something is amiss. Employees as well as managers should be consistently listening not only to the customer's actual words but also to what he or she may really be trying or wanting to communicate.

- *Ask customers about specific service issues.* A very simple, informal way to find out about any service failure is simply to ask. Managers at one hotel with a high percentage of business travellers make it a point to be at the front desk between

7:45 and 8:45 a.m. every day, because approximately 80 percent of their business travellers check out at that time. During the checkout process, managers avoid questions that can be answered with a simple "Yes," "OK," or "Fine" (e.g., "How was your stay?") and instead ask questions that force customers to provide specific feedback (e.g., "How could we have improved the technology accommodations in your room?" or "What needs to be done to improve our recreation centre?"). Asking customers very specific questions that cannot be answered with a simple yes or no may provide customers with an easy way to point out expectations that were not fulfilled.

- *Conduct short, trailer surveys.* A follow-up telephone call to a customer still in the midst of the service experience can help to identify problems in real time and thus enable real-time recovery. Enterprise Rent-A-Car Company, for example, regularly calls customers a day after they have picked up a rental car and asks the customer if everything is okay with the car. Customers who report problems, such as a broken window or a car that smells of smoke, are brought a replacement vehicle that day without any additional questions or hassle. Trailer surveys work especially well in business-to-business services in addressing problems early, before they become major issues.

┣━▶ Exercise

Think of a time you complained (or wanted to complain) to a company. Using the points discussed here, evaluate the company's ability to elicit your complaint. Consider what, if anything, might be done better, and suggest some tactics the firm may have used to improve the process.

Sources: S. S. Tax and S. W. Brown, "Recovering and Learning from Service Failure," *Sloan Management Review,* Fall 1998, pp. 75–88; O. Harari, "Thank Heaven for Complainers," *Management Review* 81 (January 1992), p. 59.

PART 3   Exercise 3

THE STARBUCKS COFFEE TERRORIST

Starbucks Coffee has set the pace in its industry—from its humble beginnings in the early 1970s, this coffee retail giant has grown to more than 5,000 outlets in the United States and over 1,000 in other parts of the world including Canada, the Middle East, Europe, and the Pacific Rim. The company and its legendary CEO, Howard Schulz, have a reputation for world-class service and outstanding employee relations and benefits. But even giants like Starbucks can stumble, and sometimes a seemingly innocent failure can escalate, as it did for Starbucks in the following story.

The story began when a Starbucks customer bought a defective cappuccino maker, which he returned for a replacement. While returning the machine, he bought another for a friend as a gift—however, he did not receive the 1/2-pound free coffee promised with the machine. And, the customer claims, the employee was rude besides. Unfortunately, the gift machine also turned out to be defective, so the customer demanded that Starbucks replace it with its top-of-the-line cappuccino machine, worth approximately $2,000 more than he had paid for the gift. The customer threatened to take out a full-page ad in *The Wall Street Journal* denouncing the company if his request was refused. The company refused. A full-page ad against Starbucks appeared in the *Journal,* with the customer soliciting others to complain through his own 800 number. When Starbucks apologized and attempted to replace both machines, the customer claimed that was not enough and made even *more* demands: that the company place a full-page ad in the *Journal* apologizing to him and that it fund his favourite charity. Needless to say, the whole issue got national media attention.

Although these types of customer terrorism are rare indeed, the example points out what can happen and the lengths some customer terrorists are willing to go to.

Exercise

At the time of this incident, a number of experts on customer service were asked what Starbucks should have done. What would you recommend? Was this complaint a gift?

Sources: "Customers from Hell: Nightmare or Opportunity," *On Achieving Excellence,* December 1995, pp. 2–3; and A. Lucas, "Trouble Brews for Starbucks," *Sales and Marketing Management* 147, no. 8 (August 1995), p. 15; www.starbucks.com.

Mini Case 1

⟶ THE WINE (TASTING COURSE) THAT WENT BAD

Recently, Paul Hersford began teaching his 10th round of wine tasting seminars (each seminar lasts two hours) in the banquet hall of a large and varied wine cellar. Unfortunately, his class participants were complaining that the class was not what they expected. Some left after the first hour without a word, and no participant took any more of Paul's classes. This was of particular concern, for each seminar studied a different variety of wine and Paul was therefore expecting more repeat customers.

Because he had recently signed up for a night class in marketing and was currently working in a group that had to identify and discuss marketing issues in a service setting, he decided to mention his concerns to the group when they next met.

Wine tasting is becoming a more familiar business in Canada. In Southern Ontario alone, where Paul conducted his seminars, everything to do with wines is trendy. With three wine regions, Ontario would seem to be perfect for a wine tasting instructor (or *sommelier*). The Niagara peninsula between Grimsby and Niagara-on-the-Lake had over 45 wineries. Lake Erie's north shore, situated at the same latitude as northern California, boasted the longest growing season in Canada. Prince Edward County, on the eastern edge of Lake Ontario, southwest of Kingston, was famous for its powerful, signature wines. And although Canadian wines weren't known (yet) as the world's best, there was no question that people in Ontario loved their wine, and increasingly wanted to know more about it.

"So, everyone, what do you think?" With these words, Paul concluded his overview of the disappointing experiences with his seminars in a meeting with marketing classmates.

Brent Valadin, who worked in the marketing department at a large packaged goods firm, was the first to speak up. "Paul, I can tell you exactly what you should do. You need to work harder on your classes. Now, please don't take offence at what I'm about to say, but I think it is pretty obvious that you don't know as much about wine tasting as you thought. Either that, or you are having trouble teaching others what you do know. The 'product' element of the marketing mix is where you are having trouble."

"I think you have a good point, Brent, but I don't think you are on the money this time," Jamie Riley offered. Jamie, a cosmetician taking the course to help her start her own business, was one of the most dedicated students in the group. "Paul, while I agree that the product issue might be an area for improvement, from what you have said, I am convinced that you need to do a better job with your advertising. You've told us that you do all your advertising in the newspaper, and yet I am convinced that you are using too narrow a selection of media. What about the yellow pages, what about the Internet, what about brochures and other material that services marketers are now using? Everyone is going to have some 'customer churn." That's to be expected. You can't avoid it. The key is to keep the new customers coming in, and the key to achieving that is to increase your overall advertising efforts. Personally, I would begin by getting into more wine tasting clubs, attending the trade shows, and getting on the Internet. In my view, the 'advertising' element of the marketing mix is what needs to be addressed first."

Marysa Jones, who was always the most quiet student in the group, hadn't yet spoken, so Paul now turned to her and asked, "Marysa, what do you think? I would really appreciate any insights you might have."

"Well, I think what Brent and Jamie have said makes a lot of sense. I would definitely follow up on both of their comments. However, I have to say that I would also worry about pricing. Given that you are not getting any repeat customers, you need to make more money out of each customer you do get. Our marketing course has talked about the importance of understanding price-sensitivity, and I think it would be fair to say that adults who take a wine tasting course are not very price-sensitive. You should give some thought to raising your prices. As Jamie said, customer churn is inevitable. It would be great if every one of your students took additional seminars from you, but realistically it just won't happen."

"Well, thanks a lot, everyone," Paul said, reflectively. "I appreciate your ideas, and your comments on the marketing mix have been very helpful. I will give some more thought to what I should do."

But later that night after the class was over, and after he had treated his group members to a glass of wine at his favourite spot downtown, Paul continued to puzzle over his lack of success. He simply couldn't agree that he didn't know enough about wine. Neither did he think that the problems were in his advertising or his pricing. But although he didn't agree with the views of the people in his group, he didn't know what else might be the issue, either.

Exercise

1. Assess the situation in which Paul Hersford finds himself. In your analysis, be sure to think about the gaps model of service quality.
2. If you were in Paul's group and were asked your opinion, what would you tell him?

PART 3   Mini Case 2

⟶ DELUXE CRUISE LINES (DCL) TRYING TO STAY AFLOAT

Deluxe Cruise Lines (DCL) was in trouble. The company, which began operations in 1984 from ports all over North America, has been realizing steady and significant decreases in sales (and profit) in each of the last seven years. In 2000, the first year that DCL saw its sales dip, the poor performance was a bit of a shock to top management. It was attributed to the poor weather that year. In 2001, the poor performance was written off as a result of North American's reluctance to travel after the September 11 terrorist attacks in the United States. But now, in 2006, the situation was dire. DCL needed to find out what was causing this sales downturn and fix it.

In the marketing department, Kevin Landry struggled with the problem and thought a fresh perspective might help. Kennedy Michaels, a recent graduate from the University of Calgary, was given some background on her first day on the job. She was told about the downturn, and that the poor performance seemed to contradict DCL's marketing research. DCL had excellent customer retention rates, and satisfaction scores among guests were high. But they did notice that guests, while they continued to buy cruises, were getting older—it was hard to attract the 24-to-35-year-old segment. Not wanting to bias Kennedy's analysis with any of his interpretation, Kevin left her alone with the reports. She had one week to prepare a report about what she thought might be the problem and recommend a course of action.

Nervous, but excited to have such an important challenge, Kennedy began sifting through the many expensive research reports the company had amassed. First, she reviewed the secondary research reports acquired from AC Nielsen. These reports, conducted from 1996 to 1997, indicated that customers thought cruises were an exciting, luxurious vacation option.

The Cruise Line also made a practice of sending customer satisfaction surveys to all its guests within 10 days after a cruise. The scores had been used at DCL since 1984 as an internal motivational tool, employee compensation at all levels being tied to customer satisfaction. As Kevin had said, there seemed to be no problem with customer satisfaction. Although not increasing, satisfaction ratings had been holding steady at about 90 percent for each of the past seven years.

On Friday, Kennedy still had not identified anything that might indicate the problem. When her friends took her out to celebrate her new job that evening, she got an idea. Looking around the table, Kennedy realized that she was looking at 10 people who fell into the 24-to-35 demographic that wasn't taking cruises. She asked, "Would any of you ever go on a cruise?" It was as though her friends didn't even need to think about the answer: there was a quick and resounding "no." Some of the replies were, "It seems so boring," "I worry that I would feel claustrophobic," "I couldn't be stuck on a ship for a week with nothing else to do," "If I'm going to spend that kind of money on a vacation, I want the freedom to see what I want to see," and "Aren't cruises for old people?" Kennedy was stunned.

After dinner, Kennedy went back to work on her report. Could it really be something that fundamental, she wondered? Is that really what DCL is missing? And if so, how could she tell that to her boss after only one week on the job?

She wanted to present a sound argument to her boss and thought of the services marketing course she had just taken. Kennedy knew that most problems in service delivery might be the result of any of four Provider Gaps, so she decided to apply the gaps model to her presentation. First, she had to determine which gap was exhibited here, and try to isolate the key factors that created it. Then she had to recommend how DCL should address the issue.

STRATEGIC GROWTH THROUGH SERVICES

Firms in many industries are discovering the value of strategically focusing on new service offerings to provide value for their customers as well as profits and growth for the firm. Using this strategic approach, services are developed to enhance relationships with customers by providing them total packages of offerings, sometimes referred to as "solutions." By adding services to their traditional offerings, firms can differentiate themselves from their competitors and frequently earn higher profit margins on the new services compared to traditional manufactured or retail product offerings. IBM Global Services is perhaps the best-known example of this type of solutions strategy (see opening to Chapter 1). Like IBM, many companies are attempting to "grow through services" in business-to-consumer as well as business-to-business markets. As they move in this direction, they quickly recognize the great opportunities as well as the complex challenges of introducing new services. Here we highlight three firms' growth-through-services strategies.

PetSmart

The pet products market is booming, and services are a big part of the growth for pet retailer PetSmart. With over 675 pet stores in North America, PetSmart's vision is to serve "pet parents" through "total lifetime care" of their pets. Although sales of pet food, toys, and pet accessories are part of this vision, total lifetime care means much more. The company also promotes comprehensive pet training, grooming, and upscale day and overnight care through its pet hotels. PetsHotel, its newest service, not only ensures pet safety and health but also promotes professional care and a total "pet experience" through daily "yappy hours" and a "bone booth," where pet parents can call in and speak to their pet. The company's success in the past several years can be directly traced to the expansion into services.

Canada Post

In a totally different realm, Canada Post (www.canadapost.ca) is also projecting growth through adding services for its customers. Through its recent partnership with eBay (www.ebay.ca) and PayPal (www.paypal.com), Canada Post offers Canadian eBay users the option of completely eliminating a trip to the post office if they so wish. The company's new online shipping solution allows customers to create, purchase, and print shipping labels from their home or office computer. And for customers shipping to the United States, the required customs forms are automatically generated. Not only is using this new service easier and more convenient, it is also more cost-effective.

Home Depot

As the world's largest home improvement retailer, Home Depot sees strong potential growth through services. Home Depot Canada president Annette Verschuren, has brought service philosophy to the company. Traditionally the relationship with the customer (who was predominantly male) ended at the checkout counter. Now there is a greater focus on the female customer, and the company offers to install what customers buy, as well as manage relationships between building and installation contractors and customers. This type of "solution" is exactly what many Home Depot customers are seeking. Because Home Depot screens and monitors the contractors it uses, customer risk is reduced and a high level of satisfaction is likely. The company has had some rough spots in moving from a pure retail mindset to a services orientation. For example, store managers were initially reluctant to put much effort into promoting services, and important service project management software was slow in development. As these barriers have been overcome, the company is projecting continued and even more rapid success through its service solutions strategy, which is currently expanding at 40 percent per year.

One way firms like Canada Post formulate new service ideas is to use the following New Service Development matrix.

Offerings	Markets	
	Current Customers	**New Customers**
Existing Services	Share building	Market development
New Services	Service development	Diversification

⊢⟶ Exercise

On the basis of your reading of the examples provided here, (*a*) classify each of the described growth strategies used by PetSmart, Canada Post, and Home Depot using the preceding matrix and (*b*) use the matrix to suggest other new and innovative services that these firms could develop.

Sources: M. Sawhney, S. Balasubramanian, and V. V. Krishnan, "Creating Growth with Services," *Sloan Management Review,* Winter 2004, pp. 34–43; R. C. Morais, "Dog Days," *Forbes,* June 21, 2004, pp. 78–89;"Stock Highlight: PetSmart," *Value Line Selection and Opinion,* July 30, 2004, p. 2192; www.petsmart.com; D. Foust, "Big Brown's New Bag," *BusinessWeek,* July 19, 2004, pp. 54–56; C. R. Schoenberger, "House Call," *Forbes,* September 6, 2004, pp. 93–94; "Canada Post Shipping Services Now Available Directly from eBay Canada and PayPal Websites," *CCNMatthews Newswire,* February 15, 2006. New Service Development matrix adapted from H. I. Ansoff, *Corporate Strategy* (New York: McGraw-Hill, 1965).

PART 4 Exercise 2

WHEN IS THE STRATEGY OF CUSTOMIZATION BETTER THAN STANDARDIZATION?

Chapter 10 focuses on the benefits of customer-defined standards in the context of situations—hotels, retail stores, service outlets—in which it is important to provide the same service to all or most customers. In these situations, standards establish strong guidelines for technology and employees in order to ensure consistency and reliability. In other services, providing standardization is neither appropriate nor possible, and customization—providing unique types and levels of service to customers—is a deliberate strategy.

In most "expert" services—such as accounting, consulting, engineering, and dentistry, for example—professionals provide customized and individualized services; standardization of the tasks is perceived as being impersonal, inadequate, and not in the customer's best interests. Because patient and client needs differ, these professionals offer very customized services that address individual requirements. They must adapt their offerings to the particular needs of each customer because each situation is different. Even within a given medical specialty, few patients have the same illness with precisely the same symptoms and the same medical history. Therefore, standardizing the amount of time a doctor spends with a patient is rarely possible, one of the reasons why patients usually must wait before receiving medical services even though they have advance appointments. Because professionals such as accountants and lawyers cannot usually standardize what they provide, they often charge by the hour rather than by the job, which allows them to be compensated for the customized periods of time they spend with clients. It is important to recognize, however, that even in highly customized services, some aspects of service provision can be routinized. Physicians and dentists, for example, can and do standardize recurring and nontechnical aspects such as checking patients in, weighing patients, taking routine measurements, billing patients and collecting payment. In delegating these routine tasks to assistants, physicians and dentists can spend more of their time on the expert service of diagnosis or patient care.

Another situation in which customization is the chosen strategy is in business-to-business contexts, particularly with key accounts. When accounts are large and critical to a provider, most aspects of service provision are customized. At a very basic level, this customization takes the form of service contracts in which the client and the provider agree on issues such as response time when clients have equipment failures or delivery time and fulfilment when retail clients depend on items being in stock in their stores. At a higher level, customization involves creative problem solving and innovative ideas (as in consulting services).

Finally, many consumer services are designed to be (or appear) very customized. These services include spa and upscale hotel visits, rafting trips, exotic vacations such as safaris, and even haircuts from expensive salons. In these situations, the steps taken to ensure the successful delivery of service is often standardized behind the scenes but appears to the customer to be very individualized. Even Disney theme parks use this approach, employing hundreds of standards to ensure the delivery of "magic" to customers.

⟼ Exercice

Think of a service encounter you have had in which the service was, or appeared to be, customized. Are there any elements of that service that would likely have been standardized? Do you think customization of that service was the best approach?

PART 4 Exercise 3

⟼ HARD AND SOFT STANDARDS AT FORD MOTOR COMPANY

In Chapter 10 we discuss two types of customer-defined service standards. "Hard" standards are operational measures that can be counted, timed, or observed through audits. The other category, "soft" standards, are opinion-based measures that cannot be obtained by counting or timing but instead must be asked of the customer. A real example of the difference between hard and soft standards might help distinguish between them. We use Ford Motor Company's Customer Care standards for service at their dealerships. Marketing research involving 2,400 customers asked them about specific expectations for automobile sales and service; the following seven specific service standards were established as most critical to customers in the service department of dealerships.

1. Appointment available within one day of customer's requested service day.
2. Write-up begins within four minutes or less.
3. Service needs are courteously identified, accurately recorded on repair order, and verified with customer.
4. Vehicle serviced right on the first visit.
5. Service status provided within one minute of inquiry.
6. Vehicle ready at agreed-upon time.
7. Thorough explanation given of work done, coverage, and charges.

⟼ Exercise

1. Which of these standards would be considered hard? Why?
2. Which would be considered soft? Why?
3. Think about your experience at the college or university you attend. Identify a variety of "hard" and "soft" service standards that, if implemented, would improve overall service quality.

PART 4) Exercise 4

⟶ STRATEGIC POSITIONING THROUGH ARCHITECTURAL DESIGN

BusinessWeek and *Architectural Record*, both McGraw-Hill publications, together sponsor an annual international competition to identify the best use of architecture that solves strategic business challenges. Company winners clearly demonstrate the impact of design on people—customers, employees, the general public, or all three. Here we present three of the 2004 award winners that illustrate the ways that architecture and servicescapes execute or reinforce strategic decisions and marketing positioning.

Limerick County Hall, Limerick, Ireland

The Limerick County Hall in Limerick, Ireland has been completely redesigned to increase efficiency and transparency and reduce its environmental impact. The new servicescape is better able to serve customers, the environment, and employees. With public service counters now lining the perimeter, customers can meet with authorities more efficiently than before. The building, constructed of glass and timber, is designed so that natural light is the primary light source, and fresh air circulates throughout, eliminating the need for air conditioning. Employees are reportedly proud of their new workspace and the "institutional identity" it suggests.

Limerick County Hall.

Source: © Michael Moran.

Humane Society/SPCA, San Antonio, Texas

We can all likely agree that most humane shelters are not terribly pleasant environments. However, that is not the case at the SPCA of San Antonio and Bexar County in Texas. The organization has overhauled its entire servicescape in an effort to increase adoption rates, reduce return rates, and make a more pleasant environment for employees. The building is now located in an affluent neighbourhood instead of on the outskirts of town, and it blends with other structures in the area and is much more welcoming. A particularly interesting element of the design is the interior layout, which was modelled after those commonly used in retail. With this change, the younger animals—the more desirable adoptees—were moved to the back of the structure, forcing prospective adopters to walk past all the adult animals first. The results speak for themselves: three times more adult animals are now being adopted.

Israeli Foreign
Ministry.

Source: © Tim Griffith.

Israeli Foreign Ministry, Jerusalem

When the Israeli Foreign Ministry sought to consolidate its offices into a single structure, the building needed to be both a model of security, so that staff members would feel safe at their job, and inviting-looking for the many dignitaries who visited. To design such a servicescape, many unique solutions have been implemented. While the building is constructed with innovative materials able to withstand explosions, it does not seem inhospitable. It is now plants, and not security barriers, that provide privacy, and the attractive central reception hall and separate entrance make for an alluring atmosphere.

Exercise

How is the service concept or strategic positioning reinforced by the architecture or servicescape in some of the organizations you have frequented?

Source: Jane F. Kolleeny and Audrey Beaton, "The 8th Annual BW/AR Awards: Design Solutions That Enhance Business Success," *Architectural Record*, 2006, http://archrecord.construction.com/features/bwarAwards/2004.asp, accessed November 3, 2006.

Mini Case 1

PROBLEMS AT SPANISH RIVER GOLF AND COUNTRY CLUB

Dawn and Curtis Burke thought they were set when they took over ownership of Curtis' uncle's 18-hole golf course in 2000. At Uncle John's request, the two avid golfers decided to move from Calgary to a more rural part of Ontario to help out when John's health began to fail. In just one year John's health had deteriorated so much that he was no longer able to run the course or advise on its operations, and so transferred ownership of the profitable business to the young couple.

When Dawn and Curtis took over, Spanish River Golf and Country Club was a well-appointed course that had operated at full membership in each of the past five years. It had a good image within the golf community as a sociable club of strong players. There was usually a waiting list for membership, as new spaces rarely became available. Dawn insisted that image must be preserved under their management, particularly given the competition in the area. Although the demand for Spanish River memberships was high, there were three other courses in a 50-kilometre radius. Eagle's Glen was a super-elite course with a full range of services, high fees, and waiting lists that exceeded two years. Barry's Par-3 offered few services and was recognized as a lower-end course catering to the neophyte golfer. Belle View was a course very similar to Spanish River in the market to which it appealed, the types of services it offered, and the fees it charged.

After reviewing the financials of the business, Curtis decided that there was certainly room to make even more money. He felt that the groundskeeping expense was excessive, but was unsure. The assistant grounds supervisor, Haley Morrison, insisted that the expense was a necessary one, but Les Campbell, the supervisor, felt that some cost might be trimmed from groundskeeping. In the end, Curtis decreased the budget by more than 35 percent. Les was a little shocked at such a decrease, but still thought that by cutting two staff members and tending nine fairways and greens on alternate days he could manage.

By 2006, the Burkes were still running Spanish River. Profit had declined substantially from 2004, the course had stopped winning awards, and the calibre of player calling Spanish River its home had decreased. Dawn, getting worried, administered customer satisfaction surveys to members at the beginning of this season and last, but did not notice any significant difference in the overall results. To isolate the problem, she called Margaret Johnson for help. Margaret found that while overall revenue and profit for the course had remained about the same in the early years, club membership was very different today. Full memberships had decreased by 8 percent. It seemed that visiting golfers paying green fees had increased substantially in the early years, and the revenue generated by them had masked any type of problem the Burkes might have found among the membership. More worrisome to Dawn was Margaret's insight that visiting golfers had also begun to trail off in the past two years. Most alarming was that an analysis of Spanish River's current member list revealed that only 65 percent of the individuals were the same as in 2001.

Exercise

1. What Provider Gap(s) are involved in this case?
2. What are the causes of this (these) gap(s)?
3. What recommendations would you make to Spanish River?

⟶ LEONARD'S DRUG STORES, LTD. (II)

"Mac" Raymond, vice-president of Leonard's Drug Stores, Ltd., was doing a store tour in one of the chain's Saskatoon locations. It was, he thought grimly, typical of the chain's western operations. And although he wasn't happy with the condition of the store, he took some solace in the recognition that at least he *knew* that it wasn't up to par. He wished more people at head office would come to the same conclusion and release more funds for renovations.

Leonard's Drug Stores had been a fixture in western Canada for several generations. It was typical of the kind of store found in rural and semi-rural areas throughout the country. The chain had been continually profitable, but had never been prioritized by head office when it came to physical changes. Customers' impressions of Leonard's started with the exterior signage and colours. From the aquamarine blue background and bright red letters in a 1960s font, to the neon lights, the store looked old compared to the recent major renovations performed by Shoppers Drug Mart, Rexall, and Medicine Shoppe.

Inside, customers might have thought they had walked into a convenience store by mistake. Candy, confections, and soft drinks dominated first impressions. Shelves were high and cluttered, the lighting was very bright with bare fluorescent fixtures, the floor was made of tile with missing and broken pieces, sales flyers and other types of promotions were everywhere you looked, and the checkout counter was filled with lottery tickets. Farther back in the store were canes, wheelchairs, reclining chairs with automatic lifts, and various other prosthetic devices. What customers couldn't see was the staff lunchroom that was filled to overflowing with supplies for the upcoming sale or the staff bathroom (there was no facility for customers) that was never as clean as it should be and often filled with incoming stock. What customers would see if they walked farther into the store was a crowded pharmacy dispensing area with a set of very high shelves facing the customer, behind which the pharmacist worked on a raised floor. No private counselling area was available, and conversations between the customer and the pharmacist had to take place over the top of the shelves that separated them.

Mac knew that the tangible elements of his store operations must inevitably be causing lower performance than the chain could otherwise deliver, but so far he had been unable to get renovation funds from head office. Sometimes, he couldn't help but wonder about the impact on both customers and employees.

⟶ Exercise

1. Which Provider Gap is discussed in this case?
2. Use the framework for understanding environment–user relationships from Chapter 11 to assess the various elements of
   a. The physical environment
   b. The likely internal responses (cognitive, emotional, and/or physiological) experienced by customers and employees
   c. The kinds of individual behaviours this servicescape might lead to

Exercise 1

➡ CUSTOMER CO-CREATION: THE NEW STRATEGY FRONTIER

Consultants, researchers, and strategists are urging companies to think about their customers in new ways. Instead of viewing customers as end recipients of predesigned goods and services, they encourage a view of customers as active co-creators of value. This view goes beyond thinking of customer involvement in idea development or design of new products, and it is more than customer participation in service delivery. Instead, this view suggests that the value customers receive is in the *co-created experience* they have as a result of choosing and combining elements of the company's offerings to create their own "total experience." This exercise contains some examples to help make the co-creation idea more concrete and the strategic possibilities apparent.

American Eagle

American Eagle Outfitters (www.ae.com), the North American fashion retailer, has an online strategy that allows customers to create their own total experience. As with many retailers' websites, visitors to the American Eagle site can shop for merchandise that will be shipped worldwide. What makes the AE site so interesting is the opportunity for shoppers to completely customize their experience. They can listen to AE Radio, choosing the songs they would like to hear, and then rate any song available. They can also download exclusive music previews and iron-ons of their choosing with their AE All-Access pass. One of the more innovative aspects of the site, and one that makes customers true co-creators of their service offering, is that visitors can customize their own flip-flops for purchase.

OnStar

OnStar (www.onstar.ca) is a service launched by General Motors Corporation (GM) to provide safety and emergency services for its automobile customers. The system can unlock a customer's door remotely when the customer is locked out of the car, assess the severity of damage to the car following an accident, and help police track down a stolen vehicle. Over time the service has been expanded to include information and entertainment. For example, the system allows customers to access location-based information on restaurants such as, "Find me the nearest Italian restaurant to my current location and make a reservation." Many providers, services, and experiences can be linked via the OnStar service, which is sensitive to time and location. Each customer thus has the opportunity to create a total and unique experience by combining elements of the system. To be successful with OnStar, GM needed to view the customer as a co-creator of value, understand the interconnected services that might be desirable within a vehicle, and have the foresight to connect the relevant suppliers and information within its system. In thinking of potential services desired within a "vehicle experience space," GM went beyond OnStar's core security offerings into a broad range of additional services that consumers can access in creating their travel experiences.

Look at the graphic from the inaugural edition of *OnStar Magazine*, Canadian Edition (on page 529). Note, in particular, the attempt by General Motors to involve/ educate their customers in this unique service.

Home Depot

Another example of customer co-creation can be seen in Home Depot's (www.home depot.ca) full range of home remodelling solutions. Historically the company simply provided a vast "do it yourself" product selection, coupled with in-store advice provided by sales associates, allowing customers to complete their own home projects. Its customers did all the work themselves. More recently, the company has expanded into complete remodelling services—from design assistance to product selection, delivery, contracting, and installation. Through actively involving the customer in all stages and even recommending alternative sources for products it does not carry, the company allows the customer to cocreate a constellation of value and a total remodelling experience. Home Depot's strategic role has been to recognize the components of the total remodelling experience from the customer's perspective and to provide customers easy access to information, prescreened services, and resources to co-create value for themselves. Each customer can thereby create an individual experience with as much or as little participation as desired. Some customers will choose to "do it themselves," whereas others will turn the entire job over to Home Depot. Still other customers will pick and choose the services they desire, resulting in a level of participation somewhere between these two extremes.

As companies begin to think about the "experience space" their customers are in and start to view the world from their customers' perspective, the possibilities for strategic innovation are endless. This approach contrasts with a traditional perspective that sees companies as producers of standardized value and customers as receivers. Instead, this view begins to look at customers as co-creators of value and companies as facilitators of this process.

Exercise

Think of an example in which you were a co-creator of a service. Was your experience positive or negative? Why? Relate your answer to the service provider's ability to close Gap 3.

Sources: C. K. Prahalad and V. Ramaswamy, "The New Frontier of Experience Innovation, *MIT Sloan Management Review,* Summer 2003, pp. 12–18; S. L. Vargo and R. F. Lusch, "Evolving to a New Dominant Logic for Marketing," *Journal of Marketing* 68, no. 1 (January 2004), pp. 1–17; A. Overholt, "Listening to Starbuck's," *Fast Company,* July 2004, pp. 50–56; C. R. Schoenberger, "House Call," *Forbes,* September 6, 2004, pp. 93–94; www.ae.com.

PART 5 Exercise 2

➤ WHICH CUSTOMER (A OR B) WILL BE MOST SATISFIED?

Scenario 1: A Major International Hotel

Guest A called the desk right after check-in to report that his TV was not working and that the light over the bed was burned out; both problems were fixed immediately. The hotel staff exchanged his TV for one that worked and fixed the light bulb. Later they brought him a fruit plate to make up for the inconvenience. Guest B did not communicate to management until checkout time that his TV did not work and he could not read in his bed. His complaints were overheard by guests checking in, who wondered whether they had chosen the right place to stay.

Scenario 2: Office of a Professional Tax Preparer

Client A has organized into categories the information necessary to do her taxes and has provided all documents requested by the accountant. Client B has a box full of papers and receipts, many of which are not relevant to her taxes but which she brought along "just in case."

Scenario 3: An Airline Flight from London to Toronto

Passenger A arrives for the flight with a portable tape player and reading material and wearing warm clothes; passenger A also called ahead to order a special meal. Passenger B, who arrives empty-handed, becomes annoyed when the crew runs out of blankets, complains about the magazine selection and the meal, and starts fidgeting after the movie.

Scenario 4: Architectural Consultation for Remodelling an Office Building

Client A has invited the architects to meet with its remodelling and design committee made up of managers, staff, and customers in order to lay the groundwork for a major remodelling job that will affect everyone who works in the building as well as customers. The committee has already formulated initial ideas and surveyed staff and customers for input. Client B has invited architects in following a decision the week previously to remodel the building; the design committee is two managers who are preoccupied with other, more immediate tasks and have little idea what they need or what customers and staff would prefer in terms of a redesign of the office space.

➤ Exercise

For each scenario, ask "Which customer (A or B) will be most satisfied and receive the greatest quality and value, and why?"

PART 5 Exercise 3

→
DELIVERING SERVICE THROUGH MULTIPLE CHANNELS: H&R BLOCK'S BLENDED CHANNEL APPROACH

H&R Block, the world's largest tax services company, served more than 19 million clients in North America and 13 other countries in 2005. With so many customers, H&R Block delivers its services through a variety of channels. H&R Block's approach, referred to as a "blended channel" approach, is a multichannel strategy delivered through various types of intermediaries that creates tremendous flexibility for its clients and the means by which they receive services. This approach allows H&R Block to offer what it describes as services with "solutions for every taxpayer." Customers may receive H&R Block's services through retail offices, through the Internet, through software programs, or through some combination of these channels. Each method of service delivery is described in the following paragraphs.

Service Delivery via Company-Owned and Franchised Retail Offices

H&R Block has approximately 10,000 offices worldwide. Customers wanting to purchase H&R Block's services through an office have three options. The Face to Face option, in which customers can either call an H&R Block office for an appointment or just walk right in, provides an opportunity for the customer to be interviewed in person and to have the company completely prepare the tax return document. Here customers are paying for a H&R Block representative to spend time with them to understand their unique situation and to do everything possible to help reduce their tax liability. Those customers wanting to use the Office Drop-off option complete a questionnaire that captures key information and informs customers of what forms and documents to bring to the H&R Block office in order to have the company prepare a tax return; the customer is then called when the return has been completed. The third option, Out-of-Office Preparation, is used by clients who find it difficult to get to an H&R location, but do not want to prepare their tax returns themselves. In these instances the company will send a representative to the client's home or office to conduct the interview and then have the company complete their return.

Service Delivery via the Internet (Online)

When it comes to preparing tax returns, a relatively large percentage of all taxpayers prefer the Do It Yourself method. Traditionally these people have completed their tax returns using pen and paper. However, H&R Block offers these customers an alternative means of doing it themselves by providing its services through the Internet. Customers who prefer to complete the entire process online can do so through H&R Block's website (www.hrblock.ca). For $19.95, individuals can use the site to completely prepare and then electronically file their return.

H&R Block's blended channel strategy provides clients with many choices as to how they would like their service to be delivered and how much of the work they would like to do themselves. At one extreme, the customer can have the task of tax preparation completed entirely by H&R Block by visiting one of its offices. Alternatively, clients can have their tax returns completed entirely by H&R Block without

Source: Image supplied by H&R Block, Inc.

ever setting foot in a retail office by exercising the Out-of-Office Preparation option. Or customers can file their returns completely independently of H&R Block employees by purchasing the ability to prepare and file their returns online. H&R Block provides clients with the ability to choose what method, channel, and products are best for them, at the time that meets their needs, and in the stage of the tax preparation experience that is relevant to them—in effect, allowing customers much flexibility by providing many choices to blend the channels of service delivery in a customized service. Thus, H&R Block has, through its blended channel strategy approach, created value for its customers by providing as much of the service as customers desire and through the channel in which the customer feels the most comfortable.

Exercise

1. Does H&R Block's multiple-channel strategy narrow Provider Gap 3—Not Delivering to Service Designs and Standards? How?

2. Think of another organization that uses multiple channels to deliver its service. Relate its multiple channel strategy to its ability to minimize or widen Provider Gap 3.

Source: H&R Block sites, www.hrblock.ca and www.hrblock.com, accessed June 12, 2006.

COMBINING DEMAND (MARKETING) AND CAPACITY (OPERATIONS) STRATEGIES TO INCREASE PROFITS

In many situations, firms use multiple demand and capacity management strategies simultaneously to obtain optimal usage and maximize profits. Because each strategy involves costs as well as potential service quality, customer loyalty, and revenue outcomes, determining the appropriate mix can be a complex decision.

Research done for a ski resort illustrates how operations and marketing data can be combined into a sophisticated model that attempts to predict the right mix of strategies. The ski industry presents particularly interesting challenges for capacity management, because the industry sees typically large fluctuations in demand based on seasonal, weekly, and even daily usage patterns, unpredictable weather and snowfall, a variety of skiing ability segments that use the resort in different ways, and demographic shifts over time. In addition, most resorts face constraints on their capacity due to environmental regulations that limit land use and parking as well as the large capital investment required for facility expansion and/or improvement. Furthermore, as ticket prices at ski resorts have continued to escalate, customers expectations have risen.

Powder Valley (PV, a disguised name), a ski resort in British Columbia, had consistently lost market share for five years to its rivals. Lack of facility improvements and increased marketing efforts by its competitors were cited as likely reasons for declining market share. To improve the situation, PV managers had proposed several marketing strategies to increase demand on slow days and increase revenue per customer. Operations strategies to improve the skiing experience and reduce waiting during peak demand periods that relied on acquisition of new terrain and new, faster ski lifts were also proposed. Each of these strategies had its associated costs and less than totally predictable outcomes. Adding to the complexity of the inherent tradeoffs in the various strategies was the fact that the resort offered multiple activities (e.g., restaurants, skiing, shopping) for customers to choose.

The researchers working with PV proposed that the optimal profit strategy would require an integrated set of approaches representing both demand and supply perspectives. Using data from the resort, they built a sophisticated simulation model to assess the impact on customer usage, waiting times, and profits of several different strategies that were being considered including:

- *Price variations.* Strategies aimed at levelling demand by charging lower prices for off-peak skiing.

- *Promotions of underutilized services.* Promotions to attract new customer segments or shift existing customers to underutilized services.

- *Information provision on waiting times.* Strategies that provide information about less-crowded periods or shorter waiting times to move customers temporarily to underutilized services.

- *Capacity expansion.* Investments in additional fixed capacity for skiing such as adding new terrain or expanding the number of lifts.

- *Capacity upgrades.* Improving or replacing existing lifts to carry more skiers and/or run faster.

As input to their model the researchers used historic data on daily demand, demand smoothing and capacity expansion options, service times for each lift, flow patterns across various lifts within the resort, travel time between lifts, customer perceptions, and customer choice data. By combining these marketing and operations data, the researchers showed that retaining the current customer mix, installing two new chairs, and providing waiting time information would maximize profits for the resort. Adding new chair lifts by replacing old ones within the existing terrain was a more profitable approach than expanding to new terrain. The simulation model showed that contrary to management predictions, smoothing demand across the day through differential pricing would actually decrease profits significantly. The model results were also useful in suggesting a priority order for the investments. The wait time signage investment was the least expensive and offered the largest single improvement for customers as well as the largest single profit impact. Upgrading at least one chair lift was the next priority.

Balancing demand and capacity can involve a complex set of decisions, and sometimes the outcomes are not obvious, especially when strategies seem to have contradictory objectives. For example in the PV simulation, a marketing objective of increased revenues through attracting more customers was contradicted by an operations objective of providing optimal wait times for lifts. As illustrated in the ski resort research, firms can combine marketing and operations data into one overall model and run simulated experiments to determine the best set of combined strategies. Of course, the quality of the decisions based on the model are highly dependent on the accuracy of the assumptions in the model and the quality of the input data.

Managing demand and capacity in ski resorts can be very challenging.

Source: Photodisc Blue/Getty Images.

Exercise

1. How have the demand and capacity strategies used by PV narrowed Provider Gap 3?
2. What, if any, impact would the demand and capacity strategies employed by PV have on the role of employees and customers?

Source: M. E. Pullman and G. Thompson, "Strategies for Integrating Capacity with Demand in Service Networks," *Journal of Service Research* 5 (February 2003), pp. 169–83.

PART 5 Mini Case 1

→ DRAMA AT REVERIE CINEMAS

Lauren Moffatt was not sure what she should do. The 19-year-old had recently begun a part-time job as a concessions stand worker at Reverie Cinemas, a national chain of Canadian movie theatres. Being a movie buff, Lauren had initially thought the job would be perfect for her, because Reverie offered employees free admission any time. And the job was a perfect fit with her college timetable. She had plenty of time after classes each day to prepare assignments before needing to go to work. However, while the job seemed to be a good fit in these ways, there was not much else about it that she liked. Now, she was trying to decide whether she should undertake another time-consuming job search during midterm exams or just stick it out with Reverie Cinemas until the end of the school term.

Lauren, ever the high achiever, had never quit anything in her life, and so she was reluctant to be giving up after only four weeks. Looking for advice, she called her older brother Gavin. After calming her down, Gavin asked, "What exactly is it about the job you don't like, Lauren?" Thinking for a moment, Lauren replied, "I never seem to know what to do." Gavin found that hard to believe. His sister was very bright, conscientious, and inquisitive, and always seemed to know what to do. "How can that be, Lauren?" Gavin asked. "Didn't you spend your first two days at Reverie in a training program?"

Lauren answered, "Yes, and I thought it was a very thorough program for the job I was about to be doing. I was given an employee handbook with all of the company's standards of service, and was continually told about Reverie's goal to be the best customer service provider among movie theatres. The training involved learning how to use the cash register and fill orders to standards in no more than 75 seconds. It also involved speakers from within the company talking about some of Reverie's service heroes. It seemed there were endless examples of how some employee went above and beyond the call of duty to provide exceptional service and we were encouraged to do the same."

"Well, how can you not know what you are doing?" asked Gavin. Lauren's answer surprised Gavin. "If I knew what I was doing, customers, managers, and co-workers wouldn't be yelling at me regularly. The first time my manager yelled at me, I had just given a popcorn refill at no charge to a gentleman whose crying four-year old had spilled hers. Another time, a customer got very upset because his snack bill totalled $30. Although he could have had the same items cheaper if he had bought our snack combos, our training program had specifically indicated not to ring in a combo unless the customer asks for it. To top it off, Mike Langille, the maintenance manager, has been rude to me since I filled out a customer complaint log about a messy washroom even though the handbook says that all employees are required to report customer complaints."

→ Exercise

1. What Provider Gap(s) are involved in this case?
2. What are the causes of this (these) gap(s)?
3. What recommendations would you make to Lauren? Reverie Cinemas?

PART 5 Mini Case 2

⊢────▶ THE PROBLEM OF NONCOMPLIANCE

Not everyone would necessarily realize that the Canadian pharmaceutical industry—from manufacturers to retailers—as well as the entire hospital system—would be better off if patients simply took their medicine as prescribed. Dr. Dale Thomas realized this, though. As head of operations at the Lloyminster, Saskatchewan, Health Authority, Dr. Thomas was aware of a number of studies that had identified noncompliance—the decision by a patient to either not have a prescription filled in the first place and/or not take it correctly and/or not take it as long as indicated—as a very serious issue.

Manufacturers clearly had a vested interest. If a patient was given a prescription to address excessive cholesterol and chose not to fill it or quit taking the drug prematurely, the manufacturer lost revenue. This same loss would also apply to the retail pharmacy that would have filled the prescription. In fact, some analysts thought that rather than fight each other for the opportunity of filling prescriptions, all retail chains in Canada would be better off if they simply worked on getting existing customers to take their existing prescriptions properly. Nor did the effects of noncompliance stop there. Dr. Thomas knew that the majority of visits to Canadian emergency departments were due to underlying conditions such as hypertension and blood pressure which, left untreated due to noncompliance, led to acute cases that required hospitalization and resulted in massive costs to the healthcare system. The issue of noncompliance was so important that the topic was being addressed by the World Health Organization.

In his role as the head of operations for the local Health Authority, Dr. Thomas was interested in having the research on noncompliance reviewed and policy recommendations developed. He was confident that if appropriate corrective action were taken, all parties would benefit: patients, manufacturers, retailers, hospitals, and ultimately, governments.

⊢────▶ Exercise

1. Which Provider Gap is at the root of noncompliance?
2. Identify the causes of this gap.
3. What recommendations, if any, would you make to Dr. Thomas?

PART 6 Mini Case 1

CREATING A STRONG BRAND WITH GEOGRAPHICALLY TAILORED IMC

How does an advertiser gain competitive differentiation and strong brand-awareness in a highly competitive market, especially given the intangible nature of services? And how does a global company create advertising that conveys the same brand image to all people, despite their very different geographies, demographics, and cultures? In the credit services industry, one answer is to create a recognizable brand that speaks to the target audience. MasterCard developed such a campaign in 1997 with its "Priceless" ads—the ones that end with "There are some things money can't buy. For everything else, there's MasterCard."

By the end of 2005, the number of MasterCard-branded cards in circulation increased to almost 748 million and were used for transactions valued at $1.7 trillion. In Canada, the number of cards being used increased 9.9 percent and the value of the transactions made with the cards increased by 13.7 percent in 2005. This growth is at least in part due to the "Priceless" campaign.

Although MasterCard is a global company, its campaign has been successful because of the ability of the company's geographic subsidiaries to produce their own communications using the same theme. On a global basis, the ads all convey the same message—that MasterCard makes it possible for cardholders to get more out of life than simply the tangible goods they purchase. But how that message is delivered is different around the world. Many of the ads are created regionally, in order to depict products and activities near and dear to the hearts of customers in the area. As Tammy Scott of MasterCard Canada states, "The ability to connect with the hearts and minds of Canadians will be the biggest issue facing marketers. Since consumers are constantly receiving numerous messages, it's essential for brands to differentiate themselves across all categories and all messages that are competing for consumer mindshare."*

Generally, the "Priceless" ads have been effective because they tie in to our daily lives. Although credit services have an intangibility component, the ads feature familiar household names and products. And MasterCard uses an integrated strategy to deliver its message. The MasterCard Priceless Index, a listing of things Canadians perceive to be priceless, was developed by MasterCard, and a complementary PR campaign was initiated to communicate the initiative.

Promotion and sponsorship are also integral to the campaign, as with the 2006 Zamboni Driver series of commercials. These

*Quoted in L. D'Innocenzo, "Top 3 New Year Predictions," *Strategy*, January 1, 2006, p. 9.

commercials (which can be viewed on the company's site at www.mastercard. com/canada/hockey) tell the story of a zamboni driver who, through the benefits of being a MasterCard holder, has been preparing his whole life to become a zamboni driver. The series ultimately ends when he is called up to the NHL to drive the zamboni.

During this part of the campaign, MasterCard Canada ran a number of tie-ins. Two contests, "Your Crew at the Cup" and "Get Closer to the Cup," gave cardholders the chance to win a trip to Stanley Cup playoff games for themselves or with friends. Zamboni gear emblazoned with the slogan "I wanna drive the zamboni" was also sold, to increase awareness, reinforce the brand, and generate sponsorship dollars for the Big Brothers Big Sisters of Canada. And rounding out this particular MasterCard Canada "Priceless" communications campaign was sponsorship that reflected the spirit of the ads, with several sporting events and organizations making the list.

Exercise

1. What do you think of the MasterCard "Priceless" campaign?
2. How does MasterCard's communication strategy help narrow Gap 4?

Sources: L. D'Innocenzo, "Top 3 New Year Predictions," *Strategy*, January 1, 2006, p. 9; T. Hanson, "Canadianizing a Global Campaign? Priceless," *Strategy*, March 8, 2004, p. 8; and www.mastercard. com/canada, accessed June 18, 2006.

PART 6   Mini Case 2

⊢───▶   VANCOUVER AQUARIUM TOURS

Verna MacDonald, the newly appointed director of operations for Vancouver Aquarium Tours, was getting more and more nervous that the company she had just joined was heading for trouble. She wasn't sure what she could do, but she felt she had to do something.

Vancouver Aquarium Tours (VAT) is a tour company based in Vancouver that is a subsidiary of privately owned Touring Canada, Inc. VAT is specifically devoted, as its name implies, to providing tours of Canada's famous Pacific-coast aquarium, located in Stanley Park in the heart of Vancouver. VAT operates a variety of tours and depends, in large part, on its marketing programs.

It was these marketing efforts that were worrying Verna, even though she herself was in operations. Recent campaigns that had attracted Verna's attention included the following:

- Advertising (print) that promised all customers would be "absolutely delighted" with their VAT experience. Brochures stated, "No customer of VAT has ever had a bad experience." This type of advertising put Verna's operations group in the difficult position of having to meet extremely high expectations.

- Telemarketing that, according to two customers Verna overheard speaking in the parking lot, assured prospective customers that the VAT experience would be constantly updated, daily if necessary, depending on the health of the animals. Verna wasn't sure how she could even get that information, let alone adjust her tour scheduling to take such information into account.

In addition to worrying about the marketing efforts, Verna knew her own department had some work to do. She noted that among many issues she was becoming aware of, tour staff usually neglected to tell customers that attendance at some exhibits (such as the "Dancing Dolphins") could result in their getting soaked to the skin if they sat too close to the water. While most customers enjoyed this aspect of the tour, many didn't. Many customers had also commented on the fact that if they had known when the feeding times were, they would have planned the timing of their visit differently.

In the light of the kind of marketing VAT was running, Verna felt increasingly vulnerable in her role as the person in charge of actually conducting the tours. The more she thought about it, the more she knew she needed to set up a meeting with her superiors to outline her concerns.

⊢───▶   Exercise

1. What Provider Gap(s) are involved in this case?
2. What are the causes of this (these) gap(s)?
3. What recommendations would you make to VAT?

PART 6 Mini Case 3

➤ ## MOVE RIGHT: AN ADVENTURE IN MOVING

Max O'Dell was excited but apprehensive. He had just graduated from the business program at Memorial University in Newfoundland, and couldn't wait to get his first real job. He had met with a number of recruiters when they visited campus during his senior year, and was certain he wanted to move to Calgary where he was promised an abundance of opportunity awaited. But with all his family living in St. John's and having only travelled as far west as New Brunswick on family vacations, he was a little worried about such a big move.

In addition, Max had real financial concerns. (At least he had already found an apartment to share with some of his brother's friends and had paid his first month's rent.) Working whenever he could while earning his degree, he had managed to save a total of $3,300 for the move. He figured he would need about $3,000 in the first month for rent ($600), a one-way plane ticket ($600), moving expenses ($750), a bus pass ($50), some business clothes to get him started ($700), and groceries ($300) before he started earning a wage. This would give him two weeks to get a job and allow two weeks before he received his first paycheque. But there wasn't much room for mistakes in any of his planning.

After watching a news exposé on fraudulent movers, Max had decided to hire a large, reputable company. He didn't have many possessions to bring, but what he did have he wanted handled with the best care, because he couldn't afford to buy new ones when he arrived.

After researching various moving companies online, he had narrowed his choice down to two. Deciding between them had proved difficult, though, since they offered comparable rates and similar services. Eventually, Max decided to go with Move Right because of the image it communicated. They were a family-owned company based in Nova Scotia that had grown to operate a national fleet, and their promises seemed genuine. Their website provided dozens of customer testimonials to the fantastic service. Max particularly liked the fact that Move Right posted its customer satisfaction scores (which had averaged 92 percent for the last three years). He also liked the fact that when things did go wrong, the company seemed to resolve the situation quickly and effectively. And, most notably, Move Right guaranteed that his possessions would be delivered on time. If not, he would be entitled to a full refund.

But despite his careful planning, Max's move was not without incident. In fact, the truck arrived four days late. Moreover, Max was having difficulty getting the promised refund. Calgary's Move Right franchise owner, Derek Jenkins, insisted he was not aware of any such guarantee, and seemed genuinely surprised to learn Move Right even had a website.

➤ ## Exercise

1. Which Provider Gap is illustrated in this scenario?
2. Can Move Right fix the situation? How?

DECISION CASE   1

———————▶   ## FedEx (Canada)*

Anita Kilgour was still upset as she mailed the letter to FedEx. The letter, Exhibit 1, detailed the problems she had encountered in shipping two packages from Kitchener, Ontario to Simpsonville, South Carolina via FedEx. Only one of the two packages, each containing one-half of a display booth, had arrived for the trade show. The show was a disaster for the dealer who was promoting their software product.

Anita, the office manager for Desktop Innovations, knew the importance of this trade show to the firm. Desktop Innovations (DI), a small software company located in Kitchener, produces the MainBoss Maintenance Software package (software designed to control a company's maintenance activities), which it licenses to dealers who market the software to end users. In this case, the dealer, Heat Treatment Services UnLimited, was going to market DI's software package to potential customers at the Greater Charlotte Plant and Engineering Maintenance Show. The dealer expected to receive around 100 potential sales leads based on DI's experience at similar trade shows. While Anita didn't know the number of leads or sales the dealer had obtained, when she talked to the dealer to confirm that half the booth was not going to arrive, he said that he thought the show would be a "writeoff."

Anita was very disappointed in the way in which FedEx had handled the situation. FedEx was known as an innovative, reliable company that had won awards for its excellent service. It had an excellent reputation for delivering "on-time, every time." (See Exhibit 2 for information on FedEx.) Anita was aware that FedEx provided a delivery guarantee, having dealt with the company for a number of years. She checked the FedEx materials she received when she set up the FedEx account and found the following statement under "Money-Back Guarantees:" "As always, we stand behind our services. FedEx offers two money-back guarantees for your shipments within Canada: if your shipment arrives even 60 seconds late, or if we can't tell you the precise status of your package within 30 minutes after you inquire, you're eligible for a full refund or credit. ... Some restrictions apply. Call 1-800-Go-FedEx or see the current *FedEx Worldwide Service Guide* for details." (Exhibit 3 provides the guarantee conditions in the *Service Guide*.)

"How could they do this?" she wondered, " And after I called FedEx to find out the best way to get the boxes to Simpsonville, allowed plenty of time to get the boxes there, kept calling them when things went wrong, and it still didn't work." "I'll be really interested in seeing how they reply to my letter, if they do."

© Gordon H.G. McDougall (Sir Wilfrid Laurier University). This case was prepared by Gordon H. G. McDougall and Keith Dorken as a basis for classroom discussion and not to illustrate effective or ineffective handling of a management situation.

EXHIBIT 1 Letter to FedEx

October 16, 1998

To: FedEx

Attn: Julie Curry
Executive Desk, Customer Service
1300 Central Parkway W., Suite 200
Mississauga, ON
L5C 4G8

From: Anita Kilgour
Office Manager
Desktop Innovations

Re: Waybill 400-3947-4352

I am writing to complain about the service my company received in shipping two packages recently. Not only did FedEx lose one of the packages for a considerable length of time, they repeatedly failed to follow through on promises they made once the package was found. In particular, several FedEx employees said they would phone me to confirm various shipping details, but not one ever actually made a phone call as promised.

Desktop Innovations is a small company whose software packages are sold by dealers throughout Canada and the United States. As part of our marketing efforts, we have put together a display booth that our dealers can set up at local trade shows to advertise our software. The display booth packs away into two boxes.

On Wednesday, October 7, I contacted FedEx about the best way to ship the two boxes from Kitchener, Ontario to Simpsonville, South Carolina. Simpsonville is the headquarters of one of our dealers: Heat Treating Services Unlimited. The dealer intended to set up the booth at a trade show in Charlotte, NC on October 14–15.

We wanted the boxes to arrive in Simpsonville by Monday, October 12. This would give the dealer plenty of time to transport the boxes on to Charlotte. The FedEx representative said that International Economy would get the boxes there by Monday.

Unfortunately, only one of the boxes made it to Simpsonville on time. According to FedEx, the other lost its shipping bill while passing through Memphis. Because the box still had our company address on it, Memphis sent it back to Toronto as a first step in getting it back to us in Kitchener. However, even though the box arrived in Toronto on Friday, October 9, no one contacted us that it was there and no one tried to send it on the rest of the way to Kitchener.

In the afternoon of Tuesday, October 13, our dealer became concerned that he'd only received one box. When he called me, I phoned FedEx and asked them to trace the missing box. They said they would check and get back to me. They never called back.

I called again before going home from work. FedEx assured me they would call and leave a message on my voice mail, telling what was going on.

That night, I checked my office voice mail. Again, no phone call. Therefore, I called FedEx from my home. At this point, I was finally told that FedEx had been unable to track down the package. (The FedEx employee said, "We don't like to use the word *lost*.") However, the person I talked to said he would continue checking and would call first thing Wednesday morning to tell what was going on.

Of course, no one called Wednesday morning. Eventually, I phoned and was told someone would get back to me within an hour. No one did.

In the afternoon, I called again. Finally, someone had found what happened to the package: that it had been sitting in Toronto all this time. FedEx promised to ship it out ASAP ... but by now, our dealer was at the trade show in Charlotte, not in Simpsonville. (And the first day of the trade show had been wasted.)

I arranged with FedEx to send the package to Charlotte rather than Simpsonville. FedEx's Charlotte office was supposed to call our dealer on his cell phone when the package came in. They also promised they would phone me to confirm that the package was on its way.

Naturally, I never got any phone call.

That night, I phoned FedEx again to see how things were going. It was important for the package to get to our dealer by 8:00 a.m. so that he would have time to set up before the trade show opened. Unfortunately, the FedEx staffer, Mike, still thought the package was supposed to go to Simpsonville. After a long conversation, I finally convinced them that it should go to Charlotte, and once again, I asked them to make sure they called our dealer and also called me to make sure things had worked properly.

No one called me. No one called our dealer. The package never showed up in Charlotte. Our dealer called the North Wendover office in Charlotte where the package should have been. Apparently, it had been shipped to the Simpsonville depot.

Since our dealer intended to leave Charlotte when the trade show was over, there was no point in delivering the package to FedEx's Charlotte office anymore. Therefore, I made one more phone call to get FedEx to deliver the package to our dealer's Simpsonville office. Somewhat to my surprise, the package eventually got there. It arrived late in the afternoon, today.

Needless to say, I was unhappy with FedEx's performance with all this. I spoke to a FedEx supervisor named Chris yesterday and asked him what FedEx intended to do to make amends. He immediately said we would not be charged for the shipping, but that hardly satisfied me—if we were invoiced, I would have refused to pay the bill. Chris said he would check with his superiors to see what else FedEx was willing to do; after all, our dealer had wasted two days and $600 booth fees at the Charlotte trade show, and I had accumulated more than three hours on the telephone trying to get things straightened out. (We also wasted $600 on the Charlotte trade show, paying for a booth that never got set up.) Chris promised to get back to me by 3 p.m. yesterday with an answer on what else FedEx might do to make it up to us ... but of course, he never did.

Today, I received a basket of chocolates and other goodies from FedEx—amusing, but not what I'd call an apology.

I understand that foul-ups happen, especially with the quantity of packages that FedEx ships every day. However, I think FedEx itself should be worried by the consistent inability of its personnel to make a single one of the phone calls they promised. Even the supervisor named Chris would rather send an anonymous box of chocolates than actually talk to a customer. Perhaps your customer relations policies need an in-depth review.

Yours sincerely,

Anita Kilgour

EXHIBIT 2 FedEx Canada—Selected Company Information

FedEx's success as the leader in the air express cargo transportation business is based on the philosophy that "when people are placed first they will provide the highest possible service, and the profits will follow."

The *people* priority acknowledges the importance of employee satisfaction and empowerment to create an environment where employees feel secure enough to take risks and become innovative in pursuing quality, service, and customer satisfaction.

Service refers to the consistent and clearly stated service quality goal of 100% customer satisfaction, 100% of the time.

A corporate *profit* should result, if the people and service goals have been met.

The people-first philosophy is implemented through a number of processes including: an annual employee satisfaction survey, promotion from within, an employee recognition and reward program, regular employee communication, pay-for-performance, an open-door program, and a guaranteed fair treatment procedure.

FedEx has been the leader in the use of high technology to improve its services including:

- COSMOS—a computerized tracking system designed to determine the exact location of a package at all times.

- DADS—a computerized dispatch system which communicates with couriers in their vans via computer screens.

- EXPRESSCLEAR—a customs clearing system which electronically transmits information to Customs so that processing can begin prior to the arrival of the actual packages.

- Call centre technology—approximately 250 customer service representatives work at three Canadian locations, responding to 33,000 calls per day. The representatives are accessible 24 hours per day, seven days per week.

- Initiated the 10:30 a.m. service commitment.

- Offered the first money-back guarantee on service commitment and is the only company to offer a money-back guarantee for the ability to track a package within thirty minutes.

- Is the first and only express transportation company to automate the entire process over the Internet.

Some facts about FedEx:

- FedEx employs more than 137,000 people worldwide and provides service to 212 countries.

- A North American radio network dispatches 25,000 couriers (nearly 1,500 in Canada), enabling fast response to customer requests and constant tracking of every shipment.

- FedEx Canada employs more that 3,500 employees in 60 facilities, who serve Canadian shipping needs from coast to coast, to the U.S., and internationally to 212 countries.

- FedEx achieves the most rigorous international standards for Quality Management and Assurance by earning ISO 9000 registration for its global operations.

- In 1990, FedEx became the first company in the service category to win the Malcolm Baldrige National Quality Award in the U.S.

- FedEx planes carry more than 2.9 million packages every night, weighing more than 2 million pounds.

Source: www.fedex.ca.

EXHIBIT 3   FedEx Money-Back Guarantee Policy

Money-Back Guarantee Policy*

We offer two Money-Back Guarantees, subject to the terms and conditions set out in this *Guide*. These Guarantees can be suspended or revoked without notice, at any time, and from time to time, in respect of all customers or any particular customer. These two Guarantees are:

(a) Service Failure

For U.S. and Canadian based payors, we will, at our option, and upon request, either refund or credit to the applicable invoice only your transportation charges, if we deliver your shipment 60 seconds or more after the applicable delivery commitment time ("service failure"). The following limitations apply:

1. Where Customs or other regulatory clearances are delayed, our delivery commitment time may be modified by adding one business day for each day (or portion thereof) that such clearances are delayed.

2. An exact delivery commitment time can be obtained only by telephoning Customer Service at 1-800-Go-FedEx, and supplying us with the following:
   - Commodity being shipped
   - Date of the shipment
   - Exact destination
   - Weight of shipment

   Any transit time published in this *Guide* or elsewhere or quoted by Customer Service without the above noted information is only an estimate and is not a stated delivery commitment time.

3. If the sender or recipient specifies a Customs Broker other than FedEx (where this service is available), notification will usually be given to the broker by 12:00 noon for FedEx® International Priority shipments and 5:00 p.m. for FedEx International Economy® shipments on the first business day the shipment is available for Customs clearance in the destination country, and such notification constitutes timely delivery. If the actual shipment is released to the broker in bond, our responsibility terminates at the time we relinquish custody of the shipment to the broker. However, if we retain custody of the shipment and are responsible for the delivery of the shipment, following receipt of the appropriate Customs release paperwork from another Customs broker, our delivery commitment time is modified by adding one business day for each day (or portion thereof) that our receipt of the paperwork is delayed.

4. For invoiced shipments and for shipments sent using an automated device, we must receive your notification (in writing or by telephone) of a service failure within 30 days from the invoice date. You must furnish with your payment the invoice numbers to which your payment applies. If an invoice is not paid in full, the reason for each unpaid charge must be noted with its waybill or package tracking number.

5. For shipments that we do not invoice (paid by cash, cheque, money order, or credit card), you must notify us (in writing or by telephone) of a service failure within 30 days from the date of shipment.

6. Notification of a service failure must include the account number, if any, the waybill or package tracking number, the date of shipment, and complete recipient information.

7. A service failure will not be deemed to have occurred if within 30 days after you notify us we provide you with:
   i. Proof of timely delivery, consisting of the date and time of delivery and name of the person who signed for the shipment, or
   ii. Service exception information reflecting that the failure to timely deliver resulted from circumstances described under "Liabilities Not Assumed."

   We are not obligated to respond if your request is not received within the time limits stated above.

8. A service failure will not be deemed to have occurred if payment is not made in accordance with the terms set out in this *Guide* and the package was held until alternate payment arrangements were secured.

continued

EXHIBIT 3—*continued*

9. Only one refund or credit is permitted per package. In the case of multiple-package shipments, this Money-Back Guarantee will apply to every package in the shipment. If a service failure occurs for any package within the shipment, a refund or credit will be given only for the portion of the transportation charges applicable to that package.

10. A refund or credit will be given only if complete recipient information was provided at the time of shipment. Complete recipient information must be provided on either the waybill or through any FedEx automated device.

11. A refund or credit will not be given for shipments delayed due to incorrect addresses or to the unavailability or refusal of a person to accept delivery or sign for the package or due to any of the causes described under "Liabilities Not Assumed."

12. A refund or credit will not be given when we have been authorized to deliver a package without obtaining a signature, but we do not deliver such package without obtaining a signature.

13. This Money-Back Guarantee does not apply to requests for invoice adjustment based on overcharges (see "Billing") or shipments to P.O. Box addresses acceptable for delivery (see "Post Office Box Addresses").

14. This Money-Back Guarantee applies only to transportation charges paid by U.S.- and Canadian-based payers and does not apply to duties, taxes, or any other charges.

15. A refund or credit will not be given to customers using FedEx automated shipping devices if incorrect package tracking numbers are applied to the subject package or shipment.

16. This Money-Back Guarantee applies only to shipments tendered using FedEx First Overnight®, FedEx® Priority Overnight, FedEx International First® and FedEx® International Economy. Contact FedEx Customer Service at 1-800-Go-FedEx® for further information.

17. This Money-Back Guarantee does not apply to undeliverable or returned shipments or any shipment containing Dangerous Goods.

18. This Money-Back Guarantee does not apply to delays in delivery caused by adherence to FedEx policies regarding the payment of duties and taxes prior to Customs clearance or at delivery.

19. See "FedEx® International Broker Select" for additional restrictions on the Money-Back Guarantee applicable to such shipments.

20. Credits for transportation charges will be applied to the payor's account only, and refunds will be made payable to the payor only.

    Written requests for refunds or credits under this policy should be directed to:

    When by mail: FedEx Canada Ltd.
                              P.O. Box 2700
                              Streetsville Postal Station
                              Mississauga, Ontario L5M 2L8

    When by FedEx service: FedEx Canada Ltd.
                              1270 Central Parkway West
                              Suite 200
                              Mississauga, Ontario L5C 4P4

(b) Package Status

At our option, we will either refund or credit transportation charges upon request, if we cannot report the status of your package within 30 minutes of inquiry (unless due to the fault of the customer). Package status is defined as the most recent electronically scanned location of your package reflected in our COSMOS tracking system. In order to qualify for this Money-Back Guarantee due to untimely package status reporting, the following limitations apply:

1. You must telephone us within our business hours and make your request within 15 days after the date of shipment.

continued

EXHIBIT 3—*continued*

2. Written requests will not be accepted.

3. The response period under this Money-Back Guarantee is 30 minutes per package. Where more than one package status inquiry is made in a call, we will respond within 30 minutes of our receiving all package related information.

4. You must provide your account number, if any, the waybill or package tracking number, date of shipment, pieces and weight, and the recipient's name, address, and postal/zip code on the first call.

5. Only one refund or credit is permitted per package. In the case of multiple package shipments, this Money-Back Guarantee will apply to each package in the shipment, but a refund or credit is only available on those packages whose status is not timely reported.

6. This Money-Back Guarantee is only applicable to shipments within Canada or from Canada to the continental U.S. and does not apply to those delivery points outside FedEx direct service areas. Call 1-800-Go FedEx for further information on FedEx direct service and extended service areas.

7. This Money-Back Guarantee does not apply to requests made to FedEx via the Internet.

8. Credits for transportation charges will be applied to the payor's account only and refunds will be made payable to the payor only.

*Offer void where prohibited by law.

Source: *FedEx WorldWide Service Guide*, Book 9, August 15, 1998, pp. 23–25.

The Train Trip

On July 21, 2006, Marianne and Robert relived their annoyance as they composed a letter to the French National Railway concerning a recent bad experience with the train system. It had been the only blight on a two-week family holiday in Europe in May/June 2006.

PLANNING THE FAMILY HOLIDAY

Marianne Ricci (aged 41 years) and Robert Dupuis (aged 48 years) were a typical professional couple with one son, Michael (10 years). They lived in a small town in Northeastern Nova Scotia. They usually took their family vacation at the same spot on the Gaspe Coast of Quebec. The summer of 2006 would be special, however. Marianne had a special leave from work, Robert was flexible in his job as an independent consultant, and Michael was now old enough to go with the flow of a "big trip."

The family initially contemplated going across Canada, going to Europe, or Marianne taking a trip to Japan by herself. However, she had not been to Europe for 15 years and had always wanted to visit France with Robert because he spoke French fluently. At this point Michael would also appreciate a different cultural setting. Robert was less keen on going to Europe; he saw it as an expensive holiday with the risk of not accommodating the whole family in a truly holiday way. (One of his sisters did not have a good time travelling in Europe. It just might be an expensive two-week nightmare!) Michael was keen and became increasingly enthusiastic as Mom described her trips to Europe, and what he might take with him and what he might see and do. After discussion off and on from November 2005 to February 2006, they came to a consensus and decided to take a trip to Europe. One of the deciding factors was that a trip to Europe would cost only $1400 more than going across Canada. As usual, they would work within a predetermined budget.

The family narrowed down their range to France and Italy. Because Marianne had taken two holidays in Europe, she felt that Robert and Michael should have first choice for places to visit. Her only requests were that they spend time in Florence, Italy and that she visit, however briefly, a friend who had moved to Milan, Italy. Michael wanted to see the Eiffel Tower, the Leaning Tower of Pisa, and Venice. Robert wanted to see the heart of Paris, Venice, and Florence. So they decided to visit Paris, Venice, Florence (with a side trip to Pisa), and Milan, spending about four days in each of the first three cities. They worked out in detail what they would like to see and do.

Marianne investigated travel arrangements with the airlines. The travelling was complicated, because they lived two-and-a-half hours from the airport in Halifax, Nova Scotia, and would have to fly to Montreal or Toronto where virtually all international flights originated for travellers in Atlantic Canada. The return trip would involve staying overnight at the Airport Hotel in Halifax. They bought their tickets from a Canadian airline that could fly them into Paris on May 26 and out of Milan on June 9 for a reasonable price. The rest of the travel would be by train, because they were not interested in driving in Europe. The routes seemed direct and Marianne's experience on the European trains was very positive; she said they were comfortable, ran on time, and had frequent departures and various routes.

Robert was particularly concerned about accommodations and how they might get from one place to another at reasonable times and at reasonable prices. To enjoy the experience everyone would need adequate sleep and time to rest. From Robert's perspective, planning this holiday was turning out to be very different from planning other major family purchases. He was especially sensitive to the fact that it was so difficult to verify, in advance, that the hotels would be suitable. He also knew that if they were unhappy with a hotel experience, they would not be able to "return" a night's stay. Nor, unlike in Canada, were any European hotels willing to guarantee his family's satisfaction. Thus, Robert spent a lot of time gathering information on where to stay and how to get around.

As the one responsible for the family's hotel arrangements, Robert's expectations were higher than they would be if he were travelling alone. So to reduce the risk that he might make poor choices, he collected brochures from tour companies and talked to travel agents. Marianne assisted with gathering this information, but Robert took primary responsibility for it. He wanted to be thorough and to have as few surprises as possible. They spent nearly $150 on travel guides, such as *Let's Go Europe* and the *Fodor's Guides*, purchasing most of them in March during a business trip to Halifax by Marianne. Robert also visited hotel and travel websites, such as Expedia.ca and AirCanada.ca, to cross-check the descriptions of hotels and room rates reported in the guidebooks. He found some of the personal testimonials helpful, but worried that they might not accurately reflect what he might find. In the end, the biggest influence on his hotel selections was the opinions of his family and friends.

Robert also wanted to know more about how the train schedule would work, so a month prior to the trip he called the French embassy for the train schedule leaving Paris for Italy. The embassy forwarded his call to a Canadian agency that looked after train passes for Canadians travelling abroad. He determined that the best route to follow would be a stay in Paris, followed by a 12-hour daytime train trip to Florence via Lausanne, Switzerland (with a bonus stopover of two hours), through Milan to Florence. After a few days in Florence, they could go up to Venice and then have a day in Milan before flying home. He carefully noted the times of arrivals and departures and took this information with him to Europe. Hotel reservations for each city were made and confirmed with deposits or full payment.

THE TRIP

The trip went very well except for the train trip between Paris and Florence on May 31. On the previous day, Robert had gone to the International Travel desk at Gare de Lyon (a major train station in Paris) and presented the schedule he had brought with him. The agent had informed him that the computer system had just been changed and that Robert's schedule was incorrect. The agent had had problems getting the tickets from the computerized setup, but finally printed them out after numerous attempts and working with various manuals. Robert paid 267 Euros for the tickets and three reserved seats (optional, unless you wanted your seats guaranteed). Although the agent seemed experienced, and seemed to know what he was doing, Robert had left still having doubts about the schedule.

The train arrived in Lausanne on time, which gave the family an opportunity to have lunch and walk around. Upon returning to the train station in plenty of time to catch their next train, however, they discovered that they had tickets and reservations for a train departure that did not exist! (In fact, the agent told Robert that the schedule obtained while in Canada was correct and that the agent in Paris had been working off the old schedule.)

An unsettling chain of events unfolded. They were able to use their tickets to get another train to Milan, but did not make their original connection to Florence because the Lausanne train arrived five minutes late. In Milan, after spending nearly one-and-a-half hours speaking to personnel at three different desks, Robert finally learned (through a half-French, half-Italian exchange) that the choice was to take a train which would arrive at 00:30 hours in Florence or buy tickets for the next train out of Milan, which was first-class only but would get them there at 22:00 hours. They chose to take the first-class train and called the pensione (hotel) in Florence to say that they would be late. The tickets cost 88 Euros plus 17 Euros for the high exchange rate at the train station. The clerk would not refund the tickets bought in Paris, because he insisted that there was no error in the system. However, he did stamp the tickets to indicate that they had not been used.

The first-class service offered no consolation. The car was filled with fashionably dressed Europeans, many working on laptop computers and doing business. Two attendants served dinner and generally looked after the passengers. Neither the other passengers nor the attendants seemed particularly pleased at the presence of the family dressed very casually, carrying backpacks and duffle bags, and asking for extra water to quench their thirst. They were hot (from August temperatures in May), tired, and annoyed. Some of their annoyance was due to the fact that they felt they had worked hard in planning this part of the trip; the mistakes did not occur because they had left things to the last minute or been careless. As they approached Florence, they realized that the train stopped only at the other end of the city from their pensione. They had chosen to stay at that particular pensione because it was a short walk from the downtown train station where they were originally supposed to arrive. They managed to find a taxi quite easily, however, and the fare they paid the skilful driver was worth it in comic relief. The three passengers found themselves in a very small automobile travelling at what seemed incredible speed through very narrow streets in a strange city late at night. They were impressed and laughing by the time they reached their pensione where they were greeted as expected guests. After a good night's sleep, they were determined to put the train ordeal behind them and enjoy the rest of the trip—which they did.

THE TRIP REVISITED

When they got home, they were reminded of the train incident every time they shared the news of their trip with friends and families. As well, the extra expense showed up in accounting for the budget for the trip. The amount was significant to Robert in particular, who looked after the family books. Both Marianne and Robert became increasingly annoyed over time. Although Robert was doubtful that anything would be achieved across such a long distance, Marianne convinced him that they should at least try to appeal for some compensation by writing a letter to the French National Railway. They composed a registered letter (shown in the Exhibit) on July 21, 2006 in English, because it would be too complicated for them to try to explain the situation in French. They felt good about having documented the events as best they could along the way and about stating their case.

EXHIBIT   Letter to the French National Railway

12 Pinevale Drive
Smalltown, Nova Scotia
Canada B0Z 4X2

July 21, 2006

French National Railway—SNCF
Departement Après-Vente
10 Place Budapest
Paris, France

Dear Sir or Madam:

On Saturday May 29, 2006 my wife, my young son, and I made reservations and bought tickets at Gare de Lyon (in Paris) to go from Paris to Florence (Italy) on Monday May 31. Our trip required that we change trains in Lausanne and Milan.

   While waiting for our train in Lausanne, we became alarmed when Train #323 leaving at 12:55 did not appear on the Departure Notice Board. We immediately spoke to a ticket agent and were informed that our train no longer existed, that a new schedule had recently come into effect, and that the train we should have been on had departed Lausanne for Milan at 11:13. The ticket agent told us to take the next train (#327) at 13:32 to arrive in Milan at 17:45. This was a second-class train and reservations were not required. The agent doubted that we would be able to catch Train #541, for which we had reservations, which was leaving Milan for Florence at 17:50. We were told to take Train #511 leaving Milan at 19:40 to arrive in Florence at 22:08 if we missed Train #541.

   Unfortunately, Train #327 was late, arriving in Milan at 17:50, and although we tried, it was impossible for us to catch Train #541 for Florence.

   The ticket agent we spoke to when we arrived in Milan stamped our reservation card (Milan to Florence) as not having been used. However, he also informed us that Train #511 from Milan to Florence at 19:40 would cost us an additional 88 Euros. Naturally, we protested, but we were forced to pay the additional fee to get to our destination.

   The ticket agent at Gare de Lyon made a mistake when he issued our tickets and reservations. This mistake resulted in lost time, a great deal of frustration, and additional costs to us of 88 Euros. We hold the SNCF responsible and hereby request a refund of our additional costs.

   You will find enclosed with this letter photocopies of our tickets, reservations, payment receipt, directions we were given in Lausanne, and our ticket from Milan to Florence with the costs indicated. Should you require the original copies I would be happy to forward them to you.

I look forward to hearing from you.

Sincerely,

Robert S. Dupuis

Sobeys Atlantic: The AIR MILES® Decision

Following a request by corporate head office, Sobeys Atlantic was considering the possible merger of Club Sobeys—its in-house loyalty program—with AIR MILES. The new arrangement, if approved, would mean that Sobeys' customers would now carry AIR MILES cards instead of their familiar Club Sobeys cards. Other changes, as described later, would also occur.

It was Barry Young's job, as Sobeys' Director of Customer Relationship Management (CRM), to review all the information and make a recommendation. Young knew that he needed to sift through all the data, meetings, and informal coffee-room conversation to get ready for the senior management team. The upsides to the merger were clear—unfortunately, there were also some significant risks. With only a few days left prior to the meeting, Young knew he had to make his recommendations on the basis of the data he had in front of him.

CLUB SOBEYS

Sobeys Atlantic is a division of Canada's second-largest food distributor. Nationally, Sobeys Canada has several well-known banners including (at the time) IGA Garden Market, Sobeys, and Price Chopper. Within Atlantic Canada, the company operates Sobeys, Foodland, Needs (convenience stores), Lawtons Drug Stores Limited, and TRA Atlantic (wholesalers).

The Club Sobeys program had begun in the Atlantic Division and was currently available only in the Sobeys stores—it was not yet available to customers of the Division's other banners due primarily to IT infrastructure compatibility. As of the third quarter of 2001, approximately 630,000 Atlantic Canadians were enrolled in Club Sobeys.

Benefits to membership included the following: special member pricing (in-store shelf tags would display two prices on eligible merchandise—one price for members and a second, higher price for non-members); cheque cashing privileges; sweepstakes and contest entries; and special prices on in-store promotions. The biggest benefit, of course, was that Club Sobeys members received points on most purchases over $20 (excluding tobacco). These points could then be redeemed for $10 discounts off a member's grocery bill. Young recalled stories of how some loyal shoppers would accumulate their points until Christmas at which time they would redeem multiple vouchers in order to dramatically reduce—even completely eliminate—their Christmas grocery bill.

From the company's perspective, the special pricing and other member benefits were naturally intended to increase shopper loyalty. An additional objective of the program, however, was to encourage heavy use of the card so that the majority of purchases could be tracked. This was integral to the creation of a comprehensive CRM database.

Sobeys staff therefore had a wealth of information at their disposal that could be used to track key performance indicators such as household penetration, shopping frequency, and average basket size. As well, the database could be queried for more detailed information such as the impact on the sales of lettuce when, for instance, the price of tomatoes was reduced; or for assessing the effectiveness of varying display arrangements or shelf location. Finally, staff were perhaps most enthusiastic over the possibility of using the database to customize the store to the needs/habits of individual shoppers. It was possible, for instance, to program the system so that coupons could be chosen and generated in real time at checkout on the basis of an individual customer's purchases. To illustrate, the first time a couple purchased diapers might signal the creation/printing of coupons that would be attached to the cash register receipt giving discounts on baby food or baby shampoo. From the company's perspective, this would encourage greater department penetration as well as increased basket sizes. From the customer's perspective, this would make the store much more relevant to their needs.

The program did not start out with this capability, however. It took a very substantial capital investment, development of a proprietary system, and countless hours of effort to make the Club Sobeys program so well known. Management considered it to be a source of significant competitive differentiation over Loblaws, who did not yet have a loyalty program of their own. Tables 1 and 2 provide awareness and membership information for Club Sobeys.

TABLE 1   Club Sobeys Total Awareness (%) Within Atlantic Region Among All Banner Shoppers, FY 2000

Total Atlantic	Sobeys	RASS*	IGA**	Co-op
90%	96%	94%	87%	90%

*Real Atlantic Super Store—a corporate division of Loblaws.
**Independent Grocers Association—a wholesale division of Loblaws (in Atlantic Canada only).

TABLE 2   Club Sobeys Membership (%) Within Atlantic Region Among All Banner Shoppers, March 2001

Total Atlantic	Sobeys	RASS	IGA	Co-op
69%	82%	73%	68%	67%

AIR MILES®

The AIR MILES Reward Program, created by The Loyalty Group in 1992, is one of Canada's best-known loyalty programs. In 2001, more than 60 percent of Canadian households (more than 11 million Canadians) were active members. AIR MILES is a coalition-based reward program, unlike the Club Sobeys stand-alone program. AIR MILES has more than 100 different sponsors across the country representing more than 12,000 retail locations. Major sponsors include Bank of Montreal, Shell, Sport-Chek (Sports Experts), A&P/Dominion, Canada Safeway, and Reitman's. In Atlantic Canada, however, there were fewer sponsors and significantly, no grocery sponsors. IGA were formerly sponsors, but when Loblaws bought the Atlantic Canadian IGA stores from the Oshawa Group it cancelled IGA's sponsorship of AIR MILES. AIR MILES was therefore very interested in obtaining a new, major grocery store for its coalition in the Atlantic area. For this reason, it was thought that AIR MILES might be especially receptive to a Sobeys Atlantic connection. It was also rumoured, though, that AIR MILES were in discussions with Co-op Atlantic, the region's third-largest grocer. This rumour gave added impetus to the review.

CONSIDERATIONS

There were, Mr. Young thought, several reasons why the AIR MILES deal was on the table in Atlantic Canada. First, the Quebec Division of Sobeys Canada—made up primarily of IGA stores—had joined with AIR MILES in October 1999. Sobeys Canada therefore had two loyalty programs—Club Sobeys in the Atlantic and AIR MILES in Quebec. Everyone knew that having two completely different loyalty programs provided less opportunity for economies of scale than would exist if the company had only one program.

Secondly, a number of new senior managers of Sobeys Canada had prior experience with AIR MILES—experience they acquired when they worked for a competing retailer. They were therefore very comfortable with the AIR MILES organization and how it worked.

Thirdly, there was always the possibility that if the Atlantic Division joined Quebec in their sponsorship of AIR MILES, there might be a chance to wrest the Ontario sponsorship out of A&P's hands when their contract expired. This would effectively make Sobeys the only food sponsor within AIR MILES for Ontario, Quebec, and the Atlantic. Such a structure might give Sobeys greater bargaining power over the arrangements with the Loyalty Group.

A fourth factor on people's minds within the Atlantic Division was the impact of any change on its customers—the ultimate decision criterion. If switching programs damaged relationships with customers, all the Division's hard work would be in vain.

On one side of this issue were the views among staff who were already familiar with AIR MILES and thought the move would have a positive impact on sales. What, Mr. Young wondered, would the expectation for sales increases be if Sobeys Atlantic were to switch?

On the other side of the issue was the fact that the AIR MILES experience in Quebec (IGA) and Ontario (A&P) was based on both chains adopting a loyalty program where none had existed before. In these examples, customers went from having no rewards program to having one of Canada's best—AIR MILES. This was not the case in the Atlantic. Sobeys Atlantic customers would be going from having one very well known program to having another very well known program. Could this lead to the same 4–5 percent sales lift as was experienced in Quebec when Sobeys Quebec joined AIR MILES?

As well, Young also knew the Division was facing a variety of issues related to their in-stock position and their financial accounting. Both issues were due, in part, to

Sobeys' well-documented conversion to SAP's enterprise resource planning program. When first initiated, Sobeys decision to move to SAP was thought to be a key competitive advantage. Over time, though, as the conversion began to take its toll, staff were hard pressed to manage the change. Would switching to AIR MILES exacerbate the Division's IT workload at this critical time?

MARKETING RESEARCH

The company undertook significant market research to reduce the uncertainty within the Atlantic Division. Although the research could not answer questions about timing and the impact on the Division's IT infrastructure, it would at least go a long way to answering questions about what impact any switch in reward programs would have on the customer base.

The following objectives were therefore set:

- Evaluate the reaction of Club Sobeys members and the impact on their shopping behaviour upon Club Sobeys joining forces with AIR MILES.

- Understand the impact upon various Club Sobeys shopper segments: High-, Medium-, and Low-Spend; loyal vs. non-loyal; AIR MILES vs. non–AIR MILES members; and finally, urban vs. rural.

- In the Atlantic, identify current AIR MILES awareness and membership within the total market; among Sobeys banner and key competitor shoppers; and among Club Sobeys members in particular.

Consumer feedback was primarily obtained through a telephone survey conducted with 565 randomly chosen Club Sobeys members. Segments were described as follows: high spenders (average spend of $100 plus); medium spenders (average spend of $20 to $100); low spenders (average spend of less than $20).

To ensure that each respondent understood exactly what was being considered, careful attention was given to the wording of the issue. There was some discussion about the way the issue should be phrased, but the eventual wording chosen was as follows:

> The Club Sobeys program that you currently are a member of will be joining forces with the AIR MILES Reward Program, one of Canada's largest shopper reward programs. This change will enable you to collect AIR MILES travel points, instead of Club Sobeys points. The only change you will notice is that, unlike Club Sobeys points which are mainly redeemed for $10 off your grocery bill, AIR MILES travel points cannot be used to save $10 off your grocery bill, but instead, AIR MILES travel points can be used towards receiving a wide variety of rewards including travel, electronic items such as cameras, CD players and entertainment, such as movie and theatre passes. In addition, for easy and fast collection, AIR MILES travel points can be collected at a number of participating retailers.
>
> While the Club Sobeys Program will be joining AIR MILES, as a special member you will continue to receive Club Sobeys privileges you receive today such as special member prices, cheque cashing privileges, sweepstake and contest entries and special prices on in-store promotions including dishes and pots and pans.

Following this introduction, Club Sobeys members were asked what they thought. These opinions and the shoppers' relevant demographics are provided in the following tables. Looking at the data he had, Young knew he had about as much information as he could reasonably expect to get. He also knew that within a very few days, he would be asked to make a firm recommendation to the Atlantic leadership team.

TABLE 3   Collected AIR MILES in Past Month, March 2001*

	Club Sobeys	Urban Club Sobeys	Rural Club Sobeys	High-Spend Club Sobeys	Med.-Spend Club Sobeys	Low-Spend Club Sobeys
Members with AIR MILES	47%	45%	48%	49%	49%	45%
Members Who Collected AIR MILES in Past Month	58%	56%	64%	63%	55%	60%

*Read column 1 as follows: 47% of Club Sobeys members are also members of AIR MILES—of this group, 58% collected AIR MILES within the past month.

TABLE 4   Club Sobeys Members' Reaction to Joining AIR MILES

	Total Sample %	Urban Club Sobeys %	Rural Club Sobeys %	High-Spend Club Sobeys %	Med.-Spend Club Sobeys %	Low-Spend Club Sobeys %
Very pleased	28	26	31	23	27	31
Fairly pleased	30	31	29	32	28	31
Neither pleased nor displeased	27	28	25	23	34	22
Fairly displeased	6	6	5	8	2	7
Very displeased	7	7	6	13	4	6
Don't know	3	3	4	1	5	3

TABLE 5   Club Sobeys Members' Reaction to Joining AIR MILES

	Total Sample %	Total Sobeys Shoppers %	Regular Sobeys Shoppers %	Occasional Sobeys Shoppers %	Loyal Sobeys Shoppers %
Very pleased	28	28	29	26	35
Fairly pleased	30	30	29	32	23
Neither pleased nor displeased	27	27	23	34	21
Fairly displeased	6	6	7	3	6
Very displeased	7	7	8	4	11

TABLE 6   Club Sobeys Members' Reaction to Joining AIR MILES

	Total Sample %	Total Sobeys Shoppers %	Total Sobeys AIR MILES Member %	Regular Sobeys AIR MILES Member %	Occasional Sobeys AIR MILES Member %
Very pleased	28	28	36	39	31
Fairly pleased	30	30	30	29	33
Neither pleased nor displeased	27	27	22	16	33
Fairly displeased	6	6	5	7	2
Very displeased	7	7	5	7	2
Don't know	3	3	2	2	—

TABLE 7   Club Sobeys Members' Reaction to Joining AIR MILES, Expected Shopping Behaviour Change

	Total Sample %	Urban Club Sobeys %	Rural Club Sobeys %	High-Spend Club Sobeys %	Med.-Spend Club Sobeys %	Low-Spend Club Sobeys %
Will shop at Sobeys:						
Much more	8	8	6	6	10	6
Little more	12	10	14	6	15	11
About the same	74	74	73	80	69	76
Little less	3	3	4	4	1	4
Much less	2	3	2	3	2	2
Don't know	2	2	2	1	3	1

TABLE 8   Club Sobeys Members' Reaction to Joining AIR MILES, Expected Shopping Behaviour Change

	Total Sample %	Total Sobeys Shoppers %	Regular Sobeys Shoppers %	Occasional Sobeys Shoppers %	Loyal Sobeys Shoppers %
Will shop at Sobeys:					
Much more	8	8	6	12	7
Little more	12	11	7	18	2
About the same	74	75	80	64	86
Little less	3	3	4	1	3
Much less	2	2	2	3	2
Don't know	2	2	2	2	1

Fraser Office Supplies

Clare Prather, Marketing Manager for Fraser Office Supplies, was concerned as she looked at the annual report. Sales had been stagnant for the past three years in spite of the different marketing strategies she had tried. Just then, Don Jardine, President and Owner, walked into her office and asked, "Have you seen the annual report?" "Yes, I'm just looking at it and I'm not happy about our results." "I agree," said Don, "Let's have a look at what we've done and figure out how to improve the situation. There's got to be a better way of increasing our sales. We have a good product selection, offer excellent service, customers can order online, we have quick delivery, but we can't seem to grow." Clare replied, "I'll go over everything we've done in the past three years and have a look at that material I have on customer relationship management and growing a small business. I'll put something together for the Monday executive meeting." "Sounds good," said Don, "I look forward to it."

BACKGROUND

Fraser Office Supplies (FOS), located in Toronto, Ontario, was established in 1964 by Ben and Linda Fraser. FOS's strategy was based primarily on catalogue sales, and focused on serving the needs of small and medium-sized businesses in the Toronto area. While FOS had a small retail store, most of their sales were generated via its catalogue. Clients phoned in their orders and FOS delivered the orders within 24 hours. Over the years, FOS had grown on the basis of the Frasers' dedication to customer service and product selection.

In 1995, the Frasers sold the business to Don Jardine, who had extensive experience in the office supply market, and retired to Antigonish, Nova Scotia. At that time, FOS's product line included, among other items: basic office supplies (binders and binder accessories; calendars and organizers; clips, rubber bands, and pins; envelopes; mailroom and shipping supplies; paper, notebooks, and pads; pens, pencils, markers, and correction tapes; Post-its, flags, and markers; staplers, punches, and scissors; ink and toner cartridges; etc.).

From 1995 to 2002, annual sales for FOS had grown from $508,000 to $1,285,000, but had then flattened and were $1,276,000 in 2004. FOS had weathered the storm of large chains such as Office Depot and Staples entering the market beginning in 1996. As the competition increased, many smaller and medium-sized office supply firms had gone out of business. However, FOS had established a strong online presence (the entire catalogue was online) and continued to expand its product line to include custom printing (business cards, business forms, promotional products, labels, etc.) and some technology items (computer supplies, computer accessories, presentation and meeting tools, etc.).

THE ANALYSIS

Clare began by looking at clients and revenues for 2002–2004. Because virtually all of the clients had accounts with FOS and most ordered online, FOS had detailed records of clients and sales since installing a database management program in late 2001. Clare noted that FOS had lost 27 percent of their clients in 2002 and 29 percent of their clients in 2003 and 2004 and added about the same percentage each year (see Exhibit 1). She was concerned at the high percentage of clients lost each year, and she decided to prepare some discussion points on this issue for the upcoming meeting.

Using the database program, Clare analyzed client revenue for 2002–2004 (see Exhibit 2). She divided FOS's clients into quartiles and calculated average revenue per client and total revenue per quartile. In 2002, 71.4 percent of total revenue was generated by 25 percent of the clients. The average revenue per client for the top 25 percent was $2,430, while the bottom 25 percent was $160 per client. Average annual revenue for the top 25 percent declined from $2,430 in 2002 to $2,050 in 2004. As she looked at the numbers she noted that the average client in the three lower quartiles was buying more on an annual basis, but it wasn't clear why.

Looking further at the data, she discovered that FOS was losing about 30 percent of the top 25 percent clients every year, which was a slightly higher percentage than the other three quartiles. She was surprised at this, because she had read that typically larger customers stay with firms for a longer period of time than smaller customers. She began to wonder what, if anything, she could do to change this situation.

Clare then examined the annual report highlights for 2002–2004 (see Exhibit 3). While sales were stagnant, marketing expenses had risen, costs of goods sold had increased slightly, and net profit had declined from $121,000 in 2002 to $79,800 in 2004, a drop of 34 percent. "I've go to do something about this," she thought, "but what?"

Clare's next consideration was the overall marketing budget. For the past three years, marketing spending, as a percentage of company revenues, had increase from 8 percent ($90,000) in 2002 to 9 percent ($111,000) in 2004, while overall revenues had not grown (Exhibit 3). The two major marketing expenditures were six half-page ads each year in the Ontario edition of *Canadian Business* magazine (Ontario

EXHIBIT 1

Number of Clients, 2002 to 2004

	2002	2003	2004
Beginning of year	1,500	1,510	1,525
New	410	435	415
Lost	400	420	430
End of year	1,510	1,525	1,510

EXHIBIT 2   Client Revenue ($) by Quartile, 2002 to 2004

Quartile	End of Year—2002 1,510 Clients			End of Year—2003 1,525 Clients			End of Year—2004 1,510 Clients		
	Average Revenue per Client	Total	Cum. % of Total	Average Revenue per Client	Total	Cum. % of Total	Average Revenue per Client	Total	Cum. % of Total
Top 25%	2,430	917,000	71.4	2,245	839,000	70.2	2,050	771,000	60.4
26–50%	511	193,000	86.4	498	186,000	85.7	590	223,000	77.9
51–75%	302	114,000	95.3	276	103,000	94.3	411	155,000	90.0
76–100%	160	61,000	100.0	182	68,000	100.0	338	127,000	100.0
Total	860	1,285,000		800	1,196,000		848	1,276,000	

circulation of 38,500) and seven quarter-page ads in the business section of the *Globe and Mail* (Toronto edition, circulation of 372,000) (see Exhibit 4).

Another marketing activity included a direct-mail campaign every year. For 2002, a mailing list of 2,000 small-to-medium-sized businesses in the Greater Toronto Area was purchased at a cost of $2 per business, and the company brochure and mailing, which also cost $2 per business, included a 10 percent discount on all office purchases for the next six months. In 2002, one hundred businesses responded and purchased a total of $6,000. Only 20 were still customers of FOS at the end of 2004. The direct-mail campaign costs increased every year due to higher postage rates and higher mailing list rates. For 2003, one hundred twenty-five businesses responded and purchased a total of $9,000; 35 were still customers of FOS at the end of 2004. The results for 2004 were similar; one hundred twenty responded, purchased $8,500, and 40 were still customers of FOS at the end of 2004.

In 2003, Clare decided to take out a larger ad in the yellow pages at an additional cost of $6,000. It was difficult to determine how many new clients were obtained because of the larger ad. The Toronto radio station that focused on business was used to help promote the two sales FOS held each year (cost range $4,000–$5,000). The "All Other" category included media expenditures on special events and other promotions.

EXHIBIT 3   Annual Reports Highlights, 2002 to 2004

	2002		2003		2004	
	$	%	$	%	$	%
Sales	1,285,000	100	1,196,000	100	1,276,000	100
Cost of goods sold	848,000	66	789,000	66	855,000	67
Gross margin	437,000	34	407,000	34	421,000	33
Marketing expenses	90,000	8	103,000	9	111,200	9
All other expenses	231,000	18	203,000	17	230,000	18
Total expenses	316,000	25	306,000	26	341,200	27
Net profit	121,000	9	101,000	8	79,800	6

EXHIBIT 4   Marketing Expenditures, 2002 to 2004

Category	2002		2003		2004	
	$	%	$	%	$	%
Sales	1,285,000	100	1,196,000	100	1,276,000	100
Magazine	31,400	35	32,100	31	32,600	29
Newspaper	16,400	18	17,200	17	19,600	19
Radio	5,000	5	6,000	5	5,000	4
Direct mail	9,000	10	10,000	10	11,000	10
Yellow pages	9,000	10	15,000	15	16,000	14
Internet/Web page	12,500	14	13,500	13	16,000	14
All other	7,000	8	9,000	9	11,000	10
Total	90,300	100	102,800	100	111,200	100

Considerable resources were spent in 1998 and 1999 to design a website that allowed clients to order online in an easy and efficient manner. In fact, FOS had won two awards for the website design and order function. In a small survey of clients, the FOS website received very positive ratings in terms of ease of use, product selection, and overall satisfaction. The website was also used to promote new products, offer specials, and provide information and relevant links for small-to-medium-sized businesses. The marketing expenditures for the Internet/Web page involved maintenance, updating, and order processing.

Over 80 percent of FOS's clients ordered online, and the online site (www.fos.com) was highlighted in all of FOS's marketing and communications activities. Typically, when an order was placed, it was delivered to the client within 24 hours. Clare wondered if she should consider offering specials for those who purchase more than $500 per year. "What would it take to increase retention rates by 5 percent?" she asked herself.

CUSTOMER RELATIONSHIP MANAGEMENT

Clare had recently taken a course on customer relationship management (CRM), and now reviewed the course materials. As she read, she was struck by the following comments:

- Someone once said: "I know I'm wasting half of my advertising money. I just don't know which half."
- It is far more expensive to attract new customers than it is to keep current customers.
- Reducing customer defections by 5 percent can increase profits by 25 to 85 percent.
- A relatively small increase in customer retention (loyalty) will drive relatively large increases in profits.
- Long-term customer value (LTV) is based on the concept of customers as streams of profitable revenue, resulting from their continued use of the product or service and the patronage of other customers to whom they recommend their service supplier.
- Attracting and keeping the highest-value customers is the cornerstone of a successful marketing program.

- Where retention rates are 50 percent or below, the average customer stays with the firm for two years or less.

Clare was particularly struck by the paper "Growing Your Business" (see Appendix 1), which had been handed out by one of the course presenters. She felt that this might be a good way to try and improve FOS's marketing approach, customer retention and sales. She also thought the paper "Long-Term Customer Value and Retention Rates" (Appendix 2) was something she could use to generate some scenarios and examples using the FOS financial and client information.

THE REPORT

Clare began by looking at the questions she had written down during her analysis:

- Why are 30 percent of our clients leaving every year?
- What are the financial implications of increasing annual retention rates by 5 percent? 10 percent?
- How can we increase retention rates, particularly of the top 25 percent?
- What does it cost to get a new customer?
- Why has the direct marketing campaign had such a low response, and why do those clients leave us?
- What role might the website play in increasing sales? Increasing client retention rates?
- If I started with a clean slate, how much would I spend on marketing and how would I spend it?

"Boy, I've got more questions than answers," thought Clare. "I'll have another look at the CRM material and come up with some ideas for the meeting." With that, she began preparing the report.

APPENDIX 1

Growing Your Business

Many small businesses use the shotgun approach to grow. They spend a lot on advertising— newspaper, radio, mail brochures, Yellow Pages—to increase their business. But for many, it doesn't work. Why? Because it's far more expensive to attract new customers than it is to keep current customers. So, if you are going to try this, remember most of the time you will have to take your new customers away from the competition.

Another approach is to get your current customers to buy more from you. Everyone from Amazon.com ("If you like that, you will love this") to McDonald's ("Would you like fries with that?") uses this strategy. The strength of this approach is that it focuses on customers that know you and apparently like your product/service offerings.

A third approach is to sell to your current customers more often, which is really about getting more of their business. Typically, consumers buy similar products from more than one supplier, and what you try and do here is to get some of that business by getting them to buy from you more often.

Many small business owners, however, concentrate only on getting new customers. This can be dangerous, for several reasons. First, it is expensive to market to new customers. This is where the advertising budget goes. Second, new customers are not yet loyal to you. It takes time to build relationships with customers. And third, it's hard to market to a cold audience. You are trying to peddle your wares to people who do not know you or your business practices. It is a leap of faith on their part to buy from you.

Smart companies focus on the customers they already have. These are the customers who have purchased from you before, know what you have to offer and like it. They know you, know your business practices and often know your premises. Buying from you is comfortable and familiar to them.

The great thing about understanding the numbers behind your business growth strategy is that it gives you power that you wouldn't otherwise have.

Making even small, incremental changes in each of the three growth areas (new customers, current customers buy more, current customers buy more often) provides you with leverage.

This means that the numerical result of all of the changes is greater than the sum of the individual pieces. Let's look at an example. Let's say we currently have 1,000 customers. On average, each customer spends $175 each time they buy from us. Our customers buy from us on average twice annually. What are our current revenues? 1,000 customers times $175 times two equals $350,000.

What would happen if we put strategies in place to make small changes in the number of customers, the average amount of each sale, and the number of times they buy from us? Let's say we're aiming for only a 5 percent increase in the customer base and a 10 percent increase in the amount of the average transaction, and that we will attract them three times a year instead of two. What's the impact on our bottom line?

Our customer base grows from 1,000 to 1,050, the average transaction grows from $175 to $192.50 and annual visits grow from two to three. Our new annual revenues would be: 1,050 customers times $192.50 times three equals $606,375.

That's a 73 percent increase in bottom-line revenues from small changes in each of the three areas of business growth. We haven't doubled our customer base. We haven't doubled our prices.

We've simply made small incremental changes in each area that add up to a leveraged result.

Some ideas on the three strategies for growth (attract new customers, sell current customers more, sell current customers more often):

Attract New Customers

How much did your customer base grow last year? If you're like many small business owners, you really have no idea. It's only when you start tracking your statistics that you get a grip on what happens when there are changes in your asset base.

Once you have a list, put a letter beside each name: either A, B, C, or D.

- A is for customers who buy lots from you, pay promptly, bring in other new customers and are pleasant to deal with. You love doing business with them.

- D is for customers who are price-sensitive and complain often. They often pay late or not at all.

- B and C are for customers somewhere in between.

This ranking gives us an idea of the types of customers we want to attract.

Clearly, we only want to attract new A customers. But strangely enough, you may find that most of your advertising targets D customers. Every time you advertise that you have the lowest price, you attract price-sensitive customers.

The problem with D customers is that you will never instill loyalty in them. The minute a competitor can come up with a lower price (and someone will always be able to do that), these customers are gone.

Now, take some time to analyze how you are going to find new A customers.

Are you in a business where trust is important? Then you will most likely get most of your new customers through referrals from existing customers. Why not send a letter to your existing A customers and offer them a 10-percent discount on their next order if they bring in a referral.

Oh no, you say. I can't afford to do that! Well, let's look at the numbers using the earlier example:

Existing customer average order:	$175
10-percent discount:	($17.50)
New customer's average annual order:	$350 (in two $175 orders)
Lost revenue:	$17.50
Gained revenue:	$350
Net gain:	$332.50

If you want to be more detailed, you would also count the cost of the stamp and paper for the letter. You would even get more mileage out of this strategy if you also implemented the other growth methods and increased the average value of each sale and the number of visits.

The key point here is to track your numbers so that you understand your business better.

Sell Current Customers More

The next strategy is to increase the average value of every transaction.

The key is to make sure customers are aware of all of the other products and services you offer. When a customer comes into your gas station to pay for gasoline, ask if they need oil or wiper fluid. If they come into your restaurant for dinner, ask if they would like dessert. Make saying yes easy. Give them choices instead of expecting them to pipe up if they want something.

Another way to keep your products and services fixed in the minds of your customers is to keep in touch with them on a regular basis. Send mailings or newsletters quarterly. Give them valuable information while reminding them you are ready to take their order.

Sell Current Customers More Often

You now have more customers coming in the door and they're buying more when they come. Next you want to have them come in more often.

Accomplishing this will be different in every industry. In the restaurant industry, for example, you can send out coupons to current customers to entice them to visit more often. In the auto repair business, you can put together a package for customers to have a lube, oil, and filter change for a set price. Send them reminders twice a year that their car is due for this service. The possibilities are endless!

Growing a business without tracking results is like running a marathon without looking at the clock. You have no indication of how you're doing and if you're achieving your goals.

Growth benchmarks should be a part of your monthly operating plan and you should track new customers, average revenue per customer, and average customer visits.

As well, you should track where your new customers are coming from. Are they visiting your business because of an advertisement you ran? Or has someone referred them to you? Knowing this helps drive your growth efforts in the future.

Source: Abridged from Angie Mohr, "Small Changes Can Have Big Results," *The Record*, September 10, 2003 and "Many Firms Target the Wrong Customer," *The Record*, October 1, 2003.

APPENDIX 2

Long-Term Customer Value and Retention Rates

Long-term customer value is based on the concept of customers as streams of profitable revenue, resulting from their continued use of the product or service and the patronage of other customers to whom they recommend their service supplier. The revenue curve is determined by the degree to which components—including customer acquisition costs, margin levels, high-volume segments, and referrals—contribute to costs or profits over time. Long-term value is likely to be significant when the following characteristics are present: high marketing expenses to obtain a new customer, reasonable margins on sales, high-volume segments exist, and high word-of-mouth referral.

Segmentation Issues

"Attracting and keeping the highest-value customers is the cornerstone of a successful marketing program." Underlying this statement are the necessary conditions that: (1) the market can be segmented and (2) identifiable segments vary in customer value. The direct way to test these conditions is to apply volume segmentation to the market. When high, medium, and low users exist and can be identified, the rewards from focusing customer retention programs on the high users can be substantial. Retention improvement for this segment can lead to significant increases in profits. As an example, in many firms, the Pareto Principle operates: 80 percent of the revenues are generated by 20 percent of the clients. As one example, volume segmentation, based on annual revenues of a firm's top 500 clients, revealed that these clients (11% of the firm's clients) generated over 90 percent of the firm's total revenues (91.7%).

Retention Rates

Average retention rates have a direct impact on long-term customer value. Where retention rates are 50 percent or below, the average customer stays with the firm for two years or less. If a firm improves its retention rates from 50 percent to 55 percent, the average retention increases to 2.2 years from 2.0 years. In contrast, if average retention rates are relatively high, in the order of 75 percent or greater, an absolute increase of 5 percent in customer retention has a far greater impact. As an example, improving retention rates from 75 percent to 80 percent improves customer retention from four years to five years. Here, long-term customer value is substantially greater and the leverage effect is more significant.

Revenues, Costs, and Profitability

A major challenge in determining the long-term value of customers is calculating client profitability. While the revenue side of the equation is straightforward, the cost side can be difficult. The obvious difficulty is assigning costs on a per-client basis. To overcome the cost allocation problem, sensitivity analysis can be conducted. The key variables in the sensitivity analysis are segment value, retention rates, and revenues and/or contribution margin, as provided in the example (Exhibit 1). When little or no information exists in assigning variable costs to clients, the firm can vary the contribution margin to assess the effects of different margins as well as segment and retention rates. In the example, revenues by segment can increase from $7,600 to $233,500 by segment, depending on the retention increase and whether revenues or contribution margins are used.

EXHIBIT 1   Sensitivity Analysis by Segment Value, Retention Rate, and Contribution Margin[1]

	Top 50 Clients			51–150 Clients			151–250 Clients		
	Current Rate 76%	Increase Rate to 81%	Increase Rate to 86%	Current Rate 59%	Increase Rate to 64%	Increase Rate to 69%	Current Rate 34%	Increase Rate to 39%	Increase Rate to 44%
Number of clients	50	53	55	100	105	110	100	105	110
Revenue increase ($000)[2]	N/A	140.1	233.5	N/A	120.5	141.0	N/A	25.4	50.8
Increase at 50% margin[3]	N/A	70.1	116.8	N/A	60.3	70.5	N/A	12.7	25.4
Increase at 40% margin	N/A	56.0	93.4	N/A	48.2	56.4	N/A	10.2	20.3
Increase at 30% margin	N/A	42.0	70.1	N/A	36.2	42.3	N/A	7.6	15.2

Notes:

[1] The example is based on an actual firm.

[2] Average annual revenue for the top 50 clients is $46,700. By increasing retention rates from 76 to 81%, for the top 50 clients (increasing the number of clients from 50 to 53) revenues increase by $140,100. Average annual revenue for the 51–150 clients is $24,100. By increasing retention rates from 64 to 69% (increasing the number of clients from 100 to 105), revenues increase by $120,500. Average annual revenue for the 151–250 clients is $12,700. By increasing retention rates from 64 to 69% (increasing the number of clients from 100 to 105), revenues increase by $25,400.

[3] Assume that variable costs are 50 percent. Increased revenues from the top 50 clients are $70.1 when retention rates increase to 81%.

Riverside Credit Union (A)

Frank Timmerman, Vice-President of Marketing at Riverside Credit Union, smiled as he sat at his desk. After months of effort, he now felt he really had a handle on Riverside Credit Union's membership. He had been in charge of the initiative to segment the membership base to improve his understanding of how different members contributed to the profitability of the credit union. He also wanted to know which members he should concentrate on for purposes of building their business to ensure future profitability. Having a better understanding of the various segment profiles, he believed, would also help his Credit Union do a better job of identifying members to target for appropriate financial products.

BACKGROUND

Riverside Credit Union is a well-established credit union with just over 100,000 retail members and a small but rapidly growing business membership of about 10,000 members. Credit unions are similar to banks in many respects, but they also have a number of key differences. Like banks, they offer many financial services—everything from savings and chequing accounts to investment advice. Unlike banks, however, credit unions don't have customers—they have members. The members are the actual owners of the credit union. Furthermore, credit unions have a strong sense of their social responsibility in addition to their financial responsibility.

Riverside Credit Union, for example, describes itself as a democratic, ethical, and innovative provider of financial services to its members. It is committed to doing business in a way that not only strengthens its own long-term success but also contributes to the social, economic, and environmental well-being of the community in which it operates.

Riverside Credit Union has been quite successful, now having almost $2.5 billion of assets under administration. Much of its success has been due to its excellent member-service culture, the regular introduction of new competitive products, and an aggressive pricing policy that ensures members are always getting some of the best rates available. Riverside Credit Union also has a good distribution network with which to serve its members. It has 15 branches, 30 ATMs, Internet banking, a call centre that is mostly dedicated to servicing members, and an Interactive-Voice-Response phone-banking system. It also has a number of Mortgage Development Managers. During the past two years, the branch sales force had been realigned to focus more on relationship selling. The sales force has placed the greatest emphasis on members with high deposit balances.

Riverside Credit Union is located in a large urban area that until recently has grown a little faster than the rest of the country. During the past year or so the economy has been slowing, resulting in much more competition among financial institutions. There is also more competition from category killers that are focusing on specific product areas, such as credit cards and mortgages. The Internet has facilitated this type of banking and that done by other "direct" financial institutions that are aggressively competing for savings and investment accounts, with rates approaching term-deposit levels. Since continuing pressure on margin has made it impossible for Riverside Credit Union to maintain its aggressive pricing policy, it has seen some erosion of its core business.

Riverside Credit Union has long prided itself on having a strong product marketing group, of which Frank Timmerman was a member. One of the tools that has been invaluable to the marketing group is the Member Database Information System (MDIS). This database had captured all of the product information (except the off-balance mutual fund business). Nevertheless, Frank knew that although there had been a lot of analysis and research on the membership, most of it focused on specific products. Little was known about the full value or nature of the relationships Riverside Credit Union had with its membership.

Thus, under Frank's leadership, a new project was launched to enable the marketing department to deepen their understanding of the membership. Frank saw it as critical that Riverside Credit Union be able to anticipate its members' needs and build long-term relationships with them. The information currently available in the database wasn't up to this task. Therefore, a detailed segmentation analysis was conducted of the entire retail membership. The marketing team hired an expert in segmentation to assist with the work. When the project started, no one knew exactly what the results would show.

SEGMENTATION APPROACH

Given the growing competition in his marketplace, Frank believed that getting this type of information was a pressing need. Since he had only a short time frame within which to complete the initial study, he decided to only use the data currently available in the MDIS for the analysis. Any external data he might want, or external research he might conduct later, could be added once he had a firmer understanding of the various member segments. Frank and the team felt that such information as "share of wallet" would be either too difficult to obtain for the entire membership or too inaccurate to be useful.

Together, then, they concluded there were three things they most needed to know about the membership: (1) profitability of the relationships, (2) behaviour of the members with regard to their usage of various Riverside Credit Union products and services, and (3) future potential. Details on each of these dimensions and on the data used in the analysis are outlined below:

Profitability was examined by summing the margin, fee, and service charge revenue for each member and then subtracting the expenses. With the assistance of Accounting, the total cost for each transaction type was identified and then divided by the total number of transactions in order to generate a per-transaction cost. With input from Sales and Branch operations, setup and maintenance costs were also determined. Expenses were subtracted from revenues to calculate profitability for each member.

Even though there were a few missing numbers, the team agreed that the calculation would represent the profitability of one member relative to another's. Profitability would be looked at by value and by decile to understand the dynamics of the membership.

Member behaviour, or the type of financial relationship the person had with Riverside Credit Union, was the next variable analyzed. To understand this, Riverside compiled all of the data it had for each member for the past year. This included transactional data, members' ages and account information, information on what channel each used, length of membership, etc. A clustering technique was used to group members so that those who demonstrated similar "behaviour" were grouped together while keeping each group as distinct as possible from the other groups.

Potential: Predictive models were developed for the core products offered by Riverside Credit Union (RRSPs, mortgages, term deposits, loans, credit cards, lines of credit, etc.). These models were created by means of statistical techniques, such as regression analysis, and were formulated using data from members who had purchased the product. Such models can then be used to predict future sales of that particular product. Having used predictive models successfully in the past to target product campaigns, Riverside was comfortable with this approach. Each member would be scored for each product and this information would be incorporated into the analysis.

SEGMENTATION RESULTS

Profitability: Table 1 summarizes the annual member profitability analysis.

TABLE 1

Profit Tier	No. of Members	Percentage	Cum. %	Avg. Annual Profit
Top 10%	300	0.3	0.3	$9,000
10 to 20	1,000	1.0	1.3	$2,700
20 to 30	1,300	1.3	2.6	$2,077
30 to 40	1,900	1.9	4.5	$1,421
40 to 50	2,300	2.3	6.8	$1,174
50 to 60	3,000	3.0	9.8	$ 900
60 to 70	4,000	4.0	13.8	$ 675
70 to 80	6,000	6.0	19.8	$ 450
80 to 90	8,000	8.0	27.8	$ 338
90 to 100	35,000	35.0	62.8	$ 77
Zero profit	19,200	19.2	82.0	$ 0
Negative profit	18,000	18.0	100.0	($ 100)
Total	100,000			

Behaviour Segments: Seven different member segments emerged from the analysis. These are described in Table 2 in order of average profitability. Each segment profile also includes a description of average Funds Under Administration (FUA) and average number of products per member.

Further analysis quickly showed that although segments 6 and 7 had the lowest average profit and did cost Riverside Credit Union money to serve, the majority of the members that had negative profitability were in segment 4 (30 percent of segment 4 generated approximately 60 percent of the total negative profit). Segment 4 members did a lot of transactions across all channels, but they did not have high enough balances or revenue to offset the transaction costs.

TABLE 2

Segment	No. of Members	Avg. Profit	Avg. FUA	Products/Member
1	12,000	$900	$150,000	4.5
Complex relationship, with multiple products, mortgage holders, with RRSPs, high lending; utilize all channels with high transaction levels.				
2	8,000	$600	$51,000	3.5
High-balance non-RRSP savers, average transaction levels, traditional channel usage (phone, branch, ATM); slightly older, low lending.				
3	13,000	$310	$27,000	2.3
Average transactions, average balances, ATM and branch transactors; older, low lending.				
4	25,000	$225	$22,000	3.2
High lending, high transactions, all channels; similar to segment 1 except low mortgage usage, high credit card penetration.				
5	15,000	$135	$10,000	2.2
Savers (RRSP and other), average balances, low transactions, limited channels.				
6	7,000	$20	$3,100	0.3
Younger savers with lower balances and average transactions.				
7	23,000	$17	$1,100	1.1
Single-product accounts; inactive, low transactions, low balances.				

Potential: All of the behaviour segments had some members who had higher predictive scores for some products. When the overall scores were combined to give an indication of relative potential, Frank was able to create an index for each segment. Under the indexing system, a score of 100 is average; anything over 100 means higher-than-average potential. Table 3 outlines the segment indexes. The segmentation analysis provided tremendous insight to the marketing department, not only about the current status of the membership but also about the future potential of the individual segments. With more knowledge about which members were profitable, they were able to develop member-focused strategies that were geared to help Riverside Credit Union either retain the member or grow the relationship through targeted cross-selling programs. The marketing department used the information to help restructure their department. Frank was convinced it would help in the transition from being product-focused to being more member-focused.

TABLE 3

Segment	Potential Index	High-Potential Products
1	125	Mortgage, RRSP, LOC, credit card
2	150	Terms, RRSP
3	140	RRSP, term
4	200	RRSP, mortgage, credit card, loans
5	100	RRSP, mortgage, credit card
6	55	Term
7	40	Low on most, some credit card

Acorn Park Hotel

The Acorn Park Hotel was opened in 1946 and is located in South Kensington, a quiet area of London, not far from Harrods and other fashionable shops, and very close to a number of museums and art galleries. With only 80 rooms, the Acorn Park is typical of the properties in the Redpath Group of Inns, who pride themselves as hotels that create a special atmosphere for their guests. It was Monday, July 17, and Geoffrey Thornton, guest relations manager, had just entered his office. The morning mail had arrived, and the first envelope Thornton opened contained the following letter.

Martha K. Stone, QC
Barrister and Solicitor
3265 Main Street
Fredericton, NB, Canada
E3B 4K6

Telephone: 506-624-7419
Fax: 506-624-8000

July 12, 2006

Mr. Geoffrey Thornton
Guest Relations Manager
Acorn Park Hotel
100 Bromley Road
London, England

Dear Mr. Thornton:

My husband and I have just returned home, having spent the past ten days in London on a combined business and pleasure trip. We decided to end our trip with a short weekend stay at the Acorn Park before returning to Canada, as your hotel had been recommended by some good friends of ours who stayed there last summer. Our friends had nothing but good things to say about the Acorn Park Hotel. But, despite the hotel's excellent reputation, the service we received during our stay was quite the opposite. I have decided to write to you to describe the treatment my husband and I received from what can only be described as your tactless and unhelpful staff.

When we arrived last Friday, we were quite tired and were looking forward to relaxing in our room for a few hours before dinner. Upon checking in we were assigned Room 216 which was, if I may say, not what one would expect of a four-star hotel. The room had not been cleaned, as items of clothing had been left by the previous guest. The window looked out on scaffolding and the room was unbearably hot. The person at the front desk, when I finally was able to get through, informed me that there was nothing she could do to find us an alternative room.

The next morning, we experienced totally unacceptable treatment when we ate breakfast in the dining room. The lady on the desk as we entered the dining room pointed out to us that, as we were not members of one of the bus tours staying at the hotel, our breakfast was not included in our room rate and we would have to pay for it! This was no surprise, as we had fully expected to pay.

We were quite surprised as we were leaving the dining room to be stopped again by this lady, who insisted that we pay either in cash or by credit card. Despite our protests that we were guests in the hotel and that she should simply put the charge on our room bill, she insisted that she had instructions to accept only cash or credit card payment from us, referring to the fact that our name was on a list that had been provided to her by the front office.

While I began the process of paying by credit card, my husband went looking for the front-desk manager, who was most helpful and responded immediately. He accompanied my husband to the dining room, where he ascertained that an error had been made and that the name opposite Room 216 on the list that had been provided to the dining room staff was not ours. He apologized and the charge was allowed to go on our room bill. The dining room staff involved were totally unaccommodating and tactless in the way they handled the matter. Needless to say, we did not eat breakfast at the hotel the following morning.

We also encountered problems with your telephone system. Shortly after arriving on Friday evening, I wanted to make an outside telephone call and dialled 9 to get an outside line. I did not get a second dial tone, but rather the line rang and rang for 15 or 20 rings with no answer. I tried two or three times before I could get an answer from the switchboard, only to be told that I should dial 9. Only when I explained that I had been dialling 9 was there an effort made to find out what had happened. Evidently, our line had been switched over in some way so that dialling 9 resulted in the telephone ringing at the front desk. Once this was rectified, I was able to make outside calls.

Checking out on Sunday morning was the final frustration. It was 9 o'clock; others were checking out, bus tours were leaving, guests were trying to have travellers' cheques cashed before their buses left, and the telephones were ringing constantly. The young lady who was working alone on the front desk was trying to deal with this confusion. Guests were becoming upset, the departure of the tours was being delayed, and your employee became so frustrated with the ringing telephones that she simply lifted them and placed them back down again, without answering them!

I do not blame the employee; she was doing her best under the circumstances. I find it totally unacceptable that a hotel would have one employee serving the front desk during what is one of the busiest periods of the day, and have her try to answer the telephones at the same time.

Despite the recommendation from our friends and the Acorn Park's excellent location, I would have to say that it is very unlikely that we will be back unless we have some assurance that the problems with customer service have been overcome. I would welcome your comments.

Sincerely,

Martha K. Stone, QC

The Orangedale Whistle

On a hot sunny day in August, 2006 Todd MacEachern sat in his office in The Creamery, a restored building on the Port Hawkesbury, Nova Scotia waterfront, trying to decide how to launch The Orangedale Whistle. The proposed new venture was a scenic recreational train ride that would depart from the Cape Breton and Central Nova Scotia (CB & CNS) tracks just outside his office, travel to the Orangedale Railroad Station Museum about 50 kilometres away, and arrive back about three hours later. Todd, the 23-year-old marketing director of the Strait Area Waterfront Development Corporation (SAWDC), had to have a draft action plan ready for presentation at the next meeting of his board of directors. As he stared at the piles of information in front of him, he wished he had an assistant who could take the raw data, analyze it, and write the launch plan so he could spend his time dreaming up, and nurturing along, other ideas for the development of the Port Hawkesbury waterfront.

Visioning the Orangedale Whistle had not been a problem for Todd. In his mind's eye he had seen it depart dozens of times. At the start of the summer, prior to the collection of most of the information, Todd imagined it would look something like this:

- It would operate from June to October with a combination of about 80 scheduled trips and an unknown number of special customer bookings. The 80 trips would be scheduled: 36 on Saturdays and Sundays in July and August, 26 on Saturdays, and Sundays in June, September and October, and 18 on weeknights throughout the season. Special customer bookings, Todd thought, might average one per week.

- Capacity of one restored VIA Rail passenger car would be 55.

- The car would be pulled by a CB & CNS locomotive. CB & CNS, a commercial/industrial short line, had agreed to discuss waiving its normal commercial per kilometre rate for pulling a car.

- The trip would pass through several scenic areas, take about an hour to reach Orangedale, include a one-hour tour of the museum—complete with oat cakes and tea if desired—and take another hour to return to The Creamery.

- Each ride would be hosted by an interpretive guide who would provide historical, geological, genealogical, ecological, and other educational information as the group wished.

- Passengers might be families who lived within an hour or so of Port Hawkesbury, their summer guests, vacationers staying overnight in the Strait Area, vacationers

© Ian Spencer (St. Francis Xavier University). The research assistance of Kelly Bonvie, BBA, is gratefully acknowledged. The material in this case is provided solely for the purposes of class discussion. It is not intended to illustrate either effective or ineffective management.

travelling through the area but not staying over, bus tour groups, conventioneers and their families, school groups, and other organized groups based in the area.

- Normal fares would be $15 for adults and $7.50 for children.

- A gift shop, if typical of the industry, might generate 20 to 30 percent of total revenue.

- The initial, tentative estimates of costs were $350 per trip (for two CB & CNS operators, diesel fuel, the interpreter and a ticket seller) plus $15,000 per year (for advertising, insurance, and maintenance) plus $40,000 one-time-only startup costs (for purchasing and restoring a used VIA Rail passenger car, signage, railroad safety improvements, uniforms, speaker systems, and interpretive research/writing).

Advertising costs were: local radio—$30 per 30-second spot, local newspaper—$150 for a 1/4-page ad, wall posters—$1 each, 4-colour brochures—$0.25 each and 1-colour flyers—$0.10 each. The Board would be responsible for obtaining the $40,000 from various development agencies. Todd, the champion of the idea, would have to make a profit—or at least break even—on the rest.

Todd also envisioned possible theme rides, different destinations and durations, and an adults-only evening trip. Possible theme trips included Canada Day, Thanksgiving, Halloween, and other holidays. Possible destinations included heading west to mainland Nova Scotia (about 1 hour) or farther east to the Highland Village at Iona (about 5 hours), or even to Sydney (a full day). (A map of Nova Scotia can be viewed at www.nsonline.com/maps.) The adults-only trip would include refreshments and entertainment on board and would conclude with a nice meal back at The Creamery.

SAWDC AND ITS INFORMAL PARTNERS

The Strait Area Waterfront Development Corporation's mandate was primarily economic development and secondarily the development of civic pride. It had a strong board of directors dominated by professionals and a track record of success. Recent projects included constructing and expanding the Granville Green Bandshell, creating the Customs House Gift Shop, upgrading the marina, creating a boardwalk, restoring The Creamery, and constructing a Pirate Ship Playground.

The Orangedale Railroad Station Museum operated from mid-June to mid-October from 10 a.m. to 6 p.m. Monday to Saturday and from 1 to 6 p.m. on Sundays. It was run by a group of retired railroaders and their families, all working as volunteers. The group hired students via summer grants to help operate the museum. The museum consisted of a restored two-storey station with some of the stationmaster's quarters on the second floor converted into a tea room. The grounds included a restored caboose, a boxcar gift shop, and a restored snowplow car. Normally visitors arrived one car at a time and went on a tour guided by one of the retired railroaders. Capacity of the museum, including the outbuildings, was about 50. Admission was by donation. In 1997 the museum hosted just over 5,000 visitors. Martin Boston, the leader of the group, realized the proposed recreational train ride would require adjustments in the museum's operations but observed to Todd, "Anything is possible."

The CB & CNS Railroad had been most cooperative, both in agreeing to supply an engine and operators and in expressing a willingness to waive its normal $27 per kilometre fee for pulling a car. Daily, except Sunday, a train left Sydney westbound for Truro. The train attempted to leave between 10 and 10:30 a.m., but waiting for coal, and technical/mechanical problems, caused departure times to vary substantially. The speed varied as well, depending upon the number of full cars. If a train left on schedule, it tended to pass Orangedale at about 2 p.m. and Port Hawkesbury at about 3 p.m. Daily except Sunday another train headed east and passed through Port Hawkesbury at about 9:30 a.m. and Orangedale at about 10:30 a.m. This train also was somewhat unpredictable. The railroad maintained several spurs and sidings, including ones at both Port Hawkesbury and Orangedale. CB & CNS owned a diesel locomotive that, part of every workday, shunted freight cars for major industrial clients in the Port Hawkesbury area. This was the locomotive to which Todd was hoping to have access. An old but functional steam engine owned by a nearby gypsum company also might be available to pull the passenger car.

Todd and his board had begun negotiations with VIA Rail to acquire one of the dozens of retired passenger cars in storage at its yard in Halifax. Given the objectives of SAWDC, Todd was hopeful they could purchase one for a token $1. The normal price would be more like $25,000.

THE RECREATIONAL RAILROADING INDUSTRY

In July Todd asked his summer intern to research the recreational railroad industry in North America. The intern discovered there are about 60 such operations and interviewed about 20 by telephone. The interviews revealed:

- Capacity ranged from 70 to 500 and averaged 325.
- Adult prices ran $8 to $12 for rides typically lasting 45 to 90 minutes.
- All offered special theme rides that seemed to be very popular, and many, including some in cooler climates, operated year-round. Many were linked to other attractions such as the Rocky Mountains or the Grand Canyon.
- A steam engine seemed to be a real drawing card and gift shops were seen as mandatory.
- Most relied heavily on volunteers.
- Budgets for advertising averaged about 12 percent of revenue. All interviewees felt aggressive marketing was a key to success.

AN OVERVIEW OF THE MARKETPLACE

Todd also had undertaken an initial examination of the potential market. He discovered that 26,000 people lived within approximately 30 minutes of the waterfront, 38,000 lived 30 to 60 minutes away, 179,000 lived one to two hours away, and 400,000 more lived two to three hours away—most in the Regional Municipality of Halifax. The average household contained 2.9 people. Every year from May to October 500,000 vacationers crossed the Canso Causeway at least twice (into and out of Cape Breton). Including vacationers and locals, 150,000 people stopped every summer at the Visitor Information Centre at Port Hastings, a five-minute drive from the Port Hawkesbury waterfront. From May to October 2005 the Strait Area's seven motels accommodated 22,000 visitor parties (about 64,000 people) in their 350 rooms. The provincial government estimated an out-of-province visitor party spent $284 per day in Nova Scotia while visitor parties from within the province spent $158.

To obtain a feel for local interest, Todd conducted a telephone survey among 50 residents using a systematic sampling approach (every *n*th listing in the "625" exchange). The survey revealed nearly 50 percent awareness of the proposed ride despite only one short radio interview Todd had given in June. Almost all respondents (84%) said they would take a ride on the train and, on average, considered $14 a reasonable price for an adult ticket. Key reasons for locals' interest were the scenery, the kids would love it, its uniqueness, nostalgia, and the allure of trains. Most (60%) were also interested in the adults-only evening ride. Half said they typically had summer guests who would be interested in riding the Orangedale Whistle.

Other market segments Todd had identified were tour buses, school children, conventions, and local organizations. He discovered about 1,000 tour buses came to Cape Breton every summer, each with about 40 passengers. About 300 tour buses spent one, or sometimes two, nights at a Strait Area motel. Most buses arrived between 4 and 6 p.m. and left between 7 and 9 a.m. the next morning. Bus tour patrons and operators were very package oriented ("Do this ... do that ... eat here ... see this ... leave") and somewhat price-sensitive. The Strait Regional School Board has about 8,500 elementary students (350 homerooms) and 4,200 secondary students (160 home rooms). Almost all lived within one hour of Port Hawkesbury. Normally students would be available from 8 a.m. to 3 p.m. Monday to Friday. Principals loved the idea but were concerned about safety and price. Most felt $5 would be the maximum price for a student ticket. Some suggested area businesses might consider sponsoring (subsidizing) student trips. Todd quickly discovered the conference market was very small. Most delegates did not travel with their families and most were not in the area to sightsee. Several hundred organizations (business, educational, labour, community groups, government) existed in the Strait Area, but Todd had not yet contacted them about their interest in special bookings or to assess their needs and interests.

→ ## Rick's Pizza Corporation

Richard (Rick) Firenze, chief executive of Rick's Pizza Corporation, looked sombre as he addressed senior executives of the North American pizza restaurant chain that bore his nickname. "We're facing yet another lawsuit for injuries due to alleged dangerous driving by one of our delivery drivers," he announced at the company's head office. "It comes on top of some very bad publicity about accidents involving our drivers in recent years."

BACKGROUND

Speed had always been a key strategic thrust for Rick's Pizza, which used the slogan, "It's quick at Rick's." The company's restaurants not only prepared pizza rapidly but also delivered it quickly. The company's promise to home-deliver a pizza within 30 minutes of a phone order or to cut $3 off the price had boosted it from a single pizzeria 20 years earlier to the status of a North American chain with thousands of outlets and over $3 billion in sales. But now a growing number of critics were saying that, in Rick's case, at least, speed was a killer.

Rick's executives argued that the system did not promote fast or reckless driving. "The speed takes place in the store—not on the road," declared a spokesperson. "We can custom-make a pizza within 10 to 12 minutes. Our average delivery area is only 2 to 3 kilometres, so there's enough time to deliver."

THE SAFETY PROBLEM

The company's own records indicated that during the previous year, accidents involving Rick's drivers had cost 20 lives, 18 of them during pizza runs. But it had declined to specify how many of the victims were employees. Randell Meins, Rick's vice-president for corporate communications, stated in a television interview that the company had always encouraged drivers to take care, had never penalized late drivers, was urging franchise owners and store managers to promote safe driving, and would soon implement a new safety course for all Rick's drivers.

Meins cited the owner of several franchises who had declared: "We never ask a driver to break the speed limit. We never want them to do anything unsafe on the road. And we always tell them to fasten their seat belts." Although acknowledging that "even one death is too many," Meins noted that with 230 million pizzas delivered last year, this works out to only one death per 11.5 million pies. "We're not minimizing the deaths by any means," Meins said. "But that's what the mathematics show."

Martine Leblanc, director of a nonprofit safety research and advocacy group, expressed outrage over the Rick's statistic. "Great!" she said. "Now we know the value of the life of a 17-year-old—11.5 million pizzas." Leblanc offered her own statistical analysis. Rick's, she said, employed some 75,000 part-time drivers. Assuming that this amounted to the equivalent of 20,000 full-time drivers—four for each of the 5,000 Rick's outlets—she claimed that 20 deaths in one year meant that the company's drivers faced a death rate between three and six times higher than that in the construction industry and twice as high as that of miners.

"The point is this," said Leblanc. "Would parents let their kids drive for Rick's if they knew they were three times more likely to die doing that job than if they were working in construction?"

Scott and Linda Hurding's 17-year-old son had been the latest Rick's driver to die, the only Rick's employee so far during the current year. Hustling to deliver pizzas in a semi-rural area in the western part of the country, Mike Hurding often covered 150 kilometres a night. His parents and classmates said that he was proud that he almost always made the delivery within the 30-minute limit and was determined never to get the "King of the Lates" badge allegedly given every week by his franchisor to the driver most often late on deliveries.

Mike died when the company-owned pickup he was driving in a delivery run skidded off a wet road and hit a utility pole as he tried to avoid another car that was braking to make a left-hand turn. A police reconstruction of the accident concluded that Mike had been driving at 75 kilometres per hour on a road with a 50 kilometre per hour speed limit, and was not wearing a seatbelt. The other driver was not charged. Rick's subsequently offered the Hurding family about $5,000 in worker's compensation to cover funeral costs. Leblanc estimated that the 20 deaths during the previous year had cost Rick's some $90,000 in death benefits. Like many other critics of the company, she argued that Rick's was unconcerned because the cost was so low. Accordingly, she had written to Richard Firenze, asking that Rick's pay $500,000 to each accident victim, abandon the 30-minute rule, and hire only drivers aged 18 or older.

Linda Hurding, Mike's mother, told a TV reporter that Rick's guarantee to deliver within 30 minutes or knock $3 off the price was just "a licence to speed." Blaming this policy for their son's death, the Hurding parents and a group of family friends had started a petition drive asking for federal restrictions on the policy. Within a month of beginning their drive, the petitioners had delivered the first batch of more than 1,500 signatures to the offices of their political representative. "We're angry and we're fighting," the Hurdings said. Meantime, another group in a separate part of the country was looking into the case to determine whether Rick's policy violated the federal Occupational Safety and Health (OSH) guidelines.

Rick's faced criticism and legal action on other fronts as well. On the west coast, the widow of a motorcyclist allegedly struck and killed by a Rick's driver nine months earlier had sued the company for damages. Farther east, attorney Anders Mundel had just filed suit on behalf of Wilson and Jennifer Groncki, who suffered neck, back, and arm injuries when their car was broadsided by a Rick's delivery truck whose driver had run a stop sign as she left a Rick's store with four pizzas for home delivery.

The Gronckis alleged that the store manager had rushed to the scene of the wreck and yelled, "Let's get this pizza on the road!" In addition to unspecified monetary damages, the suit sought to force Rick's to abandon the 30-minute rule, which the attorney called "a grossly negligent corporate policy."

Attorney Mundel was also helping other lawyers around the country to press cases against the company and had organized an information network, including a website, to coordinate the filing of cases in different jurisdictions. "Even if Rick's franchisees, managers, and executives do not actively encourage reckless driving," he argued, "the 30-minute rule acts as an inherent encouragement, putting great pressure on the drivers."

As part of her research, safety advocate Leblanc had interviewed a number of current and former Rick's employees, several of whom preferred to remain anonymous for fear of reprisals from the managers at the stores where they worked. Leblanc claimed that her research showed that "the vast majority" of the company's drivers were under 18.

Nelson Chen, a 20-year-old college student and former part-time Rick's employee who had worked in several of Rick's outlets in Ontario over a three-year period, told Leblanc that he and other drivers "speeded all the time. I would even run stop signs—anything to make those deliveries." Declining to give her last name, Sue, a 19-year-old Rick's driver from the prairies, said that managers "get uptight when pizzas are running late and start yelling at everyone to hurry up, hurry up!"

A consultant familiar with the industry agreed: "There's a lot of pressure to speed. It's not written in the manuals, but it's there. If a driver goes out with four deliveries and ends up with only a minute to make that last one but figures he's two minutes away, he's going to speed, he's going to cut corners."

RESPONDING TO THE PROBLEM

Two weeks after Mike Hurding's death, Rick's sent a letter to its corporate-owned stores and its franchisees, stating that it was company policy to hire drivers 18 or older. This directive, however, was not binding on the franchisees, which operated some 65 percent of all Rick's restaurants.

The newly filed lawsuit by Anders Mundel, together with continuing criticism of the company, had been widely reported in the media. Firenze and his colleagues were worried. Historically, the company had enjoyed a positive public image and a reputation as a generous donor to local community activities. "We definitely have a perception problem," said Meins. "We're taking a lot of heat right now." But Harry Carpaccio, the senior vice-president of marketing, warned against taking precipitous action. "The last thing we need to do is to panic," he declared. "The 30-minute guarantee is very, very important to our customers. Sales could be hard hit if we drop it."

DECISION CASE 9

Country Paws Boarding Inc.

On April 2, 1999, Jaymie and Michelle Crook, owners of Country Paws Boarding in London, Ontario, were busily working their way through the queue of dogs being brought in for boarding that Easter weekend. While the queue included a number of regulars whom Jaymie and Michelle knew and enthusiastically greeted by name, there were also a number of dogs being boarded at Country Paws for the first time. For these dogs and their owners, this initial boarding was likely to be a traumatic event. Jaymie and Michelle customarily took every opportunity to get to know each dog's likes, dislikes, behaviours, and tendencies, in order to minimize this separation trauma. This required ongoing dialogue with each dog owner and observation of each canine. Jaymie and Michelle were always eager to chat with those boarding their dogs at Country Paws, in the hope of identifying potential new services and improving existing offerings.

COUNTRY PAWS

Jaymie and Michelle opened Country Paws in September 1998, on 28 hectares of land in southeast London. A single climate-controlled building was constructed that contained facilities for "doggie" boarding, grooming, and recreation. The total cost of the land and the building was $500,000. The 427-square-metre facility contained 46 standard runs. Each run was outfitted with a doggie bed, food and water bowls, and a private doggie door. A staff of three full-time and one part-time employees sanitized each of the runs on a daily basis (and between each guest), performed grooming services, and supervised recreation activities for the dogs.* Michelle, given her business diploma, oversaw the daily operations and marketing of the kennel, while Jaymie

Jacob Cho and Professor Larry Menor prepared this case solely to provide material for class discussion. The authors do not intend to illustrate either effective or ineffective handling of a managerial situation. The authors may have disguised certain names and other identifying information to protect confidentiality.

*A standard run contained a 1.2 × 1.2 metre indoor and 1.2 × 3.7 metre outdoor suite. Each suite had an indoor area attached to a covered outdoor patio and was separated by concrete block walls. Each run provided its occupant with a private window. Several upscale, larger rooms were available as well (i.e., VIP suites). These suites came equipped with a raised soft bed, TV, radio, and window.

was in charge of facility maintenance. While neither had any previous background in starting up and running a dog kennel, both were long-time dog owners. Knowing that some professional expertise was required in managing such a business, Michelle participated by correspondence in the training program offered by the American Boarding Kennels Association. In addition to his duties at Country Paws, Jaymie continued to serve on the London Police Force.

In 1998, Country Paws joined nine other boarding kennels serving London. None of these boarded dogs exclusively; all also accepted cats and exotic animals. Jaymie and Michelle, long-time London residents, started to think about starting their own kennel after several disappointing experiences boarding their own dogs. They devised a business plan for their kennel in 1996, after having toured and benchmarked kennels in the United States. Their research showed that 25 percent of all London households had a dog. Typically, there were approximately 22,000 dogs and 12,000 cats licensed in the municipality of London. To build awareness and to reach dog owners, Jaymie and Michelle promoted Country Paws at the Western Fair, London's annual 10-day fall fair and exhibition. Additionally, they held an open house and barbeque for local veterinarians. Relying largely on word-of-mouth advertising, Country Paws was soon having to wait-list dogs for weekend boarding. Demand for overnight boarding on holidays was also high. At one point, more than 86 dogs were boarded over the Christmas holiday; some owners brought in their own crates to house their dogs. For weekends and holidays, the kennel would be fully booked several months in advance. While occupancy rates fluctuated from month to month, a number of dogs quickly became regular guests at Country Paws.

BOARDING KENNEL CUSTOMERS AND GUEST SERVICES

Dog owners sought boarding services for three primary reasons. First, they wished to have their dogs preoccupied during the normal workday hours. Second, some boarded their dogs while on short- or long-term holidays. Third, some owners wished to expose their canines to non-home environments. Many of the dogs were boarded at Country Paws while their owners were on weekend or week-long vacations. Irrespective of the reasons, most owners were concerned about the quality of care their dog received. They used a variety of cues to assess the quality of care provided, including the smell of their dog, its physical condition, receptivity upon pickup and the level of excitement upon subsequent boarding. Country Paws required that all dogs receive up-to-date annual Bordetella (canine cough) vaccinations. Dog owners were encouraged to bring their own food and medication, which the staff would administer, based on each dog's typical schedule. Further, it was strongly suggested that owners provide favourite toys and other items that might be useful to combat canine homesickness.

Country Paws' mission was "We care for dogs like our dogs." As such, Jaymie and Michelle offered a variety of traditional and nontraditional kennel services (see Exhibit 1). An array of boarding options existed, including overnight, weekend, and long-term stays. Dog owners could have their dogs pampered with a massage at Country Paws' spa. During the kennel's daily hours of operation from 8 a.m. to 6 p.m., dog owners could drop off their dogs for doggie daycare. Additionally, an assortment of doggie beds, toys, and food items were available for purchase in the Country Paws pet store. The staff routinely offered unlimited belly rubs and ear scratches free of charge.

THE "COMMUNITY PLAYGROUND" EXPERIMENT

To further meet dog owners' expectations for doggie socialization and recreation, Jaymie and Michelle were experimenting with providing all guests access to a "community playground." Under this arrangement, each dog would be allowed access several times every day to a 0.1 hectare fenced-in play area supplied with toys and, in warmer weather, a wading pool. Most of the time, multiple dogs would be allowed in the play area simultaneously for supervised frolicking and exercise.

Providing this community playground required some new operating procedures. Staff would have to ensure that only compatible dogs played together. Dog compatibility was primarily a function of dog size, breed, age, and gender. Given that the staff daily recorded each dog's routines, the sociability of each dog could be easily assessed. According to Michelle:

> The first task in making the community playground work would be to identify the grouping of playmates. We planned on having each dog's sociability classified based on the use of a colored tagging system. Dogs with a blue tag tended to be quiet and submissive with other canines. Dogs with a green tag tended to be rough players, while dogs with a red tag were identified as not being allowed to play with others at all.
>
> In some cases, "complex" dogs would have to be double tagged. For example, P.T., a three-year-old male Siberian Husky and doggie daycare regular, would receive both green and red tags since he had a tendency to be fence-aggressive, toy-aggressive, and disliked smaller dogs.

New dogs were assigned a yellow tag and would have to be separated from the regulars until their temperaments were identified. Although a rarity, dogs that were people-aggressive (i.e., that should not come into contact with people) were sometimes turned away or barred from further boarding.

Both Jaymie and Michelle realized that offering the community playground would require some changes to the current facility. Enough playgrounds would be needed to accommodate each grouping of 10 to 12 playmates. Additionally, older and less socially active dogs would require separate play areas. Jaymie had designed the playgrounds so that the dogs making up each playmates community would have easy access to their private runs. Besides changes to the facility, starting community playgrounds would require some additional staffing and operations challenges. For example, the staff would now have to interact more frequently with the dogs and be capable of breaking up any doggie clashes that might arise. Additional training and certification might be required. Further, to offer and maintain this increased level of dog socialization and recreation, additional staff and veterinarian technicians might be required.

Country Paws dog owners, once notified, were generally enthusiastic about the community playground idea. The community playground experiments conducted so far, which involved grouping of different sets of tagged dogs for up to 15-to-30-minute intervals of interaction, had progressed without major incident. Currently none of the other kennels in London offered such a service. Despite this, Jaymie and Michelle were not so sure that a community playground was the right approach to providing their guests with increased socialization and recreation. One straightforward alternative would be to double the distance of the existing 1.5 kilometre walking trail. Both wondered whether there were other alternatives worth considering and pursuing.

EXHIBIT 1

Country Paws'
Services

Boarding Services

Offering	Price (CDN$)
Indoor/outdoor suite*	14.95
VIP suite*	24.95
Late pickup charge**	9.95
Doggie daycare	9.95
1.5 km country trail walk	3.95

*A discount would be offered to second or third guest overnight stays using the same suite.
**Charge for overnight guests picked up after the 11 a.m. checkout time.

Grooming Services

Offering*	Price (CDN$)
Long-haired breeds:	
Small	30.00
Medium	35.00
Large	40.00
Extra large	50.00
Short-haired breeds:	
Small	22.00
Medium	27.00
Large	32.00
Extra large	37.00

*A full groom includes a bath, brush, nail trim, and ear cleaning.

Source: Company files.

———→ # Golden City Miniature Golf

Connor Smith and Mia Brown, two high school teachers, had just finished their analysis of a proposal for a miniature golf course in Golden City. They had initially thought of the idea after watching a miniature golf tournament on television. After collecting data on the viability of the proposal, they were discussing whether they should actually invest more time and money and make the proposal a reality. On the basis of his initial review, Connor was very optimistic about the new service, and felt the proposal would make money no matter where they located or how they priced and promoted the venture.

"Look, Mia, there's no real competition and there's lots of people who would love to play miniature golf in Golden City. I think we've got a potential gold mine on our hands. I've calculated that our maximum capacity for the course is 864 rounds per day, based on the assumption that there would be four people per hole and they would take one hour to play one round. Given that there are 18 holes and the course will be open 12 hours per day, a total of $(4 \times 1 \times 18 \times 12)$ 864 rounds could be played every day."

Mia Brown was more cautious: "I agree our initial assessment is very positive but I think there are several other important factors: location, how we communicate the idea to people, and how we price it. If we don't get the Metropolitan Mall location, I wouldn't be too keen on the idea. Also, if we don't advertise and promote miniature golf properly, there's a chance that it won't succeed. Finally, without some good pricing ideas I doubt we will operate at capacity for the whole season. I'm sure there will be times when demand and capacity are not balanced. I think we should have another look at our analysis and figure out if this idea could work and what's the best way to market it."

THE IDEA

Connor Smith and Mia Brown had often discussed ways of getting into business during their lunch hours at school. The two teachers felt they could each invest $5,000 in a business venture if they could come up with a reasonable idea. After seeing the televised miniature golf tournament, they decided to do some research on miniature golf in Golden City. The research included an analysis of competition, potential locations, consumers' needs, the Golden City market, and the costs involved.

© Gordon H. G. McDougall (Sir Wilfrid Laurier University). This case was prepared by Gordon H. G. McDougall as a basis for classroom discussion and not to illustrate effective or ineffective handling of a management situation. Revised 2006.

The Competition

A survey of the Golden City area revealed two existing miniature golf courses. The competitors were evaluated on a number of criteria (see Exhibit 1), and the general conclusion reached by the partners was that both courses were of poor quality. It was felt that if a miniature golf course was constructed of high-quality materials and offered a fair degree of challenge, it would attract virtually all of the competitions' customers. The partners decided that if they went ahead with the venture they should consider constructing the best possible course in terms of challenge, materials, and craftsmanship.

Potential Locations

After looking at a number of areas, the partners concluded that any location should be readily accessible to the public. The basic idea was to "bring the game to the people" by having a convenient location. They felt that a location in or near a shopping mall would be good because of the high traffic flows. The manager of Cambridge Investments, a company that controlled Metropolitan Mall, was contacted, and the idea of a miniature golf course located at the mall was discussed. Metropolitan Mall was considered an ideal site as it was the largest shopping centre in Golden City, with over 150 stores and services in an enclosed mall located in the southern suburbs of the city. The number of people who shopped at Metropolitan Mall each month was estimated at around 390,000. The mall had large areas of parking space (parking was available for 4,860 cars), and it was proposed that the golf course be located in the parking lot near one of the entrances to the mall. The manager, while interested in the proposal, did not commit himself to the venture. He suggested that the two partners return after they had finalized their plans. If they were allowed to locate at Metropolitan Mall, their rental fee for the land would be 20 percent of gross sales.

EXHIBIT 1   Miniature Golf Courses in Golden City

	Competitor 1 (Gateway Plaza)	Competitor 2 (Suburban Go-Kart)
Location		
Accessibility	Excellent	Poor
Built-in clientele	Very good	Poor
Price		
Per 18-hole round (single adult ticket)	$4.50	$4.00
Course		
Appearance	Fair	Poor
Challenge offered	Fair	Poor
Material quality	Poor	Very poor
Promotion		
Advertising	Little	None
Tournaments	None	None
Leagues	None	None
Incentives	None	None
Appeal to market segments	None	None
Return on investment	Fair	In the red

Consumer Analysis

The next step in the project was to conduct a consumer analysis. The partners recognized that miniature golf could appeal to many consumer segments including preteens, teens, adult males, and adult females. On the basis of this segmentation, they listed a number of needs they felt miniature golf could satisfy, and ranked them in terms of probable importance for three different consumer groups. The needs and rankings are listed in Exhibit 2. This analysis indicated the primary needs satisfied would be enjoyment, challenge, and socializing with friends or family. Further information was collected by conducting two consumer surveys.

A questionnaire was drawn up and given to students at their school. The results, shown in Exhibit 3, indicated that most students would play miniature golf at Metropolitan Mall if they were there.

Approximately 50 percent would play miniature golf on a date, and 50 percent said they would come to the mall on Sunday and play. Approximately 77 percent said they felt that $4.50 was a reasonable price for golf. Only 17 percent felt $4.50 was too high a price.

The second survey, shown in Exhibit 4, asked 100 adults if they could see any use for a miniature golf course at Metropolitan Mall. The results indicated that consumers might participate in miniature golf while shopping at the mall.

Fluctuations in Demand

Connor and Mia, after further analysis, began to realize that demand for mini golf would likely fluctuate over the season. They didn't have any firm data but they knew that they would need to make some reasonable assumptions about *who* was likely to play *when* so that they could try to balance capacity and demand.

The Golden City Market

Golden City was primarily a heavy-industry community with large automobile assembly and feeder plants. The average income in the city of 262,000 people was 5 percent above the national average and per capita personal income was estimated at $18,500 (see Exhibit 5). The proposed site at Metropolitan Mall would be within a 15-minute drive for most of the population.

Connor and Mia also collected information about the average number of days without rain between May and September (Exhibit 5). On average, there were 104 days without rain during this period.

EXHIBIT 2   Assumed Consumer Needs

	Parents and Teens	Male Adults	Female Adults
Recreational enjoyment	1	1	1
Family outing	4	4	2
Relaxation	5	5	4
Socializing	3	8	3
Challenge/competition	2	2	5
Time required to play	8	6	6
Status	6	7	7
Convenience	7	3	8

EXHIBIT 3

Student Survey Results—Age Six to Eighteen (sample size = 300)

1. Sex?

Male	144
Female	156
	300

2. Do you go to Metropolitan Mall in the summer?

Yes	253
No	47
	300

(a) If yes: Would you play miniature golf?

	Yes	No	Maybe
Male	99	12	7
Female	97	24	14

(b) If no: Would you go to the mall for a recreational activity like miniature golf?

	Yes	No	Maybe
Male	4	11	11
Female	4	10	7

3. Do you think members of your family would play?

(a) Older than yourself?

Yes	No	Maybe
85	61	154

(b) Younger than yourself?

Yes	No	Maybe
126	33	141

4. Would you play miniature golf with your date?

	Yes	No	Maybe	No Answer
Male	80	14	26	24
Female	82	10	32	32

5. Do you consider $4.50 a low price—reasonable price—high price?

	Low	Reasonable	High
Male	14	96	34
Female	4	134	18

6. Would you come to the mall on Sunday to play?

	Yes	No	Maybe
Male	70	42	32
Female	80	31	45

EXHIBIT 4 Adult Survey Results

1. (Sample size = 100; females = 50, males = 50)
2. Interviews were conducted at Metropolitan Mall and with friends and colleagues.
3. The respondents were informed of the proposal (miniature golf) and asked if they could see any use for such a service.
4. Results—most frequent responses only (response was considered frequent if it occurred 10% of the time):
   (a) I could see it as an advantage in that my children wouldn't mind coming shopping with us.
   (b) Could serve as a family activity.
   (c) Would play while waiting for my wife.
   (d) I really don't have the time.

EXHIBIT 5   Selected Statistics—Golden City Market

A. Population (Golden City)

Age Group	Male	Female
0–4	9,120	8,540
5–9	8,955	8,170
10–14	9,145	8,565
15–19	9,680	9,430
20–24	10,095	10,100
25–34	21,850	22,205
35–44	19,380	20,195
45–54	14,095	14,185
55–64	11,965	12,430
65–69	5,155	6,550
70+	8,195	13,520
	127,635	134,430

Families:	Number	70,635
	Average no. per family	3.1
Households	Number	97,305
	Average no. per household	2.6

B. Income

Average family income	$ 53,117
Average household income	$ 46,793
Estimated per capita personal income	$ 18,500

	%
Under $15,000	38
15,000–24,999	22
25,000–34,999	14
35,000–49,999	17
50,000–74,999	7
75,000–99,999	1
100,000 and over	1
	100%

C. Weather

	Rainfall	
Month	Average Number of Days with Rain*	Average Number of Days Without Rain
May	12	19
June	10	20
July	9	22
August	9	22
September	9	21
	49	104

*Based on an accumulation of at least 0.01 inches. Averaged over past 30 years. Most likely time of rainfall 3 p.m. to 7 p.m. during these months.

Sources: Statistics Canada, *Marketing Research Handbook*, Catalogue 63-224; *Financial Post*; *Canadian Markets*.

Cost Estimates

The partners calculated the costs of constructing the miniature golf course (see Exhibit 6). The total estimated cost of $21,166 (including taxes) included the cost of building the 18 holes plus a pro shop, fencing, and miscellaneous expenses. No cost was included for labour, because the holes could be built by the industrial arts class at the high school where they taught. The only operating expenses they would incur would be advertising expenses and hiring someone to run the course. The cost of hiring someone was estimated at $8,696, based on paying them $6.70 per hour (plus 4% vacation pay) 12 hours per day for the season of 104 days. They tentatively planned to have the course open from 10 a.m. to 10 p.m. every day.

While they had collected some data on advertising rates, they had not decided on any advertising campaign. The *Golden City Star*, the local daily newspaper, had a citywide circulation of 86,000. Cost of advertising for a full page, a half-page, a quarter-page, and a one-eighth page was $5,472, $2,727, $1,864, and $682 respectively. Radio advertising costs ranged from $65 for a 30-second spot on prime time on CKLW (a local rock oldies station) and $65 for an equivalent spot on CKWW (a local nostalgia rock station) to $75 for an equivalent spot on CIMX (a local teen-oriented rock station).

DECISIONS

The partners faced a number of decisions. First, they needed to set a price. They were thinking about pricing at either $4 or $4.50 per round for single adult tickets. They wondered, though, whether price could be more effectively used. Second, they needed to decide on what advertising should be done, if any. Third, they needed to decide on a promotional program. A weakness of the competition was the lack of any promotion, and Mia didn't want them to make the same mistake. Fourth, and this was related to pricing and promotion, they needed to address how to manage the expected fluctuations in demand. Finally, they had to decide what to do if the manager of Metropolitan Mall did not agree to their proposal. They estimated the total cost would probably be around $23,000, which would mean they would have to borrow $13,000 from the bank. Ultimately, the major decision had to be made. Should they invest in

EXHIBIT 6 Cost Estimates for Miniature Golf Course

Material Cost			
3⁄4″ plywood	$34.95 per sheet		
2 × 4	$0.50 per foot (linear)		
2 × 8	$1.05 per foot (linear)		
Paint	$27.00 per gallon		
Carpeting	$26.00 square yard		

Average Cost per Hole			
Material costs:			
3⁄4″ plywood, (3 or 4 sheets)	$123.00		
2 × 4, 125′	$ 62.50		
2 × 8, 60′	$ 63.00		
Carpeting (Kentucky blue grass), 11.25 square yards	$292.50		
Miscellaneous (nails, sheet metal, batteries, motors, sand, shrubbery)	$220.00		
Paint (1 gallon per hole)	$ 26.00		
Total	**$787.00**		

Labour Cost per Hole			
All construction to be done by the industrial arts class at the high school under the supervision of a qualified craftsperson			
Total cost per hole	$787.00		
Total cost for eighteen holes = 18 × $787		$14,166	
Other expenses:			
Pro shop	$ 3,000		
Fencing	$ 2,700		
Miscellaneous (putters, bails, cards, pencils)	$ 1,300		
Total	$ 7,000	$ 7,000	
Total cost		$21,166	

The Riverside Motor Inn, Bridgewater, Nova Scotia

Office of the General Manager

MEMORANDUM

October 1, 2006

TO:	Heidi Smith Senior Lounge Hostess
FROM:	Ronald Veinot General Manager
SUBJECT:	Chapters Lounge

Welcome to the staff of the Riverside Motor Inn. Your six years' experience at the Little Brown Jug lounge in Lunenburg, your infectious enthusiasm, and your strong customer/service orientation all suggest great promise for success. I am looking forward to working with you. By the way, I just moved to Bridgewater myself in March so the whole operation is relatively new to me as well.

As we discussed at your interview, in time I want you to regard Chapters Lounge as your own business. For at least the first nine months, however, I'd like to work closely with you and review and approve your plans. If everything goes well, independence, profit sharing, and promotion to manager could be just around the corner. To assist you in understanding Chapters' situation, I have assembled the following summary of operations, recent results and recent strategies. I hope you don't mind point form.

- The Riverside Motor Inn was built in 1985 and has 34 rooms on two floors all within one building. For the fiscal year ended November 30, 2005, occupancy totalled 7,800 room nights at an average rate of $85. The Inn operates at capacity (almost) during July, August and September. Our 50-seat dining room, The Sou' Wester, is open daily from 7 a.m. to 2 p.m. and 5 to 9:00 p.m. Sales last year were $175,000 and will be about the same this year. The Sou' Wester, as you may recall, is across the lobby from Chapters Lounge.

- This summer the owners invested over $250,000 creating a new front entrance and lobby area and dramatically renovating both Chapters and The Sou' Wester. Unfortunately, as I think I mentioned, Chapters had to close for almost all of May and June to accommodate the renovations.

- Chapters Lounge contains 30 seats and is open Monday to Saturday from 4 p.m. to 12:30 a.m. During the past three fiscal years, sales have been $63,300 (2003), $75,700 (2004), and $66,700 (2005). Cost of goods sold has been constant at 36 percent of sales and direct labour has been constant at about $18,000.

- Chapters Lounge offers a quiet, comfortable, relaxing alternative to "the bar scene." The seating is padded bar stools, armchairs, loveseats, and a couch. The lounge's seven square tables are solid wood. The colour scheme is burgundy and forest green with pastel accent colours dusty rose and pale green. This summer we began using the slogan "Conversation Without Shouting" to promote Chapters Lounge to guests of the Riverside Inn (signs in the lobby and notices in guests' rooms) and to residents of the community (three ads in the local weekly paper). By virtue of its name, decor, size, rich colour scheme, and overall ambience, Chapters Lounge is unique in the area.

- In fiscal 2005, sales from drinks were beer 69 percent, liquor 30 percent, and wine 1 percent. Gross profit margins (markups) were beer 60 percent, liquor 73 percent, and wine 50 percent. Average retail prices were beer $3, liquor (including cocktails) $3.75, and wine $3.25. Sales from drinks was 95 percent of total revenue. The other 5 percent was packaged food items (peanuts, chips, etc.), prepared food items (from our kitchen), and cigarettes. I suspect these figures are pretty much the same this year.

- Happy Hour at Chapters now runs from 4:30 to 8 p.m. (it used to run 5–7 p.m.). Beer is $2.80 per bottle and liquor (excluding cocktails) is $3.25 per 1½ oz shot. The three largest bars/taverns in the area also have Happy Hours:
  - Len's Place—A country and western bar/lounge (seating for 125); 4–7:30 p.m., beer $2.75, liquor $2.75.
  - Chevy's—A rock 'n' roll (50s–60s) bar/lounge (seating for 200); 4–9:30 p.m., beer $2.75, liquor $2.75.
  - Pirate's Pub—Turn-of-the-century pirate theme, German cuisine (seating for 400); 4–7:00 p.m., beer $2.75, liquor $2.75.

  All have dance floors, "pub food" type meals and feature live entertainment on a fairly regular basis.

- Chapters' revenue by month in calendar 2005 was:

Jan.	$5,055	Apr.	$6,345	July	$6,071	Oct.	$4,902
Feb.	5,133	May	6,486	Aug.	4,843	Nov.	4,673
Mar.	5,146	June	7,405	Sept.	5,273	Dec.	5,327
1st Qtr.	$15,334	2nd Qtr.	$20,236	3rd Qtr.	$16,187	4th Qtr.	$14,902

- Revenue in 2006 has been disappointing. During the seven months Chapters was open every day (January to April and July to September), revenue averaged $3,140 per month. I think most of the decrease can be traced to the departure of "D.J.," a long-time bartender who moved to Calgary in December 2005, and to the hype surrounding the opening of Pirate's Pub in January 2006.

- Volume improved modestly in August ($3,708) and September ($4,350), but it is still well below that for the same months in 2005. Recently newspaper ads have urged the public to rediscover Chapters Lounge by featuring free hors d'oeuvres (value $3–$5 per table), the new 210-minute happy hour, and the new slogan. As well, we sent out about 200 flyers to local groups suggesting they consider Chapters for group outings.

- I must confess I haven't had a chance to examine the lounge in any detail given the renovations and the need to adapt to new systems and people. It seems to me, though, that patrons will tend to be
  - Overnight guests at the Riverside Inn.
  - The 50 or so local groups that rented our meeting room (capacity 20).
  - Residents who work in or near Bridgewater (about 3,000 people) who may want to go out for a drink—usually in groups—after work.
  - Couples, or groups of couples, who want a social drink or two prior to or after some event in the community (banquet, concert, play, movie, sporting event). Bridgewater seems to be a very active community. I estimate that at least twice a week there's something going on with audiences typically from 100 to 400 but occasionally as large as 2,000 for major sporting events.
  - Members of area organizations, clubs and groups (there must be 300–400 of them) who want to go out for a drink after a meeting or special event.
  - Anybody else who might want a quiet drink (a rather poorly defined group I admit).
- Some additional numbers you may find helpful are:
  - The population of Bridgewater is about 7,500 (2,600 households), Lunenburg County (including Bridgewater) about 48,000 (13,900 households), and the Bridgewater trading area about 60,000 (20,700 households).
  - About 500,000 tourists (incremental visitors) pass by or through Bridgewater every May to October.
  - Across Canada in 2005, average annual household spending on alcoholic beverages served on licensed premises was:

	Average Expenditure per Household	Percentage Reporting Any Such Spending
Beer	$118	36%
Liquor	38	18
Wine and cider	35	25
Total	$191	49%

Heidi, I believe we can rebuild volume with good strategies and good implementation. But I'm realistic. The ambience of Chapters, the availability of acceptable alternatives, and the fact that a high percentage of social drinking is party-oriented suggests a ceiling on revenue. During the next week or so, could you please spend some time thinking about what we might do to rebuild volume. I'd be willing to invest the full contribution (after labour) from October 2006 to June 2007 if you think that would be necessary and appropriate.

Do you think we could hit $100,000 in the year 2009? I look forward to your size-up of the situation, your insights, and your recommended objectives and plans.

GoodLife Fitness Clubs

"These retention rates are poor. I need to do a better job of keeping members," thought Krista Swain, Manager of the GoodLife Kitchener Fitness Club in Kitchener Ontario, as she reviewed her retention rates for the 1999–2000 fiscal year.

As she was analyzing the report, Jane Riddell, Chief Operating Officer, entered her office. Krista looked up and said, "Hi Jane. I've just been looking over the retention rates for the clubs. I'm not happy with my numbers."

"Neither is head office," Jane replied, "and that's why I'm here today. You run one of our best clubs, and yet your retention rates are around 60 percent, the average for the 40 GoodLife Clubs. We lose 40 percent of our members each year. By improving your club's retention rates from 60 to 65 percent, based on last year's figures, gross revenues would increase by over $35,000. You are one of our top performers and you should be leading the way."

"I agree," said Krista. "We have to figure out how to keep the members enthused and show that the club offers them value."

"That's what I wanted to hear," replied Jane. "As a first step, let's both think about this and meet again next week with some ideas. Then I'd like you to prepare a retention plan that will be the model for all the clubs."

THE FITNESS MARKET

In a national study, the Canadian Fitness and Research Institute found that most Canadians believed that physical activity was beneficial in preventing heart disease or other chronic conditions, in reducing stress, and in maintaining the ability to perform everyday tasks with aging. However, physical inactivity remained pervasive in Canada, with 63 percent of adults aged 18 and older still considered insufficiently active for optimal health benefits in 1998.*

The study also revealed that for a variety of reasons most Canadians tended to "talk the talk" positively about the importance of physical activity but didn't "walk the walk." The most popular physical recreation activities were walking (86% of Canadians participated at least once in this activity within the past 12 months), gardening (75%), swimming (57%), bicycling (55%), and home exercise (50%). Exercise class/aerobics was ranked thirteenth (21%) with significantly more women (33%) than men (9%) participating.

*Canadian Fitness and Research Institute, 1998 Canadian Physical Activity Monitor.

While the overall physical activity of Canadians was relatively low, the fitness market was growing at approximately 6 percent a year. The growth was due to demographic changes (baby boomers were increasingly interested in maintaining a good level of physical fitness), marketing (increasing numbers of health/fitness clubs extolling the benefits of fitness through their programs), and individuals selecting fitness clubs over other physical activities as their choice for exercise.

Industry estimates were that about 10 percent of the Canadian population belonged to a health club. However, there was considerable "churn" (the percentage of members lost in a month or year), as many Canadians had good intentions and joined a club only to leave at the end of their membership for a variety of reasons. Industry research revealed the following major reasons for leaving: decline in interest, took too much time, too hard, and didn't like the club. It was estimated that on an annual basis the average health/fitness club in Canada lost between 36 and 45 percent of its members.

Another reason for the high average churn rates was that many clubs, referred to as "factories," did not take a professional approach in managing their operations. Typically, a sports personality (e.g. a retired hockey player), would own these "factories" and offer low initial memberships to get people into the club. These clubs had few trained instructors, frequent equipment breakdowns, and poor facilities maintenance. These clubs often failed within a year or two, leaving customers with a valid membership and no facility.

GOODLIFE

The Philosophy and Goals

In March 1979, David Patchell-Evans established GoodLife as a sole proprietorship. "Patch," as he was called, saw an opportunity—Canadian fitness clubs were largely cash- and sales-oriented with little emphasis on scientific fitness or member retention. By May 2000, Patch had built this privately owned fitness company to over 40 clubs (10 were franchises, the rest were company-owned) in Ontario and Quebec. GoodLife had the largest group of fitness clubs in Canada with over 70,000 members. (Appendix 1 provides more details on the philosophy and growth of the GoodLife Clubs. See the company website at www.goodlifefitness.com for examples of current marketing approaches.

From the beginning, the company's goal was to provide the best in equipment, facilities, and service with a well-trained staff. The goal was based on high-quality service with education and training, superior cleanliness, and programs that made the individual a member for life based on their "needs and goals." The GoodLife motto, Measurable Constant Improvement, for the company, its staff, and its members underlay its plan to grow to 100 clubs by 2004.

Head Office

The head office was located at the Galleria Mall Fitness Club in London, Ontario. Head office personnel numbered approximately 40, led by "Patch," Jane Riddell, Chief Operating Officer, and Maureen Hagen, National Director of Fitness. Head Office's main role was to provide leadership and support for the franchisees and company-owned clubs. Among the group's major activities were determining the advertising strategy, designing new fitness programs, ensuring that all clubs maintained quality standards, providing training programs for staff, and keeping all club managers abreast of the latest trends and issues in the fitness industry.

One of Jane Riddell's responsibilities was the design and management of GoodLife University, where every month 50 to 60 new associates went through a one-week program. The training included an orientation to GoodLife (basic knowledge of GoodLife and its philosophy), personal training (skills required to assist members as a personal trainer), and computer program training. When club managers hired the associates, they typically spent their first few weeks "learning the ropes" at the club and then attended the University program. Jane led some of the training sessions and evaluation of the participants, some of whom failed and left GoodLife.

Jane was generally pleased with the calibre of the participants. She rated about 70 percent of them as good to great and 30 percent as poor. In the past, the GoodLife clubs had focused on hiring Physical Education and Kinesiology graduates. However, as the economy improved in the late 1990s, these graduates chose other job opportunities, requiring GoodLife to broaden its hiring criteria. Now GoodLife hired individuals with the "right" attitude (i.e. customer-focused). However, the attitude of some new employees was that this was not a "real" job or a career. Rather it was a fun place to be for a while, a "cool," easy job until they got a "real" one. Jane felt that this was part of the issue of employee retention at GoodLife. In the past two years employee turnover had increased, and last year 600 employees (out of a total of 1,400) had left. Jane estimated that most of the employee retention problem was GoodLife's "fault"—they either hired the wrong people, or didn't do enough to keep them.

Advertising spending, at 6 percent of revenues, used a "call to action" versus a "branding" approach. The "call to action" used variations on "$99 for 99 days," "one month free," "no initiation fee," "save now," etc.

The company allocated advertising expenditures by season—winter 40 percent, summer 25 percent, and October to December 35 percent—which reflected the general interest level of people in joining a fitness club. Every month headquarters evaluated each club on sales targets—the new members obtained through internal marketing (e.g., referrals, yellow pages), external marketing (e.g., newspaper, flyers, radio, television), and walk-ins (e.g., someone walks into the club and asks about memberships). This information, along with conference calls with the regions, set the regional advertising allocation.

GoodLife's commitment to club members, staff, and community resulted in numerous awards and achievements. GoodLife was the first to bring many innovations to the fitness industry, including the Fit Fix training concept and the PUNCH program. GoodLife raised over $500,000 annually for various charities and supported a wide range of community activities.

The GoodLife Staff

GoodLife's size (over 1,400 associates) and rapid growth provided many opportunities for advancement. The career path at GoodLife could take an associate to any number of areas: group exercise classes, personal training, sales, administration, management, accounting, and even to owning one of the clubs.

Compensation consisted of a base salary plus club sales commissions and bonuses. The club sales commissions were based on the number of memberships sold per week against a target. Depending on the type of membership sold and/or specialty programs sold, the associate could receive a commission on sales ranging from 5 to 15 percent. Bonuses were based on weekly targets set for the individual club. Depending on the hours and shifts worked by the staff, if the goals were met, the staff member could earn a bonus of $15 or $25 per week. As well, there was an employee referral bonus: any current staff member who referred an individual for employment with GoodLife could receive a bonus of $100, or $200 for individuals hired on a part-time or full-time basis. Finally, there were incentive programs for good ideas—the rewards, called Patch Bucks, could be redeemed for fitness conferences.

GoodLife offered company awards on a monthly and yearly basis. On a monthly basis, awards were given to: (a) Group Exercise Coordinator (gift and plaque), (b) Manager of the Month ($200 and plaque), (c) Associate ($100 and plaque), (d) Sales Manager ($200 and plaque), (e) Sales Associate ($100 and plaque), (f) Personal Training Associate ($100 and plaque), and (g) Customer Service Representative ($100 plus plaque). On a yearly basis, awards were given to: (a) Manager (free fitness conference, valued at $2,500), (b) Group Exercise Instructor, and (c) Group Exercise Coordinator.

GOODLIFE KITCHENER

The New Location

In September 1998, the GoodLife Kitchener Club reopened on the second floor of an indoor mall in downtown Kitchener, Ontario. Prior to that it was located two blocks away in a relatively small (1,115 square metres) and poorly designed facility. The new facility was larger (2,787 square metres), and had an open concept design and an extensive range of equipment and programs. Over the next 18 months membership increased dramatically under Krista Swain's guidance. As of May 2000, the club had 3,500 members, an increase of 2,300 over the original 1,200 members who moved from the old club.

Krista, a 1995 graduate in Kinesiology and Physical Education from Wilfrid Laurier University in Waterloo, Ontario, worked for GoodLife as a fitness instructor while she was attending the university. After graduation, she joined the GoodLife Waterloo Club as a service trainer. In addition, she handled corporate sales for the GoodLife Women Only Club in Kitchener. Within 10 months she was appointed manager of the GoodLife Kitchener Club and was actively involved in the transition from the old to the new location. When asked how she had rapidly advanced to club manager, she said:

> I have a passion for fitness and I'm committed to the company. I'm convinced that the GoodLife values, mission, and philosophy are right; and I truly feel that we are helping people at GoodLife. I like working with people. My role is to be a coach and mentor, and I lead by example. I think the staff understand my goals and respect me because I respect them. Sometimes I can't believe what the staff are willing to do to help the club and the members. But I'll also say, if you are not a top performer, you won't fit in at GoodLife.

In early 2000, the Kitchener club was signing up over 230 new members per month (see Exhibit 1). At the same time, the club was losing about 100 members per month for a net gain of about 130 members. On an annual basis, the club was losing 40 percent of its members. Overall, the rapid growth in membership had a very positive impact on revenues, which increased by over 60 percent between June 1999 and March 2000 (see Exhibit 2).

The Associates

The Kitchener club's 40 associates (10 full-time, 30 part-time) worked in four groups: sales, customer service, personal training, and service:

EXHIBIT 1 GoodLife Kitchener Club, Membership by Month

Month	Members Lost During Month	Members Gained During Month	Net Members Gained During Month	Members (at end of month)	Retention Rate per Year (%)	Loss Rate per Month (%)
March 1999	—	—	—	1,900	—	—
April 1999	58[1]	163	105	2,005	63.5[2]	3.0
May 1999	61	158	97	2,102	64.0	3.0
June 1999	73	156	83	2,185	59.4	3.4
July 1999	75	155	80	2,263	60.9	3.3
August 1999	68	150	82	2,341	65.2	2.9
September 1999	70	168	98	2,423	64.8	2.9
October 1999	108	196	88	2,521	48.5	4.3
November 1999	91	220	129	2,609	57.9	3.5
December 1999	90	223	133	2,738	60.1	3.3
January 2000	103	244	141	2,871	56.4	3.6
February 2000	99	238	139	3,012	60.1	3.3
March 2000	113	234	121	3,151	56.4	3.6
Annual average					59.8[3]	3.4

1. At the beginning of April, the club had 1,900 members. The monthly loss rate for April is 3.0 percent (based on a yearly retention rate for April of 63.5% which is a yearly loss rate of 36.5%). The club lost $1,900 \times 0.03 = 58$ members in April.
2. 63.5 percent of the members as of April 1998 were still members as of April 1999; 36.5 percent were no longer members.
3. The average retention rate for the year shown is 59.8 percent; average loss rate per month is 3.4 percent ($1 - 0.598 = 0.402/12$).

Source: GoodLife Fitness Clubs.

- The four sales associates (all full-time) were responsible for getting new members.
- Customer service employees, who were primarily part-time, worked the front desk.
- Personal trainers worked with individual club members on fitness programs.
- Service employees introduced new members to the club and its philosophy through a series of programs on fitness and equipment use.

All employees were involved in selling. Although the sales associates were dedicated to selling new memberships, the personal trainers spent time encouraging members to sign up for personal training. The customer service employees would sell tanning programs and other services to members. Typically, each group or individual had sales targets and earned bonuses and commissions based on meeting those targets.

Most of the employees earned a base salary of $8 per hour, plus bonuses if they achieved the weekly targets. As an example, a sales associate might have a target of eight new members per week. If the target were achieved or exceeded, the associate could earn $1,250 or more every two weeks. Customer service staff might earn up to $25 per week if they met targets that included phoning members to remind them of upcoming events, encouraging them to use the club, and selling various club products and services such as tanning. Personal trainers might make up to $27 per hour for personal training in addition to their base pay of $8. The more members the trainer signed up, the more hours he/she spent in personal training.

Through these incentive programs GoodLife encouraged its staff, particularly the sales associates, to be entrepreneurial. As Krista often said, "The staff have to make

EXHIBIT 2 GoodLife Kitchener Club—Selected Revenues and Expenses

	June 30, 1999 Month (%)	June 30, 1999 YTD (12 months) (%)	March 31, 2000 Month (%)	March 31, 2000 YTD (9 months) (%)
Revenues:				
Membership	89.9	88.2	86.9	83.3
Services[1]	9.3	10.2	11.9	15.5
Other	1.8	1.6	1.2	1.2
Total revenues	**100.0**	**100.0**	**100.0**	**100.0**
Expenses:				
Sales wages and commissions[2]	10.5	12.1	8.3	8.9
Service wages and commissions[3]	9.0	7.1	5.3	12.3
Service and other[4]	19.4	28.6	20.4	17.1
Total direct expenses	38.9	47.8	34.0	38.3
Manager-controlled[5]	9.2	15.6	4.8	10.4
Administrative[6]	31.8	31.1	26.3	32.6
Total expenses[7]	**79.9**	**94.4**	**65.0**	**81.3**
Members	2,200		3,200	
Total revenue ($)	**120,000**	**1,004,000**	**195,000**	**1,177,000**

1. Includes personal training, specialty programs, tanning, and pro shop.
2. Related to new membership sales.
3. Includes personal training and member services.
4. Includes service staff wages and expenses.
5. Includes utilities, supplies, and services.
6. Includes advertising, administrative management, rent, realty taxes, equipment leasing.
7. Not included are depreciation, amortization, interest, and taxes.

Source: GoodLife Fitness Clubs.

things happen; they can't wait for them to happen. Both GoodLife and the staff do better when they make things happen."

As noted, GoodLife had formal training programs for new employees. In addition, Krista spent time with the new employees teaching them the technical side of the job and establishing the norms and culture of the club. By emphasizing what was important to her, Krista hoped they would understand the importance of excellent customer service. "If I can show the new employees what's important to me, and get them to trust me, they come on board and are part of the team. For example, we hold weekly staff meetings where we discuss a number of issues, including how to improve the club. People don't miss the meetings. Every once in a while, a new associate decides not to come to the meetings. The team lets him or her know that's not acceptable. Those people either become part of the team or decide to leave GoodLife."

Employee turnover at the Kitchener GoodLife Club was slightly better than the average across all the GoodLife clubs. In the past year, Krista had a turnover of about 35 percent, with the rate for full-time slightly lower than for part-time. Part-time turnover was higher, in part because many of the part-time employees were students who left to go to university or left after completing their degree programs.

Like Jane Riddell, Krista was concerned about employee turnover, but she wasn't sure what actions could improve the situation. She had noticed that some new employees were surprised at the amount of selling involved in their positions. She also felt that some employees were not satisfied with the base salary of $8 per hour.

Typically, when an employee left, Krista needed to hire a new associate relatively quickly. She would place an ad in the local paper, *The Record*, get some applications, conduct interviews, and hire the individual she felt was most suited for the position. With full-time employees, Krista was not always happy with the pool of applicants she interviewed; but there was always the pressure of filling the job, which had to be balanced against the quality of the applicants. With the economy improving and a low local unemployment rate, it was sometimes difficult to attract high-quality applicants.

The Members

Most new members joined the club through referrals. When an individual asked about joining the club, a sales associate would show them the club, discuss the benefits of membership and the GoodLife philosophy. Assuming the individual decided to join, the sales associate would ask if he or she had any friends who might be interested in joining the club and, if so, they would receive a free membership for one week. Typically, the associate tried to get five referrals. The associate would then contact these people, offer the free one-week membership, and set up a meeting with them if they accepted. The cycle was repeated with each new member. On average, the sales associates converted between one and two of the five contacts to new members. Referrals generated between 60 and 80 percent of all new members.

The price for a new membership varied depending on the promotion option. The two main options were: (1) a $199 initiation fee and the first six months free and $40 per four weeks after that or (2) the initiation fee was waived and the member paid $40 per four weeks. Payments were on a biweekly basis through an automatic payment plan that the member signed. The new member also paid a total of $54 for the membership card ($15) and a processing fee ($39). A new member could also decide to join for a three-month period for $180. Members could also decide to pay once a year and not use the automatic payment plan.

When an individual joined the club, an associate from the service group would take the new member through three programs as an introduction to the club and the GoodLife approach to a healthy lifestyle. The three programs were: (1) Fit Fix 1—an introduction to strength training, (2) Cardio—basic information about cardiovascular training principles, and (3) Fit Fix 2—adding exercises to your program. Any new member could also have a fitness assessment (resting heart rate, body fat measurements, etc.). After six weeks, the new member could also have a second fitness assessment to track his/her progress.

The club offered a wide range of cardio equipment, weights, and personal training programs. Members could participate in over 20 aerobics programs each week, from Steps 'n' Abs to Circuit Training to Newbody to PUNCH. On average, 12 members were participating in each program. Typically, members had been going to these programs for years, and few new members joined any program. The club attempted to address this issue with new members by having a "new members only" aerobics class. On average, the club would get 50 new members to sign up for the program, then 15 would show up for the first class, and it would be down to six people when the class ended in 12 weeks.

This issue reflected a broader problem common to most of the GoodLife Clubs, often referred to as the "20-20-60 phenomenon." Twenty percent of the club members were hard-core fitness and health people, who came three or more times a week, were serious about their training, and would tolerate a lot (e.g. uneven service) as long as it didn't interfere with their training. The second 20 percent were the new members. They were enthusiastic, wanted to get fit, and over time they either became committed or not. The largest group, the remaining 60 percent, were those members who came on an irregular basis. The club staff didn't know their names, these members often were not sure about how the equipment worked or what they should be doing, and they often wouldn't ask for help. Even when they stopped coming, this group kept their membership for a period until they decided to cancel. When one came to cancel, an associate tried to get her/him to stay, usually with little success.

Krista and other associates at GoodLife felt that getting members to feel that they were part of the GoodLife Club was important in retaining them. Krista believed that many of the 60 percent probably never felt they were part of the club, as they didn't know many or any of the other members or the staff. Krista remembered that while many of the 1,200 members from the old club liked the new facility (open, spacious, more equipment, etc.) they felt that the club was more impersonal. In particular, as the membership grew, the "original" members felt less at home. Krista estimated that, within a year, about 50 percent of these members had left the club.

The advertising for GoodLife consisted of an ad in the yellow pages and ads in a local free weekly newspaper, the *Pennysaver*. Local businesses were targeted with brochures offering specials. Krista felt that most of the new members came from the referral program and the other advertisements (see www.goodlifefitness.com). As she said; "The ads get the phones ringing."

While Krista believed that overall the members were satisfied with the club, she felt there was always room for improvement. For example, members sent her about 14 written complaints or concerns of members every week through the suggestion box (where members could offer comments). Every week, the front office staff received about a dozen verbal complaints. Most complaints or concerns dealt with equipment problems (e.g. equipment not working properly) and a few dealt with staff (e.g. a particular staff member was not friendly). Krista dealt with the complaints as they arose.

Competition

In the Kitchener/Waterloo (K/W) area (Kitchener and Waterloo are twin cities) there were about 15 fitness/exercise clubs serving a population base of 450,000 people. The Kitchener GoodLife Club had four major competitors:

- The two YMCAs in K/W offered aerobic programs and had workout areas. The "Y's" had a good reputation as friendly, family-oriented clubs. The annual membership fee ranged from $400 to $650 depending on the type of membership and the services requested (towel service, locker, etc.).

- The International Family Fitness Centre was also located in downtown Kitchener within three blocks of the GoodLife Club. It offered equivalent facilities to the GoodLife Club, was of a similar size, and had over 40 programs a week. Its membership rates were very similar to those of GoodLife.

- Popeye's Gym previously had a reputation as a male-oriented facility where body-builders worked out. However, the image was slowly changing to that of a men's and women's fitness club that offered aerobic programs and a variety of weight and training machines. It was located approximately three kilometres from downtown Kitchener and was open 24 hours a day. The membership fees were approximately $350 per year.

Customer Retention

As Krista prepared for the meeting with Jane, she knew that improved customer retention rates were possible but was uncertain as to what actions would be most effective. She identified three major areas that she could address; employee turnover, a new bonus system, and swipe card technology.

Employee turnover, at over 40 percent, created a lack of stability at the club. Every time a new employee started, he/she didn't know any members, then over time would learn the members' names (often those who visited frequently). If the employee left, so did the knowledge. Krista had always felt that members would have a greater sense of "belonging" to the club if the front-desk staff could greet them by name. Although many of the front-desk staff knew some of the members by name (most of these members were the hard-core regulars who came frequently), most of them were just part-time associates or had recently joined GoodLife; therefore, they knew relatively few members by name. Further, because most of the "60 percent" group came infrequently, few staff knew their names.

Krista had two ideas for reducing employee turnover—both based on increasing wages. Increasing the hourly base rate from $8 to $9 for most employees (excluding managers and sales associates) would add about $4,000 per month to wage costs. The problem was that, although she knew that employee turnover would decline, she didn't know by how much, nor did she know the effect on retention rates. A second option was to focus only on the front-desk employees who greeted members. Increasing their rate to $9 would increase monthly wage costs by about $1,000. She preferred this option, because the front-desk associates greeted all the members as they entered and swiped their card. With the increase in their wages, Krista would ensure that the front-desk staff knew that an important part of their job was to greet members by name.

Next, Krista considered introducing a bonus plan for increasing customer retention. Virtually all the targets and bonuses at GoodLife focused on increasing sales, reflecting in part Patch's aggressive growth targets. Although she didn't have a specific plan in mind, Krista felt that an allocation of at least $1,000 to bonuses for increased retention was feasible. Her initial idea was that for every percentage-point increase in retention rates per month (e.g. from 60% to 61%), staff would receive $200 in bonuses. Where Krista was uncertain was how the target should be set—on an individual or a group basis. The front-desk staff had the most contact with members, but potentially all the employees could be involved. What was important to Krista was that the associates would have a goal and a bonus attached to customer retention. She knew that this plan would get the associates to focus more of their efforts on customer retention.

Krista felt that better use of the swipe card information might improve retention. Members swiped their membership card when they visited the club. A valid card allowed a member to go through a turnstile; a card that was invalid (because it had expired) did not release the turnstile. Krista knew that other information (e.g. the number of member visits) was available, but no one at the club or head office had developed a software program to track such information. Krista contacted two software companies, one of which offered a membership management program that would provide interface with swipe scanners and provide reports on members' frequency of visits, along with a host of other member information. The cost ranged from $3,500 for a licence for five sites up to $8,500 for unlimited site use.

One of the targets for the front-desk associates was to make "motivation" calls to members each week. Associates would call a specified number of members to reach their target. The associates would begin anywhere on the member list (a binder at the front desk) and begin calling members to encourage them to use the facilities or inform them of special events. After the call, the associate would record the date called and his or her name next to the member's name. Ideally, all members were called once every six weeks but this didn't always happen.

With the new software system, reports could identify members who had not visited the club for a particular period. Staff could then contact members who had not visited for a specific time period (e.g., three weeks, four weeks, etc.). Krista felt that this would substantially improve the existing approach and would improve member retention rates.

Krista knew that there were other available approaches or tactics to improve retention rates. In particular, any activities that built a greater sense of "community" would increase interaction between members and a sense of "belonging." But it was difficult to find the time to figure it out. Managing a club with 3,500 members kept her very busy making sure everything was running smoothly and she spent most of her time "doing" not "planning."

A week later, Jane met Krista in her office. Jane started the conversation. "Let me review the situation. As I mentioned last week, if we could improve your club's retention rates from 60 to 65 percent, based on last year's numbers, gross revenues would increase by over $35,000. In this business most of the costs tend to be fixed, probably about 60 percent of revenues, so most of the revenue would be profits. If we could do that for all the clubs, it would be great for business and I think we would have more satisfied members. And just to put this in perspective, on average, we have about 2,000 members per club."

Jane continued, "In the past year, the story has been about the same for most of our clubs. For every 100 new members signed up each month, we have about 40 people who don't renew or cancel their membership. We spend a lot on marketing to get them in the door. Then we spend time with them setting up an exercise or training program. They are enthusiastic to begin with, then they stop coming to classes or exercise. Then they cancel or don't renew when their membership comes up. When they cancel, we ask them why they are leaving. The most common reasons are that they don't have enough time or they can't fit it in to their schedule. I think that about 30 percent of the time they have a good reason for leaving, such as they are moving out of town. I think that 70 percent of the time we could have done something to keep them with the club."

"From a head office point of view, we have had a number of debates about the amount of advertising we do, which is about 6 percent of revenues. That's a lot of money and sometimes we think that we should be spending more of that in staff training. Another question is—what type of training would be most effective?"

"Let me mention one other issue we are concerned about," Jane continued. "We don't use the swipe card to collect data. We need to do more with that."

"That was one of my thoughts," Krista replied. She then told Jane about the software program's capabilities and costs.

"Very interesting," replied Jane. "That's certainly something to consider." Krista then presented her other ideas to Jane. As she finished, Krista said, "I think my cost estimates wouldn't be too far out of line for our average club."

Then Krista added: "Sometimes I think that maybe we should focus more on service than sales. As an example, my front-desk staff have sales targets and other assignments as well as greeting members. Also, there are few opportunities for the staff to walk around and just talk to our members and see how they are doing. That's why I suggested a bonus plan based on increasing retention rates. We have very aggressive growth targets for each club as plan to add a lot more clubs. As an organization, we are really getting stretched. Most of our time is spent on growth, not service."

"Yes, but the strategy has worked well so far." Jane replied. "I'm not sure if we could justify adding more staff to focus on service; we would need to see a payback. But it's an another interesting idea."

Krista and Jane continued the discussion and then decided that Krista would prepare a customer retention plan for the Kitchener GoodLife Club with the goal of increasing retention rates by 5 percentage points or more within six months. I want to at least get the average retention up to 65 percent," Jane said. "As I mentioned last week, we'll use this plan as the model for all the clubs."

As Jane left she said; "Krista, I have every confidence in you. I'm going to send an assistant manager from the other Kitchener club down here to help you run the club while you work on the plan. I look forward to positive results."

After Jane left, Krista sat down and began thinking about the approaches she could take to increase retention rates. She had always liked a challenge, and knew that she would do her best to meet this one.

APPENDIX 1

Excerpts from Louise Dearden, "Muscle Mania," *Profit*, May, 1999, pp. 46–49

David Patchell-Evans may not be a natural athlete, but he's a confirmed fitness fanatic. He works and dreams physical fitness. Even his vacations are spent pursuing extreme sports such as mountain climbing or skiing. But that wasn't always the case. In his first year at university, a motorcycle accident paralyzed the right side of his body. Following extensive rehabilitation, Patchell-Evans was determined to return to full physical fitness. He took up rowing and eventually became a five-time Canadian rowing champion and a member of the 1980 Canadian Olympic team.

Those experiences taught Patchell-Evans the role health and fitness play in creating a satisfying life and fostered a lifelong commitment to sell the idea to others. In 1979 he bought a workout club in London, Ontario and began implementing his vision: to provide customers with an affordable club offering state-of-the-art equipment and, more importantly, knowledgeable staff eager to teach them how to get the most from it. "The opportunity in the marketplace," he says, "was to provide service."

In an industry notorious for dubious claims and fly-by-night operators, GoodLife Fitness Clubs has built its business on highly trained staff, innovative programming and reinvesting in its facilities. In 20 years, it has become Canada's largest health club chain, with 42 clubs, 100,000 members and 1998 sales of $40 million. In an industry that's adding new clubs and members at 9% a year, GoodLife is growing at almost three times that rate. By 2004 Patchell-Evans goal is to have 100 facilities.

To reach the goal Patchell-Evans will rely on the same philosophies on which the chain was founded: providing health, fitness and self-esteem so that people feel better about themselves. It's part of the strategy to raise the bar of service excellence and bring a new professionalism to an industry where clubs were traditionally run by sports jocks with little business training. The GoodLife philosophy of ensuring consistently high standards in every club goes a long way to building brand loyalty among the members. "When people work out, they want to know that the shower will be clean, the equipment is going to work, and the staff know what they are talking about."

That philosophy has served GoodLife well as the chain expanded, opening new clubs and buying others that were doing poorly in strong locations. "One of the ways we grew in the early days was to take over clubs that really nobody else wanted to touch," says Jane Riddell, GoodLife's Vice-President and Director of Franchising. "A classic example is our club at the corner of Queen and Yonge Street in downtown Toronto. When we took over the club, the membership was languishing around 100, and the facility was losing $60,000 a month. The club needed refurbishment and new equipment, but it had huge potential, with its high profile location in a dense work population." GoodLife invested $400,000 and the facility is one of the firm's most financially successful clubs with a membership of 3,000.

One fitness expert says; "GoodLife developed a niche underneath the well-established clubs. Patchell-Evans runs a professional organization and he has a well-honed management style that includes business and financial acumen. The old style clubs were run by squash players or golfers." One example was the innovative client billing system. While most fitness clubs demanded on up-front annual fee, Patchell-Evans debited monthly membership fees ranging from $30 to $50. Members like the system because it eliminates the needs for large up-front payments and it stabilizes cash flow for GoodLife, which is attractive to lenders and investors.

The key to any fitness club's success is attracting and keeping members. At GoodLife it starts with the staff. Some 75% of its 1,200 employees hold kinesiology or physical education degrees. In addition to competitive salaries, staff benefit from ongoing training—GoodLife's annual education and training budget exceeds $2.4 million—and recognition for individual achievement, such as a weekly top performer's list. "Good staff retention leads to good membership retention," says Jane Riddell. "Members don't have a relationship with a treadmill or a whirlpool. They have a relationship with the staff." That commitment to human resources gives GoodLife an edge, says the industry expert. "GoodLife has good equipment, but they also have a very proactive staff with an attitude that says they want to help you out. The club's employee training program is probably more extensive than any other in the industry. It's difficult for an independent operator to compete with this."

In 1998 GoodLife was recognized for its mandate to provide leading edge programs. The U.S.-based International Dance Exercise Association named the club's fitness director, Maureen Hagen, Program Director of the Year for her creative programming and leadership abilities. Hagan's innovations include Newbody, a low-impact, cardiovascular conditioning class designed for both fit and "underactive" participants.

Programming and services are also tailored to fit the demographics of each club. Some 70% of members are women, reflecting the club's focus on aerobics programs, to which women tend to gravitate. To ensure that women enjoy a high comfort level, GoodLife designated more than a dozen clubs for women only, where they are provided with such services as daycare, tanning facilities, and individual change rooms. GoodLife was one of the first clubs to develop the trend to women-only sections and clubs. As an example, GoodLife recently spent $500,000 upgrading the facility and equipment of a women's club in Cambridge, Ontario.

This formula to exceed customers' expectations is the foundation for GoodLife's aggressive growth plans for the future. Two trends will help the growth; industry consolidation, where GoodLife has achieved a critical mass, and an expanding market, where the number of people who will work out in clubs will increase substantially because the baby boomers want to stay in shape.

A challenge for Patchell-Evans is finding staff to keep pace with growth. "There was a time," he says, "when we had a bigger pool of people waiting for the next manager's job." To that end he says GoodLife will focus on giving staff the skills and knowledge they need to get to a higher level within the firm. "Staying on the cutting edge of the industry is a challenge, but it's also a passion for me," says Patchell-Evans. "Running a business is like a sport—you're driven to go fast, go hard, and find the ways you can do it better."

Shouldice Hospital Limited (Abridged)

Two shadowy figures, enrobed and in slippers, walked slowly down the semi-darkened hall of the Shouldice Hospital. They didn't notice Alan O'Dell, the hospital's managing director, and his guest. Once they were out of earshot, O'Dell remarked good-naturedly, "By the way they act, you'd think our patients own this place. And while they're here, in way they do." Following a visit to the five operating rooms, O'Dell and his visitor once again encountered the same pair of patients still engrossed in discussing their hernia operations, which had been performed the previous morning.

HISTORY

An attractive brochure that was recently printed, although neither dated nor distributed to prospective patients, described Dr. Earle Shouldice, the founder of the hospital:

> Dr. Shouldice's interest in early ambulation stemmed, in part, from an operation he performed in 1932 to remove the appendix from a seven-year-old girl and the girl's subsequent refusal to stay quietly in bed. In spite of her activity, no harm was done, and the experience recalled to the doctor the postoperative actions of animals upon which he had performed surgery. They had all moved about freely with no ill effects.

> By 1940, Shouldice had given extensive thought to several factors that contributed to early ambulation following surgery. Among them were the use of a local anesthetic, the nature of the surgical procedure itself, the design of a facility to encourage movement without unnecessarily causing discomfort, and the postoperative regimen. With these things in mind, he began to develop a surgical technique for

Professor James Heskett prepared the original version of this case, "Shouldice Hospital Limited," HBS No. 683-068. This version was prepared jointly by Professor James Heskett and Roger Hallowell (MBA 1989, DBA 1997). HBS cases are developed solely as the basis for class discussion. Cases are not intended to serve as endorsements, sources of primary data, or illustrations of effective or ineffective management.

repairing hernias[1] that was superior to others; word of his early success generated demand.

Dr. Shouldice's medical licence permitted him to operate anywhere, even on a kitchen table. However, as more and more patients requested operations, Dr. Shouldice created new facilities by buying a rambling 53-hectare estate with a 1,580 square-metre main house in the Toronto suburb of Thornhill. After some years of planning, a large wing was added to provide a total capacity of 89 beds.

Dr. Shouldice died in 1965. At that time, Shouldice Hospital Limited was formed to operate both the hospital and clinical facilities under the surgical direction of Dr. Nicholas Obney. In 1999, Dr. Casim Degani, an internationally recognized authority, became surgeon-in-chief. By 2004, 7,600 operations were performed per year.

THE SHOULDICE METHOD

Only external (vs. internal) abdominal hernias were repaired at Shouldice Hospital. Thus most first-time repairs, "primaries," were straightforward operations requiring about 45 minutes. The remaining procedures involved patients suffering recurrences of hernias previously repaired elsewhere.[2] Many of the recurrences and very difficult hernia repairs required 90 minutes or more.

In the Shouldice method, the muscles of the abdominal wall were arranged in three distinct layers, and the opening was repaired—each layer in turn—by overlapping its margins as the edges of a coat might be overlapped when buttoned. The end result reinforced the muscular wall of the abdomen with six rows of sutures (stitches) under the skin cover, which was then closed with clamps that were later removed. (Other methods might not separate muscle layers, often involved fewer rows of sutures, and sometimes involved the insertion of screens or meshes under the skin.)

A typical first-time repair could be completed with the use of preoperative sedation (sleeping pill) and analgesic (pain killer) plus a local anesthetic, an injection of Novocain in the region of the incision. This allowed immediate postoperative patient ambulation and facilitated rapid recovery.

THE PATIENTS' EXPERIENCE

Most potential Shouldice patients learned about the hospital from previous Shouldice patients. Although thousands of doctors had referred patients, doctors were less likely to recommend Shouldice because of the generally regarded simplicity of the surgery, often considered a "bread and butter" operation. Typically, many patients had their problem diagnosed by a personal physician and then contacted Shouldice directly. Many more made this diagnosis themselves.

---

[1]Most hernias, known as external abdominal hernias, are protrusions of some part of the abdominal contents through a hole or slit in the muscular layers of the abdominal wall which is supposed to contain them. Well over 90% of these hernias occur in the groin area. Of these, by far the most common are inguinal hernias, many of which are caused by a slight weakness in the muscle layers brought about by the passage of the testicles in male babies through the groin area shortly before birth. Aging also contributes to the development of inguinal hernias. Because of the cause of the affliction, 85% of all hernias occur in males.

[2]Based on tracking of patients over more than 30 years, the gross recurrence rate for all operations performed at Shouldice was 0.8%. Recurrence rates reported in the literature for these types of hernia varied greatly. However, one text stated, "In the United States the gross rate of recurrence for groin hernias approaches 10%."

The process experienced by Shouldice patients depended on whether they lived close enough to the hospital to visit the facility to obtain a diagnosis. Approximately 10 percent of Shouldice patients came from outside the province of Ontario, most of these from the United States. Another 60 percent of patients lived beyond the Toronto area. These out-of-town patients often were diagnosed by mail using the Medical Information Questionnaire shown in Exhibit 1. Based on information in the questionnaire, a Shouldice surgeon would determine the type of hernia the respondent had and whether there were signs that some risk might be associated with surgery (e.g., an overweight or heart condition, or a heart attack or a stroke in the past six months to a year, or that a general or local anesthetic was required). At this point, a patient was given a operating date and sent a brochure describing the hospital and the Shouldice method. If necessary, a sheet outlining a weight-loss program prior to surgery was also sent. A small proportion were refused treatment, either because they were overweight, they represented an undue medical risk, or they did not have a hernia.

Arriving at the clinic between 1 p.m. and 3 p.m. the day before the operation, a patient joined other patients in the waiting room. He or she was soon examined in one of six examination rooms staffed by surgeons who had completed their operating

EXHIBIT 1   Medical Information Questionnaire

FAMILY NAME (Last Name)	FIRST NAME	MIDDLE NAME	

STREET & NUMBER (or Rural Route or P.O. Box)	Town/City	Province/State

County	Township	Zip or Postal Code	Birthdate: Month Day Year

Telephone Home .... If none, give Work .... neighbour's number	Married or Single	Religion

SHOULDICE HOSPITAL

7750 Bayview Avenue
Box 370, Thornhill, Ontario L3T 4A3 Canada
Phone (418) 889-1125

(Thornhill - One Mile North Metro Toronto)

NEXT OF KIN: Name   Address   Telephone #

INSURANCE INFORMATION: Please give name of Insurance Company and Numbers.   Date form completed

HOSPITAL INSURANCE: (Please bring hospital certificates) O.H.I.P. BLUE CROSS Number Number	OTHER HOSPITAL INSURANCE Company Name _____ Policy Number _____
SURGICAL INSURANCE: (Please bring insurance certificates) O.H.I.P. BLUE SHIELD Number Number	OTHER SURGICAL INSURANCE Company Name _____ Policy Number _____

MEDICAL

INFORMATION

WORKMEN'S COMPENSATION BOARD Claim No.	Approved Yes No	Social Insurance (Security) Number

Occupation Name of Business	Are you the owner? If Retired – Former Occupation Yes No

How did you hear about Shouldice Hospital? If referred by a doctor, give name & address)

Patients who live at a distance often prefer their examination, admission and operation to be arranged all on a single visit – to save making two lengthy journeys. The whole purpose of this questionnarie is to make such arrangements possible, although, of course, it cannot replace the examination in any way. Its completion and return will not put you under any obligation.

Are you a former patient of Shouldice Hospital?   Yes   No   Do you smoke?   Yes   No

Have you ever written to Shouldice Hospital in the past?   Yes   No

What is your preferred admission date? (Please give as much advance notice as possible) No admissions Friday, Saturday or Sunday.

Please be sure to fill in both sides.

FOR OFFICE USE ONLY

Date Received	Type of Hernia	Weight Loss lbs.

Consent to Operate ☐ Heart Report ☐	Special Instructions	Approved

This information will be treated as confidential.

Referring Doctor Notified	Operation Date

(continued on next page)

schedules for the day. This examination required no more than 20 minutes, unless the patient needed reassurance. (Patients typically exhibited a moderate level of anxiety until their operation was completed.) At this point it occasionally was discovered that a patient had not corrected his or her weight problem; others might be found not to have a hernia at all. In either case, the patient was sent home.

After checking administrative details, about an hour after arriving at the hospital, a patient was directed to the room number shown on his or her wrist band. Throughout the process, patients were asked to keep their luggage (usually light) with them.

All patient rooms at the hospital were semiprivate, containing two beds. Patients with similar jobs, backgrounds, or interests were assigned to the same room to the extent possible. Upon reaching their rooms, patients busied themselves unpacking, getting acquainted with roommates, shaving themselves in the area of the operation, and changing into pajamas.

At 4:30 p.m., a nurse's orientation provided the group of incoming patients with information about what to expect, including the need for exercise after the operation and the daily routine. According to Alan O'Dell, "Half are so nervous they don't remember much." Dinner was then served, followed by further recreation and tea and cookies at 9 p.m. Nurses emphasized the importance of attendance at that time

EXHIBIT 1 Medical Information Questionnaire—*continued*

THIS CHART IS FOR EXPLANATION ONLY

Ordinary hernias are mostly either at the navel ("belly-button") - or just above it

or down in the groin area on either side

An "incisional hernia" is one that bulges through the scar of any other surgical operation that has failed to hold - wherever it may be.

THIS IS YOUR CHART – PLEASE MARK IT!

(MARK THE POSITION OF EACH HERNIA YOU WANT REPAIRED WITH AN "X")

APPROXIMATE SIZE . . .
Walnut (or less)
Hen's Egg or Lemon
Grapefruit (or more)

ESSENTIAL EXTRA INFORMATION

Use only the sections that apply to your hernias and put a ✓ in each box that seems appropriate.

NAVEL AREA (AND JUST ABOVE NAVEL) ONLY
Is this navel (bellybutton) hernia your FIRST one?   Yes ☐   No ☐

If it's NOT your first, how many repair attempts so far?   ☐

GROIN HERNIAS ONLY

	RIGHT GROIN		LEFT GROIN	
	Yes	No	Yes	No
Is this your FIRST GROIN HERNIA ON THIS SIDE?	☐	☐	☐	☐

How many hernia operations in this groin already?   Right ☐   Left ☐

DATE OF LAST OPERATION ☐

INCISIONAL HERNIAS ONLY (the ones bulging through previous operation scars)
Was the original operation for your Appendix? ☐ . or Gallbladder? ☐ . or Stomach? ☐ . or Prostate? ☐ . or Hysterectomy? ☐ . or Other? ....

How many attempts to repair the hernia have been made so far? ☐

PLEASE BE ACCURATE: Misleading figures, when checked on a admission day, could mean postponement of your operation till your weight is suitable.

HEIGHT .... ft .... ins.   WEIGHT .... lbs. Nude Recent gain? .... lbs.
                                   or just pyjamas   Recent loss? .... lbs.

Waist (muscles relaxed) .... ins.   Chest (not expanded) .... ins.

GENERAL HEALTH

Age .... years   Is your health now GOOD ☐ . FAIR ☐ . or POOR ☐

Please mention briefly any severe past illness — such as a "heart attack" or a "stroke," for example, from which you have now recovered (and its approximate date) ....
....

We need to know about other present conditions, even though your admission is NOT likely to be refused because of them.

Please tick ☐ any condition for which you are having regular treatment:	Name of any prescribed pills, tablets or capsules you take regularly: –
Blood Pressure ☐	
Excess body fluids ☐	
Chest pain ("angina") ☐	
Irregular Heartbeat ☐	
Diabetes ☐	
Asthma & Bronchitis ☐	
Ulcers ☐	
Anticoagulants (to delay blood-clotting or to "thin the blood") ☐	
Other	

Did you remember to MARK AN "X" on your body chart to show us where each of your hernias is located?

because it provided an opportunity for preoperative patients to talk with those whose operations had been completed earlier that same day.

Patients to be operated on early were awakened at 5:30 a.m. to be given preop sedation. An attempt was made to schedule operations for roommates at approximately the same time. Patients were taken to the preoperating room where the circulating nurse administered Demerol, an analgesic, 45 minutes before surgery. A few minutes prior to the first operation at 7:30 a.m., the surgeon assigned to each patient administered Novocain, a local anesthetic, in the operating room. This was in contrast to the typical hospital procedure in which patients were sedated in their rooms prior to being taken to the operating rooms.

Upon the completion of their operation, during which a few patients were "chatty" and fully aware of what was going on, patients were invited to get off the operating table and walk to the post-operating room with the help of their surgeons. According to the director of nursing:

> Ninety-nine percent accept the surgeon's invitation. While we use wheelchairs to return them to their rooms, the walk from the operating table is for psychological as well as physiological [blood pressure, respiratory] reasons. Patients prove to themselves that they can do it, and they start their all-important exercise immediately.

Throughout the day after their operation, patients were encouraged to exercise by nurses and housekeepers alike. By 9 p.m. on the day of their operations, all patients were ready and able to walk down to the dining room for tea and cookies, even if it meant climbing stairs, to help indoctrinate the new "class" admitted that day. On the fourth morning, patients were ready for discharge.

During their stay, patients were encouraged to take advantage of the opportunity to explore the premises and make new friends. Some members of the staff felt that the patients and their attitudes were the most important element of the Shouldice program. According to Dr. Byrnes Shouldice, son of the founder, a surgeon on the staff, and a 50 percent owner of the hospital:

> Patients sometimes ask to stay an extra day. Why? Well, think about it. They are basically well to begin with. But they arrive with a problem and a certain amount of nervousness, tension, and anxiety about their surgery. Their first morning here they're operated on and experience a sense of relief from something that's been bothering them for a long time. They are immediately able to get around, and they've got a three-day holiday ahead of them with a perfectly good reason to be away from work with no sense of guilt. They share experiences with other patients, make friends easily, and have the run of the hospital. In summer, the most common after-effect from the surgery is sunburn.

THE NURSES' EXPERIENCE

Thirty-four full-time-equivalent nurses staffed Shouldice each 24-hour period. However, during non-operating hours, only six full-time-equivalent nurses were on the premises at any given time. While the Canadian acute care hospital average ratio of nurses to patients was 1:4, at Shouldice the ratio was 1:15. Shouldice nurses spent an unusually large proportion of their time in counselling activities. As one supervisor commented, "We don't use bedpans." According to a manager, "Shouldice has a waiting list of nurses wanting to be hired, while other hospitals in Toronto are short-staffed and perpetually recruiting."

THE DOCTORS' EXPERIENCE

The hospital employed 10 full-time surgeons and 8 part-time assistant surgeons. Two anesthetists were also on site. The anesthetists floated among cases except when general anesthesia was in use. Each operating team required a surgeon, an assistant surgeon, a scrub nurse, and a circulating nurse. The operating load varied from 30 to 36 operations per day. As a result, each surgeon typically performed three or four operations each day.

A typical surgeon's day started with a *scrubbing* shortly before the first scheduled operation at 7:30 a.m. If the first operation was routine, it usually was completed by 8:15 a.m. At its conclusion, the surgical team helped the patient walk from the room and summoned the next patient. After scrubbing, the surgeon could be ready to operate again at 8:30 a.m. Surgeons were advised to take a coffee break after their second or third operation. Even so, a surgeon might complete three routine operations and a fourth involving a recurrence and still be finished in time for a 12:30 p.m. lunch in the staff dining room.

Upon finishing lunch, surgeons not scheduled to operate in the afternoon examined incoming patients. A surgeon's day ended by 4:00 p.m. In addition, a surgeon might expect to be on call one weekday night in ten and one weekend in ten. Alan O'Dell commented that the position appealed to doctors who "want to watch their children grow up. A doctor on call is rarely called to the hospital and has regular hours." According to Dr. Obney:

> When I interview prospective surgeons, I look for experience and a good education. I try to gain some insight into their domestic situation and personal interests and habits. I also try to find out why a surgeon wants to switch positions. And I try to determine if he's willing to perform the repair exactly as he's told. This is no place for prima donnas.

Dr. Shouldice added:

> Traditionally a hernia is often the first operation that a junior resident in surgery performs. Hernia repair is regarded as a relatively simple operation compared to other major operations. This is quite wrong, as is borne out by the resulting high recurrence rate. It is a tricky anatomical area and occasionally very complicated, especially to the novice or those doing very few hernia repairs each year. But at Shouldice Hospital a surgeon learns the Shouldice technique over a period of several months. He learns when he can go fast and when he must go slow. He develops a pace and a touch. If he encounters something unusual, he is encouraged to consult immediately with other surgeons. We teach each other and try to encourage a group effort. And he learns not to take risks to achieve absolute perfection. Excellence is the enemy of good.

Chief Surgeon Degani assigned surgeons to an operating room on a daily basis by noon of the preceding day. This allowed surgeons to examine the specific patients that they were to operate on. Surgeons and assistants were rotated every few days. Cases were assigned to give doctors a non-routine operation (often involving a recurrence) several times a week. More complex procedures were assigned to more senior and experienced members of the staff. Dr Obney commented:

> If something goes wrong, we want to make sure that we have an experienced surgeon in charge. Experience is most important. The typical general surgeon may perform 25 to 50 hernia operations per year. Ours perform 750 or more.

The 10 full-time surgeons were paid a straight salary, typically $144,000. In addition, bonuses to doctors were distributed monthly. These depended on profit, individual productivity, and performance. The total bonus pool paid to the surgeons in a recent year was approximately $400,000. Total surgeon compensation (including benefits) was approximately 15 percent more than the average income for a surgeon in Ontario.

Training in the Shouldice technique was important, because the procedure could not be varied. It was accomplished through direct supervision by one or more of the senior surgeons. The rotation of teams and frequent consultations allowed for an ongoing opportunity to appraise performance and take corrective action. Where possible, former Shouldice patients suffering recurrences were assigned to the doctor who performed the first operation "to allow the doctor to learn from his mistake." Dr. Obney commented on being a Shouldice surgeon:

> A doctor must decide after several years whether he wants to do this for the rest of his life because, just as in other specialties—for example, radiology—he loses touch with other medical disciplines. If he stays for five years, he doesn't leave. Even among younger doctors, few elect to leave.

THE FACILITY

The Shouldice Hospital contained two facilities in one building—the hospital and the clinic. On its first level, the hospital contained the kitchen and dining rooms. The second level contained a large, open lounge area, the admissions offices, patient rooms, and a spacious glass-covered Florida room. The third level had additional patient rooms and recreational areas. Patients could be seen visiting in each others' rooms, walking up and down hallways, lounging in the sunroom, and making use of light recreational facilities ranging from a pool table to an exercycle. Alan O'Dell pointed out some of the features of the hospital:

> The rooms contain no telephone or television sets. If a patient needs to make a call or wants to watch television, he or she has to take a walk. The steps are designed specially with a small rise to allow patients recently operated on to negotiate the stairs without undue discomfort. Every square foot of the hospital is carpeted to reduce the hospital feeling and the possibility of a fall. Carpeting also gives the place a smell other than that of disinfectant.
>
> This facility was designed by an architect with input from Dr. Byrnes Shouldice and Mrs. W. H. Urquhart (the daughter of the founder). The facility was discussed for years and many changes in the plans were made before the first concrete was poured. A number of unique policies were also instituted. For example, parents accompanying children here for an operation stay free. You may wonder why we can do it, but we learned that we save more in nursing costs than we spend for the parent's room and board.

Patients and staff were served food prepared in the same kitchen, and staff members picked up food from a cafeteria line placed in the very centre of the kitchen. This provided an opportunity for everyone to chat with the kitchen staff several times a day, and the hospital staff to eat together. According to O'Dell, "We use all fresh ingredients and prepare the food from scratch in the kitchen."

The director of housekeeping pointed out:

> I have only three on my housekeeping staff for the entire facility. One of the reasons for so few housekeepers is that we don't need to change linens during a patient's four-day stay. Also, the medical staff doesn't want the patients in bed all day. They want the nurses to encourage the patients to be up socializing, comparing notes [for confidence], encouraging each other, and walking around, getting exercise. Of course, we're in the rooms straightening up throughout the day. This gives the housekeepers a chance to josh with the patients and to encourage them to exercise.

EXHIBIT 2   Organization Chart

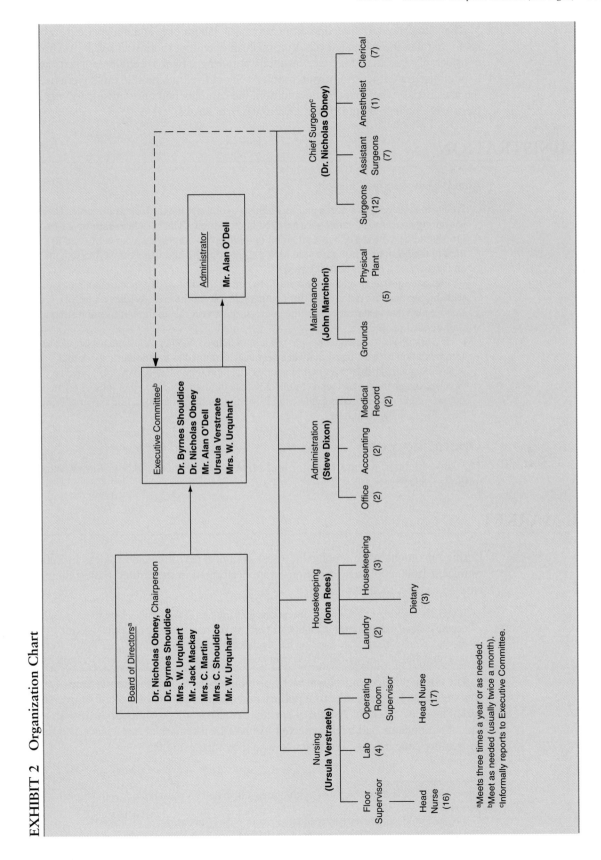

Board of Directors[a]

Dr. Nicholas Obney, Chairperson
Dr. Byrnes Shouldice
Mrs. W. Urquhart
Mr. Jack Mackay
Mrs. C. Martin
Mrs. C. Shouldice
Mr. W. Urquhart

Executive Committee[b]

Dr. Byrnes Shouldice
Dr. Nicholas Obney
Mr. Alan O'Dell
Ursula Verstraete
Mrs. W. Urquhart

Administrator
Mr. Alan O'Dell

Nursing
(Ursula Verstraete)

Floor Supervisor
— Head Nurse (16)

Lab (4)

Operating Room Supervisor
— Head Nurse (17)

Housekeeping
(Iona Rees)

Laundry (2)

Housekeeping (3)

Dietary (3)

Administration
(Steve Dixon)

Office (2)

Accounting (2)

Medical Record (2)

Maintenance
(John Marchiori)

Grounds

Physical Plant (5)

Chief Surgeon[c]
(Dr. Nicholas Obney)

Surgeons (12)

Assistant Surgeons (7)

Anesthetist (1)

Clerical (7)

[a]Meets three times a year or as needed.
[b]Meet as needed (usually twice a month).
[c]Informally reports to Executive Committee.

The clinic housed five operating rooms, a laboratory, and the patient-recovery room. In total, the estimated cost to furnish an operating room was $30,000. This was considerably less than for other hospitals requiring a bank of equipment with which to administer anesthetics for each room. At Shouldice, two mobile units were used by the anesthetists when needed. In addition, the complex had one "crash cart" per floor for use if a patient should suffer a heart attack or stroke.

ADMINISTRATION

Alan O'Dell described his job:

> We try to meet people's needs and make this as good a place to work as possible. There is a strong concern for employees here. Nobody is fired. [This was later reinforced by Dr. Shouldice, who described a situation involving two employees who confessed to theft in the hospital. They agreed to seek psychiatric help and were allowed to remain on the job.] As a result, turnover is low.
>
> Our administrative and support staff are non-union, but we try to maintain a pay scale higher than the union scale for comparable jobs in the area. We have a profit-sharing plan that is separate from the doctors'. Last year the administrative and support staff divided up $60,000.
>
> If work needs to be done, people pitch in to help each other. A unique aspect of our administration is that I insist that each secretary is trained to do another's work and in an emergency is able to switch to another function immediately. We don't have an organization chart. A chart tends to make people think they're boxed in jobs.[3] I try to stay one night a week, having dinner and listening to the patients, to find out how things are really going around here.

Operating Costs

The 2004 budgets for the hospital and clinic were close to $8.5 million,[4] and $3.5 million, respectively.[5]

THE MARKET

Hernia operations were among the most common performed on males. In 2000 an estimated 1,000,000 such operations were performed in the United States alone. According to Dr. Shouldice:

> When our backlog of scheduled operations gets too large, we wonder how many people decide instead to have their local doctor perform the operation. Every time we've expanded our capacity, the backlog has declined briefly, only to climb once again. Right now, at 2,400, it is larger than it has ever been and is growing by 100 every six months.

The hospital relied entirely on word-of-mouth advertising, the importance of which was suggested by the results of a poll carried out by students of DePaul University as part of a project (Exhibit 3 shows a portion of these results). Although little systematic data about patients had been collected, Alan O'Dell remarked that "if we had to rely on wealthy patients only, our practice would be much smaller."

---

[3]The chart in Exhibit 2 was prepared by the casewriter, based on conversations with hospital personnel.
[4]This figure included a provincially mandated return on investment.
[5]The latter figure included the bonus pool for doctors.

Patients were attracted to the hospital, in part, by its reasonable rates. Charges for a typical operation were four days of hospital stay at $320 per day, and a $650 surgical fee for a primary inguinal (the most common hernia). An additional fee of $300 was assessed if general anesthesia was required (in about 20% of cases). These charges compared to an average charge of $5,240 for operations performed elsewhere.

Round-trip fares for travel to Toronto from various major cities on the North American continent ranged from roughly $200 to $600.

The hospital also provided annual checkups to alumni, free of charge. Many occurred at the time of the patient reunion. The most recent reunion, featuring dinner and a floor show, was held at a first-class hotel in downtown Toronto and was attended by 1,000 former patients, many from outside Canada.

EXHIBIT 3 Shouldice Hospital Annual Patient Reunion Date

Direction: For each question, please place a check mark as it applies to you.

1. **Sex**   Male *41 95.34%*
                Female *2 4.65%*

2. **Age**   20 or less ___
               21-40 *4 9.30%*
               41-60 *17 39.54%*
               61 or more *22 51.16%*

3. **Nationality**

    Directions: Please place a check mark in nation you represent and please write in your province, state or country where it applies.

    Canada *38* Province *88.37%*
    America *5* State *11.63%*
    Europe ___ Country ___
    Other ___ ___

4. **Education level**

    Elementary   *5 11.63%*
    High School   *18 41.86%*
    College   *13.30 30.23%*
    Graduate work *7 16.28%*

5. **Occupation** ___

6. Have you been overnight in a hospital other than Shouldice before your operation?   Yes *31*   No *12*

7. What brought Shouldice Hospital to your attention?

    Friend *23* Doctor *9* Relative *7* Article ___ Other *4*
    53.49% *20.93%* *16.28%* (Please explain) *9.30%*

8. Did you have a single *25* or double *18* hernia operation?
    58.14% *41.86%*

9. Is this your first Annual Reunion? Yes *20* No *23* (*2-5 reunions - 11 47.83%*
    46.51% *53.49%* *6-10 reunions - 5 21.73%*
    If no, how many reunions have you attended? ___ *11-20 reunions - 4 17.39%*
    21-36 reunions - 3 13.05%

10. Do you feel that Shouldice Hospital cared for you as a person?

    Most definitely *37* Definitely *6* Very little ___ Not at all ___
    86.05% *13.95%*

continued

EXHIBIT 3 Shouldice Hospital Annual Patient Reunion Date—*continued*

11. What impressed you the most about your stay at Shouldice? Please check one answer for each of the following.

A. Fees charged for operation and hospital stay
   Very   Somewhat   Not
   Important _10_   Important _3_   Important _6_   Important _24_

B. Operation Procedure
   Very   Somewhat   Not
   Important _33_   Important _9_   Important _1_   Important ____
   _76.74%_   _20.93%_   _2.33%_

C. Physician's Care
   Very   Somewhat   Not
   Important _31_   Important _12_   Important _—_   Important _—_
   _72.10%_   _27.90%_

D. Nursing Care
   Very   Somewhat   Not
   Important _28_   Important _14_   Important _1_   Important ____
   _65.12%_   _32.52%_   _2.32%_

E. Food Service
   Very   Somewhat   Not
   Important _23_   Important _11_   Important _7_   Important _2_
   _53.48%_   _25.59%_   _16.28%_   _4.65%_

F. Shortness of Hospital Stay
   Very   Somewhat   Not
   Important _17_   Important _15_   Important _8_   Important _3_
   _39.53%_   _34.88%_   _18.60%_   _6.98%_

G. Exercise; Recreational Activities
   Very   Somewhat   Not
   Important _17_   Important _14_   Important _12_   Important _—_
   _39.53%_   _32.56%_   _27.91%_

H. Friendships with Patients
   Very   Somewhat   Not
   Important _25_   Important _10_   Important _5_   Important _3_
   _58.15%_   _23.25%_   _11.63%_   _6.98%_

I. "Shouldice Hospital hardly seemed like a hospital at all."
   Very   Somewhat   Not
   Important _25_   Important _13_   Important _5_   Important ____
   _58.14%_   _30.23%_   _11.63%_

12. In a few words, give the MAIN REASON why you returned for this annual reunion.

PROBLEMS AND PLANS

When asked about major questions confronting the management of the hospital, Dr. Shouldice cited a desire to seek ways of increasing the hospital's capacity while maintaining control over the quality of service delivered, the future role of government in the operations of the hospital, and the use of the Shouldice name by potential competitors. As Dr. Shouldice put it:

> I'm a doctor first and an entrepreneur second. For example, we could refuse permission to other doctors who want to visit the hospital. They may copy our technique and misapply it or misinform their patients about the use of it. This results in failure, and we are concerned that the technique will be blamed. But we're doctors, and it is our obligation to help other surgeons learn. On the other hand, it's quite clear that others are trying to emulate us. Look at this ad. [The advertisement is shown in Exhibit 4.]
>
> This makes me believe that we should add to our capacity, either here or elsewhere. Here, we could go to Saturday operations and increase our capacity by 20%. Throughout the year, no operations are scheduled for Saturdays or Sundays, although patients whose operations are scheduled late in the week remain in the hospital over the weekend. Or, with an investment of perhaps $4 million in new space, we could expand our number of beds by 50%, and schedule the operating rooms more heavily.
>
> On the other hand, given government regulation, do we want to invest more in Toronto? Or should we establish another hospital with similar design, perhaps in the United States? There is also the possibility that we could diversify into other specialties offering similar opportunities such as eye surgery, varicose veins, or diagnostic services (e.g. colonoscopies).
>
> For now, we're also beginning the process of grooming someone to succeed Dr. Degani when he retires. He's in his early 60s, but at some point we'll have to address this issue. And for good reason, he's resisted changing certain successful procedures that I think we could improve on. We had quite a time changing the schedule for the administration of Demerol to patients to increase their comfort level during the operation. Dr Degani has opposed a Saturday operating program on the premise that he won't be here and won't be able to maintain proper control.

EXHIBIT 4

Advertisement by a Shouldice Competitor

The
Canadian Hernia
Clinic

Hernias (Ruptures) Repaired Under local anesthesia as by Canadian method.

No Overnight Hospital Stay.

Consultations Without Charges

23061 St. Rd. 7
BOCA RATON, FLA. 33433
482-7755

Alan O'Dell added his own concerns:

> How should we be marketing our services? Right now, we don't advertise directly to patients. We're even afraid to send out this new brochure we've put together, unless a potential patient specifically requests it, for fear it will generate too much demand. Our records show that just under 1% of our patients are medical doctors, a significantly high percentage. How should we capitalize on that? I'm also concerned about this talk of Saturday operations. We are already getting good utilization of this facility. And if we expand further, it will be very difficult to maintain the same kind of working relationships and attitudes. Already there are rumours floating around among the staff about it. And the staff is not pleased.

The matter of Saturday operations had been a topic of conversation among the doctors as well. Four of the older doctors were opposed to it. While most of the younger doctors were indifferent or supportive, at least two who had been at the hospital for some time were particularly concerned about the possibility that the issue would drive a wedge between the two groups. As one put it, "I'd hate to see the practice split over the issue."

Index